PELICAN BOOKS

The Pelican Guides to European Literature

THE CONTINENTAL RENAISSANCE
1500–1600

Dr A. J. Krailsheimer was born in 1921 and has been Tutor in French at Christ Church, Oxford, since 1957. His publications are *Studies in Self-Interest* (1962), *Rabelais and the Franciscans* (1965), *Three Conteurs of the Sixteenth Century* (1966) and *Rabelais* (1967). He has also translated the *Pensées* and the *Lettres Provinciales* of Pascal for the Penguin Classics.

Professor W. A. Coupe was born in 1929, and educated at Bolton School, Emmanuel College, Cambridge, and the University of Marburg. He has taught German at Aberdeen, Exeter and Reading Universities and was recently appointed Professor of German at Southampton. His chief research has been on German illustrated broadsheets of the 17th century, but he has published on 16th, 19th and 20th century topics as well.

Dr John A. Scott has taught Italian at universities in Great Britain, the United States and Canada. Since 1961, he has spent most of his time at Reading as Senior Lecturer in Italian. He has written numerous articles – mainly on Dante and Renaissance literature – for British, American, French and Italian journals.

Dr R. W. Truman was born in 1934. He studied Spanish and French at Oxford and taught for four years at London University. Since 1963 he has been a University Lecturer in Spanish at Oxford and is a Student and Tutor of Christ Church. His interests lie particularly in the 16th and 19th centuries.

THE
CONTINENTAL
RENAISSANCE
1500–1600

W. A. COUPE
A. J. KRAILSHEIMER
(EDITOR)
J. A. SCOTT
R. W. TRUMAN

PENGUIN BOOKS

Penguin Books Ltd, Harmondsworth, Middlesex, England
Penguin Books Inc., 7110 Ambassador Road, Baltimore, Maryland 21207, U.S.A.
Penguin Books Australia Ltd, Ringwood, Victoria, Australia

—

First published 1971
Copyright © Penguin Books, 1971

—

Made and printed in Great Britain by
Hazell Watson & Viney Ltd, Aylesbury, Bucks
Set in Monotype Bembo

Contents

5

Contents

Contents

PART IV: PROSE FICTION

Contents

PART V: THE LITERATURE OF
IDEAS AND MANNERS

PART VI: POPULAR LITERATURE

Contents

Acknowledgement

As editor of this volume I take sole responsibility for its overall plan and approach, subject to the publisher's original directives regarding length and so on. Any criticism on that score applies to me alone. The three colleagues who agreed to help me accepted my scheme and then the four of us together drew up the detailed plan for the various sections. While each of us remains responsible for his own contribution, we have all treated the whole work as a common enterprise. It is a pleasure and a privilege to express my gratitude to my three collaborators, two of whom I had not even met before, for their unfailing kindness and support throughout this rewarding but often very arduous task. Setbacks caused by illness, student unrest, heavy teaching and administrative commitments and much else did not delay our agreed programme nor disrupt the almost preternatural harmony of our quartet. I for one regard this as an academic achievement worthy of record, and hardly less important than our finished product.

A.J.K.

Introduction

It is self-evidently impossible to produce a comprehensive account of the European literature written in five languages (including Latin) from 1500 to 1600 within the compass of the present volume, and even if it were possible such an account would probably be unreadable. Our aim has been at once more modest and more difficult: more modest because we have made no attempt at completeness, more difficult because the rigorous editorial demands of selection and compression are not easily reconciled with justice to the subject or to the reader. In the event the compromise on which we have agreed is represented by the title *Guide*. The map, so to speak, is composed of six divisions, very unequal in size but treated more or less similarly, and within each of these divisions there are further divisions, usually national and linguistic, the purpose of such an arrangement being to juxtapose like with like and thus facilitate comparisons and contrasts. The six primary divisions are devoted to the four principal genres of literature, with a separate section on popular literature and an introductory section on the cultural, intellectual and historical background to which the works of literature constantly allude. The omission from this volume of English literature is regrettable, but inevitable, if only for reasons of space, and that of other literature, particularly in Portuguese, Dutch and the Scandinavian languages, also became inevitable once the broad outlines of the book took shape. To avoid scrappiness as far as possible we have excluded mere mentions of authors and works and have tried to be more informative about those we have included and, hardest of all, we have had to apply a self denying ordinance of length to such giants as Ariosto, Tasso, Rabelais and Luther. Our hope is that there is enough information about all the main figures and a representative selection of minor ones to give the most inexperienced explorer coordinates with which to plot further excursions into unknown territory. We have tried too to make the narrative as continuous as possible, so that specialists in one language and culture can trace corresponding developments in others. In general we have talked about books that are available and likely to be read, and in the case of Latin works this has usually meant those which exist in translation, so that the fascinating output of scientific or occult works, as well as much neo-Latin poetry, has had to be omitted. Like any guide-book this one is somewhat arbitrary, though naturally based on the topography of the area surveyed, but the wise traveller will soon discover that reading books about books (or places) is no substitute for a personal visit. In the familiar classification of another guide, everything in this volume is 'worth the detour' and most of it 'worth the journey'.

The nature and purpose of literature, the status of the author and the number and type of reader are three basic questions which have to be answered in Renaissance terms before the following pages can be properly understood, but unfortunately it is just these questions which aroused most debate at the time. The chapter on criticism gives most of the relevant details for literary theory but it should be stressed at the outset that sixteenth-century canons of taste by no means coincide with our own, so that the test of time is something very different from that of critical orthodoxy. In the hierarchy of languages Latin and Greek towered above the vernaculars, and even when Italian, French and Spanish had firmly established their credentials (as German was not to do until much later), Classical erudition, *Litterae humaniores*, was universally accepted as the essential touchstone and preparation for literary composition or appreciation. This means that the great bulk of the works here discussed was written by, and for, a cultured élite, and incidentally explains why we have set aside a section for specifically popular literature, appealing to a mass audience. Estimates of literacy are so unreliable that it would be simply misleading to guess at percentages, but it is fair to say that at all times the cultured reading public constituted a very small numerical minority. This in its turn meant that authors, like all artists at the time, depended economically on patrons rather than on publishers (who were virtually always printers as well). Patrons frequently commissioned works, authors constantly hawked their books around seeking some wealthy or influential person who would accept a dedication in return for a subsidy. Some writers, like Bembo,

Montaigne or Marguerite de Navarre, were of independent means, and could write to please themselves, but they were the exceptions.

A whole series of consequences flows from these facts. The enormous prestige of Classical literature, and the similar prestige of Petrarch, encouraged, when it did not oblige, sixteenth-century writers to return incessantly to the same sources. Not only allusions to Classical mythology and so on, but actual imitations of Classical (or Petrarchan) models were the rule rather than the exception in poetry, drama, satire and other ancient genres. Originality in the sense of doing something completely new, and sincerity, in a simple autobiographical sense, are irrelevant concepts for most of the literature under discussion. Variations on a theme and the ability to express emotion within the strict conventions of style are Renaissance norms. Clearly this does not preclude genuine artistic originality, let alone spontaneity, any more than, say, Mozart writing on a theme by some minor composer. If it were only possible to come to Renaissance literature direct instead of through accumulated sediment of later ages one could see these qualities in all their freshness.

From imitation to plagiarism is only a step, that from following a model to wholesale borrowing, often from contemporaries. It is not sufficiently realized how modern is the idea of literary ownership, of the integrity of a text, and how inappropriate to the Renaissance. There was, of course, no copyright law, and the 'privileges' (a kind of royal *imprimatur*) simply gave authors a brief monopoly and authorization to sell their work, that is, censorship clearance, but more to the point texts were pirated, falsely attributed, cut, distorted or enlarged with total unconcern by rival authors, editors (especially of posthumous publications) and printer-publishers. Anonymous works, especially in the sensitive fields of religion and politics, were numerous, and naturally treated with complete freedom by anyone wishing to use them for his own ends. This is equally the case whether the works were designed as propaganda, entertainment, erudition or poetry.

The distribution between the various sections illustrates the great difference in priorities between the sixteenth and the present century. Poetry, with which it is proper to include most drama, was the only artistic form of literature, whether it be epic, lyric, pastoral or what you will. From being a craftsman, a maker of verse, the poet became a seer, inspired by the Muses (or God) with visions vouchsafed only to a privileged few. In Italy this development had taken place long before 1500, but in France and Spain the century was well under way before it became generally accepted. In Germany it had to wait until the eighteenth century, and that is why the only German poetry discussed in this volume comes into the section on popular literature. Poetry was seen as the ultimate test of the vernaculars, and thus the element of national and linguistic prestige was always important. Even when composed for some court entertainment, or for musical accompaniment, poetry (as distinct from mere verse or song) aimed at dignity and elegance, even elevation. In this respect tragedy manifestly belongs with poetry, while comedy, for all its ostensibly moral purpose, must be bracketed with lighter entertainment.

Fiction was purely for entertainment, and though the genre could not wholly escape the didactic zeal of the century, it was classed as reading matter rather than as literature. In this connection it must be emphasized that poetry, drama and fiction were commonly read aloud, and that both socially and stylistically the spoken word delivered to an audience remained throughout the period at least as important as the written word read privately (and it is a moot point how far silent reading was practised). Popular literature, addressed to partly or mainly illiterate audiences, remained a primarily oral phenomenon.

An exception to what has just been said, and perhaps the most striking feature of our distribution, is the literature of ideas, whose importance is grossly understated in terms of the pages here devoted to it. Scholars are by definition well read, but the gloss and commentary of the Scholastics had been designed purely for specialist consumption. The essays, dialogues, satires, histories and so on of the Renaissance humanists were directed at all, men and women, who were interested in culture for its own sake. The visionary element of poetry is inappropriate to these prose works, which all have a lesson to impart, often, indeed usually, buttressed by Classical or biblical authority. Sometimes they are propaganda for religious or political ideas, either expounded directly or in satirical form, sometimes they are repositories of assorted facts and wisdom, sometimes they are mainly concerned with teaching a moral lesson, but they are all books to be read, re-read and consulted. The borderline between treatise and literature is largely artificial, and perhaps the best criterion is the subjective one of readability. These works are usually learned, they instruct and edify, and publishers were only too glad to exploit the apparently insatiable public demand. Censors, on the other hand, at once recognized that here, not in poetry, drama or fiction, lay the real danger to the establishment of Church and State, and authors ran very considerable risks, shared, it must be said, by publishers whose profits could all too often go up in the flames of the executioner's bonfire. Much of this work was in Latin, much has never been republished, and most of it requires preparatory reading beyond the range of nearly all non-specialist readers, but it would be falsifying the picture of Renaissance literature to give this section any less space, and all of us would ideally have liked to give it more.

It should finally be said that the division too frequently drawn between Middle Ages and Renaissance, the manuscript and the printed book, is extremely misleading. It was not much before 1540 in France and Germany that the practice ceased of printing books exactly as if they were manuscripts, in black letter bristling with abbreviations, though, of course, the superb humanist type of the Aldine Press at Venice set a standard early in the century which has never been excelled. Presentation copies and de luxe works (for example, Marguerite's *Heptameron*) were still quite commonly manuscript. Medieval titles figured prominently in publishers' lists throughout the century (the most popular devotional work was the *Imitation of Christ* from the fifteenth century) and great folio volumes of Aquinas and other scholastic doctors were published side by side with new editions of the early Fathers and Classical texts. The humanists tended to exaggerate the emotional break with the past, and continuity was considerable in all fields, especially in northern Europe. For all that, the spread of printing and the revival of Classical learning make sixteenth-century literature recognizably modern as that of the previous century is not, and it could be argued that in some important respects we are today closer to it than to the literature of the intervening centuries.

PART I

The Cultural and Historical Background

ONE

Learning and Ideas

PERHAPS the most characteristic feature of the sixteenth century is its boundless enthusiasm. Neither in thought nor deed did men (or women) do things by halves. People had a prodigious appetite for learning, and were reluctant to sacrifice any one aspect of what most regarded as a single truth and wisdom, but were ferocious in their denunciation of supposed error. Consequently a respect for authority which may seem uncritical and even superstitious can often accompany and animate revolt against some other authority of apparently similar credentials. The cry throughout much of the century was 'back to the sources' and one convenient way to focus momentarily the shifting pattern of Renaissance thought is to look at some of the sources and the instruments with which they could be reached.

First and foremost of these instruments was *philologia*, the study of languages, and this meant, in an age when every educated person had to converse and write in Latin, the study of Greek and, to a lesser extent, of Hebrew. By 1500 most of the groundwork had already been done, mainly, but not entirely, in Italy, and the rest of Europe was beginning to reap the benefit. Pioneers like Lorenzo Valla (d. 1457) had been followed by such men as Gian Pico della Mirandola (d. 1494), Angelo Poliziano (Politian, d. 1494) and Marsilio Ficino (d. 1499). Their great contribution was to make available by Latin translation and commentary writers of antiquity who had been neglected, unknown or simply misunderstood for centuries. Already in Valla's day the critical study of manuscripts was helping to advance linguistic knowledge, throwing fresh light on Classical and Patristic writings and even revealing unsuspected survivals from the ancient world. Given the temper of the age it was inevitable that biblical studies would soon be affected by this mounting interest in language, and such enterprises as the Complutensian Bible in Spain (begun

1502) and Erasmus' Greek New Testament (1516) are early examples of a movement which soon extended to vernacular versions of the Bible and critical editions of the Fathers. The story of the application of philology to religion belongs to another chapter, but it must be emphasized that the humanists of the early sixteenth century neither observed nor desired any rigid demarcation between their sacred and profane pursuits. It is not even possible to separate their purely factual inquiries into the meaning of particular words or customs of the ancient world from more fundamental study of the systems of thought and belief thereby revealed. The outstanding example of this is Erasmus' *Adages*, the source book *par excellence*, in which the original quite brief explanations of ancient sayings eventually developed into a full scale commentary on every imaginable topic, from personal reminiscence to textual criticism, by way of contemporary satire. Similarly Guillaume Budé, greatest of French humanists (1468–1540), in his monumental *De Asse* (1514) ranged far and wide over Roman law and customs in discussing the value of the coin, *as*.

In the linguistic field it is easier to chart progress than in the more complex field of ideas. The shortage of reliable Greek teachers and texts which had seriously hampered the efforts of Erasmus and his contemporaries at the turn of the century was gradually overcome. The original so-called Academy of Ficino, set up in Florence in 1462, had given rise to many others in Italy, and influenced developments in France, as had the later group of *Fillelleni* (Philhellenes) set up in Venice around the great printer Aldo Manuzio. By 1530 Budé had persuaded François I to set up his *Lecteurs royaux* (later the Collège de France) in Latin, Greek, Hebrew and mathematics, to the fury of the Sorbonne, piqued at this threat to their long hegemony over the University of Paris, and similar trilingual colleges were founded elsewhere at about the same time (Corpus Christi at Oxford, and Busleiden's college at Louvain among others). Budé published a learned commentary on the Greek tongue (1529) and Etienne Dolet, erstwhile friend and publisher of Rabelais, one on Latin (1536–8). Another printer-scholar, member of a veritable dynasty, Robert Estienne, published the first French–Latin dictionary (1539) and his son Henri a Greek thesaurus in 1572. Similar progress was accomplished throughout Europe under widely differing auspices. Sometimes it was thanks to Protestants, like the Estiennes, sometimes Catholics, like the new Society of Jesus, but by 1600 the movement which had begun in Italy some 150 years before had led to the establishment everywhere of a recognized educational system based on sound command of Latin and Greek, bringing down to our own day the common cultural heritage of ancient history, mythology and wisdom. Hebrew could not, in the nature of things, compete, but it was seriously studied both by biblical scholars like Reuchlin in Germany and the not inconsiderable number of those interested in the cabbala and the occult in general, especially Guillaume Postel (d. 1581), who actually taught Greek, Hebrew and Arabic at the Collège de France before succumbing to insanity.

With so much attention paid to linguistic questions it was inevitable that the vernacular should also come under scrutiny. The easy refinement of the first Florentine Academy gave way to a more professional or, as we should say, academic approach. About 1540, for example, Sperone Speroni was the leading light of an academy (*degli Infiammati*) at Padua, which anticipated Richelieu's French Academy by a century in laying down the law about style, rules and so on in a generally neo-Classical sense. Though by no means an innovator in Italy (his ideas were not even novel in France), Speroni was a major influence on Ronsard and du Bellay, who took over his doctrine regarding the vernacular, with slight changes, in their *Defense et Illustration de la langue françoyse* (1549), somewhat ironically in view of their vigorous attack on Italian cultural pretensions. Another Italian academy (*della Crusca*) in Florence again anticipated Richelieu by bringing out an authoritative Italian dictionary (published 1612).

In the latter half of the century France saw a considerable development of academies, under the patronage of Catherine de' Medici (descendant of the Florentine family) and from such groups as that which began at the Collège de Coqueret, round Dorat, and later became known as the Pléiade, there evolved palace and other academies in which all the arts, including music and ballet, were cultivated, but which did not yet have legislative pretensions. Even here one must not draw the boundaries too sharply. The circle gathered round Marguerite de Navarre in the second quarter of the century had many of the features of the Florentine academy, and they acted plays or told stories, discussed Platonism and poetry, Evangelism and politics in a highly civilized way. Marguerite would have been the first to acknowledge her debt to Italy, where she had numerous contacts, but she never had resources comparable to those of Catherine and consequently never quite so much influence, except on individuals. In Spain, the Netherlands and the Empire there was no shortage of scholars, and the prestige of such universities as Salamanca or Louvain was immense; but while successive kings and emperors proved lavish patrons of the arts, there was nothing strictly comparable to the situation in France or Italy as regards academies.

If from the instruments one turns to the sources, it is again with Ficino that one must start. More than any other single man he is responsible for the form taken by the Platonic revival so typical of the sixteenth century. Turning his back on the Aristotelian logic of the Schools, Ficino sought to reconcile religion and philosophy, that is Christian and pagan, through a kind of mysticism in which Plato himself was not really distinguished from Plotinus, Proclus or even the pseudo-Dionysius, who has exercised an extraordinary influence on Christian mystics through the ages. All the emphasis is on synthesis, on the oneness of the vision and the truth. The curious cosmology of the *Timaeus* and above all the *Symposium*'s teaching on love were of enormous importance through the next century because of Ficino's translations, commentaries and his grand synthesis in the *Theologia Platonica*. Petrarch, it is true, had long before given poetic expression to certain neo-Platonic ideas about love, and his sixteenth-century followers, in Italy, France, Spain and England, naturally imitated their master in this, but the systematic justification for their theories they found in Ficino. The concept of rising through the successive stages of sensual, intellectual and spiritual love to mystical union with God is a commonplace of medieval neo-Platonists, like St Bonaventura, but the ennobling virtue of idealized love between human beings as described in so much sixteenth-century literature owes more to Ficino (though his own debt to Bonaventura must be recognized). The charming Androgyne myth (that every lover is really seeking the other half of what was originally created a single being), the spiritualization of love, freed from carnality, the tendency to see in earthly love a reflection and prefiguration of divine love – these are constantly recurring Platonic features in Renaissance literature. Similarly, the marked interest in the spirit world, where Christian angels, Classical daemons and miscellaneous elves, fairies and what not overpopulate the intermediate airy regions between God and man, in dreams, where the soul's brief participation in divine omniscience permits a peep into the future, and in the Ideas, or archetypes, of which earthly things are pale shadows – all this can be traced back to the rejuvenated Platonism of fifteenth-century Florence, with many medieval or hermetic accretions picked up on the way.

It is very often, perhaps too often, maintained that men in the sixteenth century were not interested in metaphysics but in ethics, but whatever the truth of such a claim, it needs to be assessed in the light of what has just been said about Platonism. It cannot however be denied that men also sought, and found, in Plato teaching of a very different kind concerned with problems of human conduct. The *Republic* was anything but metaphysical, and Renaissance Europe was ready for new approaches to the theory of government, of which Plato provided one at least as influential as did Machiavelli. The philosopher-kings, the character-building education, the cultivation of virtue rather than war, are only three of the features of the *Republic* eagerly propagated by sixteenth-century writers, with Erasmus and More at their head, and the latter did not shrink even from Plato's communism. Of all Plato's legacies, however, none proved more valuable than his portrait of Socrates. From Erasmus' challenging 'Sancte Socrates, ora pro nobis' (actually copied from a phrase of Ficino) to Montaigne's choice of Socrates as the greatest man of whom he knew, the person of Socrates was a focus throughout the century for those who passionately believed in man, with or without benefit of clergy; and he was inevitably the target for those others who as passionately believed in man's irremediable corruption without God's saving grace, and would not concede to any unbaptised pagan the smallest share of either truth or virtue in eternal terms. The sublime account of Socrates' death in the *Phaedo* inspired successive generations from Erasmus on to devise some means of reconciling their purely human with their Christian heritage.

Closely associated with this cult of Socrates was the revival of Stoicism, which in the Renaissance came to mean almost exclusively the ethics of that school, in antiquity a much more comprehensive philosophy with its own curious cosmology. The key Stoic document was the *Manual* of Epictetus, a concise and simple statement of the Stoic case which continued to be read throughout the following century. Politian's Latin translation of the original Greek (second century A.D.) was published in 1498 and long remained the standard version, but there were other important Latin translations, including one by the German Protestant Naogeorg (1554), as well as a series of vernacular translations or paraphrases, of which the best known is the French version by Guillaume du Vair (1585). In an age of continual violence, obsessed with the reversals of an apparently capricious fortune, men craved some inner moral certainty which need not depend on religious dogma, though could preferably be reconciled with it. The phrase 'contempt for fortuitous things' runs like a *leitmotiv* through the century, in writers as diverse as Budé and Rabelais, and the maxim of Epictetus 'sustine et abstine' ('endure and abstain') excellently summarizes the position of those who were striving to attain that self-mastery through the proper use of reason which would enable them to rise above events and enjoy the state of ataraxia, or impassivity. The Stoic assumption that reason is good, passions bad, clearly supported the 'dignity of man' thesis so dear to the Renaissance and so eloquently expounded in Pico's famous oration with that title (1486), and while the Christian virtues of temperance and fortitude could readily be identified with Stoic teaching, it had its vulnerable side, and was often accused of fostering arrogance, indifference to the suffering of others and excessive austerity. It is only fair to add that true Stoics taught the brotherhood of man, but then so did the officials of the Holy Inquisition. As an antidote to fear of pain and death Stoicism enjoyed a considerable vogue, and even its critics had to deal with the Stoic solution to moral questions. It is significant, and typical, that Montaigne, who was once deeply influenced by Stoicism (especially through his friend La Boétie) remained a fervent admirer of Socrates, patron saint of the school, long after he had rejected Stoic doctrines. It should perhaps be added that Epicureanism, the ancient rival to Stoicism, had more influence as a loose term of abuse for any apparent hedonists than as a moral doctrine, but came into its own in the seventeenth century with such men as Gassendi.

It was typical of the sixteenth century that men preferred concrete examples to abstract ideas. This was, of course, nothing new, in that the cult of saints, ancient or modern, had always given the faithful specific examples to follow, but what was lacking was a similar band of virtuous pagans. The enormous success of Plutarch's *Lives* (parallel biographies of twenty-three Greeks and twenty-three Romans) in the latter part of the century is due above all to the insatiable curiosity of the age regarding the conduct and motivation of great men. In Italy Plutarch was read in Latin, but in France Jacques Amyot's French version (1559), like that of North in England, made him familiar to the vast public which had little Latin and less Greek. In a quite different context, Plutarch's *Moralia* were also important, and widely drawn on by those who found in this colourful synthesis of ethics, history, demonology, Egyptology, mythology, and theories about oracles (*inter alia*) an impressive authority, enhanced by being written in Greek.

Together with Plutarch, the two most widely influential authors of antiquity were Cicero and Seneca. The humanists all admired, and imitated, Cicero's style, but some, like Erasmus, were driven to criticize the quite superstitious reverence which, for instance, precluded the use of any non-Ciceronian words in contemporary references to Christian doctrine. An acrimonious dispute, into which Dolet was eventually drawn on the side of the Ciceronians (1535), shows yet again how even questions of style could turn out to have wider implications. Apart from his style, Cicero – 'moral Tully' to the Elizabethans – was read primarily for his essays on friendship, old age, public and private duties, and on the different philosophies (especially Stoic) with which he was acquainted. The same is true of Seneca, sometimes held to have died a Christian, whose particular brand of Stoicism commended itself to men avid for pithy and quotable moral maxims, or *sententiae*. His great influence on European tragedy throughout the sixteenth century spread his ideas and sayings even beyond the already extensive reading public of his letters and essays.

It was quite normal in the Renaissance for Platonism, Stoicism and other philosophies to co-exist in a syncretism of which the aim was to preserve the best of pagan wisdom and reconcile it with Christian truth. Pico even went so far as to claim that he had succeeded in reconciling Plato and Aristotle, but for the most part the Aristotelian tradition proved the least amenable to syncretic treatment. For one thing Aristotelian logic had become too closely identified in the eyes of Renaissance thinkers with the obsolete Scholasticism which they found especially repellent, and for another St Thomas had so effectively Christianized Aristotle in the thirteenth century, when the great majority of his works became suddenly available, that it was much harder to disentangle the authentic philosopher from his Scholastic adapters than was the case with Plato, who had been almost wholly rediscovered in the fifteenth century. In the natural sciences, however, Aristotle's influence survived the general discredit of Scholasticism, and at Padua in particular there existed a tradition strongly marked by Averroes, an Arab commentator of Aristotle whose teaching on personal immortality of the soul (which he denied) and the eternal nature of the world (which he affirmed, against the Christian doctrine of creation *ex nihilo*) was undoubtedly anti-Christian.

Early in the sixteenth century Pietro Pomponazzi (1462–1525) attacked his Averroist colleagues at Padua, and evolved a system at once rationalistic and fideistic, that is, he outwardly remained a dutiful son of the Church, while denying that natural theology or miracles were susceptible of rational proof, or even acceptable to reason. He believed in the personal nature of the soul, as against Averroes's doctrine of collective immortality, but regarded it as being no more than a natural bodily function; he disapproved of appeal to reward or punishment in the hereafter as a basis for the moral life; he rejected the possibility that fate (or predestination) and free will can both exist, and in general adopted the sort of naturalistic and rationalistic approach which is usually associated with the eighteenth-century Enlightenment, for which he was indeed a much respected figure. Opinions are divided as to how far and how early his influence spread outside Italy, particularly in France, but there can be no doubt that Pomponazzi is one of the most important thinkers of the Renaissance.

Doctors in general, and Paduans in particular, were professionally committed to seeking rational explanations wherever possible for the phenomena with which they had to deal, and throughout the century many of them, like Girolamo Cardano (1501-76), combined considerable scientific distinction with ideas of a strongly rationalistic, and by no means orthodox kind, often based on Aristotle and Averroes. Some dabbled in the occult, like Paracelsus (1493-1541), some turned to scepticism, or even alternated the two, like the legendary Cornelius Agrippa (1486-1535), some chose the experimental method, though even they could fall foul of authority. Thus the study of anatomy was revolutionized by Leonardo da Vinci (1452-1519) and the Fleming, Andreas Vesalius (1514-64), but when the latter, who had become Charles V's physician, was imprudent enough to dissect a living patient he narrowly escaped being burned and died in exile. Even autopsies were exceedingly rare, and Rabelais's presence at one was thought worthy of comment as proof of his medical distinction. Men wanted to know more about themselves and the world in which they lived, and were prepared to defy vested interests and repressive authority to further their explorations. The ancient wisdom of Galen and Hippocrates, Aristotle and Pliny, Ptolemy and all the other venerable figures of the past had first to be assimilated, but then recovery was followed by discovery.

The trite phrase about advancing the frontiers of knowledge was never less trite than in the Renaissance, when with the impetus of the regained Classical heritage to fire them men advanced in thought and in deed into the heavens, like Copernicus (1473-1543) or Tycho Brahe (1546-1601), across land and sea like Columbus, Jacques Cartier or Francis Xavier, into the living mystery of man's own body, like Leonardo, Vesalius or the great French surgeon Ambroise Paré (1509-90). Evocative as it is, such a partial roll-call does scant justice to the vision and fervour of a century in which men wanted to know, and believe, everything that was to be known. Beginning with the authority of tradition and ancient authors, the pioneer spirit led them on to look for themselves and thus to pave the way for the scientific progress of later ages. The facts of their achievement are clear enough, its value more controversial. The last word may appropriately be given to one of the greatest men of the Renaissance, a man dedicated to learning, a respected physician, a writer of genius: Rabelais wrote in 1532, 'science without conscience is but ruin of the soul.'

TWO

Literary Criticism

ITALY

BOIARDO (1441–94), the first great poet from outside Tuscany, heralded the coming age, which saw the end of the Tuscan monopoly of 'Italian' literature and a new type of vernacular humanism. At the beginning of the sixteenth century, two figures dominated the cultural scene in Italy: PIETRO BEMBO (1470–1547) in the north, IACOPO SANNAZARO (*c.* 1455–1530) in the south. Their influence left an indelible mark on Italian literature, far in excess of their literary worth, while it represents the first stage of sixteenth-century criticism in Italy: the establishment of the vernacular as a literary medium on a par with Latin and a solution to the language problem, the notorious *Questione della lingua*. Bembo's *Prose della volgar lingua* (1525) offered a compromise that could appeal to the susceptibilities of Tuscans and non-Tuscans alike. In this work, one of the greatest humanists of the day transposed the principle of imitation from the Classical languages to Italian. The absence of any political unity or hegemony had deprived the Italians of a truly national tongue. Printing, with its markets throughout the peninsula, made the need for standardization more acute; it also helped to provide a solution by producing numerous editions of the great fourteenth-century Tuscan writers – the triad praised and drawn upon by Bembo in his codification of the vernacular. A further reason was provided by the general desire to 'nobilitate' the vulgar tongues: the need to impose order and unity on them, to show that they possessed their own rules like Greek and Latin, before going on to prove that they were capable of dealing with noble subjects and forms (such as philosophy and tragedy), hitherto regarded by many as the exclusive province of the Classical languages. The question was chiefly a literary one, and even Bembo is said to have avoided Tuscan frills in his speech at the court of the Medici pope, Clement VII. In literature, however, this cultural dictator adapted his strict Ciceronianism to the vernacular by establishing Petrarch as the sole model for verse and Boccaccio for prose.

But that the question was no academic matter is also shown by the treatment it received in Castiglione's *Cortegiano* (1528). Here, in the formation of the perfect gentleman, speech is discussed in no less than twelve chapters of the First Book (xxviii–xxxix). As always, the courtier must shun affectation. He must therefore avoid using archaic forms and aping Tuscan speech. Castiglione refuses to accept the divorce of the written from the spoken word, for writing is nothing but 'a form of speech, which remains after man has spoken'. Special care should be given to one's written style, but this must still be composed of words used in speech, selected for their grace and beauty. And Castiglione remarks on the absurdity of those Italians who, browbeaten by the snobbish ideal of Tuscan supremacy, feel compelled to confess their supposed ignorance of a language they have in fact learned from the cradle. His solution is to propose a *koine* based on a judicious choice from all the regions of Italy and not excluding the adaptation of certain foreign words and neologisms, such as the essential *sprezzatura*, a kind of nonchalant grace used by the perfect courtier to suppress all trace of effort in the practice of his numerous skills (I, xxvi).

This *lingua cortigiana*, as it came to be called, the language spoken at the various courts or linguistic melting-pots of Renaissance Italy was championed by GIANGIORGIO TRISSINO (1478–1550) among others. To support his stand, he called on no less an authority than Dante himself – in the form of the latter's treatise, the *De Vulgari Eloquentia*, which Trissino unearthed and translated into Italian (1529), adding his own misinterpretations of Dante's text. As early as 1514, Trissino had been expounding his view that Dante had championed the *lingua cortigiana* some two centuries before (although in the *De Vulgari Eloquentia* Dante is in fact concerned with a literary language and his unfinished work deals only with the most noble poetic style, as used in the *canzone*). This idea was put forward by him in the gatherings of leading citizens and intellectuals at the Orti Oricellari in Florence, and it led NICCOLÒ MACHIAVELLI (1469–1527) to reply in typically swingeing style in his controversial *Discorso o dialogo intorno alla nostra lingua*. This fascinating document begins with some observations on the importance of lexical and phonetic differences in language and on the desire for revenge against his fellow-citizens that had led Dante to place so many of them in Hell and to attack them on linguistic grounds in the *De Vulgari Eloquentia*. There ensues a lively dialogue between Dante and Machiavelli for the prosecution. Dante is forced to admit that non-Florentine words and expressions are rare enough in the *Comedy* and that they do not change the essential nature of his language, which remains essentially Florentine. Machiavelli goes on to make two points. First, that the myth of a *lingua cortigiana* has only been made possible by the adoption of so many Florentine forms and expressions by the rest of Italy, drawing its inspiration from the works of the great Florentine *trecentisti* – for proof, says Machiavelli, you only have to look at what was written in other regions before Dante. The second point concerns the example of comedy, more realistic than the illustrious form of tragedy. Machiavelli declares that non-Tuscans ('i forestieri') make a hash of comic dialogue, while they pay tribute by imitating Tuscan speech. He then singles out Ariosto's *I suppositi* (1509), praising its qualities but criticizing its dialogue, which lacks pith because Ariosto 'disliked the idioms of Ferrara and didn't know the Florentine ones'; as a corollary, Machiavelli quotes the examples of Bembo, Sannazaro and Trissino himself, who write well only because they follow Tuscan usage – 'which they could not have done, before you, Petrarch, and Boccaccio wrote your works.'

The three main solutions to the *Questione della lingua* were thus based on spatial and temporal criteria. The various writers either supported or opposed the claims of one region (Tuscany or, in more extreme cases, Florence). Those who accepted Tuscan supremacy were divided into two groups: on the one hand, the few who advocated the language of the present; on the other, those authors who were willing to submit to the ideal of a linguistic golden age (the *Trecento* or fourteenth century), situated well in the past and made more palatable by the obvious parallels with classical studies. The victory of the latter party was overwhelming and it was codified in the principles that governed the foundation of the Accademia della Crusca (1582) and the publication of its great dictionary (1612).

The sixteenth century is a landmark for the establishment of Aristotle as the norm for both theory and practice in literature. The first half of the century, however, was still under the influence of

Horace and the rhetoricians, as well as the ubiquitous neo-Platonism of fifteenth-century humanism. It was in this climate that Vida wrote his *Poeticorum libri tres* (published 1527). He deals with the poet's choice of tutor and studies, and devotes the whole of the second book to a discussion of the most noble genre, the epic, which replaces the drama of Horace's *Epistula ad Pisones*. This, in fact, means a detailed examination of Homer, whose excessive 'realism' constitutes a grave offence against epic grandeur, and a parallel exaltation of Virgil, who is regarded as the peak of perfection, so that even the smallest details of the *Aeneid* are transformed into essential conditions of heroic poetry. Virgil offers the poet an example of eternal truth in the treatment of human nature, exquisite harmony and balance of style, and he remains for all time the supreme model from whom the Horatian principle of decorum can be learned. Lip-service is paid to the Platonic conception of artistic inspiration, but in fact the neo-Classical view of literature as a skill whose various ingredients can be analysed and mastered in academic fashion is already well in evidence, with the consequent exhortation to the poet to provide a wealth of embellishment, variety and suspense within the Classical order. Vida's lack of interest in vernacular literature is accompanied by his condemnation of poets who abandon Classical clarity for barbaric chaos; and his obvious, unflattering reference to Dante (II, 192–202) echoes Bembo's wish that the author of the *Comedy* had not striven to appear something more than a poet with his cocktail of biblical and Classical erudition. It also points the way to the great debate which flared up after Benedetto Varchi stated in his *Ercolano* (1570) that Dante might even be considered superior to Homer and thus provided the first spark in the long-lasting quarrel of the ancients and moderns.

The importance of Aristotle's *Poetics* was only recognized after Alessandro de' Pazzi's revised Latin transcription (1536), although the work had been known in the Middle Ages in Averroes's digest and published in Giorgio Valla's Latin version at the Aldine Press in 1498. Robortello produced the first classical edition in 1548, and the following year saw the first Italian translation, by Bernardo Segni. The desire for conformity that characterized official life in Counter-Reformation Italy encouraged the adoption of a literary orthodoxy, while the setting up of Aristotle as the supreme authority in natural philosophy by the Council of Trent made the choice inevitable. Just as the Greek philosopher was seen to provide a rational basis for the Catholic faith, so now he offered a rational analysis and vindication of the art of poetry. The vindication, however, continued to be worked out on Horatian as well as Aristotelian lines, with its characteristic emphasis on the basic utility of literature, which, teaching by example, provides the most effective moral teaching in its representation of a higher reality.

SPERONE SPERONI (1500–1588), who studied under Pomponazzi, was one of the leading exponents of the new Aristotelianism, which found an intellectual centre in the Accademia degli Infiammati at Padua. In Italy, he was considered first and foremost a philosopher and orator, and his critical writings appeared rather too late on the scene to be truly influential. His great influence was on du Bellay, who made extensive use of Speroni's writings in his celebrated *Défense* of 1549. Speroni's *Dialogo delle lingue* (1542) repeats Bembo's solution of a vernacular humanism capable of raising modern literature to the level of Greek and Latin perfection by the careful imitation of antiquity based on the recognition of the peculiar needs of each language and age. It is interesting to note that Speroni was one of the first to recognize the importance of poets writing in other languages and that he especially commended Ronsard's odes. Yet, against those who, like G. B. GIRALDI (1504–73), held that certain genres such as the romance were unknown to Aristotle and that literature must reflect the changing needs of society, Speroni maintained that, while modern poets need not be constricted by all the rules prescribed by the ancients, they cannot depart from the fundamental laws of poetry, which are eternal and immutable. His tragedy *Canace* (1542), with its emphasis on *peripetia* and attempt to satisfy Aristotle's requirement of catharsis by arousing pity and horror in the minds of the spectators, sparked off a debate on the nature of Classical tragedy which lasted until the end of the century.

Minturno's *De poeta* (1559) is the first extensive manual of the new genre. In it he does his best to strike a fine balance between the Horatian aims of profit and delight. His *Arte poetica toscana* (1563) applied the same principles to Italian literature, with the addition of one or two new ingredients: for example, the restriction of dramatic performances to three or four hours in order to comply with the needs of the audience. Like Speroni, he opposed Giraldi, though he was more rigorous in upholding the eternal validity of the laws discovered and practised by the ancients.

If Minturno's method is eclectic and even confused at times, that of JULIUS CAESAR SCALIGER (1484–1558) in his *Poetices libri septem* (1561) is nothing if not orderly. This 'mouthpiece of literary Aristotelianism' did not hesitate to depart from Aristotle, as in his insistence on the cardinal tenet that poetry is imitation in verse. Nevertheless, Scaliger was in many ways the most influential critic in the setting up of Aristotle as the perpetual legislator for the fine arts ('imperator noster, omnium bonarum artium dictator perpetuus'). Like his neo-Classical successors, Scaliger believed in the supremacy of reason over the imagination and tended to regard poetry as a science, which, with the help of logical deduction, could establish a norm for every genre. A similar orderly process led to the proclamation of a hierarchy of genres, well in accord with the demands of post-Tridentine Catholicism, with its superficial recognition of the primacy of hymns and sacred compositions, and second place accorded to 'songs and odes and scolia, dealing with the praises of brave men'. Only third place is reserved for the epic, fourth for tragedy and comedy, although it was obviously here that Scaliger found his true scope. Tragedy is defined as the imitation of an illustrious event, with an unhappy ending ('death or exile'), written in verse and in a grave style. Kings and illustrious personages alone must appear, while the language must reflect the general desire to avoid everything that is plebeian. The dramatist teaches morality through action, because his audience will imitate what is good and shun what is bad. It is only fitting that in tragedy evil men should be punished, though happiness may be meted out to the good – a final impression, reinforced by the intermittent recitation of moral precepts throughout the play. Fitting subjects are 'slaughter, despair, execution, exile, bereavement, parricide, incest, conflagrations, battles, blinding, tears, shrieks, lamentations, burials, epitaphs, and funeral songs' – a list which reflects Scaliger's delight in the blood and thunder of Seneca, whom he declares the equal of any Greek for majesty. The plays of Plautus and Terence are the models proposed for comedy, which achieves its moral end through the vituperation and ridicule of vice; it is in fact the best corrective of morals and a fitting companion to satiric poetry in general. For the epic, Virgil is the touchstone against which all else must be measured. As a result, the apparent vulgarity of action and similes in Homer places the Greek poet well down the scale (below Musaeus, in fact), and the all-embracing requirement of 'decorum' forbids any departure from Virgilian example in the portrayal of character and poetic style. Behind all this is the idea that the poet may confer lustre and artistic excellence on the most trivial subject by observing certain rules in the search for elegance, splendour and proportion, while anything that smacks of common reality can render the most artistic subject worthless. Admittedly, the ancients had counselled the study of nature; on the other hand, Homer – the poet nearest to nature – is full of mistakes against art. The poet must indeed study nature (especially human nature), but he must learn to select judiciously from the abundance that nature herself provides. A great artist must create a second 'nature', and the greatest poet of all has provided a more perfect reality, in which the dross has been eliminated and which offers us all the secrets of man's activity: 'Everything that you may wish to imitate, you have according to another nature: Virgil.' Only a few voices of dissent were raised – such as Bruno's in his *Eroici furori* (1585), where he condemned imitation as the servile, unimaginative copying of those who had not enough genius to invent for themselves.

Castelvetro's *Poetica* (1570) rejected the idea that the poet attempts to discover the truths of nature and went so far as to deny any immediate moral aim to poetry. For him, poetry was intended to imitate the deeds of men and bring delight to its audience, since 'poetry was invented in order to please the ignorant crowd and common people, and not to please scholars' – an unusual enough statement in this Horatian, aristocratic age. In this, the first great vernacular commentary to the *Poetics*, Castelvetro did not hesitate to claim that Aristotle's work was little more than a series of notes, which must serve as a point of departure. And depart he did from Aristotle's text in his insistence on the needs of the audience, which came to replace the organic explanation of the work of art. The most famous example is his formulation of the three dramatic unities (formerly regarded by French critics as 'les unités scaligériennes'). The limitations imposed by the 'wooden O' of the stage, but even more by the audience's lack of imagination, called for unity of place, which excluded any change of scene, while the physical impossibility of sitting still for more than a few hours, together with the same lack of imagination, led to the restrictions imposed by the unity of time. Aristotle's only specific, and essential, requirement – unity of action – is of course mentioned, but merely as a desirable addition dependent on the other two, a mere ornament offering proof of the playwright's skill. Robortello, in 1548, had already restricted dramatic action to twelve hours, for he pointed out that people only sleep at night. This was bettered by Segni (1549), who insisted on allowing the dramatist twenty-four hours, because actions fit for tragedy – such as adultery and murder – are far more likely to take place at night, especially since wicked people will act contrary to the laws of nature. This constant search for verisimilitude led Scaliger (1561) to object to frequent shifts in space, as they were now impossible in the time allowed. It was, however, left to Castelvetro to take things to their logical conclusion and to define the three unities as they came to be understood at the time of the *Cid* controversy in France (1636) and to go so far as to suggest that even the epic would be better off for observing such limitations.

Another difficult point of Aristotelian exegesis was tackled by Castelvetro in his explanation of the notorious 'catharsis'. This purgation through the spectacle of tragedy had been explained with a greater or lesser dose of morality implied: for example, by Giraldi (1543), who asserted that in tragedy wicked men are found in such pitiable and terrible situations that the spectators are driven to avoid their vices, while Robortello (1548) formulated a homoeopathic explanation, whereby terror and pity are purged through the sight of these very same passions, and, by accustoming themselves to the tribulations of others, men are the better prepared for similar suffering. Castelvetro, on the other hand, explained catharsis as Aristotle's counter-attack against Plato's exclusion of poets from his republic on grounds of immorality: purgation is, in any case, a side-effect, even an 'oblique pleasure', and the playwright's sole concern must be to please his audience, which may of course delight in watching punishment meted out to the wicked and reward to the good.

One of the interesting aspects of the age is the interplay between practical and theoretical criticism. An outstanding example is the debate over the relative worth of ARIOSTO (1474–1533) and TORCEUATO TASSO (1544–95), whose works came to be judged by Aristotelian criteria. First, Ariosto was attacked for his apparent lack of unity and doubtful morality in the *Furioso*. His defenders claimed that the poem belonged to a genre which must not be judged by Aristotle's precepts, since it had been unknown to the Greek critic; and the poem's tremendous popularity was no mean guarantee of artistic merit. His opponents asserted the validity of the eternal laws of art, discovered in ancient times and from which there could be no departure. The debate became intense after the publication of the complete *Liberata* in 1581, and in 1585 the Accademia della Crusca published its *Difesa dell'Orlando Furioso*, which declared that the poet must invent his material and not follow history, keeping in mind pleasure as the chief goal of poetry. The two Tassos – *père et fils* – were consequently rated inferior to both Pulci and Boiardo, and the *Liberata* attacked as unoriginal and pretentious.

Tasso's *Apologia* of the same year sets out to refute these charges and is complementary to his *Discorsi dell'arte poetica* (published 1587, though written *c.* 1565). The latter is the first attempt to reconcile the strict form of the neo-Aristotelian epic with the popular appeal of the romance. Tasso points out that there are two types of unity in nature: the simple one of chemical elements and the complex unity of living organisms. The epic poet should strive to imitate the latter. As with Aristotle, poetry is an imitation of human actions; its aim is to delight. Yet heroic poetry is made up of both imitation, which produces delight, and allegory, which provides instruction and a justification for poetic licence; thus, allegory, which had been used to excuse the 'lying fables' of the poets in the Middle Ages but then discarded in the Renaissance search for absolute beauty, now returns as a passport for literature in Counter-Reformation Italy. The plot must be historical, founded on truth, since illustrious deeds are unlikely to have escaped the historian's pen. Forestalling the Romantics, Tasso would ban Classical mythology, and the poet must seek inspiration in the history of the one true, Christian religion. In this, he must take care to avoid dogma, as it would place intolerable restrictions on his imagination, even as he must avoid events too near in time, while the history of the remote past is unlikely to interest the modern reader. Tragedy portrays unexpected changes of fortune which compel horror and pity, but the epic inspires admiration for outstanding conduct and character. Characters in tragedy will conform to Aristotle's demands for a mixture of good and evil, whereas in the epic they will go to 'heroic' extremes. Like Manzoni in the nineteenth century, Tasso held that the poet's task was not to 'create', but to choose from the reality that life affords. Art can only add to what is already given by the Creator. It must seek out the natural beauty of the world and express this through the universal (things as they might or should be), drawing its inspiration from history or the particular (things as they actually were). The poet must satisfy the needs of his audience by providing variety and delight, and it is in the need to strike a balance between the claims of truth and poetic licence or adornment that lies the supreme challenge of art. Multiple plots, such as we find in the romance, are excluded, although variety must be provided. The naked truth will be adorned by novelty and surprise, which will increase the sense of wonder inspired in the reader by the use of artifice and illustrious language. And in the role assigned to the marvellous in heroic poetry we find a foretaste of the Baroque obsession with wonder and magnificence: Longinus was being added to Horace and Aristotle.

The last debate of the century began with Giason De Nores's *Discorso* of 1586, in which the critic denounced the bastard genre of tragicomedy and the incongruity of its pastoral setting, as well as its subversive morality. The final section was in fact an attack on the *Pastor fido*, although this immensely successful play is not mentioned by name and it was only published in 1590. Guarini, its author, replied immediately (1586) to the points raised by De Nores. Taking his cue from the debates on Dante and Ariosto, Guarini claimed that Aristotle was not a terminus but a point of departure, and that the taste of an audience is relative. The traditional form of tragedy has become archaic, for pity and fear are well enough catered for by Scripture in Christian times, while a modern audience is disgusted by the sight of too much blood and death. Comedy, moreover, has become corrupt and appeals only to the baser instincts. The new form of tragicomedy, on the other hand, avoids extremes of gravity and levity, as it purges the spectators' minds of melancholy – a far more desirable result than the purging of pity demanded for tragedy by Aristotle. Guarini has acted like a skilful gardener in grafting a new branch on the tree of poetry, just as nature offers us bronze and the mule as examples of completely successful fusion. And Guarini goes on to claim that tragicomedy is not only justifiable but that it is in fact the best dramatic form for modern times: another foretaste of things to come.

FRANCE

The history of criticism in the French Renaissance is inevitably a postscript to that of Italy, but with the great difference that French, probably more than any other language, underwent a kind of totalitarian revolution in the seventeenth century from which it has never fully recovered. Since one of the avowed aims of Malherbe and then of the French Academy (founded by Richelieu in 1635) was to purge language and literature of the alleged excesses inflicted on them by the Pléiade and their successors, the theories of the sixteenth century are not as important as their authors undoubtedly believed. With enthusiasm for reviving Classical standards went a deepseated inferiority complex in the face of Italian cultural achievement, so that most writers felt impelled to defend French against its detractors while advocating imitation of Classical models, and sometimes that of Petrarch. Jacques Peletier du Mans had already given some hint of this in his preface to a French translation of Horace's *Ars Poetica* (1545) and Thomas Sébillet went still further in his *Art poétique* (1548), speaking of the need for inspiration in poetry and recommending among other things use of the sonnet form. It was, however, a largely unoriginal work that made the greatest stir and has ever since enjoyed the highest reputation: the *Defense et Illustration de la langue françoyse* (1549) by Joachim du Bellay, probably assisted by Ronsard, made lavish use of Speroni's recent *Dialogo delle lingue* (1542) while affecting to despise earlier French theoretical works. This book of some seventy-five pages is divided into two sections of twelve chapters each, dealing respectively with the defence of French against charges of inadequacy and then with the means of making it illustrious (*illustration*). There are detailed prescriptions for the various forms of poetry to be practised in French, condemnation of the triviality or aridity of existing French literature, and above all very full proposals for enriching the language by incorporating words from Old French, technical terms (for example, from hunting), from dialects, and, of course, neologisms, based either on existing French words (infinitives for nouns, for example) or coined from Latin and Greek words. Little of this was really original but unlike earlier theorists du Bellay was able triumphantly to justify in practice what he had advocated in theory. In 1565 Ronsard echoed much the same ideas in still more concentrated form in the dozen or so pages of his *Abrégé de l'art poétique françoys*. In view of developments elsewhere it is particularly interesting to find him warning aspirant poets not to follow the language of the court too closely, but rather to prefer dialect words, from whatever region. In the seventeenth century critics of the Pléiade made much of their supposed Hellenization of French, when in fact much of the colour and richness of their vocabulary is of purely native origin. Jean de La Taille's *Art de la tragédie* (1572) is discussed in the section on drama, and deserves a mention here because it too is cogent critical theory written by a gifted practitioner. Finally Henri Estienne's long treatise (240 pages or so) *De la Precellence du langage françoys* (1579) must be mentioned, since it goes vigorously into the attack in seeking to establish the superiority of French over Italian or Latin with a wealth of specific linguistic examples. For readers of Renaissance literature and students of French linguistic history all these documents are of great interest, but the following century nullified much of what they were trying to accomplish.

SPAIN

The first major work of literary criticism to come from a Spaniard in the sixteenth century was Juan de Valdés's *Diálogo de la lengua*, written at Naples about 1535 and considered elsewhere in this volume. It remained unpublished, and the other two principal Spanish literary theorists of the century approached their task with the sense of filling a serious gap in Spanish letters. One was the poet FERNANDO DE HERRERA (*c.* 1534–97), who in 1580 published his *Anotaciones* on the works of Garcilaso, more briefly commented on six years earlier by Francisco Sánchez de las Brozas ('El Brocense'); the other was ALONSO LÓPEZ PINCIANO (1547– after 1627), like Scaliger a doctor, who in 1596 brought out his *Philosophía antigua poética*.

The interest of Herrera's *Anotaciones* arises largely from the fact that they combine three kinds of concern: the scholarly, the patriotic and the literary. Much space is given to identifying rhetorical figures and explaining Classical and other allusions. Sources and parallel passages in other poets are set out in a way that remains helpful to the critic, while philosophical and other terms are elucidated with more interest in the views of Plato and Aristotle than concern with the immediately intended meaning of Garcilaso. But Herrera also includes passionate apologias in the spirit of his *Ode to Lepanto* for the achievements of Spaniards in war and exploration, the creation of an empire and the defence of religion. He is much angered by the contemptuous remarks of Italians, including Bembo, regarding Spanish letters, and the acceptance of these views by Spaniards. He vigorously presses the claims of Spanish as a literary language and seeks to encourage esteem for it. To this end he holds up Garcilaso's achievement and in doing so proposes a stylistic norm for Spanish poets that owes rather more to his own ideas than to Garcilaso's verse. Insisting that poetic composition is a matter of artifice and contriving, he urges a careful selection and ordering of words and figures directed towards creating euphonious and balanced verse where dignity and strength are achieved without stiffness or pomposity and are combined with smoothness and purity of expression without falling into triviality. His highest praise is for Virgil, followed perhaps by Horace. Words in themselves must be used clearly, but obscurity arising from matters treated is to be admired. The extent to which he sees poetic composition as an erudite activity properly engaged in by 'those who know', and his censure of whatever strikes him as moral impropriety in Garcilaso's verse, set him in the neo-Aristotelian tradition of literary theorists. He makes many references to Aristotle and Scaliger, among others. But he also shows a marked independence of judgement. In approving the judicious use by poets of new or imported words, he implicitly departs from the views of Vida and Scaliger and what was to be neo-Classical orthodoxy in stressing that poetic language should not be restricted to the range found in particular 'excellent authors'. He protests against the narrowing or impoverishment of literary language. For this reason, while seeing 'imitation' as a valuable part of poetic composition, he emphasizes that it is not the whole of it. There are new things to be said on old subjects, new effects to be achieved. The Spanish language is alive and flourishing: it is still full of promise and possibilities. His desire is to help others realize these. It perhaps tends to carry him beyond the limits of his own stylistic values.

Herrera discusses modern writers, especially the Italians, whom he much admires, as well as the ancients. Pinciano restricts his comments to the latter. His work is basically a commentary on Aristotle's *Poetics*, and so one finds here a fuller consideration of such topics as *mimesis*, verisimilitude and 'admiration' (or wonderment) than Herrera provides. At numerous points Pinciano follows Scaliger. However, his own work lacks the latter's dogmatic character, being in the form of thirteen reported conversations between Pinciano and two friends. He also draws on other modern theorists. His treatment of comedy owes much to Maggi's *De ridiculis*, while he derives many of his views regarding the epic from Torquato Tasso's *Discorsi dell'arte poetica*. His studies of these two latter forms of writing are particularly valuable to read in relation to *Don Quixote*.

THREE

Fine Arts

BY the year 1500, Italian supremacy was assured in all the arts, except music. Strangely enough for later generations that were to regard Italy as the land of *bel canto*, the musical scene was dominated by the Flemish school; and, as Castiglione rightly complained, a composition's success could only be guaranteed if it was ascribed to JOSQUIN DES PRÉS (*c.* 1450–1521). Josquin brought the medieval polyphonic tradition to perfection by treating the different parts as simultaneous elements in the overall effect of grand melodic line and choral sonority. With the Reformation and subsequent strife many musicians lost their livelihood and sought greater security abroad, where Flemish composers influenced the whole evolution of European music. In 1501, the first musical press was established in Italy and rapid expansion in publishing encouraged the interest in music that was a general feature of court life in Renaissance Italy. In 1527, Adriaen Willaert founded the famous Venetian school of music, which trained scores of Italian musicians and achieved such renown that in 1581 the Venetians could boast that music had 'its very home' in their city. Such a development helps to explain an interesting detail in Veronese's great picture *The Marriage at Cana* (1563), where a group of musicians in the foreground shows us Titian playing the string bass, Bassano the flute, and Tintoretto and Veronese himself the viol. In church music, GIOVANNI PIERLUIGI DA PALESTRINA (1525–94), himself a pupil of a Flemish musician, reigned supreme throughout the latter half of the century, despite considerable opposition aroused during the Counter-Reformation against the complexities of modern music, which tended to obscure the words of the sacred text and arouse 'lascivious, impure' thoughts in the faithful. In Protestant countries, the attitude varied: there was little patronage for professional musicians, although hymn singing was passionately encouraged by Luther and psalms were accepted by Calvin, who otherwise banned the use of musical instruments in church. As the century progressed, the most significant developments took place in Italy, particularly in the sphere of profane music. The humanists had sought to revive the marriage between music and drama practised in ancient times. Gradually, therefore, the intricate compositions of the Flemish tradition were combined with the characteristic approach of Italian Renaissance artists: a quest for harmony in all things. By the end of the century, some Florentine musicians set about recreating musical drama and thus created modern opera. This unique combination of visual effects and subtle harmonies, which accompanied and heightened the impact of dramatic events enacted on the stage, had an instant and overwhelming success: only ten years separate the earliest opera (*Dafne* by Peri and Rinuccini, 1597) from Monteverdi's masterpiece, *Orfeo*. As a synthesis of the arts, the new form could not fail to appeal to the succeeding age in Italy and France, where the *ballets de cour* and general court festivities organized by Catherine de' Medici (including one to celebrate the Massacre of St Bartholomew) had prepared the way for the theatricality and grandeur of seventeenth-century music and the gradual shift from the supremacy of painting at the time of the High Renaissance to the superb achievements in architecture and music during the age of the Baroque.

The history of the visual arts in Western Europe during the sixteenth century is largely dependent on the development of these arts in Italy and their influence abroad. By the end of the preceding century, the Italians had tackled and overcome the major technical problems in Renaissance art: the adaptation of the Classical orders and symmetry to modern architecture; the use of perspective and harmonious composition in painting. It remained for the artists of the High Renaissance to consolidate these achievements and to produce masterpieces that have influenced European art down to our own day. The control they exercised over their media and the sense of balance they succeeded in imposing on their subjects have rarely been equalled and never surpassed.

The first name is that of LEONARDO DA VINCI (1452–1519). His portrait of Mona Lisa, the wife of Francesco del Giocondo, is a turning-point in the art of representing the individual, and it is difficult for us to realize that at the time of the Renaissance the art of portraiture was considered inferior to other types of painting. Gone are the harsh outlines: Leonardo's *sfumato* technique seems particularly suited to the representation of this womanly beauty, with its idealization and individuality combined in the background as hauntingly as in the subject herself – her eyes reflecting the artist's belief that the 'eye is the window of the soul', her hands creating a calm dignity in their reflexion of the landscape's transversals and offering a perfect foil to the smile that has haunted generations of bemused admirers. Leonardo's other revolutionary work is his *Last Supper*, painted in Milan (1495–7). Unfortunately, the artist used tempera on a wall surface; the result was disastrous, and what we have left must be numbered, as Malraux has pointed out, among the glorious ruins of man's achievements. It is, however, possible to reconstruct the effect it had on contemporaries. We need only compare its portrayal of the famous scene with that by Ghirlandaio, finished in 1480, just before Leonardo left Florence. Ghirlandaio's fresco shows a fine handling in the traditional manner: the eleven apostles are seated on either side of Our Lord (with St John apparently asleep, his head resting in front of Christ, so as not to disturb the symmetry, which is echoed in the stiff folds of the tablecloth), while Judas – on the other side, already deprived of a halo – is immediately identifiable to the spectator, who can allow his gaze to wander towards such charming distractions as the cat on the floor or the peacock splendidly perched on a side window. If we now turn to Leonardo's fresco, we see with what power the artist has continued the atmosphere of the monks' refectory where it was painted and where their daily bread was eaten. Leonardo's power is not drawn from mere realism, or illusionism. He has placed his whole genius in seizing the dramatic moment after Christ's revelation that one of his companions will betray him: amazement and disbelief are shown in the expressions and movements of the apostles, heightened by the static figure of Christ that is framed by the light pouring in from the window behind. There are no distractions. As in St John's account, Peter moves forward to get John to find out the traitor's name. Here, John is on Christ's side – and so is Judas, who is thus made to form the triangle Peter–John–Judas, for the apostles have been grouped into threes so as to concentrate the spectator's gaze on blocks of actors, instead of the traditional dispersal two-by-two. Judas alone does not make a gesture to speak; his is the only face bathed in shadow. Even without the religious drama, the work is a miracle of composition over which the eye may roam endlessly in search of one of the mysteries of human art. Bandello (in *novella* I, 58) describes how the painter would wait for the right moment of inspiration – not 'romantic frenzy', but the need to set down line or tone based on meditation and practice. Leonardo reacted against the Florentine tradition of theoretical study and the application of mathematics to drawing and painting. Useful as they might be, the artist's supreme guide must be the constant observation of nature, as we see from his notebooks with their numberless illustrations of anatomical, botanical and atmospheric phenomena. Experience, for Leonardo, was 'the common mother of all the sciences and arts'. His mind teemed with ideas and inventions. His contemporaries criticized him for his constant change of place and project, but without this nature, we should not have had the creator of aerial perspective in painting and a series of unique, though in many cases unfinished, masterpieces. His character came to be accepted as one of the consequences of genius. Formerly, artists had had to work to rule; they were regarded as talented craftsmen. Now, popes and princes began to realize that they must bear with the occasional eccentricities of genius – and artists such as Leonardo and Michelangelo drove the message home. They insisted on having painting, sculpture and architecture included among the liberal arts, so called because in antiquity they were practised by free men, while the humbler, mechanical arts were carried out by slaves. Leonardo also helped to kindle the discussions on the supremacy of the various arts, which continued throughout the century. Painting is superior to poetry, he claimed, because it is more real, more effective in its impact. The painter is not limited by his material like the sculptor or architect, but can create a multitude of objects and scenes and arouse every kind of emotion. In this, he possesses a divine power comparable to that of the Creator himself. The famous story of the Emperor Charles V stooping to pick up Titian's brush as a homage to this god-given quality may or may not be true. What is sure is that the King of France, François I, took the dying Leonardo in his arms in an attempt to soothe the old man's agony – something inconceivable before Leonardo's time and which illustrates the utterly different role and prestige accorded to the artist in Renaissance society.

MICHELANGELO BUONARROTI (1475–1564) acquired the epithet 'divine' during his long lifetime. His great inspiration was the human body, its beauty and power of movement. This is already clear in the descriptions we have of the battle scene he was commissioned to portray in competition with Leonardo (1504). Unfortunately, neither work remains. Michelangelo's project never got beyond the cartoon, and even that has been lost. Yet in this and subsequent works we find the language of Alberti and fifteenth-century humanism proudly expressed in Michelangelo's admiration for man's beauty. The artist, encouraged by Florentine neo-Platonism, never forgot that man was created in God's image: it was this belief that inspired the master-pieces in the series painted on the ceiling of the Sistine Chapel from 1508 to 1512. Michelangelo divided the ceiling into nine panels illustrating the story of man, from the creation to the drunkenness of Noah. The chronology is inverted, however, for as we enter the chapel we see, immediately above our heads, the figure of Noah and the degradation of the human body. The scenes were in fact painted in this order, and they increase in size and majesty until, with the Temptation in Eden, Michelangelo reaches the heroic scale that inspired the central episode of the Creation of Man and the scene above the altar, where the Creator divides light from the darkness. The whole epic of God's grandeur and Man's nobility and degradation is here expressed in terms that have remained unique. Behind the altar, however, is the only work that could match such a ceiling: the *Last Judgement*, painted between 1536 and 1541. In the quarter of a century that separates the two works, the artist had seen the confident belief in the perfectibility of man, the optimism of the High Renais-sance, torn to shreds. He had lived through years that had witnessed the Protestant revolt and the Sack of Rome; now, attracted by the moderate party of reform, his spirit was oppressed. The contrast with the ceiling is striking. On the latter, we find harmonious forms and pleasing colour. The *Last Judgement* presents us with a terrifying vision of sombre colour and anguished form. The saints lust for vengeance; Christ raises his right hand, hurling a swirling mass of figures to their doom, while, above the *Deus irae*, angels struggle to bear the burden of the cross and instruments of his passion. The influence of this epic vision has been incalculable. And yet, the *Last Judgement* in many ways rejects the canons of High Renaissance art with its neglect of natural proportion and its exclusion of mundane reality. The human figure is here twisted into a mass of shapes, obviously approaching the Mannerist obsession with the S-shaped body (*figura serpentina*). It is what other artists failed to accomplish during the sixteenth century: a truly colossal achievement. And while observing both master-pieces, we may be struck by the force of Goethe's remark: 'Unless you have seen the Sistine Chapel, you can have no idea of what one man is capable of achieving.' Soon, however, Paul IV (1555–59) was to command Daniele da Volterra to paint some draperies over certain parts of the painting which offended the new sense of de-corum; indeed, even before its completion, the master of ceremonies to Paul III complained about the indecent display of nudity above the papal altar – though this time the artist was able to get his revenge by depicting his critic as the infernal Minos – and later popes (Pius IV, Clement XIII) were similarly shocked by this temple to Renaissance art and its religious vision.

Just as Michelangelo created the popular image of God the Father on the Sistine ceiling, so the ideal figure of the Virgin was produced by RAPHAEL OF URBINO (1483–1520) during his stay in Florence. The *summa* of Renaissance painting was, however, achieved in the decoration of the Vatican *Stanze*, only a few yards away from Michelangelo's ceiling. Raphael, for long considered the supreme master, has tended to be dismissed for his sweetness and light in our search for primitive purity (the pre-Raphaelites) and, more recently, our need for terror and violence. It is perhaps difficult for us to realize the full extent of the incredible feat accomplished by this young man of twenty-six, who produced a Mozartian wealth of beauty in ten years of his brief life. The decoration of these interconnecting rooms in the Vatican was commissioned by Julius II with unusual breadth of vision and daring, for he entrusted the whole project to a young artist with practically no experience of mural painting. The first room – the Stanza della Segnatura (1509–12) – was decorated by Raphael while Michelangelo was engaged on his herculean task in the near-by chapel; and the work continued under Leo X (1513–21), when Raphael finished the Stanza d'Eliodoro and the Stanza dell'Incendio with the help of pupils. The latter extol the greatness of the Church and the papacy, while the Sala di Costantino (decorated after Raphael's death) describes the elevation of Christianity to the status of a uni-versal religion. It is, however, the first room that has attracted most attention in its pictorial rendering of the Renaissance's thirst for universal knowledge and its ideal synthesis. The walls of the Stanza della Segnatura show us the various ways in which man strives after truth: theology, justice, intellect and inspiration. The most famous of these gigantic undertakings is the *School of Athens*, the epitome of Renaissance aspirations and intellectual harmony. Beneath the majestic sweep of what is evidently Bramante's new architecture, we see two groups to the right and left of the central figures: Plato with hand outstretched towards the heaven of his ideal world; and Aristotle, pointing towards the reality of the visible world – the one characterized by the *Timaeus*, the other by his *Ethics*. The glorious composition reflects the quintessence of Renaissance humanism, with its celebration of Classical antiquity. In the right foreground we find the Geometer, Euclid, portrayed with the features of Raphael's master, Bramante, surrounded by the painter himself and Leonardo. Nearer to Plato are those who depended more strongly on emotion and intuition, gradually leading us to *Parnassus*, where poets and musicians exemplify the Platonic concept that divine inspiration has its essential part to play in human society. The painter's contemporaries, Tebaldeo and Sannazaro, accompany the great poets of antiquity, and the ideals of Christian humanism are here converted into a visual language unique in its serenity and dignity. An equally poetic approach to antiquity is evident in Raphael's fresco *Galatea* (1514), painted in the Villa Farnesina for his patron, the banker Agostino Chigi, and in scenes of *Cupid and Psyche* (begun 1518), which he was unable to complete because of his death in April 1520, some five days before that of his patron, to whom Renaissance art owed so much. In this same villa, this modern Maecenas had had his bedroom decorated by Sodoma (*The Wedding of Alexander and Roxana*), while the Galatea room contains Peruzzi's ceiling with its monumental horoscope showing the heavens on the day of Chigi's birth, and others were decorated by the same artist with friezes displaying the loves of the gods. In a different context, we owe to Chigi's munificence his family chapel in Santa Maria del Popolo and the frescoes of prophets and Sibyls in Sant' Agostino, both tasks entrusted to Raphael during the artist's stay in Rome. Whereas Raphael's treatment of historical and mythological subjects tended to open up new possibilities and his portrait of Castiglione illustrated the ideal of Renaissance nobility, the set of tapestries he designed for the Sistine Chapel, describing various episodes in the lives of the apostles, set a rigid type of religious grandeur that was to be copied *ad nauseam* and gradually petrified into academic art and sugar-icing religiosity.

By 1527, however, both Bramante and Raphael were dead, the High Renaissance was over, and the Reformation and the Sack of Rome left little money or energy for artistic patronage or the study and excavation of Classical antiquity. The latter activity, for some years supervised by Raphael himself, had yielded such treasures as the Laocoön group (1506) and the Apollo Belvedere. It is not difficult to imagine the excitement and sense of discovery caused by such finds: a true 'rebirth' of the arts, encouraged by Machiavelli's warrior pope, Julius II, who obtained both relics for the Vatican.

We must now cast a glance at other Italian cities, including the provincial town of Parma and the proud metropolis of Venice. ANTONIO CORREGGIO (*c.* 1489–1534) was undoubtedly influenced by Leonardo and ANDREA MANTEGNA (1431–1506). Fascinated by light effects, he soon exploited Leonardo's *chiaroscuro* to produce paintings which delight the eye and impel it along new lines. Adopting the technique of illusionism used by Mantegna in the Camera degli Sposi at Mantua, Correggio began that long series of church cupolas in which the spectator below is afforded the illusion of looking into a host of sunlit clouds towards the open vault of heaven. The decoration of San Giovanni Evangelista at Parma (1520–24) is a clear pointer towards the art of the seventeenth century, whereby the spectator feels himself drawn up into the very Ascension of Christ and another actor in the chorus formed by the foreshortened forms of the apostles, which emphasize the spherical rhythm of the whole composition. The vision shimmers in a light almost too delicate for the church's dark interior, but the mauve silhouettes and silvery-pearl clouds create a pleasing celestial drama, which becomes even more dynamic in the dome of the cathedral (1526–30) with the dazzling swirl of the *Assumption of the Virgin*. Like so many of his contemporaries at the beginning of the nineteenth century, Stendhal gave this art his unqualified admiration: 'Correggio combined forms more grandiose than Raphael's with a suavity and tenderness that no painter before him had achieved. He frankly wished to charm in every possible way' – something that is only too damning nowadays, but which achieved its aim in the sixteenth century and for a long time to come.

Such perfection and charm as we have seen in the masters of the High Renaissance were bound to produce a reaction, which was hastened by the collapse of the traditional religious and economic order. Unable to compete with the supreme achievements of Raphael and Michelangelo, artists turned towards the unexpected, they broke up order and symmetry in an attempt to do something different, to amaze their patrons and astonish their audiences, but also impelled by a new spiritual and intellectual order, which was the prelude to the Counter-Reformation. Michelangelo himself disapproved of the importance attributed to rules in painting, and he explicitly condemned Dürer's treatment of the human body as being too rigid. It was in fact the imitation of Michelangelo's later style or manner as well as such seminal works as Raphael's *Saint Michael* (1517–18), that encouraged the movement of 'Mannerism', which has been used to describe those artists who turned away from the High Renaissance's attempt to construct an ideal reality, based on order and harmony. Instead, they sought novel sensations in line and colour; and, from Michelangelo, we find a concentration on the nude with exaggerated muscles and artificial poses, frequently distorted by extremes of scale and proportion. Apart from Michelangelo's universal influence, one of the most formative paintings was Pontormo's *Deposition* (*c.* 1526). It shows a surprising use of pink, green, and mauve (partly due to the poor lighting in Santa Felicità, Florence), but its most striking feature is its crowded use of figures in twisted shapes, with exaggerated gestures and pathetic expressions, dominated by the *figura serpentina* of the dead Christ, whose outline is complemented by the elongated gesture of the Virgin's right arm and the unnatural twist in the female saint peering down from behind the Virgin and who is herself balanced by a wisp of equally unnatural cloud. As in the panel *Joseph in Egypt* (1515–18), the artist no longer wishes to respect the laws of symmetry and perspective or to approach his subject in an orderly, rational manner. GIOVANNI BATTISTA ROSSO (1495–1540) was the other creator of Florentine Mannerism. His altarpiece for the Hospital at Santa Maria Nuova (1518) so shocked its commissioners that they declared Rosso's saints to be devils because of their wild appearance. A similar effect is obtained in the *Descent from the Cross* at Volterra (1521), where the lighting and lines are used to one end: to create a sense of shock before the livid green body of Christ hanging limply from the cross. Everywhere, we find a neurotic obsession with the emotional impact of the scene portrayed.

Rosso was influenced by Michelangelo in Rome; so was GIULIO ROMANO (c. 1499–1546), a pupil of Raphael, who carried out the decoration of the Sala di Costantino after his master's death and then began the Palazzo del Tè at Mantua for Federigo Gonzaga (1524). Pagan eroticism characterizes his frescoes on the north side, around the Sala di Psiche, while those on the south side celebrate other favourite themes of the later Baroque: triumph, majesty and power. Of the latter series, the decorations in the Sala dei Giganti are the most famous. The room is dimly lit, to exaggerate the violent effect of the illusionist paintings. Jove, surrounded by the frightened inhabitants of Olympus, annihilates the *hybris* of the giants, who die beneath the weight of rocks and temples shattering all about them. A ruined fireplace was placed so that the flames leaped up towards the scene where the Cyclops lie crushed under Etna, adding a final touch to this temple of Mannerist art.

FRANCESCO PARMIGIANINO (1503–40) shows us the other side of Mannerism: its sensual elegance obtained, like Rosso's violence and eroticism, through distortion and tricks of perspective. Parmigianino became more neurotic with the passage of time, but his stay in Rome (1523–8) brought him under the spell of Raphael, after the formative influence of Correggio at Parma. His *Madonna dal collo lungo* (c. 1535) is another landmark in Mannerist painting. We find a Raphaelesque, but strongly elongated Madonna in the very centre of the picture. Her immense vertical is cut by the extraordinarily lengthened body of the child, and paralleled by the impossibly tall leg of the angel standing beside her. The whole of this left half and centre of the picture are in complete contrast with the right background, where a minute human figure is added against all the laws of perspective, with the sole purpose of striking a graceful poise beside the obviously artificial column. Everything is subordinated to the needs of elegant sophistication and grace, a prime requisite in Vasari's theory of painting and in many of the Italian Mannerists. Parmigianino's sophistication and glacial tones created a new atmosphere of luxury and grace, which was quickly taken up by painters in France, especially in the portrayal of feminine beauty. His influence in France was combined with that of AGNOLO BRONZINO (1503–72), who became court painter to Cosimo I, Duke of Florence. It was for Cosimo's wife, Eleonora of Toledo, that he decorated the chapel in the Palazzo Vecchio with frescoes displaying many of the attributes of Mannerist paintings: fantastic colours, weird foreshortenings, exaggerated musculature, and a certain type of frigid beauty. By now Florence and the whole of southern Italy had become a Spanish apanage, and the change is well marked in Bronzino's portraits of Eleonora and Don Garcia de' Medici, which open the way for the vapid personalities and rigid etiquette of the seventeenth-century Spanish court depicted with such mastery by Velazquez. Many of the Italian portraits were done as miniatures: twenty-four by Bronzino were in the Palazzo Vecchio and Catherine de' Medici left a collection of more than 300. They are just as typical of Mannerist taste as the gigantic frescoes by Rosso: the love of extremes.

One Italian state remained an exception to the general transformation: the Republic of Venice, which maintained a proud independence, although its days as an economic power were numbered. At the beginning of the century, GIORGIONE (*c.* 1477–1510) showed, even more clearly than Leonardo, that colour may create its own form. Colour was all-important in Venice, both in its buildings shimmering in the intense light reflected off the water and in the splendid creations of its painters. Giorgione's work remains a mystery. But there is nothing mysterious about the demonic energy and genius of TITIAN (*c.* 1477–1576). The famous *Madonna with Saints and Members of the Pesaro Family* (1519–26) breaks up the composition in a daring manner, with the figure of the Virgin raised up from the centre and the symmetry dependent on two columns that rise up out of the picture; yet it is always Titian's colour that gives unity to whatever scene he chooses to represent. It would be an impossible task merely to enumerate them – religious, mythological, biblical, and, above all, his superb portraits. Titian was never influenced by the quirks and foibles of the Mannerists. But by the creation of dazzling feasts for the eye, images that radiate brightness and vitality, he painted his own way towards Baroque illuminism, so that Vasari, while aware of the power of Titian's art, was quite incapable of appreciating the Venetian's use of colour and the 'impressionism' of his second manner.

Two other painters kept to the forefront of the Venetian scene. One was PAOLO VERONESE (1528–88), whose last work (*The Triumph of Venice*, commissioned 1578) sums up his life's achievement: the grandeur and opulence of sixteenth-century Venice. At the time of his arrival in the city (1553) he worked on the ceiling of the Sala dei Dieci in the Doge's Palace, and then went on to provide Venetian society with the religious subjects and profane décor it desired. Veronese was well suited to appreciate the way of life of the Venetian aristocracy, which he helped to enhance by his decorations at the Villa Barbaro (Maser), designed by Palladio. Although his style never developed, it never fell below its magnificent rendering of Venetian luxury, which is well reflected in the wealth of harmonious colour he gave to the world. And as Boschini pointed out, we may 'count up all the touches of his brush as if they were so many pearls, sapphires, emeralds, all the most precious jewels of the Orient.' Veronese's contemporary JACOPO TINTORETTO (1518–94) was far from possessing the same seignorial manner. For him Titian's pictures were sumptuous, but not sufficiently dramatic to make his subjects live for us through the empathy he sought to create in the spectator. In his attempts to achieve this aim, Tintoretto may be considered the greatest Italian Mannerist painter. The difference between the two artists is well illustrated in their version of *The Presentation of the Virgin in the Temple*: Titian's painting is a closed composition, framed by the ceiling and horizontal lines in the foreground; Tintoretto's picture, on the other hand, revolves around the dynamic gesture of the woman in the foreground – pointing towards the same obelisk found in Titian's static scene – and the impossible spiral movement of the temple steps, leading up to the towering elongated figure of the High Priest in the centre, while the spectator's eye moves on into the distance, impelled by the trajectory of the woman's arm. Both artists have given us dramatic renderings of the *Entombment*; but in Tintoretto's composition we are seized by the forceful diagonal lines that sweep across, while the colours are more intense and passionate and the whole group is turned at an angle to the plane of the picture, catching the eye and moving it in various directions, as opposed to the horizontal sweep of Titian's painting. Tintoretto's *Miracle of St Mark* was hailed as a masterpiece when it was finished in 1548: the figure of the saint plunging to rescue a slave is a miracle of foreshortening and the colour astonishes by its brilliance. Tintoretto had succeeded in combining Michelangelo's draughtsmanship with Titian's use of colour. He went on to equal Veronese's magnificence in *Susanna and the Elders* (c. 1560). But his most typical style was created by his speed: stresses of light and shade build up form and movement, so that even Aretino, who admired his lifelike effects, condemned his slapdash brushwork – the very means necessary to create such works 'less like painting than life itself'. In the same way, Vasari, amazed by the painter's inventive powers, thought he knew little about drawing. In 1562, Tintoretto returned to the Scuola di San Marco and painted three miracles attributed to Venice's patron saint. *The Finding of the Body of St Mark* presents us with an apparently confused scene and a long recession of silvery arches. The only figure in truly 'Venetian' colour is that of the saint in the left foreground, who raises his arm – in a receding plane – to stop the shadowy figures searching for his mortal remains. A corpse lies in vivid foreshortening at the feet of the saint. We realize that, in typical Mannerist style, the scene has been 'frozen' as though by a high-speed camera exposure. The corpse in ghostly foreshortening is, of course, that of St Mark, wrested from the infidels by the Venetians at Alexandria; and as a reward for this virtuous enterprise the saint has delivered the man on the right who had been possessed by a demon. The donor, in Venetian robes, kneels down in gratitude; and such is the perspective of the whole composition that he seems to be at its centre, whereas he is in fact at the apex of the triangle in the foreground pointing towards the strange figures silhouetted against the tiny patch of light in the depths of the vault. Tintoretto had succeeded in building up the most dramatic portrayal of a morbid hagiographical subject. The following year, he won a competition by his incredible speed of execution, putting up his full-size picture while his rivals submitted their sketches. In the cycle at the Scuola di San Rocco, Tintoretto used the full range of his dramatic genius to portray biblical subjects, of which the most famous are *Christ before Pilate*, where contrast between light and shade had never been put to greater effect, and the *Way to Golgotha*, where the Z-road to Calvary is a mass of seething diagonals, horses and bystanders, all preparing the way for the drama of Christ's passion. The last of Tintoretto's versions of the *Last Supper* (1592–4), painted some five years after the San Rocco cycle, shows an immensely long table, whose diagonal separates the sacred from the profane. The elongation, the turning figures, the swirling of the angels, the chatter of the apostles, the use of artificial lighting – all illustrate the change that had overtaken Italian painting since Leonardo's celebrated treatment of the same theme.

*

Vasari, in 1550, mentions some thirty-two architects: of these, no less than twenty-one were experts in other fields of art. Similarly, in the fifteenth century, such pioneers as FILIPPO BRUNELLESCHI (1379–1446) and LEON BATTISTA ALBERTI (1404–72) had built up theory and practice in architecture on an understanding of the needs and aims of allied arts and crafts. Despite the prestige of ancient architecture, epitomized in Vitruvius' monumental treatise, the authority of the ancients was never absolute. Alberti, for example, used Classical pilasters to unite the alternation of narrow walls and large openings at Sant'Andrea in Mantua; and this un-Roman pattern was to have an immense influence on the development of Renaissance architecture. On the façade of the Palazzo Rucellai in Florence, Alberti adapted the Classical orders (Doric, Ionic, Corinthian) by using a single order for each storey. This new sense of freedom was not only due to the judicious imitation of antiquity. It was also made possible by the fact that structural needs were no longer supreme, while architects were inspired, like Alberti himself, by an ideal of beauty which consisted in 'a certain regular harmony of all the parts' where 'nothing could be added or taken away or altered without making it less pleasing.' Buildings were erected as a celebration of man's god-like creative power, and Brunelleschi's great dome over Florence Cathedral told his contemporaries that nothing was impossible to man's genius. It was in fact the treatment of the dome that marked one of the greatest changes in Renaissance church architecture. With the example of the Pantheon and Byzantine churches before them, architects of the sixteenth century learned to create a new relationship between the drum and the dome, which prolonged the vertical elements of the façade, as we find in Bramante's Tempietto at Rome (1502–10). The architect also acquired a new status: from now on, he was able to direct or adapt fashion and impose a new appearance on the great cities of Europe. Horizontal forms and the universal search for harmony helped to achieve this and to empty the streets of medieval towns of their stagnant air and relate everything to human comfort. From the heavenward thrust of the Gothic spire, architects turned to buildings and ornaments that were related in neo-Platonic terms to the human body. This was most evident in the Classical column with its anthropometric divisions, and by using the diameter of the column as the basic element of harmonious design architects now fused the details as an integral part of the whole. The centralized church with its circular dome bore witness to the perfection of the circle and its representation of divine infinity, although the Greek and Latin crosses continued to be used. The most famous church of the sixteenth century is of course St Peter's in Rome. It is impossible to describe in detail its evolution from 1506 to 1626. In 1513, Bramante was replaced by three other architects, including his pupil Raphael. After the latter's death, the main work was carried out by Antonio da Sangallo. But in 1546, Michelangelo succeeded him at the age of seventy-one and created order out of the existing chaos. Carlo Maderna added the vast façade after Michelangelo's death, and Della Porta gave greater *élan* to Michelangelo's spherical dome, which has remained an object of admiration and wonder to all. Ironically enough, the building of the greatest church in the world helped to bring about the split in Christendom, as it was the selling of indulgences for funds needed for this immense project that encouraged Luther and other reformers to protest against the corruption of Christ's Church.

One of the results of the Reformation was the Sack of Rome in 1527 by the Protestant troops of the Catholic emperor, Charles V. Many artists fled from the stricken city. One who never returned was JACOPO SANSOVINO (1486–1570), a Florentine who took up the appointment of Architect to the Republic of Venice in 1529. His greatest buildings are the Library opposite the Doge's Palace (1536–54), the Mint (La Zecca, 1537–45) and the Loggia at the foot of the famous Campanile in St Mark's Square. He also created the monumental staircase in the great courtyard of the Doge's Palace and built some of the palaces along the Grand Canal (Palazzo Corner, 1532). His masterpiece is the Library, with two superimposed orders (Doric and Ionic) and the most elaborate decoration culminating in a balustrade crowned with statues. In all, Sansovino helped to justify

Philippe de Commines's statement (made at the end of the previous century) that the Grand Canal was 'the most beautiful street in the world'. Venice now had a fitting centre for its great cathedral and seat of government. The aristocracy was equally well served by ANDREA PALLADIO (1508–80), who provided the noble families of Venice with elegant country villas (for example, the Villa Rotonda and Villa Barbaro, the latter with Veronese's famous decorations). Raised on a base and using a temple front, such villas blended harmoniously with the surrounding landscape, while their interiors offered a symmetrical plan based on the harmonies of the musical scale, with rooms leading off from the central axis of a domed circular hall. Palladio's *villa rustica* returned to an Albertian conception of architecture, which set the model for family mansions in eighteenth-century England, while his last project – the Teatro Olimpico at Vicenza begun in 1580 and finished by Scamozzi – was to be just as influential as far as European theatre design was concerned. It was thanks to the humanist Trissino that Palladio studied in Rome (1545–7) and that on his return to Vicenza he was commissioned to build the Palazzo della Ragione in Vicenza (1549); it was even Trissino who gave him the name (derived from the ancient goddess of wisdom) that was to become world-famous. In the Palazzo della Ragione, Palladio was faced with the same problem as Alberti at Rimini: how to make the shell of an old medieval building conform to the laws of modern architectural style, based on a study of antiquity. Now, at the beginning of his career, he introduced the 'Palladian' motif: a triple opening made up of an arcade supported on two columns and flanked on either side by a rectangular opening, taken from Serlio and similar to the window arrangements in Sansovino's Library at Venice. The total effect is a remarkable sense of rhythm marked by the bold sequence of light and dark forms. Later buildings reveal a Mannerist tendency towards complex detail and even the deliberate confusion of elements from the Classical orders (Loggia del Capitano, 1571). More interesting, however, is the way in which Palladio tackled another central problem in his Venetian churches: the adaptation of the antique temple plan to the requirements and traditions of a Christian church. He found his solution by interlocking two orders: the smaller one of the aisles, with the massive order corresponding to the height of the nave. His masterpiece is the façade of San Giorgio Maggiore (1556), where he projected and raised the pediment on tall Corinthian columns on high bases, and united the whole church front by emphasizing the strong horizontal base of the lower pediment extending over the aisles. The same formula was successfully repeated in the more modest Franciscan church, Il Redentore, begun some ten years later. In 1570, Palladio published his *Quattro libri dell'architettura*, one of the most influential treatises on architecture: the first book expounds general principles, based on Vitruvius; the second deals with houses; the third with towns; the last with temples. Throughout, the author attempts to blend knowledge, particularly what he has gleaned from a study of ancient theory and practice, with individual style, requirements and good taste.

The epitome of Mannerist architecture is Giulio Romano's Palazzo del Tè at Mantua, built from 1526 to 1531 as a summer villa for Federigo Gonzaga. As opposed to Palladio's *villa rustica*, where elegance and restraint were married to utility, this exercise in flamboyance was based on the Classical *villa suburbana* and its chief purpose was to be used for court festivities. Built as a single storey round a square court, nothing could be more different than its façade and garden front. The former is squat and rusticated, with massive keystones and misused Classical details, while the garden front develops what was to become the Palladian motif. Dramatic tension is built up by the exaggerated width and violent contrasts, increased by the use of colour and the juxtaposition of heavy blocks of stone and graceful columns. Giulio's own house in Mantua (*c.* 1544) shows a similar perverse delight in contrast between plain and rough surfaces, graceful column forms and 'fortified' walls, simple Doric entablatures borne on richly decorated columns. For Serlio, the Palazzo del Tè was a 'veritable model of architecture and painting of our times' and numberless contemporaries fell under its bizarre spell.

Written before Palladio's *Quattro libri*, Vignola's *Regole delli cinque ordini d'architettura* (1562) became a manual for all aspiring architects and their patrons. JACOPO BAROZZI DA VIGNOLA (1507–73) went to work on the Villa Giulia in Rome with Vasari and Della Porta, in 1554. After this training in Mannerist architecture, he studied the ancient ruins and returned to a more austere style, based in part on Alberti's interpretation of antiquity. His reaction against Mannerism harmonized with general trends in post-Tridentine architecture and is summed up in his most famous work: the mother church of the new Jesuit Order, Il Gesù, began in 1568 but finished after his death. As had become the custom, the Jesuits specified their requirements with little regard for artistic freedom: they wanted a church with a single vaulted nave, in which everything must be subordinate to the acoustics necessary for effective preaching. Vignola modified the plan drawn up in 1470 by Alberti for Sant' Andrea at Mantua: an aisleless building with deep side chapels, leading to a transept proportioned to the wide crossing beneath the dome, with an apse behind the main altar. The domed crossing is a blaze of light and directs attention to the high altar. Otherwise, however, little of Vignola's original design remains, for his restrained interior was exuberantly decorated in the seventeenth century, and when he died in 1573 Giacomo Della Porta took over work on the façade, altering Vignola's simple plan by the use of two pediments forced one inside the other and with Albertian volutes on the sides. Il Gesù, the main church of the most militant Order, was extremely influential, for most Jesuit churches followed its basic plan in their great expansion throughout Europe and the Americas.

*

Sixteenth-century European sculpture is dominated by one name: Michelangelo. During the Renaissance, sculpture gradually broke away from its essential church setting. Donatello produced the first bronze equestrian statue since Roman times at Padua (1444–7). Then, in 1502–4, Michelangelo produced his *David*, one of the greatest expressions of High Renaissance art and a paean to youth, the proud spirit of independence, self-confidence, and the dignity of man. Only a quarter of a century separates this heroic figure from Verrocchio's statue of the elegant youth; but Michelangelo's creation represents the full realization of ideal beauty exemplified in the human body. The full range of Michelangelo's vision is best seen in the *pietà* groups, which start with the polished perfection of the version in St Peter's (1499) and end with the stricken power and pathos of the unfinished Rondanini *Pietà* (1555–64). It is, however, in one of the statues intended for the grandiose project of Julius II's tomb that we can best understand Michelangelo's approach to sculpture: one of the two 'Slaves', the one still encased in the rough block of marble, in an attitude that has given their name to the two statues. As we look at this anguished figure, we forget its antique model, the Laocoön, and realize the full force of Michelangelo's neo-Platonic inspiration. For the figure is not trying to escape: his struggle is waged against mortality, this all too solid flesh, which remains imprisoned in matter, the stone from which the artist likewise struggles to free his artistic ideal, glimpsed through divine inspiration. Small wonder that Vasari tells us that Michelangelo was never satisfied, for he could never quite reproduce the Platonic vision in his mind nor liberate the masterpiece contained in the marble he attacked with such vigour and constancy. After Michelangelo, the greatest sculptor in Florence was Giovanni da Bologna, a Fleming, born at Douai in 1529. He arrived in Florence after 1550 and learned to express the beauty and grace fashionable at the time. His *Rape of the Sabines* (1582) is an exemplary Mannerist group, intended to be looked at from all sides and achieving the greatest possible effect of drama and movement, twisting and swirling with the spectator's axis. His figure of Mercury possesses unequalled lightness of grace, while his Venuses display the Mannerist ideals of elongation and courtly elegance. His most famous works, however, are his fountains at Bologna and in the Medici villas, where we see the beginnings of fountain sculpture, soon to become one of the great Baroque arts of European civilization.

*

Germany was the nearest country open to Italian influence, especially through the trading centres of the south. Everywhere the great tradition of Gothic art resisted this influence, particularly in sculpture and architecture. Riemenschneider's stone figures of Adam and Eve betray little or no acquaintance with the anatomical studies so dear to Italian sculptors, although Peter Flötner's graceful Apollo Fountain at Nuremberg (1532) is an obvious example of Italian Mannerist influence. This sudden transition from late Gothic to Mannerist art is typical of what happened north of the Alps and may also be observed in the career of Conrad Meit, who was court sculptor to Margaret of Austria and responsible for the decoration of the famous chapel at Brou. In German architecture, little was achieved apart from the superficial application of classical motifs and orders to Gothic structures. One of the masterpieces of sixteenth-century German painting, Grünewald's Isenheim Altar (1512–15), shows a supremely Gothic ability to drive home the suffering and mutilation inflicted on Christ's body – that same body that was being exalted by the humanists and by Michelangelo on the Sistine ceiling as the cynosure of the universe. Despite the tremendous religious impact of his creations, it seems likely that the iconoclasm of the Reformers put an end to Grünewald's career as a painter. LUCAS CRANACH (1472–1553), a court painter in Saxony, illustrated Luther's Bible and produced a number of bizarre, unclassical Venuses, clad in only a hat or some thin veil of provocative sensuality, which reflected the demand for mythological subjects and nudes. ALBRECHT ALTDORFER (c. 1480–1538) was probably the first European painter to produce a landscape devoid of human figures (c. 1532): nature for nature's sake, and one of the few innovations to come from outside Italy. The great name that overshadows all others is, of course, that of ALBRECHT DÜRER (1471–1528). Fascinated by the mystery behind some figures shown him by a visiting Italian painter, Dürer strove to master the principles of Renaissance art, the way in which Italian artists had succeeded in applying mathematics and linear perspective to the representation of the human body. Like Leonardo, he studied every detail in nature; like Michelangelo, he strove to portray the human body according to the ideal proportions of Classical art (*Adam and Eve*, 1504) though in a somewhat rigid manner. After completing this engraving, he travelled south to Venice, where he boasted of the deference paid to him in one of the great centres of Italian painting: 'Here I am a lord, at home a parasite.' He visited Italy a second time in 1505–6, and learned to combine the great crafts of his native tradition with the advances in technique and composition that were now the hallmark of Italian painting. Then came the Reformation. But despite the opposition towards humanism and the arts, Dürer's prestige was such that he was able to create a Protestant iconography (for example, his *Four Apostles* of 1524, with its superb use of Venetian colour and northern realism), while his engravings helped to bring home to simple folk the beauty of religious scenes and the force of Protestant propaganda. However, the absence of religious patronage, with little to replace it, and the tense atmosphere of revolt and civil war drove Dürer's contemporary, HANS HOLBEIN THE YOUNGER (1497–1543) to settle in England in 1532. The period 1521–5, with its fine religious paintings, the title page for Luther's New Testament and the original treatment of traditional iconography in the *Dance of Death* (1523–6) and *Alphabet of Death* (1524) reflecting the horrors of the Peasants' Revolt, shows us how much was lost by Holbein's decision to spend the rest of his life as a portrait painter, however great his achievements in this field.

The Low Countries showed similar tendencies, but with greater independence in the domestic and civic architecture produced by a small nation which managed to defeat the great might of Spain – indeed, the Spanish occupation left little trace, except for a few ornamental details of Moorish origin on some Dutch buildings. The celebrated town hall at Leyden (1579) displays the Ionic order treated with an exuberance of detail that must have shocked Italian visitors. The earlier Town Hall at Antwerp (1565) had shown how the native tradition could be blended more easily with the Classical orders. But climate as well as tradition meant the general retention of high sloping roofs and large windows. JAN GOSSAERT (*c.* 1475–*c.* 1536, called 'Mabuse' from his birthplace, Maubeuge) proved what ill-digested Italian influence could do: some years after his stay in Rome, he painted his *Neptune and Amphitrite* (1516), which shows how disastrous a near-parody of mythological subjects northern artists could produce. PIETER BREUGHEL (*c.* 1520–69) visited both France and Italy towards the middle of the century, although no trace of Italian art may be seen in his realistic representations of peasant life and parables. Minor artists, on the other hand, were often overwhelmed by their first contacts with Italian art – for example, through Raphael's designs for the Vatican tapestries, which were woven in Brussels where the cartoons remained.

The French invasions of Italy in 1494 and at the turn of the century had little effect on French art. The period of Italian influence began with the reign and patronage of François I (1515–47). Architecture proved to be the most resistant art, although superficially receptive to the frills of Italian design. This was partly due to the fact that the basic design of buildings cannot be changed as rapidly as style and technique in painting or sculpture, and partly to the hostility displayed by the French master masons, who resented the attitudes of

Italian architects and the preferential treatment accorded them. Typical of this conflict is the Château at Chambord. Although designed for the king by an Italian architect in 1519, the plans were drastically altered by the French masons, so that we now have a medieval castle-keep with numerous Classical details incongruously superimposed among the forest of tall gables, chimney pots and roof balustrades. Most of François' schemes were left unfinished. But he concentrated most of his energy and resources on the transformation of Fontainebleau from a hunting lodge into a Renaissance palace. It was here that Rosso was engaged on the decoration of the Galerie François I (*c.* 1533-40), a room of quite un-Italian design but whose unclassical proportions proved eminently suitable for the Mannerist decoration produced by Rosso and his compatriot FRANCESCO PRIMATICCIO (1504-70). The latter had been Giulio Romano's assistant at the Palazzo del Tè in Mantua, and there is no reason to disbelieve Vasari's statement that it was Primaticcio, the younger artist, who suggested the combination of painting with stucco, which is such a characteristic feature of Fontainebleau. Restoration has ruined most of the Renaissance work, except in the Galerie and the Chambre de la Duchesse d'Etampes (the king's mistress and Cellini's sworn enemy). The decoration of the Galerie created a model of elaborate décor which was an instant success and was copied in Italy, England and Germany. The most distinctive feature is the strap-work, where the stucco gives the impression of pieces of leather that have been rolled and cut into fantastic shapes. The plaster decoration offers a profusion of themes, as the treatment of space between the windows is always different, combining motifs of fruit, *putti* and Mannerist nudes. After Rosso's death in 1540, Primaticcio became artistic dictator at Fontainebleau, where he produced the Grotte des Pins with its heavily rusticated Mannerism (*c.* 1543) and the Aile de la Belle Cheminée in 1568. From 1541 to 1545, he worked on the Chambre de la Duchesse d'Etampes, where we find some of the finest examples of virtually free-standing stucco nymphs, forming a frame that is far more important than the picture itself. Everywhere the forms are tall, slender and elegant, while the allegories and histories all extol the glory and virtues of the king. It is hardly surprising that such studied elegance should have appealed to French artists, like JEAN CLOUET (1510-72), whose portraits also show the influence of Bronzino and

Holbein (for example, *Pierre Quthe*, 1562), and the sculptors JEAN
GOUJON (*c.* 1510–*c.* 1569) and GERMAIN PILON (*c.* 1535–90). Their
flowing lines are evident in Goujon's nymphs for the Fontaine des
Innocents (1548–9), where the treatment of the drapery was influenced by Cellini, who had been such a troublesome visitor from 1540
to 1545 and who had executed a number of commissions for the king,
including the *Nymphe de Fontainebleau* and, of course, the famous
salt-cellar. Pilon, one of the greatest masters of the northern Renaissance, created his *Virgin of Pity* (1580–85) for the chapel at St Denis;
it reveals some of the debt he owed to Michelangelo's later *pietà*
groups, while in the same period Pilon produced a *Deposition* with
a typically Mannerist flow of line.

The year 1540 is a landmark for French architecture: Primaticcio
journeyed to Rome and brought back Vignola with him, while in
the same year or possibly in 1541 SEBASTIANO SERLIO (1475–1554)
was invited to France and PHILIBERT DE L'ORME (*c.* 1515–70)
returned after a three-year stay in Italy. Vignola did not stay long,
and the less talented Serlio was far more influential, being placed in
charge of building works at Fontainebleau and at the Château of
Ancy-le-Franc in Burgundy. His treatise on architecture was even
more influential, because he abandoned the largely theoretical
approach of his predecessors and produced the first practical illustrated handbook for architects. Philibert de l'Orme was a brilliant
architect, who had gained a thorough understanding of his art in
Rome. Soon after his return to France, he was commissioned to
build the Château at Anet (1547–52) for Diane de Poitiers. Not much
of the original structure has survived, but the gateway is famous, and
the entrance (now at the École des Beaux-Arts at Paris) shows a true
Renaissance handling of the three Classical orders. The chapel is a
centrally planned building, articulated on the inside by skilful use of
the Corinthian order and a spirally coffered dome. For some time to
come, the main art in France was architecture. It was now realized,
however, that it must be based on definite rules governing form and
proportion, such as those laid down in Serlio's treatise and Philibert's
own two books on architecture.

In 1527, François I decided to modernize the palace of the Louvre.
The medieval keep was destroyed, but it was not until 1546 that the
king commissioned PIERRE LESCOT (*c.* 1500–1578) to undertake the

rebuilding on a grand scale. Lescot visited Rome in 1556, and may have visited Italy in his youth. His fame rests mainly on the buildings he designed for the south-east corner of the Cour Carrée at the Louvre, where the proportions and use of the orders show that he had assimilated the lessons of the Italian Renaissance. The sculptures are probably by Goujon, who also worked with Lescot on the Salle des Caryatides; and it is interesting to note that, while Serlio produced a charming blend of Italian and French elements at Ancy-le-Franc (begun in the same year), Lescot did his best to give the Louvre an Italian appearance. Such grafting was at times eminently successful. However, the wars of religion during the second half of the century prevented the further development of a true vernacular tradition until the reign of Henri IV (1589–1610), when urban architecture began with the Place des Vosges and the Place Royale. Under Italian influence, architects had replaced the master masons and assumed overall direction of building and decoration. Their unifying influence and the change from medieval castle to Renaissance palace, from the haphazard urban jigsaw to modern town planning, made possible French Classicism. Indicative of the general trend in the arts was the movement in painting away from the tradition of manuscript illumination and miniature portraits towards the monumental art of the seventeenth century: the way now lay open for the portraiture of Philippe de Champaigne, the landscapes of Claude Lorrain, and the great Classicism of Nicolas Poussin.

The arts in Spain were a mixture of various styles: at the end of the fifteenth century, the universal Gothic of the late Middle Ages and the Mudéjar style from Moorish architecture. The addition of Italian influence produced the 'Plateresque' (so called from the ornate art of the *platero* or silversmith), whereby a rich variety of Gothic and Renaissance ornamentation was applied to a basically simple Classical structure. One of the finest examples is the façade of the University of Alcalá (1543). What is remarkable is the apparent ease with which architects turned from one style to the other. RODRIGO GIL DE HONTAÑON (d. 1577) designed some of the finest Plateresque buildings, but he also completed the Gothic cathedral at Salamanca (1513–60), which had been planned by his father. He modified his father's Gothic plans for the cathedral at Segovia (1525–1616), which is nevertheless the last major example of the Gothic style. The rejection of florid decoration in favour of a more restrained Classical style finds its most illustrious exponent in JUAN DE HERRERA (1530–97). His masterpiece is the immense granite Escorial, which was hailed as the eighth wonder of the world when it was completed in 1584. This complex building, which included a college, monastery and cathedral, as well as the main palace, was praised by a contemporary for the way in which 'it follows the rules and orders of Vitruvius, abandoning as vanities the pretty projections, reversed pyramids, brackets and other foolish things.' This praise shows how faithfully Herrera followed Philip II's instructions for the building of the Escorial in its austere setting, some thirty miles from Madrid: 'simplicity of form, severity in the whole, nobility without arrogance, majesty without ostentation'.

Spanish sculpture was chiefly confined to altarpieces, monuments for tombs and church decoration in general. The Florentine Domenico Fancelli arrived in Seville in 1510 and later worked on the tombs of Ferdinand and Isabella in the Royal Chapel at Granada (1518). Isabella's own taste was directed towards Flemish art, and throughout the century Spanish sculpture remained largely untouched by the mainstream of Renaissance art. The greatest sculptor of the age, ALONSO BERRUGUETE (*c.* 1490–1561), was one of the exceptions. He studied in Italy and copied Michelangelo; his Mannerist art sought out the dramatic element in his subjects, while it is to him that we owe one of the few female nudes in Spanish art, the *Eve* from the choirstalls at Toledo Cathedral. JUAN DE JUNÍ (*c.* 1507–77), a Frenchman who was influenced by Berruguete, continued the Mannerist tradition, which was gradually transformed into the Baroque.

Alonso's father, PEDRO BERRUGUETE (*c.* 1450–1504), was the greatest painter at the turn of the century. Until 1483 he worked in Italy, although his art seems more Flemish than Italian. The Spanish style first emerged with FRANCISCO RIBALTA (*c.* 1551–1628). At first, portraits and even frescoes were rare, while all through the century painting was virtually limited to religious subjects. Navarrete's *Martyrdom of St Lawrence* (1579) in the Escorial points the way to the art of Ribera and Velazquez. However, in many ways the most Spanish of all painters was 'EL GRECO' (1541–1614), who was born in Crete and may well have been trained in icon painting before his arrival in Venice, where he was influenced by Titian, Tintoretto and others. When Pius V (1566–72) decided to impose greater decorum on Michelangelo's nudes in the *Last Judgement*, El Greco offered to paint another version of the same subject, just as fine, but chaste and in accordance with the spirit of the Counter-Reformation. Such *hybris* hastened his departure for Spain, where, uninvited, he made his way to the wealthy city of Toledo, then on the verge of its decline. In 1577, although he had never tackled such large-scale composition, he painted an *Assumption* over sixteen feet high for San Domingo el Antiguo, which shows Mannerist elements in the basically Titianesque treatment of the theme. The *Espolio* was then commissioned for the sacristy although the finished picture was nearly refused by the authorities, who felt that decorum – perhaps the chief prescription of the Counter-Reformation – had been violated because the artist had placed the heads of the thieves and executioners higher than the figure of Christ. With few exceptions, El Greco worked for the Church throughout the rest of his life. And even in the field of portraiture, his masterpiece is the celebrated image of *Cardinal Guevara* (*c.* 1600), where the awesome personality of the Grand Inquisitor is cunningly conveyed in the high-domed forehead and the bespectacled eyes which transfix the spectator, while the elongated shape is balanced by the majestic swirl of the cardinal's cape. In 1586, after Philip II had rejected the *Martyrdom of St Maurice and the Theban Legion*, El Greco finished his most famous picture, which strikes us as the document of a whole epoch: *The Burial of Count Orgaz*. We witness the burial of the knight by St Augustine and St Stephen, as the dead man's soul is borne up to heaven by an angel. The theme of death is treated with a serene dignity that is reflected both in the circular composition of the saints enclosing the sinuous lifeless body and in the background of mourners with their constrained manner and faces expressive of a whole background of Spanish mysticism. Without any attempt at aerial perspective the backcloth of heaven is revealed in the upper half of the picture. The contrast with the earthly scene is forceful: a curtain has been drawn aside to show the real world of the after-life, full of life and movement and sharp colour. The shapes are even more elongated than in most Mannerist pictures, the limbs have a sinewy quality, and the whole composition is already Baroque in its theatricality. But underneath lie the intense emotionalism and religious fervour that make El Greco the greatest painter of the Spanish Counter-Reformation.

Critics have sometimes harped on the fact that the Italian Renaissance, and in particular the sixteenth century, produced little original thought or speculation. What they were seeking may be found in the visual arts, where Michelangelo's Sistine Chapel and Raphael's *Stanze* must surely be numbered among the supreme achievements of western civilization, with an intellectual depth and emotional intensity that have few parallels, even in literature or philosophy. In general, Italian artists broadened immeasurably the scope of the arts of Western Europe by discovering new techniques, but most of all by their application of the ideals of order and symmetry, harmony and the golden mean which characterized the Renaissance faith in man's powers. Following the economic and political decadence of the Italian states, there was a general decline in the arts, which coincided with the Council of Trent (1545–63) and its final decision to make the arts once more subservient to the Church and the dictates of theology. In 1573, Veronese was brought before the Inquisition in Venice on charges of having introduced sacrilegious elements into his rendering of *The Feast in the House of Levi*: German soldiers (Protestant heretics?), a fool with a parrot, dogs, dwarfs and other details that are not mentioned in the biblical account. His answer was that a painter should be allowed a certain licence to make his creation more interesting, more varied and therefore more beautiful by filling in the gaps in a large composition with the figments of his imagination. The Inquisitors were not satisfied: they ordered certain superficial changes to be made, which left the mood of the picture unaltered. Another symptom was the publication of the Index of Prohibited Books in 1564, which placed Castiglione's *Book of the Courtier* on an illustrious list of forbidden reading matter. The decline in the arts was, however, reversed towards the end of the century, when architecture and music began to occupy the central place in the Italian artistic scene: architecture, perhaps because it was here that artists could most easily reconcile the letter of religious law with their individual genius; and music, because it was the least amenable of the arts to ecclesiastical censure and prescription.

FOUR

Reform and Schism

The return to the Gospels

Verbum Dei manet in aeternum – the suggestion, implicit in the Lutheran adoption of 1 Peter i, 23 as a party motto, that the Roman Church was alienated from the word of God was never more than a half-truth. Traditionally, the proto-Protestant heretical sects such as the Cathars, the Waldenses and the Albigensians had turned from the institutionalized and 'worldly' Church to the 'simple purity' of the scriptures. Equally traditionally, the official policy of the Church – from the decrees passed by the Councils of the thirteenth and fourteenth centuries against the Bible-reading heretics of the day down to the syllabus of 1864 in which Pius IX condemned Bible societies, together with communism, socialism and freemasonry, as *ejusmodi pestes* – had regarded unguided access to the scriptures on the part of the layman as a potential danger to the latter's soul and a challenge to the Church's authority. The Church herself had, however, on occasion responded to the challenge of evangelical heresy by encouraging the circulation of 'authorized versions', usually with suitable commentaries. The frequency with which vernacular editions of the Bible appeared in the years immediately preceding the outbreak of the Reformation (eighteen in Germany alone between 1483 and 1522) bears witness not only to the widespread interest in the scriptures, but also to the readiness of the Church to countenance their dissemination. The Church, in fact, was not so much 'against the Bible' as against the 'fundamental fallacy of private interpretation' which, experience had shown, tended to go hand in hand with the dissemination of the scriptures amongst laymen devoid of theological training.

The point at issue between the old and new faiths was not the authoritative status of the scriptures, but how that authority was to be interpreted: whether, as the Council of Trent was to affirm, the scriptures could only be properly understood in the light of the sacred traditions of the Church which incorporated the inspired insights of the saints and sages who had served her through the centuries, or whether, as the Protestants maintained, the individual believer, with no help other than that of his own intellect and the guidance of the Holy Ghost, had the right and duty to interpret the scriptures for himself. The Reformers did not so much rediscover the authority of the Bible as invest the actual words of the scriptures with *independent* authority; they denied the claim that the traditions of the Church were in their own way vehicles for divine truth and, in theory at least, invited the layman to 'search the scriptures' and interpret them for himself. The natural corollary to this invitation was the great wave of Bible translation and publication which swept through Protestant Europe in the sixteenth century. (There were some 200 post-Reformation editions of the Bible in German-speaking lands, 38 in England, 15 in Holland, 12 in Denmark and 17 in France, with correspondingly few editions in the lands where the old faith was strongest: 9 in Italy and 7 in Spain.) If the scriptures were regarded as the sole means by which the believer could come to know God, then the scriptures must be made readily available in the vernacular.

The Protestant doctrine of 'sola scriptura' was not, of course, anything startlingly new in Europe: traces of such a doctrine may be found in the teachings of Marsilius of Padua (d. 1343) and William of Ockham (d. 1349), while John Wyclif (d. 1384) and John Hus (d. 1415) had both proclaimed the Bible as the only touchstone by which matters of faith and doctrine might be judged. Towards the close of the fifteenth century, however, a number of circumstances combined to endow the concept with an irresistible appeal for the intellectual aristocracy of Europe. The increasingly obvious secular ambitions of the papacy, the externalized nature of official Christianity and the general immorality of the clergy – which enabled a Borgia to sit on the throne of St Peter as Alexander VI – made it steadily more difficult for all but the most naïve believers to accept the Church as an institution which spoke with more than human authority. In face of the failure of the Church to satisfy the spiritual needs of her more demanding members, the latter – unless they were to seek solace in mysticism – were naturally forced to turn to the scriptures as the only other possible source of divine truth.

This development in turn produced an increasingly vocal demand for the pure, unadulterated text of the scriptures and so gave impetus to the task of re-editing the biblical texts and freeing them from the errors and accretions of the centuries. But even without the very genuine motive of piety, it was inevitable that the disciples of the New Learning, with their critical attitude to all authority, their methodological return 'ad fontes', their avid interest in the tongues of Classical antiquity and their passion for collating and editing manuscripts, should take a critical interest in the scriptural texts. It was now that, deriving from the techniques evolved initially in connection with the editing of the great works of Latin and Greek literature, the science of biblical criticism was born and so provided an intellectual basis from which the 're-conquest' of the Bible could take place. In the closing decades of the fifteenth century in nearly every European country Christian humanists were hard at work editing, expounding and translating the scriptures. In Italy Lorenzo Valla (d. 1457) compiled his *Annotations on the New Testament* which, when published by Erasmus in 1505, were to prove a great stimulus to biblical studies in their demonstration of the inadequacies of the Vulgate. In the Netherlands Wessel Gansfort (d. 1489), like Erasmus after him quickening the piety of the Brethren of the Common Life with the scholarship of the New Learning, was already anticipating Luther (who published Gansfort's writing in 1522) in his elevation of the authority of the Bible above that of Popes and Councils and in his doctrine of justification by faith. In Spain Francisco Ximenes (d. 1517), Archbishop of Toledo, fostered the New Learning in his newly established university at Alcalá, where the first printed text of the Greek New Testament was completed in 1514 (though not published immediately), to be followed in 1522 by the famous Polyglot Bible, in the compilation of which the distinguished human- ist, Elio Antonio de Nebrija, collaborated. Across the Pyrenees, in France, Jacques Lefèvre d'Etaples, professor of mathematics and philosophy at the Sorbonne, for whom the Bible was 'the Book of Life and only true rule for Christians', was editing the Psalter (1509) and the Epistles of St Paul (1512), before going on to produce his commentary on the Gospels (1522) and his translation of the Psalms and the New Testament (1523–5). In England, young John Colet (d. 1519) had startled his Oxford audiences and latterly his congrega- tions at St Paul's by his assertion of the exclusive authority of the scriptures and his humanistic concern to penetrate to the true meaning of the biblical texts. Similarly, in the Empire, men like Jakob Wimpheling (d. 1528) and Johannes Reuchlin (d. 1522) used their humanistic skills in Classical languages – Reuchlin was the foremost Hebraist of his day – in order to arrive at a better understanding of the meaning of the Bible, often criticizing traditional interpretations in the light of new philological insight.

It was, however, in the Greek New Testament which Erasmus edited and published in 1516 that the combination of piety and good learning which is characteristic of Christian humanism gained its finest expression. Although not free from error itself, it successfully exploded the myth of the perfection of the Vulgate, thereby challenging the authority of the Church, which had declared St Jerome's translation to be faultless; indeed, it could be argued that its completion of Valla's work by its assertion of the scholar's right to submit the most sacred documents to critical scrutiny was more important than the intrinsic value of the scholarship it embodied. However that may be, it certainly did enjoy wide dissemination, passing through six editions in as many years, and provided Protestant exegetes and translators with an invaluable tool. Erasmus' words in the preface are an apt indication of the importance which both he and his fellow humanists attached to a knowledge of the Bible:

I wish that all men might read the Gospels and the Epistles of St Paul. I wish that they might be translated into all tongues of all men, so that not only the Scots and the Irish, but also the Turk and the Saracen might read and understand. I wish that the countryman might sing them at his plough, the weaver chant them at his loom, the traveller beguile with them the weariness of his journey . . .

It was in no small measure due to Erasmus' own efforts that the Protestant Bible translators were so successful in making the wish he expresses here come true. The Reformers' appeal to the *profanum vulgus* was in practice distasteful to his aristocratic nature and the doctrine of individual interpretation was offensive to his scholarship, but in his evangelism, as in certain other aspects of his teaching, Luther, in the sixteenth-century phrase, only 'hatched the egg which Erasmus laid'.

Martin Luther

By its criticism of ecclesiastical authority and its appeal to the scriptures Christian humanism prepared the way for the Reformation: in other respects the two movements were poles apart. The humanists sought to repair the fabric of the traditional faith by the elimination of obvious abuses rather than to infuse into Christianity a radically new view of the relationship between mankind and his Maker. They believed in man's powers of ethical self-determination and saw in the human spirit a reflection of the divine: reforms, they maintained, were necessary, but would be consequent on the spread of enlightenment. For Martin Luther, however, mankind was utterly corrupt and characterized by an inherent incapacity to do good. His protest against indulgences, from which the Reformation sprang, was not so much a humanistic protest against an *abuse*, as the expression of his dissatisfaction with the traditional doctrine of the Church – a doctrine to which virtually all the humanists subscribed – that mankind could, by doing 'good works', collaborate with God and 'merit' salvation.

Luther's radically unorthodox point of view was implicit in the overwhelming sense of his own sinfulness and the attendant fear that he would be damned which had tormented him as a novice and young priest at Erfurt and had latterly emerged as a distinct theological system in the course of his lectures on the Psalms and the Epistles at the obscure Saxon University of Wittenberg, where he held the chair of biblical studies. The traditional teaching and the whole penitential system of the Church were wrong, Luther maintained, because they laid emphasis on human effort and human achievement. Basing himself on Pauline texts such as 'The just shall live by faith' (Romans i, 17) and 'we conclude that a man is justified by faith without the deeds of the law' (Romans iii, 28), Luther, following St Augustine, argued that the attempt to merit salvation by performing the 'deeds of the law' was misguided and that salvation depended on the individual's state of mind rather than his moral actions. Because of man's unmitigated sinfulness, any attempt on his part to 'put himself right with God' was vain and impertinent. Only God could put the sinner right with himself and faith in Luther's terminology is not an acceptance of the truth of certain doctrines (*fides dogmatica*), but the unshakeable conviction on the part of the sinner that though he has deserved damnation, God in his loving mercy will not demand that he pay the penalty of his sinfulness, but will choose to regard the repentant sinner as though he were in fact just (*fides fiducialis*). Since, however, faith is a gift of God and man is justified not by his own moral efforts, but by an arbitrary act of grace on God's part, since man of himself cannot do good, but must do evil (*Unvermögen zum Guten*), it follows that man is not free, but is subject to predestination: God may choose either to pardon or to damn the sinner, indeed he has already chosen before the sinner is born!

Luther's theories might have been quietly buried in the lecture notes of his students, had he not been stung into action by an event which brought his theoretical position into startling contrast with current ecclesiastical practice – the sale of indulgences in North Germany in order to raise money for the building of St Peter's and to repay the debts incurred by Albrecht of Brandenburg in respect of the dispensation for the plurality of benefices held by him (he was Bishop of Magdeburg and Archbishop of Mainz). The sales of indulgences – letters of pardon which the purchaser could present to his confessor and by which the third part of the sacrament of penance (satisfaction) was commuted into a financial contribution – had been frequently used in order to raise funds in the later Middle Ages and had frequently been attacked by orthodox theologians as a prostitution of the sacrament. Quite apart from his concern for the welfare of the simple layman, to whom a letter of indulgence must have seemed like a licence to sin, the inherent emphasis on externalized works rather than on the inner state of mind constituted a direct challenge to Luther's dearest beliefs and Luther responded by publishing on 31 October 1517 his famous ninety-five theses, in which he not only protested at the excessive claims made by the papal commissioners for their wares, but denied that the Pope had the power to remit sin or penalty either here or in purgatory and asserted that the 'merits' of Christ were freely available to all believers.

The response which his essentially academic gesture evoked both amongst the general public and in official Church circles came as a surprise to Luther. Initially he had believed – somewhat naïvely – that his position was orthodox, only to find himself arraigned by orthodox theologians as a manifest heretic and hailed by wide sections of the general public – priests as well as laymen – as a national hero and the liberator of Christianity from the monstrous tyranny of the Pope. Only gradually in the course of the next few years did Luther, largely in response to pressures coming from within the Church itself, emerge as the Reformer. Step by step in the course of his meetings and disputations with representatives of the papacy (Cajetan, Miltitz, Eck) he was led towards the radical theological position which was to be given definitive expression in the great treatises of 1520 (*On the Babylonian captivity of the Church*; *On the freedom of a Christian*; *To the Christian nobility of the German nation*). The new teaching revolved around four main ideas: 1) The Scriptures, not Councils or popes, were the supreme Christian authority and might be interpreted by the individual believer; 2) Men were justified through faith, not by virtue of their works; 3) All believers were priests with direct access to God: the difference between cleric and layman was one of office only and the cleric's power was delegated to him by the community and might be withdrawn; 4) The efficacy of the sacraments (reduced first to three and then to two, baptism and communion) was dependent on the faith of the recipient and they did not operate magically. The mass was not a sacrifice.

By 1521, when he was excommunicated and, after his refusal to recant at the Diet of Worms, put under the ban of the Empire, Luther's most important theological work had been completed and the Reformation had become a reality. The breach had been effected, the obvious abuses were in process of being removed and the new doctrines enjoyed wide support amongst all classes of society. From its original home in Saxony the Lutheran movement had spread south as far as Austria and Bohemia, north to Brandenburg and Pomerania, and east to Silesia and Poland; it had found enthusiastic adherents in Switzerland and the Netherlands and was bidding fair to establish itself in France and England. That Lutheranism did not fulfil its early promise and become the dominant Protestant faith in Europe was due in no small measure to the unmethodical and apolitical nature of its founder. Luther's central interest lay in the relationship of the believer to God: he was not concerned about theories or systems of Church government or the Christianization of the secular state – even the two great canons of Lutheran orthodoxy, the *Loci communes rerum theologicarum* of 1521 and the Augsburg

Confession of 1530, were not compiled by him, but by the more precise and systematic Melanchthon. His reformation was pragmatic rather than theoretical; reforms (for example, the vernacular liturgy and communion in both kinds) were introduced only in response to evident needs and he was happy to allow individual churches and pastors to develop their own forms of worship and church orders. In the main he found it convenient to co-operate closely with the secular authorities, who tended to carry out the functions of bishops in the Old Church through specially instituted 'consistorial courts'.

To the end of his days Luther continued to exercise immense authority over the movement he had brought into being, but after 1521 the Reformation is as much a political as a religious and spiritual fact and the fortunes of the new faith were guided and protected by the Imperial cities and the territorial princes who, apart from the sincerity of their convictions, soon acquired a vested interest in the survival of Lutheranism by virtue of their expropriation of church property. Partly owing to their efforts, partly because of the popular appeal of Luther's teaching, but principally because of the dissipation of the energies of Charles V in his world-wide empire and his numerous foreign wars, the new faith was never challenged in Germany until it was too late. When the challenge did come, in the civil war of 1547, the Emperor's military successes bore no real fruit and by skilled diplomacy and the judicious application of their revitalized military strength the Lutherans were able virtually to dictate the terms of the Religious Peace of Augsburg (1555), which at last gave the new teachings legal recognition. But although the future of Lutheranism was thus assured in its native land, elsewhere in Europe – with the exception of Scandinavia, where it has remained the official religion down to our own day – Lutheranism was destined to be out-flanked by more radical Protestant movements.

Huldrych Zwingli

The German Reformation was begotten of Luther's intensely personal struggle for the certainty of salvation, and the emergence of Lutheranism as an ideal state religion is a paradoxical result of its founder's fundamentally apolitical nature. By contrast, neither Zwingli nor Calvin had experienced Luther's 'black night of the soul' and the forms of Protestantism named after them were characterized by a less emotional, more rational element, and by a distinctly political orientation. As a disciple of Erasmus, Huldrych Zwingli (1484–1531), priest at the Great Minster in Zürich and subsequently the reformer of German-speaking Switzerland, was deeply influenced by his teacher's biblicism and his Christocentric outlook. His Erasmian concern to remove abuses was, however, quickened by a very real patriotism: his condemnation of the sale of indulgences in Zürich in 1518 was probably less the result of profound theological insights than of a concern to protect the economic interests of his native canton and thus constitutes an ecclesiastical counterpart to his campaign against the acceptance of foreign pensions and the sale of Swiss mercenaries to foreign powers. From the first he looked to the secular authorities to institute reforms, and while his sixty-seven *Schlußreden* (conclusions) of 1523 inevitably remind us of Luther's ninety-five theses, it was to the Great Council of Zürich that Zwingli appealed, not the academic republic of clerics and scholars. Equally it was the Great Council that pronounced him to be the victor in his disputations with Roman theologians and proceeded to implement the reforms he advocated.

In the main his position shows a close similarity to Luther's: like Luther he preaches justification by faith, the priesthood of all believers, the exclusive authority of the scriptures, the reduction of the sacraments to two; similarly a belief in the non-sacrificial nature of the mass and in predestination is common to them both. Like Luther too, Zwingli conducted an unremitting campaign against the radical Protestant sects such as the Anabaptists, who elevated the 'inner light' to the status of an absolute authority and sought to revive the communism of primitive Christianity, while rejecting infant baptism and the authority of the secular state. In contrast to Luther's tolerant and unprogrammatic approach to the ordering of the service and the retention of traditional aids to piety, however, Zwingli consciously aimed at a radical re-ordering of church services; and his reformation is characterized by a thorough-going puritanism: candles, pictures, organs were removed from his churches, walls were white-washed and altars replaced by deal tables. It was not his puritanism which cut Zwingli off from the German Protestants, however, but his spiritualistic view of the nature of the sacraments, particularly Holy Communion. In Zwingli's view – already anticipated by Cornelius Hoen and Wessel Gansfort – the sacraments were not vehicles of grace but signs of grace already given, and the words 'This is my body' in the communion service were to be understood as meaning 'This *represents* my body', so that the Eucharist was no more than a 'solemn thanksgiving and communion' (*Eidgenossenschaft*). Luther, on the other hand, saw the sacraments as a means whereby grace was communicated to man, interpreted the 'is' literally and, like the Roman Church, continued to believe in the real presence of Christ in the elements, while denying that they changed physically. It was on this point that the hoped-for unity of Protestantism came to grief at the Marburg colloquy of 1529, which not only set the seal on four years of acrimonious dispute, but officially confirmed the fragmentation of Protestantism into feuding factions which, in Germany at least, was to have such dire consequences in the next century.

Jean Calvin

Like Zwingli, Calvin came to the evangelical faith via humanism. A native of Picardy, he had imbibed the spirit of Erasmian humanism during his studies at Paris and Orléans before being converted to Protestantism around 1533. To escape persecution he fled to Geneva in 1536 and was immediately involved in local confessional quarrels, from which, after many vicissitudes, he emerged as the virtual dictator of his adopted city. A man of clearer, more logical intellect than either Luther or Zwingli, his great achievement was to bring the diffuse doctrines of his predecessors into sharp focus in his *Christianae religionis institutio*. Theologically he was closer to Luther than Zwingli – he subscribed to the Augsburg Confession and the first version of the *Institutio* was based on Luther's catechism. Like Luther, he saw the sacraments as a means of grace and believed in the real presence – albeit in a spiritual sense – in the Eucharist. Even more firmly than Luther, he took his stand on the literal meaning of the scriptures and scorned the Wittenberger's somewhat selective approach to the canon (Luther was inclined to dismiss out of hand inconvenient books such as the Epistle of James). Where Calvin did differ from Luther, it tended to be on a question of emphasis rather than substance. Thus the concept of the ineffable majesty of God and the attendant Augustinian doctrine of predestination is given pride of place in Calvin's system, not justification by faith, and his God tends to be the stern jealous God of the Old Testament rather than the loving Father of the New Testament preferred by Luther.

But if theologically there was little difference between Geneva and Wittenberg, the social implications drawn from theology were very different indeed. Luther was concerned to explore and explain the relationship of the believer to God and was largely content to let the State go its own way. Calvin sought to Christianize the State and society, and in his 'ecclesiastical ordinances' he imposed on the unfortunate Genevans a rule of life so rigidly controlled that it can only be described as totalitarian. (The characteristic expressions of Calvinist state-theory were the Scotland of John Knox and the England of Oliver Cromwell.) In imitation, as he believed, of the earliest Christian communities, Calvin instituted four 'orders': pastors to preach, doctors to teach 'sound doctrine', elders to maintain discipline and deacons to superintend the works of charity. The city itself was divided into a number of wards, each in the charge of an elder who was responsible for the surveillance of public and private morals. Disciplinary, in fact all real power, lay in the hands of the 'Consistory', which was made up of twelve elders and six pastors. In theory democratic, in practice, like the municipal Little Council which nominated its members, a self-perpetuating oligarchy, it controlled the purity of Genevan morals and thought, from whistling on Sundays to views on the Trinity, with a frightening, puritanical and self-righteous efficiency and did not shrink from pronouncing the most severe sentences, which were then carried out by the secular authorities.

Throughout his life Calvin was concerned to promote Protestant unity. His attempts to establish full intercommunion with the Lutherans came to grief largely because of Luther's suspicion of Swiss theologians in general – he always associated them with the Anabaptists, whose terrible excesses at Münster (1532) had made a lasting impression on him. After Luther's death the notorious 'rabies theologorum' in the Lutheran camp rendered all negotiations futile. With the Zwinglians he was more successful and it was in no small measure due to his efforts that both denominations were able to subscribe to the Second Helvetic Confession of 1566 and ultimately to merge as the 'Reformed Church'.

By 1540 the missionary zeal of Lutheranism was spent and it was from Geneva that the task of evangelizing Europe was energetically pursued. The Academy established by Calvin under the rectorship of Théodore de Bèze in 1559 provided a training-ground for the Protestant intelligentsia of Europe whence young men, well educated and thoroughly indoctrinated, returned home to spread the Calvinist creed, and it was largely thanks to their efforts that the reformed religion penetrated such widely separated lands as Hungary and Scotland, France and Bohemia, the Palatinate and Poland.

It was from the doctrine of predestination that Calvinism derived its unique drive. Far from inducing an antinomian complacency, the certainty of election generated a dynamic energy. The elect, according to Calvin, were those who openly professed their faith, obeyed the commandments and enjoyed sacramental communion with God, but the works of the faithful were 'signs of their calling from which the pious may conclude that they are of the elect', so that in practice, although it is probably a mistake to see Calvinism as being instrumental in the rise of capitalism, it gave a divine blessing to precisely those virtues which were at a premium in the emergent capitalist economies. It was, however, only in the Dutch Republic, in the lowlands of Scotland, in Cromwellian England and amongst the settlers of the eastern seaboard of North America that the combination of Calvinism and commercial activity subsequently emerged as a dominant factor in the national character and way of life. Elsewhere in Europe the role of the Calvinists was that of dynamic 'ginger groups' and in this capacity, until they were eliminated by the persecutions of the seventeenth century, they made valuable contributions to the development of the wider communities to which they belonged.

FIVE

The Counter-Reformation

WITH hindsight it is easy enough to see how Erasmus laid the egg how Luther hatched it, how Protestantism formed first one and then many rival sects, how Rome was forced to react and how, finally, the solution reached at Trent left Europe split into two irreconcilable camps and fixed Catholic doctrine down to our own day. The trouble with such a scheme is that it ignores the fact that every one of the great reformers, Luther, Zwingli, Calvin, every one of their first followers, was born and brought up as a Catholic, and that while they were attempting to reform the Church by methods which were soon denounced as heretical and led to irreparable schism, other men and women, no less enlightened, were equally alive to the problems and were tackling them by methods novel enough to provoke censure but ultimately so efficacious as to compel recognition, and sometimes canonization. Neither side had the monopoly of fervour, neither was free of complacency, but only when all the options have been closed one by one is it useful to talk of sides. Moreover the political realities of the age frustrate attempts at simple classifications like pro- or anti-papal, pro- or anti-reform. Erasmus, who can hardly be classed as pro-papal, was seriously considered for a cardinal's hat just before he died, François I combined zeal for extirpating heretics at home with diplomatic overtures to German and Swiss Protestants, and even, Most Christian King that he was, made a formal alliance with the Sultan against his Most Catholic enemy of Spain and the Empire. Complicated as the actual historical situation appears, its reflection in literature is very much more complicated – by the needs of propaganda, by passionate belief in images and stereotypes which a moment's critical scrutiny would have dispelled and, of course, by the quite random incidence of literary merit, which alone determines survival of this work rather than that.

The standard reaction to dissent of authorities everywhere, secular or ecclesiastical, was savage repression, and with only sporadic exceptions (in Poland and France) tolerance was not a live issue during the century. Princes newly converted to Protestantism were intolerant not only of Catholics, but also of rival Protestants, and in Catholic countries, especially Spain, innovation of any sort was likely to be treated as a *prima facie* case of heresy or subversion. Even when opposing parties came together for abortive colloquies, as at Regensburg (1541) or Poissy (1561), each was so utterly convinced of its own rightfulness that if exchange even got as far as courtesies it looked like progress.

If tolerance was not a serious solution, it soon became clear that inertia was not one either. From the beginning of the century successive popes had been under pressure, and had often lamely promised, to convoke a council, but even when the spread of heresy underlined the urgency of making some organized response, the long awaited meeting was postponed time after time. When it eventually met at Trent (whence the adjective Tridentine) in 1545, it could hardly qualify for the title 'universal', with its vast majority of Italian delegates, supported by some Spanish and a bare sprinkling from the rest of Europe, but by the time it concluded its arduous task in 1563, after many and lengthy interruptions, the most enthusiastic proponents of a council realized that it had in one respect done exactly the opposite of what they had hoped, for papal power emerged enormously strengthened. The disciplinary reforms effected at Trent were too few and too late to reverse the tide of Protestantism, but at least some of the more squalid abuses were removed, and the Church no longer had to defend the indefensible in such matters as the traffic in indulgences or clandestine marriages. The legislators of Trent had the sense, too, to see that priority must go to the education of the clergy if worse disasters were not to befall, and the beginnings of a diocesan seminary system were laid down, though its implementation inevitably varied greatly according to place or prelate. At the same time early in the Council's deliberations a decision was taken (1546) to perpetuate Scholastic methods and to reject those of the Erasmian humanists, especially with regard to Bible study and availability of the Bible to the laity. Professor Dickens writes: 'in no field did the fear of Protestantism leave deeper marks upon the development of Catholic religion,' and it is only in living memory that the

Catholic Church has taken a worthy part in biblical studies. Purely theological decisions affecting such issues as sacramental doctrine, and questions of faith and grace, similarly reflect over-reaction to the Protestant challenge, but here the battle was not long postponed, for the Augustinians of the next century showed by the Jansenist movement that the last word had by no means been spoken.

In the immediate context of the sixteenth century it may be said that Trent stopped the rot (or closed the stable door, depending on one's point of view) but this is not the place to discuss the longer term consequences of the Council. Fortuitously (or perhaps providentially) one development more than any other has come to be associated with the Counter-Reformation launched at Trent, though originally it was quite distinct. Traditional monasticism, whether of the true monks living in the Benedictine way or of the more recent Mendicant friars, had for many complex reasons, social and economic as well as spiritual, fallen into wide disrepute, and numerous attempts, often successful, were made in the course of the century to restore particular orders or groups of houses to something closer to their original rule. Thus the long feud within the Franciscans led in 1518 to their definitive division into the two families of Conventuals, or unreformed, and Observants, followed ten years later by a still more vigorous offshoot in the Capuchins. Similarly Benedictine and Cistercian houses began forming groups, usually on a provincial or national basis, so that those who really cared for the monastic ideal could follow it worthily, and there were few, if any, orders in which effective reform did not regenerate at least some of their adherents.

It should be emphasized that such developments were not at all an answer to Protestantism, but should rather be ascribed to the same stimuli of dissatisfaction and idealism which led others into heresy. These measures, however necessary, were only palliatives, and even leaving Protestantism out of account, the changed situation of the sixteenth century demanded a new approach to the religious life. Far the most famous of the new foundations was the Society of Jesus, but it was by no means the only one. In Italy, for example, a succession of associations, some bound by rule, some merely by common aims, but none strictly speaking monastic at all, came into being in the form of various bodies of Clerks Regular, starting with the Theatines (founded by Cajetan 1524) the Barnabites of Milan

(1533) and including the best known, the Fathers of the Oratory (1564), whose founder, St Philip Neri, was a close friend of Palestrina and thus bequeathed to posterity the word and thing 'oratorio' for the type of musical offering provided at their services. All these bodies had their roots in a specific social need or situation, and started free from the prejudices (and sometimes odium) too often found in older orders. Women were not forgotten, and as early as 1535 St Angela Merici founded the Ursulines in northern Italy, whence they spread widely, as pioneers of education for girls, while the Carmelite reform initiated by St Teresa of Avila (d. 1582) set a new standard of sanctity among enclosed orders for women. The French Carmelites in particular, introduced by Mme Acarie in 1604, constituted a spiritual élite whose force is far from spent today and the same is true of the French Oratory, not founded by Bérulle until 1611, but one of the most distinguished products of the Counter-Reformation in France.

The Jesuits were, and remain, a special case, and it requires a major effort of will to forget their subsequent history as one considers their origins. The spiritual conversion of St Ignatius Loyola (1491–1556), his elaboration of a spirituality both characteristic of himself and firmly based on existing tradition, especially that of the *devotio moderna* from the Netherlands, whose *Imitation of Christ* influenced him greatly, the slow maturation of his design at the University of Paris, and finally the solemn engagement of himself and nine companions in the old church at Montmartre on 15 August 1534, all this seems impossibly remote from what happened next. Fired, like St Francis before him, with the vision of regaining for Christ the Holy Land, which he had visited in 1523, he led his little band in dedicating himself to this end through the usual vows of poverty and chastity, together with that of absolute obedience to the Pope, and set off for Venice. Prevented by war from embarking for his goal, he made his way instead to Rome, where, in 1540, he received papal approval for his Society (or Company) of Jesus. When Ignatius died in 1556, still busily directing his Society's affairs in Rome, his original group of ten had become a thousand, and just sixty years later Jesuits throughout the world numbered 13,000.

Though the Holy Land project had to be abandoned, missionary activity on the heroic scale was from the first one of the Jesuits' principal functions. Nor was this confined to the remoter parts of the known world. St Francis Xavier (1506–52), the apostle of the Far East, is no doubt the most striking figure in Jesuit annals, but St Peter Canisius (1521–97) was equally tireless in Germany and Eastern Europe, and equally effective. Other missionaries, especially Dominicans and Franciscans, bitterly resented this competition, and the story of their sordid rivalry in Asia is saddening. No less important was the contribution of the Jesuits in the field of education. In the first decade of their existence they founded colleges in Italy and Spain, including what later became the Gregorian University in Rome, and soon afterwards founded universities in Germany, at Ingolstadt (1555) and Munich (1559), while by 1575 or so the Collège de Clermont in Paris had risen from very modest beginnings to become one of the leading educational establishments in France. The history of the *grand siècle* is largely that of Jesuit pupils, from Descartes and Retz to Voltaire. The Society's great theologians Suarez (d. 1617) and Molina (d. 1600) transformed Scholasticism without formally rejecting it, and Molinism continues to offer a powerful alternative to Thomism, going to the limit (some have said beyond) in optimism regarding human nature and free will. Another Jesuit theologian of equal ability and integrity is St Robert Bellarmine (1542–1621), a major figure in controversies with Protestants. It should be added that the excellence of Jesuit education depended in large measure on sound Classical learning and, something of an innovation, a very progressive attitude towards science, especially astronomy.

Their fervour, their competence, their mobility and their modernity would all have been ephemeral without brilliant organization and *esprit de corps*. It was not just spiritual commandoes like Edmund Campion or Robert Parsons, whose discipline may reasonably be called military, but individuals and houses and provinces throughout the world who displayed a sense of unity and cohesion in attack as in defence which the older orders could no longer emulate. The coincidence of Trent and the new society's availability for papal plans is relevant, so is the nature of Jesuit recruitment, increasingly based on their own pupils; but the survival of the Jesuits after persecution and temporary suppression in the eighteenth century to become much the most numerous religious body within the Catholic Church invites less crudely rationalistic hypotheses.

Another organization which played a conspicuous part in Catholic reaction throughout the century is unhappily at least as sinister as its legend. The origins of the Inquisition or Holy Office go back to the Middle Ages, but it was the Spanish monarchs who perfected it as an instrument of repression against Moors, Jews, suspected heretics and eventually any critic, real or suspected, of Church and State. Largely (but not exclusively) entrusted to the Dominicans, the Inquisition in Spain typifies that blend of rectitude and savagery which a totalitarian mentality demands and exalts. The infamous Torquemada (d. 1498) probably established the record for productivity of victims, but with what remnants he left his zealous successors in Spain, Portugal and their overseas empires did their best (or worst). Wherever Spanish power went, to Naples, to the Low Countries, to the New World, this regime of terror by delation, arbitrary imprisonment, torture and human degradation went with it, to the greater glory of God, as its agents would have said. Other countries were not tender with heretics, and in France, for example, the *Chambre Ardente* set up by Henri II was nothing to be proud of, but the Spanish Inquisition was universally recognized as something that excelled over all imitators elsewhere.

By their victims ye shall know them, and the list of those who fell foul of the authorities in Spain is a distinguished, indeed saintly, one, including Ignatius, Luis de León, Luis de Granada and the great Carmelites St Teresa and St John of the Cross. The fact that the Carmelite reform ever survived such opposition, or that the Jesuits themselves did not at first easily overcome Dominican hostility, is at once proof of the tenacity of Spanish conservatism and of the indomitable spirit of those Spaniards who believed that Christ must be served in other ways. For moderates like the Erasmians, or the mystic Alumbrados (a term rather loosely applied to almost any unorthodox person), there was never any real hope, and between the upper and nether millstones of Church and State only the exceeding tough could survive.

The results of Spanish policy in the Netherlands are discussed elsewhere. In America they probably achieved the ultimate horrors, reducing, for instance, the native population of Mexico from twenty-five millions in 1519 to some two millions in 1575 (disease admittedly playing its part), and against England they certainly launched their most ambitious enterprise, but in the last analysis it was in France that Spanish policy most decisively affected Catholicism and left the deepest impression. Rabelais savagely satirizing Charles V from his first book to his last (1532–52), Montaigne crying out in shame at the conduct of the conquistadores defiling the Cross with the sword, the *Satire Menippée* (1594) rallying patriots of both faiths against the imposition of an alien power and an alien form of religion, down to Pascal (1657) with his mordant satire against the Hispanic aberrations of Jesuit piety and morals, all testify to persistent French hostility to what they felt to be an integral part of Spanish imperialism. In France, heretics, when they were not fighting in the king's pay, were persecuted and, if need be, executed by order of his courts. The ancient tradition of Gallicanism made little or no distinction between the old enemy across the Alps and the newer one entrenched behind the Pyrenees and on every other land frontier. Though the King of Spain enjoyed virtual autonomy over the Church in his realms, from the French point of view Habsburg and Pope were twin foes. In 1534 the moderate Evangelicals, protected by Marguerite de Navarre, lost any hope of victory when subversive placards against the mass and other Catholic rites were affixed in public places and even at Blois, where the King was, but if this permanently alienated François from their cause, both he and his son more than once came near to a separatist Gallican solution on English lines.

Once the Wars of Religion broke out in 1562 talk of Catholic reaction is a little unrealistic. For more than thirty years Frenchmen suffered appallingly from wars which were as much dynastic and tribal as religious, and until peace came little progress could be made in any direction. When the boy François II succeeded his father in 1559, the child queen was Mary, Queen of Scots, niece of the powerful Guises, who thus found themselves legitimately at the steps of the throne. These cadets of the ruling house of Lorraine had only been naturalized French under François I, and were always regarded as foreigners by their enemies. In each generation there was a duke, head of the family, and a cardinal, either of Lorraine or of Guise, and it was Henri, the third duke, and his brother Louis, the cardinal, who went furthest in supporting Spanish policy with their Holy League. The massacre of St Bartholomew (24 August 1572) had been one way of dealing with Protestants, but once Henri III had replaced his sickly brother, Charles IX (1574), and above all once the death of the last male Valois, Anjou, in 1584 left as the only legitimate heir to the throne the heretic Henri de Navarre, the Guises decided that outright treason, in collusion with Spain, was the best way to establish themselves (they had a tenuous claim to the throne, through the female line), to destroy heresy for ever and to make the world safe for Spain and the Empire. Accordingly they led an army against the King, who goaded for once into meaningful action had both brothers assassinated at Blois in 1588, only himself to fall in 1589 to the assassin's knife of a Dominican, Jacques Clément, hired by the League. This event finally led to the triumph of the *politiques*, the party of moderates to which such men as Montaigne naturally belonged, and in the end Catholics and Protestants sank their differences to repudiate as patriots the instant threat of Spanish domination. Henri IV's tactical abjuration of heresy (1594) opened the way not only to the throne but to the great Edict of Tolerance issued at Nantes in 1598, and, perhaps paradoxically, to the great Catholic revival of the next century. The profoundly national character of French Catholicism shows both in Gallicanism and in the rejection of Spanish and Italian devotional modes by Jansenists, but Calvinism in its turn began and has always remained a minority religion in France, for political reasons, no doubt, but also for reasons deeply embedded in French psychology.

On the credit side the Counter-Reformation brought a great impetus towards charitable, missionary and educational work, for which activities many new orders of men and women were created. An undeniable legacy of humanism was a much more sensitive social conscience. In terms of administrative efficiency and doctrinal uniformity the post-Tridentine Church was stronger and more centralized, but Protestantism failed to spread more because of its own inherent weaknesses than because of any positive Catholic action. On the debit side bigotry and intolerance were given a new lease of life, in Catholic and Protestant countries alike; many reforms long overdue in the sixteenth century have had to wait until our own day, notably in the fields of liturgy and of Bible study, and such vital questions as the celibacy of the clergy and the true nature of monastic life were simply shelved, and are only now being seriously looked at. Despite all the drastic changes which have played their part through the intervening centuries, there are few problems facing the Churches today which were not susceptible of solution four hundred years ago. There was plenty of talk, but pitifully little dialogue.

SIX

The Empire of Charles V
and His Successors

THE outcome of the Imperial Election of 1519 represented both the culmination of the universal ideal inherent in the concept of the Holy Roman Empire and the triumph of the supranational dynastic ambitions of the Habsburgs. Largely thanks to the foresight of his paternal grandfather, the Emperor Maximilian I, – who had laid the foundation of a world empire by his own marriage to Mary, daughter of Charles the Bold of Burgundy, and the alliance of the son of this marriage with Joanna, daughter of Ferdinand of Aragon and Isabella of Castile – the new Emperor, Charles V (1500–1558), ruled over a vast heterogeneous collection of territories which embraced Spain and the Americas, the greater part of Italy, Austria, Croatia, Germany, Franche Comté and the Netherlands. By his international family background and by his early training and environment – he grew up in the politically, racially and linguistically rather indeterminate Netherlands and his tutor, Mercurio Gattinara, inculcated in him the principles Dante had expounded in *De monarchia* – Charles was well equipped for the universalist imperial role he was called on to play and throughout his life he struggled faithfully to accomplish his mission as the champion of a universal Church and a universal empire. It was his dogged persistence in the pursuit of supranational aims in an age which was beginning to discover the intoxication of nationalism that, in spite of his very real political abilities and apparent successes, was ultimately responsible for his failure and premature retirement to the monastery at Yuste at the relatively early age of fifty-six. But perhaps even more of a liability than Charles's fundamentally anachronistic universalism was the sheer physical size of his empire: the variety and extent of his numerous possessions, each with its own traditions and modes of government, its jealously guarded interests and privileges, combined with the slow nature of contemporary communications to make the actual government of such an empire a task of truly Herculean proportions. Charles was a man of firm principles who was capable of a determination and of an industry which command respect, but the very multiplicity of the tasks demanding his attention prevented him from concentrating fully on any particular problem. Individually neither the Turks, nor the French, nor the Pope, nor the Lutherans, nor the problems of Spain and its rapidly growing colonial empire would have defeated him; coming together, however, they were too much for any one man to cope with and bore down on him with increasing weight until finally he was forced to capitulate before them. To the end Charles remained true to his motto 'Plus oultre' (still further) – as late as 1554 in obedience to the traditional policy of 'felix Austria' he was energetically pursuing the marriage of his son, Philip II, to Mary Tudor – but his division of his empire between that same Philip, who inherited the Spanish possessions and the Netherlands, and his brother Ferdinand, who acquired Austria and, Imperial elections being what they were, the Holy Roman Empire, bears striking witness to his conviction of the unmanageable complexity of the territories over which he held sway.

The greater part of Charles's reign was dominated by his quarrel with François I of France, a legacy of the conflicting claims of Valois and Habsburg to West Burgundy and Milan. But these circumstances and the personal rebuff which François had experienced as a result of his rival candidature in the Imperial election of 1519 were only subordinate causes of a quarrel which was to persist amongst generations of Europeans as yet unborn. From the English Channel to the Mediterranean and along the whole length of the Pyrenees every French frontier was exposed to invasion by troops of the House of Habsburg – a circumstance which did not change when Charles's empire was divided between the Austrian and Spanish branches of the family – and for François, as for every French statesman for the next 150 years, it became the natural and inescapable aim of French policy to break the encircling ring of Habsburg lands which threatened to thwart France's rise to European pre-eminence.

Apart from a perennial lack of money, Charles on his accession was faced with three main problems: the rivalry with France in Flanders and Italy, the Lutheran question in Germany and the threat of the Turks on the Eastern frontier of the Empire (since the fall of

Constantinople in 1453 the Turks had swept through the Balkans and twice during Charles's reign carried their holy war to the gates of Vienna). Inevitably these problems exacerbated each other and worked together for the discomfiture of Charles and the relief of his enemies: unwittingly the Lutherans and the Turks collaborated to save France from Habsburg domination, while the Turks and the French were in large measure responsible for the inability of the Imperial authorities to implement the Edict of Worms. Similarly his difficulties with the French and the Lutherans prevented Charles from mounting the anti-Turkish crusade which was dear to his heart. But the alliance of the Most Christian King of France with the infidel and the heretic (the community of interest with the former became an actual alliance in 1536, with the latter in 1552) was not the only political paradox in this Machiavellian century. Since the Italian policies of Charles were a threat to the territorial ambitions of the papacy, Pope Clement VII entered into a military alliance with François against the man who should have been his natural protector and who undoubtedly was unswerving in his loyalty to the Church. How misguided Clement's intrigues were was revealed on the field of Pavia (1525) when Charles decisively defeated his enemies. Along with François, who spent the next few months in a Spanish prison before buying his freedom with the humiliating Treaty of Madrid (1526) – which he promptly repudiated once he was safe in France again – the Pope became the unwanted and embarrassing prisoner of the Emperor, whose unpaid mercenaries completed the discomfiture of the papal intriguer by sacking Rome in 1527 – much to the superstitious horror of their devoutly Catholic employer.

The course of the five wars which Charles waged against François and his successor, Henri II, is too complicated to be described here: the significant thing about them is that in spite of the military successes of Spanish and Imperial arms the final outcome of the struggle was ultimately advantageous to France. The Habsburg encirclement of France was not broken, but by the Treaty of Cateau-Cambrésis, concluded by Philip II with Henri II in 1559, some three years after Charles's abdication, France was allowed to retain West Burgundy, Calais and Boulogne and the bishoprics of Metz, Toul and Verdun (the price of French support for the German Lutherans), which enabled her to dominate Alsace. Spain, by contrast, was confirmed in her possession of Milan and Naples. The development of France as a cohesive political unit was thus strengthened, while Spain was allowed to continue to enjoy the burdensome prestige of a far-flung empire.

A similar failure-in-success attended almost all Charles's other policies and ventures. Because of the pressure of work and Charles's natural caution the intractable problems and crises he encountered in his various territories tended to be dealt with tardily and the apparent solutions he did manage to achieve all too often succeeded simply in concealing the real problem, which was left for subsequent generations to solve – often at the price of untold suffering and bloodshed.

In the Holy Roman Empire the major political problem was posed by Martin Luther and his teachings. As the appointed defender of the one true faith Charles did not hesitate as to which course he should follow, and the Edict of Worms (1521), which put Luther under the ban of the Empire and outlawed his teachings, made the Emperor's intentions clear to all men. Yet, partly because his responsibilities elsewhere kept Charles absent from Germany for the next nine years, partly because neither the state of public opinion nor the external insecurity of the Empire, which precisely in these years was most acutely exposed to Turkish invasion, allowed Charles's lieutenants a free hand in the matter, the Lutheran heresy flourished. When Charles finally did challenge the Protestants in earnest, it was too late to stamp out the new doctrines and in spite of the complete military defeat of the Lutherans at Mühlberg (1547) and the humiliation of their leaders, Lutheranism continued to prosper. Thanks to the military and diplomatic abilities of Maurice of Saxony, the Lutherans were virtually able to dictate the Religious Peace of Augsburg (1555) which established the famous principle of *cuius regio, eius religio* and subject to this clause guaranteed the free exercise of the Lutheran form of Christianity. Yet the Religious Peace was no victory for toleration nor even a statesman-like compromise: it was a true child of the bigotry of the age and in its refusal to recognize the rights of the Calvinists and in its prohibition of the secularization of Church lands after 1552, it sowed the seeds of future quarrels which were to break out with such virulence in the Thirty Years' War.

In his own native land Charles's policies met with greater success and during his reign the Netherlands enjoyed a period of relative peace and prosperity. As a Fleming himself, Charles enjoyed a considerable degree of popularity and although in the course of his life he became increasingly Spanish in outlook, he always had a certain sympathy for his Netherlanders – who, after all, provided over a quarter of his total income – and in the main was content to leave well alone. Here again, however, his persecution of the Protestant religion and his – admittedly relatively restrained – use of the Spanish Inquisition to enforce religious uniformity ominously anticipated the trouble and torments of the unhappy Netherlanders under the reign of his intolerant and cold-hearted son, Philip II, whose savage policy of repression was eventually to force the 'men of butter' to revolt against his bloody lieutenants and establish the Protestant republic of the United Provinces.

Even in Spain, the heart-land of his empire, the apparent success and glory of Charles's reign is deceptive. Culturally it inaugurated the Golden Age; in other respects it marks the beginning of a long period of decline. Spain's American possessions continued to grow (Mexico was added in 1525, Peru in 1532) and to send their wealth for the enrichment of the Spanish treasury, but this apparently inexhaustible wealth slipped quicksilver-like through the fingers of her rulers without bringing Spain prosperity. Quite the contrary, it brought an unprecedentedly acute inflation and a steady undermining of the Spanish economy which in 1557 culminated in the complete bankruptcy of the Spanish exchequer. Foreign wars brought glory to Spanish arms, but they also drained the country of its best manhood and the ideal of the conquistador all too often went hand in hand with contempt for the farmer, the artisan and the merchant. Further, the close union of Church and State proved to be harmful for Spain's ultimate welfare. Economically and eugenically the clericization of Spanish life – it has been estimated that in 1570 a quarter of Spain's adult male population was in orders – was a disaster, while the activities of the Inquisition and the destruction of the Moorish and Jewish communities together with the Lutheran heretics robbed the country of some of its most industrious citizens. Worse still, the rigorously disciplined fanaticism imposed on the Spanish people by the union of Church and State persistently caused them to overreach themselves and ultimately left them militarily, politically and economically exhausted and impotent. Herein, rather than in any individual reverse such as the loss of the United Provinces or the defeat of the Invincible Armada, lies the real tragedy of the Spain of Charles V and his successors.

SEVEN

The Beginnings of European Nationalism

THE political structures of the Middle Ages were dynastic and supranational: nations and national feeling had scarcely existed and it was the concept of loyalty to the feudal overlord rather than to the abstract ideal of the nation which had enabled the machinery of government to function. In the late fifteenth and early sixteenth centuries, however, a new element entered into political and intellectual life in the shape of an awakening national consciousness amongst the people of Europe – the result of improved communications, the rise of a prosperous and educated middle class and the breakup of the supranational empires of the Stauffer and the Plantagenets. In the sixteenth century this new national self-awareness was almost always recessive to other considerations of an economic or religious nature; it was still confused and for the most part inarticulate, often indeed it was barely distinguishable from the group loyalties and local patriotisms of earlier epochs, but it was an awareness which was to grow and spread until in the nineteenth and twentieth centuries it was to emerge as the dominant factor in European and world politics.

That this national self-awareness should first manifest itself simultaneously with the rise of the so-called 'nation state' in the France of Louis XI, the Spain of Ferdinand of Aragon, and the England of Henry VII, is little more than a coincidence. These monarchs did indeed establish states in which nation and body politic coincided and so provided the all-important basis on which nationalism proper, with its inevitable racialist overtones, might flourish – the absence of such a basis was largely responsible for the late and distorted growth of German and Italian nationalism; but France, Spain and England were not established as 'nation states' in response to the feeling that the nation, either ethnologically or linguistically defined, constituted a natural or mystical entity which should be given political expression. Nor did Louis, Ferdinand or Henry regard themselves as symbols of the nation: their approach was essentially dynastic, their success often due to their readiness to 'divide and rule' the nation, and characteristically they were all eager to absorb other racially and linguistically distinct nations, be they Breton, Moorish or Welsh, into the kingdoms over which they presided. Similarly their successors were not loath to offer themselves as candidates for election to the office of Holy Roman Emperor, and Henry VIII seriously considered the possibility of reviving the old claim of the English kings to the throne of France. In a word, they were as universalist as Charles V himself and it was the force of circumstance rather than political insight and a sense of national mission which threw them back into the arms of their national communities.

As the rulers, so the subjects. As the century progressed, kings and commoners alike increasingly felt themselves to be English or Spanish or French or Dutch and looked with conscious pride on the achievements of the nations to which they belonged, but for decades to come the loyalties of most Europeans were to their religion, their rulers and to their own immediate material advantage, rather than to vague imponderables such as nation or fatherland. The new national self-awareness on the part of Frenchmen did not prevent the massacre of St Bartholomew. Nor was it so much a sense of outraged Dutch nationhood as religious persecution and the imposition of taxes which spelt ruin for the industrial and commercial Low Countries that caused the latter to take up arms against Philip II. By the same sign, the Flemings' racial and linguistic affinities with the Dutch did not prevent them from deserting the latter once the worst excesses of the Spanish tyranny were removed.

One may in the sixteenth century distinguish three broad types of 'nationalism'. On the one hand we have 'popular' nationalism: in effect often no more than the group solidarity and instinctive xenophobia of previous ages writ large, which, usually in response to obvious religious or economic oppression and abuse, manifested itself as hatred of the foreigners allegedly responsible. Thus it was the long-standing resentment of most thinking Germans at the financial exploitation of their faith by an Italianate Church which protected Luther at Worms and enabled him, even in the eyes of many a devout Catholic, to appear as the defender of the 'national interest' against the hated 'Welschern'. In much the same way, at opposite ends of Europe, the identification of an alien regime with a corrupt Church

had led to the outstanding success of the Hussite movement in Bohemia in the previous century and in the 1520s enabled Gustavus
Vasa to establish himself as the king of a religiously and politically
independent Sweden. Similarly, in Spain economic xenophobia,
feeding on the natural reluctance to finance foreign empire with
Spanish gold, led to the revolt of the Comuneros against the young
Fleming, Charles V, and the attempt to replace him by his mother,
Joanna, who, if mad, was at least Spanish. In a neat reversal of the
position it was these same emotions which forty years later were at
the root of the hostility of the Netherlanders to the young Philip II.
It was, in fact, in the Netherlands that the sixteenth century saw the
nearest approach to the national uprisings of more modern times.
The draconian measures by which Alba sought to impose on the
stubborn Netherlanders a political and religious uniformity in keeping
with the wishes of his master combined with the crippling and un-
constitutional taxes mentioned above to produce a savagely anti-
Spanish reaction which united all sections of the community in a
bond of common hatred. Yet it is a mistake to see in Egmont and
Hoorn, whose execution by Alba marks the real beginning of the
struggle, sixteenth-century equivalents of Padraic Pearse or Imre
Nagy: they died because of their defence of the threatened traditional
privileges of their class rather than because of their allegiance to a
national or racial *mystique*. Initially, the Revolt was almost completely
conservative in its aims, seeking to retain the best traditions of a
'liberal' past rather than to establish a new independent nation state.
Indeed much of the literature produced by the rebels (see the *Geuzen-
liederen*, especially *Wilhelmus van Nassouwe*, which was subsequently
to serve as a national hymn and in its deeply religious inspiration
regards the Spanish tyranny more in sorrow than in anger) is anxiously concerned to emphasize their loyalty to the Spanish King. In
view of this conservative element and the characteristic quickening
of politics with religion, to which the poetry of Jan van Hout or
Marnix van St Aldegonde bears such eloquent witness, it would be
wrong to see in the Revolt of the Netherlands evidence of nationalism
as we understand the term today. However, the early years of the
Revolt *did* see the emergence of a nationally based resistance movement which the military might of Imperial Spain could only temper,
but never destroy, and from which, in the northern Provinces at

least, a sense of national identity and of justifiable pride in national achievement was shortly to evolve.

Often this 'popular' type of nationalism went hand in hand with the false, politico-religious nationalism of the rulers of the emergent nation states, one of whose obvious aims was the reduction of the power of the Roman Church in their territories. Thus the English monarchs had, long before 1529, established their virtual independence from Rome by a series of statutes (Statutes of Mortmain, 1279, of Provisors, 1351 and of Praemunire, 1393) which severely restricted the right of the Church to hold land, abolished the Pope's right to appoint to benefices, and prohibited English subjects from appealing to Rome in legal matters. Similarly, after France had lost her resident and subservient Avignon popes, the Pragmatic Sanction of Bourges (1438) had drastically curtailed the Pope's authority and his right to raise revenues in France, a state of affairs in which the papacy acquiesced by the Concordat of Bologna (1516) in exchange for the abandonment of the traditional French view that the authority of a General Council was superior to that of the Pope. Often the rulers in question could draw on a considerable fund of national feeling – or at least on popular hostility to the foreign representatives of a foreign Church – in their dealings with the papacy: characteristically, it was the English desire to have an English Church which contributed to the success of Wyclif and the Lollards. Basically, however, the concessions were fought for and won by the rulers because the latter saw in the strength of the Church a challenge to their own authority, and the destruction of the secular power of the Church in England and France is no more than an ecclesiastical equivalent to the reduction of the great feudal lords.

In Spain, by contrast, this conflict of Church and State was largely absent. The centuries-old struggle with the infidel Moors had not only conferred on the Spanish Church a certain independence, but had identified the Church with the liberation of the fatherland from alien domination and thus prepared the virtual fusion of Church and State which was characteristic of the Spain of Philip II. Spain, although invariably regarded in the history books as a 'nation state', in fact never knew that centralized unity which France and England were to enjoy – a fact to which the separatist movements of our own century bear witness – but in so far as she did know unity, that unity was the gift of the Catholic faith represented by the Church Militant. In Italy and Germany, on the other hand, the absence of any real central authority, coupled with the discomfiture of the medieval emperors in their quarrels with the Pope, had prevented the growth of national Church and allowed ecclesiastical abuses to proliferate – a fact which makes the prevailing discontent with the Church and the success of Luther in Germany more readily understandable. The Italians, the 'stateless persons' of the sixteenth century, their country divided amongst alien conquerors, did not have even the Germans' restricted means of making their discontent known, although the successes of Savonarola in Florence show to what extent they were dissatisfied with prevailing ecclesiastical arrangements.

The third type of nationalism which emerged in our period was a by-product of humanism. The greatest humanists – like Erasmus – were scholars of truly international outlook who looked with contempt on the vernacular languages which were soon to undermine the foundations of their Latin-based Republic of Letters. Yet, in their concern with Classical antiquity, Italian humanists could not fail to appreciate that they and their compatriots were the inheritors of the splendours of ancient Rome, so that in the hands of patriot humanists such as Bernardino Corio (*Patriae Historia*, 1503) the Classical art of historiography could be made to serve the national cause in Corio's exaltation of the virtues of his own people and his contempt for the alien French. Similarly, certain lessons could be drawn from Classical historians: it was in Tacitus' account of the ancient Germans that Ulrich von Hutten found confirmation of his belief in the excellence of his fellow-countrymen, and it was as a result of his return 'ad fontes' that he was able to present the Germans with their national hero in the shape of Arminius, who had defeated the legions of Varus in the Teutoburger Wald (A.D. 9). Even the new science of philology was made to serve the nascent national myth: thus Alemannic German was held to be the first tongue spoken by men ('All men's language') or alternatively the word bore witness to the virile qualities of its speakers; the very name of the Germans, according to Konrad Celtis, constituted an unsolicited testimonial on the part of Latin speakers to the close kinship of the Germans with the ancient Romans. By a similar misapplication of science, many a French humanist regarded his race as being descended from

Francion, son of Hector, and thus as having inherited the virtues of the Trojans.

Once such nationalistic sentiments existed, both national success and national disaster served only to heighten them: Luis de León could see in the growth of the Spanish colonial empire proof of the peculiar calling and divinely appointed mission of the Spanish people, while conversely it was the spectacle of Florence a prey to the foreign conqueror that moved Machiavelli to dream of a strong united Italy and to exalt the welfare of his country above all other considerations.

From Otfrid to the propagators of Erse and Indonesian, nationalists have traditionally seen in the vernacular language an outward and visible sign of national identity and correspondingly equated the cultivation of the language with patriotic virtue, and the nationalists of the sixteenth century were no exceptions to this rule. The European vernaculars had been developed simply as vehicles for communication, but now they increasingly begin to be endowed with quasi-mystical overtones. Throughout Europe cultural nationalists insistently call for the extended use of their respective vernaculars: Simon Abril and Luis de León in Spain, Antonio Ferreira and Joao de Barros in Portugal, Claude de Seyssel and the members of the Pléiade in France, Ulrich von Hutten (by implication) in Germany, H. L. Spiegel and D. V. Coornhert in the Netherlands, Richard Carew and Samuel Daniel in England, all combine ardent patriotism with a programme for ennobling the vernacular. It is this cultural nationalism of the sixteenth century which most closely anticipates the nationalism of our own day: the obvious sign of national 'otherness', the hitherto scorned vernacular language, is extolled for its indwelling superiority, which is in turn considered to be a manifestation of the superiority of its speakers.

PART II

Poetry

Introduction

AT the beginning of the sixteenth century, the impact of the humanist movement, which coincided with the rapid development of printing and the French and Spanish invasions of Italy, brought about a transformation of western European culture that was regarded by contemporaries as a rebirth of antiquity. Such a view was based on a profound admiration for the accomplishments of Greece and Rome in all spheres of intellectual life and an intense desire to assimilate the message of ancient times. This could only be achieved by imitation of the great models of the past: not sterile copying, but a living communion of form and spirit, which corresponded to the period of apprenticeship necessary in any craft and certainly did not preclude the desire to surpass even the greatest model. So, like Petrarch – and Horace before him – writers thought it their task to move from flower to flower, culling the literary pollen which they then strove to turn into their personal honey, a unique literary creation composed of the most varied elements.

Perhaps the most significant change on the literary scene was the triumph of the vernacular humanism which flourished in sixteenth-century Italy, France and Spain, and which replaced the predominantly Classical interests of Italian humanism in the preceding age. This is particularly evident in poetry: for example, in Ariosto's *Orlando furioso* (1532), which remains the finest example of a successful marriage between the vernacular and Classical traditions, while the writing of Latin verse, though still a vital factor, became increasingly didactic and often pedantic. At about the same time, the precepts of Aristotle's *Poetics*, or rather his sixteenth-century interpreters with their insistence on regularity and decorum, began to dominate literary theory and practice. The gradual abandonment of Latin and return to the vernacular led to a desire to nobilitate the latter and place it on an equal footing with the two great Classical languages. For this, both poets and critics felt that a more elevated literary language must be evolved, based on the lexical and rhetorical splendours of antiquity and far from the usage of the mob. This lofty vernacular style was to be used in a systematic attempt to fill the gaps in modern literature and to make good its shortcomings. Of these, the epic was considered the most obvious and humiliating, for Renaissance critics generally refused to accept Dante's *Comedy* as conforming to the requirements of the genre, and a similar fate befell Ariosto's master-piece. Scholars like Trissino (1478–1550) and poets like Ronsard (1524–85) struggled to produce a 'true' epic. The former, being a scholar, laboured for twenty years and finally published his abortive *L'Italia liberata dai Gotti* (1547–8), whereas the poet realized the im-possibility of completing his task and gave up when only one third of the way through his *Franciade*. The endeavour was finally successful in two countries: Italy, which produced the most famous Renaissance epic – Tasso's *Gerusalemme liberata* (1575, 1581) – and Portugal, where Camões extolled man's triumph over nature and the thrill of dis-covery in his great work, *Os Lusíadas* (1572). The century began with Ariosto's supreme achievement in the romance and scaled other heights in the very different heroic creations of Camões and Tasso. Despite the latter's deep Christian faith, however, the Renaissance failed to produce a truly great religious epic.

In their enthusiasm for antiquity, writers disregarded or repudiated their immediate predecessors, except in the field of the lyric, where they found a wealth of achievement culminating in the work of Francis Petrarch (1304–74). The vernacular tradition was undoubtedly comparable to the relatively few lyrics that had survived from Graeco-Roman times, and here at least the moderns did not suffer from an inferiority complex: it has in fact been estimated that over 300,000 sonnets were written in Western Europe during the sixteenth century; and the sonnet was of course a modern invention, preferred by lyrical poets. Some of the components of Renaissance Petrarchism were already present in Anacreon and the Greek Anthology, as well as in Catullus and the Latin elegiac poets. Nevertheless, it was to Petrarch that all modern poets turned as to the supreme poet of love, the master who had succeeded in combining Classical elegance of form with modern complexity of feeling and the paradoxes of romantic love with the attractions of neo-Platonism. It was chiefly from Petrarch's *Canzoniere* that the writers of Italy, France, Spain and Portugal drew the vocabulary and imagery for their love poetry, its poetic forms – sonnet, madrigal, *canzone* – and those figures of speech – antithesis, zeugma, oxymoron – which the first great humanist had adapted from Classical rhetoric. At the beginning of the sixteenth century, another great humanist, Pietro Bembo (1470–1547), pointed out that much could still be attempted in the vernacular, whereas the excellence of the ancient writers made emulation impossible. Bembo's great prestige helped to establish Petrarch as the virtual dictator in Italian poetry, and what is owed to his *Canzoniere* in the modern European lyric is a debt unique in literature. It did not of course fail to produce a reaction: 'disciples' like Ronsard often rebelled against their master. But though at times Petrarch's influence appears overwhelming, his greatest imitators were able to use him as a point of departure. Already in the *Canzoniere*, the sonnet had been used not only for introspection or the praise of Laura's beauty, but also to mourn the loss of a friend or to attack the corruption of the papal court. So, while the poets of the Renaissance strove to equal the concision and polish of Petrarch's favourite form, they extended its scope: birth, death, politics, religion, friendship – all the facets of human experience were compressed into its narrow compass. So, too, with poetry in general. Classical antiquity led modern writers to substitute its imagery and mythology for the allegories of medieval literature; and the examples of Pindar and Horace were particularly effective in producing a noble inspiration which had hitherto seemed a monopoly of the Classical languages. Enthusiasm and confidence generated direct emulation and rivalry with the ancients; after the epic, satire was attempted, just as the bucolics of Theocritus and Virgil inspired pastoral verse. The latter, already hinted at in the vernacular Italian tradition, became one of the favourite pastimes of Renaissance society – an escape from the sophistication and harsh realities of life towards a golden age of beauty and simplicity, idealized by art. In all these ventures, translation played an important part. Amyot's translation of *Daphnis and Cloe* (1559); Luis de León's versions of Virgil, Horace and Pindar; Annibale Caro's translations of Virgil (1563–6): all are landmarks in the history of Renaissance verse. Translation, like imitation, produced new images, words and syntactical patterns modelled on those of the Classical languages. A very different type of complexity, based on the Classical ideals of harmony and proportion, came to replace the Gothic complexities of medieval poetry.

On the debit side, we find that the attempt at the close of the Council of Trent (1563) to make the arts once more subservient to religion was paralleled by the demands for decorum and conformity made by the neo-Aristotelians and the general hostility towards Classical learning in Protestant countries. Italy failed to provide great religious poetry, which was created by Protestant fervour in Germany and France and by the Catholic Reformation in Spain. Attempts to write a satisfactory 'Aristotelian' epic were accompanied by a search for grandiose effect which was out of tune with the light, even frivolous, themes preferred by poets as the century drew to its close. The fascination of music became ever more apparent in the lyrics of Italian and Spanish poets, while ornamentation, verbal conceits, and a need to surprise the reader came to be regarded as essential ingredients in poetry. Looking at the century as a whole, we realize that the pattern of poetry in modern times was fixed in the sixteenth century, when Italian influence was supreme, although the seventeenth century went on to produce the splendours of the Spanish Baroque and of French Classicism, with the drama replacing the lyric as the symbol of a new age.

ONE

Epic Poetry

ITALY

Ariosto (1474–1533)

THE greatest achievements of Italian Renaissance poetry, Ariosto's *Orlando furioso* (*Mad Roland*, first published 1516; third, final version 1532), is derived from the Carolingian legends of the French Middle Ages. Its synthesis of dream and reality, of popular and Classical culture, has fascinated generations of readers and even inspired Charles James Fox to cry out, 'For God's sake, learn Italian as fast as you can in order to read Ariosto.' Critics have been notably less successful in analysing its charms, however, and in their attempts to reduce poetic complexity to a neat formula they have imitated Ariosto's paladins in their mad search for the elusive Angelica.

The poem's kaleidoscopic equilibrium could not have been achieved in the atmosphere of Florentine humanism, where the same basic material had inspired its antithesis in the grotesquely comic world of Luigi Pulci (1432–84), who was in part driven to react against the exaltation of man preached by the leading Florentine humanists. Pulci's material originally stemmed from the *Chanson de Roland*, whose account of the exploits of Charlemagne and his court had long ago been transplanted to Italian soil. The French poem was composed towards the end of the eleventh century, at a time when the royal power in France was crumbling and the chivalric ideals of homage and loyalty to the crown seemed almost extinct· The *Chanson de Roland* turned back to a golden age of heroic manhood, when these ideals were supposed to have governed men's lives, exalting the concept of majesty in the person of Charlemagne and of religious and patriotic devotion in the emperor's nephew, Roland. The latter's nobility is set off by his tragic flaw of pride, which he has to expiate through betrayal and death on the battlefield at Roncevaux. This unforgettable episode and climax is dropped in the Italian poems that bear Roland's name, while it was only added as an afterthought by Pulci in the enlarged version of his poem, which significantly enough is still remembered by the name of one of its popular Rabelaisian giants (*Il Morgante maggiore*, 1483).

The whole *raison d'être* of the French poem was thus destroyed. Instead, the French fashion at fifteenth-century Ferrara expressed itself in the tremendous popularity of the Breton legends, which even inspired the christening of members of the ruling Este family. So, when Matteo Maria Boiardo (1441–94) came to write his *Orlando innamorato*, he boasted that he had combined the best of both French worlds, exploiting the fame of the Carolingian heroes together with the love interest of the Arthurian cycle. The very title of the new poem would have startled Roland's original audience. They would have found it difficult enough to think of love as playing a dominant role in their hero's life, but it would have been well-nigh impossible for them to accept the revelation that the noblest champion of Christendom had lost his heart – and his wits, as Ariosto was to add – to Angelica, a pagan beauty. Boiardo's courtly audience was, however, well satisfied with the poet's ability to entertain them with the tale of Orlando's hopeless love, spiced with episodes of martial prowess, incredible monsters and magic spells. The poem was interrupted by the French invasion of 1494, the year which also saw the poet's death.

Ariosto's poem takes over at this point: Orlando and Rinaldo have come to blows over Angelica, whom Charlemagne has placed in the care of the aged Duke Namo of Bavaria and reserved as a reward for the one who shall the better serve his country in defending Paris against the pagan host. Instead of victory, however, the Christians come near to being routed and Namo is taken prisoner. Angelica seizes this opportunity to escape, and in the tenth stanza begins that series of vanishing tricks which tantalize the heroes and readers of the *Furioso*. Her elusiveness is only equalled by the perfection of her charms, and she is in part a symbol of the vision of ideal beauty that haunted the artists of the High Renaissance. Ariosto's symbols are, however, well clothed with mortal flesh, his abstractions rooted in human life and experience, so that one of the fascinations of the poem is to observe the delicate interplay of abstraction and reality, that nice fusion of idealism and naturalism, which makes the *Furioso* one of the summits of European poetry.

The opening stanzas set out three main themes: the invasion of France by the Moorish king, Agramante; Orlando's madness; and the exploits of Ruggiero, culminating in his conversion to the Christian faith and his marriage with Bradamante, Rinaldo's sister. This union between the descendant of Hector of Troy and the fairest of the Frankish Amazons is a fateful one, whose illustrious consequences are foretold in Cantos III and XIII. Their descendants, the only Italian ruling family to weather the storms of the French and Spanish conquests, were to become lords of Ferrara and patrons of Ludovico Ariosto.

The reader is quickly disillusioned if he expects the poet to keep to this neat plan. Instead, he must be ready to follow the quicksilver of Ariosto's imagination and admire the sleight-of-hand with which the author presents his tale, celebrating 'the ladies, the knights, the battles, the loves, the courtesies, the bold exploits' of those far-off times. As the poet himself tells us, many and diverse strands are needed to make up his canvas, and he compares his art to the new polyphony in music, requiring bass and treble, high and low, to produce its incomparable harmony. Thus, in the first canto, Angelica's flight is immediately interrupted by her meeting with a pagan knight, Ferraù, and his ensuing battle with Rinaldo. Angelica manages to slip away, although Rinaldo finally notices her absence and sensibly proposes a truce to his opponent. The same commonsensical attitude, which characterizes so much of Ariosto's wildest fancies, prompts the pagan to forget his hatred of the Christian champion and to offer him a lift on his horse, as they set out in search of Angelica. The poet observes his characters' actions with a smile, and comments on the 'great goodness of the ancient knights': rivals, of different faith, still aching from terrible blows, they nevertheless shared the same horse without qualms. It should be pointed out that this line, 'Oh gran bontà de' cavallieri antiqui', has received too much attention. Like alchemists with the philosophers' stone, critics have pored over this one verse, turning it in all directions, in the hope that it might prove to be the miraculous solution to their problem: in this case, the poet's attitude towards the age of chivalry. For some, it is yet another example of wishful thinking on the part of an unrepentant dreamer; for most, it indicates varying degrees of detachment from or disillusionment with the ideals of chivalry which Ariosto's characters are supposed to obey. Such critics have asserted that the age of chivalry was an anachronism and that the poet was only too well aware of the fact, as he shows in his denunciation of gunpowder, which has destroyed the glory and honour of war (XI, 26–7). The historical context, however, proves very little, for the same period also contained the chivalrous career of Bayard (1473–1524), the knight 'without fear or fault', whose single-handed defence of the Garigliano bridge against two hundred Spanish soldiers might well have inspired a medieval *chanson de geste*. History, too, has its anachronisms. Instead, we should turn to the internal evidence of the poem, remembering what Erich Auerbach wrote of the chivalric ideal: 'precisely because it is so removed from reality, it could – as an ideal – adapt itself to any and every situation, at least as long as there were ruling classes at all.'

In Canto XXXI, line 61 we find a similar, though less famous, episode when the former Saracen knight Brandimarte has finally been reunited with Fiordiligi. His joy remains unclouded by suspicion of her virtue, in spite of her numerous adventures. The poet's mischievous comment is that the men of those times were very trusting, for they allowed their women to journey afar without a chaperon and were willing to welcome them back and think them 'as good as new on their return'. It is clear that the poet does not think that men were ever like this. He no doubt believes, with Machiavelli, that human nature is constant, whatever the historical context. Jealousy, however, would complicate his tale at this point. It is therefore excluded, while a bond of complicity is created between Ariosto and his readers. The poet winks in their direction, anticipates and neutralizes any possible scepticism, and obliges his audience once more to suspend their disbelief. This has been described as Ariosto's irony. But the term requires too many qualifications, if it is not to give rise to thoughts of Cervantes and even Voltaire. Instead, we should be glad to find an author who can smile at his own characters, a smile that is unique in literature, because it is neither too broad nor too thin, but is the expression of Ariosto's geniality, while retaining some of the ambiguity of the most famous smile in painting.

Now, we return to the first canto, where Angelica overhears Sacripante making his well-worn comparison between the maiden and the rose and bewailing the loss of her virginity. She reveals herself to him and assures him that his fears are unfounded. The poet tells us that Sacripante was only too ready to believe her, adding, 'Perhaps it was true, but not however credible to anyone in command of his senses' (I, 56). In Canto XIX, on the other hand, we are told: 'Angelica let Medoro cull the first rose, which had never been touched before.' There is no contradiction, if we realize that in the first episode the author's intention is to emphasize the gullibility of lovers and to point out that, however true Angelica's statement, Sacripante is love's fool in accepting her word against appearances: 'But it easily seemed possible to him, who was lost in far greater error; what man sees Love makes invisible and the invisible is revealed by Love' (I, 56). Not irony, then, but an indulgent smile at the weakness of lovers, whose predicament is only too well known to the poet. Ariosto's wisdom and experience are not expressed with patronizing superiority, but with the conviction that nothing human is alien to him. However clear-sighted and disillusioned he may appear at times, the poet is still in part Alefo, the astrologer unable to foresee his own death (XVIII, 174–5), or Moschino, the drunkard who avoided water all his life – only to end it by drowning in the hated substance (XIV, 124).

References to pseudo-historical sources (XXIV, 44; XXVI, 23; XLII, 20–22) were already to be found in the Italian tradition. What is new is Ariosto's introduction of realistic detail into his story, which so delighted Galileo: for example, his unheroic description of the three knights' reluctance to leave the comfort of the palace and their imminent meal and go out into the cold and rain to do battle with Bradamante (XXXII, 71). 'Realism' is brought into the most fantastic situations and broadens the smile on the author's lips, as when he describes Ruggiero's world tour on the back of the Hippogriph. This paragon of strength and courage takes care to interrupt his fabulous journey at night: 'Do not think, my Lord, that he remains always on the wing over such a long distance: every evening he goes to an inn, avoiding as best he may bad food and lodging' (X, 73). In the preceding canto, Orlando had managed to impale no fewer than six of the enemy on his spear. The poet adds, as mock-proof of his veracity, 'And, since it could not hold any more, he left out the seventh, so badly wounded that he died from the blow' (IX, 68). It was, moreover, part of the stock-in-trade of chivalry that the paladins undertook their exploits for no external reward. Yet when Rinaldo sets out in search of adventure in the far north, the monks at an abbey in Scotland tell him that, although he will find adventure galore in their distant land, he would be well advised to return to a place where his feats will not risk oblivion (IV, 56). They just fail to throw in 'Or why bother?', the other side of the Renaissance cult of fame as a spur to great and noble deeds.

In Canto IX, Orlando goes right through the Moorish army, asking for news of Angelica. Ariosto is careful to pay lip-service to verisimilitude with the incredible explanation that the knight was dressed in Moorish costume 'And he spoke Arabic so fluently that he seemed born and bred in Tripoli.' This detail is not forgotten in Canto XXIII, when the poet describes the way Orlando discovers the news of Angelica's marriage with Medoro. Ironically enough, it is his knowledge of Arabic, which had helped him to abandon the Christian cause and wander afar in search of pagan beauty, that enables Orlando to read the message of Medoro's conquest and helps to unhinge his reason. Once again, the poet explains 'It was written in Arabic, which the Count understood as well as Latin: among the numerous languages that he knew so well, the paladin had this one at his fingertips' (XXIII, 110). However, the reader hardly needs to suspend his disbelief in the Count's linguistic expertise, for he is completely taken up with the magnificent description of Orlando's jealousy, as it gradually turns to madness. This is the implied subject of the poem, and the incident occurs exactly half-way through the forty-six cantos. God has decided to punish Orlando for his desertion of Charlemagne in the Christians' hour of need, a crime made worse by the fact that the object of his love is an infidel. We have already seen, however, that the multiplicity of themes makes it impossible for any one to achieve pre-eminence, and it is not long before the poet abandons his mad hero to take up the other strands of his tale, while the religious connotations of Orlando's madness are ignored by reader and author alike. The latter begins the following canto with one of his celebrated comments on life and human behaviour, pointing out that any great love is a form of madness, as he himself knows from personal experience. While it is difficult to regard Orlando's sin as having provoked divine retribution, it is obvious that it infringes the poet's ideal of the golden mean which should govern human conduct. The episode also stands out as a superb proof of Ariosto's understanding of the human heart and his ability to move the reader into compassion for the strongest man in the world, who is unable to control his feelings and touchingly attempts to destroy the poison of jealousy by telling himself that it is not *his* Angelica who has fallen in love, or again that 'Medoro' is a fiction, perhaps a name she uses in order to hide her love for him, Orlando. He is then obliged to read Medoro's paean to love, celebrating the happiness he has known with Angelica. Stunned by the blow, Orlando still tries to deny the evidence and convince himself that it is all a trick, a lie. How can he bring himself to admit the defeat of all his hopes and illusions? How can he accept the fact that Angelica, the proud Angelica who had scorned the love of the greatest champions, had made a gift of her freedom and incomparable beauty to an obscure Moorish foot-soldier? He cannot, however, stand up to the final blow when the shepherd tells the story of Angelica's nursing the wounded Medoro, her falling in love, their marriage and honeymoon spent in his hut. Orlando's mind is unhinged, his superhuman strength turned to brute force and destruction, and the greatest of the Christian paladins wanders like a wild animal, shedding his weapons and armour, while the pagan forces besiege Paris and slaughter its defenders.

Orlando is punished, his love revealed as the madness it is, and Angelica's excessive pride has also been defeated: the daughter of the emperor of Cathay is now the wife of an unknown private soldier, and her last appearance in the poem hardly befits the dignity of her preternatural beauty. In Canto XXIX Orlando comes upon Angelica and Medoro, on their way back to the Orient. In his brutish state he does not know the woman he had desired to the point of madness, while she fails to recognize Orlando in this wild animal who kills Medoro's horse with one blow of his fist. Angelica only just manages to escape by placing her magic ring in her mouth, which makes her invisible. As she does so, she falls from the saddle and finds herself 'flat on her back in the sand'. Pride has had her fall. Orlando hurries off the scene, dragging behind him Angelica's dead mare. A fitting end to a heroic passion.

Astolfo, the English knight, is the vaguely absurd protagonist of all kinds of incredible adventures. He is presented (VI, 27–53) as having been transformed into a myrtle. Liberated, he acquires a book of magic spells and a horn which puts even the most valiant to flight. After numerous exploits, he destroys the wizard Atlante's castle and takes possession of the Hippogriph. Canto XXXIV describes his descent into hell, which seems to be chiefly populated by ungrateful lovers, and his hippogriphic ascent to the mountain-top which shelters the Garden of Eden. There he meets St John, who tells him that God has decided to punish his cousin by making him mad for three months. Astolfo can, however, help Orlando by journeying with the saint, on Elijah's chariot, to the moon. The earth's satellite is an immense lost-property office for all that is lost on earth: the tears and sighs of lovers are to be found up there, together with womanly beauty, offerings made to princes, and a large mountain of bottled reason. This pile is made up of numerous phials, labelled with the owners' names, their contents having been lost through love, the pursuit of wealth, magic, philosophy, astrology and poetry. Astolfo is most taken aback to find his own reason there, which he had lost unwittingly and now gratefully recovers with Orlando's.

The pagan side is led by Agramante, king of African kings. This 'noble son of Troiano' leads the infidel host to near-victory before the gates of Paris, but is defeated when, like Charlemagne, he sees his leading champions dispersed, and he finally meets his end in the epic battle on the island of Lipadusa. Gradasso, King of Sericana, who had come to France to capture Orlando's sword and Rinaldo's horse, had suggested this trial of strength between three pagan and three Christian heroes and had managed to save Agramante by slaying Brandimarte. Orlando, however, like Achilles before the dead body of Patroclus, is seized with blind fury and avenges his beloved companion by killing first Agramante and then Gradasso, who knows fear for the first time (XLII, 1–2).

The most fearsome of the pagans is Rodomonte, who had attacked Provence single-handed. With the weapons and armour of his ancestor Nimrod, he defies not only the defenders of Paris but 'heaven itself'. In attack he is always in the van and, first to scale the walls of Paris, while 'the others make vows, he reviles God' (XIV, 117). His pride, cruelty and strength strike terror in the hearts of all who oppose him, as he leads twelve thousand men to their death. Hearing their cries of agony, 'he reviles heaven with fearful shout.' The slaughter and havoc he wreaks in the besieged capital make him appear Satan himself (XVI, 87), and he is only stopped in his attack on Charlemagne's palace by the impossible odds against him. This *Sturm und Drang* hero inspired Aretino and Desportes to portray his descent to hell, where he demands submission of the king of the underworld in a blood-curdling rodomontade. Ariosto's Rodomonte is however, like Orlando, unhappy in love. Doralice spurns him for Madricardo and he is left to listen to the tale of Iocondo's well-justified misogyny (XXVIII). Later, he is equally unfortunate in his passion for Isabella (XXIX, 25), followed by his grotesque duel with the mad Orlando. Absent from the battle of Lipadusa, he appears at Ruggiero's wedding-feast to accuse him of treachery and challenge him to a duel. His death ends the poem, as his proud, rebellious spirit leaves his body, still defying both God and man.

Ruggiero, descended from the magnanimous Hector of Troy, is a completely different pagan hero: indeed, it is hardly surprising to discover his Christian origin and destiny as future husband of Bradamante, fairest of the Christian warriors. Atlante, the magician who had looked after him as a child, vainly tries to save him from an early death. Ruggiero will have none of it. The predestined prince consort follows his glorious destiny, admittedly in somewhat tortuous fashion. His continual separation from Bradamante drives her to jealousy and the edge of despair, which she expresses in oft-imitated laments (XXX, 81–3; XXXII, 37–43; XXXIII, 60–64). She is, of course, united in marriage with her fair hero at the end of the poem. But before this happy ending Ruggiero seems only too willing to be led astray by such distractions as his magnificent toy, the Hippogriph, Angelica's naked beauty (X), or Alcina's wiles.

The episode of Alcina's magic island (VI–VII) is an example of the way in which the interplay of illusion and reality fascinated the poet and his contemporaries. Man's general inability to go beyond appearances is frequently highlighted in the *Furioso*, and this preoccupation was perhaps natural in a writer conscious of his country's defeat and the humiliating contrast between Italy's cultural supremacy and her political subservience to France and Spain. Ariosto, Machiavelli, Guicciardini and other writers who had known the golden age before 1494, were only too well aware of the need to distinguish between shadow and substance. In Canto VI, Astolfo the myrtle tells Ruggiero that the enchantress Alcina had inveigled him on to an island, which had turned out to be a whale. Transferred to a 'real' island, which Alcina had largely usurped from her virtuous stepsister Logistilla, Astolfo had become her lover. She, however, quickly tired of him as of her other lovers and, Circe-like, turned him into his present form. The allegory of lust is a traditional one. But, as always with magic or allegory in the *Furioso*, it is not forced or gratuitous like Boiardo's, for it corresponds to the poet's own experience or view of life. Alcina's lovers, who are turned into fountains, beasts, trees and stones, are almost a parody of the Petrarchists who used such metaphors *ad nauseam*, but the human significance of this episode is revealed at the beginning of the eighth canto, where the poet points out that there are many crypto-Alcinas in the world, men and women who enslave the hearts of others with 'deceits, lies and fraud'. The ring that saves Ruggiero by revealing the reality of Alcina's ugly wickedness is in fact the light of reason, which makes it possible for man to see through illusion.

Alcina's island returns in the form of Armida's garden in Tasso's poem; but in the *Furioso* we see that it is not Ruggiero's physical transgressions that represent his great sin for the poet, but his complete absorption in one woman. He, too, violates Ariosto's law, for his conduct echoes Astolfo's words, 'I enjoyed her delicate body, which seemed to me to contain every good.' Ariosto's outlook is far too sane to condemn physical or any other kind of pleasure, but excess is anathema to him. Man must retain control of his pleasure, as of his suffering, and must aim at moderation in all things. This is the criterion that governs the whole poem. It is this which condemns Orlando's love to madness, Angelica's pride to humiliation, Rodomonte's cruelty to defeat – and which causes the most fearsome heroes to be unhorsed by beautiful young ladies (XX, 130; XXXIII, 71). Life, the poet tells us, is in a constant state of flux; it is full of surprises. Man must be prepared for anything, but especially to see his ideals and desires remain beyond his reach, and smile in spite of it all. Angelica, who appears and is gone like a flash of lightning; Zerbino, who is reunited with Isabella only to die in her arms; even the happy ending of Ruggiero's marriage to Bradamante is clouded by the reader's knowledge that Ruggiero will be murdered before his son is born. This is what life is like, and man must make the best of it. As Horace Walpole remarked, life is a tragedy for him who feels and a comedy for him who thinks. Ariosto is man in his entirety.

There is a story that Cardinal Ippolito d'Este, to whom the *Furioso* was dedicated, interrupted Ariosto's reading of the poem with the question: 'Messer Ludovico, where on earth did you find so much nonsense?' Positivist critics went to a great deal of trouble to answer the cardinal's question, and some seem to have taken sadistic pleasure in proving that Ariosto invented very little in the *Furioso*. They have forgotten Pascal's observation that writers must use the same ball: it is the skill with which they place it that counts. And Ariosto's 'nonsense' is raised to artistic perfection by the way in which this supreme story-teller uses his material. His style is dominated by his need to tell a story, it is subservient to the flow of the narrative, no word or image is allowed to intrude. All is encased in the gold of Ariosto's *ottava rima*, his octaves which ebb and flow like the waves of the sea, surging on and impelling the reader toward the next poetic tide. Foscolo was right when he claimed: 'No one perhaps has borrowed more than Ariosto; and yet, there is no one who can boast greater inventive powers.'

*

The tremendous popularity of the *Orlando furioso* (154 editions before 1600) inspired Lodovico Dolce to write *Le prime imprese del conte Orlando* (posth. 1572) – an account of Orlando's youth from the time of his birth to his marriage with 'Alda la bella' – and Vincenzo Brusantino to complete Ariosto's story with his *Angelica innamorata* (1550), which tells of Ruggiero's death, revenged by Bradamante and Marfisa. Ariosto's other characters were not neglected in, for example, Antonio Legname's *Astolfo innamorato* and Marco Bandarini's *Mandricardo innamorato*, while the inevitable *Rinaldo furioso* was produced by Francesco Tromba in 1530 and anachronistically followed by Ettore Baldovinetti's *Rinaldo appassionato* in 1533.

Giangiorgio Trissino (1478–1550) and Bernardo Tasso (1493–1569)

Soon, however, the very popularity of Ariosto's poem came to be held against him and the rising tide of Aristotelianism brought charges of formal confusion and immorality. The artistic unity of the *Furioso* – which the poet had been so careful to safeguard by the exclusion of his *Cinque canti* – was denied, and a single straightforward plot was required whose verisimilitude might be assured by history. The bold emulation of Classical culture was replaced by a rigid set of formulas and the setting up of an artistic balance sheet: authors were expected to make good the entries in the debit column of the vernacular, especially under the headings tragedy and epic. For the latter, Giangiorgio Trissino set out to repair the omission and remedy Dante's and Ariosto's inability to write a true epic according to the Aristotelian norm. Trissino's idol was Homer, whose epithets and wealth of description raised him far above Virgil's attempts in the heroic field; he felt little but contempt, tinged with envy, for the *Furioso*, 'which is liked by the common herd.'

His own creations were in no danger of such a fate, for after a period of white-elephantine gestation (1527-47) the work on which he had pinned all his hopes of poetic immortality was stillborn: *L'Italia liberata dai Gotti*. It is doubtful whether the poet himself believed in the naïve hope expressed in the dedication to Charles V that the emperor, like other rulers, would find much useful information and advice regarding the art of war in his poem. On the other hand, he set great store by his historical learning, taken largely from Vegetius and Procopius and intended to provide a realistic background for his narration of the conquest of Italy by Belisarius on behalf of the Emperor Justinian in the sixth century. This same erudition leads the poet to make incredibly long lists of names and objects, as in the naming of every province of the empire with its leaders' escutcheons in Book II, or in the minute topographical description of Rome (Book X) with its two amphitheatres, three theatres, seven bridges, seven hills, eight fora, fourteen aqueducts, twenty-nine libraries, nineteen hundred baths, four hundred and twenty-four churches, and so on. The story is recounted in what Trissino considered the nearest equivalent to Greek and Latin hexameters: *endecasillabi sciolti*, the blank verse whose promotion has gained the poet more fame than readers, for its turgid monotony of tone and accent have little to recommend it. As Voltaire pointed out, Trissino imitated everything in Homer, except his genius. His attempts at Homeric realism in the descriptions of clothing and weapons are wearisome, his Christian substitutes for Homer's gods ridiculous. Angels pop up from bushes to help or impede a hero's progress, and their names quickly betray their incongruous pagan origin: the chameleon-like Palladio, Nettunio of the sea, and Gradivo the eternal substance of war. Even worse is the portrayal of God and the Virgin Mary: the mother of God requires a bloodbath as revenge for rape committed in church, which had caused her statue to turn away its gaze in modest shame (Book V). The whole religious context is in fact blurred since both sides pray to the same God, although the Goths are obviously handicapped by their penchant for heresy.

In Book I, an angel appears to Justinian to tell him that he must not be content with his recent victories in Africa: he must now undertake the liberation of Italy from the rule of the Goths. Belisario is appointed supreme commander of the imperial armies. From the very beginning, the Aristotelian stress on edification is well in evidence. So, the Conte d'Isaura decides to attend to military matters first, 'And then we shall eat; although it is better to go without food than without honour,' while Justinian is at pains to claim that he has never seen his followers 'wearied or exhausted' in his service, and nearly every character at one time or other has cause to exclaim, 'Let us die, rather than sully our honour.' The bathos that lurks constantly in wait for the poet is most obvious in Book III, when Trissino describes in great detail the empress's toilet in her efforts to win over her husband to the cause of Sophia's marriage, which culminate in some chaste imperial love-making after the 'ruler of the world' and his spouse have first made sure that the doors of their chambers are locked. However, Sophia's future husband Giustino is only just saved from drowning by the Angelo Nettunio. Sophia believes him to be dead and poisons herself. Giustino is turned upside down, all the water comes out, he discovers Sophia's fatal deed and decides to put an end to his own life. All is set right in this bourgeois drama when Sophia's sister refuses to weep like the other women and gets a doctor to administer an antidote.

Homer's Circe may have inspired the figure of Lygridonia in Book IV, but a more obvious precedent is to be found in Ariosto's Alcina. Trissino generally tries to combine the best of the Homeric and romance worlds. So we find giants in Book XXV, an Amazon who almost unhorses Turrismondo (XVIII), and Belisario in Book IX who, like Orlando, has a foretaste of what gunpowder was to achieve on the battlefield, although, unlike Ariosto's hero, he is unchivalrous enough to wish to use this undiscovered invention against the Goths. The mixture of ordered verisimilitude, historical realism and romantic adventure is disastrous. But the poet is not discouraged from relating the liberation of Naples, Rome and Milan, culminating in the contest between ten 'Romans' and ten Goths to decide the fate of Ravenna and the whole peninsula. The Goths are led by their king, Vitige, one of Trissino's more interesting creations. He nevertheless fails to take on tragic dimensions, partly because the whole story is so rigidly governed from above: the heroes are mere puppets, who have their skirts pulled by an angel to remind them of what they have to do in the thick of danger (XXV) and are driven to and fro by an omnipotent God, who is himself deprived of the devil and therefore of any possibility of creating some kind of Miltonic drama. Instead, it was left to the Italian poet to provide Milton – via Tasso's *Mondo creato* – with a model for the use of blank verse in the heroic epic, which he claimed to have been the first to introduce into Italian, but which neither the precepts of Aristotle nor the example of Homer could bring to life in Trissino's poem.

The year 1548 also saw the publication of Luigi Alamanni's *Girone il cortese*, in which the poet tried to solve the problem of artistic unity by relating the adventures of only one of the protagonists of the Breton legends – Girone, whose purity of soul was admired and helped to satisfy the outward code of conventional morality demanded by the Counter-Reformation. In 1560, Bernardo Tasso published his *Amadigi*. A letter of 1558 tells us that he had composed a first version on one 'single action', but that he had come to realize that Ariosto was right in offering his readers variety – a lesson brought home to him by the failure of Alamanni's *Girone*. Tasso further decided to recast his blank verse into *ottava rima*, the traditional form for Italian romances. The source of his tale was a work by Garci Ordóñez de Montalvo (1508), which even had the good fortune to be admired by Cervantes. Tasso's poem tells of three love stories: Amadigi, son of the King of France – it was too late when Bernardo discovered that the Spanish Gaula meant Wales and not France – who is in love with Oriana, daughter of the King of England; Oriana's brother, who loves Amadigi's sister; and Floridante, Prince of Castille, enamoured of Filidora, a magician's daughter.

Bernardo was determined to satisfy the critics and avoid Ariosto's supposedly capricious way of breaking off and taking up again the various threads in the *Furioso*. His own solution – to keep the three tales moving side by side in nearly every canto – is disastrously artificial, difficult to follow, kills suspense, and irritates the reader. A similarly ingenuous solution was found for the problem of unity. Bernardo thought his many digressions and flashbacks justified, provided they were placed in the mouth of an important character. He happily went on to interrupt his narrative with long dialogues, letters, and homilies, so that an enterprising Frenchman was able to extract these passages from the *Amadigi* and publish them as models for polite conversation and correspondence. Another bright idea was to begin each canto with the description of a sunrise and end with a sunset, on the grounds that the canto division corresponded to the diurnal unit that had originally governed the reciting of epic poetry. After some friends complained that there was altogether too much weather in the poem, Bernardo decided to do away with this neat scheme, although he still left his readers with no less than fifty dawns and thirty-one sunsets.

Lions and giants, shipwreck and imprisonment, are strewn across the path of true love, although this eventually leads to marriage. The society for which the *Amadigi* was written was evidently more refined than Boiardo's or Pulci's audiences. Adultery came to be replaced by love between unmarried persons, though marriage is generally focused on as the true end of love. Action is less important, with greater stress laid on the characters' emotions. We are moving towards the Baroque in the handling of the subject, which is often florid and delights in decorative elements, with brilliant colour and panache, at the expense of the narrative. The poem, however, earned its author a considerable reputation and continued to find admirers well into the eighteenth century.

Torquato Tasso (1544–95)

Bernardo's son, Torquato, was born in the year the Council of Trent was summoned by Pope Paul III. His upbringing was marked by numerous travels and the death of his mother (1556), which helped to create a sense of insecurity evident in his work and personality long before his breakdown and imprisonment at Ferrara (1579–86). Modern critics have reacted against romantic legends of the poet's life. It is nevertheless possible to see in Tasso's sufferings a reflection of the crisis that overtook Italian society at this time, once its cultural supremacy had been neutralized by the shock of the Sack of Rome (1527) and the Confession of Augsburg (1530). The rigorous discipline imposed in the religious sphere by the Society of Jesus (founded 1540) had its counterpart in the Aristotelian orthodoxy that began to replace the suspect interpretations of neo-Platonism in art and literature. By 1570, Tasso – at one time a pupil of the Jesuits – had witnessed no fewer than eight attempts to produce an Italian epic according to the Aristotelian recipe: all of them failures, in spite of an even greater number of theoretical formulations of this recipe. The poet himself, as early as 1562, had published his *Rinaldo*, a compromise in which unity is supposedly attained by concentrating on the loves and adventures of a single character from the *Furioso* family. Still earlier, however, the adolescent poet had found the theme which was to haunt him throughout his life: the struggle for the deliverance of Jerusalem by the crusaders in 1099.

History, for Tasso, provided a firm basis for the epic. It offered a particular truth which could be placed on the universal plane of poetry. Long before the Romantics, Tasso rejected Classical mythology and ancient history as irrelevant to the modern epic. Instead, the poet must guarantee the topicality of his theme by taking it from recent Christian history – not too recent, however, so as not to be hampered in his need to alter detail and embellish his subject. It is clear how well the First Crusade met these requirements. Sufficiently removed from Tasso's times to furnish a heroic age of Christian achievement, its topicality was assured by the continuing threat of Islam and repeated calls for a crusade that echoed through Renaissance Italy. Popular enthusiasm for this mirage reached its height with the victory at Lepanto in 1571, which also inspired the ninety-four year old Titian to paint his famous *Allegory*. The heroic aspects of the struggle against the enemies of Christ held great emotional appeal for Tasso, and the capture of Jerusalem appeared to him as the grandest epic theme since Virgil's description of Aeneas' labours to prepare for the foundation of the Roman Empire. It held a peculiar fascination for a man incapable of resolute action. Moreover, the obvious allegory satisfied the renewed demand for edification in art: poetry was to provide the sugar coating which sermons lacked and which was so necessary to the man who refused all bitter medicine in his illnesses. The imposition of morality from above sprang from the weakness of the Roman Church, undermined by the Protestant revolt and its own corruption, just as Tasso's yearning for orthodoxy reflected his own doubts and led to a search for heroic grandeur not unlike that which inspired the architecture of Jesuit churches and the pomp of the post-Tridentine papacy. It is a mistake to suppose that the heroic form and diction of the *Gerusalemme liberata* (finished 1575) were alien to Tasso's nature. Instead, we should be prepared to accept the co-existence of weakness and grandiose aspirations and understand that the failure to give artistic life to certain religious strivings may be due to the poet's limitations rather than to any lack of belief. On the other hand, the dangers of such attitudes are obvious.

Twenty cantos unfold the action of the *Liberata*. At the beginning, Tasso claims that the crusaders have been fighting for six years – a hundred-per-cent inflation inflicted on history by the poet, owing to his desire to increase the difficulties and hence the achievements of his champions, and to bring his poem nearer to the *Iliad*. As in Homer, we find ourselves in the last, critical stages of a long drawn-out war. Agamemnon's role is played by the paragon Goffredo, whose forces are disastrously weakened by the absence of a number of the Christian knights, and especially by the Achilles-like desertion of Rinaldo. Although in no way related to Charlemagne's paladin, this ancestor of the Este family has some traits in common with the hero of Tasso's first published epic. Both represent the adolescent dream and promise of boundless glory. The Rinaldo of the *Liberata*, however, is more developed as a portrayal of exceptional, heroic humanity. Having joined the crusade at eighteen, he is youth in all its power and weakness. His physical strength is all-conquering, realizing Tasso's own dream of amorous success and high renown: 'no lust for gold or empire in him, but immoderate, burning desire for honour' (I, 10). He appears as the god of both war and love (I, 58). This darling of heaven and earth must not be judged by the laws governing other mortals, as Tancredi points out to Goffredo (V, 36). Unable to bear reproof or punishment for the murder of a Christian knight, Rinaldo abandons the Christian army in its hour of need, 'his spirit intent on magnanimous deeds' (V, 52). Seduced by Armida, it is his desire for glory that is appealed to by the two knights sent to win him back to the Christian cause. They do not waste time with talk of religion or duty, but come straight to the point: 'Fortune and victory await you' (XVI, 33). His later confession and reconciliation with God and Goffredo (XVIII) are in no sense a conversion: he is still the same man as before, and his prayer on the Mount of Olives is essentially a romantic communion with nature.

Armida, who plays both Circe and Delilah to Rinaldo, is sent by her uncle, Idraote, the magician king of Damascus, to wreak havoc in the Christian camp. The aura of sensuality that accompanies her throughout the poem is immediately present in Tasso's description of her beauty, which lures men's glances to caress her body and probes towards 'the forbidden part' (IV, 31). She is a fit counterpart to Rinaldo: her beauty conquers all hearts. She appeals to the Christian knights for help to redress a feigned injustice, and embodies the fascination of the Eternal Feminine as she appeals to the strength or weakness of each in turn: truly all things to all men (IV, 87–9). Even her anger is alluring (XVII, 33). But she is more than the traditional enchantress, and in the episode with Rinaldo (XIV–XVI) Armida becomes the greatest feminine creation in European literature since Dante's Francesca da Rimini. Her first instinct towards Rinaldo is one of revenge: she would punish him for having set free her captive Christian knights. Using her magic powers, she conjures up a spirit. This beautiful, naked siren echoes the *Aminta*'s call to enjoy the fruits of life and youth, and appears as an alluring antithesis to Rinaldo's dreams of glory, telling him that fame which 'seems so fair is an echo, a dream, the mere shadow of a dream' and that the only certainty in life is offered by physical pleasure and the avoidance of care. Rinaldo is lulled to sleep, and Armida comes up to him with vengeance in her heart. His beauty, however, is too much for her and Tasso describes the change that takes place in her with superb economy: 'e di nemica ella divenne amante' ('and from foe she became a lover'). Unlike Ariosto's Alcina, she has become a woman. Jealous of her prize and bashful of her love, Armida takes Rinaldo to the Isles of Fortune, far from all inhabited land and remote from the call of battle.

The idea of Jerusalem as a symbol of stern endeavour, the earthly city pointing to its heavenly counterpart and representing man's duty in this world, is one that underlies the whole poem; but it is particularly evident in Armida's garden. Looking towards the Baroque, that supreme age of artifice and *trompe-l'œil*, Tasso condemns the scene's artificiality, while he feels the pull of its powerful attraction. The whole intricate sensuality of this episode gives us the measure of the poet's involvement with his creation, which is even more obvious if we compare it with Alcina's island in the *Furioso*. Ariosto's artistic detachment throws into relief the way in which Tasso identifies himself with the hedonism of the exotic landscape and the lovers' total absorption in each other (XVI, 18–26). In spite of the moral condemnation, its artificiality is in fact what makes the island a paradise, and his awareness that it must come to an end helps the author to convey by voluptuous sound and meaning every aspect of its refined eroticism. The artificial paradise is then destroyed, first by the arrival of two knights who bring home to Rinaldo the extent of his degradation and finally by Armida herself. Her desertion by Rinaldo is modelled on the famous episode in *Aeneid*, IV. As far as Rinaldo is concerned, the role of *pius Aeneas* is disastrous. But Armida remains magnificent above the rhetoric and, rather than her final appearance as the repentant Magdalen (XX, 136), we would remember the suppliant woman who encourages her lover to victory over her people and faith and, begging him to keep her by his side, will not, cannot, admit defeat (XVI, 47–50).

Armida's island and the enchanted forest (XIII) are the two great examples of magic in the *Liberata*. Once their siege-tower has been burnt down by Argante and Clorinda (XII), the Christians find themselves without the necessary wood. They go to the forest, which has been placed under a spell by the renegade Ismeno and is turned into a complex mass of hallucinations, not unlike those the poet himself was to experience in Sant'Anna. Ariosto's magic, we remember, is quite different: it has a natural quality about it which keeps the action going and the reader suspended in amused disbelief. In the *Liberata*, however, magic is no delightful fantasy but a dark expression of human fear and weakness. The dread that the forest inspires in the Christian soldiers is irrational: they do not even know what it is that terrifies them (XIII, 18). After the common herd has been driven away, Alcasto proudly offers himself. Fearing neither man nor death, endowed with brute-like temerity, he is nevertheless made to know fear for the first time when he finds the forest protected by huge flames which take on the shapes of castles and strange engines of war. The unexpected, the unusual quickly overcome his arrogant stupidity. It is Tancredi's turn. Struck by the apparent impossibility of fighting the fire, he none the less strides through it; the flames disappear and are replaced by a storm-cloud, which also vanishes. In the depths of the forest, he comes across a cypress, bearing an inscription that warns him not to disturb the spirits of the dead. It is now that this great Christian champion, impervious to danger, is undermined by his own nature. A strange mixture of pity, dread and pain seizes his heart (XIII, 40). With the instinctive reaction of a warrior, he strikes at the tree with his sword. Blood issues forth and Clorinda's voice is heard: 'You are a murderer, if you cut this tree.' This is in fact the voice of Tancredi's subconscious, expressing his deepest sense of guilt: he is defeated by the knowledge that he has killed the woman he loved.

The wood's spell will finally be broken by Rinaldo (XVIII), to whom it presents a scene of idyllic bliss, reminiscent of Armida's garden, and the enchantress herself appears – in vain – to dissuade him from his task. Tancredi, however, does not possess Rinaldo's single-minded strength. At the very beginning of the poem, he had been introduced to us as the greatest of the Christian heroes, after Rinaldo, because 'If any shadow of fault obscures his great merit, it is only the madness of love' (I, 45). We may imagine how different these words would have been in the context of the *Furioso*; but here it is the tragedy of Tancredi's whole life that is contained in this 'madness of love'. He desires Clorinda, who fights with the pagans and who tantalizes him from afar, a symbol of the beauty and happiness which remain for ever beyond man's reach. Her appearance distracts him during his duel with Argante (VI, 27). But the essence of Tancredi's love is to be found in Canto XII, when he comes upon Clorinda at night and attacks her as one of the pagans that had set fire to the tower. With deep irony the poet tells us that Tancredi was the only one who recognized this enemy in the Christian camp, when in fact he, of all mortals, is farthest from realizing the truth of her identity. A prey to illusion, man kills the thing he loves. So Tancredi hugs his opponent to him, rejoices in seeing her blood upon the ground, and plunges his sword into her sweet breast (XII, 64). The living death of the Petrarchists is here given a new twist in Tancredi's wounding and subsequent baptism of Clorinda. But the real significance of his love lies in its hopelessness and destructive force. Tasso was determined to prove that love could be worthy of the epic and that it 'is as heroic as war'. Tancredi's love is both heroic and tragic. It belongs to the 'strange, unhappy loves' of the *Liberata* and offers a new version of the Classical union of Venus and Mars, in which both love and war lead to death and pave the way for the romantic *Liebestod*.

In some ways, the pagan side is the more interesting. It has Armida – at least for most of the poem. Clorinda, too. Demographic reasons help to explain its monopoly of the feminine figures, which include Erminia. Her love for Tancredi is the counterpart of his for Clorinda. This Racinian situation is, however, reduced to elegiac tones in her tender, self-denying nature. The famous episode of Erminia among the shepherds (VII) shows that Tasso succeeded, however precariously, in introducing pastoral, as well as Petrarchistic, elements into the epic. The poet's own misfortunes and wanderings made him sympathetic to this pathetic creature, and the repose she finds in the sunlit world of the Jordanian countryside expresses Tasso's need to escape from the pressures of society. Before this, her words as she gazes towards the distant Christian camp (VI, 104–5) express her desire for peace and love, while they provide a magnificent justification for the poet's latinized syntax in the line 'O belle a gli occhi miei tende latine!', conveying as it does all the yearning and pathos that characterize Erminia.

For contrast, we turn to the men. Like the Christian leader, Aladino, King of Judaea, never manages to steal the limelight and he arouses the reader's interest only at the end as he bites the dust of the land he had ruled (XX, 89). Tancredi's opponent, Argante, on the other hand, is as fine a creation as Ariosto's Rodomonte. Wrathful, impatient of the gods as of human authority, his faith is in his sword. He is confident that the outcome of the war can be decided by himself in single combat. His immense strength and confidence enable him to triumph over lesser men, until he meets his end at the hands of Tancredi, whose taunts he ignores in a moving meditation on the tragedy which transcends his personal fate (XIX, 10) – a surprising facet in this formidable character, whose body remains awe-inspiring even in death and defeat. He had lived entirely for war, according to a code of primitive honour, and 'he died as he had lived' (XIX, 26). Solimano, King of the Turks, is equally impressive. Twice worsted in battle by the crusaders, he refuses to acknowledge defeat and wins our admiration for his Promethean struggle. Solimano is introduced in Canto IX, line 12: 'I will come; I will make mountains where now the plain stands: mountains of dead and wounded men; I will make rivers of blood . . .' He makes good this proud boast. And yet, the poet shows him for an instant unable to fight as he weeps over the dead body of his beloved page, Lesbino (IX, 86): 'Are you weeping, Soliman? you who with dry eyes watched the destruction of your kingdom?' Then, after a surprise raid on the Christian camp, he enters Jerusalem by night and instils new strength in the dispirited defenders of the city. When the final attack comes, he is the heart and soul of pagan resistance. At last, he sees the Christian ensign flying over Jerusalem. His one idea is to kill as many of the enemy as possible. He upbraids Aladino for being downcast and expresses defiantly, in the midst of disaster, that ideal of majesty which held such fascination for the poet and his age: 'Let hostile fate take away our kingdoms, for kingship is ours and rests within us' (XIX, 41). In his encounter with Rinaldo, Solimano feels the horror and amazement of defeat (XX, 103–7). Tasso conveys the gradual despair and realization that his strength is no match for Rinaldo's prowess. But he remains true to himself, an embodiment of pagan power and *terribilità*.

The unity of the *Liberata* is impressive. The poet succeeded in knitting together the various strands and achieved his ideal *e pluribus unum*. The subject itself was a masterly choice, as Foscolo pointed out: grandiose, in harmony with the climate of the Counter-Reformation, it was religious in the broadest sense without imposing restrictions of faith or dogma on the poet's imagination. The style is heroic, the heroes magniloquent, even the horses are magnanimous (XIX, 58). Tasso himself in later years came to feel that the conceits and artificial syntax were excessive. Paradox, the darling of Baroque poetry, is indulged in: 'Magnanimous lie, when is truth so beautiful that it can be preferred to you?' (II, 22), a description of Olindo's sacrifice which reminds us that here the sufferings of the Petrarchistic lover are for once supposed to be literally true for this suitor who 'desires much, hopes for little and asks for nothing' (II, 16). The way to the Baroque, with its love of spectacle, is even more clearly indicated in the poet's claim that a highlight of his epic is 'worthy of a crowded theatre' (XII, 54) and in his general view of life enacted on a stage, which can lead to some irritating asides (II, 31; VII, 93). Bathos is also evident (XIX; III). On the other hand, the poetic world of the *Liberata* usually vindicates the poet's use of language and incident, however forced these may seem when lifted out of context as Galileo loved to lift them in his attacks on Tasso. Episodes such as the enchanted forest and Armida's island show with what mastery the poet succeeded in exploiting the musical, sensuous effects of language. And to these we must add the magnificent descriptions of night (for example, VI, 103), the dawn of victory (XX, 5), the blinding heat and effects of the drought (XIII, 53–63), the clash of battle (VII, 38–44; XX, 51) and the peace of the countryside (VII, 3–22).

The end of the poem is an anticlimax: after the impressive descriptions of doubt and struggle, there is no compensating stress on achievement and victory. We are left with the memory of pagan grandeur and defeat rather than a sense of Christian success. This, however, reflects what was new in Tasso's poetry. The artist's strength was rooted in the weakness of the man, and it enabled him to express the poetry of defeat as the counterpart to man's noblest aspirations. It was to be expected that the same poet would find difficulty in portraying the triumphant march of faith, and scenes such as the procession on the Mount of Olives (XI) or Goffredo's glimpse of the heavenly host fighting on the Christian side (XVIII) are easily condemned for their empty rhetoric. It is, however, important to judge a work of art as a whole. In the *Liberata*'s poetic universe such defects are of little moment, and we should not follow the poet's example in his increasing preoccupation with religious scruples. Instead, we should remember that it was only after 1575 that Tasso wrote to Cardinal Bonelli, 'I know that certain love elements in poetry are like poison in fine food. I will get rid of the poison and prepare the antidote.' The antidote took the form of the *Gerusalemme conquistata* (1593), where morality and historical accuracy are primary concerns and the language is more straightforward. It is however the *Liberata* which, for generations of readers, has truly expressed 'the harsh tragedy of man's estate' (XX, 73).

FRANCE

The most significant fact about the development of epic poetry in the French Renaissance is that it did not develop, at least along traditional lines. Lively national consciousness, lavish royal patronage and desire to emulate the works of Classical antiquity should have combined to produce an epic to rival those of Italy, if not of Homer and Virgil, but even Ronsard, the most versatile poet of the age, failed in this field. The epic was one of the Classical genres specifically recommended to French poets in the *Defense et Illustration de la langue françoyse* (1549), and by about 1555 Ronsard seems to have begun the work with which he hoped to win Homeric laurels for France. His poem, *La Franciade*, was directly linked to the tradition of the Trojan epic, and was devoted to the adventures of Francus, son of Hector (better known as Astyanax) from whom the kings of France and the name of their land supposedly originated. There were to have been twelve books, starting with the sack of Troy, but the project never got beyond the four books, comprising some 5,000 lines, published in 1572. In a quatrain published at the end of the revised edition of 1578 Ronsard explains the incomplete state of his work by the discouragement he felt at the death of Charles IX (1574), but it is most likely that he was glad of the excuse to abandon a somewhat embarrassing liability. For one thing, his original choice of alexandrines had been countermanded, it is said by royal order, and he tried to compose the work in heroic decasyllabic couplets, which, though the traditional epic metre, were much less flexible by the sixteenth century than the alexandrine of which he had become a master; for another, there was too stark a contrast between the essentially artificial description of legendary or imaginary perils and the hideous reality of contemporary history, especially after the massacre of St Bartholomew. Perhaps if Ronsard had insisted on alexandrines, and made faster initial progress, he might have produced at least a partial poetic masterpiece before events overtook him, but as it is, the *Franciade*, despite some undeniably fine passages, must be entered on the debit side of his poetic balance sheet. No one else did any better in similar vein, and for expression of the epic spirit, if not of its conventional Classical form, one must turn either to the Creation epics of a Scève or a du Bartas or, above all, to the *Tragiques* of d'Aubigné, all dealt with under the heading 'Religious and Philosophical Poetry'.

SPAIN AND PORTUGAL

The least-forgotten Spanish epic of this period is *La Araucana* by ALONSO DE ERCILLA (1533–94). Ercilla begins by echoing the start of Ariosto's *Orlando* in order to show the difference between them. He is not going to write about the elegant amours of knights and ladies. It is clear from his repeated references to the subject that he would like to, partly for the very reason that, as he admits, he lacks the ability to do so, partly because he felt readers might well expect it from him, and largely because he is afraid he will bore them by writing all the time about war. His poem tells the story of the resistance of the Araucanian Indians of Central Chile to the Spaniards, who were seeking to extend their control of the area in the 1550s. It consists to a great extent of accounts of the attacks made by one side on the other. Ercilla often shows himself capable of vividly describing, sometimes with gruesome and convincing detail, battles involving large numbers and also single combat. He gives, too, a powerful impression of storms encountered by the Spanish fleet coming from Peru and the hardships suffered by Spanish soldiers pressing into the south of the country. The vividness he achieves is due in part to the fact that he was himself in Chile from 1556 to 1563 and spent some of the time at least with the Spanish army fighting the Araucanian Indians. Being able to write fluent, vigorous verse, he provides a lively and to some extent eye-witness narrative that is not too much spoilt by Classical allusions and other elevating stylistic devices. The events he recounts fall almost entirely within the period during which the *araucanos* were led by the great Caupolicán. We see him chosen by his people, gradually defeated by the Spaniards, and finally executed by them. However, while the situation thus slowly advances, the work lacks effective shape, and Ercilla's fears of boring his readers are seen not to be groundless, even though, for the sake of variety, he introduces stories of the sad loves of aristocratic Araucanian girls, visits to a magician's cave, accounts of the battles of St Quentin and Lepanto, and the 'true story' of Dido – to correct Virgil's unflattering version, as he sees it. It is Ercilla's general attitudes to his subject that are now of the greatest interest.

His broadest theme is that of the variability of fortune. The Spaniards have expended so much effort and so many lives in conquering Chile and yet have failed, in the long run, to obtain the success and reward they were seeking. Nevertheless, the Indians have been largely destroyed as a people, despite their greatness. Of the *araucanos* he writes, both in the cantos themselves and in his Prologues, with great admiration. While his picture of them is not entirely idealized, he goes to great lengths to show their bravery, loyalty, dignity and sense of honour. Indians of rank, as portrayed by Ercilla, come to possess most of the qualities admired in the European knight. As regards the Spaniards, he praises their bravery in battle and exploration – he is proud to have gone with them further into Southern Chile than anyone before – and acknowledges that some of them wish to conquer with honour. But what he stresses more is their cruelty and their motive of greed. Especially when writing of St Quentin and Lepanto, he shows he can adopt the Spanish Catholic Imperial manner, but there is relatively little of this. An Indian whom he makes us highly respect – Galbarino – declares that the Spanish claim to be conquering the land in order to spread the Christian religion is mere pretence; their real aim is to find gold. It seems clear from this and other passages that the Indian here is speaking for the author. When Ercilla tells of the Spaniards advancing into parts of Southern Chile where Europeans have never been, he shows them, in the strongest terms, bringing their own corruption and greed to a people innocent and virtuous. The myth of the Four Ages, particularly associated with Ovid and lying behind so much of the denunciation of exploration and trade with newly discovered lands that came from sixteenth-century moralists, is powerfully operative in Ercilla's thinking here.

Ercilla was in London, brought there as a member of the future Philip II's retinue in 1554, when he heard of troubles in Chile and set out to take part in the fighting. He began writing his epic soon after he arrived, when still in his earlier twenties. The first part of *La Araucana* (Cantos I–XV) was published in 1569; the second (Cantos XVI–XXIX) in 1578; the third (Cantos XXX–XXXVII) in 1590. Thus it was in his mind for over thirty years. The character of his moral interest in his subject seems to have remained essentially unchanged – and did not prevent this from being a successful work in terms of editions printed. However, it is in Part III that this moral interest receives the most emphasis and most clearly distinguishes it from the greatest epic poem to be written in the Iberian Peninsula: *Os Lusíadas*, which must now be considered, not only out of regard for its intrinsic importance but also, unfortunately, as the sole representative of Portuguese literature during this century.

LUIS VAZ DE CAMÕES (*c.* 1524–80) published his *Os Lusíadas* (*The Sons of Lusus*) in 1572, three years after Ercilla brought out Part I of his *La Araucana* and three years before Tasso completed his *Gerusalemme Liberata*. Part of it was written by 1560, when Camões just managed to save the manuscript when shipwrecked off the Mekong River on his way back from Macão to Goa. His epic is built on the story of the ten-month voyage of his distant kinsman Vasco da Gama, in 1497–8, from Lisbon round the Cape of Good Hope, up the coast of Africa as far as Malindi and across the Indian Ocean, where no ship from the West had ever sailed, to Calicut. This is the central heroic, epic feat of the work. We are shown the hardships and dangers gladly suffered by da Gama and his crew in performing what no man before them had achieved. We read of the strange places they saw, the storms they met, the scurvy they died of, and the intrigues of men seeking to destroy them. But this heroic feat is heroic service. Da Gama's greatest virtues are shown to be obedience and loyalty to the king who sent him, Manoel I, upon whom has now fallen the duty to carry on the conquest of the seas. Da Gama himself gives a long review of Portuguese history from the expulsion of the Moors to his own day. Later the feats of the Portuguese in the East down to the time of Camões are revealed to him in a prophecy. His own heroic voyage is presented as part of the greater epic of Portuguese conquest of the oceans of the world. It is thus that the work becomes the epic of the Portuguese people, the Sons of Lusus.

The central event of the work readily presents itself as the symbol of its own wider meaning. The effect is heightened by the structure of the poem, which is clearly integrated, dramatically coherent, and forms, almost to the end, a mounting climax. The passages brought in to give variety – the story of the Twelve of England and the Island of Love, particularly, belonging in different measure to the world of

Ariosto romance – are skilfully placed. Nevertheless, it may perhaps be questioned whether Camões's presentation of the wider moral significance of his subject is completely successful. He several times and with excellent effect portrays da Gama's voyage as a great new assertion of man's mastery over the physical world, and it is for this reason that this has often been regarded as pre-eminently the epic of Renaissance humanism. On the other hand, his moral view of the conquest of peoples seems narrow – much narrower than Virgil's, for example. Camões concentrates his attention much more on war and martial triumph than on the peace that follows, and perhaps keeps problems at bay by often speaking of the peoples da Gama comes upon as infidels and heathens, who are therefore due for conversion or subjection. Camões himself speaks of the corrupting effects of the desire for gold, and one of his most famous passages is that at the end of Canto IV where an Old Man, just as da Gama is setting out from Lisbon, voices a mighty condemnation of the whole enterprise. He wishes that Prometheus had never fired man with high desires. The love of fame achieved through endeavour he sees as a folly which disguises what is but cruelty and ferocity, which themselves hold life in contempt and turn an Age of Gold into an Age of Iron. But such remarks remain thematically undeveloped and somewhat unattached.

As da Gama's voyage proceeds it is now aided by Venus, now frantically opposed by Bacchus. These two represent, respectively, the forces favouring and resisting the accomplishment of da Gama's great task and clearly are intended to bear a broad moral significance. This, again, is perhaps insufficiently developed, while further difficulty may be felt in relating the significance Camões wishes them to bear to their imaginative and poetic character. It is not just a matter of the inadequacy of Camões's rather late explanation of them as angels of good and evil who have been given the Classical form agreeable to poets. Rather is it part of the broader imaginative tension that Camões creates by bringing gods and goddesses into the world where da Gama's voyage takes place while at the same time repeatedly stressing – as, for example, through the remarks of da Gama himself – the superiority of the world of fact over that of fable, whether Homer's, Virgil's or Ariosto's. In this he goes further than Ercilla. Camões's view is intelligible in relation to his own experience of travelling to India and the Far East, which kept him away from Europe for seventeen years in all (1553–70). However, within the poem it creates a measure of dissonance.

In making his voyage da Gama has done more, we are told, than Ulysses and Aeneas; Afonso I, in driving out the Moors, more than Caesar and Alexander. Camões repeatedly seeks to heighten our sense of Portuguese achievements by drawing such comparisons with figures from Classical epic as well as history. This is just one aspect of the way in which he constantly echoes the Classical verse he knew so well. In his own work this results in much poetic beauty as scenes and hours are described in terms drawn from Virgil, Ovid and others. His extended similes often possess a Homeric simplicity and clarity of effect. In general the poem has many wonderfully vivid passages, among them the scenes of arrival and reception in strange ports, with their ceremonial, colour, movement and noise; the simple, vivid pictures of shipboard activity, the storms, and on land the crash and slaughter of battle. Camões is skilled in hyperbole and laconic understatement. If he tells us that, at the battle of Aljubarrota so much blood was spilt that the very flowers changed colour, and if he remarks that, were there any more world to discover, the Portuguese would be there ('E, se mais mundo houvera, lá chegara'), he can also define da Gama's role with the splendid moderation of: 'Que êle não era mais que um diligente/Descobridor das terras do Oriente.'*

---

* 'For he was no more than a diligent discoverer of the lands of the East' (Canto VIII, st. 57).

TWO

Lyric and Pastoral Poetry

ITALY

WE are told that, after reading some sonnets by Pietro Bembo, ANTONIO TEBALDEO (1463–1537) gave up writing Italian verse and concentrated exclusively on the composition of Latin epigrams. The story is probably apocryphal. But it is a good one, for it illustrates the judgement of countless generations of critics who, whatever their estimate of his poetic powers, have regarded Bembo as the saviour of the Italian lyric and the legislator of Renaissance Petrarchism.

Tebaldeo was one of the first group of Petrarchists who flourished towards the end of the fifteenth century. They wrote sonnets after the manner of Francis Petrarch (1304–74), but excelled in improvisation and often preferred the eight-lined *strambotto*, with its musical accompaniment and epigrammatic ending, which could more easily be relied on to dazzle their courtly audiences and hide their poetic shortcomings. They wished to amuse and to impress listeners by their verbal pyrotechnics and eccentric imagery, and they now seem nearer to Baroque extravaganza than to the chaste muse of Petrarch. The latter had sung of his love for Laura in the *Canzoniere*, consisting of some 366 poems, divided into two sections: the poems before Laura's death, and those written after 1348. The art of the *Canzoniere* stands supreme. No other collection has been so widely read, so much admired and imitated. One of Petrarch's greatest achievements was to transpose many of the effects of Classical rhetoric into Italian verse, thus paving the way for Renaissance Petrarchism with its hyperbole, antithesis, periphrasis and conceits, while his unrivalled use of metaphor has left its mark on the whole of modern European poetry.

Tebaldeo and his friends were quite unable to match the great art so skilfully displayed by their predecessor: they were chiefly interested in the tinsel to be found in the *Canzoniere*. Such ornaments are fairly rare in Petrarch, but they were avidly seized upon, as in the second stanza of the *canzone Tacer non posso* (CCCXXV), where the poet tells us that Laura's soul during her lifetime had been imprisoned in walls of alabaster (her body) with a roof of gold (her hair), an ivory door (teeth), and sapphire windows (eyes) from which Love's messengers issued forth, armed with arrows and fire, to wage war upon the defenceless poet. The Petrarchists revelled in all this and drenched their poems in torrents of tears mingled with tempests of sighs. In this company, Tebaldeo distinguished himself by his extravagant imagery and exaggerated conceits: for example, he assures his readers that, when his mistress's house was on fire, he was obliged to stay away from the blaze, as the flame of love burning within his heart would only have added coals to the fire. Indeed, those who tried to put out the fire were unable to do so, for they were so burnt by the eye of the lady whose house was burning that they had to dowse themselves with all the water to hand, in order to lessen the fire now raging within their hearts. Yet, in spite of such virtuosity, Tebaldeo was eclipsed by Serafino dell'Aquila. Serafino was successful in everything he undertook, and not least in the moment of his death: the Jubilee Year 1500, when the pomp of his funeral equalled that of the most magnificent ceremonies and his sudden departure was mourned as a national disaster comparable to the French invasion of 1494. He had chosen the right occasion – generally making things much easier for Bembo and for historians of the sixteenth century – before his poems, famous for their dazzling improvisation, were published and subjected to critical scrutiny.

PIETRO BEMBO (1470–1547) had other aims, other interests. Destined to become the leading Italian humanist of the new age, he wrote eclogues and elegies, as well as the most elegant papal briefs, in Latin, had a profound knowledge of Greek and – something far more unusual for his times – was well acquainted with the works of the Provençal troubadours. His reputation as a scholar lent authority to his work as a poet: both combined to produce his Aldine editions of Petrarch and Dante in 1501, the first of the pocket-sized books that were to revolutionize European culture. Moreover we know that on 26 July of the following year Bembo finished copying by hand the whole of the *Canzoniere*: a very different approach from the superficial interest in Petrarch shown by Tebaldeo and his friends. Bembo wished to eliminate their excesses and to remove the overtly sensual tone they had borrowed from neo-Latin poetry, although his interest was always directed towards stylistic, formal elements rather than to matters of content. Thus, word-forms had to be sanctioned by Petrarchan usage, the *strambotto* was rejected, and the sonnet restored not only to the pre-eminence it had been accorded in the *Canzoniere* but also to the formal pattern and variety it had enjoyed with Petrarch. Tebaldeo, for example, had discarded the traditional construction of the sonnet by building up the whole poem to a grand climax in the fourteenth line – and in this he was to be followed by both French and English poets – whereas Bembo observed the essential characteristic of the Italian sonnet, divided into octave and sextet. By the end of the fifteenth century, the rhyme scheme of the latter had become petrified in the pattern CDC/DCD. Bembo now set it free once more, writing many sonnets with three rhymes in the tercets, offering a wealth of combinations: CDC/DCD; CDE/CDE; CDE/DEC; CDE/DED; CDE/DCE.

However preponderant the formal influence of Petrarch, it was also the great love poet that Bembo admired, especially during the early years of his poetic career, which began at the moment when Florentine neo-Platonism had reached its zenith and helped to curb the antifeminism of so many of the preceding generation of humanists. Now, Bembo felt that it was also necessary to combat the licentiousness of other humanists, like Pontano, and to restore woman to the place of honour she had enjoyed in the works of Dante and Petrarch. He was so successful in this, and so ably seconded by writers of the new age such as Ariosto and Castiglione, that this literary restoration was to have important consequences in the everyday life of the upper classes of Renaissance society.

The manifesto for Bembo's new style was written at the turn of the century and published in 1505. The *Asolani*, in the form of a dialogue, are intended to be a guide to good and bad love and to report a discussion held during a wedding-feast at the Villa di Asolo. There are three sections: the first book, with Perottino, who discourses at length on the miseries of love and gives us a caricature of the exaggerated sufferings expressed by legions of Petrarchists; the second book, where we find his opposite, Gismondo, who celebrates the joys of love and roundly declares the sufferings of most poets to be a pack of lies; then, the third, in which Lavinello attempts to provide a synthesis by declaring that love may be either good or bad, but finds his 'Renaissance' definitions of love and beauty condemned by a hermit, whose well-nigh exclusive praise of spiritual love ends the work on an ambiguous note. For, in spite of the fact that the whole of Bembo's literary career and its influence on contemporary poets proves that the last book of the *Asolani* was in no way deemed to be a rejection of the admittedly inferior love of women, the message at the end is very different from the ardent celebration of neo-Platonic doctrine attributed to Bembo in the closing pages of Castiglione's *Cortegiano*. In order to understand the paradox, however, we should bear in mind that Bembo was no philosopher, that in the *Asolani* he enjoyed debating the various problems of love rather than setting out a definitive solution, and – what is perhaps even more important – that the Aristotelian (Thomistic) distinction between love and desire (III, xiii–xiv) was only added to the second edition of 1530, at a time when the future cardinal may well have wished to demonstrate how far he had moved away from his former neo-Platonic position.

The work is interspersed with poems illustrating the arguments put forward by the various speakers – except the hermit, significantly enough, who is distinguished by poetic silence, whereas Lavinello's compromise, according to which the pure love of womanly beauty may lead man on to the love of divine beauty, is exalted in no less than three *canzoni*, Dante's most noble form. The language of the poems reflects Bembo's reform: the Latinisms dear to fifteenth-century humanists who wrote in the vernacular are banished, as are the external trappings of Classical mythology, while the poet's chief concern is to maintain clarity of style, in spite of formal complexity. The latter is evident in the short *canzone*, 'Non si vedrà' (II, vi), whose metrical innovations were immediately admired: stanzas divided into only two sections of four lines each, with two rhymes repeated in quick succession including the *rimalmezzo* in the fourth and eighth verses. The excesses of Petrarchistic jargon are avoided, although 'Voi mi poneste in foco' at the beginning (I, xvi) serves up once more the paradox of the lover living a double death, burned by the fire of love and drowned in a sea of tears. However, the most important feature of all these poems is that Petrarch is taken as the unique model for verse composition and that there is scarcely a word to be found which is not already in the *Canzoniere*.

This points the way to the *De Imitatione* of 1512, in which Bembo dealt harshly with the eclecticism practised by earlier humanists. In this reply to Giovan Francesco Pico della Mirandola, the Ciceronianism of the new age was uncompromisingly set forth and vindicated: every literary language is bound to enjoy a moment of unrivalled excellence, its Golden Age, after which decadence must surely set in. Why then be content with anything but the best? And once this has been found, it must by definition exclude all other models: for anyone wishing to write Latin prose Cicero is the sole criterion; Virgil, for Latin verse.

It is clear that Bembo's Ciceronianism did not wait until 1512 to be born. The principle of imitation had dominated Italian humanism since its very beginnings, and every aspiring humanist must have faced the problem which author or authors to imitate. Bembo's contribution was to adapt this humanistic principle to the field of vernacular poetry, and thus make the imitation of Petrarch not only respectable but an inevitable consequence, once the humanists had been won over to an acceptance of Italian as a literary language.

This was Bembo's next task, which he accomplished in the *Prose della volgar lingua* (1525). One of the great weaknesses of the vernacular was that it seemed to lack a set of rules; so that even Dante – an ardent supporter of Italian – used the term 'grammar' as synonymous with Latin, defining the vernacular as the language we learn 'without any rules' in infancy. This apparent anarchy was one of the points made to justify the claim that Italian was not only less 'noble' than Latin but unworthy to be regarded as a literary medium of any kind. Bembo now set out to remedy the situation and to provide a grammatical norm, based, as in Latin, on the usage of the Golden Age: for Italian literature, the fourteenth century, with Petrarch the arbiter for verse and Boccaccio for prose.

The *Prose* are in the form of a dialogue, supposed to have taken place at the house of the poet's brother in December 1502. The discussion is instigated by the use of the Tuscan word *rovaio* by Giuliano de' Medici. As so often happens in Italy, the word is unknown to his friends from other regions, and calls for comment and explanation. This is an opportunity for Ercole Strozzi, a celebrated writer of Latin verse, to declare his hostility to the vernacular and his regret that such a Latinist as Carlo's brother Pietro should neglect the more noble language for Italian – an obvious reference to the polemic caused by the publication of the *Asolani*. This opposition is partly fictitious, for by the time Bembo came to write the *Prose* the battle for the vernacular had already been won. And yet the problem remained: which form of the vernacular in Italy should a writer use? Owing to the geographical and political fragmentation of the country, there was no national language and – as Manzoni was to repeat in the nineteenth century – the multitude of dialects and 'synonyms' was not an asset but a linguistic and artistic handicap.

A literary tradition did, however, exist, and this was almost exclusively Tuscan until the second half of the fifteenth century, when Matteo Maria Boiardo from Emilia produced his great poem, the *Orlando innamorato*. By linguistic accident, Tuscan was also the dialect that often kept nearest to Latin forms in the preservation of syllables, single and double consonants. For these reasons, it is the model proposed in the first book of the *Prose*. Not, however, the language spoken in Florence; for Bembo insists that familiarity breeds contempt and that the Florentines, like all Tuscans, make free and easy with their precious heritage. They ignore the necessary differences between the spoken tongue and the language of great literature. Instead, like their fellow-countrymen, they should school themselves in the golden language of the Trecento – in fact, the usage of Petrarch and Boccaccio, since Dante's style was too uncouth for Bembo's fastidious taste. This taste is fully illustrated, with all its strength and limitations, in the second and third books of the *Prose*: for example, in an appreciation of the musical value of words and phrases, with a discussion of the sound effects of the five vowels, syllabic stress and metrical accent, all combining to create harmony, which is to verse what the soul is to the human body. Variety is essential, and a balance must be kept between the requirements of gravity (*gravità*) and sweetness (*piacevolezza*). This balance is struck with unique mastery by Petrarch in his lyrics, and we find the true measure of Bembo's Petrarchism in his praise of the master's *canzone*, 'Nel dolce tempo' (II, xiii), and the honour he chooses to bestow on the sonnet 'Mentre che 'l cor' (II, xvii), the only poem quoted in its entirety.

It is remarkable that Bembo's collected *Rime* were not published until the poet was sixty. That year (1530) is a landmark in the history of Renaissance Petrarchism, for it also saw the publication of Sannazaro's *Rime* and the second edition of the *Asolani*. But an earlier year (1507) had seen the composition of two diametrically opposed works: Bembo's *Stanze* and his *canzone*, 'Alma cortese'.

The *Stanze* were written for the carnival during the poet's stay at Urbino and they are a gay invitation to love, expressed in fifty octaves that tell of the visit to the town made by two ambassadors sent by Venus in order to change the hard hearts of its feminine population. The poem may be numbered among the *canti carnascialeschi* of the Renaissance, but its tone is very different from that of its boisterous companions and it is chiefly notable for its restraint and Bembo's use of *ottava rima*, which cannot have escaped the notice of Ludovico Ariosto.

'Alma cortese', though begun in 1507, is a long lament on the death of Bembo's beloved brother, Carlo, which had occurred some four years previously. The persistent sincerity of the poet's grief is obvious, and in this work Bembo sets aside the lighter theme of love, using the tragic theme of a man's nobility of character and premature death in this Dantesque attempt to rival the nobility and grandeur of Classical verse. Even the form, modelled on Petrarch's longest *canzone*, already selected as an example of *gravità* ('Nel dolce tempo'), has an element of Dante in its double *envoi* and cannot but strike the reader as an example of that tragic style which Dante reserved for the *canzone* in his *De vulgari eloquentia*. The whole work's lofty style and noble theme, unmatched since the death of Petrarch, impressed a generation accustomed to the trivialities of earlier Petrarchists and the licentious horseplay of the *canti carnascialeschi*. At the same time, 'Alma cortese' was a token of Bembo's later style, with its gradual moving away from the forms and inspiration of the *Asolani*. As an artist, the master of Renaissance Petrarchism was inspired not so much by the love story of the *Canzoniere* as by its stylistic achievements, which flattered his exquisite linguistic sensibility. It was this tendency that was responsible for one of the obvious faults of Bembo's early poetry: that discrepancy between form and content which was to become one of the chief characteristics of Baroque verse, and which the poet's mistress, Maria Savorgnan, pointed out to him in a letter of 6 September 1500, when she told him that, although a poem he had sent her was beautiful, the style seemed to her too polished for its lowly subject matter.

While this remained a constant danger, Bembo nevertheless managed to acquire immense fame as a love poet – a fame that is understandable if we think of the effect produced by such a poem as 'Crin d'oro crespo' (V), in which he skilfully attributes all physical and spiritual perfection to his beloved (possibly Lucrezia Borgia). This description was to inspire countless treatises on ideal womanly beauty in the sixteenth century: the lady's hair is gold and translucent amber, her skin snow-white, her eyes brighter than the sun, her lips are rubies and her teeth pearls through which pass sounds that enchant the listener's soul, oblivious of all other good; she possesses wisdom combined with youth, unrivalled grace, supreme beauty and virtue – she is the cynosure of the poet's universe. Another poem probably sent to Lucrezia, 'L'alta cagion' (XXXVIII), according to which God gave the poet his earthly love so that it should lead him on to the divine, is a successful expression of Bembo's neo-Platonism – an element, however, which is far less apparent in the *Rime* than either the *Asolani* or literary historians would lead us to suppose. 'Lasso me' (XLIII) is entirely constructed on the play of antithesis that had inspired CXXXII–CXXXIV of Petrarch's *Canzoniere* (hope-fear, freedom-servitude, life-death . . .), and which had been dismissed as poetic lies in *Asolani* II, viii. This, together with the fact that 'O d'ogni mio penser' (LXIV) was written for Veronica Gambara some twenty years after the poet's relationship with her, cannot fail to make the reader doubt the sincerity of Bembo's inspiration. Such doubts are reinforced by a letter of 20 March 1504, in which he tells Elisabetta Gonzaga, 'The thought of heavenly things, which you believe occupies my mind, has never occupied it overmuch, and now not at all' – at a time when the poet was preparing the publication of the last book of the *Asolani*. In another letter of 1538 regarding a love sonnet he had just written at the age of sixty-eight, he assures his friend that nothing is farther from his mind than the thought of any woman, but that he uses this pretence 'so as to have a subject for poetry'. Again, in 'Né tigre' (LXVII), he exhorts Gasparro degli Obizi to write about his love, not as an outlet for his deepest feelings, but so that he may acquire fame and glory.

We are immediately confronted with a problem that worries many readers of Renaissance literature: the divorce between theory and practice, which is apt to strike them as artistic and moral hypocrisy. Although most will readily agree that sincerity is no guarantee of artistic excellence, it is more difficult to decide whether the puritanical conscience is right in numbering this moral quality among the prerequisites of art. It seems dishonest for a poet to pretend to be in love for the sake of writing a few elegant verses – and yet, this 'pretence' or half-heartedness certainly did not prevent Tasso from writing the finest madrigals of the sixteenth century. Moreover, the contradiction that exists between the conclusion of the *Asolani* and Bembo's private life, or the fact that celebrated courtesans wrote about spiritual love, did not necessarily shock contemporaries. It is not a question of moral laxity, but rather that the revolution brought about in science and politics by such men as Leonardo and Machiavelli whereby observation of the facts became all-important, did not extend to the private moral sphere. Here, the *a priori* approach of the Middle Ages continued: no fact, no unsatisfactory part of reality could invalidate the theory or the ideal. A sinner might best express the yearning for sainthood, although his life had little that was saintly about it, and every Catholic was used to confessing *Domine, non sum dignus* as he approached his ideal. It was not until the end of the eighteenth century that 'serious' literature was no longer supposed to reflect man's longing for the unattainable ideal, with the consequence that idealists struggled to confine their dreams to what is accessible on earth, and the subsequent *mal du siècle* and satanism were a reflection of their dissatisfaction, while De Sanctis and Protestant historians pointed an accusing finger at Renaissance hypocrisy and insouciance. Certainly, however, Bembo's religious aspirations did not prevent him from celebrating Ambrogina Faustina Della Torre (La Morosina) in a number of poems, after she had become his mistress in 1513, at the age of sixteen, and after her death in 1535; on the other hand, the sincerity of his grief did not ensure great poetry – although both elements provided a noteworthy contribution in 'Donna, che fosti orïental Fenice' (CLV).

As has already been pointed out, Bembo came to concentrate less and less on love poetry, while his poetic powers were increasingly stimulated by the demands of the sonnet form. 'Re degli altri, superbo e sacro monte' (XXII), with its quintessential opening verse adapted from Petrarch, though relatively early (1506), is one of the best examples of what Bembo's *aurea mediocritas* (golden mean) could achieve within the strict demands of this form. 'O per cui tante invan lagrime' (L) also points towards future developments in the Renaissance lyric with its Classical elements – rare in Bembo – and its difficult syntax which carries the reader almost without pause through the fourteen lines of verse (compare LVIII with its hints of Baroque imagery). So, too, the enjambements found in the second quatrain of CV ('Se la piú dura quercia') and – quite exceptionally – between the seventh and ninth verses of XXXI ('Nei vostri sdegni'), where the break between 'le nostre genti' and 'diranno' ignores the fundamental division between quatrains and tercets. The sonnet addressed to Ercole I, Duke of Ferrara, and the three written to celebrate the birth of Duke Francesco Maria Della Rovere's son, point the way to a flood of flattery and occasional verse, however alien this aspect of the Renaissance lyric may have been to the temperament of a Venetian patrician. Last comes the notable series of sonnets addressed to Bembo's friends, representatives of that republic of letters which is one of the finest features of Renaissance civilization: Gaspare Pallavicino (LXXV), Niccolò Frisio (LXXIV), and Bernardo Dovizi da Bibbiena (XCI), who figure in the *Cortegiano*, Francesco Molza (CIV), Benedetto Varchi (CXXXI, perhaps the finest example), and Giovanni Della Casa (CXLI). This, the last sonnet Bembo wrote – a few months before his death at the age of seventy-six – is a fitting end to his career, giving us his poetic testament in which he sees his ideals of moral worth and Ciceronian rhetoric embodied in his friend and successor.

IACOPO SANNAZARO (c. 1455–1530) was hailed as a reincarnation of Petrarch in the Aldine edition of his *Arcadia* (1514), although his *Rime* were not published until after his death in 1530, when they confirmed the acceptance of Bembo's Tuscan formula in Southern Italy. They show us an elegiac follower of Petrarch, with his desire for solitude, the melancholy he expresses among the beauties of the Italian countryside, and his yearning for the peace the tomb seems to offer him. This melancholy, however, is attenuated by the idyllic element in the *Rime*, which well suited Sannazaro's undramatic temperament. The linguistic purity of these poems, with their rejection of Classical as well as dialect forms, is reflected in the author's refusal to display his Classical learning. An odd reference to Endymion, Tantalus, or Sisyphus, is hardly surprising; but we find that only one poem – the sonnet 'Icaro cadde qui' (LXXIX) – was directly inspired by a Classical myth. Very occasionally, we find a verse translated from Latin, but it has been skilfully transposed and camouflaged in its new context: as at the end of the sonnet 'Stando per meraviglia' (LXXVII), where the poet uses Virgil's 'Tantaene animis caelestibus irae' ('Is it possible that the minds of the gods should harbour so much wrath?') to describe his dismay when the envy of heaven tries to prevent him from gazing on the sun-like beauty of his beloved. The hybrid forms of the fifteenth century are completely rejected, and the new emotional and linguistic context is of Sannazaro's own making.

The influence of Petrarch, on the other hand, is ubiquitous. Like the poems of the *Canzoniere*, the *Rime* are divided into two parts, ending with the desire to forgo vain love and turn to God, while the descriptions of the poet's love are interspersed with poems on moral and political themes: so, for example, the impressive *canzone* 'O fra tante procelle' (XI) plays the same role as 'Spirto gentil' (LIII) in the *Canzoniere*. A very few poems are direct imitations: 'Venuta era madonna' (LXIV) from Petrarch's 'Levommi il mio penser' (CCCII); 'Le dubbie spemi' (XCV) from 'Padre del ciel' (LXII). Others are typical of Petrarchism in general, such as the sonnet describing the torments of jealousy ('O gelosia d'amanti, orribil freno' XXVII), which was imitated by Magny and du Bellay in France, Garcilaso and Góngora in Spain, Sidney and Barnes in England. Similarly, one of the *Rime disperse* ('Simile a questi smisurati monti', IV) declares that the poet sheds as many tears as there are springs in the Apennines, while Love grazes in his person as the herds do in the wild mountains: this, with its other conceits, was avidly taken up by Scève, Wyatt, and other foreign poets. There are also the notable series of 'dream' sonnets (LXII–LXVIII), two written in praise of Petrarch (LV, LVI), and the humanistic theme of the grandeur that was Rome (XCIII; *Rime disperse* V, XXVII). Other poems show that Sannazaro came nearer than any other Renaissance poet to recapturing the tone and spirit of Petrarch. There is the magnificent 'Sola angeletta starsi in trecce a l'ombra' (XLIV), which not only is the greatest example of the difficult *sestina* form in Italian after the fourteenth century, but also manages to convey something of the rapt wonder of Petrarch's 'Chiare, fresche e dolci acque' (CXXVI). The *canzone*, 'In qual dura alpe' (LXXXIII), echoes some of the rhythms of 'Di pensier in pensier' (CXXIX), just as 'Sperai gran tempo' (LXXXIX) is the only Italian *canzone* that can bring to mind Petrarch's 'I' vo pensando' (CCLXIV). Finally, Sannazaro's sonnet 'Lasso, che ripensando al tempo breve' (XIV), with its lament on the brevity of life and its simile of snow in the sun and metaphor of winged flight, is an amalgam of Petrarchan themes and images; but Sannazaro is no common Petrarchist: his imitation is personal, robust, and it enables him to produce a line which is the equal of some of the best Petrarch ever wrote – 'mi pasco d'ombre et ho la morte appresso' ('I feed on shadows and have death at my side').

GIOVANNI DELLA CASA (1503–56) added the Latin elegiac poets and his personal experience to the Petrarchan tradition. Discussing *gravità* in language and verse, Tasso writes that a great poet can make any subject appear magnificent: 'None knew better than Della Casa how to do this; for any commonplace sentiment is so ennobled by him, that it seems to be one of the most wonderful things ever said.' Della Casa thus became famous for his 'magnificent' style, which left the usage of everyday speech far behind and rejected the second ingredient (*piacevolezza*, sweetness) of Bembo's formula.

The traditional elements are most in evidence in the early poems: the praise of the beloved's beauty in 'Sagge, soavi, angeliche parole' (XI), the obsession with antithesis in 'Quella, che del mio mal' (XV), the glad submission to the suffering made sweet by love in 'Dolci son le quadrella' (X), and the whole Petrarchan repertoire displayed in 'Vivo mio scoglio' (XLII), with its description of Livia Colonna as a living rock, a flint that produces sparks to burn the poet's heart, the most beautiful of Nature's creatures who nevertheless remains a slab of cold marble, a harsh column ('colonna'), untouched by the poet's fountain of tears. 'Vago augelletto' (XXXVII) is one of two sonnets addressed to Elisabetta Quirini's parrot, in which the poet warns the lady's pet that, while learning to imitate her angelic sounds, he must remember to protect his wings from the fire of her glance. A foretaste of metaphysical poetry is found in 'Le chiome d'or' (XXX), noteworthy for its difficult syntax – a feature that became more and more common in Della Casa's verse. Repentance for the poet's sins inspires 'Io, che l'età solea viver nel fango' (XVII) and 'S'io vissi cieco' (XVIII), although the treatment of this theme remains conventional until the *canzone*, 'Errai gran tempo' (*Canzone* IV), which marks a further break with Bembo and the Petrarchism of his age. The break was characterized by a change of subject matter: the rejection of love as an inspiration for his poetry and the acceptance of the vanity of wordly ambitions, a theme that proved more congenial to the poet and which, combined with his stylistic predilections, produced some of the finest lyrics of the age.

As a young man, the poet had entered the service of the Church with great hopes and ambitions, flattered by such friends as Bembo and by his mission as nuncio to Venice, where he was charged with introducing the Inquisition on the territory of the Republic. His success, however, was undermined by the scandal caused by *Il forno* and other obscene verses which he had written as a young man. Hope of achieving his aim and becoming a prince of the Church was apparently destroyed by the death of Paul III in 1549, and the subsequent disgrace of his protector, Alessandro Farnese, in 1551. Finally, Della Casa saw his disillusionment confirmed after the election of Paul IV (1555), who, although he encouraged the poet to leave his retirement and return to Rome as Secretary of State, refused to appoint him Cardinal. This personal drama is expressed most successfully in 'Questa vita mortal' (LIX) and 'Già lessi, ed or conosco in me' (LVII), two of the summits of Della Casa's poetry, in which the grave style sets off the depth and intensity of thought and feeling. 'Già lessi' is, in fact, a vindication of Renaissance rhetoric. The use of Classical mythology, which had sprinkled the much-admired fourteen lines of 'La bella greca' (XXXV) with references to Helen, Paris, Semele, Daphne, Juno and Pallas, is here as much a spontaneous association of ideas as any other successful poetic imagery. In the first part, the poet declares that he now truly understands the myth of Glaucus – not from intellectual knowledge, but because he has seen in himself how a man may descend into the turbulent sea of life and be covered with the shells and weeds that overgrow his soul. Then, in the sextet, the point is illustrated by the myth of Aesacus, who was transformed into a diver-bird and soared aloft towards heaven, until the ballast of mortal food weighed down his wings – perhaps the most effective example of the poet's favourite bird image (compare XLV, XLVII, XLVIII, XLIX, and the *sestina*, 'Di là, dove per ostro e poma ed oro').

It was, however, Della Casa's technical innovations that particularly impressed his contemporaries. They admired his constant striving after *gravitas*, his attempt, anticipating Mallarmé, to ennoble and purify language debased by the mob, which was inspired – more than by Petrarch – by the example of Virgil, Horace and Cicero. Within the narrow compass of the sonnet Della Casa succeeded, by distorting the natural word-order, by frequent use of enjambement and the creation of strong pauses within the line of verse, in creating a unique Italian model for the heroic diction of Tasso and Milton in the grand sphere of epic poetry. His sonnet to sleep (L) was imitated by Desportes, Sidney, Daniel, Griffin and Drummond. It had the distinction of being cited by Tasso as an example of Della Casa's originality, his ability to keep the 'reader suspended in delight and wonder', and was similarly honoured by Foscolo, who compared the poet's technique to the dissonances found in music and the *chiaroscuro* of painting. Yet its stylistic and verbal amplitude, the skilful pauses that create a rhythmic *rubato* reflecting the poet's mood, his restless striving for peace – all this is absent from the works of Della Casa's imitators, even as it is absent from the general development of the Italian sonnet, which continued to follow the models set up by Petrarch and Bembo.

The lyrics of MICHELANGELO BUONARROTI (1475–1564) also occupy a place outside the mainstream of Petrarchism. In his own age, his poetry was admired by such contrasting spirits as Pietro Aretino and Benedetto Varchi, while Francesco Berni, impressed by his strength and originality, used Michelangelo as a stick with which to belabour the Petrarchists of the day. However, his position in the Italian literary canon has never been fixed, and modern critics all too often hark back to Foscolo's judgement that his poetic powers were no match for the profound thoughts he strove to express. Benedetto Croce is no exception, and Attilio Momigliano even went so far as to say that Michelangelo must be excluded from the history of Italian poetry. The reason for this negative reaction is largely to be found in the difficulties that the poems offer the Italian reader: complex thought and syntax, sprinkled with anacoluthon, zeugma and inversion, as well as those formal peccadilloes which the Italian tradition finds hardest of all to forgive.

Brought up in Medici Florence, Michelangelo came into contact with two currents that were to be of great importance in the development of his poetry: the religious fervour of Girolamo Savonarola and the neo-Platonic teachings of Marsilio Ficino. His familiarity with the neo-Platonic trends in Florentine humanism, however, and even his friendship with the great Poliziano did not lead Michelangelo to be influenced by the humanist movement in general. A remarkable feature of his poetry is its almost total lack of Classical elements, while Vasari tells us that Michelangelo rejected the fundamental humanistic principle of imitation, declaring that it prevented an artist from developing his own powers to the full. Another striking feature is his late growth as a poet: we have little that was written before the artist's fiftieth year, and only one sixth of his three hundred poetic compositions was produced before 1530. Then, in 1533, Michelangelo fell in love with Tommaso Cavalieri. This encounter stimulated his poetic powers to an unprecedented extent, which continued unabated, through his relationship with Vittoria Colonna and the religious inspiration that dominated his old age, until his eightieth year.

His early poems especially show his debt to the Petrarchan tradition. The usual comparisons are made with the phoenix and the salamander, who, like the ardent lover, live or are reborn by fire. An unfinished sonnet tells us that the poet's eyes are the entrance through which the poison and the shafts of love have struck, while his heart has been transformed into an anvil and his breast into bellows which manufacture the sighs that torment him. Baroque elements are also to be found: as when the poet prays, during the physical absence of his beloved, that his whole body may be turned into one single eye, or when he debates the question whether it is better to feel less pain in hell, comforted by his lady's presence, or to feel less beatitude in heaven, distracted from the contemplation of God by the sight of her divine beauty. In general, however, Michelangelo stood alone. He did not copy others, but took what he could gather from a few kindred spirits. It was undoubtedly a pleasing coincidence that Dante and Petrarch had sung of womanly beauty as a way up to God. Yet Michelangelo's neo-Platonism would surely have dominated his conception of love, even if he had not read a line of these poets. In 'Veggio co' be' vostr'occhi un dolce lume' (89), the poet makes an impassioned declaration of faith: the spiritual beauty of Tommaso Cavalieri leads him on to virtue and into the very presence of God – an assertion made with such poetic intensity that it has no equal among the Platonic bleatings of the age. The poet does not hesitate to use Petrarchan paradox: he shivers in the sun and is warm in midwinter, he offers us the traditional sun–moon metaphor, and constantly looks back to the *Canzoniere*. There, the clearest statement of Laura's saving influence is the opening stanza of 'Gentil mia donna' (LXXII). However, Petrarch tells us that it was *in* Laura's eyes that he saw a light illuminating the path to heaven, whereas Michelangelo claims that *with* his beloved's eyes he can see a light which remains hidden from his own and on the wings of Cavalieri's soul he is borne up to heaven – a change that is indicative of the tone of this love poetry and the intensity with which it was experienced in the complete fusion of self with the other, that symbiosis of perfect love described by Ficino in his *De Amore*. There is in fact little enough direct imitation of Petrarch. Instead, we have a reliving of experiences and attitudes shared by the two poets, while the alchemy of Michelangelo's genius transformed the base metal of tradition into the gold of poetry.

Poetry, for Michelangelo, meant confession. It is obvious why he chose the lyric. What is more surprising is that this great artist never attempted or felt the need for plastic representation in his poetry. This need was amply satisfied by sculpture, and in his poems the beloved is contemplated in abstraction from nature, just as there is no landscape in the frescoes of the Sistine Chapel. But in the poems we never find any pictorial description of the physical beauty of either of Buonarroti's great loves. The painter was but seldom allowed into the poetic universe: as in the description of pastoral beauty and happiness in 'Nuovo piacere e di maggiore stima' (67), the grotesque of 'Un gigante v'è ancor' (68), or the sonnet 'I' ho già fatto un gozzo' (5), written while the artist was working on the decoration of the

Sistine ceiling and describing his impossibly cramped position which had produced a goitre, thrust his belly under his chin, his head on his back, with his beard jutting up towards heaven and drops of paint trickling onto his face, so that the poet-painter has been turned into a twisted pea-shooter. Un-Petrarchan realism is also a feature of 'I' sto rinchiuso' (267), and typical of the poet's later vigour is the early sonnet (10) depicting Rome under the pontificate of Julius II, who has turned it into an armed camp, so that Christ, whose blood is being sold by the bucketful, is warned to stay away from the Holy City which leads men to their doom and the artist to despair.

This vigour is apparent in all his mature production, not excluding the madrigals, where at times it clashes with this light, free form and refutes a recent judgement that these are the most successful of Michelangelo's poems. The delicate arabesque of musical form is ill fitted for the titanic struggle of expression that is the hallmark of, for example, 'Non pur d'argento o d'oro' (153). At least once, however, the poet overcame these difficulties and produced one of the finest, though least characteristic, of madrigals in 'Per qual mordace lima' (161), with its magnificent close 'tomm'a me stesso e famm'un che ti piaccia' ('take me from myself and make me one pleasing to you'). Such harshness, so far removed from Petrarch's musical lines, is reminiscent of the way in which Michelangelo would attack a block of marble with such force that onlookers expected the stone to be shattered by the violence of the onslaught. So, too, the poet struggled to do violence to language, when words seemed inadequate to the task of expressing his spiritual drama. The various drafts of his poems show how relentlessly he went through them, rejecting Petrarchan words and phrases and replacing them by ever stronger, harsher, more virile forms. This style is a particular feature of 'Costei pur si delibra' (172) and related poems, where Michelangelo turns to the Dante of the *rime petrose*, in which the poet had striven to find the harsh, flinty language that should reflect his mistress's heart of stone. Michelangelo's admiration for his fellow-Florentine is expressed in two sonnets – especially the famous 'Dal ciel discese' (248) – and such an attitude was rare enough in an age when Petrarch reigned supreme. But it was coupled with a spiritual affinity that is evident throughout the *rime*: no other poet so shared with Dante his struggle with the irreducible element in language and poetry, even as Michelangelo's sculpture may be compared with what Dante achieved in his *Comedy*, the refusal to be bound by the limitations of man's nature, while expressing both its nobility and its degradation.

Michelangelo's most famous sonnet, 'Non ha l'ottimo artista' (151), speaks of the artist's task. In his Platonic conception of art, the poet describes the challenge facing the sculptor. He must liberate the idea that lies buried in the mass of stone and must remove the superfluous matter that imprisons the work of art as a creation of the spirit. This was no picturesque allegory, and the poems which describe this fundamental struggle between matter and spirit within the artist's soul are the finest expressions of truly religious feeling in the Italian Renaissance. It is indeed this dynamic conception of art, seen as a reflection of the drama of human experience, that provides a link, more essential than the year 1564, between Michelangelo and Shakespeare. Both were fascinated by the idolatry of beauty; both struggled to save the centre of their sinful earth. The conflict, for the Italian poet, ended in the apparent defeat of the artist, and already in 1552 he confessed that 'art and death do not go well together.' This is followed by 'Giunto è già 'l corso della vita mia' (285), with its admission that neither painting nor sculpture may now satisfy his soul in its total dedication to Christ's love. 'Scarco d'un'importuna e greve salma' (290), written in a shaky hand at the age of eighty, adds poignancy to the message of final defeat: the artist's equilibrium, always precarious, had been shattered, although these last poems possess a clarity and harmony of their own. However, as late as 1556, we are perhaps comforted to find the elderly poet writing to a friend that he is sure of seeing him again in heaven, 'yet before death I think it would be a good thing to enjoy one another's company on earth': an indication that this man, who once described himself as 'no stranger to any human passion', was, like Dante, never exclusive in his love of either heaven or earth.

GASPARA STAMPA (*c.* 1525–54) admired Della Casa and wrote magniloquent sonnets to such illustrious personages as Henri II of France (CCXLVI), Catherine de' Medici (CCXLVII), and Joan of Aragon (CCXC). The general tone of her poetry, however, is far removed from Della Casa's ideal and she remained a devoted follower of Petrarch in the manner of Bembo's early style. Varchi did not hesitate to call her the Italian Sappho, because of the three hundred love lyrics she wrote, telling of her passion for Collaltino di Collalto and the consolation she found in her subsequent love for Bartolomeo Zen. Even as Petrarch had first seen and fallen in love with Laura on the anniversary of Christ's death, so this woman first met Collaltino at Christmastide. In 'Alto colle, gradito e grazioso' (X), she complains of her inability to give adequate expression to the praise of her lofty hill ('alto colle'), a play on her lover's name which reminds us of the link that had existed for Petrarch between Laura's name and the symbol of poetry, 'il lauro', the laurel-tree. Similarly, 'La mia vita è un mar' (LXXII) goes back to Petrarch's 'Passa la nave mia' (CLXXXIX), the sonnet 'Beate luci' (LII) was inspired by the series of poems addressed to Laura's eyes (LXXI–LXXIII), and Petrarchan rhetoric provides ballast for 'Arsi, piansi, cantai; piango, ardo e canto' (XXVI). Finally, like Petrarch, Gaspara Stampa renounces worldly love and repents her past folly in 'Mesta e pentita de' miei gravi errori' (CCCXI).

The basic mythology of Petrarchism illustrates her hopes and sufferings in love, which oblige her to live in flames like the salamander, to be reborn like the phoenix, to waste away like Echo, and to rise up like Icarus on the winds of her passion. The reader is hardly surprised to be told that the stars at the moment of his conception showered all the graces on Collaltino: Saturn gave him his noble intellect, Mars his virile prowess, Apollo his gift for poetry, Venus his beauty, Mercury his eloquence; and yet, he cannot fail to be touched by the infinite devotion of 'Io assomiglio il mio signor al cielo' (V), where the poet tells us that her lover's face is the sun, his eyes her stars, storms beat down upon her if he is angry and springtime blossoms for her when he promises to return. These clichés are brought back to life in her poetry, which is capable of expressing both the naïve admiration of 'Mentr'io conto fra me' (XXIX) and the tremendous outburst of proud joy in 'Io non v'invidio punto' (XVII), where she exclaims that she has no cause to envy the angels in heaven, whose beatitude may surpass her own in duration but not in intensity. By contrast, the poems in which she describes her torments during her lover's absence and final betrayal are monotonous and cannot rival the paean offered up during a brief reunion – 'O notte, a me piú chiara e piú beata' (CIV) – when she sings exultantly of the joys and consolations that night has finally brought her.

Apart from that of Gaspara Stampa, the names of VITTORIA COLONNA (1490–1547: 'A che sempre chiamar la sorda morte'), ISABELLA DI MORRA (1520–46: 'Poscia che al bel desir troncate hai l'ale'), VERONICA GAMBARA (1485–1550: 'Occhi lucenti e belli'), CHIARA MATRAINI (1514–*c*. 1597: 'Com'elitropio al sole sempre mi giro') and TULLIA D'ARAGONA (1510–56: 'Se ben pietosa madre unico figlio') – ranging over all levels of society, from the noble-woman idealized by Michelangelo to the courtesan who wrote a dialogue on the Infinity of Love – give us some idea of the extent to which women participated in the culture of the Renaissance and were active in the sphere of lyric poetry.

According to the chronicler Marin Sanudo, Venice in the sixteenth century had up to 11,000 prostitutes out of a population of 300,000. These figures make it less surprising that the Renaissance should have produced its hetaerae, one of whom – VERONICA FRANCO (1546–91) – has a special place in the history of its poetry, was a friend of Tintoretto, and became something of a tourist attraction. We have two sonnets by her, celebrating the visit paid her by Henri III of France in 1574 and mentioning the portrait he took away in memory of her, just as Montaigne was to be given a collection of her letters, when he passed through Venice in 1580. Although she evidently regarded her cultural position as a status symbol and boasted of her thirst for knowledge and her wish to spend all her time 'sweetly in the academy of virtuous men', Veronica Franco was no bluestocking and her poetry has a refreshing frankness that is one of the charms of her *Terze Rime*.

Love is the main theme; but it is treated in un-Petrarchan fashion, reminiscent of the realism of certain scenes in contemporary comedy. In one of her poems, she writes to Marco Venier (II), promising him all the delights of Venus in bed, if only he will set about winning her love; she assures him that, if he is successful, his reward will be such that 'my singing and my writing are forgotten by those who experience me in that way.' The hackneyed theme of the beloved's absence (III) is saved from banality by the rejection of the sonnet's tight frame for the freedom of *terza rima* and by the longing for her native city, also skilfully evoked in XXII. In 'Non piú parole' (XIII), the woman challenges her lover to a duel. She hopes to tear out his heart and lying tongue with her own hands – unless, of course, he sues for peace, in which case she will transfer the battle to the 'amorous skirmishes of the bed'. In 'D'ardito cavalier non è prodezza' (XVI) Veronica upbraids a man for his unchivalrous conduct in attacking the poet's condition, and she challenges her opponent to a literary contest, in which she will allow him the choice of language and style: Tuscan or dialect, serious or burlesque, 'for I am well versed in the lot', she confidently warns him. The praises of the Valpolicella countryside (XXV) offer a conventional elegiac picture of nature's beauty and the delights offered by the country house of Marcantonio della Torre, with some fine passages in spite of the strain imposed by the exceptional length of this composition. The most interesting of Veronica Franco's poems, however, is 'Quel che ascoso nel cor tenni gran tempo' (XIX), addressed to a clergyman whose handsome features and eloquent sermons had set her heart on fire, many years before. On seeing him again, she finds only the shadow of his former good looks, and tells him of her vain hopes that he might have noticed and would return her love. Now, her passion has given way to a desire for friendship: 'I find pleasure and profit in being and talking with you. . . . My wild love is being transformed into friendship and, by considering your immense gifts, I reform my soul in imitation of you.' The reformation did not take place.

Veronica Franco was certainly influenced in her handling of *terza rima* by the way in which LUDOVICO ARIOSTO (1474–1533) used this form in his Satires. Ariosto also wrote a number of sonnets in the Petrarchan manner, such as 'Se senza fin son le cagion ch'io v'ami' (XXXIII) and the much admired 'Madonna, sete bella' (XXV – imitated by du Bellay, Baïf, Ronsard, and Lodge). But he is more true to his own nature when, in the *canzone*, 'Non so s'io potrò ben chiudere in rima' (I), he describes his falling in love with Alessandra Benucci. Amid the customary praise of his mistress, the poet quietly admits that this was not in fact the first time he had seen her and that he did not, even then, realize the full significance and permanence of his love. This ability to look at life and himself with detachment, to smile at the follies of men, is one of the great characteristics of the author of the *Orlando furioso*, and it is much in evidence in the Satires.

These are on a variety of topics and are to some extent inspired by Horace, the poet for whom, with his dislike of any kind of excess and his mellow view of life, Ariosto felt most affinity.

'Io desidero intendere da voi' (I) was written in 1517, after the poet had refused to follow his patron, Cardinal Ippolito d'Este, to Hungary. He asks his brother and a friend to tell him whether the cardinal is still angry with him and whether any kind word is spoken in his defence, although the poet well knows that 'Anyone is mad who tries to contradict his lord, even if he were to say that he has seen the day full of stars and the sun at midnight.' He goes over his reasons for refusing to leave Ferrara: the terrible effects of the cold on his health, the drinking habits of the Hungarians, their highly-spiced food – and let no one suggest that he could have had special meals prepared, because Apollo and the Muses have not brought in even enough to buy himself a cloak. Ariosto tells of the ways in which his lord rewards his followers for their services, but has no gratitude for the poet who has sung his praises: 'he says I have done so for my pleasure and in my spare time; he would rather have had me at his side.' The satire then turns into a hymn to liberty: the personal freedom of a man who complains that he is incapable of practising the courtly arts and declares, 'more than riches, I want peace.' If the cardinal will be served in the way Ariosto knows best, he will raise up his name to the skies. But 'if the holy Cardinal thinks he has bought me with his gifts, I will not hesitate to return them and win back my former freedom.'

The second satire was written in the same year and addressed to Galasso Ariosto. The poet tells his brother to prepare a modest, clean room for his visit to Rome. He describes the Holy City as he will find it, with its drunken priests, Spanish hirelings and their masters who would turn away Peter, Paul, John and Christ himself from the doors that hide their secret vices from the world. He speaks of his business: a benefice that has been left him, which he will farm out to some worthy priest, for the poet has always refused to be bound by irrevocable vows, whether of celibacy or matrimony. The Church, everyone tells him, opens the way to a magnificent career. 'Let everyone think as he pleases; this is my opinion: that, if freedom is the price to be paid, I am not interested in the richest hat in the whole of Rome.'

In satire III (1518), the inventor of the hippogriph and narrator of Ruggiero's fabulous adventures and Astolfo's flight to the moon proudly proclaims himself a stay-at-home. He has seen Tuscany, Lombardy and the Alps: that is enough for him and he will be content to visit the rest of the world with Ptolemy's atlas, while without fear of storm or tempest he will cross strange seas safely – by turning over the printed page. In the fifth satire (c. 1519), Ariosto complains that his friend, Annibale Malaguzzi, had not told him of his intention to get married, and proceeds to give him good advice on how to choose a wife. He must not wait too long, lest he find himself either a cuckold or surrounded by bastards. Nor must he choose a woman of higher station, for she will be accustomed to luxury and ruin him with her extravagance; not too beautiful, or others will be constantly attempting to seduce her, and not too ugly: 'I have always praised mediocrity, always condemned extremes.' She should be ten or twelve years younger; devout, but not to excess; and satisfied with the face God gave her. He must love her and try to make her his true friend and companion. All this should procure him a faithful wife, though all he can do is to hope for the best, since nothing, Annibale is warned, can stop a woman bent on betraying her husband. The sixth satire (1524–5) is addressed to Bembo, asking the famous humanist to recommend a tutor for his son, Virginio: 'May he have learning and goodness, but especially goodness' and may he lead his son to Parnassus and those ideals of moderation and humanity that inspired the satires of Ludovico Ariosto.

'In spite of everything he lived happily, and was never too serious or sad. He was well liked by people (all the lords at court loved him), because he was witty and recited poems about chamber-pots and eels and others of his meagre works that were held to be strange vagaries.' So FRANCESCO BERNI (1497–1535), described himself in his revision of Boiardo's *Orlando innamorato* (III, vii, 41), adding that he was a frank, loyal friend, who disliked serving others, loved horses but could not afford to keep them, and that his greatest pleasure was to lie naked in bed, doing nothing, restoring body and soul by looking at the woodworm in the ceiling. Born at Lamporecchio, he had the capricious humour and linguistic agility for which Tuscans are famous, while he continued the province's tradition of comic and realistic verse which stretched back, through Pulci and Burchiello, to the thirteenth century. As a young man, he set out to try his fortune in Rome, but his hopes were dashed by the death of his patron in 1520, followed by the election of a Dutchman (Adrian VI) as Pope in 1522. This aroused a storm of xenophobia in Berni, and in his *Capitolo di papa Adriano* he hurled abuse at this 'scoundrel, drunkard, peasant' who dared to lord it over 'the glorious Latin name' and threatened to have insolent poets thrown into the Tiber. It was only prudent of Berni to leave Rome for a time after this outburst and possible accusations of sodomy, which would seem to be justified by the *Capitolo a Messer Antonio da Bibbiena* and the *Capitolo d'un ragazzo*. Apart from moral connotations, these early poems show us the direction that most of Berni's significant work was to take: the burlesque use of Dante's *terza rima* in his *Capitoli*, which became the standard model for Italian comic verse, and the predilection for the *sonetto caudato* ('tailed' sonnet), whose series of tails reflects the hiccuping nature of Berni's inspiration.

As mentioned in his self-portrait, many of the *Capitoli* were written in praise of such unorthodox subjects as eels, chamber-pots, gudgeons, thistles (an acquired taste, like caviar), and peaches (Margutte is reproached for having omitted them from his 'Credo' in Pulci's *Morgante*). Later ones celebrated Cardinal Ippolito de' Medici's dwarf, Aristotle (whose glory would have been complete, if he had written a treatise on the art of cooking), and the ambiguous virtues of the needle. The most famous are the *Capitolo* addressed to Fra Bastian dal Piombo, which expresses his boundless admiration for Michelangelo and contempt for the colourless followers of Petrarch, and the *Capitolo del prete da Povigliano*. In the latter, the poet describes a visit to Povigliano, where the parish-priest turns out to be a hypocritical know-all, boasting of the excellence of his wine and food and inflicting his hospitality on his victims, who suffer a night of torment among the fleas, bugs and other inhabitants of the granary.

One of Berni's tailed sonnets was written to commemorate the beard of Domenico d'Ancona, when his lord, Giovanni Matteo Giberti, Bishop of Verona, announced that all aspiring ecclesiastics must in future be clean-shaven. Giberti, a prelate with a strict sense of duty, was Berni's patron from 1524 to 1532, the most fruitful period in the poet's life. Pietro Bembo had addressed a sonnet to him –

'Mentre navi e cavalli e schiere armate' (CXIII) – in which the elegant humanist expressed his detachment from the cares of state and his absorption in his studies. Written at one of the most critical moments in Italian history, just before the Sack of Rome (1527), the sonnet was hardly welcome to Giberti and his entourage, and Berni set out to parody Bembo's self-centred world in 'Né navi né cavalli o schiere armate'. Another of Bembo's sonnets – 'Crin d'oro crespo' (V) – was satirized in 'Chiome d'argento fino, irte e attorte', where Berni proudly proclaims that his lady has pearl-coloured, squinting eyes, snow-white lashes, a mouth as wide as the gaping vault of heaven, and rare teeth of ebony through which pass sounds of indescribable harmony. This, together with the burlesque use of Petrarch's 'Chi vuol veder quantunque pò natura' (CCXLVIII) in the tailed sonnet describing the Archbishop of Florence, gives Berni a leading role among the anti-Petrarchists of the sixteenth century. His *Dialogo contra i poeti* (1526) describes poets as a band of thieves, though with far less verve than Niccolò Franco's violent satire of the Petrarchists in his *Piacevoli dialoghi* (1539).

The occasional revolt against the tyranny of Petrarchism in the Renaissance lyric was, however, a sporadic affair. It was inspired by writers who were nothing if not men of letters, opposing one literary tradition with another. And it should be realized that Berni's most extreme attitudes reflected literary topoi that were as much part of Tuscan literature as the clichés of the Petrarchists. Not for nothing does Berni wish he had Burchiello's wit in 'S'i' avessi l'ingegno del Burchiello'. In 'Non vadin piú pellegrin o romei', when the poet inveighs against his mother, aunts and uncle, who refuse to die and apparently intend to set up in competition with the gods of Ancient Egypt and the antiquities of Rome, he is certainly aware of the literary formula and precedent found in the work of Cecco Angiolieri, the *poète maudit* of thirteenth-century Sienna. So, too, 'Cancheri, e beccafichi magri arrosto' – probably his best sonnet – with its long list of woes capped by the assertion that 'the worst of all ills is to have a wife', is an amusing expression of literary misogamy. One need only think of the disastrous results of Berni's rewriting of Boiardo's *Innamorato* according to the standard criteria of his day, to understand that the poet's 'revolt' against Petrarchism was not inspired by any great artistic originality, but rather by a shrewd estimate of his own limited powers. These are seen at their best in the poems mentioned above: the thumbnail-sketch of the Pope weighing his ducats in the *Capitolo di papa Adriano* and the description of the two brothers caught in the flood (*Capitolo del diluvio*), the satirical account of Clement VII's vacillating character ('Un papato composto di rispetti') or the caricature of medical learning in 'Il papa non fa altro che mangiare', where the poet assures us that the Pope shows all the signs of good health, 'but the doctors want to kill him off, because it would be an affront to their honour if he were to get out of their hands alive, once they have said: "He's finished, he's going to die". . . . They'll murder him, in spite of everyone.' Within these limits, Berni set the pattern for Italian burlesque poetry, which is often referred to as *la poesia bernesca*.

TORQUATO TASSO (1544–95) wrote nearly two thousand lyrics, although his consummate mastery as a lyric poet is perhaps best displayed in his pastoral drama, *Aminta*. The poems are usually divided according to subject: love, praise of famous men and women, religion. The love poems show that the chief influence in the second half of the century is still Petrarch, and this influence is particularly strong in the early years of Tasso's career. The usual fidelity and adoration of the Petrarchan lover are displayed in the poems written for Laura Peperara and are accompanied by the play on Laura's name ('aura' = air; 'oro' = 'gold'; 'lauro' = 'laurel'), although in Tasso it has lost the basic connection that had existed between the myth of Apollo's love for Daphne and Petrarch's love poetry; instead, it has become mere ornament, picturesque detail. It is indeed the differences with Petrarch that are most interesting for the way in which they illustrate the Baroque elements in Tasso's poetry. So, for example, he takes from the *Canzoniere* (CLXXX, 9) the opening line of his sonnet 'Re degli altri superbo, altero fiume' (83) and uses Petrarch's verse as a solemn invocation to the river Po. The context, however, is different and this early sonnet shows that discrepancy between hyperbole and trifling subject matter which was to become one of the plagues of Baroque poetry. Here, the poet's lady has left Ferrara for Comacchio, at the mouth of the Po. He accuses the marine deities of rape and calls upon the river to wage fierce war upon the Adriatic by mobilizing its numerous tributaries and using the thousand streams that pour forth from the eyes of so many disappointed lovers.

Tasso spent many years at court, and his poetry reflects the gallant, witty, often superficial, aspects of court life. He writes of masked balls, stolen kisses, his beloved's handkerchief, a mosquito killed on her breast, and his delight in being allowed to hold her mirror as she combs her hair. Yet Tasso's temperament was anything but superficial, and in many lyrics we find a strong vein of melancholy and an emphasis on suffering and renunciation. A whole series of poems describe the torments of jealousy – a theme excluded from the *Canzoniere* – and death is even used as a metaphor for the act of love. The treatment, however, is never dramatic and lighter themes prevail. In 'La man, ch'avvolta entro odorate spoglie' (677) the poet complains that her glove keeps his lady's hand hidden from his sight. Rather than torture him in this way, her beautiful yet cruel hand should take his life and place the epitaph above his grave 'Faith lives on, where the body is dead.' And the exaggerated conceit is matched by the description of her hand, which is more scented than the perfumed glove and causes the very snow to turn red with shame when confronted with her dazzling whiteness. It is hardly surprising, then, to find that, in his commentary on his sonnet 'D'aria un tempo nudrimmi' (159), the poet somewhat ingenuously points out that he wished to amaze the reader with his assertion that he had fed on air: we are already close to the Baroque belief that one of the artist's chief aims is to arouse wonder and surprise. The religious lyrics are even more Baroque, with their insistence on the sufferings of Christ and the saints, often expressed with erotic undertones ('Diva, che su la rota aspri tormenti', 1650).

Tasso was not sparing in his praise of the great of this world. His *rime encomiastiche* are modelled on Pindar and Horace for their lofty tone and Classical allusions, but they are not free from padding and monotony. In some, however, we find a strongly personal note, such as the pleas for help addressed from the prison to which he had been confined for paranoia (667–8). It is in these lyrics that we find again one of the great poetic themes of the *Gerusalemme liberata*: the insistence on man's frailty, his inability to overcome the blows of fate, the sufferings that confer an elegiac note to the drama of the poet's life. His imprisonment even inspired him to write a parody of his encomiastic style: 'Come ne l'ocean' (980), in which he appeals to one of the prison cats to turn her eyes towards him, while he looks to them for light and guidance as the mariner looks towards the stars in heaven.

Tasso admired Della Casa, but rejected the harshness and complexity that characterize some of his greatest sonnets. Instead, Tasso's lyrics are outstanding for their musical flow, and the revision of his poems shows how important this was to him. At times, this musical element tends to swamp everything else and the ear is lulled by the rhythm and melody of words whose meaning is expendable (for example, 'E lieta primavera': 481). At others, however, this musical quality enabled Tasso to produce perfect madrigals, masterpieces of Renaissance verse. This gift is reflected in the fact that, while he wrote over a thousand sonnets, he also composed hundreds of madrigals, sixty *canzoni*, thirty ballads, and two *sestine*: ratios indicative of the main trends in the late sixteenth century, which show the great popularity of the madrigal and the relative decline of the *canzone*. Tasso's skill in using the madrigal form is already evident in the series *Vaghe Ninfe del Po* (175), but it continued to develop until he was able to write the diaphanous 'Tacciono i boschi e i fiumi' (498), the elegiac lament of 'Qual rugiada, o qual pianto' (324), and the superb ballad 'Io v'amo sol perché voi siete bella' (357). Between Petrarch and Leopardi, no other poet was able to rival Tasso's expression of the musical genius of the Italian lyric.

*

Italian pastoral poetry of the sixteenth century is summed up in a single work by the Neapolitan humanist, JACOPO SANNAZARO (*c.* 1455–1530). His *Arcadia* (1504) looks back, beyond the allegories of Boccaccio's *Ameto* (1341–2), to the mixture of verse and prose in Dante's *Vita Nuova*, Boethius and Petronius, together with a host of Classical influences, the most important of which were undoubtedly Virgil's *Eclogues*. It was Virgil who had set two of his bucolic poems (7 and 10) in an idealized Arcadia. This region of Greece had in fact been known for its barbarous customs; but in Virgil's portrayal it became a land of eternal youth, love and music, which gave new life to the Greek idyll.

Arcadia consists of twelve poems, set in a prose account which tells of the hopeless love of Sincero (Sannazaro) for Phyllis. Like Virgil's Gallus, Sincero journeys to Arcadia, where he is enchanted by the simple life and charming customs of the shepherds. He manages to turn away from his own unhappiness to listen to the description of the misfortunes of others – and, quite exceptionally, their good fortune – in love, while all compete in games and song, offering up sacrifice to the woodland deities. In the prologue, Sannazaro expresses the hope that, even as the song of wild birds is more pleasing than that of caged songsters, so his readers will enjoy the 'rustic simplicity' of the eclogues he had heard sung in Arcadia. The fiction is transparent, and the poet certainly has no intention of being bound by simplicity or reality; instead, he succeeds in creating an artefact, a literary mosaic, which was admired and imitated for well over two centuries in Western Europe. A succession of scenes describes the highly artificial life of Arcadia; they lack dramatic unity, but are bound together by the author's exquisite sense of harmony, his rejection of excess and ugliness in life and nature. The only variety lies in the multitude of pastoral themes, which alternate between idyll and elegy, adding poignancy to the one and grace to the other, finding their *raison d'être* in the expression of love. This is obvious from the beginning, where the first eclogue tells of Ergasto's falling in love, and unusual *rime sdrucciole* (dactylic feet) are cunningly changed to the normal flow of *rime piane* (trochaic), with *rimalmezzo*.

In the seventh chapter, Sincero tells the shepherds his story, which is based on Sannazaro's own love for Carmosina Bonifacio in Naples. Like Dante, he explains that he had fallen in love in his ninth year. Unable to find the courage to tell her of his love, Sincero had thought of suicide and had finally decided to leave Naples and the sight of his beloved. Their parting only redoubles his sufferings, however, for, like Petrarch before him, the unhappy lover is reminded of his lady's beauty by every 'grotto, stream, valley, hill, and wood'. So the Pathetic Fallacy, whereby nature reflects the poet's state of mind and echoes his complaints, became part of the pastoral tradition. Sannazaro goes on to describe his unhappiness in the fine *sestina*, 'Come notturno uccel', where the poet displays his mastery of this highly elaborate verse form. The poem ends with the boast that Sincero is the happiest man alive or dead, because his beloved has appeared to him in a dream and has called him to her side. After a subterranean journey, however, Sincero returns to Naples, only to hear of his lady's death.

Arcadia was frequently revised and elaborated, until its publication some twenty years after its original composition. It is a story of unhappy love and exile. It is, however, idle to speculate on the degree to which Sannazaro's personal experience influenced this world of art. What was immediately seized upon was its elegant harmony, including the author's elimination of his Neapolitan dialect in his masterly use of literary Tuscan. Like so many pastorals, Sannazaro's *Arcadia* was written by an accomplished courtier, whose life had little to do with the hard labours of shepherds. Unlike most, on the other hand, its landscapes were described by a poet who had spent his childhood in the countryside, where he had learnt to love the woods and streams that were to provide the setting for his masterpiece. It is, of course, an idealized vision of country life, in which nature is always temperate and bountiful. During the day, the shepherds never have to contend with the more arduous task of caring for their flocks; instead, they are able to indulge in sport, music-making, and such leisurely occupations as the carving of crooks or flutes, while the rustic deities to whom they offer sacrifice look down benignly on their amorous tribulations. The landscape is idyllic. Among other things, it is never described in too much detail: it remains picturesque, while the soft breeze protects it from the rigours of summer and moonlight inevitably lightens the nocturnal scene. Nothing rough is introduced: ploughmen and peasants are banished from Arcadia, where the inhabitants lead a life characterized by their moral uprightness, their simplicity of dress and manner. Significantly, the genre was born in Alexandria, the great metropolis of the ancient world: it was to lead to the *fêtes champêtres* in the Petit Trianon at Versailles, the most sophisticated of modern courts. Yet, in Sannazaro's *Arcadia*, it represents not so much an escape from reality as a heightened vision of certain facets of life and art. It does not yet oppose this vision to the corruption and artificiality of town and court life, nor has it assimilated the complicated intrigues of the romance. For this, we must wait another fifty years and turn to Spain, or wait for the emergence of pastoral drama in Italy.

*

The great outburst of Latin poetry in the preceding age continued well into the sixteenth century, producing verse that is in some ways more varied than its Italian counterpart, while it is interesting to notice the different aspects of a poet's personality in the two languages. Bembo and Della Casa are freer in their Latin lyrics, where they do not have to reckon with the Petrarchan tradition of constancy and reticence; even Tebaldeo appears less artificial in his Latin verse, while Berni's often sentimental tone is quite different from the hard, satirical humour we associate with his name. The mastery acquired made Latin into a natural instrument, and one is frequently surprised by the personal touches, such as the autobiographical details and celebration of family life – excluded from the Classical tradition – which are found, for example, in the lyrics of GIROLAMO FRACAS-TORO (1487–1553) and in the poem MARCO GIROLAMO VIDA (1485–1566) wrote about his dead parents and the memory of his happy childhood. BALDASSARE CASTIGLIONE (1478–1529) wrote a Latin elegy in the form of a letter, which he pretended to have received from his wife Ippolita when he was Federigo Gonzaga's ambassador in Rome. In a touching manner, Ippolita expresses her dismay at his lengthy absence and the temptations that surrounded him; she adds that her only comfort is to talk to their baby son and show him his father's portrait, painted by Raphael.

Ariosto began his poetic career by writing Latin verse, a habit which he cultivated fairly intensively for ten years and which produced an original ode on the death of his father, although he is best remembered in this field for the nonchalant way in which he treated the news of the French invasion in *Ad Philliroem*. He also wrote the famous epigram that he had placed over the entrance to his house in Ferrara, beginning 'Parva sed apta mihi' ('Small, yet just right for me') and reflecting his ideal *aurea mediocritas*.

The Latin lyrics of Sannazaro are redolent of Naples and its beautiful landscapes, with their Classical associations. Sannazaro introduced the piscatorial eclogue, based on Virgil, in which Neapolitan fishermen replace the shepherds of Arcadia, although the basic theme of love remains unchanged. Another variation on the Classical model was the sacred eclogue, which placed episodes taken from the Bible and the lives of the saints in a rustic setting. Unlike Sannazaro, GIOVANNI COTTA (1480–1510) was unable to master both literary languages, and his few Italian poems are far less successful than his Latin love lyrics. He was described as the Catullus of the sixteenth century and his elegy *Ad Lycorim* has some of the passionate intensity that characterizes his great predecessor. ANDREA NAVAGERO (1483–1529) is another poet whose Italian production lacks intrinsic worth, although it is of historical importance because it inspired Boscán to use Italian verse forms in Spanish. Navagero's love poems, *Lusus*, are among the best of neo-Latin lyrics. His *Florentes dum forte vagans mea Hyella per hortos* has been translated more than once into English, and his *Invitatio ad amoenum fontem* inspired one of Tansillo's greatest lyrics, *E freddo è il fonte*.

The neo-Classical elegance of these poets was not the only style represented in the Latin poetry of sixteenth-century Italy. It was indeed the successful attempt made by humanists like Bembo to re-capture the Classical purity of the language that made their Latin un-able to meet the requirements of everyday life and hastened its death as a literary medium. The *latinus grossus* of scientists, lawyers and doctors, on the other hand, survived with all its inaccuracies and bar-baric accretions and was parodied in student jargon and the 'Maccher-onics' of various writers. This caricature is remembered today, thanks to the work of TEOFILO FOLENGO (1491–1544), who defined these maccheroni as 'a kind of coarse, rustic pudding made of flour, cheese and butter' - a description which hardly does justice to the linguistic skill with which their defiantly heterogeneous ingredients are compounded. In this pudding, the syntax and most of the words are Latin in form, although we find words used with an Italian meaning ('toti' = 'all', 'omnes'); Italian constructions ('sedereque fecit Barones' = 'and he made the Barons sit down'); and schoolboy howlers ('sequivit' = 'secutus est'). Folengo's style is fascinating in its variety, which extends from the nobility of humanistic Latin to the sink of linguistic vulgarity, culled from the dialects of Northern Italy. Baldus, for example, expresses his grief over the dead body of Leonardus in purely Classical terms (*Baldus*, XVII, 692–708) - so, too, the epitaph for Leonardus is in unadulterated Latin (XX, 14–19). And Leonardo himself was too saintly a character to use anything but correct Latin (XVII, 74–8). All this only heightens the comic contrast when, in XVII, 80, Pandraga chases this embodiment of virginity, shouting 'Me aspetta puellam' ('Wait for me – I'm a girl!', where the italianate 'aspetta' is a strange bedfellow to 'Me puellam'). In another episode, apart from such Maccheronic forms as 'vecchium', 'guardare', 'cridabant', 'fazze', pure Mantuan dialect is introduced. Barba Tognazzo has been making up to Baldus's wife, egged on by Cingar. The latter causes his clothes to fall off: 'Concurrunt nudum vecchium guardare vilani. "Day, day" cridabant, "hay, hay, che cosa da rider!" Foeminae fazze partem voltantur in altram.'*.

Folengo pretends that the *Baldus* was written by a certain Merlinus Cocaius, whose name is explained in the following way: 'his mother gave birth to him while looking for the bung of a barrel ['cocaium botazzi'], and his surname was inspired by this incident. The reason why he was called Merlin was because a blackbird ['merla'] used to bring him some food every day in his cradle, since his mother drowned herself, when he was still a babe, in a wine vat.' The poem begins, according to Classical example, with an exposition of the subject and an invocation to the Maccheronic Muses. A descendant of Charlemagne's Rinaldo elopes with Baldovina, daughter of the King of France. They find shelter in a poor peasant's hut in the imaginary village of Cipada, near Mantua. Baldovina is soon left alone to give birth to Baldus. His head full of the romances of chivalry, the feats of the paladins inspire his battles with the local urchins and his obviously epic destiny. The descriptions of country life in the first part are among the best in the poem: remarkable for their sympathetic realism, they form a contrast with the idealized pictures found in contemporary pastoral literature. Baldus is marked out to be a champion of justice. But his path is not smooth, and he finds himself surrounded by a mixed band. There is the giant, Fracassus, descended from Pulci's Morgante, who cracks horses like nuts as soon as he gets into the saddle and reaches mock-epic proportions in his superhuman struggle with a whale. Pulci's Margutte is also represented – by Cingar, liar, thief, an attractive rascal with the gift of the gab, who is one of Folengo's best creations and whose ditching of the sheep inspired a similar episode in Rabelais's *Fourth Book* (vi–viii). In Book X, Cingar dresses up as a monk (the author, a Benedictine, indulges in some intermittent, but fierce, satire of his kin). He sets Baldus free to roam the wider world and become a champion of chivalric heroism, a symbol of truth in its fight against error. A battle with some pirates,

*'The peasants all rush up to see the naked old man. They were shouting, "Di, Di, Hi, Hi, what a joke!" The women turn their gaze elsewhere' (VII, 340–42).

a tempest, and other obstacles do not prevent Baldus from arriving at a magic island, where he meets up with his father. Baldus and his companions then wage a tremendous fight against the powers of darkness and go on a journey through the underworld. Finally, the poet appears in person and is imprisoned in an enormous pumpkin, where those who tell lies – in particular, poets and philosophers – are tormented by having their teeth pulled out 'quottidie quantas illi fecere bosias' ('daily as many times as they have told lies'). It is perhaps fitting that a Renaissance poet writing in Latin should remind us that – as both Dante and Rabelais pointed out – laughter is the distinguishing mark of man.

FRANCE

Clément Marot (1496–1544)

The French poets who flourished in the late fifteenth and early sixteenth century are now usually known as the *Grands Rhétoriqueurs*, though recent scholarship has shown that the title is a nineteenth-century invention. Most of them were court poets, whether of Burgundy (Chastellain, d. 1475, and Molinet, d. 1507), of Brittany (Meschinot, d. 1491) or of France proper, and their work is characterized by excessive formalism, tortuous verbal ingenuity and lack of any discernible feeling. The best of them was Jean Lemaire de Belges (1473–*c.*1525) from Hainault, who served in the courts of both France and Burgundy, but he is more interesting for his humanism and historiography than for any great poetic originality. His *Illustrations de Gaule* (in prose) helped to stimulate interest in a French epic, and in his *Epitres de l'Amant vert* (1505), supposedly addressed by a dead parrot to its royal owner, he brings a light and fresh touch to an essentially artificial genre, but he is very much a transitional writer and it is only with the son of Jean Marot, one of the last *Rhétoriqueurs*, that the French Renaissance lyric can really be said to begin.

Clément Marot belonged to exactly the same generation as Rabelais, François I and Marguerite d'Angoulême (later Navarre). He entered Marguerite's service in 1519, and thereafter owed her his livelihood and, on more than one occasion, his life. Unlike his more gifted successors of the Pléiade, Marot never suffered eclipse; even

Boileau speaks approvingly of his 'élégant badinage', but paradoxically that part of his work which is furthest from badinage is the most famous. His translations of the Psalms (13 in 1539, 30 in 1541 and finally 50 in 1543) were adopted by Calvin (in preference to his own) and with his *oraisons* (rhymed versions of prayers, the creed and so on) succeed remarkably in combining the simplicity required for popular appeal with poetic skills acquired in quite different genres.

His concern in such religious poetry is functional rather than aesthetic, that is to say he seeks to express his faith in a language and style accessible to all in order to promote piety, and it is hardly a coincidence that his longest, and arguably best, poem was also the product of verifiably genuine feelings. In 1526 he found himself imprisoned in the Châtelet in Paris on an ecclesiastical charge (his actual phrase 'for eating bacon in Lent' may be literal, or just a periphrasis for unorthodox behaviour). Convinced of the injustice of his sentence and the iniquity of contemporary judicial practice, he composed a poem of some 500 lines, *L'Enfer*, in protest (not published until 1541). He identifies the prison with Hades, and in transparently allegorical terms reviews its departments, officers and inmates in a strikingly effective exercise in sustained satire. He manages to combine humour with real indignation, for example in denouncing the use of torture, and the result is impressive both as poetry and as a personal document. *L'Enfer* more than once recalls Villon in theme and tone, and it is interesting evidence of Marot's taste, and further proof that badinage is not the whole man, that he edited Villon in 1533.

The scanty facts of his biography reveal as little consistency in his life as in his works. In 1532 he published his first collection of mainly light verse, as *L'Adolescence clementine*, and two years later, despite Marguerite's protection, had to leave the country for alleged Evangelical sympathies. These did not deter him from inaugurating while in exile in Ferrara a new fashion in erotic verse with his *Blason du beau tétin*, imitated by many other poets whose treatment of feminine attributes showed more detail than discretion. He himself composed several of these *blasons*, ranging from the mildly sensual to the frankly obscene. In 1536 he was allowed back to France after formal abjuration, and went on writing light verse, but after *L'Enfer* and the Psalms were published had to flee again, in 1541, this time to Geneva. If his Psalms gained him an entry permit, his incompatibility with puritan rules soon earned him expulsion, and he died in 1544 in Turin, not apparently as a Protestant.

Most of his work is occasional verse, often written to order in the name of one patron or another, and he was fortunate in having such facility as to earn his keep, but this was guarantee of fluency rather than quality. It is a historical accident that his translations from Petrarch at his master's orders make him almost certainly the first Frenchman to use the sonnet (he only wrote four original ones), it was economic necessity that inspired his dozens of *étrennes* (something like the legend found in modern greetings cards). On the other hand his *Epîtres* (more than sixty) include a number of very accomplished examples of the begging letter, redeemed from triviality by some ironic twist or incongruity, often reminiscent of Villon. Thus in the delightful one addressed to Pierre Vuyart he laments the loss of a horse, begs the Duchess of Lorraine for a replacement, but suddenly reveals at the end that he does not want a plodding hack or mule but a fiery steed on which to prance in glory. Similarly in his *Epître au Dauphin*, pleading to have his banishment rescinded, he asks to be allowed to return for 'half a year' or, if that is too much, 'six months', 'Non pour aller visiter mes chasteaulx. Mais bien pour veoir mes petits Marotteaux.'*

Like Villon again, Marot was much addicted to puns, outrageous rhymes and facetiousness, and this is nowhere more apparent than in the long, utterly pointless, versified riddles known as *coq-à-l'âne* of which he is an acknowledged master. At the same time his impish sense of fun is often most effective. A foolish feud with the poetaster Sagon got him into serious trouble, but the sprightly *Epître de Frippelippes* (1537), supposedly addressed to Sagon by Marot's valet, shows no resentment in its robust deflation of his enemy's pretensions. Even in an *Epître au Roy* (1535) asking for pardon, Marot refutes charges of Lutheranism with a subtle mixture of irony and sincerity. These chatty and familiar poems are of very varied length and quality, but they have a naturalness which makes them readable and sometimes memorable.

Marot generally kept to traditional metres, especially eight- and ten-syllable lines, and forms, like the *rondeau* (more than sixty), the

* 'Not to visit my castles but to see my little Marots.'

chanson (forty-two) and the *ballade*. Even when he has little or nothing to say his craftsmanship usually enables him to write verse that is witty, musical and gay. From the poets of his father's generation, whom he always respected, he inherited a propensity to verbal virtuosity for its own sake, but he never lapses into their all too frequent pedantry or obscurity. He was not a very erudite man, though he translated some of Ovid and evidently knew Virgil well, but recent research has tended to show that his debt to Italian and Classical influences was more than used to be thought. The Pléiade accused him of writing rhymed prose, and it is true that he seems to show more concern for form than content, but he followed his predecessors in that he rejuvenated an essentially French tradition, with some help from foreign models, where the Pléiade deliberately tried to break with the immediate past and incorporate alien elements wholesale into French literature. No one could speak of Marot's high seriousness, but his levity is at least entertaining and graceful most of the time, while his religious poetry and *L'Enfer* show that he was quite capable of expressing deeper emotions and higher truths when the need arose.

Maurice Scève (c. 1500–1560)

Although only a few years younger than Marot, Scève is clearly on the other side of a frontier which is as much geographical as chronological. He represents the culture of his native city so faithfully that for once it makes sense to speak of a Lyonnais school, including him, the two women poets who were his friends, Pernette du Guillet and Louise Labbé, and perhaps Pontus de Tyard, who was also in the orbit of the Pléiade, apart from many lesser names. There has been a great revival of interest in Scève in recent years, and one must be careful to distinguish between mere ephemeral fashions in academic criticism and genuine reappraisal. It is a pity that virtually every writer on Scève feels obliged to refute the longstanding charge that he is a difficult poet: it is in many ways the best thing about him that he should be so. Life is not all roses, nor poetry all song. If facility is at once Marot's charm and weakness, it must also be remembered that it earned him his bread and butter. Scève, on the contrary, was under no financial pressure, and could afford to please himself how, or how much, he wrote. That said, it is still true that neither differences of economic situation, nor even of temperament, fully explain the vast gulf between the two poets, which can be seen even more clearly in their less talented imitators.

The atmosphere of Lyon, at a political, economic and cultural crossroads, encouraged interchange of ideas on every plane, and while it is technically true that Marot made use of Italian models (and to a greater extent than was realized until recently) Scève is so steeped in Italian culture that it is less a matter of borrowing than an attitude of mind in his case. His first published work was a translation of a Spanish continuation of Boccaccio's *Fiametta*, his first claim to fame was his alleged discovery of the tomb of Petrarch's Laura near Avignon. Both as a student at Avignon (full of papal officials from across the Alps) and at home in Lyon he was in constant contact with Italians and their culture. It is therefore self-evident that his own work should be influenced by Italian poetry, but absurd to enumerate all the lines, images, echoes or what you will reminiscent of this or that Italian poet, and then call him derivative. In one respect, however, it is hardly open to question that but for a specific Italian example (and French patriotism) it would not have occurred to him to write his chief work in the form in which he did. *Délie* (1544) is in fact the first sequence of love poems, *canzoniere*, in French to follow the Petrarchan model, and it may be that by choosing to write in *dizains* Scève reduced the impact of his innovation, for only a year or two later French poets were taking on the Italians at their own game and writing sonnets with great success. At any rate *Délie* is not only a landmark in literary history, but, more to the point, poetry of remarkable quality.

Putting aside the frequent, but somewhat misleading, comparisons made with modern poets like Mallarmé or Valéry, and the more apposite ones with Donne, one can see in *Délie* the poetic expression of much that is familiar in the art of the Renaissance. Without the conventions of image, proverb, myth and the like there would be no sequence at all, and much of the initial difficulty of comprehension felt by modern readers results from general ignorance regarding such conventions today. The sequence is organized into 449 *dizains*, with an introductory *huitain*, and grouped into sections of 9, each prefaced by a woodcut emblem, except that the first 5 have no emblem and the last emblem is followed by only 3 *dizains*. The resultant formula $(5 + (7^2 \times 3^2) + 3)$ has not failed to engage the attention of critics, some of whom have offered ingenious cabbalistic interpretations. In view of Scève's known interest in number symbolism (shared by most of his contemporaries) the arrangement can hardly be accidental, but in the present state of our knowledge provides no key to the sequence that the words and emblems do not themselves already afford. These emblems (fifty in all), covering a wide variety of motifs from mythology to husbandry, have negligible artistic merit, but their interest lies in the motto they contain and illustrate, and which is usually repeated in the following *dizain*. There are cases where the emblem interrupts an otherwise continuous flow of ideas across sections (for example, 203 and 205) and not infrequently the emblem has no more to do with the section following than have the nine *dizains* with each other. This is, then, no rigidly organized emblem book, but even less is it an artificially unified anthology of occasional pieces.

The theme is love and the poet's response to his own emotions, often expressed in moral or intellectual terms, overlaying, but never supplanting, sensual experience. It follows that, for all his use of maxims and *sententiae*, Scève remains above all a personal poet. Because of the Platonic themes included (together with much else) in *Délie*, it was once thought that the title was intended as the anagram of *L'Idée* in the Platonic sense, and while this fact must have occurred to Scève himself, it is perfectly clear (for instance, from the importance of sun–moon images) that he was thinking of Diana, like her brother Apollo associated with Delos, and most probably of Pernette du Guillet, married to another man but still the object of his affection. The sequence is full of the antithesis between light and dark, presence and absence, union and separation, and contains a certain amount of the erotic casuistry that Ficino and Leone Ebreo had made familiar, but Scève's exploitation of these, and other, themes already associated with Petrarch and his later disciples never gives the impression of mere exercises in style. The sequence does not exactly tell a story, at least in the autobiographical sense, though there are references to personal and external events of several years back, but it relates the course of a passion from the peace of early days, through the anguish and turmoil of frustration and separation to the recovery of a new peace, enriched by the intervening experience of love. The language is strikingly original, the imagery, at times excessively involved, is often brilliant, and if compression is sometimes achieved only at the price of obscurity, there is always the impression of vigorous force under tight control. The legacy of the *Rhétoriqueurs* is plain to see, as in such untranslatable lines as: 'Voulant je veulx, que mon si hault vouloir / De son bas vol s'estende à la vollée, / Ou ce mien vueil ne peult en rien valoir . . .' continuing throughout the *dizain* with similar variations, but neither here nor elsewhere degenerating into verbal acrobatics. Similarly while melting ice, polished alabaster and ivory, and other Petrarchan ornaments are common enough, there is nothing but Scève himself in this quatrain, describing the lover's return after a month's absence:

> Car en mon corps: mon Ame, tu revins,
> Sentant ses mains, mains celestement blanches,
> Avec leurs bras mortellement divins,
> L'un couronner mon col, l'aultre mes hanches.*

Without the emotion there would be no poetry, but without the self-discipline the emotion would have run to waste in triteness or babbling. There is admittedly an intellectual problem to be solved in much of Scève's poetry, often arising from his odd syntax, but it is not just a riddle (like Marot's *coq-à-l'âne*), but an intricate pattern of allusion and symbol, revealing deep and genuine feeling. Scève's language and culture are today too remote for instant appreciation to be possible for any but the expert, but he has something to say, he says it in truly poetic manner, and the effort required of the reader rapidly diminishes, as one *dizain* illuminates the next.

Scève's friends, PERNETTE DU GUILLET (*c.* 1520–45) and LOUISE LABBÉ (1524–65), can hardly be denied their place in the short list of Renaissance poetesses. The tale of the former is brief and pathetic: beautiful, cultured, entertaining, she fell in love with Scève when she was barely sixteen and is generally thought to have been the inspiration of *Délie*. Her family rapidly married her off to a husband who seems

---

*'For to my body you, my soul, returned, feeling her hands, celestially white, with their arms, mortally divine, one wreathing my neck, the other my waist.'

to have behaved with gentle tact, but the affair with Scève continued on a spiritualized and poetic plane, nourished by constant meetings in society. She died in 1545, and her husband at once had her poems published, in the same disorder in which they had been left. These *Rimes* include a number of *dizains*, and longer poems of various forms and metres, nearly all on the subject of love. Scève's influence, and even his name in anagrammatic form, is obvious, but the poems in their way are as personal as his, and thus essentially feminine and wistful where he is robust and vehement. There is no doubt as to the intensity of her love, nor of her intention to keep it free from gross contamination ('. . . d'amour saincte/Chastement au cueur suis attaincte')*, but the very tight rein occasionally relaxes and she longs for the one she calls her 'Jour' in unequivocal terms. In 'Combien de fois ay-je en moy souhaicté' ('How often have I inwardly longed') she dreams of meeting him by the stream, 'Et toute nue en l'eau me gecterois,'† enticing him on with her lute, but keeping him from actual contact by throwing water in his eyes. Subdued as the tone is, she is frank about the joys and pains of love, and has a curiously appealing dignity despite her youth.

Louise Labbé, 'la belle cordière' (her father was a rope-merchant), was a little younger than Pernette, and could hardly have been more different. Pernette, to judge from her poetry, was no bluestocking, but did maintain the social proprieties; Louise openly rejected them. Her life was the subject of much slander and gossip, some, no doubt, invented, but it is abundantly clear that she was not content to establish just the cultural rights of women, but their sexual rights as well. The three elegies and twenty-three sonnets available in modern editions may not be poetry of the highest order, but are undeniably effective in their burning affirmation of feminine passion. No shrinking maiden, she sighs and tosses, seeking 'Dans le mol lit le repos désiré‡ (VII), only to be reminded of the imperious needs of the flesh. Such a sonnet as 'Oh, si j'estois en ce beau sein ravie . . .'§ (XII) makes no concessions to convention or reticence. In form and expression she owes much to Petrarch, but the content derives wholly

---

*'Chastely stricken in the heart with holy love.'
†'And I would throw myself naked into the water.'
‡'The longed-for rest in the soft bed.'
§'Oh, were I but enraptured on that fair breast.'

from the consuming ardour of her own extraordinary nature. The intensity and individuality of her verse would hardly be remarkable in a man, but in a woman of the sixteenth century are astonishing. 'Baise m'encor, rebaise moy et baise' is an echo of life, rather than an exercise in the style of Catullus; such fire owes nothing to artifice.

*

Between the poets of Lyon, where his work was published, and those of the Pléiade, who much admired him, is as appropriate a place as any to mention a neo-Latin poet who fits into no convenient category. Jean Everaerts, known as JOHN SECUNDUS (1511–36) was born at the Hague, studied in France, worked in Spain, fell seriously ill on an expedition to Tunis, and returned to die a few months later near Tournai. In the course of this brief and eventful life he found time to compose a slim volume of poetry which had an influence out of all proportion to its bulk. Published posthumously in Lyon (1539) his *Basia* (kisses) fill a mere sixty-one pages, and were followed in 1541 by a complete edition, adding *Elegia* and *Odes*. M. A. Muret and Théodore de Bèze (before his Calvinist conversion) imitated him in Latin, Ronsard, du Bellay, Baïf and Belleau, to name only the most famous, in French. Roman models, notably Catullus, are easily recognizable in the *Basia*, nineteen poems written in very varied style, but there is nothing of the pastiche about these brilliant and graceful erotic verses. He writes of unhappy love affairs (as in some of the *Elegia*) with frankness suggested by the title, but always with the lightest of touches. The second of the *Basia*, 'Vicina, quantum vitis lascivit in ulmo' ('As the vine embraces the neighbouring elm'), was a particular favourite with French poets. Even in translation his work is delightful, and no account of Renaissance lyric would be complete without a tribute to this regrettably neglected minor master.

The Pléiade – Joachim du Bellay (c. 1522–60) and Rémy Belleau (1528–77)

A year or two older than Ronsard, but fated to live little more than half as long, Joachim du Bellay is certainly not one of those Renaissance poets for whom excuses need be made by his admirers. He is not a 'difficult' poet like Scève, he is not a 'facile' one like Marot, he is just very good. All, inevitably, is not equally successful in his work, nor is this very copious, but at his best he offers delights and satisfactions only equalled by those of his friend Ronsard. Bursting boisterously into print with his *Defense et Illustration de la langue françoyse* (1549) he at once hoisted the standard of patriotism and claimed a privileged status for poets. Scève and Marot were no doubt as good Frenchmen as he, but did not make such a fuss about it; Scève, though probably not Marot, recognized the exalted calling of the poet, but did not make this the subject of a manifesto. With du Bellay and his brother poets of the Pléiade, poetry became part of a programme, and their extreme self-consciousness regarding their self-imposed task of rehabilitating the French language invests their activity with a new, and not unwelcome, sense of purpose. They may have fallen short of their lofty aspirations, but they certainly tried.

In the same year as the *Defense* du Bellay published fifty sonnets of *L'Olive* as an earnest of his intentions, to be followed next year by sixty-five more. These early sonnets represent a not very convincing foray into the familiar country of Petrarchan love poetry, and though not without technical competence, suffer all too visibly from the lack of any genuine feeling (or at least the ability to communicate it). For all that, du Bellay was clearly a young man to watch, and even in this genre might, with time, have produced a sequence as good as the best in *L'Olive* and a few posthumously published sonnets of even higher quality. As it happened his life and art took another course. Never very robust, he fell seriously ill, became deaf (perhaps totally), found himself in severe financial embarrassment and in 1553, somewhat restored in health but not in fortune, joined his distinguished kinsman (and Rabelais's former patron) Cardinal Jean du Bellay at the French Embassy in Rome. There he stayed for four years, and this experience inspired all his best work. On his return in 1558 he published a collection of Latin verse, the sprightly *Divers Jeux rustiques* (largely imitated from the neo-Latin poet Navagero) and the two sonnet sequences, *Les Regrets* and *Les Antiquitez de Rome*, on which his reputation firmly rests.

Two aspects of the patriotism which inflamed so many French writers of the Renaissance are resentment at those cultural snobs who believed that anything worth saying should be said in Latin or Greek, writing often very accomplished works in those languages, and envy and dislike of the Italians who, in French eyes, combined moral depravity with infuriating cultural superiority. As the spokesman for the new Brigade, as the Pléiade was first called, du Bellay was the last person who might have been expected to write in Latin, or closely to imitate Italian models, though in fact he did both. The point is that like Ronsard, du Bellay was an excellent Classicist, thanks to the brilliant example of their master, Dorat, and as keen as anyone to display his erudite credentials, though not at the expense of his own language. Moreover for all the Pléiade and their sympathizers Rome was the object of an almost religious awe, and to be in the Eternal City, walking the streets where once Ovid, Catullus and the rest had gone before, was an inspiration as potent as that of French patriotism. This explains the Latin verse, and without these considerations the two sonnet sequences lose much of their point. As for the use of Italian models, the watchword of the Pléiade was, as they put it, to cull their literary harvest like bees from any honey-bearing flower. The distinction between imitation, plagiarism and assimilation is a very fine one, and never more so than in the Renaissance, but it is fair to say that slavish imitation is not du Bellay's practice, and what he writes he has fully made his own, except, perhaps, in *L'Olive*.

The inspiration for the thirty-two sonnets comprising the *Antiquitez* is inner melancholy rather than specific ruins, and the contrast is one of mood rather than spectacle between the glory that was Rome and the sad reality she has become. It is remarkable that in the earlier love poetry, just where the personal note might be expected, it rarely breaks through the technical exercise, except in the thirteen *Sonnets de l'Honneste Amour*, whereas here, where nothing more human than shattered marble appears to be involved, the poet's inner grief and disillusionment runs as an unspoken refrain throughout. The sombre majesty of these sonnets, some in decasyllables and some in alexandrines, shows du Bellay at his monumental best, writing from the heart about things he feels deeply, and embellishing with appropriate Classical allusions verse which never becomes top-heavy with erudition. It is not surprising that Spenser should have felt impelled to produce his own version of the sequence.

Even the *Antiquitez*, however, are more limited in their range and less personal an achievement than the admirable *Regrets*, for which it is hard to find a parallel in French. This sequence of 191 sonnets treats the theme of exile, as the title (taken from Ovid's *Tristia*) suggests, but in an astonishing variety of ways. There are the expected poems of nostalgia, some naturally based on Ovid, and including some of the finest in the French language; there are brilliant satirical sketches of what would now be called café society in Rome; there are messages for absent friends; and above all there is the chatty, almost colloquial record of his daily life. The justly famous 'Heureux qui comme Ulysse a fait un beau voyage' (XXXI) gains from being seen in its context of disgust and cynicism at the pox-ridden prelates and prostitutes and parasites of Rome, of longing for a simpler life at home by the little Loir, of shame at the constant humiliation of being found poor, and dull, and foreign. Even on the way home, passing through Venice and Switzerland, his bitterness does not leave him: 'Rome n'est plus Rome' ('Rome is no longer Rome'). The weapon is no bludgeon, but a stiletto; thus, on the dignitaries of the papal court: 'Mais les voyant pallir lorsque sa Saincteté / Crache dans un bassin et d'un visage blanc / Cautement espier s'il n'y a point de sang, / Puis d'un petit soubriz feindre une seureté'* (CXVIII). Of the Roman Carnival he writes: 'Il nous fauldra demain visiter les saincts lieux, / Là nous ferons l'amour, mais ce sera des yeux, / Car passer plus avant c'est contre l'ordonnance'† (CXX). He wrote too truly: 'La louange, Bizet, est facile à chacun. / Mais la satyre n'est un ouvrage commun'‡ (CXLIII), for the conventional tributes with which the sequence ends fall far short of the satirical sonnets, and short too of the poignant cry of exile: 'Je regrete les bois, et les champs blondissans, / Les vignes, les jardins, et les prez verdissans, / Que mon fleuve traverse . . .'§ (XIX).

Du Bellay's poetic baggage is not heavy, nor of uniform excellence, but he stands worthily beside Ronsard as a writer who perfected the French language for poetry and truly made it illustrious.

The other members of the Pléiade may seem of minor importance

---

*'But seeing them grow pale when his Holiness spits into a basin and white-faced peep slyly to see if there is any blood, then feign confidence with a little smile.'

†'Tomorrow we must visit the holy places, there we will make love, but only with our eyes, for to go further is against regulations.'

‡'Anyone can praise, Bizet, but satire is no ordinary task.'

§'I miss the woods, and the golden fields, the vineyards, gardens and verdant meadows through which my river runs.'

compared to Ronsard and du Bellay, but to disregard them for that reason would be unjust in view of their joint contribution to French poetry. Etienne Jodelle (1532–73) is best known for his tragedies and comedies on the ancient model, but he also wrote verse much admired in his own day. Jean-Antoine de Baif (1532–89), who accompanied Ronsard on the poetically recorded *Voyage de Tours*, spent much of his time on unsuccessful experiments with *vers mesurés*, but is best remembered for his leading role in the development of academies of all the arts. Pontus de Tyard (1521–1605) was an early associate of Scève, and his first works, *Les Erreurs Amoureuses* (1549), show many of the Petrarchan and Platonic features of his master, but he later came into the orbit of the Pléiade, of which he is usually reckoned a member. He far outlived the others and found himself at the end of a long life enjoying favour as one of the Petrarchan old guard. Jacques Peletier du Mans is another of the seven, so is Dorat, the great Classical scholar at the Collège de Coqueret to whom they all owed so much, but after Ronsard and du Bellay the place of honour must go to Rémy Belleau.

Perhaps Ronsard's closest friend among the company, BELLEAU is a writer of limited, but highly individual talent, who achieved something very close to perfection in his chosen medium. He published a version of pseudo-Anacreon in 1556, accompanied by what he called *Petites Hymnes de son Invention*. These miniature compositions (of some 100 lines) are more like odes than the full-scale *Hymnes* of, for example, Ronsard, and deal with such subjects as *Le Papillon* (*Butterfly*), *L'Huitre* (*Oyster*), *Le Coral*, but also with *L'Heure* (*Hour*), *L'Ombre* (*Shade*) and so on. The grace and delicacy of these octosyllables has a distinction that marks a decisive advance on the *chansons* of Marot, in both vocabulary and imagery. Even more remarkable is his last collection, *Les Amours et nouveaux Eschanges des Pierres précieuses* (1576), where he uses both octosyllables and alexandrines to form a treasure-house of (literally) precious stones. Mythological tales, vivid pictures of natural beauty, sparkling with life and colour, these poems show a mastery of style that saves them from precosity or formalism. The awareness of nature and its bounty was, of course, no new thing, but here it is neither didactic nor merely enumerative. Belleau clearly owes much to the miniaturist technique of the *blasons*, and his work also has affinities with some of the cosmological and encyclopaedic poetry of the age, containing as it does much of the pseudo-scientific lore of the traditional lapidaries. Like all the other members of the Pléiade, Belleau lived with all his senses sharpened, and is hardly inferior to Ronsard in his ability to depict the world around him, a world of purling streams, leafy glades, twittering birds, flashing jewels and lovely men and women.

Though death cut short his career at forty-nine, when he showed no sign of flagging for lack of inspiration, he achieved a substantial output, even if in range he cannot compete with Ronsard or du Bellay. Apart from the works mentioned he also produced a collection of prose and verse, largely inspired by Sannazaro, entitled *La Bergerie* (1565 and 1572), including with much else of lesser merit the exquisite poem *Avril*. Two adaptations of biblical themes appeared in 1576. His outstanding qualities are grace, sensitivity and lightness, but a high degree of craftmanship always accompanies the apparently effortless spontaneity and fluency. His acute awareness of nature in its impact on all his senses, his musicality and refinement of taste make him at his best a delightful and, in some respects, unique minor poet.

Pierre de Ronsard (1524–85)

In sheer bulk the work of Ronsard dominates that of his companions and establishes his position as their leader, but it is not the least measure of his leadership that he never swamped or discouraged the talent of the others. He was, indeed, intensely vain, and resented bitterly the rivalry of Desportes in his later years; but while he may have aroused the envy of some (like du Bellay) no one could deny that he acted as a stimulus to those around him. In a real sense his success was their success, and that is equally true in reverse; poetic laurels and inspiration must always be personal but the members of the Pléiade formed too corporate and enthusiastic a joint enterprise for the parts to be properly independent of the whole. In so far as they were brought together in the first place by a desire to do something about the status of French as a literary language and the status of poets in society, Ronsard's success, if confined to himself alone, would have had to be accounted a failure.

It is inevitable that Ronsard should today be best known and admired for his lyric poetry, especially his sonnets, though all his love poetry together composes barely a third (if that) of the 2,000 pages or so of his collected works. He aimed at nothing less than conquest of all the Classical genres, from epic to epigram, from Pindaric ode to Petrarchan sonnet, and on any showing the results are spectacular. Leaving for a later section his longer, and public, poems, we are left with the three great love sequences: to Cassandre (including 229 sonnets), to Marie (81 sonnets, including pieces added later), and to Hélène (141 sonnets), and with five books of *odes* (except to Hélène, Ronsard also wrote *odes*, *chansons* and other forms in honour of his mistresses). In more than one sense Ronsard did not know where to stop, although the substantial number of rejected pieces (*pièces retranchées*) shows that he was not afraid to admit error. Thus his fondness for diminutives ('tendrelette', 'doucerette', etc.) tempts him sometimes into excess, his Classical erudition sometimes threatens to turn the smooth progress of his verse into a pedantic procession, his habitual sensuality can go far beyond the bounds of good taste (even for his frank age) and so on. None the less, he knows what he is about, and no one was a severer critic of his work than he himself, as any variant edition abundantly bears out.

His inspiration was essentially personal, though it was put to the service of France and the French tongue and, in later years, all too often whipped up by some royal command, and his poetic excellence corresponds with the wide range of feelings of which he was capable. He believed with what can almost literally be termed a religious conviction in his poetic vocation, in his role of prophet and priest of a cult and truth regained by the Renaissance. In everyday terms he writes best when he writes of love and death, 'Car l'Amour et la Mort n'est qu'une mesme chose',* but his attitude to these twin themes is conditioned by his belief in the unique part the poet as such has to play in both. He was quite able to write of sexual activity with the insouciance of a Marot (witness the *Gayetés* and *Folastries*) but even at its best this sort of thing displays ingenuity and a sense of fun, not poetry. On the other side of the medal, he can be intolerably precious and pompous when writing exercises in the Petrarchan mode to Cassandre. Much more often the fusion of genuine feeling and

*'For Love and Death are but one and the same.'

careful craftmanship produced just that poetic excellence for which the *Defense* had called.

Ronsard's first published work was the *Odes*, of which four books came out in 1549. A recent critic has said that they show Ronsard from the outset possessed of a 'gift for vivid metaphor; sometimes striking, perhaps too facile, but literally inexhaustible'. The long and famous *Ode à Michel de l'Hôpital* consists of twenty-four strophes, antistrophes and epodes on the Pindaric model, combining a full-scale treatment of mythological themes with the customary compliments to his patron and other great persons. Like much of Ronsard's poetry, this was intended to be (and was in fact) set to music, and its ceremonial character and evocation of ancient rites makes it more than usually difficult to judge from the printed page. Opinions are bound to differ as to the merits of so ambitious a work, but there can be no doubt that Ronsard did for French poetry what such artists as Jean Goujon or François Clouet did for sculpture or painting in taking over and acclimatizing Classical (or Italian) themes in a work of adaptation, even imitation, but definitely not plagiarism.

Since it appears, with other Pindaric odes, in the 1552 edition of the *Odes*, it would be artificial to separate the *Ode à Michel de l'Hôpital* from the far greater number of a less formal and more intimate nature written in the style of Horace (or Catullus) rather than that of Pindar. Where the monumental gives way to the rustic, even homely, strain of such brilliant adaptations as the *Ode à la Fontaine Bellerie* (from Horace's *Fons Bandausiae*) Ronsard is endearing, not overwhelming, and inspires no such reservations as he does in the more complex work. He is always at ease with the native woodnote wild, and it is not hard to see that the nymphs of the Vendôme countryside struck a truer echo from his lyre than the marmoreal muses of Pindar. This may well be a reflection on modern taste rather than on Ronsard's art; his command of rhythm, language and sheer sound is consistent, and compels admiration even when apparently put to unsuitable ends. One feature of his *Odes*, found too in many of his longer poems, is the intensity of the pagan evocation. Partly, of course, this is the direct consequence of choosing for this type of verse almost exclusively pagan sources, partly it is the expression of a very real enthusiasm felt by the Pléiade and their followers for the antique world which had inspired the supreme examples of their art.

To the question 'did they believe in pagan gods and spirits?' it is hard to reply with an unequivocal negative, just as it is impossible in the face of the evidence to deny the sincerity of Ronsard's Christianity. In a sense they were all playing a part in the self-conscious re-creation of a bygone age and culture, with their famous picnic at Arcueil, for instance, deliberately imitating Bacchic revels, but in another sense they became identified with the role and certainly believed in the immortality of their poetry.

Cassandre is herself the subject of more than one of the *Odes*, notably the famous 'Mignonne, allons voir si la rose', and many of them (like that one) appeared in various editions under the classification both of *ode* and *chanson*, but it is with the first book of *Amours*, the *Amours de Cassandre* (1552) that Ronsard shows what he can do with a single subject and virtual homogeneity of style, for only at the end of the series of decasyllabic sonnets do *chansons* and *élégies* make their appearance. The fiery darts, ivory, alabaster, coral and the rest are all there, so is a lot of Classical mythology, and it must be admitted that only the most stylized image of the lady emerges, but the sensual delight with which Ronsard writes of love leaves one in no doubt that real passion, whether for Cassandre alone or for others too, is the source of his inspiration. He was quite capable of poetic sublimation, but in the often too rarified atmosphere of Renaissance poetry it is reassuring to find a poet whose affective credentials carry complete conviction. There is a thin thread of narrative in this sequence, as in most others inspired by Petrarch: we learn that it was in 1546 (unless the rhyme dictated the date) that the poet first saw the golden-haired girl of fifteen at a dance, that his passion has endured six years, that she may (or may not) have accorded him her favours, that she is now unattainable, but none of this is of any great importance. It is interesting to know that Cassandre Salviati has a historical identity, and she remains the nominal heroine of the story, even if in reality she may have been no more than a catalyst for the powerful emotions of the young poet, but if she – and indeed the poet too – were anonymous it would make little difference to our appreciation of such marvellous poems as 'Soit que son or se crepe lentement', 'Je veulx bruler pour m'envoler aux cieux', or 'Je voudray bien richement jaunissant'. The allusions to mythology and philosophy are there (for example in the two latter sonnets), but it is playful pedantry at worst, and it is our loss, not Ronsard's fault, if Jupiter's golden rain or Hercules' fiery apotheosis strike no echo.

When Ronsard came to write his second sequence in 1555, this time to Marie, he was ready for a change. He himself recognized that a certain artificiality could easily creep into the more stylized type of verse for which Cassandre's social status called, but the biographical question of his actual relations with Marie (or Cassandre or anyone else) is probably insoluble. On internal evidence Marie was a country girl from Bourgueil, aged fifteen, in whose honour Ronsard decided to write 'd'un beau stile bas',* as he says in his address to his book, for 'Il suffist qu'on luy chante au vray ses passions/Sans enflure ni fard, d'un mignard et doux stile.' He claims that if Cassandre had been more forthcoming he would have continued to sing her praise, but that if Marie proves similarly haughty ('orgueilleuse et rebelle') he will waste no time before once more transferring his affections. However all that may be, there is a marked difference in tone and treatment; for one thing, Ronsard now uses alexandrines to court his 'petite pucelle Angevine', for another, the real, rather than the literary, countryside is the scene of his love. There are a number of *chansons*, *madrigaux* and other poems included in the sonnet sequence, and the musical element is as marked as ever. The enchanting 'Marie levez-vous, ma jeune paresseuse' is unfortunately an early stage in an affair which was to turn out as yet another example of unrequited love, so that he regrets ever having left his 'grave premier stile' for so heartless a mistress ('Marie, tout ainsi que vous m'avez tourné'). The success of this second book is only relative: it is not homogenous in either style or content, and Classical allusions do not always harmonize with rusticity; the songs and other poems are often delightful, but they detract from the effect of the sonnets, of which in any case by no means all are concerned with Marie. The best is splendid, and the experiment richly rewarding, but not without a sense of poetic, as well as amorous, dissatisfaction.

The postscript to this sequence was not appended until 1578: four years earlier Marie de Clèves, deeply loved by the future Henri III, had died, and Ronsard was obliged to write 'sur la mort de Marie' a number of poems, including twelve sonnets to mourn his patron's

---

*'In a fine simple style. . . . It is enough to sing one's passions sincerely, without pomp or paint, in a sweet and delicate style.'

loss. That his own Marie came also into his mind is certain; certain too that he knew of her death, but it is impossible to affirm that any particular one of these poems (except the *Epitaphe de Marie*, which appears as a thirteenth sonnet) was written with the Angevine wholly or mainly in view. 'Comme on voit sur la branche au mois de may la rose' may seem too personal to be a command performance, but the general excellence of the rest of the collection is a salutary warning against condemning poetry written to order as necessarily insincere or artificial.

Nowhere is this warning more appropriate than in Ronsard's last sequence, the two books of *Sonnets pour Hélène*. Bidden by Catherine de' Medici, as it seems, to compose these poems in honour of a young, apparently unattractive, bluestocking lady-in-waiting, Hélène de Surgères, nettled by the successful challenge of Desportes and worried by awareness of his own lost youth and charms, Ronsard embarked on this venture (in 1578) with most things against him. In 1584 he added some more sonnets (thirty-four) to the collection, and died soon afterwards, so that it does indeed represent his last word on love. Opinions have been very sharply divided as to the merits of these poems, some regarding them as the typical Petrarch-izing preciosity of a poet laureate, others preferring them to his earlier work, and even judging the whole sequence to be his finest achievement. It is true that there are more poems of a specific nature in this than in previous sequences, true too that the chagrins of middle age are no less productive of deep emotion than the enthusiasm of youth. None of Ronsard's skill has deserted him, so that technically these later sonnets benefit from earlier experiments and maturer wisdom. For all that most people will prefer the careless rapture of youth, however awkward at times, to the more objective or reflective mood of age.

Much the best known of these poems is 'Quand vous serez bien vieille', which constant repetition in anthologies has not made stale, but more typical of the prevailing mood are those poems which speak of the poet's own head, already bald and grey, like the opening sonnet of Book Two which reminds us: '. . . tousjours un vieil tison/ Cache un germe de feu sous une cendre grise.'* Some of the poems look back to more carefree days: 'Adieu belle Cassandre, et vous

*'An old ember always hides a spark of fire beneath grey ash.'

belle Marie . . . Maintenant en Automne encores malheureux/ Je vy comme au Printemps de nature amoureux',★ but most are concerned directly with the actuality of his relationship with Hélène. Sometimes, in fact often, he plays on the Homeric associations of her name (also of course appropriate to Cassandre), sometimes he is simply playful: 'Cousin, monstre à double aile, au mufle elephantin;'† sometimes the weight of years is too much for him: 'Au milieu de la guerre, en un siècle sans foy . . . Grison et maladif r'entrer dessous la loy / D'Amour, ô quelle erreur.'‡ Grey and cold do not exactly predominate, but provide a recurrent theme, as in the striking sonnet 'Le mois d'aoust bouillonnait d'une chaleur esprise / Quand j'allay voir ma Dame assise auprès du feu/ Son habit estoit gris.'§ This is far indeed from the stylized conventions of so many of his other poems, and numerous other examples of the same realistic precision could be cited: how he climbs panting up the stairs to her lofty room in the Louvre; finds her looking out towards the heights of Montmartre; how he is visited by her when he has just been bled, and many more. It is always hazardous to assert literary priority, but it is safe to say that the *Sonnets pour Hélène* represent an intensely personal and individualistic treatment of love which, for all the debt to Classical or Italian models, is not only original, but unmatched until the nineteenth century.

Ronsard's title of 'poet of love and death' is justified from his earliest works by an acute sense of the impermanence of beauty, whether human or natural, but usually (as in 'Quand vous serez bien vieille') this feeling is balanced by an equally strong conviction of the immortality of a poet's name and work. It is thus all the more impressive to find in the last dozen or so poems written as he lay dying a profound realization of the imminent reality of death, together with Christian hope of immortality. The sonnet 'Quoi, mon âme, dors-tu engourdie en ta masse?' is a long way from the

---

★'Farewell fair Cassandra, and you fair Marie. . . . Now still unhappy in autumn I live as in spring amorous by nature.'

†'Gnat, two winged monster with elephantine trunk.'

‡'In the midst of war, in a faithless age. . . . To return grey and ailing to the thrall of love, oh what a mistake.'

§'The month of August was boiling hot when I went to see my lady sitting by the fire, dressed in grey.'

earlier calls to wake up, but bears the same unmistakable stamp of a man who wrote because he felt.

Full assessment of Ronsard's achievement must await consideration of the *Hymnes, Discours* and other longer poems, which add another dimension to his work, but if he had written nothing but lyric poetry he would have earned his place among the greatest of French poets. More than anyone he was successful in forging the idiom in music and imagery which we can see as the predecessor to seventeenth-century Classicism, and for which the Pléiade had striven.

*

After Ronsard the remaining lyric poets of the century inevitably come as an anti-climax, yet one of them, PHILIPPE DESPORTES, seriously rivalled Ronsard for a decade or more, and was his un-challenged successor. A whole generation younger (1546–1606), he might have been expected to revivify the Petrarchan tradition on which the Pléiade had built and then advanced, but the contrary is the case. An early visit to Italy opened his eyes to his future career, and he soon became the favourite poet of the circle presided over by the maréchale de Retz, as well as ingratiating himself with the future Henri III. He sometimes acknowledged his debt to Italy openly, as in his *Imitations d'Arioste* or the later *Muses de France et d'Italie*, but for the most part was content to exploit it quietly. He wrote three main sonnet sequences, the *Amours de Diane, Amours de Cléonice, Amours d'Hippolyte* (1572–3), all on behalf of distinguished patrons, the last addressed to Marguerite de Valois, supposedly on behalf of Bussy d'Amboise, and has excited so much adverse criticism over the centuries that he is no doubt due to benefit from one of those regular fits of critical remorse. A. M. Schmidt speaks of his 'circonspection immorale d'un arriviste lucide',* but however antipathetic his personal record, his work cannot be ignored. His outstanding quality is seemingly effortless fluency, and a regularity of diction that suggests a well-oiled machine. This is not to say that he lacks charm or skill, simply that he utterly fails to convey to the reader any convincing depth of feeling. Flames, torches, ice, poison, all the stock images of Classical mythology and Petrarchistic poetry are combined in nicely calculated doses, and if it cannot truthfully be said that

---

*'Immoral wariness of a lucid opportunist.'

Desportes often falls into banality or dullness, he does not often thrill either. Work so close to mechanical preciosity was bound to provoke a reaction, and Malherbe's exasperation in the next century unfortunately led to the indiscriminate condemnation of Desportes and his far greater predecessors.

SPAIN

Juan Boscán (1487/92–1542)

The beginning of the history of Italianate lyric poetry in Spain is marked by the publication in 1543 of *Las obras de Boscán y algunas de Garcilasso de la Vega repartidas en quatro libros*. Largely prepared by Boscán himself, this collection was brought out by his widow six months after his own death and rather over six years after that of Garcilaso, his devoted friend. It is a work that enables the reader, as he goes through it, to trace with remarkable clarity the process by which the language of the greatest lyric poetry of sixteenth-century Spain was established.

'In the first book are the first things that Boscán wrote, which are Spanish *coplas*', says the Preface. These are numerous short poems about the exquisite agony of love. The lover is dazzled by his lady's radiance and helplessly silent in her presence. He is her prisoner; he bears the wounds of his anguished love and is the victim of its madness. He is full at once of desire and fear, of inner strife. He is in a state of crisis from which there is no escape. His lady deals death even as she inspires life; she brings pain and joy together. The lover would not have it otherwise: the greatest pain is to be without pain, for his lady is all his life. These sentiments are expressed for the most part in poems of two brief stanzas. Such brevity contributes to the intensity that is the effect chiefly sought for. This is achieved still more by the manner of exposition. The lover's feelings, themselves of extreme intensity, are set out in subtle, tight, analytical argument which is based on word-play and aimed above all at producing an effect of paradox – which is the paradox of the lover's emotional situation. Some of the poems give a pleasing sense of deft and elegant concentration of thought and feeling, but too often they give, to the modern reader at least, an impression of empty ingenuity, of cliché-ridden narrowness of range, and are reminiscent of the amorous subtleties whose attempted unravelling helped to drive Don Quixote mad.

In Book II Boscán declared that he had done better. For this contained poems written not 'in the Castilian manner' but 'in the Italian': ninety-two sonnets and ten *canciones*, mingled together. This was impressively new, although not wholly without precedent. Sporadic interest had been taken long since by Castilian poets in the hendecasyllabic line, which was, most notably, the measure used by Dante and Petrarch and not a usual Castilian form. Boscán had an important forerunner in Iñigo López de Mendoza (1398–1458), first Marquis of Santillana, who had written forty-two sonnets, 'fechos al italico modo'. But he established no tradition, and Boscán does not mention him. This was not simply because Boscán was eager to emphasize his own role as innovator. Indeed, he was clearly affected by the tendency of his age to dislike novelty and condemn it as new-fangledness. He is anxious rather to place his sonnets and songs in a tradition – that which, as he claimed, went back through Petrarch, Dante and the Provençal poets to Latin and even Greek. He explains that he had undertaken the attempt to write poetry in Castilian employing the sonnet form and others 'used by the good authors of Italy' in consequence of a conversation at Granada, during the marriage celebrations of Charles V (1526), with the illustrious Navagero, Venetian ambassador, eminent humanist and friend of Bembo. He may well have long been disposed to admire Italian poets since he was the esteemed pupil of the Italian humanist Lucio Marineo Siculo, who spent many years in Spain and probably taught Boscán at the court of Ferdinand. And very soon he received decisive encouragement in his endeavours from his admired friend Garcilaso. He himself justifies his interest in the Italian hendecasyllable by stressing its adaptability to any kind of matter 'o grave, o sotil, o dificultosa, o facil', and its ability to embody 'any style of those found among the ancient approved Authors'.

Boscán's Book II does represent an extension of the range of expression possessed by Spanish lyric poetry in so far as it gives us a large number of sonnets and *canciones* all expressing the feelings of the lover. Santillana had possessed a copy of Petrarch's *Sonetti e Canzoni in morte di madonna Laura* but had written his own sonnets mainly about public events, such as the Fall of Constantinople and the civil strife current in Spain. Thus Boscán did give Spanish poetry something new. However, the novelty was in the form rather than the substance. When one has read Boscán's lengthy Introduction to Book II, it comes as a surprise to find how similar the poems it contains are, in matter and tone, to what is found in Book I. The lover is 'still nailed to his torments', still mad, his lady's vassal, her prisoner, on fire with the love he cannot forget. Time and time again he declares how his heart and hopes have deceived him: Fate is against him; there is no escape. He dramatizes his situation; it is his wish to display his wounds, inflicted by love, though people will tremble who behold him, or weep, or mock. The feelings expressed are still remarkable chiefly for their extreme and intense character, and the principal aim of the poems is to communicate this. The inner anguish of the poet continues to be expressed largely through the device of paradox.

The character of the emotions expressed here probably owes much to the influence of the greatest of the fifteenth-century Catalan lyric poets, Ausias March (*c.* 1397–1459), of whom Boscán says that, were he to start praising him, he would not soon stop. Certainly, one feels oneself far from Petrarch. The latter's descriptions of his lady, his evocations of a pastoral countryside, the element of reflectiveness and melancholy in his verse, are almost entirely lacking here. His presence is felt rather in the formal characteristics of Book II, and in Boscán's attempt to write verse possessing less emphatic and more subtle rhythms, a more muted tonality, than had been known before in Spain. Boscán tells us that these attempts were soon noticed, and criticized. People complained that it was hard to tell if such writing was prose or verse. These critics, replies Boscán, are clearly unable to react to anything more subtle than rhythms which drive their way in through one ear and out the other. And yet their criticism seems not ill-founded when one reads such lines as 'Yo estoy atento a ver qué ha de ser esto'* and 'No tardé en entender luego el engaño',† and many others of the same kind. It is true that Boscán on occasion achieved notable success in creating verbal music new in Spanish, as when he begins a sonnet: 'Solo y pensoso en páramos desiertos/Mis

---

*'I am watching to see what this will prove to be.'
†'I was not slow then to see the deception.'

pasos doy cuidosos y cansados'* (which is a version of Petrarch's 'Solo e pensoso i più deserti campi ...'), or 'Vime al través en fuertes peñas dado,/Casi sin vida, y lo demás perdido',† or 'Cargado voy de mí doquier que ando',‡ but such successes are far too rare. Despite Boscán's advantage of familiarity with Catalan poetry, with its rhythms closer than Castilian to those of the Italian hendecasyllable, and despite sustained effort, his most striking failure in Book II is his inability to create a rhythmic texture capable of embodying the substance and movement of the emotions to which he tries to give poetic statement.

Book III is different in a number of respects. It has the interest of containing poems, sometimes long ones, written in further metres not employed in Spanish by Boscán or anyone else before. There is the *Leandro*, which consists not only of the story of Hero and Leander but also of that of Aristaeus and Proteus. This work is almost the first to bring blank verse into Spanish, though it does so with conspicuously unimpressive results. The extreme rhythmic poverty of the verse, combined with the awkwardness of the structure, in which the stories from Musaeus, Virgil's *Georgics* and Bernardo Tasso's *Favola di Leandro ed Ero* are linked in a singularly unconvincing and ineffective way, makes it hard for the reader to respond to the underlying enthusiasm for love stories of Classical antiquity and Boscán's bold, innovatory spirit. The other main work in Book III is called simply *Octava Rima*, and brings the Italian form of this name (consisting of hendecasyllabic lines rhyming ABABABCC) into Spanish for the first time. Its 135 stanzas represent, in the main, an extended reworking of a carnivalesque poem of Bembo's, dating from 1507, in praise of love, though Boscán seems also to have drawn on a celebrated poem by Poliziano, written in the same form: 'Vagheggia Cipri un dilettoso monte ...' This work, which has the character of an allegory, is, like the *Leandro*, a poem in praise of love rather than itself a lyric poem. Boscán's Book III does, however, contain lyric poetry. Some of the most effective of this is found in a poem cast in

---

*'Alone and pensive, in desert wastes I direct my steps. Weary they are and full of care.'

†'I found myself abandoned and struggling amidst rugged crags, almost dead; for the rest, lost.'

‡'I am a burden to myself wherever I go.'

the style of a Horatian Epistle. But there are also the 'Capítulos', and an 'Epístola', all written in the Italian tercet form. These again express the lover's feelings for his lady. They are essentially the same feelings as those voiced in Book II, though now experienced with a less immediate intensity. There is a stronger note of melancholy, of plaintive resignation. This is communicated in verse which is among the most smoothly and gently flowing that Boscán ever achieved and fulfils, as far as any of his verse ever did, the aims he set before himself in the manifesto that opens Book II. At no point in his work does he stand closer to the achievement that is peculiarly Garcilaso's.

Garcilaso de la Vega (c. 1501–36) and his successors

Boscán had been a close friend and admirer of Garcilaso since they had met in 1522, both having joined an expedition whose purpose, never fulfilled, was to go to the help of the Knights of Jerusalem, besieged by the Turk on the island of Rhodes. Boscán was then between thirty and thirty-five, and Garcilaso only about twenty-one. The latter, in the next decade, became known as an outstanding embodiment of those qualities and aptitudes which Castiglione attributed to his ideal Courtier in his book of that name. Fittingly, it was Garcilaso who, in 1533, gave a copy of this work, first printed in 1528, to Boscán, and persuaded him to translate it into Castilian. He continued, subsequently, to live the life of a courtier, man of letters and soldier (his home now chiefly Naples) until 1536, when, having gone to Provence with the army of Charles V, he was fatally wounded in circumstances of exasperating triviality.

His earliest work dates from about 1526, when Boscán was first attempting to write Castilian verse in Italian forms. Garcilaso, who encouraged him in this, himself undertook the writing of sonnets and *canciones*. The first *canción* is like so much of Boscán's verse: Petrarchan in form rather than mood. The form of its stanzas is that of Petrarch's *canzone* beginning 'Ben mi credea passar mio tempo omai', but the mood is that noted in Boscán's sonnets: one of anguished reproach and despairing self-abandonment to love: 'Yo estoy aquí tendido/ mostrándoos de mi muerte las señales,/y vos viviendo sólo de mis males'.* The second *canción* again laments the lady's indifference, but the mood is now more gentle: it is chiefly one of melancholy sorrow. Two of the earliest sonnets illustrate a similar difference. In sonnet 4, the lover's alternation between hope and despair resolves itself into a furious determination to see his lady again: 'Muerte, prisión no pueden, ni embarazos,/quitarme de ir a veros, como quiera,/desnudo espirtu o hombre de carne y hueso.'† In sonnet 26 a more reflective sadness predominates. After *Canción IV*, with its allegorical contest between Reason and Desire, its scholastic analysis of emotions and anguished vehemence, the two moods noted in these earlier works are brought together and given notably balanced expression in the 'third' *canción*, probably Garcilaso's last work before his move to Naples late in 1533. Garcilaso had, for complicated domestic reasons, fallen from the favour he had enjoyed with Charles V. Having gone to Germany, with his friend the young Duke of Alba, to join the Emperor, now preparing to save Vienna from the Turks, he found himself confined for a time on an island in the Danube, probably near Regensburg. Here he wrote this poem, lamenting his misfortunes and protesting a lover's grief within the framework of an evocation of island and river remarkable for its gentle and finely controlled musicality. The debt to Petrarch is plain; the form of the verse strongly recalls that of the celebrated 'Chiare, fresche, e dolci acque', and the note of melancholy sorrow is largely that which was to predominate in Garcilaso's greatest work, written after he had moved to Italy.

He was allowed to go to Naples, which belonged to the crown of Aragon, as the equivalent of going into exile, and it was fortunate for him, as a poet, that this was so. Being a close friend of the newly appointed Viceroy, he was quickly admitted to an active and important group of literary men and humanists residing in the city. Soon he was writing in a much wider range of Italian forms, and using some of them, in all probability, before Boscán did. Within a year or so, he had composed his *Second Eclogue*. By far his longest work, it consists mainly of tercets (eleven-syllable lines rhyming ABA/

* 'Here I am, stretched before you, displaying the marks of my death, while your life is wholly in my affliction.'

† 'Neither death, prison nor any other hindrance can prevent me from coming to see you, be it as bare spirit or a man of flesh and bone.'

BCB/...) and of lines written with the Petrarchan *rimalmezzo*, formed between the tenth and eleventh syllables of one line and the sixth and seventh of the next. This was quite new in Spanish. The rest of the *Second Eclogue* consists of stanzas very similar to those of the second and third *canciones*. Soon Garcilaso was writing a poem in blank verse – his *Epistle* to Boscán, who had not yet attempted this. Also, he was writing more sonnets. These are always constructed according to the Petrarchan pattern, and in all nearly forty of them survive. At the same time (1534 or early 1535) came Garcilaso's so-called *First Eclogue*, written throughout in a fourteen-line stanza similar to that of *Canción I*. Two *Elegies* followed, both in tercets. Some time between 1533 and 1536 Garcilaso wrote his *Canción V*, one of his most famous works, in a stanza form (aBabB: 7, 11, 7, 7, 11) taken over from Bernardo Tasso and subsequently known in Spain as the *lira*. The last of his works, the *Third Eclogue*, was written throughout in the Italian *ottava rima*.

It is already clear that Garcilaso applied this wider variety of forms to a broader range of subjects. The lover's complaints which, until Naples, had made up almost the whole of his poetry, continued to be prominent in his work: his achievement lies largely in the extraordinary expressiveness he gave them. But other subjects now make their appearance. More than a third of the long *Second Eclogue* consists of a eulogy, in the heroic manner, of successive dukes of Alba, and particularly of Garcilaso's contemporary and friend. His *Epistle* to Boscán is written to express the friendship he felt for him, and echoes Aristotle and Cicero on the subject. The first of the *Elegies* is a solemn piece composed for the consolation of the Duke of Alba on the death of his brother; the second, which dates from the late summer of 1535, is in the nature of an epistle and tells Boscán of the new love that Garcilaso has for a lady. His *Third Eclogue*, more than any of his previous poems, expresses a delight in the world of Classical mythology, and probably moved Boscán to undertake his *Leandro*.

In Naples, where he arrived only a few years after the publication of Bembo's *Prose*, and just three years after his and Sannazaro's *Rime*, Garcilaso wrote perhaps the majority of his sonnets. Their tone now is less intense than before. A prominent theme is quiet resignation to the inevitability of falling a victim to love. (This is particularly well expressed in sonnet 30, though also in numbers 7 and 28.) The power of feeling they contain finds expression not so much through direct statement as through allusions to Classical mythology, in which Garcilaso now shows a much clearer interest. Thus, in sonnet 12, one reads that the lover's feelings are such that even the warning examples of Icarus and Phaethon are incapable of restraining him. The thirteenth sonnet describes the lover's grief felt by Phoebus for Daphne, now transformed into a tree; the twenty-ninth, Leandro's prayer to be allowed to be with Hero again before he is drowned. In sonnet 11, a sad lover invites river nymphs to hear his sad tale; sonnet 23 represents Garcilaso's most celebrated treatment of the *carpe diem* theme, so much loved by sixteenth-century poets. In these last two sonnets, especially, Garcilaso's debt to previous poets is manifold: he draws on Virgil's *Georgics*, Sannazaro's *Arcadia*, Bernardo Tasso's 'Mentre che l'aureo crin' ondeggia in torno', Horace's *Ode to Ligurinus*, and Ausonius. They show how far he has become disposed to create poetic effect by evoking overtones of earlier works, and how, having at first, almost to the exclusion of description, devoted his efforts to the expression of love's anguish, he now made some of his very finest poetry out of the evocation of beauty and the expression of a lover's gentle, reflective melancholy, itself embodied in the evocation of beauty and the subdued musicality of the verse.

All this is found at much greater length in Garcilaso's *Eclogues*. The literary group with which he associated at Naples had been accustomed to meet in the house of Sannazaro, who had died there as recently as 1530. It was probably now that Garcilaso first read the *Arcadia*. Garcilaso's own pastoral poetry dates almost entirely from this time. In the first major work he wrote there, the *Second Eclogue*, 500 lines give a version of part of the *Arcadia*, closely modelled on the original. It was Sannazaro above all whose example persuaded Garcilaso to portray material beauty in his verse, and to embody in this his response to that beauty. Adjectives, previously rare in his work, now become numerous; the details of the pastoral scene are lovingly described. Not that Garcilaso piles up details of this as Sannazaro does. His descriptions of the pastoral scene are more simple than the Italian's; his colours are less vivid and varied. The reason for this was that, in general, he portrayed the pastoral scene primarily because it served to embody and evoke a mood – a mood of elegiac melancholy, of wistful regret and longing. This is the case, above all, in the *First Eclogue*, in which the pastoral scene is used to establish and amplify the mood of the shepherds, of whose laments the poem consists. To the same end, and again under the influence of Sannazaro, Garcilaso now much enriched the musicality of his verse. By taking the Petrarchan hendecasyllabic line, with its stresses either on the sixth and tenth, or the eighth and tenth, syllables, and combining it with the heptasyllable in complex stanzaic forms, all with the sensitivity of his musician's ear, he created a new kind of music in Spanish verse, more supple and subtle in its movement, more richly capable of matching rhythm and sound to the particular nuance of feeling being expressed. Spanish poetry before Garcilaso does not afford anything like the stanza that introduces the first of the shepherds' laments in the *First Eclogue*:

> Saliendo de las ondas encendido,
> rayaba de los montes el altura
> el sol, cuando Salicio, recostado
> al pie de un alta haya, en la verdura,
> por donde un agua clara con sonido
> atravesaba el fresco y verde prado,
> él, con canto acordado
> al rumor que sonaba
> del agua que pasaba,
> se quejaba tan dulce y blandamente
> como si no estuviera de allí ausente
> la que de su dolor culpa tenía;
> y así, como presente,
> razonando con ella, le decía: ...*

Thus Garcilaso was able, in a quite remarkable way, to write poetry that leaves the strongest impression of personal utterance, of deep, intimate feeling. Perhaps sonnets 10, 23, and 25, and the *First Eclogue* are the finest examples of this. This personal note is

*'The dazzling sun, rising from the waves, was shining on the tops of the mountains. At the foot of a tall beech Salicio, reclining in the grass where clear waters went murmuring by across the fresh, green meadow, was singing, matching his song to the ripple of the water as it passed. He sang of his woes, so sweetly and gently that it seemed that she who bore the blame for his sorrow could not but be there. And so, as though she were present, he addressed her thus:...'

generally explained by Garcilaso's love for one Doña Isabel Freire, who, having been the object of Sá de Miranda's praise in Portugal, came to Spain in 1526 with the Portuguese princess who was to marry Charles V. Doña Isabel Freire was herself married before Garcilaso left Spain for Italy in 1529; she died in 1533 or 1534 giving birth to her third child. Just what Garcilaso's relations with her were is uncertain, but he says enough in his work to show that he felt deep devotion to her and was grief-stricken at her death. It seems very likely that those of his poems strongest in personal feeling would not have been so but for his love for this lady. Nevertheless, even if he is sometimes willing for his readers to appreciate what he writes in relation to his personal situation, he increasingly seeks to set the emotional matter of his poems at a distance from himself, and to present it in such a way that it may be the object of aesthetic appreciation.

This is clearly seen in the *First Eclogue*, which of all his poems is the one with the strongest personal reference. It seems to have been written shortly after he had learnt of Doña Isabel's death, and it is right to respond to it as a moving expression of Garcilaso's grief. But not simply so. He does not speak directly of his own feelings, but only through the two shepherds – Salicio, who laments the in-difference to his love displayed by his lady, who went off with another shepherd, and Nemoroso, who laments his lady's death. Even the shepherds are sufficiently removed from the actual experience of their misfortunes and unhappiness to give to these the expression of 'sweet lamentation'. They are to be thought of as expressing their sorrows in song. Each stanza of Salicio's ends in a sweet and melancholy refrain. Moreover, each shepherd's lament is of the same length: twelve stanzas. The pattern of the emotional pitch of each lament closely parallels that of the other, while, together, they produce an effect of sustained crescendo. Each lament is followed by a single concluding stanza. Just one stanza sets the pastoral scene. Moreover, we learn that the sun is rising as Salicio begins his lament, and is setting as Nemoroso concludes his. In such ways Garcilaso reveals his desire, even in a poem with so personal a meaning for him, to create a work possessing, both in its details and main structure, the qualities of balance and harmony. It is a desire that recalls the ideals of composition of the Florentine painters. Garcilaso invites the reader to respond to the griefs of the shepherds – and of Garcilaso himself – as part of a total fabric of beauty.

This beauty is difficult for the modern reader to catch fully since it depends on familiarity with Classical and Italian Renaissance verse. Garcilaso accepted the principle, so notably insisted upon by his admired and admiring Bembo, and by Vida in his *Ars poetica*, that it was desirable to take over material, whether entire passages or particular expressions, and to take advantage of its echoes and associations in the creation of poetry possessing a fresh and yet richer character. Thus, for example, Nemoroso's final appeal to the departed Elisa, in the *First Eclogue*, needs to be responded to, as Herrera pointed out, in relation to similar examples of apotheosis in Virgil (*Eclogue V*) and Sannazaro (*Eclogue V* and his first Latin piscatorial eclogue). Otherwise much of the harmony and counterpoint goes unheard. This technique is much employed in Garcilaso's other *Eclogues*. Of these, the 'second', despite fine moments and a concern with balanced form, is much less well integrated than the 'first'. The third is, musically, probably the finest, and its portrayal of the pastoral scene, with its large debt now to Classical mythology, the richest. However, it is in the *First Eclogue* that one sees Garcilaso's essential achievement most clearly – in its combination of formal excellence and personal feeling in a unity possessing a power unique in Spanish secular, Italianate verse of the sixteenth century.

The example set by Boscán and Garcilaso was quite soon eagerly followed by others in Spain. Among the more interesting of the many who attempted the newly introduced forms were DIEGO HURTADO DE MENDOZA (1503–75), friend of Boscán and Garcilaso and Spanish ambassador in London, Venice and Rome, and HERNANDO DE ACUÑA (1518–c. 1580), who is best known for his sonnet 'To our Lord the King', beginning: 'Ya se acerca, señor, o es ya llegada/la edad gloriosa en que promete el cielo/una grey y un pastor solo en el suelo,/por suerte a vuestros tiempos reservada'* – he is addressing Charles V. Another poet is GREGORIO SILVESTRE (1520–69), organist of Granada cathedral, whose claims to attention,

---

*'The time is at hand, my lord, or even now has come – that glorious age promised by heaven, when there shall be one flock and one shepherd alone upon earth, happily reserved for your day.'

both for his sonnets and his *Elegy on the Death of Doña María Manrique*, have recently been urged by Professor A. Terry. Like Silvestre, FRANCISCO DE FIGUEROA (1536–*c*. 1617) showed a welcome ability to put new life into what could easily become pale common-places of convention. Two other poets may be mentioned rather more fully.

*

GUTIERRE DE CETINA (1514/17–1554/57), who went with Hurtado de Mendoza to the first session of the Council of Trent and spent some years as a soldier, was, by virtue of quality and quantity alike, perhaps the most important of Garcilaso's early followers. The new rhythm and movement in Spanish verse brought about by Boscán and Garcilaso seem to have been successfully mastered by Cetina from the beginning. He shared the taste of his day for writing imitations of other poems, and it is interesting to compare his sonnet on Leander ('Leandro, que de amor en fuego ardía') with that of Garcilaso, on which it is based, as one may compare also his 'Al dulce tiempo por mi mal pasado' with Garcilaso's 'O dulces prendas por mi mal halladas'. His sonnets are particularly noteworthy for the vividness, appositeness and range of the similes with which the unhappy lover gives expression to his grief, as in the sonnet 'Como está el alma a nuestra carne unida'. Examples of Cetina's art at its best are the sonnet 'Por vos ardí, señora, y por vos ardo' and 'Horas alegres que pasáis volando'.

Of the life of FRANCISCO DE LA TORRE nothing is known. His work was first published by Quevedo in 1631. Its character suggests strongly that it was composed in the 1560s and 1570s. There are 64 sonnets, 6 *canciones* and 8 eclogues, as well as 11 odes, and 10 *endechas*, in the older Spanish form of six-syllable quatrains. The subject matter is almost always – save in the odes – the lamenting of a lover over the indifference of his lady. This is often expressed in tones of remarkably gentle melancholy, and in verse of outstandingly melodious fluidity: for example, Book I, *Canción I*, and *Egloga II* ('Salía ya la Aurora ...'). It is a highly unusual feature of Torre's poetry, among Spanish Petrarchists, that the lover not infrequently addresses himself to the night as to an intimate friend, sympathetic, in its stillness and silence, to his sorrows. This is seen well in Book I, sonnet 20, and Book II, sonnet 15. However, Torre's verse is far from being always of this kind. The lady is sometimes described and worshipped in terms drawn from neo-Platonism: for example, Book I, sonnet 24; and Book II, sonnet 23. Her beauty is of the kind so generally found in Petrarchistic poetry, but more vivid and richly coloured, and more sensuously perceived, than in Garcilaso (see Book I, sonnet 11). Moreover, the troubled and despairing state of the lover is often powerfully expressed in verse in which the movement of the lines does much to intensify the force of the statement (Book I, sonnet 29; Book II, sonnets 30, 31). There is a marked tendency to dramatize the lover's feelings and situation. In this respect, as in the re-presentation of scenes from Classical lore – more frequent than in Garcilaso – and in the sometimes strikingly Latinate syntax (for example, Book I, sonnet 18), and the insistent architectural structure of some of the sonnets (for example, Book I, sonnet 22), Torre's work looks forward to Herrera and even to Góngora.

Fernando de Herrera (c. 1534–97)

The collected works of Boscán and Garcilaso were immediately an enormous success. By 1557 not less than seventeen editions had appeared. In 1569 Garcilaso's poetry was published separately for the first time. It appeared with regular frequency up to 1632. By 1574 he was being treated as a Classical writer: in that year, Francisco Sánchez de la Brozas ('El Brocense') published an improved text of his works, with abundant annotations, pointing out Garcilaso's debts to the ancients and the Italians, and prefaced it with his famous assertion: 'I do not hold that man to be a good poet who does not imitate the excellent poets of former times.' In 1580 came Herrera's extensive annotations on Garcilaso's works. Herrera is the next major poet in the Spanish Petrarchan tradition after Garcilaso.

The emotional situation typically treated by Herrera is different from that of Garcilaso. It is true that the later poet did compose a few works expressing melancholy and wistfulness (see sonnets 28, 65, 67) but the characteristic mood of his poems is one of emotional drama seen as a present reality: the lover knows his love is hopeless, but persists in it. He hopes in his despair; he despairs but never repents of loving: 'la dura ostinación de mi porfía/no cansa, ni se rinde al dolor fiero;/mas siempre va al encuentro de mi muerte' (sonnet 54).* The mood is nearer to that of Boscán.

Herrera's poetic technique seeks to communicate the force of the lover's anguish. This is done very largely by means of metaphor. The metaphors used are most often of a highly traditional kind and are much repeated. The radiance of the lady's beauty is continually hidden from the lover by the clouds and mist that cut him off or envelop him; time and again the blaze of the lover's passion does combat with the ice of the lady's indifference, and the latter, in turn, is often linked with the hard and bitter winter which cuts short and sets itself against the warmth of summer (for example, sonnet 22). Thus the lover's feelings are often embodied in a vivid picture. His fruitless persistence is described in terms of a man struggling to climb a mountain, weighed down by a great burden and for ever slipping back to where he started (sonnet 26). He may be portrayed as a sailor in a stormy sea, pressing on, despite the rocks and the sight of whitening bones, to the place from which there comes the sirens' song (sonnet 6). In such poems, where the lover's feelings are embodied in an extended metaphor, emotion is given a concrete, externalized expression, and the effect is to dramatize and amplify it.

One may ask how far the feelings thus expressed were actually felt by Herrera himself, in a particular emotional relationship. It has been repeatedly claimed that his work possesses an important auto-biographical significance and that his personal feelings largely motivated the writing of his poems. Certainly, Herrera was one of the group of Sevillian men of letters regularly received by the Conde de Gelves, Don Alvaro Colón y Portugal, great-grandson of Columbus, who, in 1559, when Herrera was about twenty-five, had brought his beautiful young wife to his house on the banks of the Guadalquivir. There is a little evidence to suggest that, as late as 1575, Herrera enjoyed the close personal trust of the Condesa, and that, among his friends, he was regarded as feeling what was described as a platonic attachment to her. He seems not to have written lyric poetry before he met her, or after her death in 1580. Moreover, a number of his poems can easily be read as expressing the poet's own feelings and even invite this view of them. Among these *Elegy III* is the most

---

*'The hard stubbornness of my persistence does not grow weary nor does it surrender to fierce grief; but always presses forward towards my death.'

striking, though most of the other elegies contain material of a comparable kind, and a whole series of sonnets may appear to possess a similar significance (see 1, 13, 20, 40, 49–51, 58).

On the other hand, Herrera never mentions the Condesa's name and his apparent references to a relationship between them are too vague for one to be at all sure what it may have been. In any case, as portrayed in almost all his poems, the relationship between the lover and the lady seems to have been human on one side only: the lady exists solely as a creature of icy indifference, yet of a beauty beyond the reach of telling. This beauty, like the whole situation as it is described, is highly conventional: with her hair like gold, her eyes of purest sapphire and cheeks of roses, her ivory skin and teeth like pearls, she is the lady hymned by so many Petrarchists (see sonnets 10, 27, 33, 71, etc.). Telling us almost exclusively of the lady's beauty, Herrera seeks to portray it in the most vivid terms. His descriptions are hyperbolical. Her pure beauty is more lovely than the dawn's, her eyes are equalled only by the stars; her radiance dims that of the sun. She is, indeed, her lover's sun. To intensify the impression of the lady's beauty, the poet speaks in terms drawn from neo-Platonism, so rich in aesthetic appeal. The lady is most commonly spoken of as 'Luz' – Light. In her is seen the First Uncreated Light, the eternal beauty and harmony of the heavens, the realm of Love. In the light with which she is radiant the lover burns; to that realm of love he seeks to ascend (sonnets 4, 5, 38, 42, 61, 73). The effect of all this is heightened further by the poetic language that Herrera created by introducing many neologisms drawn from Latin, rich, magnificent and emphatic in meaning and sound, and frequently repeated.

This portrayal of the lady's beauty, like the portrayal of the lover's anguish, may well appear to the modern reader rather unattractively exaggerated, overstated and unconvincing. Although a more personal note is not infrequently conveyed by the verbal rhythm united to a particular utterance, and while some statements suggest powerful emotion by a dense brevity, this poetry on the whole lacks the accent of personal experience that gives Garcilaso's its lasting appeal. Herrera's sonnets can hardly be enjoyed with reference to whatever personal experience lies behind them. To an exceptional degree they must be enjoyed with the taste that made them what they are. It is the taste that finds extended expression in Herrera's *Annotations* on

Garcilaso, as also, for example, in Abraham Fraunce's *The Arcadian Rhetorike* (1588), where the poems of Boscán and Garcilaso, among others, 'Greeke, Latin, English, Italian, French', are praised for the tropes and figures of rhetoric which they embody and which are here picked out for the reader's admiration. In reading Herrera's poetry, one has to enjoy poetry as finely contrived artificial composition. One must share his respect for erudition and obscurity of idea in verse (with which he satisfies a much more learned taste than Garcilaso did), his acceptance of the principle of imitating and borrowing from the Classics (including the Italians), and his intense personal concern to achieve, on the basis of imitation, something new and yet more beautiful, in a poetic language comparable with those of the Italians and the ancients. One must take pleasure in the careful and sometimes highly contrived working out of ideas (a good example is sonnet 16) in verse where idea and rhythm are often linked in a highly effective way.

A number of Herrera's eleven *Elegies* are more immediately appealing. *Elegy III* has been mentioned. *Elegies II, V* and *VII* express a helpless, despairing, resigned love. The passions of the lover dominate his life, weary him, cause him deep unhappiness, and yet he cannot bring himself resolutely to reject them, 'so sweet is the pain of this my wound'. Nevertheless, three other *Elegies, IV, VI* and *XI* describe, or embody, an attempt to do just this. The poet reminds himself of the truths traditionally urged to induce contempt of the world: time is passing like a fast-flowing river; nothing can resist its destructiveness; earthly beauty and the works of men soon fade and vanish; they are a vain shadow, mere smoke and dust. The Stoic philosophy provides such remedy as there is. Virtue alone should be desired; the wise man will seek it, separating himself from the vices of men, placing his inner self beyond the reach of the blows of fortune and finding an ordered tranquillity of spirit. And so he exclaims: 'Mas ¡ô si ser pudiese qu'este punto/de breve vida alegres en sosiego/gozássemos sin miedo i dolor junto!'* And yet the lover, despite all the lessons he rehearses to himself, cannot effectively learn them; love's hold continues: 'nosotros, turba vil . . ./puestos en desear y

---

*'And yet, if only it could be that we might find joy in this fleeting moment of life, happy in tranquillity and without fear and sorrow together!' (*Elegy* VI).

amar estamos/y en servir a este bien perecedero.'* These three elegies are among the most interesting and human statements of inner emotional conflict that sixteenth-century Spanish poetry affords.

It is, however, for his least personal verse, for his poems on great national and public events, that Herrera is best known. Up to about 1560 his ambition was to write epic poetry. The one work of this kind that he wrote has been lost. However, this general inclination of his, together with his inclination, already noted, to dramatize and amplify situations, found expression in a number of his *canciones*. Sometimes these are in praise of great noblemen of the day who had taken part in famous battles. One (*IV*) congratulates Don Juan of Austria on his defeat of the *moriscos* in the Aljuparras in 1570, and is chiefly remarkable for its rodomontade. Another (*VI*) celebrates the interment of the remains of the sainted Fernando III of Castile in its fine new tomb in the cathedral of Seville (1579). The best known are *Canción II*, a lament on the death of Don Sebastián of Portugal at the battle of Alcazar Kebir (1578), and *Canción I*, a hymn of praise to God for the Spanish victory over the Turks at Lepanto (1571). In these latter poems he achieves a note of solemn magnificence equalled by few, if any, other Spanish writers. It is highly reminiscent of the Old Testament, and from this Herrera here borrows extensively. *Canción I*, in particular, breathes a spirit of exultant confidence in the glorious destiny of Spain as the upholder of the Faith against the Infidel. Herrera wrote a number of sonnets of a similar character (for example, 9, 56, 60, 64, 69). However, it is in the *canciones* that he is able to express these public attitudes with the greatest force and that the poetic gifts peculiarly his find their fullest play. *Canciones I* and *II* probably remain his best and most impressive, if not his most interesting, works. It is fitting that Herrera wrote a Life of Sir Thomas More.

Luis de Góngora (1561–1627)

In the closing decades of the sixteenth century, the sonnet became, in Spain as also in England, the vehicle of Italianate lyric poetry to a still greater extent than it had been previously. Lope de Vega's

*'We, the base crowd , . . are resolved to desire and love and serve this good which one day will perish.'

Rimas humanas (1602) contains 200 sonnets, written in the sixteenth century but more conveniently considered together with his other later work. Góngora certainly wrote nearly 400, and probably almost a hundred more than this. Of those which can be ascribed to him without doubt, just on fifty were composed in the sixteenth century, and of these something must be said here.

A very few are cast in the heroic manner. In one of them, probably written in 1589, the Escorial, completed five years earlier, is celebrated as the eighth wonder of the world. Another sings the praises of Córdoba, where Góngora was born and spent most of his life. A few others are of a purely jocose character, or paint satirical pictures of life at court. But most are concerned, again, with a lady's beauty and a lover's woe. The beauty is of the kind already noted in Francisco de la Torre and Herrera; the woe has, in general, rather more of the former's melancholy than the latter's drama. The Classical pastoral setting is now more prominent and more feelingly portrayed than it has been in most Spanish sonnets so far. The verse flows smoothly, and contributes largely to the elegance and lyrical freshness that many of these sonnets possess. But beyond this, these sixteenth-century sonnets of Góngora's include at least two of the best ever written in Spanish. The first is the one that begins: 'Mientras por competir con tu cabello.' The lady's beauty is described: burnished gold gleaming in the sun cannot compete with the colour and loveliness of her hair; the whiteness of the lily is less fair than that of her brow. Her lips and neck are described with similar hyperbole. Then comes the exhortation:

> goza cuello, cabello, labio y frente,
> antes que lo que fué en tu edad dorada
> oro, lilio, clavel, cristal luciente,
>   no sólo en plata o víola troncada
> se vuelva, mas tú y ello juntamente
> en tierra, en humo, en polvo, en sombra, en nada.*

The technique employed to stress the lady's beauty recalls that found in Herrera's sonnet 10; the architectural structure recalls both this

---

*'Rejoice in that throat of yours, your hair, your lips and brow, before what in your golden age was gold, lilies, carnations, gleaming crystal, not only is turned to silver or becomes like a violet snapped off, but you and all this, together, are reduced to earth, smoke, dust, shadow, nothing.'

same poem and the sonnet of Francisco de la Torre's which begins: 'Claro y sagrado sol, que con la viva/lumbre.' But, here in Góngora, the closely integrated structure, with its two parallel and related series 'cuello, cabello, labio y frente' and 'oro, lilio, clavel, cristal luciente', is much more emphatic than in those other works, and serves to intensify the force of the poem's climax as a third series of nouns is added in the concluding line: 'tierra, humo, polvo, sombra, nada'. It is a statement far more brutal and overwhelming than is found, for example, in the well-known poems of Ronsard and Herrick on the same subject, or in Torre's first ode in Book I of his poems, or in Garcilaso's renowned sonnet 'En tanto que de rosa y d'azucena', concluding:

> coged de vuestra alegre primavera
> el dulce fruto antes que'l tiempo airado
> cubra de nieve la hermosa cumbre.
> Marchitará la rosa el viento helado,
> todo lo mudará la edad ligera
> por no hacer mudanza en su costumbre.*

Góngora's statement is more stark and harsh than anything to be found in Horace or Ausonius, the two chief sources of this theme. Its power, in Góngora, seems not to be attributable to any particular emotional crisis in the poet's life. He was only twenty-one when he wrote this poem, and not of a markedly serious disposition. The sense of death and dissolution which he voices was to be found on all sides in the earlier seventeenth century. In Spain at least, it runs back into the fifteenth century, and finds vigorous expression in works where the ever-present imminence of death is stressed and the impressive or comely aspect of men and women in life, and especially in youth, is harshly contrasted with the foul and obscene things they will become in tomb and grave. A fifteenth-century English poem declares:

> The joye of this wretched world is a short feeste:
> It is likned to a shadewe that abideth leeste . . .
> Thou that art but wormes mete, powder and dust,
> To enhance thysilf in pride sette not thy lust ['heart'].

* 'Pluck the sweet fruit of your happy spring-time before angry time covers your lovely head with snow. The icy wind will wither the rose and fleeting time will change all things, lest it should vary its accustomed way.'

Perhaps one might say that Góngora has applied this kind of tradition to the lady of Petrarchan verse; her lover echoes the warning, 'Memento mori', but inverts its moral sense. Moreover, Góngora was largely helped to give his poem the power it possesses by the fact that he shared the conviction of his contemporaries that written works fell into a well-defined scheme of different styles, and that writing meant adopting a particular style, treating a given subject in the manner that befitted it according to this scheme, and establishing a particular tone and mood in the course of following the techniques of rhetoric. The modern reader is thus called upon to respond to the significance and excellence of the statement that is the poem in itself rather than to attempt to evaluate it in terms of the nineteenth-century concept of literary 'sincerity'.

The message of the other outstanding sonnet of Góngora's in this period ('Ilustre y hermosísima María') is the same: 'antes que lo que hoy es rubio tesoro / venza a la blanca nieve su blancura, / goza, goza el color, la luz, el oro.'* Though it is worked out in a less complex way than the first, its dazzling portrayal of the lady's beauty in terms of the dawn, the sun and gold brings out well an important fact about the imagery employed in all the Spanish poetry considered so far: that the poets were less concerned with rendering a scene or feature with sensuous accuracy than with imparting a sense of value. In this particular sonnet, it is right to enjoy contemplating the lady's beauty, but it is more important for the poet's purpose that one should form a sense of the desirability of that beauty. It is at this that his technique is principally aimed. Thus the poet comes to link his poem to the scheme of reality generally, itself seen as essentially expressive of related series of values. Here, in this poem, and generally in sixteenth-century poetry, the element of intellectual, evaluative connection between simile or metaphor and the thing described is of high importance to the total meaning and effectiveness of the work. The effectiveness of these intellectual connections increases as the reader becomes aware of a whole structure of argumentation embodied in the texture of the poem. The poetic value of such argumen-

---

*'Before what is today your golden treasure outdoes white snow itself in its whiteness, enjoy, enjoy the colour [of your cheeks], the light [of your eyes], the gold [of your tresses].'

tation can be clearly seen in such sonnets as Góngora's 'Varia imaginación, que en mil intentos' and that of Cetina's already mentioned: 'Como está el alma a nuestra carne unida'. It was a technique that became still more important in Spanish poetry of the seventeenth century.

THREE

Religious and Philosophical Poetry

ITALY

SONNETS of repentance, expressing the poet's renunciation of earthly love in imitation of Petrarch's last poems, as well as whole groups of *rime spirituali*, are one of the less interesting features of the sixteenth-century Italian lyric. Other religious poetry was mainly written in Latin, owing to the prejudice that the supposedly greater nobility of this language was more suited to the noble themes of religion, but perhaps in part because of the fear that the Holy Office would concern itself more closely with works accessible to the mass of the faithful.

Paul IV's placing on the Index in 1559 of the scurrilous *Vendemmiatore* of LUIGI TANSILLO (1510–68) encouraged the poet to try to make amends with his *Lagrime di San Pietro* (posth. 1585). This attempt to transfer the spiritual lament of the Middle Ages to the field of epic poetry was imitated by Malherbe in France. Otherwise, this account of St Peter's self-reproach and remorse for his betrayal of Christ is a wearisome tribute to the lachrymose piety of the Counter-Reformation. It failed to sustain even the author's interest in his subject, which was left unfinished. Too often, however, it has been taken for granted that the Italians' inability to write great religious poetry at this time was due to a lack of profound faith, which could not make up for their readiness to follow the dictates of the Council of Trent. Instead, we should realize that Tansillo's failure is typical, because it was caused, not by an inadequacy of religious feeling, but more directly by the essentially lyric nature of his limited poetic powers. Proof of this is the fact that, whereas he was incapable of sustaining a grand religious theme, he was not precluded from writing religious sonnets – successful within the bounds of the ideal *mediocritas* – such as 'Pensar ch'il corso de la vita è breve' (inspired by the death of his son) and the youthful 'La vita manca e l'alma ognora s'empie'.

The first example of French influence in Italian literature since the fourteenth century is afforded by du Bartas's *La Sepmaine ou Création du Monde* (1578), which, together with many Classical and patristic writings, inspired Tasso's writing of *Il Mondo creato* (1594). After the poet's efforts in the *Conquistata* to make his epic more acceptable to the pundits of the Counter-Reformation, he could now feel that he had found a subject beyond ecclesiastical reproach, totally dedicated *ad maiorem Dei gloriam*. Like the French poem, Tasso's was intended to be a Christian answer to the materialistic view of the universe propounded by Lucretius in his *De Rerum Natura*. From his multitude of sources, the Italian poet attempts a final synthesis of pagan and Christian earning: everything must be sifted and judged according to the 'sacred laws' of orthodoxy. The encyclopaedic task was, however, too much for the ailing poet. At times he misunderstands his sources; at others, he produces a cocktail of heterogeneous information; and his scientific understanding left much to be desired. As was to be expected, this hymn to the perfection of the universe is man-centred. But, rather than the dignity of man, extolled as the fairest of God's creatures, it is his weakness and helplessness, his utter dependence on God that dominate the poet's vision; the poet's essentially subjective reaction to the grandeur of God's creation and the goodness of the Creator is well illustrated in Book VII (especially lines 1,099–1,127). Any idyllic fragment is avidly sought out by the reader among the poem's 8,750 verses, divided into seven books, describing the seven days of creation. The best-known episode is that of the phoenix (Book V), a symbol of Christian regeneration, which is based on the *Carmen de Phoenice* attributed to Lactantius and which has even been published separately. The influence of the *Mondo creato* on Milton and Klopstock is its greatest claim to fame: especially Tasso's use of blank verse in a religious epic. But, however skilful the poet's technique, the music of the *Liberata* has passed away and with it most of the poetry.

GIORDANO BRUNO (1548–1600) entered the Dominican order in 1565, left it in 1576, was excommunicated by the Calvinists in Geneva, and spent the last eight years of his life in the prisons of the Inquisition. In 1600, he was burnt at the stake for believing in the eternal and infinite nature of the universe, the annihilation of the individual soul, and the Copernican hypothesis of the earth's motion. The last of the six philosophical treatises in Italian which he published in 1584–5, *De gli eroici furori* (dedicated to Sir Philip Sidney), contains over seventy poems, of which four are by Luigi Tansillo, one of the speakers in the first of the two parts. One of Tansillo's love sonnets 'Poi che spiegat'ho l'ali al bel desio' is quoted (I, 3) and explained in an allegorical manner reminiscent of Dante's *Convivio*. Tansillo's sonnet is made to illustrate the flight of the soul towards God. A forerunner of Spinoza, Bruno tells us that God is present everywhere in the universe: the divine light surrounds our senses and only asks to be admitted through them to enter into union with the soul and be converted into the God that is within us. The *furor divinus*, or heroic madness, is an all-conquering impetus of the mind which, 'on the wings of the intellect and the will, is borne up to the godhead', where it is immune from fear and baser pleasures alike and becomes part of the divine harmony of the universe. Bruno's vision of life is marked by flux and heroic struggle. In a universe composed of an infinity of worlds, matter, like all creation, is eternal: 'everything changes, nothing is annihilated.' Only God is unchanging. And divine harmony and unity are the goals towards which all things strive, through discord and diversity.

Bruno rejected both Aristotle and Petrarch. The former, because rules are derived from poems and not poetry from rules; the latter, because his preoccupation with the love of a woman was too trivial for a mind seized with the *eroico furore*. It is, however, difficult for the modern reader to ignore the Petrarchan elements in Bruno's sonnets, compared by him to the Song of Songs which 'beneath the shell of ordinary loves and sentiments likewise contains divine and heroic madness.' Petrarchan antithesis is the hallmark of, for example, 'Io che porto d'amor l'alto vessillo' (I, 2), which is clearly modelled – except for Bruno's idiosyncratic sonnet-form with the ninth and thirteenth verses containing only seven syllables – on Petrarch's celebrated 'Pace non trovo' (cxxxiv) and even has the line 'Altr'amo, odio me stesso' ('I love another, I hate myself') from Petrarch's 'Et ho in odio me stesso, et amo altrui'. The dialogue-form of 'Pastor! che vuoi? che fai? doglio. Perché?' (I, 2) may remind us of the worst excesses of Serafino. On the other hand, Bruno's pantheism perhaps justifies his allegorical approach to poetry, and one of Tansillo's verses, 'Ma qual vita pareggia al morir mio?' ('But what life can be compared to my dying?') inspired Bruno's prophetic utterance: 'Certainly a worthy and heroic death is better than an unworthy and base triumph.'

A fellow Dominican, TOMMASO CAMPANELLA (1568–1639), spent almost thirty years in prison and feigned madness in order to escape the death penalty in 1599, after the discovery of his conspiracy to overthrow the Spanish authorities and set up a theocracy under his leadership in his native Calabria. Even in prison, he continued to produce poetry and to write philosophical works. The failure to gain popular support in Calabria inspired him to write the sonnet 'Il popolo è una bestia varia e grossa', in which he tells the people that they do not realize their own power: to them belong all things between heaven and earth, but they kill the prophet that tells them this truth.

Campanella played the role of prophet in all his works. His *Città del sole* puts forward communal ownership of all property: 'the community makes all rich and poor: rich, because they have and possess everything; poor, because they do not strive to serve things, but everything serves them.' The citizens of this utopia 'laugh at us who call artisans ignoble and call those noble who . . . live in idleness and keep in idleness and vice so many servants to the ruin of the state.' The voice of the reformer is heard loud and clear in the sonnet 'Io nacqui a debellar tre mali estremi', in which the three great evils of the world are tyranny, sophistry and hypocrisy, generated by ignorance and love of self, and opposed by Cato, Sophocles and Christ respectively. 'Credulo il proprio amor' tells us that it was self-love that made man think that the elements and stars are deprived of sense and love, that they revolve for him alone, and led him to despise other peoples as barbarians and imagine that God could be the monopoly of one people; finally, it had led to a denial of Providence and the very existence of God. Instead, man must realize the brotherhood of the whole of creation, as St Francis preached ('Questo amor singolar fa l'uomo inerte'), and learn that Nature, 'guided by God, created the universal comedy in space, where every star, every man, every animal, every element has its own part to play' ('Natura, da Signor guidata'). In 'Il mondo è il libro dove il Senno eterno', the poet tells man that he must put away false knowledge and return to a contemplation of Nature. In another sonnet ('Da Roma ad Ostia'), he brings up to date the parable of the Good Samaritan, who now appears as a Lutheran who helps the wounded man, while a bishop and a cardinal pass by on the other side of the way. Campanella also translated the Lord's Prayer into Italian, as well as Psalm cxi.

He rejects the myths of Classical poetry. In *A' Poeti* he tells his colleagues to give up their 'fictitious heroes': 'the works of Nature are more wonderful than your fables.' As a poet of the modern age, Campanella sings of Columbus, far more daring than the Argonauts, and of Venice, Poland and Switzerland, whose cult of liberty he admires so much, 'for all things belong to the free.' In the age of the Divine Right of Kings, Campanella asserts, 'Man is not born with a crown on his head' and that only the man who knows how to govern is fit to be king. Campanella admired Dante; the flinty style of the latter's *rime petrose* is echoed in 'Convien al secol nostro abito negro', while Campanella's impressive madrigals (for example, 'Si come il ferro di natura impuro') remind us of those written by that other Dantesque figure, Michelangelo Buonarroti. Like both these poets, Campanella reveals himself to be a solitary figure, conscious of the nobility of his efforts to rise up towards God and eternity ('Sciolto e legato, accompagnato e solo'). With his death, we arrive at the death of Italian religious poetry.

*

PALINGENIUS (Pier Angelo Manzolli, 1500–1543) wrote *c.* 1536 his *Zodiacus vitae*, a work in hexameters, divided into twelve books corresponding to the signs of the zodiac. In this work, which was placed on the Index in 1558, Palingenius revived the medieval Averroistic 'double truth': the distinction between the truth of revelation and the acquired truth of philosophy. And so, while professing orthodoxy, he taught the creation of the world *ab aeterno* and God's indifference to the sufferings and even the sins of man. The *Zodiacus* was admired by Bruno, who must have warmed to such verses as 'Vix paucis novisse datum, quo tendere tutum,/qua sit iter, per quod vera et bona summa petantur.'* The way to truth is not

---

*III, 62–3. 'It is only given to a very few to journey towards the goal and to know the path whereby the highest truth and good may be sought.'

revealed by law, medicine, or any of the practical branches of knowledge, for which Palingenius expresses nothing but contempt. It is
wisdom alone that opens the way as man's true guide and teacher.
Palingenius felt some sympathy for Luther and his poem is notable
for the violence of its diatribes against the corruption of the clergy,
'faex hominum, fons stultitiae, sentina malorum':* no vice is forgiven
to these seducers of women and boys, who sell the things of heaven.
Such attacks led Scaliger and Gravina to place the *Zodiacus* in the
satiric genre.

MARCO GIROLAMO VIDA (1485–1566) was a very different figure,
who became Bishop of Alba and took an active part in the Council
of Trent (1545–63) and the reform of the Church. It was Leo X who,
flattered by the idea that he might play Maecenas to a Christian Virgil,
admired Vida's Latin poems on chess and the silkworm and suggested
that he should write a poem on the life of Christ. The *Christias* (1527)
opens with the raising of Lazarus and Christ's coming to Jerusalem. It
ends (Book V) with the Crucifixion and Ascension: the dawn of a new
age. In Books III and IV, the poet gives us flashbacks of Jesus's past
life, placed in the mouth of Joseph and John and inspired by Aeneas'
tale of the fall of Troy in *Aeneid*, II. The mixture of pagan elements
with the Gospel story shocked Erasmus and bores the modern reader
with its padding of the superb realism and bareness of the original
text.

JACOPO SANNAZARO finished his epic *De partu virginis* in 1526. The
difficult theme of the virgin birth had already been treated by Gaguin
(1433–1501) in France. This time, it took the Italian poet thirty years
to write less than fifteen hundred elegant Latin verses. The Gospel
story is again puffed out in epic style and length: a good example is
the scene in the stable, where the ox and ass are made to genuflect
before the newly-born Christ and the stark simplicity of Bethlehem
is transformed into the discordant grandeur of Renaissance pagentry,
watched over by God on high, who remains the *Jupiter tonans* of the
Classical Olympus. The poem was admired by Erasmus, who nevertheless wished that Sannazaro had treated the theme in a more religious
manner, and it is inevitable that someone familiar with the biblical

*V, 589, 'The dregs of humanity, source of folly, and pit of all evil'.

account should be shocked by the incongruous style and imagery.

Sannazaro's grand failure is typical of the fate that befell attempts to write Latin verse on religious and philosophical subjects, during and after the Renaissance.

FRANCE

Marguerite de Navarre (1492–1549)

In the history of French literature the case of Marguerite de Navarre is strange, and probably unique. The most influential patron of the day after her brother, François I, and a good deal more knowledge-able, her name would have survived in the grateful tributes paid by writers including Marot, Des Periers, Rabelais and even Calvin if she had never written a line herself. Moreover her protection was sought and enjoyed by almost all those of reforming sympathies for a quarter of a century, and the Evangelical movement owed her an immense debt. Paradoxically her chief literary work was unknown in her lifetime (except perhaps in manuscript to a select few) and neither in prose, verse, nor drama did she have any direct influence or recognition except as patron.

Her first published work was religious: *Miroir de l'âme pecheresse*, a long, rather tedious poem, condemned by the Sorbonne on its appearance in 1531 for its overtly Evangelical tone. This was accom-panied by a few short prayers in verse, and in 1533 followed by the curious *Dialogue en forme de vision nocturne*, representing a discussion on some quite advanced points of the Christian faith between Marguerite and the soul of her niece Charlotte, who had died aged eight some years before. In 1547 her secretary, Antoine du Moulin, published a collection of her works under the punning title *Marguerites de la Marguerite des Princesses*,* comprising some dramatic works, both sacred and profane, a long poem, *La Coche*, and a large number of shorter poems. On this not inconsiderable evidence Marguerite is shown to have had a taste and some talent for the dialogue form, dramatic or otherwise, and a striking ability for translating her own deep piety into simple unpretentious verse like that of the *Chansons Spirituelles*. Her technical mastery is slight, but simple piety makes

* *Marguerite* also means 'pearl'.

only modest demands on virtuosity and she consistently strikes the right note. And there her reputation as a poet would rest but for the discovery and publication in 1896 (by Abel Lefranc) of a further 12,000 lines of her *Dernières Poésies*, at once recognized as containing her finest poetry. More verse dramas, a long poem (some 1,500 lines) in the by no means fashionable *terza rima* on the death of François, entitled *La Navire*, and above all *Les Prisons*, completely changed her status as a writer when revealed nearly 350 years after her death.

Apart from constituting her masterpiece, the 6,000 lines of *Les Prisons* are extraordinarily informative about her most intimate feelings. Cast in three cantos in the allegorical mode, the poem constantly recalls earlier poetic fashions, so that, after an opening passage describing the actual stone walls and iron bars of her, or rather his, first prison (for the poem is written in accordance with a not unusual convention in the first person masculine), it comes as no surprise to meet Dame Crainte (Fear) or Madame Hypocrisie. The first prison is in fact that of human love, in which the author's disappointment is made clear, though without bitterness. The second is that of worldly ambition, for riches and for renown, and in both these cantos the imagery seldom goes beyond the chains, fetters and so on of the prison motif, together with the sun of liberty (that is, disillusionment) piercing the darkness of the cell, and some miniature landscapes reminiscent of those seen through the window of many a late medieval picture. The echoes of the *Roman de la Rose* are unmistakable, though in tone rather than in direct imitation, but even more interesting is the conclusion of the second canto, in which a wise old man delivers a long and warm encomium of Dante, whom the author is exhorted to read – together with St John the Divine.

The last canto, some two thirds of the whole, is by far the most remarkable. The third prison is knowledge, represented by pillars made of books, and this gives the opportunity for an extensive survey of human learning through the ages, chiefly notable for a long eulogy of Socrates, whose wisdom and noble death are held up as an example to Christians. Indeed the Platonic element, barely perceptible before, is now very marked, and includes the Androgyne myth (from the *Symposium*) and the famous comparison (originally from a medieval neo-Platonist) of God with the circle whose centre is everywhere and circumference nowhere. From the beginning of this canto the refrain is of 'Celluy qui est' (the 'I AM' of *Exodus*) in all his manifestations, in the Old and New Testaments and in the saints. This leads by a natural transition of thought to the repeated antithesis between *Rien* (the creature) and *Tout* (God), which itself has neo-Platonic overtones. The last section of the canto suddenly interrupts the somewhat abstract contemplation of philosophical and scriptural truths with a startlingly realistic description of the deaths of four of Marguerite's closest relatives: her mother-in-law, Marguerite de Lorraine, her first husband, Charles d'Alençon, her mother, Louise de Savoie, and her brother, François. The intensity of feeling in these passages, all of course linked with the theme of liberation from corporeal bonds, reaches a still higher degree of mystic exaltation when she returns after the last to contemplating the longed-for union, in spiritual ecstasy, of her *Rien* with God, *Tout*, whose love alone brings complete release.

No bald account can do justice to the cumulative effect of these hundreds of flat decasyllabic couplets, clumsy as the rhyme often is, stilted and archaic as the language may be. The fusion of Evangelical piety with Platonic idealism is typical enough of humanists, but what is untypical, and perhaps unique, is the combination of such elements with passages as personal as the deathbed scenes. Marguerite's technique is curiously old-fashioned (her praise of Dante is contemporaneous with the composition of the *Defense*), but more than anyone else, even Ronsard, she convinces the reader that she has something of literally vital importance to communicate, even if her means of expression are barely adequate for the task. When one thinks of the thousands of lines of virtuoso verse, in every style, written throughout the century, empty alike of meaning or inspiration, Marguerite's comparative clumsiness seems noble, and despite all, effective. Apart from the emotion conveyed, *Les Prisons* provides an exceptionally successful synthesis of all the main currents of thought in the Renaissance: the Bible, theology, Plato, theories of love, human and divine, a smattering of mathematics and science, statecraft, everything finds a place in this commodious gaol. She may fall short of absolute greatness as an author, but she can stand comparison with anyone of her day, man or woman, as a personality of wonderful richness and complexity.

Inspired or commissioned by Marguerite, other writers also tried their hand at themes both pious and Platonic. Marot was one such, Des Periers and Héroet two others. Apart from some stilted religious verse, Des Periers also composed a poem, *Queste d'Amitié*, to accompany and more or less paraphrase his translation of Plato's *Lysis* (published posthumously 1544), while Héroet wrote both a poetic version of *Androgyne* (from the *Symposium*) and a much better known poem on the same subject, *La Parfaicte Amye de Cour* (1542), by Castiglione out of Ficino. These, and other examples of amorous casuistry, are by no means badly written, but they remain in every sense academic, illustrating the very limited aspects of Platonism seized on by Renaissance poets and demonstrating the great superiority of Marguerite, whose personal involvement is as obvious in her Platonism as in her piety.

Maurice Scève (c. 1500–c. 1560)

Scève, too, was well acquainted with Platonism, and is known to have made extensive use of Speroni's prose dialogues in the last sections of *Délie*, but it is with his two longer poems that we are concerned here. In 1547 Pernette had been dead for two years, and Scève's *La Saulsaye, Eglogue de la Vie Solitaire* of that year is thought to reflect the poet's actual retirement to the country near Lyon. The pastoral theme hardly suited his talents, and the poem's main interest is historical, as his contribution to a very popular Renaissance genre. Much later, in 1564, Scève published his ambitious *Microcosme*, where in 3,000 lines he recounts the history of the world from the Creation, using the familiar dream device to describe man's scientific and cultural achievements since the Fall. In his description of God before Creation Scève uses neo-Platonic concepts as well as biblical ones, and in the rest of the poem draws on a motley collection of authorities, ranging from Josephus to Polydore Vergil. The result is a rich quarry for historians of ideas, but extraordinarily muddled and with too little poetic quality to make it much more than an encyclopaedia in verse. The poem has been not inaptly called Scève's *Légende des Siècles*, but the comparison cannot be extended beyond the similarly grandiose conception of a total epic.

Guillaume du Bartas (1544–90)

Much better known is the similar enterprise of Guillaume de Salluste du Bartas. A Protestant, and protégé of Marguerite's daughter Jeanne, he achieved a now almost incomprehensible fame with his epic on the Creation, of which the *Première Semaine* came out in 1578 and the *Seconde Semaine* (an unfinished account of events since the Fall) in 1584. He influenced Milton, and had in his turn been influenced by the Bible and all the encyclopaedists of previous centuries. It cannot be denied that his religious fervour is ardent, and that his torrents of alexandrines have considerable picturesque value, but his verbal exuberance makes him oscillate wildly between majesty and absurdity, sometimes anticipating the mock solemnity of La Fontaine at his satirical deadliest. Addressing the remora, for example, he says 'Di-nous, Arreste-nef',* and he describes the ostrich as 'l'oyseau digere-fer'.† In moderation this sort of thing is, as the Pléiade preached and practised, excellent, but on the scale used by du Bartas it cries out for parody. He is certainly not as dull as Scève is in the *Microcosme*, but equally he lacked the power to produce anything as good as *Délie*. Unmistakably of his age in his enthusiastic piety and his language, in his relentless determination to put in everything, and draw the proper lesson from it, du Bartas is heir to the long tradition of encyclopaedic works like the *Roman de la Rose*, for all the change of purpose and emphasis.

Pierre de Ronsard (1524–85)

Any system of classification is bound to be arbitrary, and this is especially the case with Ronsard, who frequently transferred poems from one category to another in successive editions. The criterion of length is not by itself very helpful; already in the *Amours* of 1560 he had included a narrative poem of more than 300 lines in the bucolic style derived from Theocritus, *Le Voyage de Tours* (in the company of Baif), and another amorous adventure, this time with a Parisian girl called Genèvre (and initially involving Belleau), is described in three similarly long poems entitled *Discours*, published with his *Elégies* (I and II in 1563, III in 1571). These works plainly belong with his

*'Tell us, ship-stopper'. †'The iron-digesting bird'.

love poetry. Similarly a number of his *Elégies* or *Poèmes*, both short and long, deal with the sort of subject treated by Belleau in the jewel poems already discussed, and even when they go into some philosophical detail (as in *Le Chat*, where pantheism is discussed) are more usefully taken with his lyric verse. There are, however, two groups of poems which stand out quite clearly from the rest: the *Hymnes* (from 1555) and the *Discours* (from 1562).

The *Hymnes* belong to the class of cosmic or philosophical poetry practised by the ancients and recommended in the *Defense* but there is nothing slavish or mechanical in Ronsard's treatment of a theme as common as, for example, that of the four seasons. The poet's vision of the fertility of nature, the progress of time and above all his own vocation (notably in the *Hymne de l'Automne*) achieves a synthesis of tremendous vitality and originality, whatever its diverse sources may have been. These seasonal *Hymnes* have indeed been seen by some critics to mark a turning-point in Ronsard's poetic development, and to the extent that they represent a successful break with the Petrarchan conventions of his early love poetry while continuing to express the poet's deeper feelings, such a view makes sense. Another *Hymne* of particular interest is that addressed to Cardinal de Châtillon (Coligny's brother, and soon to be a Huguenot himself) under the title *Hercule Christian*, in which a specifically Christian inspiration is invoked ('Car c'est ce Dieu qui m'a donné l'esprit / De celebrer son enfant, Jesus-Christ')* for an extended comparison between Hercules and Christ, in which the labours of the one are set against the miracles of the other. Equally remarkable in a different way is the *Hymne* called *Les Daimons*, in which Ronsard gives an encyclopaedic account of the spirit world, not only of Classical antiquity, but of Christian angelology, Germanic and Celtic folklore and even of his personal experience in routing hostile spirits with his sword. The fantastic medley of traditions here presented is no poetic exercise, but a real expression of the unquestioning acceptance by Ronsard and his contemporaries of a spirit world always about them. Finally the *Hymne de la Mort* must be mentioned for its similarly personal synthesis of beliefs: 'Et Charon, et le chien Cerbère à trois abois / Desquels le sang de Christ t'affranchit en la Croix', and its closing apostrophe: 'Je te salue, heureuse et profitable Mort, / Des extrêmes douleurs,

*'For it is this God that inspired me to celebrate his son, Jesus Christ'.

medecin et confort.'* As a body of verse these two books of *Hymnes* (some 160 pages) range widely through the universe of things seen and unseen, while never degenerating into the mere catalogue of phenomena to which all too many Renaissance writers are addicted. Nor is Ronsard's personality ever for long in the background, whether in the *Hymnes* to the seasons where richly sensual passages betray the author no less than those where he speaks openly of himself, or in others on more metaphysical subjects, where a profession of faith or record of experience stamps the poetry with the seal of personal involvement.

Of somewhat the same character as the *Hymnes* are some of Ronsard's longer official poems, for example some of those addressed to Mary Queen of Scots (whom he accompanied to Scotland for a visit of several months), and others collected under the loose title *Elégies* or *Poèmes*; but the *Discours* are quite different in inspiration and tone. As court poet Ronsard had frequently to refer to contemporary events in his verse, and as a patriotic Frenchman, of noble birth and traditional loyalties, he reacted vigorously to the threat of sedition and national disunity which took concrete form with the outbreak in 1562 of the Wars of Religion whose end he did not live to see. The first two of these poems, *Discours des Misères de ce temps*, are addressed to Catherine de' Medici, and others continue the theme under various titles, the longest being the *Remonstrance au Peuple de France* (800 lines or so) and the *Reponse aux Injures et Calomnies* (more than 1,000). Inevitably, as the latter title suggests, indignation breeds indignation, and but for the national tragedy it is most unlikely that Ronsard would ever have had any occasion or desire to exploit this emotion. The result is interesting both for itself and for the influence it had on later polemists. As a Catholic, and as a tonsured holder of benefices (a minimally clerical status) Ronsard was naturally not favourably inclined towards the Huguenots, but he was ready to admit that improvements could and should be made in the Church, and there is as much sorrow as anger at first. Later, when he has to answer personal attacks, his language becomes more and more violent, but the predominant note is always of grief and indignation

*'And Charon, and Cerberus, the triple barking dog, from whom Christ's blood freed you on the cross . . .' 'I salute you, happy and profitable death, physician and comfort of the final pains.'

that his beloved France should suffer for the fanatical excesses of those who call themselves Christians. The taunts of militancy launched at Bèze and other leaders, going to preach with a sword in their belt, are grossly unfair: the Huguenots had suffered persecution for a generation by fire and sword before they retaliated in kind. Here, though, poetry, not justice, is the point at issue, and lines like 'Un Christ empistollé tout noirci de fumée'* may not be fair, but they are undeniably fine. By no means all the ninety or so pages comprising this section are first-rate, and such rhetorical devices as personification and apostrophe tend to pall with repetition, but Ronsard's polemical poems show that satire was well within his range, even if the cudgel of his scorn never rivals the deadly thrust of du Bellay's sharper sonnet form.

Happily Ronsard went back to the sonnet after these topical pieces, and those addressed to Hélène are his maturest work; but without the *Hymnes* and *Discours* a major part of his immense contribution to French poetry would be lost. The title 'prince of poets' may be hackneyed, but Ronsard's contemporaries bear abundant witness to the sense of solemn mourning engendered by his death. It remains astonishing that a poet who wrote so much should so rarely approach bathos, even if much is inevitably pedestrian or merely competent. The abortive epic of the *Franciade* is probably his only major failure, and that was not all his fault.

Agrippa d'Aubigné (1552–1630)

Though he did not die until 1630 (and was Mme de Maintenon's grandfather), d'Aubigné clearly belongs in spirit to the sixteenth century. His first poems (only published in 1874) provide a curious literary link with the past, for they were addressed to Diane, niece of Ronsard's Cassandre, with whom he had a passionate affair before he was twenty. These poems, known as *Le Printemps*, were written about 1574, and already show considerable poetic mastery, combining originality with a sometimes extravagant display of emotion, expressed in stanzaic and other forms. His almost miraculous escape from the massacre of St Bartholomew (1572), nearly fatal wounds, and enforced opportunity for reflection (not to mention the obstinate

*'A pistol-wielding Christ all black with smoke'.

opposition of Diane's parents to his suit) led him very soon to turn his attentions to something more serious than love poetry, and in 1577 he began his masterpiece, *Les Tragiques*, which was not published until 1616, though all but the finishing touches must have been put to it long before the turn of the century.

Now that the events are so remote it is possible to judge the work almost wholly on its literary merits. One says 'almost' because some of the alleged history is so patently absurd that no erudite footnote is needed to expose it, but as the history of sectarian feeling it is self-affirmative, and is incontrovertible proof of prejudice just when it is furthest from fact. Ronsard's indignation in his *Discours* was genuine, because he was a patriot, and also because his integrity had been impugned, but it was neither the only nor even the main driving force in his work, as his successful return to love poetry soon showed. It is otherwise with d'Aubigné: his is the burning, moral indignation that feeds on religious faith and in its turn rekindles it. He loved France no less than Ronsard did, but he loved his faith much more, and explicitly rejected the luxury of a mere poetic inspiration for the vocation of a prophet.

The plan of the work is simple enough: the 10,000 or so alexandrines comprise a record of the suffering and faith of the Protestants, an indictment of their persecutors and enemies and finally a judgement, first earthly, then apocalyptic, on both elect and reprobate. In his own foreword to the reader he says that *Misères*, the first book, is more or less narrative, in 'style bas et tragique'; the next, *Princes*, is more satirical, and *Chambre Dorée* similar, followed by *Feux* in 'style tragique moyen' and *Fers* 'style tragique élevé, plus poetic et plus hardy que les autres'; finally comes *Vengeances*, 'theologien et historial', and *Jugements*, 'd'un style élevé, tragique'; in these last two books, and by implication in the whole work, he faces the possible accusation of partisanship, but says that his aim is to move the reader, though so long after the events as to constitute no incitement to action.

Early on in *Misères* he invokes 'Melpomène en sa vive fureur', the tragic rather than the epic muse (Calliope), and a little later he apostrophizes his compatriots: 'Voyez la tragédie . . . Vous n'estes spectateurs, vous estes personnages' (actors). Indeed the sufferings of France, personified as a mother torn and bleeding from the fratricidal strife of her children, is the general subject of the first book, into which he inserts a long and 'tragique histoire / Car mes yeux sont temoins du sujet de mes vers.'* The atrocity which he then describes, perpetrated on a peasant family in the Dordogne, makes one almost glad to revert to the more generalized tale of blood which it so horribly illustrates. Nothing is spared: mutilation, massacre, cannibalism, the whole catalogue of human beastliness is recited, and serves as an effective introduction to the authors of these abominations: according to d'Aubigné, the Cardinal of Lorraine and Catherine de' Medici. She, 'l'impure Florentine', the Jezebel, has contaminated France with corruption imported from her native Italy. Accused of a comprehensive and imaginative list of crimes, she is particularly charged with witchcraft, mixing a brew strangely similar to that in the witches' cauldron in *Macbeth*. Indeed, in many ways d'Aubigné does recall Shakespeare at his most sombre (rather than Corneille or Racine), and with the constant repetition of the themes of blood and national calamity it is not surprising that *Les Tragiques* should echo the blackest of Shakespearian tragedies.

From the mother the transition is easy to the sons: the short-lived François II; Charles IX, charged with personal complicity in the massacre of St Bartholomew; that other François, duc d'Alençon (and later Anjou) whose double-dealing in the Low Countries cost his allies more than his enemies; and finally Henri III, surrounded by his infamous *mignons*. Logically enough, in d'Aubigné's eyes, those who perverted the course of nature by their atrocities against the land and people of France are just those whose personal vices are the most monstrously unnatural, and thenceforth the theme of Sodom recurs throughout the poem. *Princes* elaborates the charges in the most biting and specific terms: unhappy those who lie in bondage 'Soubs une femme hommace et soubs un homme femme',† Catherine is accused of acting as bawd for her sons, and they of incest with their sister, Marguerite de Valois. Henri's proclivities are historically attested, and it is not hard to see how d'Aubigné's raging indignation at the death and shame of his co-religionaries should be still further exacerbated by Calvinist horror of unnatural vice, almost obsessively so indeed.

Chambre Dorée gives an allegorical picture of Justice, personified

---

*'For my eyes are witnesses to the subject of my verse.'
†'Under a mannish woman and an effeminate man'.

as a woman in direst need seeking redress at the throne of God for crimes committed in her name, and is the least effective because the most strained. Much of his anti-legal satire is traditional and embellished with examples from the Bible and from history, ancient and modern; but his fury goes even beyond that of Marot in *Enfer*, for he is protesting in the name of others no longer able to protest for themselves.

When neither prince not magistrate can, or will, defend the innocent, evil has a free rein, and in *Feux* and *Fers* the long martyrology of the faithful few is unfolded, with their hideous deaths, by fire and sword, and worse, in the first, and in the wars in the second. The account goes far in time and space, back to the Albigensians, to Wyclif and Hus, and on to include with all too many French martyrs those of England, like Cranmer, Gardiner and Jane Grey.

By the end of this long recital the reader has supped full with horrors, and indignation has given way to pity, pity to impotent grief, so that he is ready for some sign that divine justice can repair the crimes of men. *Vengeances* is another atrocity story, but this time describing the dreadful punishment meted out to wrong-doers through the ages by a God whose wrath can still make men tremble. From Cain, through the people of Sodom, Jezebel, the Herods, to the Roman persecutors of the Christians, on to modern times, the execution of God's judgement is shown in lurid detail. D'Aubigné seems to have felt a particular fascination for the physical agents of corruption, and dwells with relish on the worms and lice that devour Herod and others.

With *Jugements* the scene shifts from this world to the next and the roles of victim and executioner are at last reversed by the eternal judgement of God. The note of protest gives way to a song of triumph ('L'homme à sa gloire est fait'*) and quite unexpectedly to neo-Platonic themes such as have already been met in Marguerite. 'Prototype, idée, exemplaire' all occur in the lines immediately preceding, and Hermes Trismegistus a little later, with a detailed exposition of his celestial hierarchy. Even more unexpectedly comes a kind of preview of the resurrection of the body, a version of a traveller's tale, which describes how there is a place near Cairo where bodies annually rise from the ground. Finally the last section opens

*'Man is made for his glory.'

with the celestial vision: 'C'est fait: Dieu vient regner; de toute prophetie / Se void la periode à ce poinct accomplie.'* The wicked wail and gnash their teeth in everlasting torment, their pangs increased as they hear the blessed chanting their 'Holy, holy, holy'. Overcome by so much glory the poet ends: 'Le coeur ravi se taist, ma bouche est sans parole: / Tout meurt, l'ame s'enfuist, et reprenant son lieu / Extatique, se pasme au giron de son Dieu,'† echoing once more the mystic ecstasy of Marguerite.

Rooted in the history of its own times, stretching back into antiquity and forward into eternity, d'Aubigné's *Les Tragiques* differs from other religious or cosmic poems of the age by the sense of urgency and the sheer power of the emotions sustaining the seven books. It would be epic were it not for the tragic (and personal) immediacy of the subject, and no doubt d'Aubigné would have reduced the repetition, and thus monotony, of seemingly endless horrors had he been more concerned to serve a poetic than a prophetic vocation. As it is the poem stands as a monument to one of the blackest chapters of French history, and nobly concludes the roll of protest inaugurated by Marot's *Enfer* and Marguerite's *Prisons*. So much sound and fury was not to be seen again until the nineteenth century, but it never signified so much.

SPAIN

Luis de León (1527–91)

By far the greater part of the verse of Luis de León consists of translations. These testify again to the interest of the age in taking over and recreating admired pieces of writing. In part, they also bear witness to the deep devotion of this Augustinian friar and learned Hebraist to biblical literature, especially that of the Old Testament. He made renderings of the Song of Songs, nearly half the chapters of Job, and thirty of the Psalms. These versions are evidence of a desire, deriving largely from the Erasmian movement in Spain, to make both

* 'It is done: God comes to reign; at this point the fulfilment of every prophecy is seen.'

† 'The rapt heart is silent, my mouth is speechless: everything dies, the soul takes flight and, resuming its place of ecstasy, swoons in the bosom of its God.'

word and spirit of the Scriptures accessible to those who were ignorant of the ancient tongues. They show also Luis de León's interest as a poet in form and technique. His renderings of the Psalms (of which he sometimes made more than one version) display a marked variety of stanzaic form and tone. They possess a fluidity, polish and eloquence which are effective and artistically attractive in themselves even if they result in a somewhat milder effect than one quite expects. Luis de León's verse translations as a whole show the range of his poetic interests and sympathies. They include the ten *Eclogues* of Virgil, Books I and II of the *Georgics*, and over twenty of Horace's *Odes*. There are a few renderings of Petrarch, Giovanni della Casa and Bembo.

Luis de León published neither this work nor his own twenty-five or so 'Original Poems'. His verse was first brought out by Quevedo in 1631. (This fact, with others, has made the dating of this verse very difficult.) But neither did Garcilaso or St John of the Cross have any of their poems printed. If Garcilaso wished to preserve the pose of an amateur, Luis de León himself probably felt that, beside his weightier works, poems would appear to be lacking in due seriousness. In the prologue to a manuscript collection of his verse, Luis de León shows himself eager at once to stress the high principles he has tried to follow in his translations and to make it clear that his verse has been the work of idle moments and of no importance to him.

The largest group of his 'Original Poems' consists of those in which the poet voices his concern with the importance of living one's life rightly and wisely. Repeatedly he speaks of the foolishness of greed and avarice, and writes of the city with its self-seeking, its wearying rivalries, its deceitfulness and false values. In contrast to this he sets the countryside, together with the life of virtue, true understanding and peace that the wise man can live in it. His particular debt for the grouping and balance of ideas here appears to be to Horace's *Epistles* (see especially I, x, xiv, xvi; II, ii), though his poems have sometimes a more general reference to the central ideas of Stoicism, as when he praises the power of 'the constant spirit, armed with truth' to overcome hostile circumstances, or speaks of the happiness of the man who seeks life's joys within himself and, regarding as 'alien' whatever is not within his breast, puts himself beyond the blows of Fortune. However, the tone of these poems is, in the main, far from being one of quiet philosophical reflectiveness. What gives them their power is the angry scorn of Luis de León's denunciation of city life and all it stands for, the vigour with which he rejects it, the intensity of his longing for the life of wisdom and peace in the countryside, with its trees and streams and flowering bushes, and the note of calm but deep joy that is heard as he pictures it. This is much less the poetry of philosophical generalization than of personal emotional need and satisfaction. The best and most famous of these poems is that which begins: '¡Qué descansada vida . . .!'

The desire to escape, to find freedom and tranquillity of spirit, achieves perhaps still more powerful expression in those other – fewer – poems of Luis de León's where his desire is to escape not from the town to the country but from the prison of the body, from this world as a whole, 'sunk in sleep and forgetting', and to soar up to the Empyrean, to know the joy of the souls who contemplate the First Truth, which is God. His own soul is filled with longing as he looks up at the stars, arranged in a wonderful order and moving with harmonious motion in a realm of pure light and beauty. Here is satisfaction and peace. This is the substance of the poems beginning 'Cuando contemplo el cielo' and '¿Cuándo será que pueda, / libre de esta prisión, volar al cielo?'*

Luis de León thinks and feels in terms of the Ptolemaic universe, with its stars and planets set in concentric spheres, each more pure than the last as one moves outwards from the centre, the earth, the 'dregs of the universe'. As the spheres revolve in their different directions they create a music which, in its intervals and mathematical relationships, is expressive of the perfect harmony found in the structure of the universe and characteristic of the being of its Creator. Luis de León builds the third and finest of these poems, 'El aire se serena', on these ideas derived ultimately from Plato and given great importance for medieval and even later times by their transmission through Boethius's *De musica* in the sixth century and their incorporation into the medieval university course in arts. Luis de León probably had a special debt here to his friend Francisco Salinas, to whom this poem is dedicated. In his *De musica* of 1577 this celebrated blind professor of music at Salamanca had described how the music of instruments not only appealed to the senses but led the mind on to

*'When shall I be able, free from this prison, to fly up to the heavens?'

an apprehension of the greater heavenly harmonies. This is the experience described by Luis de León in this poem. His soul is lifted upwards until it feels itself in a sea of sweetness and experiences a sense of union with the divine such as occurs only once in Luis de León's poetry:

> ¡Oh desmayo dichoso!
> ¡Oh muerte que das vida! ¡Oh dulce reposo!
> ¡Durase en tu reposo,
> sin ser restituído
> jamás a aqueste bajo y vil sentido!*

But the experience soon passes: Luis de León in these poems remains the poet not of union and fulfilment but of aspiration and longing. In this the unity and greatest appeal of his 'Original Poems' lie.

Although this second group of poems has a more religious character than the first, the terminology employed in them is not specifically Christian. Luis de León did sometimes use such terminology, as in his poems in praise of the Virgin, or St James, patron of Spain, or the saints of the Church, or in his poem on the Ascension, where he expresses grief at being left behind in this world. But in the other poems where he speaks of his desire to escape to the heavens, the Christian significance is implicit rather than explicit. His imaginative and emotional experience was far from being restricted to what was peculiarly Christian. He responded to, and expressed himself in, ideas that had been given prominence in the statement of Christian thinking and experience but which derived from pagan sources and retained in some degree their own associations and power of attraction. When he writes of his longing to break out from the prison of the body and soar into the heavens, he employs ideas found in Plato and the neo-Platonic tradition, in Seneca, in Cicero's *Dream of Scipio* and Macrobius's *Commentary* on it, and Boethius's *Consolation of Philosophy*. This is why disputes over whether or not he is a 'Renaissance poet' involve difficult questions of definition.

While his use of erudition could enrich his verse with overtones

---

*'Oh happy oblivion! Oh death that givest life! Oh sweet repose! Would that I might remain in your repose and never be restored to this base, low world of sense.'

and undertones, it was not without its dangers. His 'Alma región luciente . . .' is related to a whole body of religious and devotional pastoral poetry written in this period. Ideas of Christ and the Christian heaven are mingled with others belonging to the world of pastoral poetry and neo-Platonism. This technique could sometimes be effective, but here it perhaps results in some uncertainty of intellectual and emotional focus. There are other poems of Luis de León's where the pleasure he found in bringing his Classical learning into his verse led to some diminution of impact. The urgency and power of the poems 'Cuando contemplo el cielo . . .' and '¿Cuándo será que pueda . . .?' are rather seriously dissipated after their magnificent openings. But Luis de León is often at his best in beginning poems. The note of protest, repudiation or longing that comes over so strongly at the start of so many of his poems often arose, no doubt, from his own experience of life, with its pressing activities, its professional and ecclesiastical rivalries and hostilities, culminating in his imprisonment by the Inquisition. But it also derives much of its power from Luis de León's mastery of the *lira* stanzaic form, with its five lines of seven and eleven syllables and its capacity to give expression to both the relaxed movement of calm joy and the more urgent rhythms of intense and violent emotion, and to swing rapidly from the one to the other. It is this accent of personal utterance that often gives so moving a character to his expression of his central poetic concern.

Francisco de Aldana (1537–78)

This writer of extraordinarily powerful philosophical and religious verse composed, in his earlier years, some scarcely less noteworthy love poetry. Having grown up in Florence, he came first under the influence of Benedetto Varchi and Della Casa, and his sonnets about love should probably be seen mainly in relation to the Italian tradition. Among sixteenth-century love sonnets written in Spanish, with their general refinement and idealization of erotic emotion, Aldana's are sometimes remarkable for the intensity with which they express the physical desire and intoxication of lovers as they embrace and kiss. The use of brief utterances in direct speech contributes much to the effect. Among the most powerful of these sonnets are those beginning: '¿Cuál es la causa, mi Damón . . .?', 'De sus hermosos ojos dulcemente' and 'Mil veces digo, entre los brazos puesto/de Galatea'.

In 1567, at the age of thirty, Aldana went to the Low Countries with the new Spanish governor. He spent all but about three of his remaining years there, engaged in the war that had begun in 1566. He did not pay his first visit to Spain until 1571, the year of Lepanto, and then went with Don John of Austria's second expedition against the Turks. Back in the Low Countries, he was severely wounded at Alkmaar in 1573. It was perhaps then that he wrote his fine sonnets expressing weariness with the world. The one beginning 'Mil veces callo que romper deseo/ el cielo a gritos' and ending 'cuanto en mí hallo es maldición que alcanza, / muerte que tarda, llanto inconsolable, / desdén del Cielo, error de la ventura'* at once recalls Boscán and looks forward to Quevedo. Perhaps the best of these poems is that 'On the Vanity of the World', with its wonderfully expressive rhythms: 'En fin, en fin, tras tanto andar muriendo' (34).† To withdraw from the world and have the satisfaction that comes from victory over self and the service and love of God are now the only things to be desired.

In another of these sonnets he longs, in his weariness, that his soul, breaking free of its veil of flesh, might ascend to the region whence it came. The neo-Platonic element that makes itself heard here, and which was already present in various of his love sonnets, was to provide the basis for his greatest achievement in philosophical poetry. Probably when still in Florence, he had written, 'Otavas . . . sobre el bien de la vida retirada'. Living in the country a life of the kind especially recommended by Horace, the poet ponders the succession of the seasons and the regular movement of moon and sea. This passage (lines 144–59) is remarkably similar to parts of Luis de León's *Ode to Felipe Ruiz*. For Aldana, here, all things in the beauty of nature provide him with steps by which his spirit may ascend to the 'Lord of the supernal hierarchies'.

These ideas and desires are expressed again and at much greater

---

*'A thousand times I am silent when I want to shatter heaven with my shouts. . . . All that I see within me is a curse that holds me, death that delays, a weeping beyond consolation, heaven's scorn and good fortune's aberration.'

†'At last, at last, after so long walking into death'.

length in Aldana's major philosophical poem, his *Epístola VI*, one of the chief poetic expressions of neo-Platonic ideas in Spanish. Aldana was writing at Madrid in 1577, within a year of at last getting away from the Low Countries. The soldier's career 'rewards the soul with two hells': he will now concern himself with the inner man. Man as such is the 'horizon' between the worlds of imperfection and perfection. In the universe, where the creative power of God reaches down 'to the foulest, least thing', there is a Jacob's Ladder ascending from this world by which men may rise to 'the castle of high heaven'. He writes with ecstatic delight of his sense of the operation of the divine in the soul, and of the latter's discovery of God: '¡Oh grandes, oh riquísimas conquistas/de las Indias de Dios, de aquel gran mundo/tan escondido a las mundanas vistas!'* He desires that his soul may rise to the realm of Eternal Beauty and the First Cause of things, where it can feel itself submerged in 'the sea of the divine'. Yet, rather than anxious aspiration, Aldana recommends quiet openness of spirit and thankful acceptance of the created order. His wish is to practise this in San Sebastián, where he had obtained the governorship of the fortress. With his characteristically powerful response to material things, he speaks now of the sea in its different moods, and describes shells with their rich and varied colours, flashing in the sun and gleaming rainbow-like on the sand as the water runs back down the beach (lines 365-432). It is an extraordinarily fine expression of his sense of the wonder of creation, displaying the Divine Beauty. This he invites his friend Arias Montano, the great biblical scholar and Christian humanist, to share. He had probably met Montano at Antwerp when the latter was working on the revised edition of the Polyglot Bible. Aldana repeatedly expresses in his work the keen pleasure, reminiscent of what one finds in the literature of Classical antiquity, that he took in the company of close friends. In this poem, addressed as it is to Montano, this pleasure, or the wish for it, finds its strongest statement.

In Aldana's religious poetry, neo-Platonic ideas again play an important part. This is clearly seen in sonnets 36 and 37, the latter with its cry: '¡Oh patria amada!, a ti sospira y llora/esta en su cárcel

---

*'Oh conquests great and rich beyond measure of the Indies of God, of that great world so hidden from worldly sight!'

alma peregrina,/llevada errando de uno en otro instante'.* Much of
Aldana's religious verse is theological, dealing with the work of
Christ and the Eucharist (see especially *Poema XX* and sonnets 38,
45). Even when it is not primarily dogmatic in character and treats
of subjects that have tended often to evoke a chiefly emotional,
pietistic response, such as Christ's tomb and the Blessed Virgin
(sonnets 42, 41), this religious poetry inclines to develop on the basis
of argumentation, where feeling and intellectual apprehension are
closely bound together. Aldana writes, in sonnet 39, about the mosque
of Córdoba, now a church. God has entered it under the form of
bread. How well for King Almanzor, who built it, if he had received
God likewise! God, having built for himself the angelic structure of
the heavens, descended, in Christ's incarnation, to the base centre of
the universe, the earth. Now, this mosque-church, made by mere
man, is changed from hell to heaven by God, sacramentally present,
whom it hides within it. The clear and condensed formulation that
Aldana gives to precise ideas, and the way in which he orders them
in a structure of argumentation, often embodying antithesis and
paradox and moving in a concentrated progression to a final climax,
combine intellect, imagination and feeling in a highly effective
manner.

Aldana's longer religious poems are marked by a similar control
of emotion. *Canción IV*, a lament on the death of Christ by his
Mother, owes its moving character largely to its restrained lyricism.
Canción III ('To Christ Crucified') is noteworthy for its modification
of the kind of emotion so often expressed in relation to this subject.
Aldana, contemplating Christ dying on the Cross, desperately wants
Him, even at this late moment, to hear and speak to him, to him in
particular, that he may have guidance and hold on to that which
Christ's death procures. His sense of urgent need leads him to address
Christ in tones of brutal ruthlessness: 'I know you are there on the
Cross, dying for my sake. Your sufferings are beyond measure, but
you must suffer even more by listening to me. When I throw mud
at your face, as I am doing, I am giving you the thing I am capable
of giving. You cannot escape me, nailed to the Cross as you are.

*'Oh beloved homeland, my soul — a pilgrim abroad, though in prison —
sighs and weeps for you, carried along from one instant to another.'

Both you and I will see the kind of thing you have loved and are dying for, but listen to me and speak.'

Aldana, despite his bitter and ironic treatment of war, in sonnet 30 and elsewhere, was capable of voicing feelings of religious nationalism and of commending war in the service of Spain and her religion. This is most extensively done in *Poema XVII* ('Otavas dirigidas al rey don Felipe, nuestro señor'). Writing in 1577, and employing a basically allegorical device, he enumerates the dangers threatening Spain and Philip's empire. He adds his voice to those urging Philip to resolve the situation in the Low Countries by invading England. He also spoke of the threat to Spain from the north African Moors. The next year, he accepted the invitation of the King of Portugal to go with him on his crusading campaign to North Africa. Like the King, Aldana died in the battle of Alcazar Kebir.

St John of the Cross (1542–91)

San Juan de la Cruz died only four months after Luis de León, and many attempts have been made to establish contacts between the lives and works of these two greatest masters of religious verse in Spanish. Near the end of their lives they may well have met, but if Luis de León read the writings of San Juan, it was after 1586, when he had written nearly all his own work bearing on mystical experience; and if San Juan knew the works of Luis de León, it would, so far as is known, have been the *Exposition of the Song of Songs*, first published in 1580, and the *Names of Christ* and *Perfect Wife*, which appeared in 1583, rather than Luis de León's verse, which, though it circulated in manuscript form, was first published in 1631 by Quevedo. The greater part of San Juan's major poetic work was probably written by 1580 or shortly afterwards, and the poems of neither poet offer any tangible internal evidence of being influenced by those of the other.

So far as the surviving testimony goes, San Juan appears to have begun his career as a poet by starting quite suddenly to write some of the finest poetry in Spanish while he was being held as a prisoner. As a devoted supporter of Santa Teresa's Reform, he had incurred the censure and enmity of the unreformed Carmelites of the Mitigated Observance, who were seeking to put an end to Santa Teresa's movement and certain of whom carried him off from Ávila to Toledo, where they kept him prisoner in their house for nine months, until he escaped. His capture took place at the end of 1577, when he had just spent five years as spiritual director of the Convent of the Incarnation at Ávila, where Santa Teresa had been a nun before she began her Reform and where, in 1571, she returned as prioress. This period may have been important for his poetic work in more than one way. In prison he composed a number of poems in popular forms (these include nine *romances* and the *canción* '¡Qué bien sé yo la fonte que mana y corre/aunque es de noche!'), and his interest in the popular tradition of Spanish verse may owe something to its cultivation among the nuns of Santa Teresa's Reform. It has been argued that during these years San Juan also came to know two printed collections of poems related to the Italianate tradition of Spanish verse and which made an important contribution to the form and matter of his three great mystical poems especially: a version of the poems of Boscán and Garcilaso adapted by one Sebastián de Córdoba so that they speak not of secular love but of religious themes and situations (published in 1575), and a Spanish translation of the poems of the Italian Franciscan Jacopone da Todi (published in 1576). The position regarding San Juan's literary sources is still not completely established. Clearly they include the Song of Songs and the courtly love and pastoral traditions. What is also evident is that the five years at the Convent of the Incarnation gave San Juan an opportunity to deepen and reflect on his spiritual experience. The most astonishing result of this is his *Cántico espiritual (Spiritual Canticle)* which, containing as it does some of the most beautiful as well as some of the most profound verse in Spanish, was another of the works composed in prison, when he was being kept in a cramped, dark cell, the object of severe physical ill-treatment, and for six of his nine months there without writing materials. The title of *Cántico espiritual* is not San Juan's; he spoke simply of 'these songs', and it appears that the poem as we have it was not brought into being as a closely integrated whole. However, San Juan arranged the 'songs' so as to describe the same search of the soul for God, its spiritual betrothal and marriage, as Santa Teresa had portrayed in her *Interior Castle*, completed the month before San Juan's capture. He then began writing commentaries on these *canciones*, expounding his spiritual teaching in relation to them. This was a matter partly of setting down what was consciously in his mind when he composed them, partly of elaborating or adding to this. Like the poem itself, the commentaries were not written straight off. The first thirty stanzas of the *Cántico* (as far as 'jOh nymphas de Judea!' in San Juan's first ordering of them [Recension A]) were those composed while he was a prisoner; the remaining ones were added later, and his commentaries began with stanzas 17–26. Subsequently, San Juan revised the sequence of his *canciones* (Recension B) in order to make them a more lucid and coherent statement of his teaching. He also reworked the commentaries.

As regards his other most famous poems, the *Subida del Monte Carmelo* (*Ascent of Mount Carmel*) was probably written a short while after his return to liberty. In this work ('En una noche oscura') he again speaks of the ascent of the soul to God. In his *Llama de amor viva* (*Living Flame of Love*), written at Granada about 1583–4, which would be soon after Santa Teresa had died and between the first and second recensions of the *Cántico espiritual*, he devotes himself almost entirely to describing the soul's experience of union with God. These poems too are accompanied by extensive commentaries. In his own day San Juan, like Santa Teresa, not only suffered years of ecclesiastical antagonism but also came under suspicion of heresy. Some wanted the Inquisition to proceed against him. When his works were published in 1618, forty propositions were extracted from them by a group of people at Salamanca, whose names are lost, and referred to the Inquisition as heretical or unsound. Nevertheless, San Juan was beatified in 1675, canonized in 1726 and declared a Doctor of the Church in 1926.

All three of his great mystical poems largely owe their being to the fact that San Juan sought to overcome the difficulties (to which he repeatedly alluded) of communicating knowledge of a profoundly analysed mystical experience by resorting to allegorical and symbolic statement. They all have the twofold character of spiritual or mystical statement and poetic evocation. It is extraordinary that the two functions should work so well together. The *Subida del Monte Carmelo* illustrates this especially clearly. It most immediately presents itself as a story told by a young woman of how she stole out in the night to meet her lover and gave herself to him. In recounting this, she vividly relives the whole episode; that is, the poet himself enters deeply into it, so that the whole poem comes to convey the girl's experience in the fulness of its reality. At the same time the poem is seen to be a detailed allegorical account of the stages by which the soul, passing through spiritual purgation, arrives at the union it seeks with God. It is because all the details of the girl's account are for San Juan so deeply permeated with a symbolic and allegorical significance that he is able to present her human experience so openly and evocatively, even in its erotic and sensuous character, and make this evocation of human experience and emotion the expression of his own response to that which essentially lies beyond human emotion. It is a paradoxical situation where it is because San Juan is not ultimately concerned with human emotion for its own sake that he is able to accept and portray it so fully, as it were in its own right. This poem, with its commentary, could not be further from giving an impression of frustrated sexuality in religious disguise. Like San Juan's other works, it gives rather the impression of a work in which the emotional and literary aspect, without losing any of its reality and power, is transmuted or transfigured. The way in which, as in San Juan, the imagination and sensitivity of a poet, on the one hand, and the intellectual activity of a theologically trained mystic, on the other, operate simultaneously and interact on each other, is complex and mysterious. What can be said is that it drew its strength from his deep conviction that the beauty of God is seen and known through the beauty of the created order and our joy in it.

PART III

Drama

Introduction

THE sixteenth century saw the birth of modern drama and the gradual rejection of the only types of dramatic performances officially tolerated by the Church: mystery plays and religious pageants. Perhaps no other genre, not even the epic, shows such a direct and overwhelming influence from Graeco-Roman example. This began with translations of what was left of ancient drama: little enough, when compared to the riches of antiquity, but sufficient to open up a new field of literary and social activity in the Western world, which has occupied some of the most creative minds and exerted an almost universal appeal over the past four centuries. The remains of Greek tragedy were scant (some thirty-three tragedies written in the fifth century B.C.), but it was especially the difficulty of language and dramatic conventions that made Renaissance playwrights turn to the Roman stage. It was in fact to Rome that twelve of Plautus' lost comedies, discovered by Nicolas of Cusa, were brought in 1429; but the birthplace of the modern theatre was to be Ferrara at the end of the fifteenth century, when its rulers encouraged dramatic spectacle as a courtly entertainment. It was this impulse, provided by one of the leading families of Renaissance Italy, that paved the way for the development of theatrical activity. Wealth, leisure, an interest in the multifarious actions of mankind, pagan and Christian, historical and contemporary, in exotic lands and costumes, the contemplation of human grandeur and folly, the problems of society – all these characteristics of Renaissance culture helped to produce the great age of modern European drama and the conviction that all the world's a stage, even as the theatre provided one of the best examples of the modern preoccupation with illusion and reality, once the beliefs of medieval times had begun to crumble.

Comedy was first off the mark, with the plays of LUDOVICO ARIOSTO (1474–1533) written in Italian and performed at Ferrara at the beginning of the sixteenth century. The haphazard construction of medieval farce was abandoned for a more or less unified plot, following the Classical pattern of five acts, and lasting some two or three hours – as opposed to the brief sketches and interminable cycles of the medieval stage. Stock characters were taken over, like Plautus' *Miles Gloriosus* (Braggart Soldier), and the entertainment provided was theoretically justified by Horace's dictum that comedy is the scourge of vice through laughter. The hierarchy of Renaissance society was respected in the rule that only men of low and middle station could be suitable targets for ridicule and subjects for commonplace action.

Decorum likewise demanded that personages depicted in tragedy should be of high rank and noble birth, accustomed to expressing their emotions in elevated style. Here, too, the mould was taken from ancient example: five acts laid out according to a well-defined pattern of exposition, conflict, and *dénouement*, eventually submitting to the requirements of the 'three unities' (time, place and action). Only unity of action had been called for by Aristotle, but the addition of the other two was not merely due to the whim of pedants, as we tend to assume; it was in fact the result of a general search for order and a realistic approach to the problems of stagecraft after the chaotic kaleidoscope of medieval drama. Another Aristotelian ingredient was the notorious 'catharsis'; and, although no standard recipe could be found, everyone agreed that catharsis turned the spectators of tragedy into better citizens by the purgation of possibly harmful feelings – everyone, that is, except for a celebrated eccentric like Castelvetro, who believed that pleasure was the sole purpose of all literature.

Italian and English blank verse was derived from Trissino's adaptation of the Classical hexameter in the first regular tragedy of modern times, his *Sofonisba* of 1514–15 (published 1524), where he also reintroduced the chorus of Greek drama. The fact that this 'Greek' chorus is made to utter Senecan *sententiae* reflecting appropriate moral judgements on life and human actions serves as a pointer towards the general direction of Renaissance tragedy, which failed to understand the true nature of Athenian drama. Seneca's para-Christian moralizing was but one of the reasons for his immense popularity. His nine plays showed an entirely personal treatment of Greek myths, which proved to be far more accessible and congenial to Renaissance playwrights than the originals. Madness, mutilation and murder mingled with incest and tyranny to provide an irresistible formula, which inspired not only an avalanche of horrific bombast but also such creations as Marlowe's Tamburlaine and Shakespeare's ghosts. Indeed, as Polonius tells (*Hamlet*, II, ii), when he presents 'The best actors in the world, either for tragedy, comedy, history, pastoral, pastoral-comical, historical-pastoral, tragical-historical, tragical-comical-historical-pastoral, scene individable, or poem unlimited: Seneca cannot be too heavy nor Plautus too light', the great formative influences in sixteenth-century comedy and tragedy were Plautus and Seneca. Polonius' speech is also an occasion for caricaturing the fixed and hybrid genres of Renaissance drama. Only in England and Spain were comic scenes introduced in tragedy, where they provided variety, relief of dramatic tension, and a picture of life in the round which would have been unthinkable in Italy or France. Italian dramatists, on the other hand, exercised considerable freedom over their choice of plot, which might be drawn from either history or the contemporary *novella* (the latter a technique put to good purpose by Shakespeare in *Romeo and Juliet* and *Othello*).

The stage was obviously the place to portray exotic lands and picturesque customs. This tendency, combined with the tremendous popularity enjoyed by pastoral poetry, led to the creation of pastoral drama, which in turn produced the new genre of tragicomedy and, with Guarini's *Pastor fido* at the end of the century, one of the greatest box-office successes of all time. A very different type of comedy, the *Commedia dell'arte*, appealed to every section of society. Its relationship to the *Commedia erudita*, however, has led us to place it – with the German *Fastnachtspiel* – in the section on popular literature. At another level, the desire to explore new combinations, allied with the humanists' wish to rediscover the essential link that had existed between music and drama in ancient times, also gave rise to that most fascinating of irrational entertainments: modern opera. By-products included masques and other pageantry, which were fed by and encouraged the delight in spectacle that came to characterize the society which ushered in the most theatrical age ever known in Western Europe: the pomp and circumstance of the seventeenth century.

The immediate popularity of the new drama, which led to the setting up of professional troupes of actors and increasingly complex scenery and costume, was the signal for the discarding of the temporary platforms used in medieval drama and the building of the first permanent theatres since the great age of Classical drama. This impulse coincided with the humanists' omnivorous interest in every aspect of ancient life and the innovations in Renaissance architecture brought about by the publication of Vitruvius' monumental treatise in the 1480s, with its section on ancient theatres. Theory and practice combined in Bramante's stage designs at Milan and in the building of various theatres during the sixteenth century, usually made of wood, with the sole exception of the stone construction built by Falconetto at Loreo in 1528. The passion for the antique culminated in the magnificently preserved Teatro Olimpico at Vicenza (1580–85), designed by Palladio and completed by Scamozzi. The overall effect is one of symmetry and dignity that adds an illusion of permanence to the fleeting moment of drama, and Palladio's masterpiece stands as a monument to its age. It was, however, superseded by contemporary innovations in Florence, where the visual and acoustical advantages of a large rectangular hall were preferred and a stage-curtain with plenty of space behind the proscenium arch afforded ample scope for the complex machinery and décor required for the staging of the grandiose spectacles that had become so popular. Here, the pattern of theatrical design was set for centuries to come. As for the immediate consequences, we may claim that, if ever life is given to imitating art, then the wig of the Baroque age was a sure reflection of the impact of modern drama, while Versailles was the grandest continuous theatrical performance ever staged.

ONE

Italy

TRAGEDY

By the beginning of the sixteenth century tragedies in rhyme, medieval in their syncretic handling of Classical themes, could no longer appeal to the fastidious taste of humanist scholars; and it was these *literati* who set the pattern for Renaissance neo-Classical tragedy.

Seneca had been studied throughout the preceding age. Early in the sixteenth century, however, printed texts of Aeschylus, Euripides and – most significantly – of Sophocles became available, while translations into Italian appeared before the middle of the century. This return to Greek models was ensured by the influence of GIAN-GIORGIO TRISSINO (1478–1550) and the literary dictatorship of Aristotle. Trissino, in fact, dismissed Seneca and devoured the remnants of Greek drama. His tragedy, *Sofonisba* (1514–15), unlike its predecessor by Del Carretto (*c.* 1502), afforded a structural model that was to be performed in France and twice translated into French, before it was imitated by Jean Mairet in the first French 'regular' tragedy, his *Sophonisba* (1634).

The story is taken from the thirtieth book of Livy's *History of Rome* (with traces of Petrarch's *Africa*, V): a somewhat surprising choice in a scholar so totally dedicated to Greek culture. It tells of the capture of Sophonisba, Queen of Carthage, and her immediate marriage to Masinissa, to whom she had been betrothed in youth. In spite of his bold oath to protect her, Masinissa is unable to sway the stern judgement of his Roman allies, who demand that the Queen be taken to Rome as part of the spoils of victory. He therefore offers her the only alternative, suicide, but is all too naïvely distraught when she takes him at his word, instead of waiting for nightfall, when he would have arranged for her escape. He does, however, entrust her son to the faithful Ermina, as the chorus ends the play bewailing the misery of human hopes and fortune.

Although never performed during the author's lifetime, the influence of Trissino's *Sofonisba* was immense. The unity of time is observed by depicting the action as it reaches the culminating moment of catastrophe, while Sophonisba's opening speech, in *versi sciolti* (blank verse), sets the tone for this tragedy of suffering. The rejection of rhyme was justified by Trissino on a number of occasions: in his *Poetica*, where he shows a greater familiarity with Aristotle, and in the earlier dedication to Leo X, where he stresses the need for verisimilitude, which is in turn necessary to 'arouse compassion', because the type of speech which usually provokes it is born of suffering; suffering expresses itself in words that are not thought out – hence rhyme, which reveals thought, is indeed contrary to 'compassion' (one of the two ingredients in Aristotle's catharsis). Blank verse is therefore used for most of the dialogue, while rhyme is reserved for certain lyrical passages and the choruses. The latter are another important part of the play; used as another actor, according to ancient Greek practice, they give rise to some of the most typical features of 'regular' tragedy, with Senecan moralization at the appropriate cues ('Uneasy lies the head'; 'As ashes to ashes, and dust to dust'). The third choral ode is significant for another reason: in that it invokes the god of love and is modelled on the chorus in Sophocles' *Antigone* (line 781 ff.): this soon became the archetype for Italian dramatists intent on dealing with the all-important theme of romantic love, which had been virtually excluded from ancient tragedy. Apart from its obvious formal importance, however, Trissino's play has generally been roughly handled by critics, although it does contain fragments of poetry, especially in Sophonisba's last speech to Erminia and the final chorus.

The supremacy of Greek culture was not accepted by the leading dramatist of sixteenth-century Italy, GIAMBATTISTA GIRALDI (1504–73), although Trissino had cast the mould for many of the formal elements in Italian neo-Classical tragedy. Giraldi, who wrote and worked at Ferrara, admired Seneca above all other dramatists, while he was far more concerned with the actual staging of plays and entertainments at the ducal court. His *Orbecche* (1541) was the first regular Italian tragedy to be performed. In it, the Senecan influence returned with a vengeance and it was to be followed by a spate of blood and thunder, horror and cruelty on the Italian and, of course, the English stage. As recent critics have remarked, this is unfortunate for Giraldi who spent most of his career writing and defending the happy endings of his later *tragedie miste*. The fact remains, however, that this first play was by far the most influential – hardly surprising in an age when plot seemed to override all other considerations. Here, as so often in Renaissance tragedy, we have a variation on the theme of a secret marriage between personages of different – and in terms of sixteenth-century society unbridgeable – rank (for the archetypal *novella*, see *Decameron*, IV, 1). The sadistic elements, reminiscent of the House of Atreus and Seneca's *Thyestes*, fall thick and fast at the end. Oronte's hands are cut off by Sulmone, his father-in-law, who then has him witness the murder of his children. Orbecche is presented with the mutilated remains of her husband and offspring: she is able to seize the knives and hack off her father's head and hands. The chorus finally withdraws, as Orbecche appears onstage, bearing these trophies of poetic justice. The play ends with her suicide, while the chorus delivers a fitting dissertation on the fragility of human fortune and the need to seek eternal happiness.

It was in fact Giraldi's desire to bring home to his audience the moral significance of the actions witnessed, which led to the controversial interpretation of Aristotelian catharsis and the insistence on the peculiarly moral function of tragedy in the second half of the sixteenth century, an element much in accord with the cultural climate of the Counter-Reformation and which led to the inclusion of tragedy in the Jesuits' teaching orbit. So, for Giraldi, 'tragedy . . . purges the minds of the audience from their vices and induces them to adopt good morals': excessive punishment of a tragic hero provokes pity and horror, which lead men to avoid the terrible examples set before them.

Soon, however, Giraldi's conception of tragedy broadened. No doubt influenced by the contemporary debate on the importance of good works as opposed to the Lutheran doctrine of justification by faith, he became more and more attracted by the possibility of punishing vice and rewarding virtue (the happy ending), while retaining the essential tragic framework. For this, he agreed with Trissino that blank verse was the best equivalent of the Greek form, since, like the iambic tetrameter, it could be made to reproduce the rhythms of everyday speech. Unlike Trissino, he followed Horace and Renaissance practice with Seneca's tragedies in dividing up his plays into five acts, with a separate prologue. He also differed from Aristotle in his choice of plot. Whereas Greek playwrights had made use of history or traditional myths, Giraldi took his subject matter from his own fiction, the *Ecatommiti*, thus exploiting picturesque romantic material for the stage and setting an example for numberless Renaissance playwrights (including Shakespeare, whose *Othello* and *Measure for Measure* were ultimately derived from this same source). A fictitious plot is used in no less than seven of Giraldi's nine tragedies; the other two (*Didone* and *Cleopatra*) were suggested by the Duke of Ferrara and were failures.

Despite Aristotle's 'tyranny', the playwright was determined to abide by the taste and judgement of his modern audience, and – probably encouraged by similar statements made by comic dramatists – he boldly announced his right to adapt his works to the customs of the age, the spectators, and the novelty of his subject matter. Nevertheless, everything must be ruled by decorum, which required that only personages of royal rank should perform tragic actions and that their speech and behaviour should be in keeping with their lofty station. This led to a slight dilemma, for, while decorum required majesty of bearing and language, verisimilitude made it impossible for the protagonist to indulge in flights of rhetoric when under great emotional stress. The solution, for Giraldi, lay with the messenger, who can report the sufferings and deaths of others with such force and in such a grand style that his speeches will arouse 'all the horror and compassion which are the pith of the play'. He also refused to accept the limitations of decorum in showing virtuous women onstage. His tragic heroines are in fact his best characters: they give their names to eight of his nine tragedies, and in this 'cult of the feminine soul' they point the way towards Racine, just as his *tragedie miste* were a step towards tragicomedy, and his ghosts and depiction of horrific scenes foreshadowed Jacobean excess.

SPERONE SPERONI's *Canace* (1541–2; publ. 1546) is only one of the numerous imitations of Giraldi's *Orbecche*. Its author was particularly proud of having brought in the Aristotelian ingredient of *peripetia*, the sudden change in fortune which was lacking in *Orbecche* and which was calculated to produce terror and compassion (catharsis). Such a change was, of course, usually accompanied or provoked by a sudden recognition scene. It is no chance that Speroni cites *Oedipus Rex*, or that the theme of his play is one of incestuous love, drawn from Ovid's *Heroides*, XI. Here the play is mentioned because it sparked off a critical debate, almost as important in its time as the controversy over Corneille's *Le Cid* in the next century. The attack was published anonymously in 1550 (*Giuditio sopra . . .*), after circulating for some years in manuscript form. Its author may well have been Giraldi, although until recently Bartolomeo Cavalcanti was the favourite candidate. In the form of a dialogue, it claims that *Canace* is no tragedy because the writer has not digested the *Poetics* with due care (a bold enough attack against the leading representative of Paduan Aristotelianism!). Everything about the play is wrong: the plot, for example, which shows us wicked persons whose miserable end cannot arouse pity and terror (as opposed to Aristotle's requirement that they be neither wholly good nor bad – Oedipus had sinned unwittingly); it has no chronological verisimilitude and violates the rule that the stage should never be left empty. Speroni, moreover, has sinned against the rules of decorum. His counsellor is not sufficiently wise, he has introduced the death of a nurse, a character far removed from the elevated status of tragedy, and, incredibly enough, Canace speaks in public about the sordid subject of childbirth. Speroni's versification also reverses current practice in that he uses the traditional hendecasyllable far less than the shorter lines, while he uses rhyme far too often. Speroni's reply was only published posthumously (1597), although others were not slow in taking sides.

Two other tragedies may be singled out for comment: PIETRO ARETINO's *Orazio* (1546) and TORQUATO TASSO's *Torrismondo* (1587). The first is – surprisingly enough – one of the most successful of Italian Renaissance tragedies. The action follows Livy's account of the battle between the Horatii and Curiatii (I, 24–6). The sole survivor, Orazio, returns to Rome in triumph, where he meets his only sister, Celia; enraged by her lamentations over the death of her betrothed, he kills her and is condemned for the murder. Their father, Publio, implores mercy for his remaining child – but in vain, until Orazio appeals to the Roman people, who absolve him on condition that he submit to the yoke of penance. He obstinately refuses, until Jove's voice is heard from above and, following the divine command, Orazio brings the tragedy to an end. Despite the title, there is no Cornelian conflict in Aretino's play: Celia is utterly taken up with her personal calamity, and the meeting between brother and sister (Act III) is of two irreconcilable forces. In spite of the pity shown for his adversary, Orazio is a wooden figure. Nevertheless, Aretino went a long way towards making his tragic characters more human. There are no irrelevant mythological allusions, little bombast, fewer messengers, no soliloquies, and the reduction of the role played by the chorus is significant. Instead, we have the first real attempt at portraying the grandeur and ideals of Republican Rome on a modern stage: ideals which remain abstract in the spokesman for the *popolo romano*, but which take on dramatic life in the tragic figure of Publio. An interesting detail is to be found in the dedication to Pope Paul III, where Aretino compares the great duel of Roman history to the divinely-led struggle against the Lutherans: another sign of the times.

Tasso's play (originally conceived long before its publication) is the most famous imitation of *Oedipus Rex*, set in a barbaric northern world, whose strange landscapes were supposed to reflect the deviations of romantic passion. In his dedication to the Duke of Mantua, Tasso told his patron that his play would conform to the canons of Renaissance Aristotelianism in offering some pleasure and much utility. The unities are observed, so that the moment chosen is the climax – which also means a great deal of more or less contrived exposition of the past. We learn that Torrismondo, Prince of the Goths, has obtained the hand of Alvida, daughter of the King of Norway, secretly on behalf of his friend Germondo, King of Sweden, and formerly Norway's enemy. In leading her to her future husband, Torrismondo is cast on a deserted beach with Alvida; they become lovers. The first act opens with Torrismondo's expressions of remorse at having betrayed his friend and Alvida's despair at the coldness of her lover. In the fourth act, after the two friends have agreed to exchange brides, Torrismondo finally learns that Alvida is his sister. In the last act, Torrismondo reveals the terrible truth to Alvida and begs her to accept Germondo as her husband. The news of her father's death and her refusal to believe Torrismondo's story lead to the double suicide of brother and sister. In Tasso's tragedy, the role of the chorus is mainly restricted to rhymed odes at the end of each act, and, as in the *Aminta*, these contain some of the play's greatest poetry, which is here concerned with the lack of justice and happiness in this life. *Torrismondo* shows the total victory won by the Classicists in the second half of the century, even over the romantic genius of one of Italy's greatest lyric poets; whether Tasso could ever have been a great dramatist remains an open question.

The final result of Italian Renaissance tragedy was to bequeath to the playwrights of Western Europe a well-organized plot, divided into five acts, rising to a dramatic climax, but with breaks in between which made possible the use of musical entertainment and paved the way for Italian opera. And whereas Aristotle thought scenery and costume to be of little importance, the Italians began to mount an increasingly elaborate, magnificent spectacle, often placed in an exotic setting. The theatre of Greek democracy was reborn as a courtly entertainment, with sufficient moral justification to be accepted in the post-Tridentine age. The influence of Aristotle and Seneca was, of course, paramount. But the impact of another ancient writer, Vitruvius, must not be forgotten. His *De Architectura* influenced numerous architects and scenographers, and the changing scene typical of medieval plays gave way to a single set and visual perspective, which created a completely new relationship between actors and audience. Eventually, one of the greatest of Renaissance architects, a friend of Trissino, Andrea Palladio (1508–80), began his work for the theatre, which culminated in the famous Teatro Olimpico at Vicenza, reflecting the aspirations and achievements of Renaissance tragedy in Italy, soon to be bequeathed to the great playwrights of England, France and Spain.

COMEDY

Two factors influenced the development of modern comedy in Italy: humanism, and the sophistication of court life, with its search for entertainment and delight in spectacle. The centre of this new culture was Ferrara, where plays by Plautus and Terence were translated and performed in Italian at the end of the fifteenth century. As opposed to tragedy, comedy was supposed to deal with people of low or middle station, avoid the grand style, and portray everyday life, while using a fictitious plot. It offered a unique opportunity to poke fun at the strict forms of contemporary society, although after the middle of the sixteenth century the bridle of the Counter-Reformation was avoided by escape literature, including pastoral drama, rather than by direct confrontation. To be respectable, comedy needed two things: to be bolstered by the authority of the ancients and to receive moral justification as a genre. The latter was achieved by using arguments put forward by Donatus and Servius, the Latin commentators on Terence: comedy portrays reality and teaches us what we must avoid; in Horace's famous dictum, it attains its end (the chastisement of vice) by means of laughter. The former meant abandoning the formless naïvety of medieval farce and religious drama, while it followed the humanistic principle of imitation. The modern reader must understand that Renaissance comedy was based on plot, and not on a study of individual character. As far as plot was concerned, Donatus provided the modern playwright with a threefold mould: *protasis*, the exposition (usually Acts I and II); *epitasis*, the introduction of complications and intrigue (Acts III and IV); *catastrophe*, the reversal of the situation necessary to bring about a happy ending, usually by means of a recognition scene. For characterization, Latin comedy also provided the basic types: the servant, frequently the hub of the whole action; the greedy parasite; the foolish man, usually a miser; the courtesan; the nagging wife; the cowardly, boastful soldier; and the young lover – young ladies of good reputation were not allowed on stage.

It is fitting that the birth of modern comedy should be due to the fertile imagination of the author of the *Furioso*, LUDOVICO ARIOSTO (1474–1533), who translated ancient comedies before producing his first original comedy (*La cassaria*, 1508) in prose. The plot of this play is more complex than any in Plautus or Terence and points the way to the use of *novella*-type action, which delighted Renaissance dramatists and audiences alike. As ancient comedy had been composed in verse, Ariosto later decided to 'embellish' his play by turning the dialogue into unrhymed *versi sdruccioli*, where the proparoxytone (accent on the ante-penultimate syllable), relatively rare in spoken Italian, is hardly convincing as a sample of everyday speech. Although not taken from ancient comedy, there is little enough that is original in Ariosto's plot. It does, however, mark the first attempt to write a modern 'regular' comedy. *I suppositi* (1509) was translated by Gascoigne in 1572 and indirectly exploited by Shakespeare in *The Taming of the Shrew*; this time, although the play is set in Ferrara, nearly all has been borrowed from Plautus' *Captivi* and Terence's *Eunuchus*.

Of Ariosto's five comedies, *La lena* (1529) is the best and most original. In the prologue, the author claims that he has attempted something almost unheard of in comedy – the invention of a new plot – as the comic writers of Rome had undoubtedly borrowed their material from Greek models. In fact, Ariosto's work owes a great deal to a tale by Boccaccio (*Decameron*, VII, 2). Flavio's servant Corbolo fails to raise the twenty-five ducats needed to bribe the bawd (la lena); and yet, his part is not the mechanical device of ancient comedy, for, as he himself explains (III, 1), he needs all the cunning 'such as I have seen acted sometimes in comedy' to outwit a miser (Ilario, Flavio's father); but, he moans, 'what shall I do, since I haven't a gullible old man to deal with, like Cremetes or Simon in Terence or Plautus?' This is supposed to be real life, with all its difficulties, where Corbolo has to prove 'a better liar than any poet' and the bawd herself is given some humanity in the description (II, 2) of her plight, hemmed in between a greedy pimp of a husband and her miserly lover on whom she plans a dual revenge. Her husband finally suggests that Flavio hide in an empty wine cask. The bailiffs come to seize it, and her rich lover offers to keep it in his house until the dispute is settled. After a bumpy journey, Flavio finds himself dumped in the place where he has always desired to be, Licinia's house, and the parents of the young lovers have to accept the *fait accompli* and arrange for a wedding feast. The characters on the whole are more satisfying than the usual types, and the single plot makes do without the usual recognition scenes and other artifices of the comic tradition.

One of the most typical and influential plays of the century is *La Calandria* (1513) by Bernardo Dovizi better known as BIBBIENA, (1470–1520): typical, because it is based on Plautus' *Casina* (father and son rivals in love) and his *Menaechmi* (identical twins), while the protagonist, Calandro, is modelled on Boccaccio's famous simpleton, Calandrino (*Decameron*, VIII, 3, 6; IX, 3, 5). This fast-moving play reveals a typical Renaissance delight in complicated intrigue. The master-mind is Fessenio, the servant; but his schemes are constantly hindered by the new twist added by Bibbiena to the *Menaechmi* theme in making his twins identical but of different sex (cf. *The Comedy of Errors* and *Twelfth Night*). The girl, Santilla, has eventually returned to Rome, disguised as a boy, but finds herself affianced to the daughter of her patron. Unknown to all, the boy Lidio has also escaped from the Turks, arrived in Rome, and fallen in love with Calandro's wife, Fulvia. Fessenio suggests that Lidio dress up as a girl, pretend to be his lost sister, and thus get access to Fulvia's house. The scheme works so well that Lidio not only makes Calandro's wife his mistress, but, disguised as a girl, he also becomes the object of the old man's passionate advances. A necromancer is called in at various critical moments, and, although he is obviously incapable of solving certain anatomical problems, everything turns out well when brother and sister finally meet in the last act.

Calandria was first performed at Urbino in February 1513 – appropriately enough, when we remember that Castiglione entrusted Bibbiena with the section on witticisms in the *Courtier*; less appropriately, when we learn that Bibbiena was elevated to the rank of cardinal shortly afterwards and that this portrayal of a veritable love epidemic entertained the papal court in the following year. Castiglione produced the first prologue to the play, as the author's had not arrived on time. In it, he vindicated the use of prose, because comedy represents things done and said in an informal manner, spoken in Italian so that everyone should understand, and, though based on ancient models, thoroughly modern in spirit and verve. Bibbiena's own prologue (written for another performance) shows us the author's whimsical inspiration, which enabled him to turn the traditional prologue to his own, essentially comic, ends. He tells us that he had been dreaming of Angelica's ring and its power to make him invisible, so that he had stolen money from all the misers of the neighbourhood, and then gone round to see what the various ladies were doing before coming to the theatre; one is being hurried off by her husband, who can't wait to get his hands on the young maid, and another pinches her child to make him cry so that she can send her husband off to the play and stay at home with her lover. We have some pointed remarks about the ladies' preparations, and then a desperate appeal to them to fascinate the men in the audience, to take their minds off the play and ensure its success.

ANGELO BEOLCO (1502–42), better known as 'Ruzante', was the illegitimate son of a noble Paduan family, passionately devoted to his native countryside and dialect. The prologues to his comedies are mainly variations on a theme first introduced in *La Betía*: the need to follow nature and abandon artifice in dress, behaviour, food, and language. A cultured man, his three prose comedies follow the Classical pattern, but his whole work is steeped in his feeling for the poverty and suffering – comic though it may appear at times – of the Venetian countryside, especially after the devastation resulting from the League of Cambrai (1508). His sympathy was in no way patronizing, and he went so far as to identify himself with one of his own peasant characters, Ruzante. Nothing could be farther from the aristocratic Venetian culture of Pietro Bembo or the idyllic world of Sannazaro's *Arcadia*.

Beolco's first theatrical venture, *La Pastoral* (1520), presents a dramatic clash between the literary tradition of the pastoral eclogue and the world of peasant reality: for example, in the eleventh scene, where the shepherd Arpino meets Ruzante and addresses him according to the custom of Arcadia in words that are quite incomprehensible to the peasant, who is concentrating all his skill on trying to catch a bird to fill his empty stomach and who now inveighs against this fool who has disturbed his prey. The divorce between the two worlds is in fact reflected in speech (Arpino's literary Tuscan and Ruzante's Paduan dialect). Arpino exclaims to Pan, the god of nature, while all that Ruzante can make out is the word *pan* (bread), so that he mistakes this for an offer of food. This is no mere pun. It is an eloquent illustration of the two forces – hunger and sex – that drive the world of nature, as opposed to the idealizations of Arcadia. Here, to die of hunger is no figurative phrase; the test of friendship lies in one's willingness to share a crust of bread; proof that one is alive (as in Ruzante's dream) is provided by the act of eating; and, in *La Betía* (1523–5), when Nale pretends he is a spirit just returned from hell, his wife's first question is how they manage to eat down there. In the *Parlamento de Ruzante* (c. 1528), the protagonist has just returned from the wars. He had enlisted not with the intention of killing men but of stealing a horse or a cow. However, he remains a tool, the 'object' never the 'subject' of life. He has now managed to crawl back to Venice, poorer than ever, and fails even to act the part of the braggart soldier. He is in fact a total failure, rejected by his wife Gnua, who goes off with her bravo, justifying her action by peasant morality: 'Don't you know that here you can get a square meal every day?' In Ruzante's last play, *La Vaccaria* (1533), he based his plot on Plautus' *Asinaria*; but he makes the parasite and servants use the same language as Ruzante, while in the Prologue he makes no bones about having changed many of the details to fit in with the modern Paduan setting, claiming that Plautus himself 'would not write differently, if he were alive today'. Even as the saying 'homo homini lupus' is derived from the *Asinaria*, so Nale tells us in *La Betía* 'If God created fools, it's our duty to make fools of them.' Ruzante's comic vision is set off against a background of cruelty and crude reality, best portrayed in the rough language of country speech.

Linguistic realism of a very different kind is to be found in NICCOLÒ MACHIAVELLI's cosmic masterpiece, *La mandragola* (1518), which a recent English critic considers 'a disappointment'. I doubt whether many would agree. Machiavelli followed the usual pattern, restricting events to the span of a single day and using only one fixed street scene. In his Prologue, the author explains that he tries to while away the time as best he may during his enforced exile, which has forced him to turn to a subject hardly worthy of anyone who wishes 'to appear wise and grave'. Too much has been made of this apology, as of supposed links between the comedy and *The Prince*. Machiavelli's translation of Terence's *Andria* and his other comedy, *Clizia* (1524-5, based on Plautus' *Casina*, but with its memorable portrayal of Nicomaco's tribulations), should warn us to avoid any search for political allegory in *La mandragola* – or anything else, beyond a comic masterpiece which could not accomplish more with such economy of means. No word, no action is wasted, and each act is finely constructed with due regard to what Corneille was to call 'la liaison des scènes'.

In the first act, Callimaco explains to Siro that he has been away in Paris some twenty years. He has, however, been lured back to

Florence by accounts of the extraordinary beauty of Lucrezia, wife of Messer Nicia, whom he has found even more beautiful in reality – but, unfortunately, as chaste as her Roman namesake. The situation seems desperate. Nevertheless (and here the author of *The Prince* certainly cannot be forgotten), Callimaco has analysed all the elements and found three possible flaws: Nicia's gullible nature, the couple's frustrated desire to have a child, and the lax ways of Sostrata, Lucrezia's mother. Act II shows us the meeting between Nicia and Callimaco, introduced as a famous doctor by Ligurio, a parasite who bears little resemblance to his kin on the Renaissance stage – all thought and action, Ligurio never bores us with the usual paeans to the belly. Callimaco's Latin immediately convinces Nicia. The 'doctor' then goes on, with some reluctance, to reveal his infallible cure for sterility: a potion taken from the mandrake, which has, however, the unfortunate consequence of bringing sure death to the first man to have intercourse with the woman who has drunk it. This difficulty can, of course, be overcome (as Nicia somewhat readily agrees) by kidnapping a young man and leading him to Lucrezia's bed. The real obstacle lies in Lucrezia's virtue. Ligurio once again provides the solution, this time in the person of Fra Timoteo, a confessor who can be bought for twenty-five ducats. Timoteo, who is presented in all his casuistic glory, is no mere caricature, as we well see from his soliloquies (III, 9; IV, 6; and V, 1). His 'Machiavellian' lecture to Lucrezia in Act III, scene 11 is a masterpiece, culminating in the admonition that 'the end must be considered in all things: your end is to gain a seat in paradise and make your husband happy.' Act IV describes the preparations, highlighted by Nicia's eagerness to make himself a cuckold. In Act V, scene 2, Nicia tells Ligurio how he had assured himself of the success of the enterprise *de manu*, after placing the disguised Callimaco in Lucrezia's bed. The latter, conquered by her young lover's resourcefulness, 'my husband's stupidity, my mother's foolishness, and my confessor's wickedness', has decided to let her senses speak and to accept Callimaco as her lover. The latter is handed the key of the door by Messer Nicia himself, while the play ends in general rejoicing. One of the shortest learned comedies of the century, the plot of *La mandragola* owes little or nothing to Classical antiquity: it breathes the spirit of Boccaccio and the mordant wit of Machiavelli's native city.

Nothing could be more different from Machiavelli's linear action than the comedies of PIETRO ARETINO (1492–1556). For a glimpse of the writer's personality, the reader is invited to turn to Aretino's published letters, which are full of theatrical scenes and possibilities and which have gained for him the title of first journalist of modern times. Aretino rebelled against the tyranny of literary conventions and, like Ruzante, claimed to take nature as his only guide. Of the five comedies in prose, written between 1525 and 1542, two are especially noteworthy, each reflecting in its own way the author's experience of life at court.

The *Marescalco* is set in Mantua, where Pietro stayed in 1526–7. It is little more than a long drawn-out jest played on a minor official (the 'marescalco' or equerry), such as we can find in a hundred contemporary *novelle*. Its protagonist is a most unwilling one, since he, a woman-hater, finds himself obliged to prepare for his wedding, while the person who pulls all the strings – the Duke – is completely absent from the stage. The play is kept alive by the author's verbal skill, the endless sea of words that drown the poor victim in the praise of matrimony (IV, 5) or echoes of his own misogyny (II, 5), by the satire of pedantry and the language and atmosphere of a provincial court – until the happy ending, where the unwilling bridegroom finds to his delight that his bride is none other than Carlo, the page.

La Cortigiana (1525) has a quite different rhythm and perspective. The playwright makes use of the traditional street scene. But what a street this is: with its pedlars, whores, Jews, snobs, and all the bustle of sixteenth-century papal Rome. Aretino's play, with no less than 106 scenes, is very much lacking in Classical symmetry and economy; instead, it reflects the disparate unity of life itself, life in the busy street of a capital city, as Rosso claims in the final scene, with the numerous characters meeting, chatting, quarrelling and parting with the brio of a modern revue. The play is constructed on two parallel actions: the pretensions of Parabolano, courtier and self-styled lady-killer, and the foolishness of Maco, a citizen of Sienna, who has come to Rome to become a cardinal but has decided that he must first become a courtier. Parabolano goes to an amorous encounter with a Roman beauty who ignores his very existence and is replaced by the wife of Arcolano, the baker, thanks to the machinations of Rosso the Greek and Alvigia the bawd. Maco is taught to swear and speak ill of everyone. He is then boiled in a cauldron, and, thinking he has been transformed into the perfect courtier, he goes to the 'house of Lady Camilla' and gets a thorough beating from some Spanish bullies.

In Aretino's *Cortigiana* we find a perfect backcloth for Cellini's autobiography, in the same way that it serves as a foil to Castiglione's celebrated *Courtier*: the latter seen through the distortions of the comic mask, from which reality is never far away. The antithesis is most clearly revealed in Act II, scene 6, where Sempronio, the old man, recalls the courts of his youth, where all the noble qualities and virtues flourished, while Flaminio counters with a lengthy disquisition on the wicked ways of the modern court, which have already been part of Maco's 'education' in Act I, scene 22. Long before Beaumarchais's Figaro, Rosso, the servant, points out that masters are generally far more stupid than their servants, who have to live by their wits (I, 11). Alvigia, the bawd, is perhaps Aretino's greatest creation: her mumbling and intermingling of obscene inducements with bits and pieces of Latin orations (IV, 8–9) is undoubtedly the finest of such scenes in Renaissance comedy, while her verbiage reflects the general breakdown of Roman society. For, far from having punished the Romans for their sins, the famous Sack of the Holy City (1527) has not altered them one whit; indeed, as Valerio points out (II, 10), the wars, plagues and famine that have afflicted Italy in the past years have turned her into a sink of promiscuous iniquity.

GIORDANO BRUNO's *Candelaio* (c. 1582) marks the end of learned comedy in sixteenth-century Italy. Its structure is even freer than anything in Aretino. Set in Naples, it portrays the misadventures of Bonifacio, enamoured of a whore, who sets out to get her by incantations rather than money – and is duped by an all-too-willing necromancer, Scaramurè. Bartolomeo is in love with alchemy and boys; tricked by Cencio, he loses all his money. The pedant Manfurio completes the trio of gulls; representing all that Bruno hated most in the culture of his times, he loses his clothes and undergoes a prolonged beating at the hands of the fake police. The gypsy Scaramurè and the painter Bernardo (Bonifacio's wife's lover) are as much in charge of the action as anyone, although Bruno's animated verbosity tends to run riot and his essential melancholy shows through in this picture of love and learning – those mainsprings of Renaissance culture – as forms of human aberration. It is the last example of Boccaccio's and Machiavelli's comic world, glimpsed through a distorting mirror of hypocrisy and general corruption.

To conclude, the Italian playwrights underwent a rapid apprenticeship in their imitations of Plautus and Terence. It is nonsense to regard this as a vital handicap which prevented the emergence of a universal comic genius like Molière. Admittedly, the stereotyped plot and characterization of Roman comedy became insipid. Nevertheless, without this apprenticeship modern comedy would not have produced such a masterpiece as Machiavelli's *Mandragola*. And in this same play we see the tremendous vitality that derived from the compression of the comic action into the space of a few hours, while the setting in a Florentine street helped to produce the verve of local colour in brilliant, untiring dialogue. As time passed, Italian dramatists came to assert their independence of ancient models with greater confidence, until in the second half of the century such claims were legion. One of the most fascinating results is the Prologue to *La strega* by ANTON FRANCESCO GRAZZINI ('Il Lasca', 1503–84). Here, with a device anticipating Pirandello, we have a discussion between the traditional Prologue and The Plot. With Florentine clarity, Lasca used this situation to make various points on comic practice: his rejection of the music and pastoral settings in the interludes, long-winded speeches, soliloquies and incredible recognition scenes. What about moral edification, asks the Prologue. If you want that, you had better turn to religious books and sermons: 'Aristotle and Horace saw their own times, but ours are different: we have different customs, a different religion and another way of life, and so we must write comedies in another way.' No critic succeeded in writing on comedy in such a lively way. It was left to the great comic playwrights of Spain, France and England to illustrate the lesson.

PASTORAL

Pastoral drama, incorporating the myth of the Golden Age, was a creation peculiar to the Renaissance, although based on the bucolic idylls of Theocritus and Virgil. The rediscovery of Classical drama gave rise to the idea that modern playwrights might imitate Virgil's love themes, set in Arcadia, and satisfy both the taste for picturesque scenery and costume and musical interludes, and the increasing need to escape from a world of rigid social and religious restraint. Indeed, the whole process had begun with the first 'play' of the Renaissance, Poliziano's *Orfeo*, which had been produced at Mantua (1480), set in pastoral surroundings and with secondary characters that included shepherds and a satyr.

The real landmark, however, as Guarini himself acknowledged, was *Il Sacrifizio* by AGOSTINO DE' BECCARI (d. 1590), produced at Ferrara in 1554. The scene is Arcadia, the actors in the drama, shepherds. Erasto is in love with Callinome, who has vowed her chastity to Diana; Carpalio loves and is loved in return by Melidia, though their union is opposed by her brother; Turico loves Stellinia, who is hopelessly in love with Erasto. With the help of magic, all turns out well for the three pairs of lovers. The formula is made complete with a priest who addresses a hymn to Pan (III, 3), a couple of old men who remember the happiness of their youth, and a wicked Satyr who tries to lay hands on all the nymphs. There is even a chorus of shepherds in Act III, scene 3, although Guarini claimed that Beccari had produced the first true pastoral play 'with all its necessary parts, except the chorus, which was added later by Tasso'.

TORQUATO TASSO's *Aminta*, written in 1573, is a masterpiece produced by the greatest Italian lyric poet of the century. None of his other works is so spontaneous and free; in *Aminta*, Tasso achieved a balance between nature and art, which he was never to recapture. In the Prologue, Cupid, disguised as a shepherd boy, announces that he has escaped from his mother Venus in order to enjoy the delights of Arcadia: 'wherever I may be, I am Love, among shepherds no less than among heroes.' Aminta is in love with Diana's niece, Silvia, who is jealous of her virginity and loves only the pleasures of the hunt. Act I, scene 1 shows her sentiments, while her companion Dafne tries to warn her that she repents a similar attitude; she now regrets 'all the time that is not spent in loving' and admits that the darkness of one brief night had shown her 'what the long hours and light of a thousand days' had kept hidden from her: the pleasures of love, who is lord of all, as she sings in a hymn to the supreme power of nature

(213–57). The two depart, and leave the scene clear for Aminta to tell Tirsi the story of his unhappy love. Together as children, Silvia and he had been close friends; then had come the unconscious flowering of his love and passion for her. One day, Silvia's friend Fillide had been stung on the mouth by a bee; Silvia had applied her lips and taken away the sting from the wound. Still only half-aware of his love, Aminta had pretended to have been stung in the same manner, but Silvia's kisses had only made his wound hurt all the more – until he had declared his love and been banished from her sight, some three years before. The act, a masterpiece in itself, closes with the famous chorus in which the poet sings nostalgically of the freedom and pleasures of the Golden Age, when honour had not yet come to disturb the innocent happiness of love. Instead, nature's law had reigned supreme: that all pleasure is good ('S'ei piace, ei lice'). The end of the chorus is in some ways the swan-song of the Renaissance's preoccupation with love: inspired by the theme 'gather ye rosebuds', the mood has changed from Lorenzo de' Medici's ebullient call to happiness, in spite of the uncertainty of the morrow (*Triumph of Bacchus and Ariadne*); here, that same uncertainty casts a shadow over Tasso's exhortation to love, 'for human life is not spared by time, and is wasted' (719–20).

In Act II the villain of the piece, the Satyr, is introduced. In a monologue, he tells us that he too has been spurned by Silvia but is bent on revenge. Then, in the second scene, Dafne discusses the hopeless situation with Tirsi. Her observant gaze has, however, noticed that when she had come across Silvia alone and seen the girl gaze at her own image reflected in a pool, Silvia's nascent coquetry had been revealed as she adorned herself with flowers and exulted in her triumph over the beauties of nature. Dafne only wishes that Aminta were a little bolder in his behaviour. But the third scene shows his respectful fear of offending Silvia, when he refuses to follow Tirsi and surprise the girl bathing naked near by. The third act opens with Tirsi's description of Aminta's despair. He tells us that the Satyr had seized Silvia and tied her naked to a tree. Aminta had come to her rescue, just in time – but all in vain as far as he is concerned for, without a word of thanks, the blushing girl sets off for a new set of clothes and the hunt once more. Aminta is then told by Nerina of Silvia's supposed death, devoured by wolves. Act IV, scene 1 sees Silvia return unscathed, only to learn of Aminta's suicide: the news of her death has led him to throw himself over a cliff. The girl's compassion gradually gives way to remorse and deeper feeling. Realizing too late that she had loved him, she sets off to bury Aminta's body before putting an end to her own life. Act V consists of one brief scene, in which Elpino tells us how Aminta's fall had been broken by some bushes, and that when Silvia had applied her lips in a farewell kiss Aminta had returned to his senses and new-found happiness.

The dialogue is in unrhymed verse, rhyme being used in the choral odes. In a sonnet, the poet expressed his belief that in *Aminta* he had produced something worthy of 'the ancient Greek laurels with new art'; and in the Prologue he had already asserted his originality in pastoral drama (76–7). As in all of Tasso's poetry, we find a delight in language for language's sake, which was later to lead to Baroque excess; here, however, it may be used to paint a picture (401 ff.) where part of our delight is the lack of detail, which nevertheless conjures up an image of Botticellian beauty. There is the usual play on words, the conceits (194–6; 1,848–9), all part of the poetic atmosphere; and when the poet likens Fillide's cheeks to a flower (443–9), the conventional comparison becomes part of a game whose rules we accept from the very beginning, creating a vision of the whole of nature bound together by youth and love. The disillusionment that is apparent in the *Liberata* is nowhere to be seen in *Aminta*, and critics have too often made the mistake of taking Dafne's words out of context – 'The world grows old, and, growing old, gets worse' (891–2) – and attributing them to the poet. They do not in any way reflect the playwright's world, which is rooted in the essential happiness of love, its gradual awakening in Aminta's young heart and the much slower, dramatic development of Silvia's true feelings.

We are told that one of Tasso's friends once asked him what he thought of GIAN BATTISTA GUARINI's *Pastor fido* (1585). The poet answered that he liked it very much, although he wasn't sure why. The friend immediately replied that what pleased him was surely what he recognized to be his own. Guarini, who succeeded Tasso as court poet at Ferrara in 1577, never attempted to deny his debt, whereas his intention was quite clearly to compete with Tasso's pastoral drama. In this, Guarini was aiming rather too high: there is not the great poetry of *Aminta* in his work, and we have only to compare the opening scenes to note two obvious defects: the lack of subtlety and over-elaboration. The *Pastor fido* is much longer than *Aminta*, and its plot is too complex – although it is impossible to deny the tremendous success of the play and its appeal to audiences in many lands. The story is based in part on Pausanias. Diana has set a curse on Arcadia, because of a nymph's infidelity. In retribution, she requires the annual sacrifice of a nymph, and any other found guilty must be punished by death, until the marriage of two descendants of the gods. Such is the situation at the opening of Guarini's play.

Silvio, the first character we see, is the counterpart of Silvia in *Aminta*: consciously modelled on Hippolytus, he is only interested in hunting. Like Silvia, however, he ends up by loving Dorinda, whom he has accidentally shot. Mirtillo, the other male lead, is the 'faithful shepherd', who has snatched a kiss from Amarilli by dressing up as a girl. He is madly in love with her; but Amarilli is promised to Silvio, as both are of divine stock, and she cannot reveal her love for Mirtillo. The villain of the piece is, of course, the Satyr. We also have a villainess, Corisca, who invents a story about Silvio's infidelity and leads Amarilli to a cave. In this third act, Corisca manages to trap Mirtillo by leading him to the cave, where she claims he will find Amarilli with her lover, and the villainous Satyr leads up to a 'tragic' climax by blocking the entrance to the cave with a huge rock. In the fourth act, Arcadian society is shocked by the incredible news that Amarilli has been found with a lover on the very day of her marriage. She is destined to die, when a messenger announces that Mirtillo has offered to give up his own life to save her. As Montano is about to execute him, Carino arrives and explains that Mirtillo is not his son: he had found him as a child, hidden in a thicket of myrtle (hence his name). It is now the servant Dameta's turn to confess that he had tried to save Mirtillo's life, because of a prediction that the child would die by his father's hand (cf. *Oedipus Rex*). Montano must now perform his duty as priest and executioner, and kill his eldest child. The required 'reversal of fortune' is, however, achieved in Act V, scene 6, when Tirenio, the blind soothsayer, reminds Montano that Diana will relent when a faithful shepherd of divine race marries a nymph of similar station. The condition can be met by Mirtillo and Amarilli. Meanwhile, Corisca appears on the scene, confident that her rival Amarilli has been dispatched. Instead, she learns that Amarilli and Mirtillo are married. She repents and congratulates the couple, who magnanimously pardon her. Apart from the Counter-Reformation taste for Mary Magdalens, Guarini pointed out that her continued wickedness and frustration would have ruined the comic end to the play. Now, in the last scene, the chorus of shepherds, Mirtillo and Amarilli bring the play to its happy close, while the Chorus ends the play in the Classical manner with a short sententious ode: 'True joy is that which comes from virtue after suffering.'

Guarini obviously went out of his way to appeal to a politer age: the Satyr, for example, no longer tries to rape the woman he loves; he is little more than a comic buffoon who inveighs against venal love and women's make-up. In his notes to the play, Guarini tells us: 'The comic scenes are the games, Corisca's deceit and the Satyr's tricks. The tragic ones are ... [inspired by] Amarilli's virtue and greatness of soul, Mirtillo's faith and constancy, his decision to kill his rival and then himself.' The formula was successful enough with audiences, but it was immediately attacked by Giasone De Nores, who published a *Discorso intorno alla poesia* (1587) in which he rejected pastoral tragicomedy as a monstrous abortion, since it had not been included by Aristotle in his classification of genres. Guarini replied in two stages (1588 and 1593), which were later combined in his *Compendio della poesia tragicomica* (1601). In the latter work, he points to a number of successful fusions in nature: bronze, hermaphrodites, mules and other animals listed by Aristotle, while, if we turn to art, painting is made up of differing colours, music of varying harmonies. Tragedy is supposed to achieve catharsis by means of horror and compassion. Horror is obviously out of place on the comic stage, but there is no reason why compassion should not blend and mingle with laughter. The great examples in antiquity are Euripides' *Cyclops* and Plautus' *Amphitryon*. Nowadays, tragedy has become a sadistic bloodbath, while comedy has once more degenerated into vulgarity and obscenity. The golden mean can, however, be achieved through tragicomedy, which retains the dignity of tragedy while it offers the box-office appeal and verve of comedy. Decorum must, of course, be observed. But it is no offence to show shepherds on the stage, since cities had not yet grown up in the Golden Age, and even such exalted personages as Moses and David had led pastoral lives. Decorum also requires that, while tragic and comic scenes may be juxtaposed, tragic and comic features must never be revealed in the same person: Mirtillo is always honest and faithful, the Satyr always bestial. Moreover, times and customs have changed. Whereas the ancient Greeks and Romans may have felt the need for spiritual improvement through catharsis, such medicine is superfluous for modern audiences, who can turn to the holy precepts of the Christian religion. The great need nowadays is to be purged of the excesses of melancholy, which may even lead to suicide – and no better way can be found than through the effects of laughter on the soul. The end of tragicomedy is therefore 'to imitate with dramatic apparatus a fictitious action, composed of all those tragic and comic parts which can be blended together with verisimilitude and decorum, brought to one single dramatic form, in order to purge the audience's sadness by means of delight.' In fact, Guarini claims that tragicomedy is a more noble genre than either tragedy or comedy and that it is the best dramatic invention, because it avoids the excesses of other genres and appeals to all ages and tastes.

TWO

France

TRAGEDY

THE history of French Renaissance drama underlines the paradox inherent in the consciously élitist programme of the humanists: as literature a play is a book like any other, but as theatre it also involves a social phenomenon. At the beginning of the sixteenth century the traditional mystery, miracle and morality plays, as well as more ephemeral farces and *soties*, were still drawing enthusiastic audiences. PIERRE GRINGOIRE (1475–1538: best known for Victor Hugo's anachronistic and fanciful portrait of him in *Notre Dame de Paris*) was a writer of considerable talent, whose *Vie de Saint Louis* (*c.* 1507) is a still readable dramatization in several 'days' of major episodes in the king's life, while his *Moralité* (1512) satirizing Julius II shows great verve. In the more spectacular mystery plays the scenic and mechanical effects were often as important as the text, as revivals have shown in recent years. The brothers Arnoul and Simon Greban, masters of the genre in the fifteenth century, wrote an *Actes des Apôtres*, extending over thirty-five days, which was performed until as late as 1541 in Paris; but such productions were popular, for the people, and as such despised by humanists. In the event it was the social, rather than literary, significance of these works that decided their fate, for with temperatures mounting in the religious controversies, theatrical audiences could too easily degenerate into riotous assemblies; and on 17 November 1548 the Paris Parlement forbade any further performance of mysteries by the Confrérie de la Passion (who held the monopoly), an order later followed in most large towns. Miracle plays, which were in any case less flourishing, soon petered out too, and only the morality survived in one form or another.

The traditional popular theatre would no doubt have changed considerably as, for instance, it did in England, to meet changing tastes, but this edict abruptly created something of a theatrical vacuum.

Unlike the situation in Italy, there were no courtly or other patrons to give a strong lead; as late as 1547 Marguerite de Navarre was writing and producing so-called *comédies*, one, for example, on the death of her brother, François I; but despite their great literary interest these are dramatized dialogues in the morality tradition rather than plays. Early in the century Latin translations of Euripides and Sophocles, by Erasmus among others, had aroused interest in humanist circles, and the general desire to revive antique culture prompted numerous productions of Latin plays, including one by Marc-Antoine Muret (1526–85) on *Julius Caesar* and another very popular one by the expatriate Scot George Buchanan (1506–82) on *Jephthes*. In the scholarly context of such productions, usually in schools and universities, the audience was preselected and almost bound to be favourable, but in terms of theatrical (as distinct from rhetorical) technique little or nothing was achieved. At the same time, Italian influence was less than might have been expected. Mellin de Saint-Gellais adapted Trissino's *Sofonisba* for performance at Court in 1556, and there must have been other isolated performances, as well as publications, but apparently Catherine de' Medici did not encourage any more tragic experiments.

At all events, half the century was past before the first tragedy in the vernacular was performed in France. Following du Bellay's appeal in his *Defense et Illustration* (1549) to practise all the Classical genres, including tragedy and comedy, in order to enhance the dignity of French language and culture, ETIENNE JODELLE (1532–73), a member of the Pléiade, wrote *Cléopâtre Captive*. He staged it, in the presence of Henri II, at the Hôtel de Reims, town house of the Cardinal of Lorraine, in late 1552 or 1553, and then, to the rapturous applause of senior and junior members of the University, at the Collège de Boncourt a few weeks later. This work by a lad of twenty created such a stir that its conspicuous defects must be set against its historical significance. Henceforth French tragedy *existed*, and the only problem was how to improve it.

The play has five acts, in alexandrines, punctuated with choruses in lyric metre, dozens of *sententiae*, every rhetorical cliché imaginable, virtually no action, and yet, bad as it is, undeniably belongs to the tragic genre. In Act I Antony's ghost soliloquizes at length, Cleopatra recounts her dream to her attendants and makes it clear that she is determined to follow him; in Act II Octavius and Agrippa discuss the ways of fortune and the impending ceremonial triumph; in Act III Cleopatra appeals to Octavius for mercy, wins the life of her children and ends with a tirade against the unmoved Octavius; in Act IV she rages again at the prospect of being humiliated in the triumph and then goes to Antony's tomb, where she says she will die; Act V is occupied with a recital of her death, the whole interspersed with observations from the chorus on grief, pride, reversals of fortune and the like. Jodelle had made the point: tragedy was to be, like the rest of the Pléiade's works, accessible only to a cultured élite, and was to be dignified, moralizing and regular in form. In print *sententiae* were typographically distinguished lest they be overlooked. Inevitably the result constituted an exercise in rhetoric, not theatre, and the fact that most such plays were acted by scholars and students did nothing to raise professional standards.

A very much better exercise of the same kind is the *César* of JACQUES GRÉVIN (1538–70), performed in Paris at the Collège de Beauvais in 1561. Grévin acknowledged his debt to Muret's Latin play, but surpassed his model, and composed a quite convincing tragedy on the familiar theme. Long political discussions by Caesar, and by Brutus and his accomplices, are balanced by more intimate speeches by Calpurnia, there is a genuine moment of crisis, when Caesar nearly heeds her appeal before eventually going to meet his death in the Senate, and the play ends on a climax, with Antony's impassioned appeal for vengeance. The chorus, of Roman soldiers, is duly sententious, the style sometimes descends into bathos, as in Act IV, when the messenger rushes in to break the fatal news to Calpurnia, who cries, 'Hè! nourrice il est mort,' and faints, but Grévin has much more sense of theatre than Jodelle.

Meanwhile a parallel, but distinct, tradition had been inaugurated in 1550 in Lausanne, where the Professor of Greek, THÉODORE DE BÈZE (1519–1605), Calvin's deputy and successor, wrote a play for his pupils on the biblical theme of *Abraham sacrifiant*. His aim is explicitly didactic, his chorus of shepherds sing the divine praises, and an epilogue condemns those who put reason above faith. In his preface he regrets that French scholars do not turn their talents to glorifying God instead of indulging their fancy; and, unlike those (for example, the Pléiade) who 'thinking to enrich our tongue, dress it up in Greek or

Roman style', he prefers to use language which is not 'too remote from ordinary speech'. In fact he does not divide his work into acts, nor use alexandrines, and in this recalls mysteries of the older pattern, but his Classical training is reflected in his characterization of Abraham. His Satan is dressed as a monk, and with charming anachronism is used to pillory monastic vices: his Abraham, Isaac and Sarah show perfect faith and obedience; but despite the polemic and didactic content, Bèze achieves some outstanding effects, notably in a very touching scene between father and son, which even impresses Satan. He remains true to his declared aims, but he had enough sense of style and culture to select the human and psychological details most appropriate to a dramatic effect.

The propaganda value of biblical plays was obvious, but to succeed tragedy had to be regular. Even the Protestant JEAN DE LA TAILLE (1540–1608) criticized Bèze in his *De l'Art de la tragédie* (1572) for choosing a theme unproductive of true tragic emotion and for failing to follow Classical form. For La Taille, tragedy should properly deal only with 'piteuses ruines des grands seigneurs, que des inconstances de Fortune' ('piteous downfall of the great, with reversals of fortune'); its sole intention should be to move, and to this end all irrelevant matter should be suppressed. He requires five acts, a chorus and what came to be called the three unities – of time, place and action. Perhaps most interesting is his wish that real tragedy (and comedy) could be put on, properly acted, in a theatre which he would like to design, for it is clear that for all his appeals to Aristotle and Horace, what animates him is desire for living theatre. His own *Saül le Furieux* (written *c.* 1562, published 1572) is a remarkable, rather uneven play. Like its indifferent sequel, *La Famine ou les Gabéonites* (modelled on the *Troades*), *Saül* shows Senecan influence in its emphasis on rhetoric and horror, but what makes the play stand out is the treatment of the very complex psychology of its eponymous hero. We see him in the first act, already intermittently deranged, setting upon his sons, consulting the witch of Endor in Act III, dying with Jonathan in Act IV, and mourned by his successor, David, in Act V. War with the Philistines is the sombre background to Saul's mental torment, but La Taille has most skilfully handled external action so that it never distracts attention from the spiritual and inner drama of Saul, one of the elect who has incurred

God's wrath. There is, inevitably, moralizing, but none of the theological discourse which La Taille had condemned in Bèze and others. All the elements of the tragedy are to be found in the Bible, it is true, but *Saül* offers the best character study of the century, and is only marred by clumsy and uninspired poetry.

The outstanding playwright of the century is undoubtedly ROBERT GARNIER (1545–90), whose seven tragedies and one tragicomedy demonstrate progressive mastery of the genre. Only three of his plays are actually taken from Senecan themes, but Garnier may not unfairly be described as a Senecan dramatist. Largely because Greek was just too difficult for any but experts, but also because Seneca gratified the century's insatiable appetite for moralizing, and as a further attraction was commonly believed to have died a Christian, he was the preferred model for French Renaissance tragedy. From him they got plenty of *sententiae*, his gruesome horrors and inflated rhetoric matched rather than inspired their own taste, and his themes included the best known Greek subjects. Unfortunately, and this they do not seem to have known, he was not writing for a live theatre, but 'closet-dramas' for private play-readings, and was thus the worst model they could have chosen in their attempt to replace rejected popular genres with something of unimpeachably Classical ante-cedents. True, from 1562 onwards the present horrors of civil war overshadowed purely literary considerations, and like many others Garnier explicitly states in his prefaces that his tragedies are meant to be relevant to the anguished state of France. *Porcie* (1568), *Cornélie* (1574), and *Marc-Antoine* (1578) all deal with various phases of Roman civil strife; *Hippolyte* (1573), *La Troade* (1579) and *Antigone* (1580) all have Greek subjects used by Seneca. In almost every case major political questions are discussed at length, such as the nature of monarchy and justice, the evil of war, civil or foreign, or the rights of the individual. *Hippolyte* deserves study as a distant anticipation of Racine's *Phèdre*, and is by no means a slavish imitation of Seneca. All the plays contain good speeches and scenes, but none is much more than competent.

His last two plays are different. *Les Juives* (1583), the only biblical tragedy by this Catholic magistrate, admirably conveys the deep emotions roused in both parties by a Bible in which they passionately believed. It deals with Nebuchadnezzar's treatment of the Jews after Zedekiah's (Sédécie) disobedience. The prophet (Jeremiah) and chorus fill up the whole first act with foreboding and lamentation; Act II begins with a Tamburlaine-like swagger from Nebuchadnezzar (Nabuchodonosor) which later became almost proverbial: 'Pareil aux dieux je marche. . . . Nul ne se parangonne à ma grandeur royale' ('I walk the equal of the gods. . . . None can rival my royal greatness'), and goes on with a topical discussion on the powers and duties of kingship, between the vindictive tyrant and his more moderate adviser. This long act continues with alternating laments between Amital, mother of Sédécie, and the chorus of Jewish women, until the Queen of Babylon appears on the scene, listens to Amital's pleas for mercy and promises to intercede with her husband if she can. In Act III she does her best, but Nebuchadnezzar is set on revenge ('Qui n'est cruel n'est digne de royauté' – 'Only the cruel are worthy of a crown'), but silences her by promising to spare Sédécie's life. Amital and her followers then come in to make their own supplications, and are eventually given the same promise, in sinisterly ambiguous terms. Act IV at last confronts Sédécie with his captor, and he is dragged off after a stormy interview, defying him to do his worst, then a scene full of tragic irony shows the Jews receiving the order to hand over all the royal children as hostages for their father. The mothers' long and affecting farewells increase the tension, broken only in the last act, when the prophet reappears to describe the hideous vengeance of their captor: Sédécie has been forced to see all the children slaughtered before having his own eyes put out. The final scene shows the blinded Sédécie confessing that he has sinned, but imploring God's mercy on his people, and closes with the prophet's reassuring promise of salvation and ultimate redemption through Christ.

The construction of the play is not very skilful, but the confrontation scenes, particularly those in which the aged Amital figures, are powerful and dramatic. Ten years after Saint Bartholomew the bloodthirsty tyrant and the consequences of disobedience were all too topical, and the historical context illuminates the play. Most critics agree that *Saül* and *Les Juives* are the best tragedies of the century, and it is no accident that the strongest emotion in each case is roused by a biblical theme of contemporary significance rather than by some Classical tale of more remote misfortunes.

Garnier's other great success was *Bradamante* (1582), one of the first tragicomedies, and a good one. Taken from the *Furioso* (canto 43 ff.) it tells of the winning of Bradamante by Roger, whose true identity is only established at the end of the play, just as an embassy comes to offer him the crown of Bulgaria, thus making him eligible in the eyes of the bride's insufferably snobbish parents. These two, Aymon and Beatrice, come near to supplying comic relief, and the old man's testy insistence on family honour in Act II contrasts incongruously with the imperial dignity maintained throughout by Charlemagne. Here, as in *Les Juives*, Garnier takes obvious pleasure in a certain ranting excess, and the play's success with audiences in the next century shows how well he had come to gauge public reaction.

After Garnier the last tragic writer of note before 1600 is ANTOINE DE MONTCHRESTIEN (1575–1621). After *Sophonisbe* (1595) he published four more tragedies in 1601, presumably written before the end of the century. One of these, *L'Escossoise*, deserves mention for it deals with the execution of Mary Queen of Scots (1587), brings in the characters of both Mary and Elizabeth, and is the best example of an indeterminate number of plays drawn from recent, rather than biblical or antique sources. There is very little action, the tone is elegiac rather than dramatic, but the play stands comparison with those discussed above. For the rest, the vogue after Garnier was more and more for irregular tragedy, with sundry atrocities, severed limbs, rape and the rest, and in the generation before Corneille the theatre became lively at the expense of literary merit; it also, of course, became popular again.

COMEDY

It is not surprising that comedy lagged far behind tragedy in quality; Corneille claimed, with some justification, to have created (with *Mélite*, 1629) a comedy that did not depend on ridiculous characters. Already in 1561 JACQUES GRÉVIN (1538–70) introduces his comedy *Les Esbahis* with a critical preface, appealing to the authority of Plautus and Terence for his own contribution to the comedy of manners. This five-act comedy in verse concerns the amorous intrigues of old Josse, supposedly a widower, who hopes to marry

Magdalène, daughter of his elderly friend Gérard; but she is loved by a young lawyer. With the aid of crafty servants, a cunning bawd and a comic Italian, Panthaleone (given to lengthy quotations from the *Furioso*), the action moves to its inevitable happy ending. Josse's wife turns up, after several years of disreputable grass-widowhood, and the young people are free to marry. This pattern is almost constant in comedies of the period; old men are absurd, and deceived, young people are amorous and succeed, servants are wily, bawds passably obscene and so on. Jean de La Taille also wrote a comedy, *Les Corrivaux* (1574), on very similar lines, probably the first to be written in prose. The most prolific writer of comedies was PIERRE DE LARIVEY (1540–1612), a canon of Troyes, of Italian extraction, who published six comedies in 1579 and three more (written much earlier) in 1611. As Larivey himself explains in his prefaces, these are close adaptations in prose, rather than translations, of Italian comedies, mostly by secondary authors, and cannot properly be regarded as a contribution to French comedy. Finally Adrien Turnèbe (1538–81) in his prose comedy *Les Contens* (published 1584) seems to have gone to the *Celestina* for the model of his bawd Françoise, and is another who portrays amorous affairs in a realistic way. Dealing as it did with everyday life and with less exalted classes than tragedy, comedy relied for its appeal more on plot and witty, often obscene, dialogue than on character of any deeper literary value. As social and linguistic documents Renaissance comedies cannot be disregarded, but they are at best minor literature. It should be added that the great popularity of Italian comedians at the end of the period, with their use of mime, scarcely encouraged indigenous production.

THREE

Spain

IF liturgy was important among the origins of the secular drama, liturgical drama itself remained important in Spain in the sixteenth and seventeenth centuries. After the Council of Trent and the reformed breviary of 1568 it was particularly associated with the feast of Corpus Christi, for which special dramatic pieces, or *autos sacramentales*, were composed in allegorical form on religious subjects bearing some more and some less closely on the Blessed Sacrament, especially honoured on that day. It became usual for *autos* to be performed on a platform on either side of which was placed a cart bearing scenery and apparatus. The carts would move from place to place, broadly along the route of the day's procession; performances would be given to the civic authorities as well as the people at large. It was in Seville and Madrid, where three or four *autos* were performed each year, that this type of drama was particularly cultivated, especially from the time of the appearance of professional actors and the financing of these performances by the municipal authorities. After Corpus Christi the *autos* could also be produced commercially.

In technique they were indebted to the tradition of pageant and spectacle that spread into the south and Castile from Catalonia and the Levant. Public events were often marked by festivities involving triumphal arches, cars bearing richly arrayed allegorical figures or tableaux, and all manner of spectacle. In 1571 Anne of Austria, on her way to marry Philip II, was welcomed at Burgos with a sea-battle played out by ships on wheels in the city square, the whole performance being based on parts of *Amadís de Gaula*. Tournaments were themselves frequently turned into spectacular enactments of episodes from romances of chivalry.

There was a learned, largely Latin theatre. In the Jesuit colleges religious plays were presented by the pupils, often with impressive display and effects, for the general edification, while in the universities students gave regular performances of plays by Terence and Plautus (often as required by statute) and also of plays written more or less in imitation of these. In the 1520s Pérez de Oliva, later Rector of Salamanca University, made what were among the earliest vernacular versions of the *Electra* of Sophocles and the *Hecuba* of Euripides.

Court theatre developed only in the time of Philip III. A century before the latter's accession, JUAN DEL ENCINA (1468–*c.* 1529) had written eclogues to be performed in the houses of great families, as perhaps the dialogue section in the middle of Garcilaso's *Second Eclogue* was intended to be performed. BARTOLOMÉ DE TORRES NAHARRO (*c.* 1480–1530), six of whose nine plays were published in 1517, wrote in Italy for a similar audience. His *Comedia Tinellaria* was played in the presence of Pope Leo X. In Spain private perform-ances were given by LOPE DE RUEDA (*c.* 1510–65). But Rueda, who wrote plays, acted and ran his own troupe, mostly put on public performances, not only of *autos* but also of secular plays, performed in town squares or the yards of inns. Himself one of the first profes-sional actors in Spain, he travelled about the country with his players for perhaps twenty-five years down to 1565 and did more than anyone to create a professional drama in Spain, modest and makeshift though his own productions were. Remembered now for his *pasos*, or one-act comic pieces involving peasants, servants, thieves and simpletons, he also wrote plays based on the contemporary Italian comedy. Like JUAN DE TIMONEDA (d. 1583) and others, he was glad to take over plots from both the Italian plays and the *novelle* of such people as Bandello, mixing the serious and the comic. Italian troupes of actors travelled about Spain from 1548 onwards, when one such presented Ariosto's *I Suppositi* at the marriage of the Infanta María at Valladolid. Italian actors had much to do with developments in the organization of Spanish theatrical performances. It was in the 1570s that theatres were established in various cities. These were *corrales*, or unroofed yards with a platform at one end, equipped at least with trapdoors and a rear curtain, whose importance was not only that it gave actors a place in which to don or change costumes and provided, at either side of it, two entrances on to the stage, but also that it could be thrown aside and provide the 'discoveries' or dramatic disclosures that were so prominent in the *comedia*. A gallery above the stage was often used for such things as upper-window or siege scenes. Costume was colourful. What were long to be Madrid's only two theatres were opened in 1579 and 1582, at about which time Lope de Vega began to write for the stage. By 1585 Madrid had become the centre of important dramatic writing. While theologians and moralists were not lacking who expressed unease or worse regarding theatrical performances and women actresses, local municipalities were generally well disposed, remembering that actors were needed for the *autos* at Corpus Christi, which were matters of great civic pride. Moreover, the *corrales* were often set up and managed – as were those in Madrid – by brotherhoods who sought to raise money for the hospitals they ran. Audiences included the clergy as well as the rest of society, who occupied different places in or around the *corral* according to wealth, social position and sex.

The main interest of the early Spanish drama attaches now to those of its aspects in which one can see similarities or approaches to what the *comedia* was to become as developed by Lope, whose important plays date from about 1610 onwards. Already in Torres Naharro one finds a mixing of the tragic and the comic. While watching the pains and trials suffered by lovers before finally finding happiness, we also meet entertaining and irreverent servants. There is an elementary comic sub-plot in the *Comedia Himenea*, which, moreover, rests largely on the notion of family honour. Already one reads that 'for the sake of reputation life is well lost' – which here means 'taken'. The theme is found again in plays of JUAN DE LA CUEVA (*c.* 1550–*c.* 1610), fourteen of which were performed in Seville between 1579 and 1581. Even amidst his Senecan melodrama one finds crudely comic episodes provided by servants. Torres Naharro had devoted whole plays to presenting pictures of society at its lower levels: Spanish soldiers in Italy (in his *Comedia Soldadesca*) and life below stairs (in his *Comedia Tinellaria*). Cueva was the first to make plays out of episodes of Spanish national history or legend rendered famous by ballads – as in his *Siete Infantes de Lara*. As Juan de Valdés, in Naples, noted, Torres Naharro was good at writing dialogue for his humbler characters – lively, vivid, colloquial, with much use of proverbs and word-play. Cueva was fond of the grand, orotund, Latinate manner. Nevertheless, he also attempted to match the tone and mood of speech to situation by employing various verse forms in a single work. Both Torres Naharro and Cueva were largely unconcerned with the dramatic unities; they were also generally unsuccessful in giving their plays effective pattern and coherence of structure. Torres Naharro's plays have five acts; Cueva's have four. Lope began by writing four-act plays but soon took over the three-act scheme, which was to become the standard form of the *comedia*. The latter he established largely by bringing together and ordering many of the elements already mentioned. In his plays different levels of society are presented; manner and form of speech are adapted to the person speaking and the matter spoken of; the comic and the tragic are mixed in plays whose most frequent themes, perhaps, are honour and social order; their most immediate emphasis is on action (each act is given to a single day) and movement, in the presentation of a situation often set in Spanish history and of a kind to appeal to (and not offend) a socially mixed audience. (It might be added that Torres Naharro's plays, not performed in Spain but several times printed there, were placed on the 1559 Index, probably less for their bawdy element than for the freedom with which they treat religion and its forms.)

FOUR

Germany

IT would have been surprising if the Reformers with their instinct for propaganda had failed to realize the potentialities of the drama as a means of spreading Evangelical doctrine, and German sixteenth-century drama does in fact consist largely of didactic Protestant plays. Yet, partly because of the distrust of popular assemblies, relatively little use was made of the polemical drama in Germany proper until long after Protestantism was already established: in the early years of the Reformation controversialists tended for preference to use the dialogue and the tract. In Switzerland, by contrast, perhaps because of the inherently more democratic atmosphere, popular drama was very early applied to polemical purposes.

The most remarkable of the Swiss dramatists was the Bernese painter-poet, NIKLAUS MANUEL (1484–1530). His slightly older compatriot, Pamphilius Gengenbach, had developed the traditional *Fastnachtspiel* or Shrovetide farce (cf. p. 509) in the direction of serious moral satire and religious polemicism, and Manuel's earliest polemical *Fastnachtspiel*, *Vom Bapst und siner Priesterschaft* (*About the Pope and his Priesthood*, 1523) draws heavily in its opening scene on Gengenbach's *Die Totenfresser* (*The Eaters of the Dead*, c. 1521), which had with crude logic attacked the clergy as necrophagous, since the layman's death was a source of income. Manuel's play, in which the old review technique is still strong, presents us with a series of seven disconnected scenes: the Pope and cardinals feast on dead bodies in the style of Gengenbach's play; the Pope rejects an appeal for help from the beleaguered garrison of Rhodes – he is too busy fighting the Emperor to fight the Turk; peasants tell of the lies of indulgence-sellers; the Swiss guard express their satisfaction that the Pope finds them plenty of employment, and so on. The aim of these tableaux was clearly not to convince the spectator by the enactment of a *drama*, but rather to impress by what was said and revealed in the context of a spectacle: the huge and richly varied cast with its fifty speaking parts and over one hundred silent ones and the careful staging – in unprecedented fashion Manuel writes detailed stage directions – cannot have failed to impress the good burghers of Bern in the quickening of religious polemicism with a visual content similar to that which throughout the Middle Ages had given the Passion and Easter plays their appeal.

Manuel's second polemical play, *Von Bapsts und Christi Gegensatz* (*On the Antithesis of the Pope and Christ*, 1523), is equally derivative and static and makes a similar visual appeal. It is a translation into dramatic terms of the familiar theme, which derives via the Hussites from Wyclif, of the antithesis between Christ and his Vicar. In the Reformation period this had commonly been expressed pictorially – as we find it in the *Passional Christi und Antichristi* of Cranach, Melanchthon and Luther (1521) – in terms of the poverty-stricken Christ on his donkey and the richly clad Pope on his horse, Christ accompanied by barefoot disciples, the Pope by well-shod cardinals. Manuel's play consists simply of the representation of the two processions and a dialogue between two peasants, who comment on the contrast thus represented.

But if in his earliest works it is the painter's interest in visual effects which predominates, Manuel's most celebrated polemical *Fastnachtspiel*, *Der Aplasskremer* (*The Indulgence-seller*, 1525), is entirely dramatic. The action – the torture and confession of an indulgence-seller by peasants from whom he had extorted money on a previous visit to their village – is made to speak for itself. Gone are the commentators of tradition and the static descriptive element of the earlier plays; here one action begets another, one peasant's outrage naturally evoking a response in his fellow. The crux of the whole play – the confession of the rascally indulgence-seller with its shocking recital of forged relics, seduced peasant women and cynical exploitation of naïve faith, and its final admission that the grace of God is a freely bestowed gift which can be earned by neither works nor gifts of money – is extracted from him by a process of slow, repeated interrogation rather than being an artificial self-condemnation in the standard fashion of the times.

By contrast with Manuel's extremely popular style, the greatest polemical drama produced by German Lutheranism, THOMAS NAOGEORG's *Pammachius* (1538), is unmistakably directed to a learned audience. Naogeorg (i.e. Thomas Kirchmair, 1511–63), an Evangelical preacher whose obstinately individualistic outlook in an age of narrow orthodoxies caused him endless difficulties, was motivated primarily by an almost pathological hatred of the papacy. His monumental Latin polemic sets out to present within the context of a realistic political drama a symbolical account of the papacy's betrayal of Christ and is a curious blend of elements taken from Greek and Latin drama and popular German tradition in which historical fact and caricature, allegory and realism, satire and tragedy are united. In four lengthy acts and an epilogue by way of a fifth we are shown how Pammachius, the archetypal Pope, and his rascally adviser, Porphyrius, throw in their lot with Satan in exchange for worldly power, reduce the Emperor, Julian, to vassalage and impose on Christendom the monstrous servitude of Roman abuses: seven sacraments, communion in one kind only, indulgence, and so on. But the seeming victory of evil is only part of God's plan for the salvation of the elect; Satan and his agents are no more than means by which true believers can be separated from the rest of the community and, just when Pammachius is at the height of his power, in distant Saxony a certain Theophilus (Luther) is inspired by Christ to challenge the papal tyranny, which will, however, as the epilogue tells us, never vanish completely until the Day of Judgement – which cannot now be far off.

When told thus in bare outline the plot seems clumsily contrived and painfully obvious in its indebtedness to the Antichrist legend and in its reckless anachronistic juxtaposition of the Constantine donation, the quarrels of papacy and Empire and the outbreak of the Reformation. In fact, however, Naogeorg has written a play which attains a dramatic effectiveness rarely paralleled in the sixteenth century in its carefully engineered structure, its convincing motivation, its skilful use of dialogue and the grandeur of its conception. The argumentation by which Pammachius comes to his decision to abandon God and serve Satan and the central political drama in the conflict of Pammachius and Julian, with the latter's incredulity and proud defiance slowly worn down by the religious pressures Pammachius is able to bring to bear, are entirely convincing – as is Pammachius's pact with the devil or even the anachronistic introduction of Luther. This latter allegory, like the introduction of figures such as Veritas and Parrhesia, or Christ and the Apostles, who at times give an almost Lucianic air to the proceedings, is not at all disturbing. Only the utilization of Gengenbach's *Totenfresser* motif in Pammachius's feast in Act IV strikes a discordant note in this essentially classicizing play, whose popularity is testified by three editions and four translations in almost as many years and the fact that as far away as Cambridge the students of Christ's College gave it a public performance in 1545.

Compared with the polemicism of Manuel or Naogeorg and their lesser and forgotten associates, the treatment by BURKHARD WALDIS (*c.* 1490–1556) of the story of the Prodigal Son in his Low German *Fastnachtspiel*, *De parabel vam verlorn Szohn* (*The Parable of the Lost Son*, 1527) sets a more strictly didactic tone, which was to be characteristic for the mass of German sixteenth-century drama. The intention here is not to castigate and denigrate the Roman Church and its less reputable representatives, but to inculcate in the audience the central Lutheran doctrine of Justification by Faith and provide living proof that God saves us, as Waldis puts it, 'Alleyn dorch gnade vnd blote gunst, Idt helpt keyn arbeyt, werk offt kunst' ('Only through grace and simple favour, No work or deed or skill is of any help'). This doctrine was, of course, ideally exemplified in the story of the Prodigal. The Prodigal returned home not trusting in his own non-existent merits, but relying entirely on the love and mercy of his father, and was welcomed by the latter; the self-righteous brother, by contrast, claimed to have merited his father's esteem by his exemplary behaviour and was rebuked accordingly, and Waldis brings out the Lutheran meaning of the parable with unmistakable clarity in the commentaries he appends to both of the play's two acts. Waldis's play is as unconvincing as its biblical source in its suggestion that the elder brother's sense of grievance is entirely unjustified, but in other respects it represents a remarkable advance in the treatment of a biblical subject and is far from being a simple rendering of the Gospel story into dialogue form equipped with a Lutheran gloss. The recriminations between the brothers and between the father and his elder son show for their time impressive suppleness in the handling of dialogue, and the central scene in the brothel is effectively realized. The ideological element does, however, finally obtrude in rather disturbing fashion when, not content with his two theological commentaries, Waldis makes the father answer the elder son's complaints with the voice of God and talk about his eternal grace and the bread of heaven. Given this translation of the play into universal allegory, however, the final contrast between the elder son as a strict monk, still intent on meriting salvation by works, and the repentant brothel-keeper, who had formerly cheated the Prodigal and now comes to God trusting solely in God's grace, is highly effective and rounds the play off neatly.

Waldis described his drama as a *Fastnachtspiel*, and it was first produced in Riga in February 1527, but there is clearly little similarity between it and the traditional Shrovetide play – even as developed by Gengenbach and Manuel or later by Sachs. Waldis's intention, as stated in the prologue, is to provide a serious and edifying alternative to Terence and Plautus, and he is clearly using the term *Fastnachtspiel* simply in the sense of 'comedy', and a comedy of some literary aspirations at that. The unpretentious nature of the language, the use of four-stressed doggerel and the inclusion of proverbs indicate Waldis's nearness to popular tradition, but perhaps even more striking and significant is the fact that this is a serious play of didactic intent produced in a church by a company which included schoolboys. Further, for the first time in the history of German literature a play was divided into acts and scenes. Taken together with the biblical subject matter, these factors are sufficient to entitle the play to be regarded not so much as a *Fastnachtspiel*, but as a precursor of the vernacular school drama.

The humanistic school drama was conceived less as *drama* than as a pedagogic aid in the teaching of elegant Latin and as a means of developing self-confidence, public speaking and a courtly bearing in the schoolboy actors – hence the stipulation in the statutes of many a grammar school that plays be produced once or twice a year as a sort of practical extension of the syllabus. Often enough the schools were content simply to produce plays by Terence or Plautus, and inevitably the schoolmasters who wrote original plays tended to see their function as being an essentially imitative one – 'ut apte possit verba et phrasin veterum auctorum imitari', as Nikodemus Frischlin, the foremost neo-Latin dramatist of the century, put it. Naturally they imported into their plays the Classical division into five acts, the chorus and often a prologue and epilogue, and sought to represent an elevated theme in a dignified manner. In spite of their rather esoteric appeal, the plays, as instruments of education, naturally shared the common sixteenth-century tendency to satire and biblically oriented didacticism: Reuchlin's *Henno* (1497) is the first neo-Latin drama to be written for performance by scholars and seems to augur well for the establishment of a tradition of lively comedy. It treats the widespread anecdote, best known from its appearance in the medieval French farce, *Maître Pathelin*, of the dishonest advocate who taught his client to make meaningless noises before the court, in order to convince the judge of his unfitness to plead, only to find that the client subsequently used the same technique against him when he tried to prosecute his client for the fee the latter refused to pay. But it was not Reuchlin's comedy of the 'cheater cheated' which provided neo-Latin school dramatists with a model, but Wilhelm Gnaphaeus's *Acolastus* (1529), on the theme of the Prodigal Son, which applied classicizing techniques to biblical subject matter in a way which was to become normative in the following years. The limited appeal of the Latin drama was widened, first by providing German synopses of the action, then by following each act with a German translation, and finally by producing plays entirely in German.

For a variety of reasons the school drama tended to be largely a Protestant affair: the Protestant disregard for sacred legends – Luther described them as 'Lügende' ('liars') – left a gap which urgently needed to be filled; the *Fastnachtspiel* was commonly felt to be a rather improper and 'Catholic' genre and school statutes often prescribed the performance of a play at Shrovetide in an obvious attempt to supplant the *Fastnachtspiel*; Luther himself had in his preface to the Books of Judith and Tobit (1534) specifically recommended the dramatization of sacred history and this naturally tended to encourage his co-religionists (and discourage his opponents) to build on foundations already well and truly laid and establish a distinct Protestant tradition.

Amongst the host of patient, dedicated and often rather pedestrian schoolmasters who, year in year out, varied their productions of Plautus and Terence with dramatized accounts of the fortunes of ʃoseph, Tobias, Ruth, Rebecca, etcetera, NIKODEMUS FRISCHLIN (1547–90) an irascible and ill-starred professor of poetry and history in Tübingen, stands out as a man of wider interests and sovereign wit.

In the words of the statutes of the Speyer grammar school of 1594, which recommended that his plays or those of the Classical dramatists be produced annually, 'though he did not equal the ancients Frischlin came nearer to them than anyone of the present age.'

Altogether the 'German Aristophanes', as he was known to contemporaries – partly because of his sardonic temperament, partly because he translated five of Aristophanes' comedies into Latin – completed some twelve dramas, which exhibit a considerable range of modes and themes. The Aristophanic satire *Priscianus vapulans* (1579) pillories the greed and ignorance of academics and describes the horse-cure administered to the medieval grammarian Priscianus in order to cleanse him of his impure Latin. *Phasma* (1580), which celebrates Luther and his local representative, Dr Brenz, and consigns Zwingli, Karlstadt and the whole Council of Trent to hell, represents an excursion into confessional polemicism, while *Rebecca* (1576) and *Susanna* (1577) treat stock themes of school drama. *Hildegardis magna* (1579), a Genoveva theme (the pure woman accused of adultery and banished but eventually vindicated after years in the wilderness) set at the time of Charlemagne, and the Germany comedy, *Frau Wendelgart* (1579), a treatment of a tenth-century *Heimkehrer-motif*, both draw on native German tradition. Nor does Frischlin neglect the concern which German humanists from Wimpheling onwards had shown for the honour of their fatherland: Caesar and Cicero in *Julius redivivus* (1585) are amazed at the literary elegance (as represented by Eobanus Hessus and other neo-Latin poets) and the technical skills (as represented by gunpowder and the printing press) of the Germans, and while the author does not omit the traditional castigation of the insobriety of the Germans, the latter are favourably contrasted with their western and southern neighbours in the shape of a Savoyard merchant and an Italian chimneysweeper.

As Scherer remarked, Frischlin's *œuvre* thus subsumes the threefold struggle of the German sixteenth century to establish good Latin, the true faith and German excellence. But while these serious topics are clearly important for him, Frischlin is by nature neither a moralist nor a propagandist: the often quoted comparison of him to Hutten is misleading and he is probably more akin to Heine than to any of his close contemporaries. The dominant element in his make-up is an Aristophanic love of the ludicrous and the burlesque and Frischlin is at his best where this element is given fullest expression. Characteristically, his tragedies are his weakest works: *Dido* and *Venus* are little more than dialogue versions of *Aeneid*, I and IV, divided into acts and provided with a chorus, and were probably intended, like *Helvetiogermani*, which does the same for *De bello gallico*, I, as memory exercises for Frischlin's pupils. Even in the comedies, although like all writers of school drama Frischlin makes his plays a vehicle for ideas and moral lessons, it is not on the ideological content – the purity of Christian marriage, the excellence of the Germans and so on – that he lavishes his greatest care, but on the scurrilous minor figures of the sub-plots. The latter are often remote from the main action ; the Ismael sub-plot in *Rebecca* has no real connection with Eleazar's wooing of the heroine, any more than the somewhat immodest actions of the coward Thrasimachus and Thusnelda meretrix have anything to do with Caesar's campaigns in *Helvetiogermani*. But in every case, in spite of the indebtedness to Terence and Plautus – parasites, braggarts and rascally servants abound – it is in these minor figures, the tramps and beggars in *Frau Wendelgart*, Talandus and his parasite in *Hildegardis*, the Savoyard merchant in *Julius* or the superbly realized loud-mouthed, peasant-beating, gluttonous *Junker* Ismael in *Rebecca*, that the true dramatic interest lies. From a formal point of view, this leads to an inversion of priorities, of course; all too often one simply tolerates the main action for the sake of the comic interludes with their spivs, whores and cheats – larger than life perhaps, but thoroughly alive and amusing. Serious though this fault may be – and it is one of which even Shakespeare could be guilty – it is thanks to it rather than to the rhetorical skills, linguistic jokes, puns and stock situations of the main plots that Frischlin's comedies so notably transcend those of his contemporaries.

By comparison with Frischlin, GEORG ROLLENHAGEN (1542–1609) Rector of the Magdeburg gymnasium and one of the best known exponents of German school drama, is a rather heavy-handed pedant. As in his *Froschmeuseler* (cf. p. 508), the pedagogic intention conditions everything he writes and the didacticism of his three biblical plays, *Abraham* (1569), *Tobias* (1576) and *Von dem reichen Manne und armen Lazaro* (*About the rich man and poor Lazarus*, 1590) is only rarely relieved by the lighter touches which occasionally

give his mock epic considerable charm. Like so many school dramatists Rollenhagen is not really a creative writer: in the accepted
fashion of the times he incorporates whole scenes from earlier dramas
into his own productions, although with greater honesty than many
a more famous writer acknowledging his *honestum furtum* in the
preface. Thus his *Abraham* is heavily indebted to Hieronymus
Ziegler's *Immolatio Isaaci* of 1544, *Tobias* is based on Thomas Brun-
ner's *Historia von dem fromen und Gottsfürchtigen Tobia* (1569), while
Von dem reichen Manne takes over some twenty scenes from Joachim
Lonemann's tragedy on the same subject (1564) – which Lonemann
had, however, similarly borrowed from Georg Macropedius'
Lazarus mendicus of 1541!

The 'structural alterations' by which Rollenhagen does in fact
considerably modify the character of these plays consist mainly in
expanding the relatively modest models in order to accommodate
new roles – no less than seventy-five in *Von dem reichen Manne*: a
school with 1,600 pupils needs plays with a big cast and his *Abraham*
has some fifty parts to offer, while the later plays double this figure.
Concomitant with the preference for large casts – and a surprising
capacity to handle the logistic problems involved without creating
chaos on the stage! – is a love of spectacle which could almost be
described as baroque: the most famous example is the ornate funeral
procession of his Dives (Porphyrius) in *Vom dem reichen Manne*, but the
marriage celebrations in *Tobias* with their songs and dances, and even
the donkey and sheep in *Abraham*, point in the same direction.

In the main Rollenhagen's characterization is unconvincing and
stiff: his Lazarus is an impossible masochist who is duly grateful
for his misfortunes and with whom one feels little sympathy, while
Porphyrius and Tobias are little more than conventional stereotypes.
Only the minor characters, the poor widow, the braggart soldiers,
or the doctors in *Vom dem reichen Manne* or the gossiping maids and
the rather endearing Asmodes, the devil whose job it is to disrupt
marriages, and Unrath, the demon of domestic waste and disorder,
in *Tobias*, seem to be possessed of any real independent life and interest. Rollenhagen is, however, concerned to provide motivation
for his characters, transferring the dream which foretells Tobias's
coming from Sara's mother to Sara herself, for instance, in order to
make the sudden marriage more credible. The pedagogic element is

still as strong as it was in the drama of Manuel or Waldis, but now at the end of the century the didacticism is ethical and social rather than theological. Abraham, and indeed Lazarus, can be construed as embodiments of fiduciary faith, but if Rollenhagen is a Protestant, he is also a member of the North German bourgeoisie, and the ideals he seeks to inculcate are their ideals: a quiet sober faith in God, and a life of industry, domestic harmony, moderation and charity to those less fortunate than oneself.

No review of the main tendencies of German drama in the six-teenth century would be complete without some mention of that remarkable and many-sided prince, Duke HEINRICH JULIUS VON BRAUNSCHWEIG-WOLFENBÜTTEL (1564–1613), whose plays – even though they did not exercise any strong immediate influence – seem to anticipate future developments. To Heinrich Julius belongs the honour of establishing the first regular court theatre in Germany – for the production of his own plays! – and it was in large measure his enthusiasm and patronage which made it easier for the English strolling players, with their rather debased Elizabethan repertoire, to enjoy a moderate success and, ultimately, considerable influence.

Heinrich Julius began his career as a dramatist with an adaptation of the German version of Frischlin's *Susanna*, developing the peasant scenes and introducing – as one of the earliest German writers to do so – dialect for comic effect; but he rapidly abandoned biblical drama for a more realistic and modern type of play. For the most part, however, he continues to regard his plays as vehicles for a moral message: the subtitle of his tragedy *Von einem Buler und Bulerin* (*About a paramour and his mistress*, 1593) reads: 'How their whoredom and lewdness, although concealed for a time, yet was finally revealed and was punished in fearful fashion by God. Diligently presented to instruct and warn everyman'; and the terrible fates which overtake his adulterers – one is carried off by the Devil in *Von einer Ehebrecherin* (*About an adulteress*) and one hangs herself in despair in *Von einem Buler* – are clearly intended to underline his own legislative efforts in this connection. This evident moral didacticism stamps Heinrich Julius as a child of the sixteenth century, as does his occasional use of traditional motifs culled from the *Fastnachtspiel* or the traditional anecdote: *Von einem Weibe, wie dasselbe ihre Hurerey für ihren Ehe-*

mann verborgen (*About a woman, how she concealed her whoredom from her husband*) takes up the old motif of the adulterous wife who is able to bluff her way out of compromising situations, the husband in the end meeting the lover who, not knowing him, jestingly tells him how he has been deceived. But for all these sixteenth-century attitudes, Heinrich Julius is very much indebted to the new drama of the English players: he prefers a rapidly developing plot with a manageable cast of not more than twenty-four; he writes a rhythmic prose which breaks with the doggerel of tradition in an attempt to approximate to the blank verse of the English stage, and he introduces into his plays Jan Bousset, the clown-commentator developed by the English players in order to explain the action to non-English speakers. Equally he borrows their realism and even outdoes it: he tends to portray the world of the middle class and frequently draws on material which in our day would find its way into the more lurid Sunday newspapers: murders, adultery and marriages ruined by drink are his preferred themes, and in his celebrated *Von einem ungeratenen Sohn* (*About a spoilt and undutiful son*) which clearly sets out to emulate the horrors of *Titus Andronicus*, Nero is made to kill his son, drink his blood mixed with wine and then roast his heart and eat it – all on the stage!

While Heinrich Julius was thus very much open to new influences, his most successful play, *Vincentius Ladislaus* (1594), draws on more venerable traditions than those imported from Elizabethan England. The comedy, possibly under the influence of Talandus in Frischlin's *Hildegardis*, introduces us to a *miles gloriosus* and allows him to strut his little hour upon the stage for our amusement, before finally deflating him by having him fall into a cold bath instead of the hoped-for marriage bed. The new-found liberty conferred by the use of prose is, in baroque fashion, exploited to the full in order to make comic capital out of the linguistic accumulation associated with the high-sounding titles Vincentius arrogates to himself, titles which find a parallel in the tall tales, mostly culled from familiar collections of *Schwänke*, by which the braggart seeks to establish his credentials. The play on the conflict of appearance and reality and the deflation of unjustified pretension as a source of comedy – even the figure of the braggart himself – were to be favourite devices of the seventeenth century, but it is not so much these factors which make *Vincentius*

Ladislaus especially noteworthy. In spite of the ludicrous garb in which the hero is dressed and the crude slap-stick of his final humiliation, the play turns on the concept that comedy is to be found in character rather than farcical situation or social satire, and it is this concept, together with the purely incidental nature of any moral element, which entitles the play to be regarded as heralding a new departure in German dramatic literature.

PART IV

Prose Fiction

Introduction

WHILE the different types of poetry and drama in the Renaissance fall easily enough into categories, the same is by no means true of prose fiction. Neither the novel (in the modern sense of the term) nor the short story enjoyed the prestige of the genres established in antiquity, and even when a didactic element was introduced their primary function of entertaining the reader militated against such precise formal prescriptions as were applied to other literary genres. A further complication arises from the fact that already in the Middle Ages there had existed prose versions of verse romances, and in the Renaissance the distinction between works in verse and prose continued to be one of form and prestige rather than of content. It is therefore not surprising to find that Italy should have produced no major work of prose fiction to rival the epic masterpieces of Ariosto or Tasso, or that the greatest works of this kind in France and Spain should each fit most uneasily into this class. Rabelais's book is a descendant, at several removes, of the epic tale of knightly deeds, the *Celestina* is a long tale in dialogue, and ostensibly dramatic, form, for which it is not easy or helpful to find an analogue. If these two unique works are included in this section it is simply for convenience.

The other works discussed offer fewer problems. The phenomenal success of the *Amadís* story, both in France and Spain, is only the most obvious case of the continued popularity enjoyed everywhere by romances of chivalry. Though, or because, unashamedly archaic, such stories provided a ready means of escape from the realities of everyday life, and were still doing so by the time the Romantics gave them a new lease of life. At the other end of the social scale the beginnings of picaresque literature in Spain and of bourgeois novels in Germany show that the taste for adventure stories did not exclude low life and realism.

The short story reflects almost exactly the same tendencies in smaller compass. Here too the distinction between what can be said in prose and in verse is far from absolute, and Ronsard, for instance, wrote bawdy tales in verse. The two principal traditions continuing throughout the century are those represented by Boccaccio on the one hand and by the *exemplum*, anecdote or *fabliau* on the other. The purely humorous story of any age seldom aspires to great literary excellence, but France, Italy and Germany all produced collections in the sixteenth century which are still well worth reading. The Boccaccio tradition led to a considerable degree of psychological refinement in such writers as Marguerite de Navarre and Bandello, but a cruel and morbid streak became more pronounced in the course of the century. Not a few of these tales of unrequited love supplied dramatists, especially in England, with their plots, of which that of *Romeo and Juliet* is only the best known.

In general it may be said that fiction, so often equated with lies, and especially prose tales, long or short, never became fully respectable in the sixteenth century. There was evidently a voracious public for fiction, whose tastes are reflected in what they read, but most of the authors discussed here would have been astonished that one day their works would rank as literature.

ONE

France

RABELAIS (*c.* 1492–1553)

FEW adjectives are more misleading than 'rabelaisian'. With its dismissive implications of mere bawdy excess and taproom ribaldry it invites misunderstanding and prejudices true appreciation of one of the world's great comic writers. The nature and difficulty of Rabelais's work are not unlike those of Shakespeare's; his language is exceptionally hard, even for Frenchmen, and resists close translation, but, despite the astonishing breadth and depth of his thought, his appeal is immediate and remarkably catholic.

To characterize Rabelais's work as narrative fiction is not to invite comparisons with similar works, for, strictly speaking, there are none. He embodies elements of many traditions and transcends them all. From a formal point of view his work consists of five books linked by the loosest of narratives and dealing ostensibly with the deeds and words of Gargantua and his son Pantagruel. The first book in order of composition is *Pantagruel* (1532), followed in 1534 by *Gargantua*, but ever since the collected edition of 1542 the two books have been printed in order of chronology, with father preceding son. In 1546 appeared the *Tiers Livre* (*Third Book*), then in 1548 a partial edition of a *Quart Livre* (*Fourth Book*), published in full in 1552. Rabelais died next year (1553), but in 1562 a sequel appeared under the title *L'Isle Sonnante* (*The Isle of Bells*), purporting to be authentic, and finally in 1564 a complete *Fifth Book*, incorporating most, but not all of this sequel, came out. This last book is finished in the sense that the story comes to a logical conclusion, but is clearly unfinished in that numerous inconsistencies, and even meaningless passages remain. Almost all critics agree that much of this posthumous book (especially the earlier chapters) represent Rabelais's own draft, that several chapters are crude translations or paraphrases of work by other authors which he may well have intended to incorporate but for some reason never adapted properly, and that the rest may be the work of an editor doing his best with work abandoned by Rabelais in varying stages of completion. Happily the literary problem of the last book is more a puzzle for scholars than crucial to an understanding of the rest.

When he came to write *Pantagruel* Rabelais was about forty and looked like settling down to a respectable career as a doctor and Classical scholar at Lyon, where he had begun publishing a series of learned works on such subjects as ancient law and medicine. His early training as a Franciscan had, however, not reconciled him to poverty, even if it had given him plenty of practice in it, and his very late vocation to the field of popular literature was most probably motivated by financial need. As he says in his Prologue, his book is intended as a sequel to an enormously popular chapbook relating the adventures of the giant Gargantua (this indeed existed in several versions, variously entitled *Grandes Chroniques, Chroniques Illustres,* and the like) and because of inexperience in the genre, and also for commercial reasons, it would have been unwise of him to diverge too far from his model. Such chapbooks were often the work of educated men, but their literary value is usually slight, depending on exaggeration, improbability and repetition to a degree which soon renders them as monotonous as the rough woodcuts with which they are generally illustrated. Here, at once, Rabelais distinguished himself from his predecessors, indeed asserting supremacy with a command of language seldom equalled and never surpassed.

The helpful analogy has been drawn more than once between Rabelais and Bosch. Not only do they both display a literally fantastic complexity of composition, but they reveal in each of their countless details the same richness of invention accompanied by sureness of execution. There is nothing approximate about Rabelais's style, any more than there is in Bosch's pictures; in each case the teeming canvas gives an immediate impression of life and colour, but its full intricacy can only be appreciated after meticulous inspection. There are undeniable lapses; to modern taste some of the catalogues and litanies may well seem tedious, some of the puns atrocious, some of the farce too cruel or too crude, but Rabelais's torrent of words is on the gigantic scale and carries all before it.

The first two books follow the traditional epic pattern in recounting the birth, youth, education and first feats of arms of their eponymous heroes, but whereas the giants of the chapbooks had spent their time riding gigantic steeds, combatting gigantic foes, taking seven league strides and so on, Rabelais soon tires of mere magnification. Already in chapter vi of *Pantagruel* he introduces a scene of purely verbal humour, in which Pantagruel terrifies a pretentious scholar out of Latinized jargon into his native Limousin dialect, and the next chapter soon abandons narrative in favour of an extensive catalogue of the books alleged to be in the great Library of St Victor in Paris. Such academic humour was no less traditional than the gigantic theme, though obviously less accessible to the ordinary reader, but the combination is typical of Rabelais's transformation of existing elements. In chapter ix we meet the character who after the giants is to play the principal role: the immoral and ingenious Panurge. The Mercury of, for example, Lucian's satire somewhat resembles Panurge, perpetual trickster and artful dodger, but more recent figures like the apocryphal Villon of many oral tales, or Eulenspiegel, or local rascals like Pierre Faifeu of Angers and similar popular anti-heroes all contribute their part, though perhaps the closest model is Cingar in Folengo's remarkable mock-epic of Baldus. Once presented Panurge soon occupies a position in this first book sometimes more prominent, and never less so, than that of Pantagruel. Many casual readers have thus come to associate his often distasteful exploits with those of the hero, who is in fact absent entirely from several of the chapters devoted to Panurge. He causes dogs to befoul a lady who rejects his advances, he raids the poor box in numerous churches, and in general conducts himself in a malicious and only intermittently diverting way.

This point needs emphasis, because the character of Pantagruel is not sufficiently well drawn in this first book to dominate that of Panurge, and because the final injunction to readers to live like good Pantagruelists 'in peace, joy, health, always enjoying good cheer . . .' is too vague to make any real distinction between the two men. There is, however, one chapter which stands by itself, and which in the light of the later books gives some hint of Rabelais's as yet undefined purpose. In chapter viii Pantagruel receives a letter from his father which is a justly famous example of Renaissance prose. After an opening passage in praise of paternity, Gargantua launches into a review of the current intellectual situation and his recommendations for his son's studies. Often called a humanist manifesto, this letter is a stirring hymn to the New Learning based on the recently restored Classical tongues, and championed by Rabelais's heroes Erasmus and Budé. This embraced not only the whole of the antique wisdom enshrined in Greek and Latin authors, but led directly to study of the Bible in the original, for which Hebrew and Syriac are also to be mastered. The style and content of this letter (some half dozen pages long) are of such sustained solemnity that they create the most striking impression, sandwiched as it is between the burlesque Library of St Victor and Panurge's first appearance. While all the other chapters show Pantagruel as a giant, albeit uttering sentiments of notable sagacity from time to time, this one alone is on a purely human scale, and it is serious.

The implications of this strange intrusion into a book of comic fantasy are to be seen in *Gargantua*. By 1534 *Pantagruel* had become such a success that Rabelais's second hero (and original model) could be presented as 'father of Pantagruel' and set in a context very different from that of the chapbook. He still, it is true, has a giant mare, hangs the bells of Notre Dame round her neck and periodically indulges in sundry excretory excesses, but the theme of education, wholly alien to the chapbooks, is greatly expanded from the single chapter of 1532. Above all, the strongly religious note of the letter, echoed only occasionally elsewhere in *Pantagruel*, becomes a major and recurrent motif. The earlier book had already shown a fair amount of topical comment and satire, for instance on the absurdities of the legal system, but in *Gargantua* this plays as great a role as the traditional fantasy. Outmoded habits in education and religion are satirized, positive programmes based on the New Learning and moderate Evangelism are seriously propounded, and several whole chapters are devoted to such matters as pacifism, international relations and moral freedom, concluding with the long episode of Thélème.

Together with this increased proportion of serious matter goes a considerably increased emphasis on the giants themselves. One or other of the giants is almost constantly in the foreground, and the relationship between father and son becomes all the more realistic for being transferred from the fantastic landscape of folklore to the small area round Chinon where Rabelais spent his own youth. An immediate consequence of the topographical realism is that the giants become persons, as Pantagruel had scarcely done, and what is more, they do not have to face competition from so strongly marked a character as Panurge. Frère Jean, one of Rabelais's most endearing creations, plays a prominent part indeed, but he is never allowed to steal the picture.

Something like half the book is taken up with the war against King Picrochole, but while *Pantagruel* describes an epic struggle between giants in an imaginary land, *Gargantua* depicts a campaign waged in the Chinon countryside, based on an actual feud involving Rabelais's father (probably the model for Grandgousier) and a neighbouring landowner, and full of references to identifiable persons and places in the region. Vast armies execute their manoeuvres over fields and hamlets, a squabble between cake-makers and shepherds escalates into global war, Gargantua picks cannon balls out of his hair like so many lice, but supporting all these brilliant and bewildering changes of scale is Rabelais's loving recreation of his own home background. Grandgousier warms himself in front of the log fire in the modest farmhouse of La Devinière (now a museum), even if his son does swallow six pilgrims sheltering under a lettuce leaf in the garden, the battling monk Frère Jean routs an invading army with the stave of the processional cross from the abbey of Seuilly just down the road, Picrochole plans world conquest from the unpretentious manor of Lerné near by, and when his victors divide the spoils it is in the lush water meadows between Loire and Vienne that the abbey of Thélème is established for Frère Jean. 'Do as you will' is the motto of this improbable foundation, where young men and women of good birth and comely appearance live together in almost intolerably cultured refinement and harmony, and where giants would seem as incongruous as the lusty, lewd and lovable monk who is their nominal superior.

Gargantua is still boisterous, with a fair amount of violence, urinary deluges and cheerful obscenity, but without Panurge it is free from the element of malice and nastiness which makes *Pantagruel* somewhat uneven. Rabelais's style shows more assurance, and he blends the different ingredients of serious and comic, gigantic and realistic with greater success. There is the same prodigious erudition as in the first book, but the balance remains heavily tilted on the side of action rather than thought.

All this changes completely with the *Third Book* of 1546. No longer disguised by the anagrammatic pseudonym of Alcofribas Nasier, no longer competing with anonymous chapbooks, but now continuing his own work under his own name, Rabelais decisively tips the scales from action over to words. The title page drops all reference to horrendous exploits, and simply promises: 'The deeds and words of the good Pantagruel'; almost the whole book is in the form of discussions. There is a formal link with *Pantagruel* in that the book opens with the colonization by Pantagruel's subjects of the territory conquered in the earlier book, but consistency of narrative never mattered much to Rabelais, so that we find Gargantua, whose death had provoked the war fought by his son, alive once more, while his companion, Frère Jean, is added without comment to the entourage of Pantagruel, together with Panurge, despite the generation's gap between them. Early in the book Panurge shows signs of disquiet, and confides to Pantagruel that he feels it is time he got married, but fear of cuckoldry (of which he has hitherto been a wholesale dispenser) deters him. From then on the book is nominally devoted to a long series of inquiries into Panurge's problem, which remains unresolved at the end of the book, when they decide to embark on a voyage to the Oracle of the Bottle, only reached in fact at the end of the *Fifth Book*. The matrimonial preoccupations of Panurge turn out to be little more than a pretext for a wide-ranging review of different methods of acquiring knowledge. Dreams, divination, soothsayers and fools, Platonism and Pyrrhonism, with much else besides, are the real subjects of this, Rabelais's densest book. It is even more difficult than the others because of the astonishing technical expertise displayed over an encyclopaedic range of subjects, and this inevitably affects the language, in which there is much more of the polysyllabic, Latinate style, with extremely involved syntax, as well as the usual crop of inventions, neologisms and dialect words.

For all its difficulty this is a very rewarding book, and adds a philosophical dimension to a hero whose gigantic stature is almost wholly forgotten. Pantagruel is now unmistakably the hero, even more so than his father before him, and time after time the others defer to his superior wisdom and authority. In coming down to human size Pantagruel gains enormously in moral stature. Already in chapter ii we are told that he practises the Stoic virtues of self-discipline and detachment, because fortuitous events beyond our control should never be allowed to shake our composure, and by the end of the book he is being described as the 'archetype and exemplar of all joyous perfection'. The uncertainty of his earlier relationship to Panurge is now removed, and while he never abandons his friend, always treated with good-natured tolerance, on more than one occasion he rebukes him (and Frère Jean, too) for overstepping the limits of reverence, not decency. His philosophy is Stoic as to morals, Platonic as to epistemology, and is accompanied by a firm Christian faith solidly buttressed by scriptural teaching, especially that of St Paul. It must not be supposed from this that gravity replaces fun, but it is true that there is very little horseplay, and a great deal of satire, irony, parody and other more cerebral forms of humour. Compared to the earlier books there is a consequent loss of simplicity, perhaps even innocence, but this is more than outweighed by the gain in sheer humanity. It is no accident that the father-son relationship so successfully portrayed in *Gargantua* after the brief sketch in *Pantagruel* is here continued, even though it necessitates the resuscitation of Gargantua, and one of the most eloquent chapters in Rabelais is that in which father and son discuss marriage. Rabelais's views are by no means agreed upon by scholars, but broadly speaking he seems to have attached almost obsessive importance to the begetting of children in marriage (it must be remembered that as a priest he was denied this privilege, though he is known to have had at least three illegitimate children), and to have respected the rights of women as wives and mothers only in so far as they did not distract man from his prime duties to friends and public affairs. On medical grounds he shared the general belief of his age that women were naturally inferior creatures, but he was no fanatic.

Tiring as he always did of the last theme or style attempted, Rabelais turned in the *Fourth Book* to a very different formula. From Homer's day the voyage had been part of the epic tradition and the form suited Rabelais's purpose very well, for it enabled him to string together self-contained episodes on land or sea, of varying length, and connected only by the general quest for the Oracle – not that loose ends had ever caused him concern. As a result the *Fourth Book* is the most heterogeneous of all. Classical mythology, pure fantasy, allegory and metaphysical profundity succeed one another, and are indeed intermingled. Unity of a sort is provided by the hero, still a man rather than a giant, but the resemblance with Bosch is nowhere more apparent. Some of the chapters would even in isolation earn Rabelais a place among the world's great writers, but the cumulative effect of the book must be felt, it cannot be described. The episode of Panurge and the sheep (borrowed from Folengo), the magnificent setpiece of the tempest (owing much to Erasmus), the deeply impressive discussion on immortality with Pantagruel's concluding affirmation of Christian faith in the Pan chapter (xxviii), the riotous fun of the Andouilles (Chitterling) war, the brilliantly obscene *fabliau* of the peasant and the devil, the satire of the Decretals, the riches are too many even to be listed. It is particularly noticeable that the constant shift of scale which contributed the main technical resource of Rabelais's fantasy in the first two books has by now become a virtuoso performance, not merely in degree of magnitude, but over the whole gamut of satirical, allegorical, topical, realistic, reflective and other notes.

The verbal inventiveness which had marked his book from the beginning here reaches a crescendo, and Rabelais frequently launches into tumultuous cadenzas of words, as in the extraordinary anatomy of Quaresmeprenant, the spirit of Lent (standing for Charles V), and even the sonorous litany of Diogenes' tub-rolling in the Prologue to the *Third Book* is surpassed by the sustained dramatization of the storm. Considering Rabelais's age (at least sixty) when he wrote this book, and the bitter disappointment he and his moderate friends had had to endure since the happy days of *Pantagruel*, one must equally admire the literary genius and the unshakeable faith in man.

In retrospect it is easy enough to trace the stages of this work composed over twenty years, but the facts of the case impose caution in attributing to Rabelais intentions which may fit the situation but are not necessarily the only ones to do so. *Pantagruel* was obviously experimental, *Gargantua* as obviously the exploitation of success, the *Fourth* and *Fifth Books* are explicitly prepared for in the *Third*, and written so soon afterwards that a loosely continuous plan is more probable than not, but the change between 1534 (or even 1542) and 1546 is a considerable one and can hardly have figured in the original project. In the last analysis Rabelais is one of the world's great comic writers not because he is funny, though he is that, but because he combined an unmatched mastery of language with a comic vision embracing mankind and nature. Like Shakespeare with Falstaff, he uses farce to go beyond farce and illuminates the human situation with dazzling clarity in episodes where it is almost presumptuous to seek a hidden meaning; but the key to his unique creation is undoubtedly the role of Pantagruel and the other giants. All the funny things that happen to or around Panurge and Frère Jean, let alone the grave pronouncements on religion, ethics or philosophy, would remain just anthology pieces were they not joined together and integrated into the noble philosophy of Pantagruelism, where triviality and even obscenity are invested with relevance. The quest for the Oracle is clearly an allegory of Rabelais's own quest, and the ideal character whom he took twenty years to shape embodies all the wisdom and goodness to which he thought men should aspire and could attain. No experience is too base, no ideal too lofty for Pantagruel to deal with in word or deed. Rabelais the doctor, priest and scholar, Rabelais the countryman, the fugitive from justice, the father of bastards, combine in Rabelais the writer to give one of literature's rare pictures of the whole man of the Renaissance.

His influence on French prose was considerable in his own century, and even in the next La Fontaine versified one or two of the tales, but the refinement of the Classical Age put an end to that sort of exuberance, and only in the nineteenth century did he come into his own again with Balzac and the Romantics. Abroad he has enjoyed very variable fortunes, and while Latin countries do not seem to have taken kindly to his genius, the Fleming, Marnix, recaptured his style brilliantly at the end of the sixteenth century, Germany soon had its own version, and in England, where Sir Thomas Browne was a notable devotee, Urquhart's splendid translation in the seventeenth century made him widely accessible. It is remarkable that Rabelais studies are today a major industry, while he continues to give delight to thousands who would never call themselves scholars.

SHORT STORIES

French fiction in the sixteenth century is so dominated by Rabelais that other writers are unjustly neglected. It is true that longer works tend to be mere adaptations of older models, whether romances of chivalry or burlesque fantasies like the prototype *Gargantua*, and the century's best-seller was in fact Herberay des Essarts's free translation of the Spanish *Amadis de Gaule* (1540–48), which is at least as notable for its traditional account of knightly deeds and amorous dalliance as for any more modern features. It is essential to realize that people went on reading (into the eighteenth century indeed) the old medieval favourites suitably dressed up; but such versions, however competent and however valuable as indications of taste, add nothing to the development of the narrative genre. For this the writers of short stories must take most credit, and their work is of considerable historical interest as well as of literary merit.

Rabelais must be mentioned in this connection, for many of his stories, especially in the later books, are self-contained and would earn a place in any anthology, but it is not pedantic to exclude him from the ranks of story-tellers proper. Under the form of *exempla*, anecdotes, and *fabliaux* the short story had always existed in France, oral or written, but only with the advent of printing and Italian influence does it begin to qualify for serious consideration as art. Already in the late fifteenth century collections like Poggio's *Facetiae* (in Latin) or the *Cent Nouvelles Nouvelles* (in French) show great technical advances; wit increasingly replaced coarse humour, style improved enormously, but story-tellers were always primarily regarded as entertainers and showed few inhibitions when it came to dealing with sexual or scatological themes.

A number of writers had already tried to imitate Boccaccio, whose *Decameron* had conclusively shown how a collection of tales can be transformed into an integrated whole, greater than the sum of its parts, through skilful use of a framework narrative.

MARGUERITE DE NAVARRE so admired the *Decameron* that she commissioned a translation by Antoine le Maçon (1545) and then started on a work, interrupted by death, specifically conceived as the French answer to the Italian challenge. Some early manuscripts refer to this as the *Decameron* of Marguerite, but ever since the first complete edition by Gruget (1559) it has been known as the *Heptameron*, because the seventy-two extant tales are arranged in seven 'days'. The Prologue explains her scheme, and lays down the rules: a party of five men and five women are marooned by floods in a Pyrennean abbey and agree to pass the ten days before a bridge can be built by each telling a story a day. Stories must be authenticated by the narrator, and may not come from a literary source, men and women will alternate as narrators and as presidents for each day, a serious tale is to be followed by a gay one, and on their return to Court the resultant collection will be offered to their friends by the amateur authors. These rules are so closely observed that special permission has to be given for the only avowedly literary tale (LXX, from a fourteenth-century poem) and for a break in alternation of presidents. Modern research has shown that twenty or more stories are historically verifiable, while only a bare half dozen can be conclusively traced to a written source. Marguerite probably collected her tales over a number of years, composing some and editing all, and they clearly include court gossip, oral tradition and versions of popular anecdotes, often based on fact.

Her ten narrators bear pseudonyms sufficiently transparent to reveal the identity of close friends, including herself as Parlamente, her second husband, Henri de Navarre, as Hircan, and her chaplain, Dangu, as Dagoucin. There are three married couples, and the others are either single or widowed, so that the lively discussions constituting the framework show widely divergent attitudes to the sex war, the book's principal theme, as well as revealing the development of interesting relationships between members of the group, evidently intended for the private amusement of the Court circle to which all belonged. Closer in this to Chaucer (whom she did not know) than to her model Boccaccio, Marguerite uses both tales and framework narrative to advance and, on occasion, dramatize the debate between opposing factions. Her dialogue in the linking narrative has been plausibly described as a somewhat stylized version of contemporary Court conversation, and certainly contrasts strongly with the wooden rhetoric offered as dialogue in most of the stories.

The majority of the tales deal with sexual relations of one kind or another, ranging from rape and incest to conjugal fidelity and spiritual love. The longest (up to thirty pages) seem to reflect Marguerite's personal literary taste, all being romantic tales of starcrossed lovers in the courtly tradition, showing a high degree of psychological delicacy. Such are the Spanish tale of Floride and Amadour (X), the Breton one of Rolandine (XXI) and the Burgundian version of the fourteenth-century poem on the Châtelaine de Vergi already referred to (LXX). The shortest, of a page or less, are usually the crudest (see the scatological XI) or relate a brief incident (the superstitious old woman of LXV), but the average length is some five or six pages, and there is great variety of subject. Many stories attack the friars for their lechery, ignorance or hypocrisy, many treat the perennial theme of cuckoldry, but there are also accounts of historical events, like an attempted plot against François I (XVII) or the honeymoon of Marguerite's daughter Jeanne (LXVI). The geographical setting covers most of Western Europe, and even Canada (LXVII), but Marguerite is not interested in description or local colour, but rather in the moral or psychological implications, normally discussed after the story, which is sometimes shorter than the discussion. This emphasizes her use of the framework narrative not merely to provide literary continuity but also to convey her didactic aim.

Though love, in its broadest sense, is the ostensible theme of the debate and most of the tales, closer inspection soon reveals that behind this theme there lies a religious one. Each day opens with Scripture reading and commentary from Oisille, a pious widow and doyenne of the party, they all attend services daily in the abbey church, and in discussing religious topics, like the friars or superstition, show unusual unanimity in supporting Evangelical views. More than once in the course of discussion someone makes the point that human love is a stepping stone to divine love, and that love of God must be accomplished by love of men. Here indeed is the key to the *Heptameron*. Marguerite takes great pains to represent and balance all points of view, from the lustful brutality of Hircan and his cronies to the dreamy Platonism of Dagoucin or the pious detachment of Oisille, but her own conclusion gradually emerges (not only through Parlamente's utterances) and would no doubt have been more explicit if she had lived to complete her book: the Christian whose faith is based on the Bible will practise the sort of love therein enjoined. In other words faith and charity are inseparable. In her terms this means that the flesh must be controlled but not denied, and despite her own often discouraging experience Christian marriage is her chosen solution. Such an interpretation of the *Heptameron* explains the presence of so much that is coarse and violent, for only by facing up to such realities could Marguerite hope to convince her audience that her remedy was practical. Her aim was undoubtedly to entertain, but to instruct as well. The *Heptameron* is not just a *Decameron manqué*, and for all its flatness of style constitutes a remarkable attempt by a Renaissance princess to synthesize ideals and reality into a viable way of life. Fictional in form, entertaining in fact, the book is most interesting for the light it throws on the complex personality of Marguerite herself and through her on her circle.

The contrast between Marguerite and her protégé BONAVENTURE DES PERIERS (c. 1512–c. 1543) could hardly be more marked. After causing a scandal with his satirical dialogue *Cymbalum Mundi* (1537) Des Periers behaved more cautiously, and it was left to friends to publish some of his verse and prose as a posthumous tribute in 1544. Only in 1558 did his *Nouvelles Récréations et Joyeux Devis* appear, a collection of ninety tales of reasonably certain authenticity, though later editions add another thirty which are by another hand. Marguerite, writing from an aristocratic point of view, tended to ignore material realism in favour of psychology; Des Periers, on a lower social level, is noticeably realistic in external details. The *Heptameron*'s stories are ostensibly true and original, the *Joyeux Devis* makes no such claim, nor does it have any framework. Above all Des Periers in his Prologue insistently disclaims any serious moral or philosophical purpose.

Instead the book bears out the Prologue's injunction to 'bene vivere et laetari' ('live well and rejoice') by stressing the comic side of life and diverting attention, at least momentarily, from ever-present ills. Des Periers is no propagandist now, and true to his declaration aims at laughter, not correction. Thus the numerous tales about clerics avoid all serious criticism, and are always good humoured, poking fun at parish clergy for their illiteracy, at friars for their gluttony, at prelates for pomposity, but never drawing religious conclusions and even on occasion praising a pope (VII) or cardinal (XIV), precisely for good sense and good humour. The earlier satirist almost never shows through. Similarly in dealing with sex he is much less concerned than most story-tellers with cuckoldry, and not concerned at all about pointing a moral. For him sexual activity is meant to be enjoyable, not solemn or tragic, and he has no more patience with romance than with lechery. He is often extremely funny, and very bawdy, but like Rabelais, whom he resembles in many ways, his excesses are those of high spirits, not calculated obscenity, let alone what we should call pornography.

After the Church and sex, Des Periers's other main themes concern lawyers and assorted tricksters. In wealth and self-importance lawyers formed a privileged class, and offered Des Periers ample scope for his favourite device of deflation, but without malice. Similarly the various tricks played in the stories, very often by students, do no real harm to the victim beyond deflating pomposity or exposing stupidity, and not infrequently we see the biter bit.

Most of the stories are very short, some less than a page, on average four or five pages, and, as no discussion precedes or follows them, they must get off to a flying start and make their own point at the end. In many cases this is a verbal one, involving some pun or witty retort, but in all it is conclusive, and the whole story builds up with no slackening of pace to the denouement. This makes the comic device of deflation particularly suitable, and an epilogue superfluous. Though Des Periers only uses description functionally, never for its own sake, the tales are full of fascinating insights into sixteenth-century habits, meals, furniture and so on, and we are always told enough to visualize locality or appearance, and to imagine speech habits or other salient characteristics of those involved. As is so often the case in the period, the style is primarily oral, and in such tales as that of the stammerer (XLV) or those concerned with dialect the best effect comes from reading aloud.

The apparent discontinuity of the ninety tales is deceptive, for the great majority are loosely linked either by similarity of theme (the first two concern jesters, the next two choristers) or place. There are at least three sets of four so linked, and numerous trios and pairs, often using a 'that reminds me' technique, so that while each tale remains an organic whole, the sequence and balance of the collection is such that additions or omissions would be noticed, as is indeed the case with later expanded editions. The sources of many of the tales have been identified with Latin, Italian and French analogues of different periods, but the majority derive either from personal experience or more likely from the inexhaustible fund of oral tradition. For sheer skill as a raconteur Des Periers is second only to Rabelais, and as a stylist not far behind. It is interesting that La Fontaine admired him enough to versify one of his tales together with some by Rabelais, but more interesting to see a highly educated man making literature out of what had previously been a poorly regarded popular genre.

Yet another formula for the short prose tale was exploited by NOËL DU FAIL (c. 1520–91). He spent his whole working life as a lawyer at or near Rennes in his native Brittany, but just before settling down after some turbulent years as a wandering and not very studious scholar he published two small books, *Propos rustiques* (1547) in twelve chapters and *Baliverneries . . . d'Eutrapel* (1548) in five, and the year before he retired returned to the genre with a much longer work in thirty-five chapters, *Contes d'Eutrapel* (1585: Eutrapel was his pseudonym), of which five seem to have originally been intended for the youthful *Baliverneries*. Du Fail is unashamedly derivative, borrowing for example not only Rabelais's style but even some of his proper names, and drawing on a comprehensive catalogue of authors ancient and modern, including Cicero, Pliny, Erasmus, Guevara and Des Periers, but he is capable of real originality and in his inconsequential way surprisingly often hits the target.

The best of his books is the first, which purports to be an edited verson of talk (*Propos*) by a small group of elders on the village green, overheard when the author came home to settle. To this end du Fail provides a loose framework, mainly of reminiscences and banter between members of the group, which includes the former schoolmaster and some solid farmers. His ostensible purpose, declared in a pretentious preface, is to set down for posterity a first-hand account of the good old days before the swelling tide of urbanism sweeps away what is left of the pastoral idyll. Much of the book is therefore an exercise in rhetoric, an apology for country against town largely copied from other authors, but when du Fail decides to tell a story or describe a scene for its own sake he suddenly brings the picture remarkably to life. He had a good ear for dialogue (though he uses hardly any regional forms) and a photographic eye for detail, so that such chapters as those describing a rustic banquet (III) or a village feud (IX) or, best of all, a practical joke played on bullying neighbours (X) are entertaining and strikingly evocative of rural life, always, of course, seen through the eyes of the young squire.

The *Baliverneries* (and certain chapters of the *Contes*) do not employ the same framework device, but by bringing in the same three characters (du Fail, his brother and a legal friend) in supposedly autobiographical anecdotes provide some continuity. A very realistic account of a local wrestling-match (II) and an extraordinarily detailed description of a farmhouse interior (IV) testify to remarkable powers of observation, and there can be no doubt that du Fail's real talent was for journalism, not invention, and his besetting sin disorder and irrelevance.

The *Contes d'Eutrapel* contain much brilliant material, but the constant digressions and sententious comments, not to mention an almost unbelievably tortuous syntax, severely try the reader's patience. Despite the title, these are really essays, by turns anecdotal, moralizing and autobiographical, not unlike some of Montaigne in certain respects, but without a narrative line, and without a coherent moral theme, few of the pieces come off as well as the more modest youthful efforts.

In their very different ways these three authors cover a considerable range of prose fiction, and show the futility of attempting to fit the short story into narrow categories. There are of course other names, and some other tales have been republished in recent years. Jacques Yver's *Printemps* (1572), Bénigne Poissenot's *Eté* (1583), Tabourot des Accords's *Bigarrures* (1583) and Guillaume Bouchet's *Sérées* (1584–98) all offer some interest to the specialist antiquarian, and occasional trophies for the amateur literary archaeologist, but they are not in the same class as the authors discussed, and specifically show too clearly their undigested debt to predecessors, including especially Bandello (translated 1559) and Straparola (translated 1560) among the moderns. Though Italian influence on this genre has sometimes been exaggerated, there would have been no French Renaissance at all without Italy, and in the short story, as in most other things, the best French writers are those who learn the lesson from Italy and then develop their own originality.

TWO

Italy

SHORT STORIES

THE *novella* has been a characteristic of Italian literature, from the *Novellino* and Boccaccio to the present, reaching the height of its popularity in the sixteenth century, as we see from the multitude of collections and isolated masterpieces like Machiavelli's *Belfagor*, as well as various episodes in Ariosto's *Furioso*, Tasso's *Liberata*, and Castiglione's *Cortegiano*. The word itself, *novella*, suggests something new, strange or wonderful, a substitute for the news of modern mass media. For Renaissance writers, the greatest example of the genre remained Boccaccio's *Decameron* (*c.* 1350), with its elegant setting in the Tuscan countryside where well-to-do young men and ladies escape the dangers of the plague in Florence and while away ten days in telling one hundred stories famous for their style and wit. The Renaissance *novella*, though a frequent source of inspiration for foreign playwrights, never quite succeeded in recapturing the spirit of the *Decameron*. As an entertainment, however, it was one of the chief features of court life and polite society, and one of the basic rules was that it should be easily understood and therefore written in Italian. The only exception was Girolamo Morlini's Latin *Novellae*, published in 1520. Despite various Classical sources, the *novelle* of the sixteenth century reflect the pastimes and interests of contemporary Italy. Predominant, of course, is the theme of love; next, the satire of churchmen and fools, cuckolds and knaves, with occasional excursions into the world of exotic lands and chivalry.

GIOVAN FRANCESCO STRAPAROLA (*c.* 1480–1557) published the first part of his *Piacevoli notti* in 1550: it contained twenty-five *novelle* and was followed by the forty-eight of the second part in 1553. The usual 'frame' borrowed from the *Decameron* is provided by the *salon* of Lucrezia Gonzaga during carnival time in Venice: five ladies-in-waiting are chosen by lot each evening, after some dancing and the setting of a riddle – with some atrocious verse thrown in. Most of the tales are far removed from other Renaissance favourites and many are frankly medieval in conception (for example, IV, 5; VI, 4). Straparola is, on the other hand, known to literary historians as a pioneer in the elaboration of fairy tales, such as the story of the Swine King (II, 1) and the Singing Apple Tree and Green Bird (IV, 3). The first part of the *Piacevoli notti* is the more original, for the second was borrowed wholesale – from Morlini, among others – with little or no attempt at a personal touch, and the stories lessen in both quality and quantity (XIII, 4) as the end is reached on the thirteenth tale of the thirteenth night. Two tales stand out, both written in dialect: V,3, in Bergamask, and V,4, where the exchanges between Marsilio and Tia, written in Paduan dialect, are reminiscent of Ruzante's popular comedies.

Boccaccio's heirs were, naturally enough, to be found in Tuscany. In the *Ragionamenti* of AGNOLO FIRENZUOLA (1493–1543), we find the usual setting modelled on the *Decameron*: a villa near Florence, where six young men and women find delight in an idyllic setting and decide to spend six days in exchanging stories during the spring of 1523. Of the thirty-six stories planned, only eight were written: all of them, with one exception, are on the subject of love, and nearly all in striking contrast with the celebration of Platonic love that opens the discussion. This opposition, so obvious and perhaps shocking for the modern reader, was evidently taken for granted by the author and his audience, conditioned as they were by the debates on the superiority of spiritual love on the one hand and the realities of everyday life on the other. It is best mirrored in the contrasting personalities of the Queen (Costanza Amaretta), who typifies the refinements of Renaissance culture, and Folchetto, the somewhat sceptical male who expresses the realistic attitude of the Italian middle classes. Both are more successful creations than any of the characters in the stories and well served by Firenzuola's elegant Florentine style.

Far more interesting, however, are the *novelle* of ANTON FRANCESCO GRAZZINI ('Il Lasca', 1503–84), where the speech of Florence adds a freshness and vigour unmatched by any other sixteenth-century writer of short stories. The *Cene* – written some time between 1540 and 1547 – remained unpublished until the eighteenth century. Lasca's original turn of mind produces a new twist in the

Introduction, where we are told that the story-telling was due to a snowstorm on the last day of January, instead of the customary spring-time idyll. A wealthy young widow and her brother have been entertaining some friends. As the snow lies thick on the ground, five young men run down into the courtyard to make the best of the opportunity. The merry widow suggests to her four companions (all married, but with husbands conveniently absent) that they should go up on the roof and bombard the men below. The surprise is complete: the young men get the worst of it, until supplies run out and the ladies go back to the warmth of their drawing-room, leaving their opponents wet through and with a desire for revenge. Their counter-attack fails, however; they are left outside locked doors, and have recourse to singing five-part madrigals by 'Verdelot and Arcadet'. Unable to make out the words, the ladies become curious and peace is made, as they all settle by the fire with the 'fables of Giovanni Boccaccio, rather, of San Giovanni Boccadoro' (Saint John of the Golden Tongue). After an argument over which part to choose from the *Decameron*, the widow invites them to dinner (*cena*) and suggests that they should tell their own stories, which, though unable to match Boccaccio's art, will at least have the virtue of novelty. She then invites the company to dinner on the same evening of the next two weeks. A stylistic scale is introduced under an ingenious pretext: for the first evening, lack of preparation will necessarily lead to a humble style; the following week should produce a more ambitious collection; while the last Thursday before Lent will provide a fit setting for the most noble examples of the story-teller's art. For once, the group decides not to elect a king or queen, but 'to act as a republic', with names drawn by lot.

Only two tales of the final day have come down to us, both illustrating Grazzini's stylistic pretensions: they are four times as long as the stories of the First Day, while the Second Day is roughly twice the length of the First. The best known of the *novelle* are I, 9 (the madwoman, Biliorsa, intent on executing her pumpkins by night) and II, 2 (Falananna – 'Gobybyes' – with his baby talk and pathetic attempt to take Christian doctrine literally and reach the good life through death). Another landmark is I, 5, where the death of an alchemist, brought about by his wife's accusations, is followed by her murder of their two children and suicide, and where – long before the Romantics began to labour the same point – the writer tells us that this pitiful happening 'though it did not occur in Greece or Rome, nor to persons of high lineage or regal descent, nevertheless took place as I have described it: and you will see that tragic fury may lodge in humble and lowly dwellings as well as in great palaces and beneath a roof of gold.' The streak of cruelty in Grazzini's work is best seen in II, 5, where the wife of the Lord of Fiesole and his son by a former marriage are discovered in adultery by the wretched Currado, who has their eyes and tongues wrenched out, their hands and feet lopped off. He then places the lovers in the bed where they had sinned and where their dismembered bodies still seek each other in a final embrace – a scene that provides a foretaste of an important element in the literature of the Counter-Reformation: its morbid fascination with incest and the horrific.

Whereas Grazzini's linguistic and geographical horizons remain purely Florentine, the most famous and prolific short-story writer of the century, MATTEO BANDELLO (1485–1561) ranges over much of the Italian peninsula in his 214 *novelle*: Milan (I, 9; II, 31); Ferrara (I, 45); Mantua (I, 30); Verona (II, 9); Venice (III, 31); Rome (II, 51); and Naples (II, 7). It was in Naples that Bandello's uncle, General of the Dominican Order, died in 1506, after fairly extensive travels undertaken with Matteo, whose natural curiosity was obviously stimulated by new experiences. After many vicissitudes, he settled in France, at Bassens near Agen, in 1541, where he remained for the rest of his life and where most of his *novelle* were elaborated. All the usual subjects are to be found in Bandello's pantechnicon; one misguided critic has even attempted to give a comprehensive list: illicit love, 66; clergy, 25; unfortunate love, 19; jests, 14; trials of love, 13; historical-biblical, 10; virtues, 10; vices, 9; justice, 9; *piacevolezze*, 8; chastity, 7; *bons mots*, 7; stupidity, 5; professions, 1; wisdom, 1; supernatural, 1; miscellaneous, 9. Certainly, this Dominican priest was not afraid of criticizing his peers (for example, in I, 38; II, 3; and III, 14) or even his superiors – as when he upbraids the late Pope Leo X for ignoring the dangers of Luther's heresy until it was too late, while praising the German for his 'fine intellect' and ascribing the good advice of his counsellor to 'friarly envy' (III, 25). His interest in the contemporary scene is best illustrated by the letter of dedication accompanying III, 62, where his pen ranges over recent developments in Syria, the capture of Belgrade, Rhodes, Hungary, and the siege of Vienna by the Turks, thanks to the internal weaknesses of Christendom, rebellion in Spain and France, disunity in Germany, the break-away of the Anglican Church from Rome, the decline of Venice, and the horrors of the Sack of Rome. Henry VIII's lechery and impious tyranny became one of Bandello's favourite targets (II, 37; III, 60 and 62), while a good many of the kings of England are tarred with the same brush in the dedication of II, 37.

The problem of Bandello's sources was much debated some fifty years ago. The whole question has lost its sting, as we gradually rid ourselves of the Romantic yearning for originality at all costs. Admittedly, it is interesting to note that, while borrowing heavily from Marguerite de Navarre's *Heptameron* and Jean Bouchet's *Annales d'Aquitaine* in I, 39, he ascribes to Philip of Burgundy and the previous century certain events in the life of François I, just as he feels quite free to change the details of Henry VIII's amorous adventures in III, 62. On the whole, however, Bandello insists on the accuracy and verisimilitude of his accounts (I, 51; II, 11); and he was conscientious enough in following his historical sources, such as Machiavelli's *Istorie fiorentine* in his description of Lorenzo the Magnificent's hazardous voyage to Naples (II, 52). A personal touch is provided in the ancient story of Lucretia (II, 21), where Bandello makes the Roman heroine confess that she had experienced pleasure, much against her will, as Sextus Tarquinius had raped her. Marguerite's *Heptameron* provided material for a number of *novelle*: some (II, 24 and 35) are better in the original; others, like IV, 10, are more effective where Bandello displays greater concision and psychological finesse. The latter quality is evident in Bandello's most famous *novella* (II, 9), which retells the story of Romeo and Juliet based on the version by Luigi da Porto published *c.* 1530, and where his compassionate humanity shines through in Juliet's lament and Romeo's final speech, providing a not unworthy basis for Shakespeare's play. Other dramatists inspired by Bandello are Lope de Vega, who praised his *novelle* above those of Cervantes, John Webster (I, 26), and Alfred de Musset (I, 21). It was especially the tragic tales that were admired and translated into French and English in the sixteenth century, and into Spanish at the beginning of the seventeenth. Launay, whose French translation appeared in 1559, admired Bandello's precision as a mirror to his age, and his enthusiasm was later shared by such diverse personalities as Stendhal, Burckhardt, and Symonds.

Although the historians' dependence on the *novelle* has been criticized, it would be difficult to find more revealing descriptions than those he gives us of the house in Rome belonging to the courtesan Imperia (III, 42), customs at Caldero (II, 9), Pompeio's bedroom (I, 3), or the portrayal *à la Balzac* of a noble mansion in Milan (IV, 25). This realism, which together with his understanding of human passion provides a firm basis for his narrative, is especially reflected in casual remarks made in the dedicatory epistles accompanying each story; for example, on social life and entertainments, music, the pleasures of travelling in France (IV, 15), and the custom of reading aloud from the works of various authors, such as Petrarch (I, 41), Boccaccio (I, 21) and Machiavelli (III, 55). Bandello's involvement with his age and his Terentian curiosity give us a fascinating gallery of contemporary figures, including Machiavelli himself (I, 40), Leonardo da Vinci (I, 58), Bembo (II, 10), Scaliger (II, 24 and 32), Galasso Ariosto (IV, 17), Marguerite de Navarre (IV, 19), Veronica Gambara (III, 59), Castiglione (I, 44) and the Court of Urbino with Elisabetta Gonzaga, Emilia Pia, and Giangiorgio Trissino (IV, 11), either as protagonists or recipients of the *novelle*. We may pick up such marginal information as the name of one of the great wine merchants of London – Edmund of York (III, 66) – who regularly visited the famous vineyards of Aquitaine in time of peace, or notice the changed attitude towards women and marriage after the misogyny of so many fifteenth-century humanists (I, 27; II, 25; III, 64; IV, 18), with the caution about the effects of licentious literature – including the *Decameron* and *Orlando furioso* – on the behaviour of young women (I, 34).

That Bandello himself was sensitive on this score is shown by his frequent protestations that evil is to be found in deeds and not in any description of man's behaviour, which may well serve as a terrible warning against sin, because examples taken from life are far more effective than any exhortation to virtue. At the very beginning, however, the author declares that he has arranged his tales without regard for chronology, edification, or the embellishment of the vernacular, 'but only in order to keep a record of things that have seemed to me worthy of being written down' (I, 1). Bandello's chief concern is with neither style nor morality. With regard to the former, he repeatedly acknowledges the fact that he is a Lombard by birth, incapable of writing good literary Tuscan and certainly far inferior to Boccaccio as an artist. Nevertheless, he is convinced that his subject matter contains sufficient interest and variety to delight his readers 'even though it were written in Bergamask dialect' (IV, 23). He is equally devoid of an inferiority complex where the achievements of Graeco-Roman antiquity are concerned. His intention is to concentrate on modern times, which are in no way inferior in painting, sculpture, poetry or warfare, but only in the dearth of writers able and willing to celebrate the things that happen every day (I, 8; II, 21; III, 24). Bandello's purpose is a humble one: to be a chronicler and to entertain his audience, while participating fully in Renaissance society. Ignoring the traditional framework, the letters that accompany the stories are a good example of this participation, dedicated as they are to over two hundred patrons and friends, and avoiding the pitfalls of morality in the body of the *novella*, even as they reflect the passion for letter-writing and friendship that quickened the Republic of Letters in Renaissance Europe.

GIAMBATTISTA GIRALDI published his collection of *novelle* (*Gli Ecatommiti*) in 1565. From the frontispiece to the last page, their author insists on the moral edification to be derived from his tales, designed to bolster the truths of the Christian religion and papal authority. Like the *Decameron*, Giraldi's work is prefaced by the description of a catastrophe: the Sack of Rome in 1527, from which ten men and women escape by sailing to Marseille. Already in the portrayal of the horrors perpetrated in Rome by the 'enemies of the Christian religion' we feel the pall of the Counter-Reformation, with its trumpeting morality and underground sadism and sensuality: the rape of young virgins on church altars, the slaughter of the innocents – these and other spectacles of violence have an obvious fascination for the professed moralist. In the opening of the First Day, Flaminio derides the casuistry of Platonic love while the author insists on the virtues of matrimony, the only type of earthly love that can bring peace to man. The Fifth Day is most properly devoted to tales of conjugal fidelity, the Third Day to its opposite (providing us, paradoxically, with the story of Othello: III, 7). The usual themes – wit, fortune, adventure – are offered, with a notable tendency to avoid the traditional satire of churchmen. The work ends, like the *Decameron*, with the grand theme of Chivalry – and a bonus of thirteen tales added for good measure. Behind the obvious moralizing, opportunities for excursions into occasional lasciviousness are not lost, while Giraldi's famous horror tragedy, *Orbecche*, has its origin in the early *novella* related in II, 2. The publication of the *Ecatommiti* signals the end of the Renaissance genre and ushers in a new era. Morality has returned with a vengeance.

Spain

'LA CELESTINA'

TOGETHER with *Don Quixote*, the *Celestina* is frequently spoken of as being one of the two greatest works in Spanish. Written in dialogue form, it appeared first, in a sixteen-act version, in 1499 or 1500 and again in 1501, under the title *Comedia de Calisto y Melibea*. Fernando de Rojas, who died in 1541, introduces this version with the explanation that, having come upon an anonymous piece of writing in dramatic form (that is, Act I), he was so impressed by it that he built on it and wrote the remaining fifteen acts himself. This account of the matter, after much debate, is now widely regarded as probably true. Rojas soon afterwards inserted five new acts near the end of the first version and called this revised form the *Tragicomedia de Calisto y Melibea*. Although six editions of the latter bear the date 1502, Mr F. J. Norton has recently shown that not one of them belongs to that year. The earliest known edition of the twenty-one-act *Tragicomedia* dates from 1507. By 1640 it had gone through more than thirty editions and been translated into all the major languages of Western Europe.

Quevedo, writing in praise of Spanish literature, spoke of the *Celestina* as an 'exemplary tragedy'. Much in the work invites one to see it as teaching a lesson. Calisto, a prosperous young man of good family, is seized by an overpowering passion for the beautiful, highly-born and unresponsive Melibea. Through a servant, Sempronio, he obtains the services of Celestina, a procuress now old but of vast experience and renown. Through her efforts his desires are fulfilled, but only after he has become a slave to his often blasphemous passion, put himself into the hands of his servants and Celestina herself, squandered his money in rewarding them, withdrawn from his social activities and responsibilities, and jeopardized his reputation. Moreover, one night when Calisto has gone to visit Melibea in the orchard of her father's house, he climbs out over the wall, slips from his high ladder and is killed, only moments after we have heard him and Melibea telling each other of the physical rapture that is now theirs. Melibea, seized with grief, throws herself to her death from the top of a tower of the house. Meanwhile, Celestina has refused to share the reward she had had from Calisto with her two accomplices, Sempronio and his friend Pármeno, another servant of Calisto's, and is murdered by Sempronio, with Pármeno urging him to 'finish her off' now that he has started. Hearing that officers of the law are coming, the two of them leap from the window of the room in Celestina's house where they have killed her, and, badly injured, are arrested and executed almost at once. Thus insane passion and greed lead to dishonour and death.

However, the *Celestina* is anything but a facile morality. Rojas reveals a remarkable psychological penetration into a whole range of character, and his art of revealing this little by little, showing us even the gestures and actions of the people we meet by means of descriptive details slipped into the dialogue, adds strength to our impression that the world he shows us is the concrete world of space and time. The extent to which his book communicates a sense of complex, living individuals and their relationships may well remain surprising, so opposed to verisimilitude are certain features of his technique. The language he uses is to a great extent that of rhetoric, highly formal and marked by extended elaboration. One of Rojas's greatest achievements is his success in using this kind of language to convey great intensity of emotion while combining it with popular turns of phrase, particularly proverbs, in such a way as frequently to make it emerge out of, and run back into, speech of a colloquial kind. Moreover, this work stands in the tradition of the Italian humanistic comedy, written by the learned for the learned. There is much book-learning in the *Celestina*, and it is the regular practice of Rojas to put Classical allusions and the aphorisms and arguments of moral philosophy into the mouths of characters such as Sempronio, Pármeno and Celestina herself, who could never have been instructed in such things. On the other hand, Rojas makes highly effective use of this practice in his portrayal of character. It gives his principal figures a considerable degree of intellectual understanding. They are able to reflect, analyse, and use words not only to express themselves with power and exactness but also to exercise persuasion on others. It often gives them an air of intelligent malice. The dramatic power that Rojas derives from the elaborate misuse of the concepts and arguments of moral philosophy is well seen when Celestina persuades Pármeno to abandon his moral principles and loyalty to his master, and when Calisto, after Pármeno's death, persuades himself that it is not wrong to continue with his passionate pursuit of Melibea. At such times we are given a vivid picture of conscious, intelligent moral corruption.

Rojas's greatest achievement in characterization is the procuress herself, Celestina, who so soon gave her name to the book. Certainly, moral evil is deeply rooted in her, as her treatment of Pármeno and Melibea, in particular, shows. But this very evil is of an immensely fascinating kind since she is herself a richly complex human being. She is insistently and genuinely proud of her professional skill and renown. This is especially important to her now that she feels herself to be an increasingly frail old woman. Her eagerness to arrange a successful conclusion for the wealthy Calisto's wishes owes something to her sense of the need to provide for her old age. On the other hand, the thought and, indeed, the spectacle of sexual pleasure give her the most intense delight. This, however, despite its corruption, seems to involve an element of genuine concern for the happiness of others. She speaks with a strangely simple sincerity of the sociability and good-fellowship of the gatherings in her brothel, especially in the good old days. She learnt the best of her art from the late Claudina, mother of Pármeno, and for her she still feels an admiration and affection that easily bring her to tears. Several times she commends her to God's keeping. Words of piety are for ever on her lips, and her religious feeling is clearly, though paradoxically, a real part of her make-up.

She is also a witch, human enough to wonder whether her spell on Melibea will work but, nevertheless, a long-practised and in this case successful one. For the modern reader it is hard to take this side of the work with the seriousness with which witchcraft and magic were regarded in sixteenth-century Europe. Even Pármeno fails to understand that Melibea's very rapid change from cold aloofness to a raging passion for Calisto that matches his for her is due to the spell that Celestina casts; and yet it is made quite clear that this is so. As a witch she becomes at times larger than life, a demonic figure serving the dark powers that operate particularly through sexual passion. This she repeatedly sees as all-present and all-powerful, holding all human kind, and indeed all living creatures, in its sway. Human beings may try to resist it, but they will fail. It is too sweet to refuse.

Her insistence on this presses the problem of the moral significance of the book. As a whole the story seems to illustrate the rightness of her view. The author goes to great lengths to show us how passion and sexual desire take hold of people and then, directly and indirectly, destroy them. In this the moral of the book might be expected to lie, and it is the case that the author lays stress on the fact that each person who dies in the course of the work does so 'without confession'. We are also, on occasion, invited to think of Celestina, Sempronio and Pármeno now paying for their sins. One may well accept it that Rojas was attracted to the writing of this work at least in part by the opportunity to warn, as the *Incipit* says, against disordered passion and the treacherous procuresses and evil, flattering servants through whom passion largely works its destructive effects. Nevertheless, the book displays a most striking lack of emphasis, almost a total absence, of positive moral or religious statement. Melibea, on the point of suicide, remarks that the improving books she has been given to read are of no help to her in her present crisis. Her father Pleberio, in the concluding lament over his daughter's death, says that he thought, when young, that there was a moral order in the world at large and in human life, but now he sees that existence is 'a labyrinth of errors, a hideous desert', a place where one finds the meaningless violence and conflict of which Rojas's Prologue makes so much. The work as a whole suggests that this final outburst of Pleberio's, which is its emotional climax, is not merely the expression of his grief, the error of a man who knows nothing of the bewitching of his daughter, but is a statement of what is true.

One character after another reflects that passion tempts with the promise of physical joys which last but a short time and are followed by destruction. A whole series of people create a web of greedy, self-centred passions in which they are all caught and suffer. Rojas often takes over from certain of Petrarch's Latin works his observations on the working of hostile Fortune, but in doing so gives them a still more pessimistic and even hopeless tone. Indeed, in a great many details he emphasizes the extent to which the deaths of his characters result from the ironic workings of Chance. For example, near the start of Act I, Calisto fears lest his own unhappy love for Melibea should bring him to the same end as Pyramus came to through his love for Thisbe. One recalls that the love of Pyramus and Thisbe for each other resulted in their double suicide and that this itself followed from a mistake brought about by a purely fortuitous happening. This story from Ovid is carefully echoed by Rojas, many acts later, in the speech that Melibea makes just after Calisto has fallen to his death, when he has misunderstood the cause of the disturbance outside the garden, and immediately before she throws herself to her own death. What Calisto had feared might happen, recalling Pyramus and Thisbe, has come to pass, and in a way that in essence closely resembles their fate. Repeatedly Rojas contrives this effect of irony. Celestina frequently declares that Fortune helps those who help themselves. She enters into league with Sempronio in order, ultimately, to obtain money from Calisto. To this end she wins over Pármeno both to herself and to Sempronio. But this involves corrupting him morally, and in consequence of this he joins forces with Sempronio against her and helps to bring about her death. In the interpolated Acts the ironies of the developing situation receive added stress. In Act XVI we learn that Pleberio and his wife had at last seriously set about arranging their daughter's marriage at the very time when she responded to the desires of Calisto. The destructive ironies of the work can even arise out of morally good acts. It is a desire to show Christian compassion that helps put Melibea into the power of Celestina. It is the desire of Calisto to go to the aid and protection of his servants waiting outside the garden that is the immediate cause of his death. Such pervasive irony leaves one not so much with a sense of a moral lesson presented as with a tragic awareness of a situation where individuals necessarily cooperate with forces and circumstances beyond their control in working their own destruction.

The many-sidedness of the *Celestina* and the measure of ambiguity that remains in the effect it produces on the reader make it difficult to say precisely why it enjoyed such great popularity. Much in its pessimistic view of life could well have found a response in the Senecan Stoicism that went so deeply into the sensibility of the age. Many readers, it seems clear, found it very satisfying as a work preaching an acceptable moral by arranging that all those who do wrong in the story meet a violent death. This is the view Vives took in his *De disciplinis (Concerning Studies)*. On the other hand, he had earlier declared, in his *Education of a Christian Woman*, that the work was corrupting and should be banned. The Index of Prohibited Books prepared for the Council of Trent displays what looks like a similar uncertainty of response. The draft of the document condemns the *Celestina* as 'obscene' and puts it in the company of Lucian, Aretino and Martial, but, unlike them, the *Celestina* disappears from the final version. Juan de Valdés praised Rojas for his skill in characterization, especially as regards Celestina herself. Rojas, in his Prologue, himself suggests that, for many, the appeal of his work lay principally in its account of the erotic love of Calisto and Melibea. He says he was asked to extend this, and, in the course of adding his extra Acts, did so. Not less intriguing than the reasons for the popularity of the *Celestina* is the fact that it is the work of a Spaniard of Jewish origins who had accepted baptism, wrote this work when still in his twenties and wrote nothing else during the nearly forty years that remained to him. These he spent in a successful legal career and, as it seems from his library, indulging a taste for romances of chivalry.

'AMADÍS DE GAULA' AND THE ROMANCE OF CHIVALRY

No other form of fiction was so popular in sixteenth-century Spain as the romance of chivalry. From 1508, the year of the earliest edition known to survive of GARCÍ RODRÍGUEZ DE MONTALVO's version of *Amadís de Gaula*, down to the 1590s, the romances of chivalry came from the presses in almost uninterrupted succession. Charles V, Francis I, Juan de Valdés, St Ignatius Loyola, St Teresa of Jesus, Vives – all read them. The *Amadís*, source and model for so many other romances, suggests a number of reasons for the enormous success of these works.

Montalvo's *Amadís* tells of the birth of its hero, his dubbing, his devotion to the lady Oriana, and of his exploits across north and central Europe, from England to Constantinople, where he fights other knights, giants, enchanters and monsters, before finally marrying his lady. The style and presentation are largely those of a story told aloud, and this probably had an appeal of its own in an age when even reading to oneself was, probably, not an altogether silent exercise and when romances of chivalry were in any case very often read to groups of people. The scene-setting for the numerous battles is frequently done with real dramatic effect, and the battles themselves are presented with a verve and vividness that make one think of the modern western. The laconic nonchalance that Amadís himself sometimes displays is at least worthy of James Bond. Amadís, too, is a handsome superman, defeating knights feared far and wide when he is a mere fifteen. But beyond all this, the appeal of the *Amadís* was due to the fact that it presents a world of values and of manners. The values are, most fundamentally, those of heroic bravery, loyalty and love. The loyalty is to good kings, fellow knights and one's lady. Here it becomes part of the courtly love that is the kind of love portrayed here. Even away in Bohemia, Amadís, disguised as the Knight of the Green Sword, has ever in his mind the image of his lady Oriana and still lives for her service. He will spend all night weeping for love of her. Such emotionalism is prominent in the work. Knights are moved to tears by each other's declarations of loyalty as well as by love for their ladies. And yet this emotion is expressed in a manner which is characteristically determined by a sense of style, elegance, formality and 'courtesy', which are felt to be essential to the business of living. One sees this clearly in the exchanges of Amadís and Oriana when they speak of their love for each other with that highly-wrought elaboration which Cervantes was later to parody so superbly.

The values of this literary world are, to a great extent, Christian, or at least not apparently opposed to Christianity. People pray, devoutly hear Mass, and show respect to holy hermits. Knights regard their dubbing as a Christian act, and people often express a pious belief in the workings of divine providence. The work contains passages of explicit moral reflection. Amadís himself time and again confronts evil, defends the right, and protects the weak. When he thinks he is dying, he offers an exemplary death-bed prayer. On the other hand, the way of life he follows is based on a highly conscious dedication to the ideals of valour, loyalty, honour and courtesy, and these, to say the least, are not specifically Christian values. This was a matter of all the greater moment in an age when ideas of what constituted Christian virtue were clear-cut and systematized to a high degree. More important still is the fact that Amadís finds his central inspiration in his lady and the love he feels for her. This courtly love, however refined its eroticism, was a further ground for attack in a period when erotic love, even within marriage, was frowned upon as dethroning reason. In this situation it becomes intelligible that, if the romances of chivalry were popular to a unique degree in sixteenth-century Spain, no other form of fiction was so much attacked. Juan de Valdés and Vives, like Loyola, look back upon their devotion to the romances as an aberration to be repented of, and join the many who made the endlessly repeated charges that the romances offered no profitable moral instruction and that reading them was a reprehensible waste of time.

These charges related also to theoretical difficulties keenly felt regarding fiction as such. If, in a work of fiction, one made a statement that was not true in the realm of fact and history, in what sense was this not a lie and therefore a thing to be condemned on moral grounds? The concept of 'imaginative truth' unrelated to actual facts and an accepted moral scheme was long in achieving a theoretical standing of its own. Juan de Valdés declared that 'those who write lies (i.e. fiction) must do so in such a way that these lies will approximate to truth as far as possible'. He, together with Vives, Andrés de Laguna and very many others, protested that the romances of chivalry did not do this: they tell not little lies but big ones; they depart from reality, probability and even possibility. Such a view may help to explain why the Inquisition did not ban the romances even though it was urged to. The Inquisition concerned itself primarily with works that made what were intended to be statements of the truth and which had a bearing on the Faith. It was when a writer undertook to use the convention of the romances as the vehicle of Christian allegory that the Inquisition took an interest.

The charges made by Valdés and the rest are not the same as those which a devotee of the nineteenth-century novel might make against 'unrealistic' works, nor are the interests and aims of the romances of chivalry at all those of the modern novel. To call these works 'novels' at all is confusing. They stand in the tradition of the late medieval French Arthurian romances, of Chrétien de Troyes and of the *Lancelot*. In Spain the earliest form of the *Amadís* goes back to the early fourteenth century. It was arousing great enthusiasm at the

Castilian court in the 1370s. By about 1490 Montalvo had three versions to draw on when he prepared his own and added a fourth book. It is from the Arthurian romances that the superhuman and love-lorn knights like Amadís derive, together with their heroic deeds performed in a remote past and in remote lands where marvellous and magical events occur. Whatever the literary theorists and moralists might say, people at large seem to have taken great pleasure in these features of the Spanish romances. It is surely significant that the much more realistic *Tirant lo Blanch*, first published in 1490 at Valencia, had only one edition in Spain in the sixteenth century, even though Cervantes was to praise it so highly.

If realism was not enough to make a romance successful, it remains to be asked just how unreal the world of *Amadís* and the like appeared to sixteenth-century Spaniards. In the previous century there had still been in actual fact many knights errant, challenges, jousts and tourneys. In the 1520s the chivalric diplomatic forms involving Kings of Arms still had great importance for Alfonso de Valdés, even when religious ceremonies had lost so much of their significance for him. Such forms were still observed when the Armada met the English fleet off Plymouth in 1588. Garrett Mattingly says that the snap judgements of the Armada's commander-in-chief, the Duke of Medina Sidonia, 'tended to stem rather from romances of chivalry than from military common sense.' It has been suggested that the conquistadores were spurred on by the exploits of knights in these works, as Henry the Navigator had been. The men with Cortés looked upon the Aztec city of Mexico and thought of the enchanted lands of the *Amadís*. California is the name of an island in the *Sergas de Esplandián*. Much remains to be discovered in the matter of why the romances of chivalry had such a wide and deep-reaching appeal for sixteenth-century people. At least it is clear that these works have a great deal to tell us about the whole question of the relationship of fact and imagination in their minds.

THE PICARESQUE NOVEL

The description 'picaresque novel' is given to a series of prose narratives, written mainly in the first half of the seventeenth century,

The general distinguishing features of which tend to be that in them a man (or, more rarely, a woman) recounts the story of his life, beginning with his birth to lowly-placed and disreputable parents, his early life of struggle against adversity, the tricks and deceptions to which he was driven in order to survive, his endeavours to improve his lot, and the success or failure that concluded his efforts. Just as the origin of the word *pícaro* continues to be a problem, so also regarding the number of these works agreement is lacking, since definition here involves questions of interpretation: but perhaps up to a dozen or so Spanish works have commonly been regarded as 'picaresque'. They include three of the most impressive prose works in Spanish: Quevedo's *Vida del Buscón*, written early in the seventeenth century, and – in the sixteenth – the anonymous *Lazarillo de Tormes*, published in 1554, and Mateo Alemán's *Guzmán de Alfarache* (Part I, 1599; Part II, 1604), known in its own day simply as *El Pícaro*.

'LAZARILLO DE TORMES' consists of only five main chapters, and even these are quite short. Few prose works of such brevity can have at once aroused such admiration for their artistry and posed so many questions concerning authorship, date of composition, and meaning.

By common consent, this is one of the most immediately delightful works in Spanish. Its author had a wonderful skill in delineating types of character, capturing it in situation, gesture and speech. Each of the portraits (or rather, sketches) he gives us of Lázaro's former masters – the blind beggar, the parish priest, the squire and the seller of papal Bulls – lives in the mind with extraordinary vividness. The comedy of character and incident is handled with superb deftness. (Throughout, the book displays the art which hides art.) Well might a seventeenth-century Englishman find it 'for the number of strange and merry reports, very recreative and pleasant'. There are the various battles of wits between Lazarillo and his succession of masters. There are also the wonderful displays of mock piety by the Blind Man and Pardoner, the social antics of the Squire, and the grand gestures of generosity of the miserly Curate of Maqueda, as when he gives Lazarillo bare bones to eat and says as he does so: 'Take, eat, rejoice, the whole world is there for you. A better life you have than the Pope himself.'

However, it is at such a point that the central problem of the book makes itself felt. Is comedy the sole or principal aim of the work, or has it, at its centre, the intention of social and moral criticism? Are we, in this case, to laugh at the absurdity of the Curate or to condemn him for cruel miserliness? Is one to read the chapter about the Pardoner as a highly comic account of the tricks played by an accomplished rogue or to condemn him as an agent and representative of the corruption of the Church? Any chapter of the book raises what is in essence the same question, and one may well be led to take the serious view of the book if one concludes, as a good deal of evidence might suggest, that the adult Lázaro, in writing his autobiography, is explaining how he learnt from his masters that the ways of the world can bestow material well-being, and is showing how he has succeeded on the basis of this lesson. He does in the end marry the mistress of an archpriest because the latter, to suit himself, will look after him materially, and he does conclude his life-story with the comment: 'It was then that I was in prosperity and at the summit of all good fortune.' If this is the shameless and even boastful acceptance of his own moral degradation that it appears, it becomes very plausible to interpret the work as a study of the way in which an individual is corrupted by society – that society being represented in its various parts by Lázaro's successive masters.

However, to accept this view seems to imply that one sees the comedy of the work as being largely unrelated to its moral intention and central concern, except in so far as they come together in the function of satire. Certainly one cannot say that there is no satire here. The portraits of the men of the Church, for example, showing the difference that exists between the face they present to the world and the moral reality of their characters, were no doubt not without satirical significance and effect in the sixteenth century. The problem is to decide how much interest the unknown author took in this aspect of his work.

One fact about him that is still becoming ever clearer is that he based his work to a very large extent on material already existing in literary form and oral tradition. It has long been known that the blind man and his boy appear quite often in medieval French dramatic works, and that incidents involving them identical to those found in the *Lazarillo* are represented in the margins of a fourteenth-century manuscript. It has only recently been discovered that the episode where Lazarillo concludes to his horror that the funeral procession is coming to the house of his master the Squire because that too is a 'house where they never eat or drink' was a popular story deriving from an Arabic work. It is evident that, whatever interest the author of the *Lazarillo* had in contemporary Spanish society, his interest in the work he was composing was to a high degree a literary one.

This literary interest seems to have led him to take over a particular tradition of writing which, through the treatment it receives from him, may help one to find out more about the way in which he regarded his book. This is the very old tradition of praising the low-born man who, by his virtue, ability, energy and public concern, overcomes his disadvantages and difficulties in life, achieves public regard and renown, and acquires for himself the true nobility that is based on virtue rather than ancestry and is within the reach of all men. These ideas were sometimes, in the fifteenth and sixteenth centuries, set out in the form of speeches in which the low-born man vigorously defends his own achievement in life. The *Lazarillo*, in its main structure, appears to be a comic parody of these ideas thus expressed. Thus the basic progression of the work comes to be seen, at least in part, as a literary game or joke, based on the comic technique of inversion and the attitude of irony. This in turn leads one to see the comedy of the book as central to the concern of its author. Moreover, it encourages one to see in his repeated portrayal of the incongruities between a man's public image and his real character an expression of an ironic amusement at the inconsistencies of life which, at the least, exists alongside any more condemnatory attitudes. It may also lead one to see Lázaro, the fictitious author, as sharing not a little of his creator's own irony.

On the other hand, Lázaro, at the end of his story, is in a situation of moral ignominy which, moreover, is in many ways strikingly similar to the situation in life from which he started, when his mother was the mistress of a Moor. This would seem, again, to be a pattern which largely derives from the author's vision of the comic irony of things. It may also possibly express some sterner moral observation. The modern reader, at least, is unlikely, when he reaches this point, to be entirely without a sense of ambiguity.

MATEO ALEMÁN (1547–*c.* 1613) was born in the same year as Cervantes and died only about three years before him, in Mexico. But if Cervantes gives us, in *Don Quixote*, a whole world of living characters, Alemán, in his own enormous work, *Guzmán de Alfarache*, concentrates on one figure: Guzmán himself, showing us his life as a *pícaro*, and, in the end, his moral conversion. The form of the narrative is autobiographical, and this here determines the tone and moral character of the work. It is true that sometimes Guzmán finds amusement as well as grounds for professional pride in recalling his past skill in the role of thief and deceiver; but there is relatively little comedy. For much more of the time the repentant Guzmán portrays his past life as an example of the way in which a man grows in the ways of evil and sin, and how, amidst and even by means of the sorrows and afflictions that this brings upon him, God can lead a man to repentance and salvation.

The narrative tells how Guzmán was born to disreputable parents, left home and took to the road, how eventually he went to Rome, where he served in the households of the Spanish ambassador and a cardinal, and how, after more adventures, he returned to Spain, went to Alcalá university, married, returned to his native Seville and got himself sentenced to the galleys. This story extends over more than 1,200 pages in the standard modern edition, but by no means fills them. Much greater in bulk is the amount of moral reflection, exhortation and Christian preaching that the work contains. Alemán stressed the didactic character and intention of his book. It was to serve as a 'watch-tower' from which one could look out on all kinds of wickedness and warn against them. The responsiveness of the age to didactic and homiletic writing at once recognized and welcomed it here. The First Part of the *Guzmán* appeared in 1599. By the end of 1604, when the Second Part came out, at least twenty-three editions had been produced. In England, where five editions of James Mabbe's translation appeared, the moral side of the work was singled out for praise by, among others, Ben Jonson.

That this side of the work will be as readily received by the modern reader is unlikely; but he will still respond to Alemán's mastery of language which, according to Gracián, quite soon led many to regard him as the best and most Classical writer in Spanish. As his treatise of 1609 on *Castilian Orthography* shows, literary composition well performed was in Alemán's eyes a matter for high praise. He took a professional interest in writing, set himself high standards in matters of euphony, vigour and clarity, and took a particular pride in Castilian as a literary medium. In the *Guzmán*, what might so easily have been tedious moralizing is given force, point and vividness. He handles with equal success the ample, cumulative construction and the condensed phrase, concrete images and proverbs. Comparing the lots of rich and poor, he can observe (in Mabbe's words) that 'money warmeth the bloud, and maketh it quick and active: Whereas he that is without it, is but a dead body that walkes up and downe like a ghost amongst the living.' To carry out the suggestions of his own disposition, says Guzmán,

I had force enough; to seeke out occasion of sinne, abilitie sufficient: to persevere in them, an untired constancie: and in not leaving them, a firmenesse not to be removed. I was as well acquainted with all manner of vice, as I was a stranger to all kinde of vertue. And to lay the fault upon Nature, I have no reason for it in the world. For I had no lesse abilitie for good, than inclination to evill. The fault was mine own; for she [Nature] never did any thing out of reason ... she was never defective in what was fitting, but as she hath beene corrupted since through sin; and mine [=my sins] were so many, that I produced the cause of this bad effect, and became my owne hangman. [Part I, Book iii, Chapter 9.]

These lines are representative of a good deal of what we find in *Guzmán*. Alemán describes him (to use Mabbe's words again) as 'a man of cleare understanding, holpen by Learning, and punished by Time, making benefit of that idle time, which he had in the Gallies.' Each of these facts about him is important. Guzmán, we are told, has studied Latin, Greek and Rhetoric well: he possesses book-learning, the power of moral reflection and the power of expression. That is, Mateo Alemán, in a way that is remarkable for his age, contrives to give verisimilitude to the relationship between the tale and its teller. Guzmán, having had the experiences here described, might well have reflected on them and written about them in the way one finds done in this book. The coherence of this relationship between the point of view of the alleged narrator and the story that is told, when its effect is combined with that of the language, produces on the reader a strong sense, for much of the time at least, not of a sermon preached *in vacuo* but of a living person writing in the fulness of concentration, scrutinizing his past experiences and responses from his present stand-point and composing an acutely intelligent and deeply felt piece of moral and spiritual self-analysis, and, on the basis of that, exhortation.

Even so, this is still not a fully developed psychological novel. Alemán's interest is in the teaching of his book rather than in the mind of Guzmán, and in Guzmán as an exemplar rather than as an individual. In particular, the final conversion of Guzmán may well now seem to be inadequately treated and to rest too much on a religious assumption – the assumption alluded to by George Herbert when, in his poem 'The Pulley' he makes God say to heedless man: 'If goodness leade him not, yet wearinesse / May tosse him to my breast.' On the other hand, it is a major part of Alemán's concern to induce in his readers a particular kind of weariness with the world, to bring them to undeceive themselves as regards the false and unreal attractions and values that belong only to this world. Over against the latter is the world everlasting, the world of truth, and only in the way that leads to this can men find real and enduring satisfaction. Alemán never writes with more powerful eloquence than on the theme of the falseness and fleetingness of the things that are merely of this world (see for example, Part I, Book i, Chapter 7; Part I, Book iii, Chapter 1). However, the otherworldliness of this view, in so far as it goes beyond a preoccupation with the need to escape from the moral deceptiveness of this world, is implicit rather than explicit, and the book as a whole may leave one uncertain as to how far its pessimism about life in this world is theologically based and controlled.

So far as Guzmán's account of his past life involves the ideas that human nature is not wholly corrupted by sin and that man, even while sinful, has a certain freedom of will in nature to choose and do what is good, it is on the side of the Council of Trent as distinct from that of Luther. On the other hand, the popularity of this work in seventeenth-century Anglican and Puritan England indicates the difficulties that arise if one interprets it as, in an *exclusive* sense, an expression of the Tridentine Counter-Reformation. Moreover, it would be easier to decide how far the pessimism of this work derives from theological and philosophical sources at all if one knew more about the life of Alemán, who, after all, published Part I of this work, which was his first, when he was fifty-two. There is, for example, the fact that in 1593 he had been sent as a fairly minor judicial official to the mercury mines run by the Fuggers at Almadén to inquire into charges of excessive harshness and brutality suffered by the galley-convicts who worked there. The appalling facts he discovered on this visit may well have made a deep impression on him. Again, he sometimes speaks of the self-seeking, rivalry and deceiving ways of men in terms reminiscent of Machiavelli, while the motto he made his own and put into his books was: 'Against ambush no prudence avails' ('Ab insidiis non est prudentia'). On the other hand, Alemán does not always write pessimistically about this world. In his *Castilian Orthography* he praises the powers, inventions and achievements of men, including those of his own age, in terms of optimistic enthusiasm which recall the famous words of Rabelais. However, regarding the large measure of pessimism in *Guzmán* which did derive from religious and philosophical sources, one may wonder how far it is an expression of that pessimism associated with the writings of St Augustine which pervaded so much of sixteenth-century thought and continued to do so in Roman Catholic Europe even after the Council of Trent, with its different doctrinal emphasis. Again, Alemán's *Life of St Antony of Padua* (1604) shows how well he knew the Bible, and his debt in this matter to Job, Ecclesiastes and Ecclesiasticus may well have been great. There is also the Stoic teaching of Seneca, with his obsessive and vividly expressed sense of time for ever passing, bringing men nearer with each breath to the grave and reducing objects of even the most alluring appearance to mere dust. A sensitivity to this fact of life, derived from various sources, had been a prominent feature of the fifteenth century, and it is perhaps a question how far one might properly see in *Guzmán de Alfarache* a remarkable statement of a feeling about life which, though highly typical of late sixteenth-century Spain, had come down out of the fifteenth century and, as it seems, had haunted men in all parts of Western Europe throughout Alemán's lifetime.

THE PASTORAL NOVEL

The pastoral novel was, to a great extent, the creation of sixteenth-century Spain. Its history there begins with *Los siete libros de la Diana* of JORGEDE MONTE MAYOR (*c.* 1520–61), which very probably first appeared in 1559, when its author was about thirty-nine. This remained the most renowned and, in various ways, the normative example of the type. By 1600 not less than twenty-six editions of the Spanish had appeared, and eleven of French translations. Sir Philip Sidney was much indebted to it for his own *Arcadia*, which itself remained the most popular work of fiction in English until well into the eighteenth century. After Montemayor's *Diana*, the most important works of the kind in sixteenth-century Spain were GASPAR GIL POLO's sequel to it, the *Diana enamorada* (1564), and CERVANTES's *La Galatea* (1585).

The appeal of such works was largely based on the fact that they brought together a number of elements already much in favour. Each work is made up, above all, of a series of stories about the adventures and situations into which shepherds and shepherdesses, as it usually is, are drawn by their loves and the workings of fortune. These stories are, for the most part, highly complicated, often interlock with each other, and were well calculated to satisfy the taste of the sixteenth century for episodic narrative. In technique they recall, and probably owe much to, Heliodorus's *Aethiopica*, itself so enormously successful at the time and later imitated by Cervantes in his *Persiles y Sigismunda*. The love of these shepherds and shepherdesses for each other is essentially courtly love, to varying degrees as modified by Petrarch. It combines extremes of passion (devotion, aspiration and despair) with elegance, courtesy and refinement of behaviour and statement. Their amorous pursuits and conversations take place in the setting of a pastoral countryside where shady woods, cool glades and clear, running streams form a world whose harmonious beauty matches that of the young men and women who live in it. The background mood is one of sustained lyricism, and this is heightened by the typical mingling, in these works, of prose and verse. While echoes of Garcilaso, especially, are found in both the prose and the verse, the authors, in writing their verse, took pleasure in composing in a wide variety of forms. In a way that is characteristic of sixteenth-century Spain, the poems embrace both the Italianate tradition and the national, popular one.

The individual novels differ from each other in a number of ways. Montemayor's *Diana*, for example, achieves a unique degree of consistency in its creation of an imaginative world, even though, at one point, in response to the current of taste that produced the *romances moriscos* and Pérez de Hita's *Guerras civiles de Granada* (1595), Montemayor brings in the story of El Abencerraje, where the courtly love situation is translated into Moorish terms. The prose of the *Diana* is marked by what is, even among these works, an extraordinary musicality and rhythmic subtlety – qualities related, perhaps, to the fact that, while Montemayor was a Portuguese writing in Castilian, he was also a professional singer who had gained entry to the courts and chapel choirs of Portugal and Spain through his ability as a musician. The creation of an imaginative, literary world enclosed within itself and distinct from that in which we live is less complete in the *Diana enamorada*, while in *La Galatea* the intermingling of the two – which, in the *Quixote*, was to be central to Cervantes's highest achievement – too often produces a troubling ambiguity of reference. In Sannazaro's *Arcadia*, published in Spanish in 1547, the pastoral setting plays a much greater part than the portrayal and analysis of emotion. Montemayor, who about 1560 brought out a translation of the poems of Ausias March, reverses this emphasis. Within the convention of courtly love he traces the feelings of his shepherdesses, especially, with great acuity and delicacy – with too much in the opinion of some, whose criticism of the *Diana* and similar writing, including Garcilaso's verse and the romances of chivalry, suggests that they feared this type of literature encouraged young women to bring to earthly love a degree and subtlety of interest that were properly kept for religion. The most celebrated example of this criticism is found in *La conversión de la Magdalena* (1588) by the Augustinian Malón de Chaide.

Montemayor shows little desire to undertake a theoretical consideration of the nature of love. At one point he gives us what is in fact a translation of part of the *Dialoghi d'amore* (printed 1535) by LEONE EBREO, a Jew born at Lisbon about 1460 who left Spain in 1492 for Italy, where he practised as a physician and wrote this very famous work. The section Montemayor translates argues that extremes of emotion, beyond the control of reason, can be characteristic of virtuous love as well as of morally corrupt love, and thus the passage justifies in general terms what we find portrayed in the book at large. In the *Diana enamorada*, however, Gil Polo not only shows a much greater interest in discussing the same question but also displays a strong inclination to condemn passionate earthly love, even though his book is largely based on it. At the start of the *Diana enamorada*, the shepherdess Alcida rejects the view that the love symbolized by Cupid is in truth a god, a force from outside which cannot be resisted. Its strength is rather the weakness with which men and women surrender their freedom of mind and will; it is a disordered appetite which will-power and sound understanding can and should overcome. Her ideal is virtue's Golden Mean. These views find support from 'the wise Felicia', the lady who arranges happy endings for the loves of the shepherds and shepherdesses. Having done this she rather surprisingly declares their amorous ardours to be 'extremely hateful' to her. She urges them to abandon this love which is the enemy of reason and virtue, and to give themselves instead to a love of things that are high, perfect and heavenly. Both she and Alcida make us look at the poetry of courtly love from the outside, and speak of its most characteristic vocabulary of lovers' pains only to invert its meaning or deprive it of any.

La Galatea contains a many-sided approach to the same question. In particular, a neo-Platonic view of love leads Lenio to reject and condemn passionate love, especially as developed in the courtly love convention, while it leads Elicio to defend it, and in this he is joined by Tirsi, who bases himself on more roundabout arguments. The long speeches in which Tirsi and Lenio expound their views in Book IV are extensively drawn from Italian Renaissance treatises on love. However, the issue of these speeches is inconclusive, and so is the lesson of the work as a whole, despite Lenio's capitulation to the love he has condemned, for, like the *Diana* and Gil Polo's sequel, it is un-finished. The *Galatea* was Cervantes's first book, published five years after he was ransomed from the Moors. On his death-bed he was still saying he intended to complete it.

These works, then, keep before us a number of questions centred on that of the proper relationship between passionate love, rational understanding, and the will. Their frequent references to *desengaño* (that is, the undeceiving of oneself) with regard to the deceits of passionate love sometimes suggest the possibility of a connection be-tween such references and the exhortations to *desengaño* regarding all merely earthly pleasures and values which are so frequently to be met with elsewhere. The interest these works display in the question of the nature of true love gives rise to many questions relating to their artistic coherence and success; but it also extends their range and interest, and points towards the discussions of the passions which were to be so important in France in the late sixteenth century and in the seventeenth.

*

To complete the record of Spanish fiction in the sixteenth century a note should be added on the short stories. The best known of these appear in longer works: *El Abencerraje* in Montemayor's *Diana* (1559) and the four extraneous stories introduced into *Guzmán de Alfarache* (1599–1604). But if the short story did not flourish in sixteenth-century Spain, there was still a taste for it. The *Decameron* was printed several times in Spanish in the first half of the century but thereafter was allowed to circulate only in the expurgated Italian version of 1573. Still later than this came translations of works by Straparola, Bandello and Giraldi. A model *novella* is presented in Gracián Dantisco's *El Galateo* (1582). The most important collection of short stories published in Spain in the century (if one does not count *Lazarillo de Tormes*) was Juan de Timoneda's *El patrañuelo* (1567), where thirteen of the twenty-two stories derive from Italian sources. (The title comes from *patraña*: fable, tale, trick.) However, it was only with Cervantes's *Novelas ejemplares*, published in 1613, that the short story in Spain acquired major importance.

FOUR

Germany

GERMAN fiction in the sixteenth century embraces a number of distinct narrative traditions. Quantitively, undoubtedly the most successful tradition was that represented by the chivalric novel. Many of these novels – for the most part translations and adaptations of French originals (*Hug Schapler, Loher und Maller, Pontus und Sidonia, Melusine*), but including prose versions of medieval German epics and historical romances (*Wigoleysz vom Rade, Tristrant, Alexander*) – had circulated originally only in manuscripts intended for aristocratic readers. Towards the end of the fifteenth century they began to appear in print, initially in de luxe editions clearly intended for a wealthy clientele and latterly – an inevitable consequence of the democratization of literature consequent on the invention of printing – in editions which were conspicuous only for their cheapness and technical inferiority. Since Görres and the Romantics first developed an interest in popular literature, it has been customary to speak of these romances as *Volksbücher* (folk-books). The term is misleading in its suggestion of a false analogy with the *Volkslied* (folk-song) and they are more correctly described as *Ritterromane* (novels of chivalry). Unlike the folk-song, they were in no sense the anonymous expression of the literary genius of the people, never having been subjected to the process of modification by oral tradition, nor did they, like *Volksbücher* of the type of *Eulenspiegel* or *Faust*, embody popular elements. They were the last degenerate descendants of an aristocratic literary tradition and they were popular only in the sense that they were read by the people.

The literary qualities which speak from the pages of these chivalric novels are slight. Like the modern thriller or Western, their function was to excite and to entertain – hence their proscription by contemporary clerics and later by the eighteenth-century Enlightenment as *pestiferi libri*. Occasional moralizing notwithstanding, the interest of the audience lay in the events narrated: the adventures of the gallant knights, the trials of their ladies, the heroic exploits against heavy odds and the moving spectacle of sorely tried but constant true love. Character development, 'fine writing' and philosophies expressed in images were at a discount. In the sixteenth century itself, the chivalric tradition brought forth a number of belated children (*Magelone*, 1527; *Fierabras*, 1533; *Die Haymonskinder*, 1535) which soon joined the established favourites amongst the lists of sixteenth-century best-sellers, and as late as 1578 the Frankfurt publisher, Sigmund Feyerabend, brought out an omnibus edition of some thirteen *Ritterromane*. But for all its popularity, it was not the chivalric novel, but the *Schwanksammlung* or collection of humorous anecdotes which was to emerge as the characteristic genre in German narrative fiction in the sixteenth century.

The anecdotal tradition of the sixteenth century unites two disparate elements, which for convenience we may describe as 'learned' and 'popular'. The 'learned' – prose – tradition looks back to the *Gesta Romanorum*, the medieval collections of *exempla* and to the more recent translations of Boccaccio (Heinrich Schlüsselfelder's translation appeared in 1472 and a second, revised edition in 1535) and the humanist *facetiae*. The earliest fifteenth-century representatives of this tradition were the four volumes of *Facetiae* published by the humanist Heinrich Bebel between 1508 and 1514 which, although not translated into German until 1558, constitute a seminal work in their rootedness in Swabian village life, their genial good humour, their awareness of both the shrewdness and the gullibility of the peasant (in the fictive village of Mündlingen Bebel presents us with a Swabian Abdera), and their merciless satire of clerical humbug. On a somewhat different level Johann Pauli's collection of 700 preachers' *exempla*, published under the title *Schimpff und Ernst* (*Jest and Gravity*) in 1522, although notably lacking in Bebel's immediacy and closeness to real life, were to prove a perennial source of amusement and inspiration – especially when purged of the heavy didactic conclusions which the learned Franciscan drew from his stories.

It was, however, JÖRG WICKRAM's *Rollwagenbüchlein* (*Coach Book*) of 1555 which gave decisive impetus to the vogue in the vernacular anecdote. As the title suggests, the collection was conceived simply as literary entertainment to lighten the tedium of contemporary travel. Himself a child of the rising bourgeoisie – he came of a prosperous merchant family and worked as a goldsmith in his native Colmar (Alsace) before taking up a post in the civil administration – Wickram prefers an urban setting for his anecdotes and rarely bores us with moralizing. His style is concise almost to a fault and bears witness to a determination to write simple, natural German – which is in striking contrast to the often stilted style of his longer works. The stories usually depend on a verbal *pointe* for their effect, although they are by no means free from the crude and cruel humour of the age – especially when it is a question of satirizing the Roman clergy or the peasantry. The success for the *Rollwagenbüchlein* was sufficient to produce a crop of imitations and continuations. The most important of these were: Jacob Frey's *Die Garten Geselschafft* (*The Garden Company*, 1556), Martin Montanus's *Wegkürtzer* (*Journey Shortener*, 1557; notable chiefly for its introduction of an eroticism reminiscent of Boccaccio) and Michael Lindener's *Katzipori* and *Rastbüchlein* (*Rest Booklet*; both 1558; also characterized by a strong erotic element, but remarkable chiefly for a prose style which anticipates Fischart in its predilection for puns and love of piling up synonyms).

The older, 'popular' anecdotal tradition was somewhat different from the humanistic *facetiae* in that it aimed at bringing together amusing incidents and witticisms associated with one or other of the waggish heroes of folk-mythology. As a literary tradition, this type of *Schwanksammlung* looks back to Der Stricker's *Der Paffe Amis* (*c.* 1225) and the latter's late medieval descendants such as *Der Pfaffe von Kalemberg* (*The Parson of Kalemberg*), *Neidhart Fuchs* and *Salomon und Markolf*, which began to appear in print towards the end of the fifteenth century. Although written in verse which testifies to their medieval origin, these 'wags' biographies' remained popular throughout the sixteenth century and even inspired occasional imitations: Achilles Jason Widmann's *History Peter Lewen, des andern Kalembergers* (*The Story of Peter Lew the Second Kalemberger*) appeared in 1560, while in 1572 Fischart produced a rhymed version of *Eulenspiegel*. Translated into prose, however, the episodic form and the love of the scurrilous anecdote associated with an antisocial hero were to exercise a decisive influence on the two most memorable works of prose narrative in the sixteenth century: the 'biographies' of Till Eulenspiegel and Dr Johann Faust.

Ein kurtzweilig lesen von Dyl Ulenspiegel (*An Amusing Account of*

Dyl Ulenspiegel), published anonymously in Strasbourg in 1515 and probably drawing on older sources now lost, is an account of the career of the celebrated Low German wag and layabout who died about 1350. The author presents us with some ninety-five anecdotes in which Till Eulenspiegel, in accordance with his name (Low German 'ulen' = 'to clean', 'Spegel' = 'rear', 'back-side'; 'Eulenspiegel' = 'Owl-Glass' is a piece of folk etymology), cocks a snook at the whole of contemporary society from the local baker to the King of Denmark. A classless vagabond, albeit of peasant stock, Eulenspiegel wanders about the country in search of amusement, a victim of the arrogance, greed and prejudice of his more settled fellows, and in turn exacting a merciless waggish vengeance from both innocent and guilty for the insults to which he is subjected. Although an evident satirical intention, somewhat reminiscent of the picaresque novel, occasionally makes itself felt in the mockery of the stupidity, dishonesty and hypocrisy of many of Till's victims (for example, in chapters 14, 27, 50, 62), most of the anecdotes are clearly intended to amuse rather than to instruct. The individual stories are of unequal quality: tales conspicuous only for their triviality, crudity or pointlessness jostle anecdotes of perennial charm and even profundity. The humour is generally unsophisticated and often more than a little robust, proceeding either from a curiously naïve and uninhibited coarseness, usually of an excretory nature (Till serves his master excrement instead of mustard; he excretes in bed and persuades his host that a priest is responsible, etc.) or from Till's standard device of taking orders in the strictly literal sense (he is told to grease the cart and covers the whole thing with grease; as a tailor's apprentice he is told to sew so that his stitches cannot be seen and so does his sewing under a tub, etc.). But for all the crudity and naïveté it is impossible not to be captivated by the robust vigour of the hero or to laugh at the sheer exuberance of many of his pranks. Not surprisingly, in an age which did not suffer from the over-refinement of modern taste, the *Volksbuch* was a great favourite and passed through numerous editions, translations and adaptations and down to our own day has continued to provide inspiration for generations of writers and musicians (Sachs and Fischart in the sixteenth century, Nestroy, Hauptmann, Wedekind, de Coster, Richard Strauss and Reznicek in the last 100 years).

The other great figure which the sixteenth-century *Volksbuch* gave to literature was Dr Faust. His biography, *Historia von D. Johann Fausten, dem weitbeschreyten Zauberer und Schwartzkünstler* (*The Story of Dr Johann Faust, the Famous Magician and Necromancer*) written by an unnamed author and published by the Frankfurt book-seller Johann Spies in 1587, is constructed from a variety of traditional legends and anecdotes variously attributed to other magicians, but which, long before 1587, had increasingly accreted round the highly unsavoury necromancer, Georg Faustus (*c.* 1490–*c.* 1540). For no very obvious reason the author divides his account of the life and death of Faust into three parts. The first deals with Faust's early years, his thirst for knowledge and consequent conjuration of and pact with the devil, who in exchange for Faust's soul is to serve him for twenty-four years. In the second part, Mephistophilis, the devil's agent, continues Faust's instruction in astronomy and meteorology; Faust descends into Hell and explores the heavens and then embarks on a grand tour of Europe and the near East. In the third part Faust visits the courts of several princes, plays tricks on an assortment of bishops, knights and peasants, conjures the shade of Helen of Troy and has a child by her and finally, the twenty-four years of his pact having elapsed, is killed by the devil, all attempts to turn him from the wicked error of his ways having failed.

As it stands, the final result is a pretty obvious piece of book-making which subsumes a variety of disparate elements without ever resolving them into a unified whole. The fortunes of Faust, the impious searcher after knowledge, are frequently lost from sight in the welter of geographical detail in the travelogue (mostly cribbed from Sebastian Münster's *Cosmographia*) and the devout Lutheran author occasionally forgets his horror at Faust's wickedness in his desire to remind us of the pernicious nature of the Church of Rome – Mephistophilis appears as a monk and insists that Faust remain celibate, and during the visit to Rome even Faust is disgusted by the immorality of the Roman clergy. For the greater part of the second and third parts, too, we are caught up in a *Schwanksammlung* where Faust, as an academic wag and trickster, a sort of Eulenspiegel with magical powers, plays pranks on all and sundry, conjuring a pair of horns on a knight's head, eating a cart-load of hay belonging to an obstreperous peasant, selling a dealer a horse which turns into a bale of hay, etc.

It is obviously unfair to look at the Faust *Volksbuch* with literary hindsight, but even so one cannot help feeling that the author was conspicuously unaware of the tremendous possibilities of his theme. Except in the *Schwänke* he clearly has little sympathy for his hero: there is no trace of Marlowe's feeling of pity for the 'branch that might have grown full straight', no attempt, even in the occasional thoughts of repentance, to evoke the tragic conflict of the two souls in Faust's breast, nor is there any sense of the Promethean nature of Faust's pact with the devil or awareness of the poetry inherent in his association with Helen. Precisely those qualities which have most excited and inspired subsequent generations are for Faust's first biographer the most reprehensible and it is easy – and by no means unusual – to seize on the undoubted anti-intellectualism and obscurantism of the book as evidence of the darkening of the human spirit under the influence of narrow and oppressive Lutheran orthodoxy. Certainly, the author is no humanist concerned to see in the search for knowledge a search for God. Fundamentally he denies the individual's right to pursue scientific truth uninhibitedly: the unrestricted pursuit of knowledge, he suggests, should never be an end in itself. Indeed, in some matters ignorance is infinitely preferable to knowledge, and a man may pay too high a price for what he learns. Like his descendant in Goethe's drama, Faust has exhausted all natural means of acquiring knowledge, and his pact with the devil enables him to tear aside the veil behind which a wise Godhead has hidden those things we should not know. As a child of the Enlightenment, Goethe could see in the urge to strive after knowledge, even at the price of eternal damnation, something great and noble, a manifestation of the divine in man – hence the ultimate salvation of his hero in spite of the latter's crimes. The stern Lutheran author of the Faust *Volksbuch* is a stranger to such humane optimism, however, and for him Faust's desire to 'investigate all causes in heaven and on earth' is an example of impious and frivolous curiosity which is bound in the end to plunge Faust into catastrophe. At first sight the modern 'liberal' reader may find this attitude and the attendant belief in the physical existence of the devil quaintly naïve: Goethe's sophisticated demons who, for all their negation, ultimately work for good are undoubtedly more congenial than the full-blooded Lutheran devil who speaks from the pages of the Faust *Volksbuch*. Yet despite its seeming naïveté and obscurantism the message of the book is startlingly modern. Behind all the demonological trappings and anti-intellectualism, the author is simply saying that, emancipated from a controlling morality which can give ethical direction to scientific investigation, the pursuit of knowledge is ultimately an evil and self-destructive thing. And in the mid twentieth century it would be a very foolish reader who would seek to disagree with such a claim.

*

It is one of the commonplaces of German literary history that the sixteenth century represents a middle-class interlude before the restoration of 'courtly' values in the absolutist seventeenth century; yet so far we have seen little evidence of this in prose narrative. The writers of the *Schwanksammlungen* were, like most sixteenth-century writers, indeed members of the middle class, but few of them were concerned to advance a specifically middle-class point of view. This is true even of the *Volksbuch* entitled *Fortunatus* (1509), commonly held to be the first middle-class novel in German literature, which gives an account of the way in which Fortunatus and his two sons pass, as it were, 'from clogs to clogs' in two generations. Middle-class elements play a considerable role: the anonymous author is clearly a product of a mercantile environment (he is usually considered to have been an Augsburg merchant) who takes care to note 'commercial' details such as the role of the Lombard bankers in London and the importance of Alexandria as an international market, while the geographical range of the story between Palestine and Ireland is evidence of a cosmopolitan outlook quite appropriate to a citizen of an international banking centre. Equally, an undoubted Micawberish note creeps in when the author writes of the importance of living within one's income, and from time to time the nobility is shown in a highly critical light. Yet it is ultimately the fairy-tale element which predominates: as a penniless youth the hero is given a gift of fortune in the shape of a never-empty purse, to which is subsequently added a magic hat which will transport him wherever he wishes, and it is around the purse and the hat that the whole story revolves. Interpreters have commonly played down the magical element and seen in the hat and the purse symbols of the cornucopia which can be created by middle-class activity and of the world-wide interests of the mercantile bourgeoisie. Apart from their inherently improbable nature (the purse is not given to Fortunatus as a reward for his industry, and he acquires the hat by trickery long after he has become prosperous) such interpretations fail to take into account the moral the author himself is at some pains to point out, namely that the pursuit of wisdom, not the acquisition of wealth, should be the real aim of a man's striving: for the unwise even the most lavish gifts of fortune are ultimately useless, and far from being a source of true prosperity the never-empty purse, by attracting the envy of the less fortunate, is the source of 'suffering bitter as gall' for its unwise possessors. For all its middle-class elements *Fortunatus* is thus in no sense an expression of bourgeois self-confidence: the rising middle class had to wait for almost half a century before their outlook gained unqualified literary expression in prose fiction in the novels of Jörg Wickram, and even in his case it was only in his last novel that he emerged as the uninhibited advocate of the middle-class ethic.

JÖRG WICKRAM's earliest novels (*Ritter Galmy*, 1539; *Die Historie von Reinhart und Gabriotto*, 1553), with their faithful knights and chaste ladies of high birth who are separated by an inimical fate until finally reunited – albeit in the latter case in death – clearly derive from the chivalresque tradition and, not surprisingly, they were included, along with *Tristrant*, *Wigoleysz* and *Magelone*, in Feyerabend's *Buch der Liebe* (1578). Even in this obviously chivalric milieu, however, Wickram's characteristically middle-class concern with social distinctions plays a role: his lovers' difficulties are largely caused by the fact that they love across the barriers between the higher and lower nobility. His next two novels *Der jungen Knaben Spiegel* (*The Young Boys' Mirror*, 1554) and *Der Goldtfaden* (*The Golden Thread*, 1557, but written earlier) are also indebted to a number of romantic devices. In *Der Goldtfaden*, for instance, the golden thread is the gift of the heroine and is preserved in an open wound in the hero's bosom, while a tame lion plays quite a role in the story. But in spite of the romantic trappings Wickram's social preoccupations and middle-class loyalties predominate in the unambiguous assertion that native intelligence, industry and integrity are more important than pedigree or inherited social position. *Der jungen Knaben Spiegel* compares two children and their development, the one the son of a shepherd, the other of noble lineage, and shows how the shepherd's son is in all respects superior to the nobleman; *Der Goldtfaden* is the story of a scullion who eventually wins the hand of a countess. Yet both these works reveal a certain sense of insecurity in their preoccupation with the need to compete with the aristocracy on its own terms, and characteristically absorption into the nobility is accepted as the natural goal of the lower-class meritocracy. Only in his last novel, *Von guten und bösen Nachbarn* (*Of Good and Evil Neighbours*, 1555) does Wickram stop looking nervously over his shoulder at the upper classes and, with admirable self-confidence, portray the world of the commercial middle class as being sufficient unto itself.

The novel takes us through three generations of a prosperous merchant family. In order to escape from the animosity of a quarrelsome neighbour Robertus moves his home and his business from Antwerp to Lisbon, where his family is henceforth able to live in close and mutually beneficial amity with their new neighbours. His only daughter marries the Spanish merchant, Richardus, whom they had met on their voyage to Portugal and whom they nurse back to health when he falls sick. Subsequently, when Richardus is attacked by robbers, he is saved by the intervention of a certain Lazarus. The latter becomes a close friend of the family and accompanies Richardus on a trading journey, during which he is abducted and sold as a galley slave, but is in turn rescued by the timely intervention of Richardus. Latterly, Richardus's daughter, Cassandra, marries Lazarus's son (also called Lazarus), after the latter has spent his journeyman's years abroad and, amongst other things, survived an attempt on his life by a thieving inn-keeper in Venice.

Other 'sagas' of this kind, from *Fortunatus* to the family chronicles of Mann and Galsworthy, have tended to social criticism or cultural and moral pessimism, but Wickram's merchants are paragons of goodness and moral rectitude: their fortunes move in a steadily ascending line and are troubled only by minor vicissitudes which in the end turn out to have been for the best and serve to add a certain interest to the novel by contrasting the safe stronghold of orderly bourgeois existence with the dangers and chaos lying in wait for the unwary in the wicked world outside.

Within the limits of their class, Wickram's burghers are internationalists, free from any taint of national or racial prejudice, at home everywhere they can pursue their business interests without hindrance; they live a life characterized by industry, moderation, practically conditioned respect for the rights of their fellows, charity to those less fortunate than themselves and friendship based on mutual respect and mutual advantage. Despite the middle-class setting, Wickram is not a realist interested in recreating the material reality of the milieu and activities of his characters. Nor is he interested in presenting us with remarkable human beings: unlike the author of *Fortunatus*, he makes no attempt to differentiate between his merchants except in terms of name and function, and his characters only have significance as vehicles for the middle-class ethic he is at pains to communicate by example and exhortation. He is a child of his age in seeing in literature above all a means to a didactic end: the inculcation of certain standards of behaviour in his readers by showing them an idealized picture of middle-class values in operation. In other respects, however, Wickram transcends his age. His importation of middle-class subjects from other genres into prose narrative was perhaps a natural, but nevertheless unique development: what is more important, however, is that this new subject matter is treated in a way which betokens a new sense of the possibilities and dignity of literature. Alone in the sixteenth century, Wickram shows a keen interest in states of mind – particularly love – which, in anticipation of the seventeenth-century mode, are explored by means of letters, soliloquies and dreams. Further, Wickram is unique amongst the fiction writers of the sixteenth century in his conscious attempt to write in an elevated style both in the dignified diction of his burghers and in the 'poetic' nature descriptions. That this style today strikes an almost ludicrously forced note should not be allowed to obscure the very real advances it represents over that of his contemporaries: however clumsily and hesitantly, it is being demonstrated that prose style is not simply a matter of communicating plain facts.

But although Wickram points the way forward, his work awakened little response in Germany: it was not his idealized picture of middle-class life which was to be decisive for coming generations, but the *Amadis* cycle (translated in 1567), and it is only in a chronological sense that he can claim to be the 'father of the German novel'.

A similar remarkable, but ultimately sterile, experiment is represented by the adaptation by JOHANN FISCHART (1547–90) of Rabelais's *Gargantua* under the title *Affentheurlich Naupengeheurliche Geschichtklitterung* (1575, 1582, 1590). For all his prolific output, Fischart did not possess a particularly inventive mind and almost all his writings are adaptations and translations of other men's work. It was not entirely accidental, however, that it should be Rabelais who provided the inspiration for the novel for which Fischart is primarily remembered. As a convinced Protestant, Lutheran by upbringing, Calvinist by conversion, Fischart lacks Rabelais's scepticism and has a tendency to moralize; in other respects, however, especially in his highly developed sense of humour and his distinctly satirical bent, in his love of the monstrous and the grotesque and above all in his creative approach to language, he has obvious affinities with his model.

Fischart retains the outlines of Rabelais's story: the birth and education of Gargantua, the war between Grandgousier and Picrochole and the foundation of the monastery of Thélème, but these outlines are no more than a starting-point for Fischart's own peculiar contribution. As a translator he is inferior to Urquhart – his rendering of names, for instance, is notoriously weak – but Fischart does not regard himself as a translator: his purpose, as he explains in the preface, is to adapt Rabelais 'to the German meridian' and although he frequently follows his model literally, he also modifies and expands the original as fancy takes him, and his version is three times the length of Rabelais's. For both authors the satirical element – the castigation of scholasticism and monasticism, the mockery of human folly in all its forms and the literary burlesquing of the chivalresque novel – is important, but for Fischart as for Rabelais the main purpose of the work is to amuse the reader. Fischart retains the grotesque incidents of the original story virtually unchanged, but seeks to surpass his model in his linguistic humour.

It is in this latter respect that both the strength and the weakness of Fischart's version lie. The linguistic effects in his case emancipate themselves from the original humorous purpose and become an end in themselves, so much so that in reading the *Geschichtklitterung* the English reader is reminded perhaps more of *Finnegans Wake* than of *Gargantua*, for like Joyce Fischart is fascinated to the point of obsession with the sounds and associations of words. The story for Fischart is less important than the words he uses to tell it: the function of narrative and language are reversed, the former serving merely as an excuse for the latter, which is endowed with an almost magical, independent life of its own and sweeps the reader along with veritable cascades of puns, proverbs, quotations, allusions and synonyms which seem more calculated to overwhelm than enlighten. The expansion of the French original is not so much due to the insertion of new material as to Fischart's intoxication with words. As Wolfgang Stammler remarks, 'where Rabelais has a word, Fischart composes a list; where Rabelais composes a list, Fischart compiles a catalogue.' The celebrated passage from chapter vii (Rabelais's chapter iv) is an extreme, but entirely characteristic example of this tendency. When Rabelais wants to tell us that the guests danced he uses one word, 'dancèrent'; Fischart, however, renders it as follows:

dantzten, schupfften, lupfften, sprungen, sungen, huncken, reyeten, schreieten, schwangen, rangen: plöchelten: füßklöpffeten: gumpeten: plumpeten: rammelten: hammelten: voltirten: Branlirten: gambadirten: Cinqpassirten: Capricollirten; gauckelten: redleten, bürtzleten, balleten, jauchtzeten, gigageten, armglocketen, hendruderten, armlaufeten . . .

Similar lists of untranslatable synonyms, consisting often of neologisms which testify to Fischart's philological interests, recur frequently. Fischart loves to construct words and names for people and things, punning on them, twisting them, allowing his imagination free rein, calling up and mixing associations in order to achieve grotesque effects. The title of the work, for instance, mingles 'abenteuerlich' = 'adventurous' with 'Affe' = 'ape'; 'Naupe' = (amongst other things) 'vexatious difficulty', 'whim', 'peculiarity'; 'geheuerlich' = 'safe', 'gentle'; Geschicht(e) = 'story'; 'Klitterung' = 'hotch-potch', 'blot', 'scribbling'. The result of such 'creative' use of language is not easy to read; often it becomes downright unintelligible – for the modern reader as it must have been for Fischart's contemporaries – so much so that one needs a specially compiled glossary to penetrate the screen of verbal ingenuity hiding Fischart's meaning, which even then often remains obscure. Not surprisingly, for all its linguistic ingenuity – or more probably because of it – Fischart's masterpiece did not long survive him as a work of living literature. Nor did it exert any immediate discernible influence on the development of German prose fiction, although the fantastic allusiveness and suppleness of Fischart's style remained a striking monument to the potentialities dormant in the German language and to the peculiar genius of Fischart himself.

PART V

The Literature of Ideas and Manners

Introduction

PARADOXICALLY it is the authors discussed in this section who were regarded in their own day as pre-eminently the men of letters, in no way inferior to poets and far superior to writers of prose fiction. In Italy the Renaissance had been under way for so long before 1500 that the situation there is best studied separately, though from Machiavelli through to Bruno the men and their writings profoundly affected the rest of Europe. Outside Italy Erasmus is unquestionably the point of departure from which almost everything else stems. His heritage is expressed as much in his opponents as in his followers; all had to reckon with the movement of which he is the most distinguished representative. It would be possible, though artificial, to break down this long section into smaller units, but they would all have to refer to Erasmus. The arrangement by countries helps to bring out the interplay, often in the same man, of the different elements of Erasmus' work: learning, piety, satire.

Most faithful to him is his intimate friend Thomas More, and then, perhaps, the Spaniards Vives and Alfonso de Valdés. In Germany Reuchlin and Hutten each in his own way expresses one or other side of Erasmus' work, while Luther, though an enemy, once thought Erasmus an ally. Still further away, to the left, as it were, come such men as Paracelsus and Franck. The Lucianic satire popularized by Erasmus has its exponents in France, Germany and Spain, usually, though not invariably, on the Protestant side, but his Evangelical piety was no less influential. Some of the Spanish Erasmians stayed recognizably close to their master in their quest for spiritual renewal; others, like Loyola or St Teresa, found him inadequate and went as far to the right away from him as some Germans had gone to the left. In France Erasmians like Rabelais and Marguerite de Navarre tended to express themselves, so to speak, parenthetically, largely owing to the polarizing effect of Calvin, and then the religious wars. The French writer who in one respect owes most to Erasmus is

Montaigne. What may be called the essay-tradition (Montaigne invented the word) had begun with the *Adages*, but among other source books those of Mexía and Guevara must also be mentioned, though the latter owed little to Erasmus. It is indicative of Erasmus' unique importance that even when no direct influence need be postulated one must thus constantly refer back to him to understand how Reformers and satirists, humanists and mystics came to write as they did. In conclusion it must be stressed that the sample examined in the following pages is only a minute fraction of an output so vast that even today it is not properly known. It is better to omit altogether than to attempt to squeeze writers of such complexity (and often prolixity) as Bodin, Ramus, Melanchthon and so on into the space available.

ONE

The Literature of Ideas and Manners in Italy

Niccolò Machiavelli (1469–1527)

'AND my good faith should not be doubted, because, having always kept faith, I cannot now learn to break it; and anyone who has been faithful and good for forty-three years, as I have, cannot change his nature': so wrote Niccolò Machiavelli to Francesco Vettori in 1513. It is one of the ironies of history that his name should have come to mean an 'unscrupulous schemer ... practising duplicity in statecraft or in general conduct' (Oxford English Dictionary).

We know almost nothing about Machiavelli's early years, until June 1498 when he was elected Second Chancellor of the Florentine Republic and then delegated to the Ten of War (*Dieci di Balia*). For the next fifteen years he devoted his untiring energy and rapier intelligence to putting into effect the most un-Machiavellian policies of Piero Soderini, which led the city and himself to disaster. Living and working through the traumatic years of the French invasions and the later Franco-Spanish conflict, Machiavelli acquired the practical experience which drove him to make a realistic assessment of political behaviour and to note the gulf that divided practice from theory. Highlights in his career were his missions to France (1500 and 1504), Cesare Borgia (1502), Rome (1503), the Emperor Maximilian (1507), and the disastrous Pisan war, which, because of Florence's military weakness, continued almost non-stop for thirteen years (1496–1509). In his major works he was to stress the complementary nature of this practical experience and the knowledge acquired from a study of ancient history. The former taught him the bitter lesson of Florence's ruin – that 'unarmed wealth is a prize for the poor soldier', as he was to put it in his *Art of War* (1520) – while the latter left him with a lifelong admiration for the discipline and heroic virtues of republican Rome.

His most famous work, *The Prince* (1513), was written shortly after his exclusion from politics, brought about by the return of the Medici to Florence in 1512. All too often, *The Prince* has been read as if it were a treatise on political theory, instead of being considered primarily an impassioned answer to a particular historical situation. Admittedly, Machiavelli believed that historical situations repeat themselves and that good solutions may also be repeated. This does not, however, alter the fact that *The Prince* was written at a time of grave national and personal crisis and must be understood in the light of such events. In March 1513, Medici power was further enhanced by the election of Cardinal Giovanni as Pope Leo X, so that the family seemed to have gained control of the major part of Tuscany and Central Italy. At this point, the difficulties plaguing the King of France, and the possibility that a strong Italian power might be able to play off France against Spain, evidently encouraged Machiavelli to pour forth his 'knowledge of the actions of great men' in a passionate appeal to the Medici to rid Italy of the barbarians.

After a typically trenchant opening, the author states that his subject will be the 'new' state that characterized the Italian scene. The third chapter gives us a penetrating analysis of the six mistakes made by Louis XII of France during his Italian campaign (1499–1503): 'King Louis lost the north of Italy, then, because he did not observe any of those conditions observed by others who have taken provinces and wished to keep them. Nor is this any kind of miracle, but something very ordinary and rational.' In this statement, two things stand out: the belief in certain immutable laws governing history and the actions of men, and the desire to substitute rational, scientific analysis for the 'miraculous' so often used to explain the extraordinary series of conquest and defeat witnessed in those years. Miracles and the working of divine providence are banished from Machiavelli's view of history, which is again illustrated in chapter XII, where he ascribes the 'ruin of Italy' to the use of mercenary troops. Referring to Savonarola, he attacks: 'And the one who said that our sins were to blame spoke the truth; but they were not in fact those he had in mind, but the ones I have just mentioned. ... Because such arms give rise to slow, tardy and weak gains, and sudden and miraculous losses.'

Machiavelli was never satisfied with conventional opinion: the attack continued in his *Discourses* (II, xxx), where the same scorn is poured on mercenaries and their 'miraculous losses and miraculous gains. Because when men have little *virtú*, fortune shows the extent of its power.' *Virtú* is the power a man must use to oppose the blows of fortune, according to humanistic terminology, and its virile qualities – which have little to do with the Christian conception of virtue – are the despair of translators. An outstanding example of *virtú* in modern times is the career of Cesare Borgia (*c.* 1475–1507), son of Pope Alexander VI, who succeeded in establishing law and unity in Central Italy and learned to discard mercenary and auxiliary troops and to depend on his own forces. Critics have tried to excuse this unsavoury choice by claiming that Machiavelli is no more concerned with moral issues in his analysis of political action than a scientist is when describing the behaviour of the praying mantis. That this is not quite so, that morality does in fact cross Machiavelli's horizon, is shown in the very next chapter (VIII), where the interference of traditional ethics with his scientific outlook is evident in his description of the career of Agathocles, who 'accompanied his wicked deeds by so much *virtú* of mind and body that . . . he became praetor of Syracuse.' After mentioning Agathocles' demonic energy and courage, however, even the supposedly amoral *virtú* is judged by moral standards: 'Yet you cannot call it *virtú* to kill your fellow citizens, betray your friends, be without faith, without pity, without religion; which things can make you win power, but not glory.' In complete contrast, the very next sentence begins, 'Because if you were to consider the *virtú* with which Agathocles faced and overcame danger', while the paragraph ends, 'It is not possible then to attribute to fortune or *virtú* what was obtained by him without either.' Apart from the contradictions, it is interesting to see the wicked tyrant, the Cesare Borgia of popular imagination, condemned by our supposed scientist.

Morality, therefore, is not excluded from *The Prince*. It is, however, an ideal, a desideratum, all too frequently in violent opposition to human actions. After the first fourteen chapters devoted to the types of state (I–XI) and military forces (XII–XIV), we find the notorious central section (XV–XIX), in which the reality of political action is described. In XV, Machiavelli reacts against the whole tradition of medieval and humanistic political theory, which was concerned with things as they ought to be and not with things as they are:

And many have imagined republics and princedoms which have never been seen or known to exist; because how people live is so removed from how they ought to live, that anyone who leaves what is done for what ought to be done learns to destroy rather than to preserve himself; because a man who wants to be good in all respects must come to grief among so many who are not good. It is therefore necessary for a prince who wishes to keep his state to learn not to be good, and to use this or not according to necessity.

The dilemma is clear enough, although for those determined to make Machiavelli synonymous with evil, such statements must have been made with cynical glee at the dialectical skill with which he put over his perverse doctrine. On the other hand, it is difficult to read these central chapters with their litany of 'Nevertheless . . .' introducing harsh reality as opposed to utopian idealism, without being struck by the depths to which the lessons of experience had struck. So: 'although it would be a good thing to be considered generous. . . . In our times we have seen great things accomplished only by those who were considered parsimonious; the others have been destroyed.' This is the message of life, of experience, repeated in the most notorious chapter of all – 'How Faith Should be Kept by Rulers' (XVIII) – where it is the head of Christendom himself, Alexander VI (1492–1503), who 'never did anything else, never thought of anything else but how to deceive men, and he always found a subject to work on. And there was never a man who asserted anything more effectively or affirmed something with greater oaths, and observed it less.' Dante had pointed out much the same thing: the world was corrupt, because its spiritual head led the world to corruption; but Dante, of course, was preoccupied with setting things right. Machiavelli, on the other hand, is concerned with survival in the political jungle, where one must have the strength of a lion and the cunning of a fox. He has been accused of giving his Prince *carte blanche* in the field of morality. In fact, he stresses the need for a ruler to do all in his power to avoid the hatred and contempt of his subjects (XVI, XIX): he must not touch their women or their property, but must provide them with 'good laws, good arms, good friends and good examples' (XXIV, XII). But Machiavelli is not concerned with the precepts of absolute morality, nor with morality for morality's sake; instead, he asks his Prince to examine the effects of that relative morality which governs human actions, and in so doing he will learn that a virtuous quality, such as pity, can be disastrous in its consequences, and that good intentions are not enough: 'Cesare Borgia was thought cruel; nevertheless, his cruelty had brought unity, peace and good government to the Romagna. If properly considered, this will be seen to have been far more compassionate than the Florentine people; who, in order to avoid the stigma of cruelty, allowed Pistoia to be destroyed.' It is necessary to distinguish not simply between vice and virtue, but between these qualities well or badly applied (XVII). Christian precepts are not ignored: they are judged inadequate as a guide to human conduct, and, in particular, the conduct not only of the Pope but also of the Most Catholic King of Spain, who 'never preaches anything but peace and good faith, and is an enemy to both; and either of these qualities, if he had ever observed it, would more than once have deprived him of his reputation or his kingdom.' A prudent ruler must therefore 'not depart from the good, if possible, but know how to enter into evil, when forced' (XVIII). Ten years earlier, Machiavelli had observed that, while laws and contracts make private citizens observe good faith, only force can make princes do so – and, seven years later, in his *Life of Castruccio Castracani*, his summing up of Castruccio's character was to remain faithful to the formula set out in *The Prince* and dictated by reality: 'He was good to his friends, terrible to his enemies, just with his subjects, unfaithful towards others.'

After this shake-up of conventional morality, Machiavelli goes on to warn his Prince that fortresses are of doubtful value, 'Because the best fortress is not to be hated by the people' (XX), that he must choose his advisers with the greatest care (XXII) and avoid flatterers (XXIII). Then come the three final chapters with their indictment of the suicidal policies pursued by the rulers of Italy and the exhortation to free Italy from the barbarians (XXVI). Here, the tone rises to a climax of biblical fervour with its promises of redemption and its appeal to the redeemer to heal Italy's wounds: 'the sea has opened up; a cloud has shown you the way; the rock has given forth its water; here manna has rained down; everything has prepared the way for your greatness. The rest is up to you.' How far this is from scientific accuracy and from that 'reality of things' which Machiavelli prided himself on observing is shown by the concluding rhetorical flourishes describing universal enthusiasm for this task and ending, appropriately enough, with a quotation from Petrarch. All of the writer's practical experience must have told him that this was nothing but wishful thinking, which he despised, and that the Italians would continue to be rent by jealousy and strife. Yet his fiercely Florentine spirit could not resist the lure of his ideal – a strong, united state in Italy, capable of overcoming the foreign oppressors. This state would be a new one, and its ruler would have to obey the rules for survival set down in *The Prince*.

The *Discourses* (1513–21), inspired by a reading of Livy's history of Rome, are quite different in conception and they in fact offer the long-term political solution that is not to be found in the *Prince*. The preface to the First Book returns to the humanistic principle of imitation, already discussed in *The Prince* (VI, XIV). Here, Machiavelli points to the gap that exists in the lesson drawn from antiquity; for, whereas modern art, medicine and law are all based on the great examples of antiquity, modern politics and warfare ignore ancient practice, and men read history for mere pleasure 'without ever thinking of imitating it, since they judge such imitation not only difficult but impossible.' The same message is repeated throughout the work: men must learn from the past, avoiding the mistakes and imitating the achievements of the ancients. And it is especially the virtues of republican Rome that Machiavelli admires so fervently and opposes to the corruption of the modern world, in which the French, Spaniards and Italians are the dregs, and only the German and Swiss have kept alive some small spark of the ancient *virtú*.

The *Discourses* give us Machiavelli's republican theory of good government, while they repeat many of the lessons of *The Prince*: for example, that 'money is not the sinews of war' (II, x), that men should learn to adapt themselves to circumstances (III, ix), and – most important – that states must train and rely on their own soldiers (I, xxi and xliii; II, xx). The suicidal use of mercenaries had been encouraged by the temporal ambitions of greedy churchmen (*The Prince*, XII); but now (I, xii) Machiavelli condemns the popes even in the spiritual sphere, for 'those people who are nearest to the Roman curia, the head of our religion, have least religion.' Even worse are the political effects of religious decadence, since the state is deprived of an essential foundation that should guarantee discipline and self-sacrifice among its subjects. In Italy, moreover, 'the Church has kept and keeps this land divided': too weak to impose unity, but able enough to prevent any other Italian power from achieving hegemony, the papacy is responsible for the chaotic weakness of the peninsula, 'And truly no land was ever united or happy, except under the control of a single republic or ruler.'

An even more radical attack is made against the practices of modern Christianity in II, ii, where the greater love of liberty displayed by the ancients is attributed to their virile religion, which only glorified 'men full of worldly glory, such as generals and heads of state'. Christianity, on the other hand, chooses to exalt 'humble and contemplative men rather than men of action. It has also placed its greatest good in humility, abjectness and contempt for human things: the other placed it in greatness of spirit, strength of body, and all other things that make men strong.' As a result, Christian theory and practice have left 'the world a prey to wicked men'. Nevertheless, true leaders are capable of restraining human weakness with good constitutions and laws (I, xliii) and by leading institutions back to their original goodness and strength (III, i). The pessimism of *The Prince* (XV–XIX) is balanced by the paean to virtuous rulers in I, x, where the balance sheet of imperial Rome is unhesitatingly drawn up in favour of the good emperors, whose example will make the reader 'if he be born of man, shun all imitation of evil times and be inflamed with an immense desire to follow the good.' On the other hand, Machiavelli's ideal republic inspires the call to ignore personal considerations, 'because where it is a question of life and death for one's country, one must not give the slightest consideration to whether one is called just or unjust, pitiful or cruel, praised or reviled; instead, putting aside all else, stick to the course that can save its life and preserve its liberty' (III, xli).

Recent attempts to revise the traditional dating of the *Discourses* have been encouraged by the supposed contradiction between Machiavelli's two major works. By assigning republican ardour to a second phase (post-1515) in the writer's career, a more scholarly explanation is given for what was formerly attributed to the worst form of Machiavellian hypocrisy: the contrast between the 'tyrannical' formula of *The Prince* and the democratic spirit of the *Discourses*. The latter is well illustrated in I, lviii, where the author does not hesitate to challenge the judgement of Livy and 'all the other historians' by proclaiming that 'government by the people is better than government by princes.' To understand the divergence, we must first realize that this is an optimum choice, not one that can be applied to all conditions.

Nothing shows the modernity of Machiavelli's approach better than his readiness to change his theory according to the facts. Medieval thought had been typically aprioristic: it had sought to apply a single, unvarying solution, based on first principles; whereas the modern scientific attitude began with such thinkers as Machiavelli, who attempted to alter his theories to make them fit the particular problem and to keep as his one great objective 'the reality of things as they are'. So, in the *Discourses* (I, lv), we are told that it is impossible to put a solution into practice indiscriminately and that it is unrealistic to introduce republican government where there is great inequality and feudal power. The examples chosen are Rome, Lombardy, the Romagna, and the Kingdom of Naples – four fifths of the Italian peninsula – and 'the reason is this, that where the matter is so corrupt that laws are not sufficient to keep it in check, it is necessary to supplement them with greater force; namely, the authority of a monarch, who with absolute and excessive power may curb the excessive ambition and corruption of the magnates.' Already at the beginning of the work, it had been pointed out that one man alone must be in charge of the setting up or reform of any state. We therefore have two reasons for the different formula expounded in *The Prince*. The first is that the subject of the earlier work is 'the new state'; and this, according to *Discourses* I, ix, can best be organized by the individual. The second is that the avowed aim is the freeing of Italy from the barbarians; and here the example of the Roman *dictator*, elected at a time of national emergency for the duration of the crisis, again points to the greater efficacy of the individual in the circumstances that led to the writing of *The Prince*. Far from contradicting each other, the two works are in fact complementary in the way they illustrate different aspects of Machiavelli's thought. Few, indeed, surpass the famous Florentine in his consistency or his insistence on certain fundamental themes: the papacy's fatal policy of *divide et impera* in Italy (still to be found in the *History of Florence*, though the work was dedicated to Pope Clement VII in 1525); the folly of using mercenary forces (which led to the *Art of War* in 1520 and vain hopes of organizing the defence of Florence in 1527); above all, the need to learn from the past and to consider the present in its often harsh reality. And it was no less a Roman Catholic than the historian Lord Acton, who judged the whole of later history to be 'the *Commentarius Perpetuus* of the *Discorsi* and *The Prince*'.

Francesco Guicciardini (1483–1540)

'How wrong men are who quote the Romans at every step! You would need to have a city exactly modelled on theirs, and then follow their example: and this, for anyone who has the wrong qualities, is just as wrong as to try to make an ass run like a horse.' So Francesco Guicciardini wrote in one of his *Ricordi* (110), in obvious polemic with his friend. In pointing to another of Machiavelli's weaknesses – judging by example (117) – Guicciardini expressed the crisis of Italian humanism, with its basic canon of imitation, just as his famous *History of Italy* was to illustrate the crisis of Italian politics, with its precarious balance of power, in the first quarter of the sixteenth century.

A brilliant lawyer, Guicciardini began his lifelong devotion to his *particulare* (self-interest) by opposing his respected father in marrying Maria Salviati (1508). It was a dangerous move, for Maria's father was an enemy of the Florentine *Gonfaloniere*, Piero Soderini; but, as Francesco noted, the Salviati were wealthier and more influential than any other Florentine clan since the expulsion of the Medici. The gamble paid off, and in 1511 Guicciardini was sent as the Republic's ambassador to the King of Spain, though officially under age for such a post. Some time before this he had begun his career as a historian with the *Storie fiorentine* (1509), although throughout his life he remained too prudent a politician to have his writings published.

The *Storie* begin with the Ciompi Revolt in Florence (1378) and stretch as far as the year of composition. One of the basic themes is Guicciardini's abhorrence of popular government (*Ricordi*, 140) and his contempt for its representative, Soderini, though he is equally embittered by the tyrannous rule of Lorenzo the Magnificent (1469–92) and his son, Piero (1492–4): both lead inevitably to the ruin of the state. The famous parallel between the two Medici popes in the

Storia d'Italia is foreshadowed by the comparison drawn between Cosimo and Lorenzo de' Medici (IX), while typical features are Guicciardini's comments on the outcome of the Pazzi conspiracy (1468), which only served to strengthen Lorenzo's hold on the city and eliminate a possible rival in his brother Giuliano (IV), and the historian's attempt to understand the essentially alien figure of Savonarola (XII, XVI).

During his stay in Spain, Guicciardini wrote the brilliant *Relazione di Spagna* (1514), in which he analysed the proud, quarrelsome nature of its inhabitants and their skill at guerilla warfare, while admiring the machinations of Ferdinand, their 'Most Catholic King', only too ready to break his word and utterly devoid of Classical education. In the same year, Francesco returned to Florence, once more under the control of the Medici family. His first Medici pope, Leo X, soon made use of his outstanding administrative skills as governor of Modena (1516) and Reggio Emilia (1517–22). His career reached its zenith under Clement VII, who made him President of the Romagna (1523) and then (1526) Lieutenant General of the forces of the anti-imperial League of Cognac. Disaster soon followed, however, when the League's forces proved incapable of defending Rome itself or the pontiff's person, and the Sack of Rome (1527) sounded the knell for Guicciardini's ambitions. Exiled in March 1530 by the dying Florentine Republic, he made only a brief come-back in 1531 and after Clement's death in 1534 became ever more disillusioned with the Medici tyrants of Florence.

The dialogue *Del reggimento di Firenze* (1526) discusses the best form of government for Florence, supposedly reporting views expressed in 1494, immediately after the expulsion of Piero de' Medici. Guicciardini's father takes part, but the author's mouthpiece is the host, Bernardo del Nero, hitherto a staunch supporter of the Medici. Once more, Guicciardini, though willing to consider the example of antiquity, characterizes the crisis of contemporary Italian culture by placing his words in the mouth of one who disclaims all pretensions to Classical learning and asserts that it was far easier for Plato to banish the lust for power from his utopia than for anyone with experience of politics to witness this happy state of affairs. The author's distrust of modern democracy was similarly based on his belief that the desire to dominate others was predominant in man.

This attempt to put aside theoretical considerations and to consider the purely practical effects of man's behaviour is an important and obvious feature of the dialogue from the very beginning, where Bernardo insists that a government must be judged by its results, not its principles, and also by the peculiar needs of each state. In the Second Book the Venetian system is exalted as 'the finest and best government not only in our times, but even perhaps of any state in antiquity, because it partakes of all forms of rule, by one man, by the few and by the many, in such proportion that it contains most of the good enjoyed by any form and avoids most of the ills.' The Venetian model is therefore proposed and adapted to Florentine conditions. An interesting aside is concerned with Genoa's treatment of the Pisan prisoners in 1284. They were never set free and thus set the seal on Pisa's ruin. Guicciardini makes Bernardo confess that in this the Genoese acted cruelly and against conscience, 'but I must add that anyone nowadays who wishes to maintain his dominion and power must, where possible, use pity and goodness, but where it is impossible to do otherwise, he must use cruelty and act against conscience.' And in truly Machiavellian terms, he speaks of the need to have war waged by 'men who love their country more than their own souls, because it is impossible to govern states ... according to the precepts of Christian law.'

His extraordinary fellow-citizen was frequently in Guicciardini's thoughts, and Machiavelli's *Discourses* did in fact inspire his *Considerazioni* ... of 1530. Francesco took exception to his friend's admiration for republican Rome, his over-fondness for generalizations, and the *Considerazioni* show Guicciardini at his pedantic best. He strongly denies that the struggle between the people and the senate was responsible for Rome's freedom and greatness (I, 4); he points out that, while the Church has kept Italy disunited, this condition is more 'natural' and has made possible a greater diversity of wealth and industry (I, 12); and he accuses Machiavelli of wishful thinking in imagining that a man will ever give up supreme power of his own accord (I, 10). At times, the reader may be tempted to share De Sanctis's annoyance at Guicciardini's hair-splitting 'truths of the present' and turn instead towards Machiavelli's 'truths of the future'. The same attention to detail, however, combined with Guicciardini's psychological penetration of man's motives, is one of the fascinations of his *Ricordi* (1512–30). The genre was to be brought to perfection in seventeenth-century France, but in an atmosphere of court and *salon* society. Here, on the other hand, we have the private thoughts of a disillusioned man, convinced that he would not live to see the realization of his greatest hopes – the establishment of good government in Florence, Italy freed from the barbarians, the world rid of priestly tyranny (9) – and forced by self-interest to strive for the temporal greatness of churchmen, whose greed and corruption were so odious to him that, if it had not been for his *particulare*, 'I should have loved Martin Luther as myself' (28). This regard for self was bitterly condemned in the nineteenth century, when the men of the Risorgimento came to look on Guicciardini as a representative of Italian decadence, the typical bourgeois incapable of sacrifice or superior loyalty. The famous maxim just quoted must, however, be tempered by number 218, which speaks of those who do not understand what their best interests are: 'that is, who think that these always consist in monetary gain, rather than in honour and in safeguarding their reputation and good name.' Other maxims show Guicciardini's moderate scepticism regarding miracles (123, 124), moral causes in human affairs (33, 147), theological debates (125), and the outcome of revolution (169). Men, on the whole, are bad (41, 201) and one must behave accordingly, guided by prudence and discretion, 'which you can hardly ever learn from experience; and never from books' (186).

Guicciardini's masterpiece, the *Storia d'Italia* (1537–40), is the first work to treat the history of Italy on a national plane. The vast canvas deals with the crises of the recent past, from the death of Lorenzo (1492) to the election of Paul III (1534). The tragedy, in which Guicciardini himself played a not insignificant part, is heightened by the description of the 'golden age' Italy had enjoyed during the career of Lorenzo, who far from the tyrant of the early *Storie fiorentine* is now regarded as the linchpin of Italian peace. The Florentine vision of the *Storie* is replaced by a 'national' outlook, which justifies both the relatively sparse discussion of 'local' figures like Savonarola and the inclusion of French, Spanish and English affairs (XI, 6; XII, 1). The evil omen of Roderigo Borgia's election as Alexander VI, four months after the death of Lorenzo, is followed by the folly of Lodovico il Moro's destruction of the balance of power by bringing the oppressive might of France into the Italian peninsula. The portrait of the French king, Charles VIII, with his lust for gain, scant intelligence and fickle character, serves to highlight the injustice and whims of fate, no longer regarded as a supernatural element in history, but considered in purely human terms. The moral and physical calamities brought about by the French invasion (I, 9) are complemented by technical considerations on the French army and its revolutionary use of artillery (I, 11; XV, 6). The invasion of 1494, undertaken 'with temerity, not prudence', goes on to upset the whole European scene and transforms Italy into a prize to be fought over by the barbarians of France and Spain. The Italians themselves and the policies of successive popes are just as much to blame, however – as may be seen in the disastrous League of Cambrai of 1508 (VIII, 1). The origins of the Church's temporal power are discussed in Book Four, with a slighting reference to that notorious forgery, the Donation of Constantine, and a fierce denunciation of the popes' ambition, their accumulation of worldly treasure and their misuse of spiritual weapons for political ends. Yet one of Guicciardini's great virtues as a historian is his grasp of the complexities of life and human nature – mirrored in his complex prose style – which leads him to recognize the positive efforts and achievements of those he otherwise condemned: such is his description of Julius II (1503–13), the 'fateful instrument of Italy's woes', whose lion-hearted reaction to the disaster at Ravenna (X, 14) must be set off against the final judgement in XI, 8.

Once more, the Florentine statesman's admiration for Venice shows through – this time because of the courage displayed by the Venetians when they stood alone 'against the whole world' after the League of Cambrai: their determination is embodied in a speech made to the senate by Doge Leonardo Loredano and recounted in the grand manner by Guicciardini (VIII, 10). Although such set speeches were a part of traditional historiography and often a pretext for wild rhetoric, they are usually vindicated in the *Storia* by Guicciardini's psychological insight and his understanding of historical situations (especially XVI, 14). His greatest portraits are found in the weighing up of his two Medici protectors (XVI, 12), where the successful right-hand man of Leo X, the efficient executor, is seen unequal to his task as Clement VII. In charge of Church policy at a time of great national crisis (1523–34), Clement's irresolute nature made him act tardily and against his will, while his good intentions were doomed to failure. They led to the cataclysmic Sack of Rome in 1527 (XVIII, 8), which marked the end of any attempt at an independent Italian policy and left the country at the mercy of Spanish power, with Florence under the control of Medici rulers who were not slow in getting rid of their honest counsellor, Francesco Guicciardini.

Baldassare Castiglione (1478–1529)

If we now turn to Castiglione's *Cortegiano* (*Book of the Courtier*), we may feel that we have left Guicciardini's reality far behind and, struck by the irony that the book was first published (1528) immediately after the catastrophe of 1527, imagine that we have entered the fanciful world of contemporary utopias. That this is not the whole truth is proved by the book's tremendous popularity and influence on Renaissance society, as well as by the personality of Castiglione himself. The fact that reality, as Machiavelli and Guicciardini observed, is composed of both good and evil should not blind us to either component; nor should it prevent the true courtier from applying himself to his ideal. Far from indulging in mere wishful thinking, Castiglione ridicules those who 'would like every good to exist in the world without any evil at all; which is impossible' because both are necessary to the dialectic of life, whereby 'the one upholds and fortifies the other' (II, 2). He is only too conscious of the opprobrium attached to the Italian name, because of the weakness and decadence of many of his compatriots (IV, 4); but the shadows in the picture are a further incentive to set things right, and Castiglione has no hesitation in proclaiming the superiority of his own age over the recent past in every form of intellectual and courtly activity.

The *Cortegiano* looks back to a golden moment in Castiglione's varied experience as a courtier: the years spent at Urbino under Guidobaldo da Montefeltro, on whose behalf he journeyed to London in 1506 when Henry VII conferred the Garter on this Italian princeling. The same year provides the setting for the book, which describes the galaxy of talent and beauty assembled at Urbino after the visit of Pope Julius II. Federico Fregoso, a Genoese nobleman, proposes that the court entertainment should be 'to form a perfect courtier with words, explaining all the conditions and particular qualities required to deserve such a title.' Every member of the illustrious company is free to take part in the debate, which is led on the first day by Ludovico di Canossa, when it deals with the various physical and moral virtues possessed by the perfect courtier; by Fregoso himself on the way to display these gifts (Second Book); by Giuliano de' Medici, concerned in the Third Book with the ideal lady at court; and by Ottaviano Fregoso, who discusses the relationship between the courtier and his prince in the Fourth Book, ending with Pietro Bembo's famous paean to Platonic love.

The first condition is that the courtier be of noble blood; his chief qualifications are swordsmanship and the craft of battle. But then come the accessories – and what a seemingly endless list they make! Never had the Renaissance ideal of the universal man been stated in quite so much detail. He must practise all virile sports, such as hunting, swimming, running and riding, shun anything that smacks of the mountebank, and above all he must avoid affectation and 'observe a certain *sprezzatura* (ease of manner), which will conceal his art and show that what is said and done is accomplished without difficulty and almost without thinking about it.' The resulting quality of grace will be admired by all, for 'everyone knows the difficulty of such rare accomplishments.' The courtier's aim must be to hide his skill and display grace of manner and person in everything he does (I, 26). He must also adapt himself to circumstances, and leave the ways of the battlefield behind when he enters the courtroom and the presence of ladies. Here, he must laugh and dance gracefully, become a skilful raconteur and be quick at repartee. He will, of course, possess the 'natural' virtues of prudence, justice, temperance and fortitude; but these moral qualities need to be accompanied by the study of literature – 'although the French only recognize the nobility of arms, and have no regard for anything else . . . they greatly look down on all men of letters; and they think it a term of great abuse to call anyone a *clerc*' (I, 43). An outstanding exception is their king, François, munificent patron of the arts and a personification of Renaissance magnanimity. Castiglione then returns to his courtier, to ensure his knowledge of the humanities, his ability to write both prose and verse – especially in Italian, for the delight of the ladies. The latter's sensibility calls for musical proficiency, since their presence makes the souls of the listeners 'more receptive to the sweetness of music', which in turn stimulates man's virtues by its harmonies.

Harmony is indeed the key to the universe. And it is just as important in the courtier's ideal companion, the *donna di palazzo*, whose complementary virtues are even more difficult to achieve with their perfect balance between prudish and lascivious behaviour. The effects of the liberal education for girls championed by the great humanist teachers of the fifteenth century are to be seen in the call for a similar wide-ranging education in music, literature and painting. Gaspare Pallavicino plays the part of the traditional misogynist, but Giuliano de' Medici (brother of Pope Leo X) confidently replies 'that everything which can be understood by men, can also be understood by women.' Proof is sought in examples of virtues displayed by women and drawn from both history and contemporary experience while the whole tradition of courtly love lies behind the assertion that no court, however great, may enjoy true renown or splendour without the company of ladies, and that men strive to excel in order to win their favour:

Who tries to dance gracefully, except in order to please women? . . . Who writes verse, at least in the vulgar tongue, unless he wishes to express sentiments that are caused by women? . . . would it not have been a great loss if Francis Petrarch, who wrote in such a divine manner about his love in our own language, had concentrated exclusively on Latin, as he would have done if his love for Madonna Laura had not occasionally compelled him?

From the same tradition springs the discussion on the manner of choosing one's beloved, whether openly or not, although the medieval idea that marriage and love are incompatible has disappeared. Instead, all is subject to the Renaissance ideal of harmony and the avoidance of excess.

In the debate on the relationship between the courtier and his lord, treated in the Fourth Book, we remember the earlier warning that the former must exercise great care in the choice of his prince, 'because everyone assumes that he who serves good men is himself good, and he who serves evil men, evil.' The courtier must therefore obey his master 'in all things that are useful and honourable, not in those that are harmful or shameful' (II, 23). Here (IV, 19), the conventional question is broached, whether a kingdom or a republic is the better form of government. Bembo, the Venetian aristocrat, defends republics, but Castiglione's own choice is for the rule of a good prince, as this is more akin to nature and God's rule over the whole universe, though tyranny is worst of all. As for the size and prosperity of the state, once again the law of the golden mean is applied: citizens should avoid both extreme poverty and extreme riches 'because excessive wealth is very often the cause of great ruin; as in poor Italy, which has been and still is a prey to foreigners, because of bad government, as well as the many riches in which she abounds' (IV, 33).

The last part of this Book is the most famous (IV, 50–70). It is given up to an impassioned discourse on the neo-Platonic conception of true love, which was undoubtedly the source from which the average Renaissance reader gained his ideas on the subject. The editions and translations of the *Cortegiano* that flowed through Western Europe in the sixteenth century not only taught the barbarians of France, Spain and England the manners and accomplishments of a superior civilization; they also made popular the ideas on human and divine love that Ficino and the Platonic Academy had broadcast in their synthesis of pagan and Christian thought. Bembo here defines love as the desire to enjoy beauty. Beauty is inseparable from goodness – it was left to a later age to search for artistic gold among the mire. Now, the Renaissance credo is vigorously proclaimed: that 'beauty is born of God, and is like a circle of which goodness is the centre: and, just as no circle can exist without a centre, so no beauty can exist without goodness: so that it is very rare to find an evil soul dwelling in a beautiful body, and hence outer beauty is a true sign of inner goodness' (IV, 57). Man is a microcosm, his beauty a pointer to the divine. It is his duty to yearn for the ultimate; but, on the way, he may indulge his desire to kiss his beloved, not 'for any dishonest reason', but because a kiss 'may be said to be a union of the soul rather than of the body' – and the Song of Songs is quoted to prove the future cardinal's point. Bembo waxes ever more eloquent over the need to rise in the scale of universal values, to leave behind the desire and admiration for created beauty in total dedication to its Creator, to ascend from the individual to the universal spirit of the world-mover. The fire of love will purify man, and 'even as terrestrial fire refines gold, so this most holy love destroys and consumes all that is mortal in man's soul, while it enlivens and increases the beauty of that heavenly part which was previously mortified and buried.' This sacred love is the bond that unites all things: it forms the link between heaven and earth and remains the source of all true pleasure and virtue.

Such is the force of Bembo's impassioned speech that Lady Emilia has to bring him back to earth by catching hold of his cloak and warning him not to allow 'these thoughts to separate your soul from your body just now.' A charming detail, well matched by Bembo's down-to-earth gallant repartee: 'My Lady, it would not be the first miracle that love has brought about in me' – a tone that was to be admired and imitated, for its urbane intermingling of spirit, matter, and *esprit*, in countless gatherings throughout the history of Western Europe and, most notably, in the *salons* of French society. In this, as in so much else, France was to prove how great the debt was to the way of life formulated in Renaissance Italy and regarded as an ideal, not only by writers like Castiglione but also by their countless readers who strove to put it into practice.

Giorgio Vasari (1511–74) and Benvenuto Cellini (1500–1571)

Giorgio Vasari's *Lives of the Most Excellent Painters, Sculptors, and Architects* (1550 and 1568) is another canonical text, this time in the field of art history, where it established the pattern for later generations with its portrayal of decadence after the age of Constantine and the gradual 'renaissance' of the fine arts beginning with Giotto and culminating in the supreme mastery of Michelangelo. Vasari's extraordinary wealth of information, however, is nothing like as rich as the fascinating autobiography of Benvenuto Cellini. After Castiglione's Courtier, we may turn to Cellini's Artist for a different type of idealization – one which gives us the flavour and panache of an age that proves reality more fascinating than the wildest flights of the Romantic imagination.

Cellini dictated most of his *Life* (not published until 1730) to a young assistant. In it, he speaks 'Of moving accidents by flood and field; Of hairbreadth scapes. . . . Of being taken by the insolent foe' –

murders, quarrels, revenge, honour and disgrace: little, except modesty, seems to have escaped his omnivorous appetite for life. Typically, he begins by tracing back his ancestry to a mythical 'Fiorino da Cellino', supposedly one of Julius Caesar's generals who gave his name to Florence, Cellini's birthplace. Fiercely loyal to his origins, Cellini is passionate in everything he undertakes; so that there is good cause for an ambassador from Lucca to exclaim, 'My Lord, your Benvenuto is a terrible man' and for his patron to reply, 'far more terrible than you think.' His overriding passion is the desire to break every possible record. He is a better shot than anyone else in the papal army during the Sack of Rome, he cures himself of a fever in spite of the doctors, makes better surgical instruments, knows more about Dante than any literary critic, is an intrepid sorcerer, and even attempts to rival the saints and mystics during his imprisonment, when he sings 'psalms all day long and many other compositions ... all addressed to God' and finally has a vision of Christ in glory, which leaves him with a halo 'obvious to all those to whom I have wanted to show it, who have been very few.'

Such extraordinary ability is largely incidental, however: Cellini's real concern is with his art, which is to him what politics were to Machiavelli – his whole *raison d'être*. So he answers the Florentine exiles in Rome after the murder of Duke Alessandro (1537), 'You fools, I am a poor goldsmith, who serves anyone who pays me.' He has no time for politics and little enough for conventional morality. Indeed, the slogan 'Art for art's sake' might well have been invented by our picaresque hero, who declares his virtue and innocence before prince and prelate alike and looks upon divine intervention as his due: even when he is guilty of murder his artistic excellence leads Pope Paul III to declare that 'men like Benvenuto, who are unique in their profession, are above the law.' It is the great ones of this world who are obliged to recognize his supremacy: Clement VII is made to declare that 'Benvenuto's shoes are worth more than the eyes of all these other fools put together', while François I is moved to exclaim, 'If Paradise had doors, it would have no finer than this' and to boast, 'Truly, I have found a man after my own heart', as he wonders whether his own good fortune in having found such an artist is not greater than Cellini's in having such a munificent patron. The villains of the piece are Madame d'Etampes, the king's mistress,

Pierluigi Farnese, the Pope's bastard, and, in a minor key, his various rivals at the ducal court in Florence. Only once does Benvenuto confess he was at fault (II, 34), adding, 'If I did not admit that I did wrong in some of these events, those others where I claim that I did right would not be thought true; and so, I admit that I was wrong to want to revenge myself in such an extraordinary way on Pagolo Miccieri' – whom he forced at sword-point to marry his model, afterwards delighting in cuckolding him and pummelling her.

The highlight of Cellini's artistic career was the casting of the statue of Perseus (II, 75–8), which is still to be seen in the Loggia de' Lanzi in Florence. Few dramatists could equal Cellini's skill in keeping his readers' interest at boiling point during his description of the great fever that laid him low and almost brought about the failure of his great enterprise. News of imminent defeat resuscitates him, however, and lion-hearted he feeds the furnace until it explodes and finally reveals his miraculous achievement to his assistants, 'who rejoiced, giving thanks to God for all that had occurred, and said that they had learned and seen things which had been thought impossible by other masters of the art.' For once, his rivals are silenced. They are even forced to join in the universal acclaim that greets the unveiling of the statue. Cellini's own satisfaction at having 'accomplished what no one else had ever done' is well expressed in his claim to Duke Cosimo that Michelangelo himself – the only master he could bring himself to recognize – would have been unable to produce such a masterpiece in his old age.

The other highlights show us Cellini the man of action: for example, at the siege of Rome (I, 34–8), during which he claims *à la Dumas* that he saved both Pope and cardinals, killed the enemy general, and wounded the Prince of Orange. Amid all the excitement, however, Benvenuto feels certain twinges of conscience, which are finally set to rest by the Pope's blessing and his promise to forgive 'all the killings I had ever done and all I should ever do in the service of the apostolic Church.' Comforted, despite his supposed familiarity with Dante (cf. *Inferno*, XXVII), he is forced by art and modesty to admit 'if I were to describe all the fine things I did in that hellish cruelty, I should astound the whole world; but I will omit them for brevity's sake.' More than ten years later, there is his imprisonment in the redoubtable papal fortress, Castel Sant'Angelo, with its *opera buffa* description of the governor seeing himself as a bat in this angelic belfry. The famous escape (I, 109–10) begins with the formidable logic of Benvenuto's prayer: 'O God, help me, for I have right on my side, as you know, and because I help myself.' He describes his difficulties in reaching the ground without a sufficient length of knotted sheets, and his subsequent recapture, despite the Pope's admiration for his courage, magnanimously compared with his own. Cellini, on the other hand, is bent on setting the record straight by pointing out that, while it was true that the Pope had escaped from the castle as a young man, the handicaps had been very different, for 'Farnese was placed in a basket and lowered to the ground by rope' and the outer walls had not yet been built. Then comes the stiletto-thrust: 'moreover, he had been imprisoned justly, and I unjustly.'

Benvenuto, of course, went on to survive various attempts on his life, his mystical phase, the jealousy of rivals, further imprisonment, and the parsimony of unenlightened patrons, the whole described in the powerful idiom of Florence, which was to delight a host of modern readers as a refreshing tonic amidst the academic formalism of so much sixteenth-century prose. The only episode omitted is perforce the great flood of 1966, which damaged so much of the Ponte Vecchio, although it left Cellini's bust unscathed – a detail that would have delighted, but not amazed, the hero of the first great autobiography of modern times.

Giordano Bruno (1548–1600)

On a different level, the life of Giordano Bruno was only slightly less adventurous. In 1562 he became a Dominican, and he remained an eccentric member of the Order for eleven years. In 1576 the persecution began that was to hound him for the rest of his life: his subsequent travels took him to Geneva, where he was particularly opposed to Calvin's doctrine of predestination and was arrested in 1579; to France, where the bitter strife of religious faction strengthened his belief in the need for tolerance; and to England, where he came into conflict with academic formalism at Oxford but enjoyed the protection of Leicester and Sidney. After his return to France, this Faust-like figure proceeded through Germany back to Italy, where he took up residence in Venice under the protection of the patrician Giovanni Mocenigo. After a quarrel, Mocenigo denounced Bruno to the Inquisition in 1592. The following year his trial began in Rome, where he was accused of holding such heretical opinions as the belief in the annihilation of the individual soul, the movement of the earth round the sun, pantheism, and the infinity of the universe. After a brief recantation, Bruno held firm and was sentenced to death in December 1599. Although it is unfashionable to regard Bruno, with his interest in the Cabbala and the Hermetic tradition, as a martyr to the cause of scientific progress, we should not underestimate his scientific curiosity or his importance as an inspiration to later generations. We should also remember that, at a time when the optimism of the Renaissance, with its celebration of the dignity and achievements of man, had been replaced by the Counter-Reformation's submission of the individual to authority and Calvin's annihilation of man's will, Giordano Bruno stands out as one of the last champions of man's ability to control his (intellectual) fate and develop his god-like qualities.

In 1584 and 1585 Bruno published the six dialogues that make up the body of his philosophical writings in Italian. One of these – the *Spaccio de la bestia trionfante* (*Expulsion of the Triumphant Beast*, 1584) – portrays the liberation of man's soul from vice, the beast which 'oppresses his divine part'. The work places the science of morality within man's social context, far from medieval absolutes. Sin is to be judged by its effects on others, just as man's virtues are sterile unless put into action. Hence, the worst sins 'are those which are harmful to the commonwealth, less grave are those harmful to another individual, minimal that which occurs between two consenting persons, and of no consequence what gives rise to neither bad example nor bad effect.' Laws must be inspired by prudence and justice, while, based on human reason, they must help to depose tyrants and protect the weak. Bruno attacks the Calvinists for their denial of human freedom and Roman Catholics for their superstitious practices. Most striking perhaps is his affinity with the Protestant–Calvinist belief in the sanctity of work: 'Ozio' (Leisure) echoes the Classical myth of a Golden Age of happiness and equality, so popular during the Renaissance. 'Sofia' (Wisdom), however, opposes man's divine gifts and his duty to exploit them to the full – an aim that can only be achieved through mental and physical activity; so that in the Golden Age men 'were not more virtuous than the animals have so far shown themselves, and they were perhaps more stupid than many of these.' Through enlightened action man can achieve freedom, and by practising justice and clemency, industry and the arts, he can bring about a better social order.

De gli eroici furori (*The Heroic Frenzies*, 1585) looks at man's place in the whole universe. It insists on the full range of his intellectual development, illustrated by the myth of Acteon, who surprised the goddess Diana as she bathed naked in a stream and was punished by being turned into a stag and devoured by his own hounds. For Bruno, Acteon signifies man's 'intellect bent on the hunt for divine wisdom'. He is led by his hounds (the cognitive faculties) to become the prey of the beauty and wisdom that he first seeks without, but then discovers within himself. Although it is impossible for man to see the full revelation (Apollo), he can nevertheless perceive its 'shadow, its Diana, the world, the universe, nature, which is in things, the light that exists in the opacity of matter', and Acteon's death implies the destruction of the 'mad world' of the senses and the beginning of his true intellectual life, whereby he participates in the 'life of the gods'. In this work Bruno asserts a doctrine that was fundamental to his whole vision: the infinity of the universe, composed of elements that are both eternal and subject to change. Such beliefs were not new: they had been held in antiquity by Anaxagoras and Democritus, as well as in the modified Epicurean philosophy of the Roman poet Lucretius, whose style had an important influence on Bruno's own. For the latter, the infinite universe contains innumerable worlds, all reflecting the divinity of which man and, nature are integral parts. Everything is subject to change; nothing is lost: a chain of reaction is set up, with a 'vicissitudinal revolution' between the various levels of being. Bruno himself admits the conflict with theological doctrine; for, 'among the theologians, Origen alone, like all great philosophers . . . dared to say that this revolution is vicissitudinal and eternal; and that everything which rises up must come down again; as may be seen in all the elements and things that exist on the surface or in the womb of nature.' Although he admits the utility of the theologians' view of man's single passage through life with reward and punishment at the end, he does not hesitate to 'accept and affirm' the beliefs of those few good and wise men 'who speak according to natural reason.' Knowledge, for Bruno, is ultimately the ability to place every aspect of being in its true place on the ladder of existence. Man is led to seek this knowledge by a heroic madness, which, far from the irrational trance cherished by the opium eaters of modern times, is based on a fervent desire for rational and intellectual fulfilment. This in turn leads man through the mysteries of magic and the truths of nature to total awareness and participation in the harmony and symmetry inherent in all things.

Three other works published in London in 1584 – the *Ash-Wednesday Supper*; *On Cause, Principle, and Unity*; *The Infinite Universe of Worlds* – reveal the influence of Nicolas of Cusa and Copernicus. They show us a universe, animated by a cosmic yet individual soul, in which the earth moves round a revolving sun, part of a planetary system that is merely one among an infinite number of celestial bodies, where time and motion are essentially relative in their infinity. In all this, Bruno's method was far from scientific, as his conclusions were based on neither experiment nor scientific tools. Yet, he must surely figure among the great 'Sleepwalkers' of modern science. Even today, the observation of an expanding universe has not ruled out the steady-state explanation of the origin and development of the universe, while the famous law of the conservation of matter, which has played such a fundamental role in modern physics, is likewise akin to Bruno's belief in the indestructibility of a changing, but infinite universe. Once again, ideas that originated or were developed in Renaissance Italy were to be exploited elsewhere and brought to fruition by later generations. Although it is impossible to consider Bruno a scientist, his fate boded ill for the future of science in Italy. It is moreover ironical that this man, whose work comes near the end of the chapter on Italian Comedy in this book, should conclude this chapter in the history of Renaissance thought with his death at the stake in the first year of the century that was to witness the tragedy of Galileo's abjuration.

TWO

Erasmus (c. 1466–1536)

Two judgements passed on Erasmus by David Knowles, a historian notable for moderation, strikingly emphasize the difficulties confronting modern students of the Renaissance period. He writes: 'Perhaps Voltaire is the only writer and thinker in the modern world whose influence in his generation during his lifetime has been so widespread,' and 'Erasmus, like Voltaire in a later age, was a revolution in himself.' That a person of such stature should today be so comparatively little known is at once inevitable and a sad reflection on the fragmentation of knowledge which he would have been the first to deplore. Out of the many volumes of his works only one average-length book and one very short one are at all well known, and even the growing number of good modern translations is unlikely to popularize much more, yet the history of literature and ideas in Europe of the sixteenth century is largely that of his influence. The success of his revolution is best measured by the degree to which it is now taken for granted. Ironically enough, the Latin that made him truly a European, makes him in these post-Classical times barely more accessible than if he had written in the obscurity of his native Dutch and condemns him to the hollow celebrity of the unread.

If Latin ensured him an international public, the coincidence of his birth with the beginnings of printing in Europe made him the first author to enjoy and exploit a mass medium, which he soon came to understand from first-hand experience of the work in a printer's shop. When he published his first little book, the Paris *Adages* of 1500, he was a Dutch Austin canon in his mid-thirties, with friends and contacts in England, France and the Low Countries, but to all intents and purposes a scholarly beggar, terrified of being sent back to his remote monastery. When he died in 1536 he had recently refused a cardinal's hat, commanded the respect of popes, Emperor and kings, and treated the adulation of scholars everywhere as no more than his due. Though never short of enemies, he presided unchallenged over the Republic of Letters, and towns like Louvain, Freiburg and Basle vied for the honour of his residence.

In the thirty-six years of his working life he published editions running into many volumes of Fathers of the Church (Jerome, Augustine, Chrysostom and others), paraphrases and commentaries on Scripture, editions of Classical authors (Lucian, Terence), polemical works against Luther and others, and he wrote vast numbers of letters. When all is said and done, however, his literary fame, as distinct from his scholarly reputation, rests on the *Adages*, the *Enchiridion*, the *Praise of Folly* and the *Colloquies*, to which might be added the brilliant pamphlet *Julius Exclusus*, ascribed to and never disowned by him. The *Querela Pacis* (*Complaint of Peace*), the *De Ratione Studii* (*Method of Study*) and shorter works on marriage and piety were very influential in their day, but are of less literary significance and add little to the ideas contained and illustrated in the other four works.

The original edition of the *Adages* was a small inexpensive volume of some 800 adages, or proverbial sayings, culled from Classical literature. When Erasmus went to Venice he published (1508) at the Aldine Press (whose owner was his host) a fourfold expansion of the original work under the title *Adagiorum Chiliades* (from the Greek word for 'thousands': the 3,260 adages were arranged by thousands and centuries). Continuing to expand what was to be his life's work, he next published in Basle, with Froben, in 1515 an edition enriched by 150 new ones, including some of the best known, for example the *Sileni*, the *Scarabeus* (*Beetle*), and above all the *Dulce bellum inexpertis* (*War is sweet to those who have never known it*). Later editions continued to grow, until the last, published the year of his death, exceeded 4,000 (to be exact, 4,151). A similar collection of *Apothegmata* (pithy sayings) had appeared in 1531, and the treasure store of Classical learning comprised in these two collections enabled countless writers to parade an erudition which though genuine was not their own.

As the name suggests, the *Adages* were originally intended as a sort of handbook of Classical tags, with explanations, references, comparisons and so on, something like the entries in a large dictionary written up in connected form. Already in the Venice edition of 1508 Erasmus begins to expatiate, and in a recent excellent English translation two of the more interesting entries are nearly twenty pages long (the *Festina lente* or *Make haste slowly*, and *Labours of Hercules*). As well as Classical anecdotes, personal observations and reminiscences began to find a place, Greek became ever more important as Erasmus' mastery of the language grew, and references to the Bible, at first kept to a minimum for prudential reasons, become quite frequent after 1515, when his ecclesiastical position was regularized (14 to the Old Testament, 59 to the New). With the 1515 edition, too, some of the *Adages* become virtually full-length essays: *Scarabeus quaerit aquilam* (*The beetle looks for the eagle*, the typical bully and supposedly her sworn enemy) extends to thirty-two pages full of wildly improbable zoological anecdotes and fables, with an outspoken attack on tyrants; *Sileni Alcibiadis* (a reference to boxes fashioned like the grotesque Silenus, but opening to reveal delicately carved miniatures of gods) is nearly as long, with a very serious discussion of true religious and moral worth contrasted with the appearances which so often deceive the world; *Dulce Bellum*, of forty-five pages, is a full-scale pamphlet on pacifism, immensely influential and often reprinted separately. From this highly developed form of essay it was only a step to Montaigne's perfection of the genre.

These editions enjoyed phenomenal success partly because of public demand for an easily accessible key to Classical literature, though others, especially in Italy, had to some extent paved the way, partly because of the possibilities offered by presses as famous as those of Aldus and Froben, but above all because Erasmus' Latin style is so superior to that of most of his contemporaries. His comments on wars of aggression, on tyranny, on the obscurantism of academic institutions, on the pharisaism of so many religious persons and practices, his fluent and colloquial manner of recounting anecdote and fable, and his omnivorous erudition sufficiently explain the respect in which he was held.

In connection with this erudition it is interesting to see the use he makes of the different authors of antiquity. A leading Erasmus scholar, Mrs Margaret Mann Philips, has compiled a list from all the editions which shows Cicero as easily first, with nearly 900 quotations, Homer second with 666, with Plutarch (618) and Aristophanes (596) close behind, Plautus and Horace tie for fifth place (475) and Plato comes sixth (428). When one remembers the incessant appeals to 'Tully' in Elizabethan literature, Ronsard's devotion to the divine Homer and Montaigne's declared preference for Plutarch, these figures show that Erasmus's choice was endorsed by his successors.

The *Enchiridion* (composed 1501, published 1503) was as popular as the *Adages*, but for somewhat different reasons. Before 1515, as already mentioned, Erasmus tended to keep Classical, that is pagan, erudition distinct from Christianity in the *Adages*, and thus for some time this little manual of some 150 pages was the best-known source of what came to be known as the 'philosophy of Christ' (it ran into thirty editions in twenty years). Its brevity and direct appeal made it literally the handbook of thousands, and the adverse opinion of men as diverse as Luther and Loyola would have been less violent if the book had been less influential. Ethics during the Middle Ages had been treated in the context of theology, but the new interest in pagan thinkers enabled Erasmus and his contemporaries to treat the subject on its merits. Professor Knowles sums up the 'philosophy of Christ' as 'one in which a wide culture and a humanistic moral outlook form the basis of a life modelled on the Gospel teaching presented in a purely human fashion; ... a kind of "low-tension" Christianity, a de-spiritualized religion.' In the third section Erasmus discusses the Christian's armoury (Enchiridion means both manual, handbook, and small dagger) and picks out two special weapons: prayer and knowledge. 'Prayer, of course, is the more potent ... but knowledge is no less necessary.' He goes on in the same chapter to urge the importance of pagan literature and philosophy as a preparation for study of Scripture. It is true that he warns against stopping there, but there is no mistaking the emphasis, the more so as he unfavourably compares those who plunge straight into theology with those who have properly equipped themselves by a humanistic education. He naturally does not rely on his own authority, but quotes the Fathers, especially Jerome, his favourite, in support of the principle of despoiling the Egyptians to adorn the Lord's temple. Homer and Virgil he particularly recommends among the poets, the Platonists among the philosophers (he refers to 'a divinely wise Plato') and he frequently comments on moral problems from a Stoic, Platonic or other pagan point of view. When he comes on to the rules, twenty-two in all, which occupy about half the book, the emphasis is on moral conduct, rather than spiritual fervour, but the virtues he preaches are authentically Christian and the sentiments are both sensible and noble. Already here two of Erasmus' most revolutionary doctrines can be seen: virtuous pagans are held up as an example for Christians to follow, and the value of the monastic life, while not categorically denied, is reduced to a matter of personal taste rather than spiritual perfection, an idea already implicit in the *Devotio Moderna*. More traditional is his insistence on personal, private devotion as against mere ritualism. Later works took all these ideas much further.

After the *Enchiridion* came his most popular work, the *Praise of Folly* (1509), the only one to enjoy anything like a wide public to this day and from a literary point of view his masterpiece. He conceived this little book (about the same length as the *Enchiridion*) to beguile the time during his journey back from Italy to stay with his friend More in London, where he finished it, and it is noteworthy that without his books, under conditions of enforced leisure, he produced a brilliantly homogenous piece of satire, informed by learning but not overburdened with references. The bantering tone of the book (the very title involves a pun on his friend's name: *Encomium Moriae* in the original) does not disguise its serious implications, and for once style and content are evenly matched.

In form the work is an exercise in paradox, a declamation in Lucianic style, delivered by Folly herself from the pulpit to an attentive audience of faithful followers. Theoretically, of course, all that is most warmly praised by Folly should be condemned by reasonable men, but quite often Erasmus abandons consistency and, through the mouth of Folly, directly attacks what he should logically have damned with loud praise. Besides that, his definition of folly is not fixed. To begin with the cap and bells of the traditional Fool set the tone, but towards the end the true folly of the Christian, the Pauline folly of the Cross, comes in to blur the picture. At first the parade of folly contains no great surprises; philosophy and marriage, youth and age, war and medicine, and so on are subjected to the more or less good-humoured irony of Folly. About half-way through Folly strikes a sharper note when she addresses those gullible enough to believe in miracles, in the protection of saints, like Christopher or Barbara for travellers and soldiers respectively, in indulgences and other alleged superstitions. Later on theologians are exposed to ridicule, and caustic comparisons are made between the simplicity of the Apostles and the subtlety of the schoolmen, illustrated by some niceties of the teaching on transubstantiation. From then on the attack, for this is what it has now become, switches to monks. They are accused of ignorance, mechanical and meaningless devotions and parasitism, and their ceremonies and rules are described as a new form of Judaism. The Mendicants are singled out for specially scathing criticism (Erasmus' opponents were particularly numerous among these orders) for the bad taste of their sermons and the absurdity of their teaching methods. A brief interlude on princes separates this long section on religious orders from another, equally outspoken, on prelates, in which neither cardinals nor popes are spared. There follows a detailed discussion of various scriptural texts, working up to the Pauline idea of folly and in fact quoting Christ himself as preaching and practising this divine folly even to the Cross. The conclusion passes from a comparison between Plato's teaching and that of Christian belief concerning eternal bliss to a final identification of the beatific vision with the folly of ecstasy.

The revolutionary nature of such a satire, the distinction of author and dedicatee, and the great elegance of style, irrevocably identified Erasmus with a programme of reform which henceforth took his name, and drove his opponents to ever more savage retorts. Eight years before the emergence of Luther one cannot talk meaningfully of Protestantism, nor, in fact, is there much positively in common between the religion envisaged in the *Enchiridion* or *Praise of Folly* and that to be preached by Luther. None the less, in a negative way, Erasmus prepared the ground for schism as well as for much needed reform through the destructive influence of such brilliant satire. More than anything else he combined the purely academic claims of the New Learning with the quite separate demands of those who wanted to reform the Church in its head and in its members. His edition of the Greek New Testament (1516) is not now very highly regarded by scholars, but its significance in its own day is that it showed how the Classical study, the *Philologia*, of the New Learning could be used to sap the foundations of entrenched scholasticism. Inaccuracy in the Vulgate can be established from objective linguistic criteria, while no amount of logic chopping or interpretation *ex cathedra* can have the authority of the word of Scripture thus authenticated. Paradoxically, too, this champion of the Classical tongues, who wrote in no other, was also strongly in favour of the vernacular in Bible and devotions for uneducated people.

In the same year as the New Testament in Greek appeared Erasmus' fourth popular success, the *Colloquies*, like the *Adages* greatly expanded in later editions. Originally intended simply as a guide to learning Latin, with exercises in vocabulary and idiom arranged by subject, the *Colloquies* developed even more than the *Adages* into brilliant essays in dialogue form on matters of the widest interest. Erasmus was not slow to protest that the use of dialogue made identification of the author's views with those of the speaker both unjust and dangerous, but he can hardly have expected to deceive anyone with so disingenuous a plea. The educational value of the dialogues on games, kindred and affinity, travel and the like is exactly that of modern phrase books (with none of the 'the postilion has been struck by lightening' type of oddity) but those dealing with social and religious questions correspond rather to leading articles in newspapers or periodicals. He has a lot to say about education and parenthood; mothers should feed their own children, corporal punishment is to be avoided, sound (that is, Classical) learning should be instilled as soon as possible, and religious education should not consist merely of the mechanical recitation of set prayers. In the conversation *A Child's Religion* (*Pietas Puerilis*) he offers as the basis of Christian faith 'I believe what I read in Scripture and in the Apostles' Creed, and seek no further, leaving theologians to dispute and define the rest if they wish', acknowledging in this simple formula the teaching of his old friend John Colet, Dean of St Paul's. Another dialogue between an abbot and a learned woman rather unexpectedly in an anti-feminist age commends the latter for her studious ways, and discloses that the abbot has sixty-two monks in his monastery but not a book in his cell, for he disapproves of monks learning Latin lest it lead to argument.

Probably the most famous phrase in all Erasmus' works occurs in the *Religious Banquet* (*Convivium Religiosum*). Conversation has turned to the nobility displayed by pagans, notably Cicero, Cato and Socrates, and the guests agree that Christians can hardly surpass such virtue. One of them says, referring to Socrates' dying speech: 'When I read things of this kind about such men I can scarce forbear to say: "*Sancte Socrates ora pro nobis.*"' The phrase crystallizes the Renaissance dilemma on pagan virtue, and heralds a debate which lasted for two centuries or more. On a very similar point, the next dialogue, the *Apotheosis of Reuchlin*, raises the question of sanctity in an acutely topical form. Reuchlin was an eminent German Hebraist who had been victimized by jealous enemies, notably some Dominicans of Cologne, and whose cause all humanists espoused with a fervour comparable to that of Dreyfusards in a later age. He died in 1522, and the dialogue relates how a Franciscan had had a vision of Reuchlin's triumphant entry into heaven. It concludes with a collect composed in anticipation of Reuchlin's official canonization, an exceedingly remote contingency, thus emphasizing the discrepancy between true sanctity and its official recognition.

The Mendicants are the inevitable butt of much of Erasmus' satire, and several dialogues are devoted to them. A particularly virulent one, *Merdardus or the Sermon*, lampoons a friar who had had the temerity to question Erasmus' interpretation of Magnificat and, as the very title suggests, shows that on occasion Erasmus was quite capable of scatology. Another called the *Rich Beggars* speaks for itself. Two more, the *Seraphic Obsequies* and the *Funeral*, satirize the alleged cupidity and superstition of the friars, who taught, for instance, that to die in Franciscan habit was a sure passport to paradise. The latter, in particular, gives a striking contrast between the death of one man, plagued to the end by squabbling friars, and that of another, quietly attended by his parish priest and dying in calm meditation. Rabelais was to remember this and borrow extensively for the burlesque deathbed scene in the *Third Book*.

On a slightly different topic, the vivid *Shipwreck* also inspired Rabelais (in the tempest in the *Fourth Book*). This describes the reactions of passengers to shipwreck on the Channel coast, and again makes the point by contrast: on the one hand are those who frantically surround the priests on board for confession, vow anything to saints in their panic (and will forget the vow if saved) and recite prayers and litanies; on the other, two men quietly confess their sins direct to God, and then, commending themselves to his mercy, swim to safety. Other important dialogues are the *Fish-Eaters*, in which Erasmus presents a very restrained case against the purely arbitrary practice of abstinence, pointedly illustrated with anecdotes of the rotten Lenten fare served at the Collège de Montaigu in Paris some thirty years earlier; the *Soldier and the Carthusian*, where even Erasmus' dislike of monastic life takes second place to his hatred of war; and the *Pilgrimage of True Devotion* (1526), which is of outstanding historical interest, describing as it does two pilgrimages made by Erasmus a dozen or so years before, one with Colet to Becket's shrine at Canterbury, the other to Walsingham, where the Virgin's milk was the principal exhibit. At the time of the visit, and even more at the time of writing, such pilgrimages had had their day, and Erasmus paints an unattractive picture of somewhat seedy piety, with the rapacity of the guardians and implausibility of the relics duly highlighted. Calvin and Voltaire adopt almost exactly the same arguments and the same tone for their very different reasons in attacking Catholic credulity and abuses, but the timing of Erasmus' attack distinguishes it from any subsequent one. Such irony and scepticism were weapons of which anti-Catholics were not slow to avail themselves, and if Erasmus died protesting his orthodoxy, he cannot avoid the responsibility (or credit, depending on one's point of view) for forging such arms. It is no defence of his position to quote his controversy over free will with Luther, or the very late dialogue *Cyclops* (1529), in which he satirizes the excesses of the self-styled Evangelists; he had started a fashion and set an example.

A final assessment of Erasmus' literary contribution is peculiarly difficult. Apart from the very early *Enchiridion* and *Praise of Folly*, the bulk of his work was editorial or occasional. The *Adages* and *Colloquies* were known everywhere, and each collection includes a good number of essays which can still be appreciated, even when translation has robbed them of their style and time their actuality. His influence was exercised at least as much through his voluminous correspondence and, of course, conversation, as through published works, and when he died in 1536 it is no exaggeration to say that all educated Europe felt the loss, whether with grief or relief. His cultural legacy is still being enjoyed four centuries later, and Classical studies owe as much to his inspired advocacy as to his actual scholarship. In the last analysis, though, the revolution he inaugurated is more than cultural. Like so many intellectuals throughout the ages he personally detested violence, but by his intemperate language and bitter sarcasm inevitably helped to provoke it. In the works discussed in this chapter, and in other polemical writing, he constantly called in question practices and beliefs which were not in themselves essential, but on which the fabric of authority rested. Tyranny, superstition, ignorance, extravagance and hypocrisy are proper targets for the critic, but all too often one feels that Erasmus enjoys attack for its own sake, that he is more interested in demonstrating his own brilliance at the expense of his victims than in righting wrongs. Even his piety seems at times to be more the product of a literary brief than a devout heart. Petulance is an enduring, and not endearing, characteristic of his work, and his personal preferences coincide rather too conveniently with the high principles he enunciates. Perhaps his stomach did rebel at Lenten fare, but his attack on fasting would be more convincing if he did not thus try to justify it. Monastic orders were no doubt in a bad way at the time, but his own uncanonical breach of vows makes some of his pleading suspect. The works and letters reiterate his longing for simple pleasures, gardens, good food and wine, civilized friends, and, above all financial independence, while Holbein's familiar portraits show the typical scholar, with more than a hint of waspish, querulous wit. His values are visibly those of the mind, but behind the often distasteful egoism there shines forth a truly humane concern for the underdog, for women, for children, for the poor, and for the victims of war and oppression. He was no hero, but the lifelong friendship of a man like More is proof enough that he could evoke affection and admiration from the noblest hearts. After the great figures of the Italian Renaissance, no single figure rivals Erasmus as the leader of the Renaissance in the north.

THREE

Utopia

THOUGH English writers as such are excluded from the present volume, to omit More's *Utopia* would be to rob Europe of a work international alike in language and influence. The book was composed during More's embassy to the Low Countries in 1515, and first published (in Latin) with Erasmus' backing at Louvain in 1516. Numerous editions followed, and it was also widely translated (into French in 1530, but only in 1551 into English). The ideas represented in this little book of some 150 pages are to be found in most humanists, especially Erasmus, but it is their shaping by More's personality and highly individual cast of mind that makes it the masterpiece it is.

The book is divided into two unequal parts, the first, rather more than a third of the whole, written last. More had originally produced a discourse by one Raphael Hythlodaeus, a fictitious Portuguese sailor, describing the 'best state of a commonwealth', namely that of the island of Utopia; but he then added an opening narrative in dialogue form, giving it a historical context and raising some very pertinent questions about European politics in general and those of England in particular. He begins by recounting his visit to Antwerp, where the town clerk, his scholarly friend Peter Gilles, one day introduced him to Hythlodaeus (coined from the Greek for 'trifle'), a veteran of Vespucci's voyages, of which a record was first published in 1507. More, Gilles and Hythlodaeus then start discussing political theory and practice. Personal reminiscences of Cardinal Morton, More's first patron, form the background to some outspoken but oblique (because uttered by Hythlodaeus) criticism of the savagery of English justice, which hanged men in scores for petty theft while the policy of enclosures turned sheep into 'devourers of men', whose livelihood and land they appropriate. Human life is more valuable than property, and capital punishment should be replaced by hard labour for life. In writing this More, who had only just become Sheriff of London, could hardly have foreseen that he himself would perish on the scaffold (1535) after attaining the highest legal office in the realm. In the next section an imaginary royal council is used as a pretext for powerful attacks on contemporary international morality, warmongering and bad faith, and on the dangers of a materialism based on the profit motive. Hythlodaeus concludes this first part with praise of the egalitarian and communistic system of Utopia of which he promises a fuller description, in fact the second part.

An earlier suggestion that Hythlodaeus could help to improve the existing state of affairs as councillor to kings is then abandoned, for his stay in Utopia (Greek for 'nowhere') has convinced him that communism is the prerequisite for the ideal state. Book II begins with a detailed description of this ideal land, physically resembling England, and organized with a daunting precision of town and country planning. There is constant interchange between urban and rural populations, so that all citizens are versed in agriculture, as well as some craft, like weaving or building. Self-sufficiency at every level from family to state is the keystone of their economy, but must not be won at the cost of the unreasonable toil of a few, but by the equal and moderate labour of all (six hours a day). This ideal situation is contrasted with that obtaining in Europe, where women, religious, aristocrats and beggars swell the ranks of the unproductive. Scholarship is encouraged, but only a tiny minority are exempted from manual work in order to devote themselves entirely to study.

The social organization of Utopia is firmly based on the family and, more remarkably, on the existence of a slave class who do all degrading and dirty work (for example, butchery). Hospitals, communal kitchens and refectories, and crèches are all provided in the towns, and would also be in the country but for the more dispersed population. Travel is subjected to official sanction, freely given, but no opportunity is afforded for the useless vagrancy so prevalent in contemporary Europe.

In a somewhat whimsical account of the Utopians' contempt for precious metals and jewels, he tells how they use gold for such things as chamber-pots and give gems to children as playthings. This reversal of normal European values is ironically illustrated by a description of a visiting embassy, mistaken for beggars because of their sumptuous adornments.

Utopian education is advanced, especially in such sciences as astronomy, but scholastic methods are unknown. The Utopians are not Christians, but hold a natural religion consistent with reason. Their philosophy leads them to accept, on the one hand, the immortality of the soul and reward or punishment hereafter, and, on the other, the enjoyment of pleasure as the supreme good in this life and virtue as conformity with the dictates of nature. Reason, Hythlodaeus claims, leads men both to worship God and to desire the happiness of all as a necessary condition for the pleasure of each. Human solidarity is asserted as a fundamental principle throughout the book, and is expressed in the belief that charity is a natural instinct, not an optional moral extra. Such simple and virtuous pleasure is again contrasted with the values of Europeans, with their desire for elegance, titles, wealth and so on, their gambling and hunting and all their other corrupting and senseless pastimes. Utopians, on the contrary, derive positive pleasure from the satisfaction of bodily needs and from good health itself, but rate much higher the delights of the mind and the practice of virtue.

Some of the features next discussed are not only odd, but proposed rather tentatively by Hythlodaeus. Euthanasia, for instance, is allowed if authorized by the priests, though unauthorized suicide is strongly condemned. Pre-marital intercourse and adultery are severely punished, but among precautions taken before marriage is inspection by each party, suitably chaperoned, of the naked body of the other (not to test mutual attraction but to ensure that disease should not go undetected). Matrimonial breakdown is recognized, and remarriage to other parties sometimes permitted. Laws are few and simple, lawyers nonexistent. Treaties are never made, and there is an ironic comment on their supposed sanctity in Christian Europe, where popes set the example.

Though the Utopians detest war, they must sometimes fight in defence of themselves or their friends, or even to remove tyrants, and all regularly train in case of emergency. In war they try to minimize bloodshed by superior intelligence and instead of making helpless subjects pay for the evil policies of bad leaders, actively seek the elimination, by assassination if need be, of the tyrant and his advisers. Other details of their views on war include condemnation of mercenaries, like the Swiss, recommendation of lenient treatment for captives and defeated enemies and generally imply criticism of contemporary European theory and practice.

The last section describes the Utopians' reception of Christianity, which many (but not all) adopt in place of their natural monotheism. A particularly audacious speculation arises from the lack of any priest to administer the sacraments the Utopians now desire, for Hythlodaeus thinks they may eventually elect one of their number to priesthood. Religious tolerance is a vital feature of Utopian life, and no intemperate proselytizing is permitted. Only those who deny the immortality of the soul are discriminated against, and then not by persecution but by being judged unfit for public office. Those Utopians who follow a religious life spend their time doing such hard work as will win leisure for others, and while there are a few celibate ascetics, others perform such labour when married and otherwise leading a normal life. The priests (non-Christian) enjoy immense moral authority and superior education, but are debarred from civil office lest it interfere with their spiritual functions.

After describing a Utopian religious ceremony, Hythlodaeus finally reverts to their happiness and equality, secured by their communism, and contrasts it with the gross social injustice of Europe, based on the exploitation of many poor workers by the few rich idlers. All the ills of contemporary society and its failure to follow the true teaching of Christ he ascribes to a single cause: human pride. The last word is left to More himself; he privately dissents from some of the views he has heard, particularly on communism and the absence of money, but politely admits that it is all worthy of further thought.

As has been said, almost all the main ideas of *Utopia* can be paralleled in some earlier, often Classical, writer, but the pattern of the whole is More's own. Individual details, like the golden chamber-pots or pre-marital inspection, catch a reader's fancy, even if they do not convince, and it is obviously a mistake to identify More with Hythlodaeus in every respect. The real lessons of the book are, first, the reasoned, but often indignant, protest against the social, political, economic and religious abuses of the day, and, second, a picture of what might have been but for the Fall. It is not a blueprint, or even a pipedream, but a logical design drawn from certain premises concerning human nature. Reason is the only remedy for pride; it strengthens faith, identifies true pleasure, brings the passions under control and leads man to promote human solidarity in this life while preparing him for an immortal reward in the next. Long before his execution gave the work a fortuitous odour of sanctity, More had given a new word to Europe. Erasmus constantly echoes *Utopia*, Rabelais's hero writes to his son 'from Utopia' and puts More's theories into practice in peace and war (1532), Montaigne finds in his 'cannibals' some of the innocent virtues of the Utopians. As for the book's later history, it has never ceased to inspire political idealists, and sometimes, alas, cranks and fanatics have twisted its message to their purpose. The sheer nobility and compassion of More's humanism are compelling; setting aside his tragic end, one must never forget that it was no armchair theorist but a man professionally committed to law and statecraft who wrote *Utopia*.

FOUR

German Satire

Johannes Reuchlin (1454–1522) and 'Epistolae Obscurorum Virorum'

It was no accident that Erasmus should devote one of his most memorable dialogues to his older contemporary, Johannes Reuchlin (see p. 394), for perhaps even more than Erasmus himself Reuchlin, in the period immediately before the outbreak of the Reformation, had come to symbolize the New Learning and its conflict with the latter-day schoolmen who spoke for official Christianity.

Johannes Reuchlin was one of the formative spirits of his age. A lawyer by profession who latterly taught Greek and Hebrew at Tübingen and Ingolstadt, he composed successful Latin comedies (*Sergius*, 1496; *Henno*, 1497), published a popular Latin textbook (*Vocabularius breviloquens*, 1475), and translated Lucian, Xenophon and the *Batrachomyomachia* into Latin and Demosthenes into German. In three outstanding works of Hebrew scholarship (*De mirifico verbo*, 1494; *De rudimentis hebraicis*, 1506; *De arte cabbalistica* 1517) he laid single-handed the foundations of all future study of Hebrew amongst non-Jews. This pre-eminence as a Hebraist was to prove Reuchlin's undoing.

In 1509 Johannes Pfefferkorn, a converted Jew who enjoyed the support of the Dominicans of Cologne, managed to secure the Emperor's authorization to confiscate and destroy all Hebrew books in the Empire. The understandable protests of the Jewish community that this constituted a breach of their dearly-bought privileges and charters, caused the Emperor to hold his hand and call for opinions from the universities of Cologne, Mainz, Heidelberg and Erfurt and from certain individuals, including the Dominican Grand Inquisitor, Hoogstraaten, and Reuchlin. Reuchlin alone stood out against the proposed piece of startling obscurantist vandalism; his views, expressed in the *Rathschlag* (*Advice, Opinion*) of 1510, show a characteristically humanist approach to the problem: only down-right scurrilous works should be destroyed, but if the Talmud, the

Cabbala or the scientific works of the Jews contained errors, these should be studied and demonstrated to be errors to the satisfaction of all concerned – including the Jews; to destroy them would be a 'bachanten-argument', an argument worthy of an ignorant under-graduate, which would convince no one of anything. Reuchlin's courageous stand involved him in an unedifying exchange of pamph-lets with Pfefferkorn and culminated in his citation before Hoogs-traaten to answer charges of heresy. An appeal to the Pope, who appointed the Bishop of Speyer as adjudicator, seemed to be on the point of settling the matter in favour of Reuchlin, but a further appeal by the Dominicans caused the case to be transferred to Rome, where it dragged on until 1520 when Reuchlin, partly because the issue had become confused with the Reformation controversy, was condemned.

Not surprisingly, the trial of Reuchlin was seen as a test case in which the right of the scholar to pursue truth independently was threatened by the narrow intolerant authoritarianism of the latter-day schoolmen; every German humanist rallied to Reuchlin's defence and in 1514 Reuchlin was able to publish, under the title *Clarorum virorum epistolae*, a collection of letters from distinguished scholars assuring him of their support. It was the title and form of this publica-tion which were to suggest one of the most celebrated satires of the age: in the autumn of the following year a collection of forty-one *Epistolae obscurorum virorum* appeared, which purported to be letters written by simple, unknown clerics and scholars to Hortuinus (Ort-win) Gratius, one of the leading Dominicans of Cologne and com-monly assumed to be the man behind Pfefferkorn, assuring *him* of *their* support. A further seven letters were added in the edition published in 1516, and a second volume of sixty-two letters followed in 1517. It is now generally agreed that a variety of humanists may have contributed items and ideas, but that Crotus Rubeanus was largely responsible for the first volume, while the second one is the work of Ulrich von Hutten (see p. 405).

The basic idea was delightfully simple: since the opponents of Reuchlin were clearly ignorant and stupid, how better could they be discredited than by being made to speak for themselves – and it was not unknown for contemporaries to take the letters at their face value and regard them as genuine – and alienate opinion by the demonstration of their ignorance, fatuity and immorality? The letters, which achieve their effect by a combination of parody, traditional anti-clerical jokes and themes taken from popular *Schwänke* and Classical satirists, do not all deal directly with the Reuchlin controversy: many of them are taken up with requests for advice on a variety of problems or simply tell Gratius of the doings of his old pupils and friends, and the two volumes – the second of which, as one would expect from Hutten, is much more polemical and anti-Roman in tone – constitute a full-scale attack on the ignorance, superstition, greed and incontinence of the representatives of the ecclesiastical and academic establishment.

For the *viri obscuri* Classical antiquity has been rediscovered in vain: they continue to write in barbarous dog-Latin which is happily innocent of anything Ciceronian or Virgilian – the only Classical work they seem to know is the *Ars amandi* – and in their occasional flights of poetry they produce the most wretched doggerel. Their style is German rather than Latin, with a marked tendency to parataxis. Where their Latin vocabulary lets them down, they simply put Latin endings on German words in much the same way as they have latinized their improbable German names, which in established satirical fashion indicate their nature and mentality: Herbordus Mistladerius (Dungloaderius), Conradus Dollenkopffius (Fatheadius), Franciscus Genselinus (Littlegoosus), etc. Although many of the letter-writers are neatly differentiated (Magister Johannes Hipp is a professional humanist-baiter, Conrad of Zwickau a ladies' man, Padormannus Fornacificis a sycophant, etc.) their key-note is fatuity. They greet their revered master with absurd salutations: 'Tot salutes . . . quot in uno anno nascuntur pulices et culices' or 'Salutem quam mille talenta non possunt equivalere in sua gravitate'.* Aristotle is quoted in large matters and small as an unimpeachable authority and they love to open their letters with a scriptural quotation, usually from the Psalms or the Books of Wisdom, which is then given an absurd or disingenuous application, as when the notorious Conrad of Zwickau quotes Ecclesiastes xi, 'Rejoice, young man, in thy youth' to justify his escapades with the ladies of the town. They talk uninhibitedly about their amorous adventures, their feasts and wine-bibbing and seem to spend a great deal of time in empty and arid

---

*'As many greetings as there are lice and fleas born in a year'. 'Greetings which a thousand talents cannot equal in gravity'.

disputation – for instance, as to whether 'noster magistrandus' or 'magister nostrandus' is a more suitable title for a potential doctor of theology. Such problems of conscience as trouble them are equally revealing: one has greeted two Jews in long cloaks thinking they were doctors of theology and now wonders whether he needs special dispensation; another has ordered an egg at an inn on a Friday only to find that it contained a chicken, which he gulped down to avoid paying for it, and now suffers similar pangs of conscience.

Anecdotes such as these, together with the linguistic satire and the delightful caricatures of the *viri obscuri*, ensured that the letters enjoyed great popularity in the academic community for which they were intended and no doubt helped to complete the destruction of the authority of the ecclesiastical establishment; but for all their rootedness in the contemporary situation, the appeal of the letters was a timeless one, and they have continued to be reprinted and translated down to our own day.

Ulrich von Hutten (1488–1523) and the satirical dialogue

Not the least of the things which the Reformation owed to the humanists was the satirical dialogue, which in the years immediately following the breach with Rome emerged as one of the most effective vehicles of Lutheran propaganda. The popularization in Germany of the Lucianic dialogue was in large measure the work of that wayward scion of the Franconian nobility, Ulrich von Hutten, whom we have already met as the author of the second part of *Epistolae Obscurorum Virorum*.

Paradoxically, although he will always be associated with the Reformation Hutten was not motivated by religious considerations; he uses the language of religious controversy, but fundamentally his fight against Rome does not spring from pious regret at the corruption of Christ's teaching, but from the burning conviction of the irrevocable opposition of the Roman Church to the economic and political interests of the German Empire, which he sought to restore to its ancient glory on the basis of the Emperor and a reinvigorated knightly class. Characteristically, when it became evident that Luther was not a suitable agent for the hoped-for *restitutio imperii*,

Hutten abandoned the Wittenberg connection in order to pursue his will-o'-the-wisp ideal in association with Franz von Sickingen and the Imperial Knights. The failure of the Knights' rebellion in 1522 led to his exile and probably hastened his death the following year.

As a student in Italy, Hutten had been introduced to Lucian and like most of his generation had been delighted by the Syrian's attacks on the hollowness of Greek religion, the dishonesty of philosophers and the fatuity of mankind in general, and when, a decade and more later, Hutten launched his attacks on the Roman Church, the dialogues of Lucian provided him with a ready model. Many of Lucian's apparently polemical pieces were rhetorical exercises rather than the proclamation of personal convictions, but the techniques he had evolved could readily be adapted for the denigration of the Roman Church and its representatives, and this Hutten proceeded to do. He lacks Lucian's highly-developed dramatic sense and lightness of touch, and often his dialogues seem inordinately long: the initial curiosity at the Roman triads in *Vadiscus sive trias Romana* (1519) – 'Three things are held in high esteem in Rome: pretty women, handsome horses and papal Bulls. . . . Three things are common in Rome: carnal lust, fine clothes and inordinate pride', etc. – is rapidly exhausted in the course of over a hundred closely-printed pages in which the 'dialogue' often consists only of prompts followed by long rhetorical speeches. In most of the dialogues, however, the influence of Lucian is everywhere apparent. Like Lucian, Hutten introduces allegorical figures – his sickness (he died of syphilis) appears in *Febris I*, where Hutten seeks to persuade her that she would be better off settling down with Cardinal Cajetan, the papal legate, whose wealth and manner of life would guarantee her a good home; *Febris II* describes her experiences, the opportunity naturally being taken to 'expose' the scandalous nature of her new host's private life. Like Lucian, too, Hutten localizes the action, introduces Classical quotations and references and treats the Gods as familiars, and in *Inspicientes* he borrows not only the manner and situation but even the sub-title of Lucian's dialogue (*Charon*). Phaeton and Apollo look down on the Augsburg 'Reichstag' of 1518 in the same way as Charon and Hermes look down on earth in Lucian's satire, and Hutten, of course, launches a savage and scurrilous attack on Cajetan, while singing the praises of the Germans.

Not content with modernizing a Classical genre for the edification of his fellow-humanists, however, Hutten in 1520 proceeded to put four of his most virulent anti-Roman dialogues into German (*Fieber das erst, Fieber das ander, Vadiscus oder die römische Dreifaltigkeit, Die Anschawenden: Fever I, Fever II, Vadiscus or the Roman Trinity, The Onlookers*) in order to widen the scope of his appeal to include the whole German nation. The appearance of the dialogues in a collected edition under the title *Gespräch büchlin (Book of Dialogues)* in 1521 is in its own way almost as significant as Luther's appeal from the Pope to the laity in the Reformation treatises of the previous year: learned Latin controversy is being shifted on to the popular, vernacular level; that mysterious, hypothetical figure, the common man, begins to move to the centre of the stage and is recognized as a person to be appealed to via the new mass medium of the printed word. As the 'first political German' Hutten was destined to evoke little response amongst his contemporaries, but he had created in the vernacular dialogue an eminently suitable vehicle for the dissemination of anti-papal propaganda, and learned humanists now vied with each other in the production of a host of dialogues, often more lively and persuasive than Hutten's own, which sought to convince the simple layman of the rightness of the Lutheran cause. Parsons and bailiffs discuss the sad decay of the Christian Church; peasants and monks debate the nature of the monastic vocation and the problem of celibacy; Franz von Sickingen talks to St Peter and St George before the Pearly Gates about the pope's claim to be Peter's successor; Karsthans (Jack Mattock) vanquishes Dr Murner in open theological debate and listens to Luther expound his doctrine; Hans the Shoemaker outdoes the local canon in his theological knowledge, and two peasants discuss conditions at the local university, where the papists have tried to suppress the study of St Paul, etc. For all the inherent improbability in the situations envisaged, these dialogues frequently have considerable dramatic effectiveness, especially where opposing views are confronted: the papist, usually a priest, is allowed to state an emasculated case, which is then demolished by the Lutheran, who is usually an embodiment of the Lutheran concept of the *bibelfester Laie* (a layman well read in scripture) – a peasant, a shoemaker, or even a brothel-keeper.

From 1521 until 1525 the Protestant polemicists flooded the market with dialogues. The satirical dialogue continued to be used from time to time after that date, of course, but in 1525, partly as an inevitable consequence of the hardening of the denominational fronts, partly as a direct reflection of the bloody disaster of the Peasants' War and the progressive alienation of the humanists, output dwindled and the first great propaganda exercise of modern times comes to an end. But for all the disillusionment of 1525, the Reformation was a fact, and the satirical dialogue had in no small measure helped to make it so. Naïve and contrived though the dialogues often appear to the modern reader turning the pages of Schade's or Berger's anthologies, their contemporary significance was immense. Their naïveté was of a piece with that of their audience, for whom they possessed real and independent life: their apparent realism enabled the reader (and listener) to participate vicariously in the great debate of the age, to share in the victory of 'truth' over 'falsehood' and to take heart at the rightness of the Evangelical position, as demonstrated by the scriptural texts the protagonists quoted in such profusion. Perhaps even more than tract or sermon, they were, in Berger's phrase, the front-line troops in the battle for the hearts and minds of men.

FIVE

Martin Luther (1483–1546)

THE range of Luther's published work is immense and in its variety reflects the many-sided nature of his concerns and personality: German and Latin interpretations of the Psalms, Epistles and the Prophets, for his students and parishioners; translations of fables by Aesop; editions of works by medieval mystics; socio-economic tracts on marriage, civil obedience, education and permissible rates of interest; savage polemics – including crude illustrations and doggerel verses – against the Roman Antichrist and the Protestant sectarians; some 2,800 letters in Latin and German embracing highly official correspondence with princes and bishops, tender familiar letters to his wife and son and simple messages of comfort to bereaved friends which, together with his children's hymns, reveal a mind of rare delicacy and sensitivity; profound theological treatises which changed the concept of God throughout the greater part of western Christendom; and a collection of bilingual table talk – as recorded by the students who lodged with him – which has justly been compared to Dr Johnson's and in which a highly developed feeling for external nature and the omnipresence of God jostles barrack-room crudity and an outlook (such as on the dangers of child-birth) which frequently can only be described as barbaric. Yet, with the exception of a few hymns and his translation of the Bible, virtually nothing written by him has survived as a work of living literature. Protestantism is in unique measure the creation of Martin Luther, but there exists no devotional work or compendium of Protestant theology, no collection of sermons or spiritual diary which keeps his name alive amongst his co-religionists and most of them would have difficulty in ascribing a single title to him – so much so that professional theologians are from time to time moved to complain of a positive oblivion of Luther (*Luthervergessenheit*) in his native country.

Paradoxical as it might seem in the light of the monument which Protestant filial piety and German scholarship have erected to him in the ninety-odd bulky volumes of the Weimar edition of his works – begun in the 1880s and still incomplete – this state of affairs is entirely as Luther himself would have wished it. Literary and linguistic skill was in his eyes a precious gift of God and a fit cause for rejoicing, but only in so far as the gift was applied to the furtherance of the Giver's work and the proclamation of his purpose. For Luther literature, like all other intellectual occupations, was the servant of theology: his books were conceived merely as a preparation for and elucidation of the Word of God, to be consigned to oblivion once their purpose had been achieved, or, at the most, as the preface to the first volume of the edition of his Latin works (1545) has it, to be preserved as evidence of the 'causes and times of things done' ('causas et tempora rerum gestarum').

Even in the light of this historical approach to his own works and the historical significance Luther the Reformer was to acquire, the common tendency to think of Luther's writings simply as milestones in religious or political history is mistaken. The great bulk of Luther's literary output was only indirectly concerned with the establishment of the new faith, but was a direct expression of the pastoral preoccupations which never deserted him. We tend to think of the years 1517 to 1521 as the great period of reforming activity which, beginning with the publication of the ninety-five theses, was to culminate in the publication of the classic statements of the Lutheran faith in 1520: *De captivitate babylonica ecclesiae preludium*, which destroyed the sacramental system of the old Church; *Von der Freyheyt eyniß Christenmenschen* (*On the freedom of a Christian*), which established the doctrine of Justification by Faith; *An den Christlichen Adel deutscher Nation von des Christlichen standes besserung* (*To the Christian nobility of the German nation on the improvement of the Christian estate*), which proclaimed the priesthood of all believers and the concomitant right of individual interpretation, and put theory into practice by appealing to Caesar. Yet precisely at the time when controversy raged most fiercely and the charge of heresy, with all its possible consequences, was being levelled against him by a host of strident opponents, Luther continued at a truly remarkable rate to produce non-polemical, devotional works which met with unparalleled success, partly no doubt because of his popularity due to the indulgence controversy. Between March 1517 and July 1520, no fewer than thirty such works appeared – commentaries on the Lord's Prayer, sermons on the Passion, on how to reconcile oneself to imminent death, on baptism, on marriage, etc. – which altogether ran into something like 370 different editions!

The great mass of Luther's numerous lectures and sermons were, of course, written in the line of duty; but apart from these 'bread-and-butter' works, it is remarkable how almost everything he wrote was, like the ninety-five theses and the actual reforms themselves, produced in response to an external stimulus, be it an evident need on the part of his flock, a challenge from an opponent, or a request for guidance coming from friends and followers. For all his aggressiveness when roused, Luther only rarely yielded to the temptation to engage in gratuitous controversy. Thus his earliest vernacular statement of his position in the indulgence controversy, the highly successful *Sermon von dem Ablasz und gnade* (*Sermon on indulgence and grace*) of 1518, which was to pass through twenty-two editions in the next two years, was published in order that the lay public should have access to an authoritative vernacular statement of the ideas behind the ninety-five theses rather than the current garbled versions. The *Sendbrieff von Dolmetzschen* (*Letter on Translation*, 1530) was written to explain to a friend his apparent mistranslation of Romans iii, 28 ('ex fide' appears as 'by faith *alone*'), while *Widder die reuberischen vnd mördisschen rotten der bawren* (*Against the robbing and murdering bands of the peasants*, 1525) was similarly a reply – in its intemperate and blood-thirsty tone a very unfortunate reply – to the excesses of the peasants who rose in revolt in 1525 and had named Luther as a judge of the rightness of their cause. Often it was only thanks to such external stimuli that Luther was moved to review his own position and give his own attitudes considered expression – as was the case in *De servo arbitrio* (1525), in which he replied to Erasmus on the subject of free will, a pamphlet which incidentally completed the breach with humanism. Even the great Reformation treatises – occasionally, as Wilhelm Maurer has shown in the case of *Von der Freiheit eines Christenmenschen*, embodying the results of Luther's academic teaching over the previous decade – were on the whole not written as deliberate and unprovoked challenges to orthodox Catholicism, but in response to pressures coming from a variety of quarters: the activities and accusations of Eck, Emser and their associates, for instance, made Luther's reply in *De captivitate babylonica ecclesiae preludium* unavoidable, while *Von der Freiheit eines Christenmenschen* was written at the insistence of Miltitz and court circles around Frederick the Wise, in order to anticipate the threat of excommunication and to take the wind out of Eck's sails. That the result achieved was vastly different from the one envisaged is in the present context immaterial.

As the first and foremost of polemical journalists in European history, often working under intense pressure, with the printer's apprentice waiting under his window to rush the next page off to the waiting compositor, Luther had little but scorn for the carefully elegant Latinity of his humanist contemporaries. His task was to proclaim the truth and the truth had no need of Ciceronian Latin or recondite allusions to help it to prevail; referring to Erasmus in a famous letter of 1522, he writes: 'Potentior est veritas quam eloquentia, potentior spiritus quam ingenium, major fides quam eruditio.'* This is not to say, of course, that Luther's German – or his Latin, for that matter – is crude, clumsy or even lacking in elegance, and he was far from being the stylistic and literary vandal such quotations can make him appear. One has but to compare almost any of his vernacular writings with those of his opponents or to read a few sentences of his Bible translation to see that – truth or no truth – he was possessed of a unique and consciously applied sensitivity to the rhythms of the German language and a rare ability to evoke its peculiar strength. In translating the Bible, when faced with a choice between meaning and euphony, he naturally chose the former – even at the risk of doing violence to the German – but meaning for Luther was not divorced from aesthetic, stylistic considerations. Language (if we may modify the plural he uses in the *Letter to the Councillors of all German Towns, that they should establish and maintain Christian Schools* of 1524) was the scabbard in which the sword of the Spirit was kept, the casket in which the jewel (of God's word) was carried, and was to be respected accordingly. In producing his translation of the Bible, Luther did not set out, as his predecessors had done, merely to render the meaning, but to produce a German equivalent for the originals before him, and to a man of

* 'Truth is stronger than eloquence, the spirit stronger than wit, faith is greater than learning.'

Luther's linguistic sensitivity this meant two things. First, he must write in German which really was German and not German seen through a palimpsest of alien syntax·and idiom: as he puts it in his celebrated *Letter on Translation*:

> The Latin letters are a great hindrance to the writing of good German. . . . One should not ask the letters of the Latin language how one should speak German, one should ask the mother in the home, the children in the street and the common man on the market place and listen how they speak and translate accordingly; then they understand it and realize that you are talking German to them

– a point of view which, however obvious it might seem to us, constitutes a revolution in the philosophy of language in its recognition that each language has its own peculiar idiom and cannot readily be translated literally. Secondly, however, the desire to create a native German equivalent to the Hebrew, Greek and Latin Bible, meant producing prose which would rank as poetry in its own right. This double aim involved Luther on the one hand in such things as having a butcher explain the details of his calling so that he could translate Leviticus correctly, and being prepared to incur the wrath of opponents and the perplexity of friends by translating 'Ave Maria, gratia plena' as 'Gott grüße dich, du liebe Maria' (literally, 'God greet thee, thou dear Mary'): he eventually came down in favour of 'Gegrüsset seistu holdselige' (literally, 'Be greeted, sweet one'). On the other hand Luther's ambitious aim also presupposed a capacity for instant inspiration and sustained revision: it was only after years that, in the often-quoted examples, the opening words of Psalms 23 and 42 finally achieved the euphonious strength they have in the edition of 1545: 'Der Herr ist mein Hirte, Mir wird nichts mangeln. Er weidet mich auff einer grünen Awen, Und füret mich zum frisschen Wasser. . . . Wie der Hirsch schreiet nach frischem Wasser, So schreiet meine seele Gott zu dir.'

Luther's basic stylistic criterion of ready intelligibility – enunciated in the *Letter on Translation* solely with regard to the Bible – applies to all his writings and is a natural corollary to the doctrine of the priesthood of all believers and the right of individual interpretation. When compounded with Luther's linguistic powers, the doctrine of the priesthood of all believers was to have profound effects on the whole future development of the German language. By moving controversy into the vernacular in order to appeal to his fellow 'priests', Luther compelled his opponents to do likewise. More important still, the excellence of his translation of the Bible led them, as Luther put it, to 'steal his language' and publish translations, as Emser did in 1527, which were little more than 'corrected' versions of Luther's own, so that the most common German book – for countless thousands of Germans the only book they ever saw – was written in *Lutherdeutsch*. This is not to suggest, however, as admirers of Luther sometimes claim, that Luther created standard German from nothing. As a Saxon teaching in Saxony Luther was fortunate in that his own East Central German dialect occupied a middle position in the scale of German dialects, embodying – thanks to the colonists of the later Middle Ages – a mixture of Franconian and Central German. The various chanceries – including the politically very important Saxon chancery (Albrecht of Meissen had become Imperial Chancellor in 1480) – had for over a century been moving towards a 'common German', and it was the language of the Saxon chancery that Luther, as he tells us in a famous passage in the *Table Talk* (70), took as a norm. What Luther did was to take the phonology and morphology, the sounds and inflections, of the local chancery and enrich them with the vocabulary and rhythms of everyday speech in order to fashion an instrument for the communication of the word of God. The result was a language which, constantly revised until Luther's death in 1546, was in strength and dignity – and ultimately in influence – in every way comparable to that of the Authorised Version, so that many a German atheist in the mid twentieth century continues to use idioms and proverbs, phrases, metaphors and even individual words which, unknown to him, he owes to Dr Martin Luther.

In view of the remarks on elegance quoted above, it is not surprising that the most characteristic feature of Luther's style should be its unadorned simplicity and directness. Basically, although he wrote so much, Luther is not interested in literary forms and genres. Just as in the sermons he preached he replaced the heavily didactic allegorical and *exemplum*-laden style of the late Middle Ages by the straightforward commentary and exegesis of the Bible, so too in his other works we find no trace of the descendants of the dramas, *specula*, didactic poems, visions and other allegories beloved of medieval authors. Nor are the humanist encomium, *oratio* or dialogue represented in his *œuvre*. The characteristic forms in which his writings appear are the printed sermon and the open letter in which he lets the 'truth' speak for itself by simply enumerating the points he wishes to make (Zum ersten. . . . Zum andern. . . . Zum dritten . . .). But if it seems surprising that Luther should avoid, for instance, the dialogue, in which so much contemporary controversy was carried on, he is too much of a preacher and teacher ever to forget that he is communicating with an audience. As Heinrich Bornhamm remarks, Luther does not write dialogues, he conducts them – with God through the Bible, with his opponents and with his friends. Luther's 'we' is not a royal plural, but a genuine invitation to participate in his search: 'So that we shall be able to understand what a Christian really is . . .' Friends and opponents are addressed directly and possible objections met by anticipating questions arising in the reader's mind: 'But if you ask what this word is which gives us such grace and how we may use it, my answer is . . .'

Luther was far from sharing the hostility to pictures which was subsequently to characterize many Protestants; as he admits in *Wider die himmlischen Propheten, von den Bildern und Sakrament* (*Against the heavenly prophets, on pictures and the sacrament*, 1525), he naturally tended to think in visual terms, and his writings abound in concrete images. Very occasionally these are of Classical provenance; the triple wall with which the papacy is declared to have surrounded itself in the opening paragraphs of *An den Christlichen Adel*, which derives from the triple wall of Tartarus (*Aeneid*, VI, 549), is the best-known example. More frequent are references to fables about, for example, the wolf and the lamb (with himself in the latter role, of course!) or the mouse who had to bell the cat (what he did to the papacy!). As was natural for a man who was not afraid to make the speech of the sixteenth-century equivalent of the man on the Clapham omnibus one of his principal linguistic criteria and who was, one suspects, congenitally more at home in the earthy German idiom than in the refined elegance of humanist Latin, Luther makes great use of the rich concrete imagery contained in the proverbs and metaphors of a rural people. The difficulties in the way of the translator are 'Wacken und Klötze' ('boulders and logs') which must be dug out before the field can be ploughed; as one working by the road-side, he recognizes he will have many critics and advisers, his opponents look at the words 'allein durch den Glauben' ('through faith alone') as a cow looks at a new gate; he does not need their criticism, for he has known for the past seven years that the nails in horses' shoes were made of iron, etc.

Luther's satirical vein gave the sixteenth century two memorable works of pictorial polemicism: the *Passional Christi und Antichristi* (*The Passion of Christ and Antichrist*) produced in collaboration with Melanchthon and Cranach in 1521 and based on the Wyclifian conceit of the antithesis of Christ and his Vicar, and the *Abbildung des Papstthums* (*The Papacy Depicted*) of 1545, which contains Luther's *testamentum coram toto mundo* in the shape of ten anti-papal and for the most part obscene cartoons. In his writings, however, his satire tends to exhaust itself in short bursts of heavy sarcasm and irony such as the statement in the preface to *De captivitate babylonica ecclesiae preludium* that the numerous ingenious and learned arguments of Eck and his associates have finally convinced him that he has been understating the anti-papal case – for which insight he is duly grateful to them. Frequently too he loves to pun, often by way of a deliberate 'Freudian slip': 'Drecketen – Dekreten wollt ich sagen' ('Excretals – decretals I mean'; 'Dreck' = 'filth', 'excrement'), and in much the same way he ran Eck's doctoral title together with his name to produce 'Dreck' or, with less wit, referred to Cochläus as Dr Rotzlöffel ('Snot-spoon'). Luther was not alone in this interest in names, of course, and the whole century shared the pseudo-cabbalistic belief that *nomen est omen*. For his admirers Luther himself was 'Luter' ('pure') and for opponents 'Luder' ('carrion', 'sod', 'slut'), and even the refined Erasmus could not refrain from vilifying an opponent called Medardus by the judicious insertion of an 'r' in the first syllable of his name. Even so, Luther, when roused, did indulge in a crudity which would make a drill instructor blush: thus in *Wider Hans Worst* (*Against Punch*, 1541) he not only seeks to infuriate the noble Heinrich von Braunschweig (the Hans Worst of the title) by addressing him with sovereign contempt as 'Heintz' ('Harry', but the emotive connotation is closer to the modern English 'Jack'), but gives him the following advice: 'You shouldn't write a book until you have heard a fart from an old sow; you should open your mouth towards it and say "Thank you, sweet nightingale, I hear a text suitable for me."'

In so far as it is possible to divide Luther's writings into periods, the division inevitably coincides with the Reformation itself. The pastoral concerns we have noticed accompanied him to the end of his life, but by 1525 the great reforming period was over: the epoch-making programmatic treatises had all been published and the new faith established theologically and politically. After 1525 the need and the intention was to confirm and consolidate what had been achieved, be it by providing a German liturgy (a German mass and order of service appeared in 1526, a catechism in 1529), translating and commentating the full text of the Bible (the New Testament had appeared in 1522, the Old Testament followed in 1534), giving pastoral advice, or ensuring that the Protestant representatives at the Diet of Augsburg (1530) did not compromise on fundamental issues (being under the ban of the Empire, Luther could not participate personally and kept an anxious watch from Coburg just within the Saxon frontier). Everything which Luther wrote at every stage of his career, is, however, informed by his biblicism and the central doctrines of the ineffable majesty and righteousness of God, the direct access of the believer to God, and the incapacity of man to justify himself except through fiduciary faith alone. Running throughout the apparent – and misleading – simplicity of these basic tenets, however, there is, as Gerhard Ebeling has recently demonstrated in his penetrating study of Luther's thought, a dialectic tension between the extremes of the Law and the Gospel, the letter and the spirit, the kingdom of God and the kingdom of the world, *Deus revelatus* and *Deus absconditus*. This naturally produces a tendency to move in paradoxes and apparent contradictions which are seldom so satisfactorily – not to say conveniently – resolved as the famous paradox which Luther makes his point of departure in *Von der Freiheit eines Christenmenschen*, where the freedom and the servitude he ascribes to the Christian are seen as applying to the inner and the outer man respectively. These are, however, problems which are more properly reserved for the theologian rather than the literary historian. From the latter's point of view the importance of Luther lies in the linguistic and literary achievement inherent in his translation of the word of God. Perhaps even more momentous was the service he rendered to the words of men. In all conscience, the volumes of the Weimar edition represent something more than 'a new song's measure', but nevertheless, virtually single-handed, one man had broken the authority of the mightiest intellectual and spiritual power the world had yet seen – and he had done it essentially with tools which were available to all: his native language, a pen, paper and the printing-press. Luther may have freed men's minds from one tyranny only to impose on them a new servitude, blighting the rich promise of Renaissance Germany with an orthodoxy which became increasingly more narrow and intolerant as the century progressed, but after Luther the world could never be the same again, and for all their unfortunate side-effects, his writings represent a great leap forward in the history of the human race.

SIX

Paracelsus (1493–1541) and
Sebastian Franck (1499–1542)

In literature as in life, Luther and the religious controversy he
unleashed dominated the sixteenth century, but while Luther in a
very real sense was the father of modern German prose non-fiction
and the language in which it was written, his achievements as a
writer did not mark the beginning of a golden age of prose writing.
On the Catholic as well as on the Lutheran side, the rapidly hardening
dogmatism reduced almost all non-fiction to the level of a vehicle
for theological bickerings. It is a significant commentary on the
orthodoxies of the age that it was not they, but the 'third reformation' of the sectarians, which claimed the allegiance of the most
remarkable men the century brought forth – men like Thomas
Müntzer, Hans Denck, Caspar von Schwenkfeld and Valentin
Weigel, whose independent spirit cried a plague on both Rome and
Wittenberg and sought a personal way to God outside the established
confessions. The intention here is to treat only two of these remarkable men, Theophrastus Bombastus von Hohenheim, better known
as Paracelsus, and Sebastian Franck.

The edition of PARACELSUS' works, started by K. Sudhoff in 1922
and continued subsequently by K. Goldammer, will run to something
like thirty large volumes when completed; yet Paracelsus himself, in
this respect like Luther, regarded his writings with some indifference
and often did not even bother to find a publisher for them, so that
many of the works bearing his name appeared only after his death
and are occasionally of questionable authenticity. Paracelsus was
intensely proud of his calling as a doctor and his writings were in his
eyes merely by-products of his real activities, with which the profession of letters could not compare. Even so, no account of German
writing in the sixteenth century would be complete without some
mention of this remarkable man. His numerous pamphlets on

medicine, religion and occult philosophy curiously compounded of neo-Platonism, mystical traditions, popular magical and gnostic elements and original insights, enabled him to exercise a powerful effect on his own age and continued to influence a variety of later writers and movements from Böhme and the 'Pansophists' of the seventeenth century down to Goethe and the homeopaths of our own day.

The scion of an impoverished noble Swiss family, Paracelsus studied medicine in Italy and for a brief spell held a professorial chair at Basle, where he adopted the unusual course of lecturing in the vernacular. Paracelsus' natural restlessness and unconventional approach to his subject combined with his irascible temperament to render it impossible for him to stay for long in any one place, however, and for the greater part of his life he led a poverty-stricken existence devoted to his scientific researches and the care of the poor and the sick.

As the *Lutherus medicorum* it was fitting that Paracelsus should command a German style which, at its best, bears comparison with the Wittenberg Reformer's in its rugged, rough-hewn quality and sheer vigour. Much of Paracelsus' work was, however, written under highly unfavourable conditions – occasionally it seems to have been dictated to half-educated *famuli* whose mistakes the printer often incorporated into the full text – and these circumstances manifest themselves not only in the often colloquial tone, but also in the frequently rambling structure of his sentences. This, combined with the abstruse and technical nature of the subject matter – which necessitates a specialized vocabulary – can make Paracelsus one of the most difficult writers of his age.

Scientifically, Paracelsus does not have the significance of a Vesalius or a Harvey, but in seeking to replace the doctrinaire authoritarianism of medieval medicine, with its heavy reliance on Aristotle, Galen and Avicenna, by a more empirical approach based on experience, experiment and individual judgement, he heralds the onset of a new epoch. Further, in an age not noted for the high moral standards of medical practitioners, he evolved a code of medical ethics (*Ius iurandum*, cf. interpretation of seventh and eighth Commandments and Psalm 128) which has justly been compared to that of Hippocrates. On the strictly practical plane he was amongst the first to recognize that exogenous factors played an important part in the origination of disease. Similarly his advocacy of hydrotherapy, his use of ether as a sedative, and development of medical chemistry by his work on the detoxification of metals strike a distinctly modern note.

Paracelsus' modernity is, however, only one aspect of his complex personality, and in the last analysis he is a neo-Platonist and natural philosopher rather than a scientist in the strict sense of the word. His scientific writings (*Von der Frantzosenkrankheit* (*On Syphilis*), 1527-8; *Paragranum*, 1530; *Volumen parmirum*, 1531; *Philosophia sagax*, 1536; *Die große Wundartzenei*, 1537) are full of remarkable insights, but ultimately these insights are subordinated to a neo-Platonic, speculative view of the world which inevitably strikes the modern reader as quaint, not to say patently misconceived. The cosmos is held to be of threefold 'construction', consisting of the spiritual, celestial and elemental. In the archetypal Godhead all phenomena exist as ideas; these ideas become 'powers' in the spiritual sphere, 'forces' in the celestial one and in the elemental sphere take on denser phenomenal forms. Every thing in the created universe has a definite place in one of the various 'chains of command' which thus link in one single order the most primitive and the most sublime forms of existence, each phenomenon being allocated to a particular chain on the basis of an ingenious system of alchemical and symbolical correspondence: for instance, beneath God and the angels, Venus, whose day was Friday, ruled over the elements of air and water, the metal copper, the plants maiden-hair, rose, myrtle, etc., animals such as the goat, the dove and the swan, etc., and, in the microcosm of man, the uro-genital tract. It was particularly this idea of man as a microcosm which interested Paracelsus. Since the *limes terrae* of which man was made is the quintessence of creation, it follows that man embodies in himself the whole of creation, a point which gives Paracelsus' scientific studies a metaphysical significance. Since man is a microcosm, however, he necessarily contains within himself the 'seeds' of all possible diseases, which manifest themselves under the *impressio* of the astrologically conditioned life-force, so that it is this latter which must be treated, by a process akin to sympathetic magic, rather than the patient's body or alien 'germs'. Sickness itself is regarded as a manifestation of a disharmony of the saline, sulphuric and mercuric elements in man and can be brought about in various ways. God may, for instance, in a development of a traditional concept, work through astrology to punish us for our sins; alternatively sickness can be produced in magical fashion by 'imagining': the evil thought of a menstruating woman or even an inadvertent curse of a woman in child-birth can, because of her condition (Paracelsus has a primitive superstitious attitude to both conditions), 'poison' the upper heavens and return to earth in the form of the plague.

Paracelsus' principal non-medical work, the *Philosophia magna*, brings together a number of tracts written during the years 1528–32. The first part, which in established Paracelsan fashion gives a Latin title to the German text, *De divinis operibus et secretis naturae*, ranges from considerations of madness and somnabulism to studies of the nature of ghosts, but consists mainly of a series of investigations and speculations on the subject of the forces which control human destiny either naturally or preternaturally. Again sophisticated ideas, like the suggestion that luck is not a 'force' but the manifestation of innate capabilities and attitudes of mind, jostle primitive superstitions, such as a belief in the existence of sylphs and salamanders and the possibility of breeding minute soulless test-tube babies by keeping sperm (not a fertilized ovum!) at a constant temperature. The second part, *De vita beata*, is probably Paracelsus' most satisfying work in its freedom from scientific speculation and in the incontestable sincerity of the ideas put forward. After a semi-mystical consideration of the highest good, Paracelsus sets forth his most dearly held convictions: the 'blessed life' is here and now (in the sense that those who are not blessed on earth will never achieve blessedness in the hereafter), and its components are modesty, humility and selflessness. Idleness is equated with theft, men should live in the fashion of Psalm 128, verse 2, by the work of their hands, aiming at retaining from their work no more than a bare sufficiency. Acquisitive society is seen as unmitigated corruption; poverty, by contrast, is a gracious gift of God. Those on whom this grace is not bestowed, however, should rejoice that they can at least imitate the poor in dress and food and show charity to those less 'fortunate' than themselves.

These unorthodox views, which culminate in a vision of a restored, but mystic Apostolic community, find echoes in Paracelsus' more obviously theological works, the lengthy *Interpretation of the Psalter* and the seven pamphlets on the Lord's Supper (*Auslegung des Psalters Davids*, III and IV – I and II are lost – and *Libri VII De coena Domini*, both *c.* 1530). Not surprisingly Paracelsus rejects all contemporary forms of religion: 'He who stands on the Pope stands on a pebble, he who stands on Zwingli stands on a hollow thing, he who stands on Luther stands on a reed.' The Pope, the Anabaptists, Luther and Zwingli are four pairs of trousers cut from one piece of cloth ('vier Hosen eines Tuchs') and are all equally ready to persecute the truth. The true Apostolic community is a thing of the spirit, a Church Invisible, rather than an established community: significantly, the Lord's Supper is seen less as a sign of community than as a seal set on Apostolic calling. Christianity means that 'we should all be equal, of one song, live our life in God and conclude it in God and do as we would be done by.' 'We should walk in the path of God (and ignore) all the Church Fathers, patriarchs, priests, Levites, churches and temples of Saints.' All instituted religions, 'Stone Churches' as he contemptuously calls them, are equally corruptions and perversions of the truth and constitute fetters on the free life of the spirit. The word of God is not to be found on the lips of a priest or even the pages of a Bible, it is an inner thing, something God fashions from the believer who thus acquires knowledge of God without need of an external mediator. Yet while Paracelsus thus in keeping with other spiritualists carries Luther's doctrine of the Priesthood of all Believers to its ultimate mystical conclusion, in other respects he is nearer to Rome than to Wittenberg. He shares the common Protestant awareness of the gulf between man and God and lays due emphasis on faith, yet clearly a man who could write so movingly in praise of the necessity of the 'free, blessed liberality towards the poor' and whose whole life was a conscious *imitatio Christi* – who, as Paracelsus pointed out, was also a doctor and equally had no fixed abode – could never relegate 'works' to a subordinate position. Characteristically Paracelsus held the Epistle of St James, which Luther scorned as a 'letter of straw', in high esteem and equally characteristically he postulated the possibility that by leading the good life a man might be able to reconcile himself with God.

In spite of the mystical overtones, the fundamentally ethical view of religion expounded by Paracelsus is probably nearer the religious mood of our own age than the views expounded by his more orthodox contemporaries. In his scientific and philosophical speculations he is almost entirely alien to us, just as indeed he was ultimately out of step as far as his own age was concerned. At precisely the time when medical and scientific studies were beginning to concentrate on making advances on narrow specialist fronts, Paracelsus continued to think in terms of a genuinely universal system and to erect an edifice of thought and speculation which was shortly to be shown to rest on totally inadequate foundations. But even though the edifice was built on sand and was full of curiously-shaped rooms, twisting stairs and passages which ended in blank walls, it nevertheless testified to the grandeur of the concept which inspired the architect.

Like Paracelsus, SEBASTIAN FRANCK bore witness in his own life to the intolerance and vindictiveness of the orthodoxies of the sixteenth century and their incapacity to retain the loyalty of some of the best spirits of the age. He studied at Heidelberg and entered the Roman priesthood in 1524, but almost immediately was converted to Protestantism and for a time was active as a Lutheran preacher. Anabaptist influence soon eroded his new allegiance, however, and by 1528 he had forsaken his parish and moved to Nürnberg, which at this time, although officially Lutheran, was a hot-bed of sectarian activity. Here Franck came into close contact with some notable members of the 'left wing' of the Reformation – Paracelsus, Denck and the 'godless painters', Pencz and Beham (whose sister Franck married). However, like all sectarians, Franck was never tolerated for long in any one place, and the next ten years saw him in Strasbourg, Ulm, Esslingen and Basle, variously employed as a soap-maker, printer and free-lance essayist, writing indefatigably in spite of his extreme poverty, and everywhere harried and persecuted by the local Protestant clergy as a man who posed a serious threat to their own narrow orthodoxy.

As a religious thinker Franck stands in the tradition established by the late medieval mystics and carries their spiritualization of religion to its ultimate conclusion. The most succinct statement of Franck's religious views is contained in the letter to Johannes Campanus of 1531 which, although not intended for publication, circulated in Dutch and German translations. For a full understanding of his position, however, this needs to be supplemented by the Introduction to the *Ketzerchronik* (*Chronicle of Heretics*), which constitutes the third book of the third part of the long history of the world he published under the title *Chronica, Zeytbuch und Geschychtbibel* (*Chronicle, Time-book and History-bible*, also 1531), and the *Paradoxa* of 1534, in which he develops in a series of some 280 paradoxes his views on the mysterious and esoteric nature of religion ('The world does not believe what it believes', 'Nothing is stronger or weaker than God', etc.). The true Apostolic Church ended with the death of the Apostles and its declared successor is a servant of Antichrist. The evangelical Reformation, by contrast, seeks merely to replace papal servitude by Mosaic tyranny based on the dead letter rather than the living spirit. Scripture is not a source of revelation, but solely a means of confirming what God pours into the heart of the believer. God does indeed speak through the Scriptures, but he speaks in riddles and paradoxes which can only be understood correctly by those who have been illumined by the divine spirit. There is only one true baptism, that of fire and spirit, and this baptism unites all the members of the incorporeal true Church which is scattered throughout the whole world and includes not only Christians, but Turks, Jews and barbarians, who may be touched by the spirit even though they may not have heard of Christ! The world, being material by nature, is necessarily incompatible with the spirit and consequently must persecute true religion – hence the claim in the *Chronicle of Heretics* that those condemned as heretics were in fact true Christians. Organized churches, being of the world, are temples of Antichrist rather than houses of God. All hopes for a restoration of the original Apostolic Church are vain: God alone knows his children, and the members of the Church Spiritual thus can never recognize each other and must necessarily lead a life of spiritual isolation, which will, however, in view of their incapacity to know who is God's child and who is not, be a life of tolerance and charity towards their fellow men.

Much of this is standard spiritualist teaching; where Franck differs from his fellow sectarians most obviously is in the plea for tolerance and the generally enlightened attitude which informs almost everything he writes and gives his work a distinct modernity. Not surprisingly, while Luther and his opponents were still talking in terms of the *bellum iustum*, Franck emerged as a powerful advocate of pacifism in his *Kriegsbüchlein des Friedens* (*War-book of Peace*, 1539), and Franck has often deservedly been celebrated as an embodiment of humane charity, as an enlightened man in a dark age. Yet there is in Franck's tolerance – indeed, in his whole complex personality – an undeniably ambiguous quality. Franck wrote voluminous history books (*Chronica*; *Chronicon Germaniae*, 1538) because, as is indicated by the title of the *Chronica*, history is a source of religious revelation, 'a living Bible in which you can study the art of God and learn His will'. Yet Franck is also imbued with the pessimistic awareness that the whole of human history is also 'God's Shrovetide farce' ('Gottes Fastnachtspiel') from which men learn nothing unless touched with the spirit of God – which makes them independent of such learning. Similarly, in his social pronouncements, he can declare hereditary nobility and class distinction to be 'an alien thing' or a 'foolish pagan thing' in Christendom, but yet look with contempt on 'Herr Omnes', as he, following Luther, called the common people, whose wisdom he none the less lovingly commented and edited in the important collection of German proverbs he published in 1541. In much the same way, his patriotism and anti-Catholicism almost invariably shine through whenever Germany or the papacy are under discussion and not infrequently give the lie to his declared intention 'to be a writer and not a censor of other men's actions and words . . . and to write neither for nor against anyone, but to describe good and bad as history presents them.' It is on the basis of texts such as these that critics have often been moved to celebrate the objectivity of Franck's historical writings and his freedom from prejudice, yet the readiness to operate with terms like 'good' and 'bad' conflicts oddly with the declared unwillingness to act as a censor, and Franck is far too strong and independent a spirit not to have very decided views on the great issues of his own and earlier ages. Thus in his treatment of the Reformation in the *Chronica*, he lets the sources speak for themselves in best Ph.D. fashion by quoting Erasmus, Hutten, Luther and the sectarians, but roundly condemns the Roman Church for its abuses, castigates Luther for his obstinacy in the matter of the Eucharist, refutes the doctrines of the Anabaptists and lodges a plea for tolerance in religious matters, apportioning praise and blame according to his own lights. Occasionally, indeed, Franck's strength lies precisely in the fact that he *is* prejudiced: without the paradoxical conviction that the world is a place where fair is foul and foul is fair, he would never have arrived at the inversion of the traditional framework of ecclesiastical history for which the *Chronicle of Heretics* is famous, nor been moved to regret, in apparently modern fashion, the disappearance of the heretics' writings. Not infrequently, too, one gains the impression that Franck's tolerance is perhaps more the result of disillusionment and ironic detachment than of warm human sympathy: the world is totally corrupt and all nations and almost all men are equally depraved actors in God's farce.

Appropriately for a man, one of whose chief works bears the title *Paradoxa*, Franck on the one hand occupies a theoretical position in which he needs must become a spiritual hermit, while on the other hand in practice eschews any temptation to cut himself off from human society, and from his early publication *On the Vice of Drunkenness* (1528) to the end of his life he was concerned to improve and convert his fellow men. The bulk of his writings consists of popularizing works on history and geography written in a relaxed, almost conversational German and representing compilations and syntheses of older works rather than the fruit of original researches. The *Türkenchronik* of 1530, for instance, is an updated version of the *Libellus de ritu et moribus Turcorum* of 1480, the *Chronica* of 1531 is heavily indebted to Hartmann Schedel's *Weltchronik* of 1495, and the famous *Chronicle of Heretics* is based on Bernhard of Luxemburg's *Catalogus haereticorum* of 1522. In much the same way in the *Chronicon Germaniae* of 1538 he drew not only on Tacitus and Suetonius, but also on a host of modern humanist historians such as Beatus Rhenanus and Johann Böhm, while the *Weltbuch* of 1534 (originally conceived as the geographical fourth part of the *Chronica* of 1531) is openly proclaimed to be a synthesis of 'credible, experienced geographers, a handbook incorporating many long volumes'. Franck's unashamed compilation and popularization of history not unnaturally provoked the contempt and anger of humanist circles, who regarded him, in Melanchthon's famous phrase, as 'indoctae conditor historiae'. But the 'unlearned' nature of his histories is not the least of Franck's claims to modernity, and even though professional academics might look askance at his work, his vernacular history books for decades remained some of the most effective disseminators of enlightenment amongst a general public whose thirst for knowledge and interest in the world in which they lived had never been so intense. In this sense, the histories constitute remarkable documents of the democratization of knowledge, in their own sphere as significant as Hutten's or Luther's democratization of political and religious controversy, and their 'unlearned' author may in a practical – if not, alas, in a moral – sense justly claim to be an important educator of his people.

SEVEN

Jean Calvin (1509–64)

As a young man Calvin saw the spread of first generation Protestantism in France to the point where the possibility of something like an Anglican solution looked by no means impossible. By 1533, when he had completed his studies and became converted to Protestantism, the cause of moderate reform, sponsored by Marguerite de Navarre, was prospering, but only a year later (18 October 1534) the posting in public places (and even in the King's bedroom) of violently anti-Catholic placards changed the course of French history literally overnight, and for ever precluded the possibility of victory for the Reformers. Yet Calvin's début as a writer, apart from his commentary on Seneca's *De Clementia* (1532), is a firm expression of hope.

Obliged to flee, first from Paris, then from France, as a consequence of the placards, he published in 1536, at Basle, a book of 520 pages, in six chapters, simply entitled *Christianae Religionis Institutio*. The book is prefaced by an open letter in French to the King, in which he refutes charges of subversion and heresy made against so-called Lutherans, and exhorts François to protect rather than persecute these his loyal subjects. That Calvin believed what he said is beyond doubt; that he expected François to believe it is not, in 1536, wholly impossible. This first modest confession of faith was soon sold out, and in 1539 he published a second edition at Strasbourg, whither he had been obliged to move after a brief and stormy interlude at Geneva. This new presentation (with the title now in the familiar order *Institutio Christianae Religionis*) was three times as long as the first, in 438 folio pages, expanded into seventeen chapters covering the whole range of Christian doctrine as he thought it should be taught, amply supported by scriptural references. Though in Latin, the 1536 edition had been meant as a guide for all true believers, with chapters on the Law, the Creed, the Lord's Prayer, the sacraments of Baptism and Eucharist, the five others, now rejected, and Christian liberty, while in 1539 extensive additions brought in the knowledge of God, the Old and New Testaments, predestination and providence, and Christian life.

Reluctantly reinstalled in Geneva, Calvin published in 1541 his French translation of the 1539 Latin, entitled *Institution de la Religion chrétienne*, reverting to smaller format and smaller print so that this volume of 822 pages could have the widest diffusion. Several further editions in each language followed before the final Latin version came from Estienne's press in Geneva in 1559, now nearly five times as long as the 1536 work, comprising eighty chapters in four books, followed next year (1560) by the final French version. In some respects these last two editions, while undeniably authoritative, are top heavy and from a literary point of view the French edition of 1541 is Calvin's masterpiece, a work of prime importance both in itself and in its implication.

The authority and clarity with which Calvin expounded the faith as he saw it lost nothing through his use of the vernacular. It has been suggested, and never conclusively disproved, that Calvin wrote a French version of the *Institutio* just before or just after 1536, but, however that may be, it is certain that only two years after the Edict of Villers-Cotterets made French the official legal language of France (1539), the 1541 edition proved French equally capable of expressing the highest religious truths. A word of caution cannot however be omitted: nothing in French is more deceptive than its clarity, as the long history of Cartesianism shows, and Calvin is no exception. In his excellent book *The History and Character of Calvinism*, J. T. McNeill speaks of Calvin's 'resourcefulness ... not overmastered by an anxious consistency' and finds that 'Calvin formerly stirred debate because people agreed or disagreed with his teaching. Recently men have been in disagreement with regard to what his teaching was.' It is salutary to reflect that Calvin's enemies have always blamed him for a damnable consistency over such matters as double predestination or the relations of Church and State, just as the Jesuits very early acquired their proverbial reputation as masters of equivocation. Such misunderstandings nurture wars, and even now it is hard to look back at the texts with objectivity, remembering how much blood was shed and how much prejudice thereby consecrated.

Calvin's personal experience is closely reflected in his thought and style. The essential facts are obvious enough: he was a Frenchman condemned to spend more than half his life in exile; he was the acknowledged leader for a quarter of a century of French Protestants, but never at any time had serious hopes of heading a national Church as Luther had done; he had the example of the Anabaptists and other extremists before him to accentuate his temperamental dislike of dissent; and above all his insistence on the moral obligations of Christian life meant that he and his teaching were inevitably to be judged on the evidence of life led in Geneva. In point of fact he only became unchallenged leader, even in that city state, after Servetus' execution for heresy (1553), and for years after his return in 1541 had to face one dispute after another. All this meant that an exceptionally strong sense of purpose, a rigorous theology of election, and the practical difficulties of operating within a small political unit whose citizens were by no means docile under the puritan yoke, reinforced in him a spirit of contrast, to which he seems in any case to have been inclined. The reason for which he endured exile, and induced others to follow him, was his belief that we are citizens of no earthly kingdom, but once the elect are gathered together, as in Geneva, they must show by the example of their daily lives that Christianity demands total commitment, from which none can be exempt.

His work is full of antitheses, nowadays recognized as a dialectic rather than a static and sterile set of mutually exclusive categories. The many and the few, this world and the next, superficial piety and true faith, the physical and historical Church and the invisible body of the elect through the ages, these are among the most frequent of his contrasts. One literary consequence is the high seriousness so characteristic of his work, and the accusations of levity and frivolity made against opponents. Such humour as he shows is naturally more prevalent in his directly polemical works, and is invariably destructive, ridiculing people, practices and beliefs different from his own. It would be unfair to represent him as a doom-laden killjoy, and there are numerous passages in which he lyrically describes the joys of the elect or praises a merciful Creator, but it is true that most of the attitudes associated with Puritan and Presbyterian visibly derive from him.

Calvin advances his arguments point by point, like an advocate, appealing at least as often to the heart through emotive language as to the mind with compelling logic. His French is generally regarded as being well in advance of his day, and closer to that of Pascal or Bossuet in both syntax and rhythm. It inevitably preserves the stamp of the Ciceronian Latin on which he had been brought up, but the simplicity of the Bible and the influence of a lifetime spent preaching the word to ordinary folk were equally decisive. Although his teaching was treated as dogma in his own day, modern critics deny that he ever intended to do more than expose error and offer his personal interpretation of the word of God in Scripture.

The dignity and coherence of his exposition did for French what Luther's Bible did for German, but it is significant that it was Marot's Psalms, and not his own, which were adopted for worship. If he had a gift for imaginative use of language he seldom showed it. It is relevant to recall that for most of his ministry he suffered from chronic ill health, especially migraines, was grossly overworked, never eating or sleeping enough, and was under continual pressure in all he did; if he enjoyed the reputation for never wasting a word in speech or on paper, this was the effect of such pressures. Thus he is very sparing with imagery and prefers that of a concrete and direct nature, he does not indulge in complex or syllogistic argument, and, by sixteenth-century standards, avoids rhetorical and syntactical flourishes.

The grave and measured prose of the *Institution* was not Calvin's only style. Reports of his sermons (he published hardly any himself), his vast correspondence and his polemical works show considerable variety, always within a range which excludes the poetic or merely entertaining. As a satirist in Latin and French he was successful and influential, and quite often achieves comic effects at the expense of his victims. The *Traité des reliques* (1543) shows his destructive logic at its best. Setting out to compile a systematic catalogue of relics, in order of sanctity, he shows that in many cases multiplicity (for example, John the Baptist's head), or flagrant anachronism (some of Christ's alleged garments), or inherent improbability (the Virgin's milk) defy credibility and encourage superstition or, worse, total scepticism about religion. In very similar vein is the *Traité contre l'Astrologie judiciaire* (1549), in which the pretensions of astrologers to explain and predict individual human destinies is caustically challenged. Calvin was not the first to write such pamphlets, but their rationalistic approach foreshadows the Calvinist Bayle (1647–1706) and the Enlightenment.

A very different sort of work is the *Excuse aux Nicodémites* (1544), addressed to the various classes of fainthearted believers, who are compared to the Scriptural Nicodemus, who dared only to come to Our Lord by night. This very important work is very typical of Calvin in its condemnation of compromise and its call for all or nothing. He is particularly harsh about courtiers and others of high rank who publicly go through Catholic motions while inwardly professing the Gospel of reform. God's service may call us to exile or the stake, but, for Calvin, it cannot be performed with half measures.

The Latin treatise *De Scandalis* (1550) has fortuitously come to be known better than any of the others because of its personal attack on Rabelais. This work examines the various scandals or stumbling-blocks in the path of true religion, and is not directed against the moderates for whom there is still hope, but against the impious, for whom there can be none. Some have gone so far in their attacks against Rome as to bring all religion into disrepute, some, like Rabelais and Des Periers, are accused of having turned to derision the Gospel truths they once acknowledged, others, even worse, are dubbed atheists, or, as we should say, rationalists or materialists, denying immortality of the soul. The vigorous reaction of Rabelais in the *Fourth Book* (1552) is sufficient proof that Calvin had drawn blood.

For all the rest of Calvin's work, catechetical, educational and legislative, his monument lies around him, in Geneva, in Holland, in South Africa, in Scotland, in New England, wherever the Reformed Church has spread and flourished. There is no gainsaying his greatness, and his literary achievement alone would have assured him of a place in history. More forbidding, less human than Luther, who was so openly inclined to fleshly weakness, Calvin was what French Protestantism needed in a situation demanding individual initiative and courage from each convert and organizing ability from its leader. One could wish that a propensity to anger had not been the chief fault to which he owned, but his personality and policy have been vindicated by events. It was not the moderation of a Bucer or a Melanchthon, but the ruthless singlemindedness of Calvin and his successor, Bèze, that enabled the Huguenots to survive war and persecution, to force the Edict of Nantes (1598) and finally to preserve their identity and faith after the Revocation (1685).

EIGHT

French Satire

In so violently controversial an age as the sixteenth century it is a little unreal to treat satire as a mainly literary phenomenon. Poets like Marot, du Bellay, Ronsard and d'Aubigné all wrote satirical poems, discussed already, which remain interesting primarily as poetry, but in prose, with the obvious exception of Rabelais, the propaganda content is usually more interesting than the form. However, amid the flood of polemical reading-matter one or two genuine works of literature stand out and may usefully be classified under the broad heading of satire; committment can often make up in inspiration what a writer may lack in talent.

One of the Classical authors rediscovered by the Renaissance was the second-century (A.D.) Greek Lucian whose satirical dialogues criticizing religion and other established ideas were first edited by Erasmus (from 1500) and visibly influenced his own satirical works. This particular form of mocking banter proved an extremely effective weapon in the hands of humanist critics of sixteenth-century institutions, and it was not long before the accusation of 'Lucianism' was being levelled with equal vehemence by both Catholics and Protestants against those who impartially attacked all extremists. The best French example of Lucianic dialogue is BONAVENTURE DES PERIERS's *Cymbalum Mundi* (published anonymously, 1537). Des Periers had been closely associated with the early French Reformers, having collaborated with Calvin's cousin, Olivetan, in the Waldensian Bible of 1535, but became disenchanted with the Protestant cause and consummated the breach with this enigmatic little pamphlet of some forty pages. The book was at once condemned, seized and destroyed by the authorities, and though very few copies can ever have been in circulation (only two or three survive) it was taken seriously enough to earn its author (together with Rabelais) special obloquy from quarters as diverse as the Sorbonne, the crazy polymath Guillaume Postel (1543), Calvin (1550) and Henri Estienne (1566). The ritual charges of atheism and Lucianic impiety have recently been challenged but it is incontrovertible that contemporaries regarded the *Cymbalum Mundi* as an exceedingly dangerous book.

Disagreement over the meaning of the title (probably a reference to the tinkling cymbal of 1 Corinthians xiii) does not assist interpretation of the four loosely-connected dialogues. These contain enough action to make them dramatic rather than rhetorical, and much depends on vexed problems of identification. In the first dialogue we meet Mercury, sent to Earth by Jupiter to have a new binding put on a book containing the history of creation, the plan of future events and the register of those destined to immortality. This clearly refers to the Bible and religious innovation. At an inn Mercury falls in with two bibulous rogues, representing the seamier side of Catholicism, who threaten him with severe penalties for alleged blasphemy and then ironically enough (Mercury was god of thieves) rob him of his book. In the third dialogue we learn that they have substituted another, and are rapidly becoming rich by selling information from it (a reference to indulgences). The second dialogue shows three philosophers, actually Luther, Erasmus and Bucer in transparently anagrammatic disguise, fighting for fragments of a shattered philosophers' stone which, we learn at the end, never really existed. Luther in particular is harshly satirized for his arrogant claim to a monopoly of truth, and the other two are more mildly censured for relying on mere words. The latter part of the third dialogue introduces a talking horse, and the fourth dialogue is between two talking dogs, and whatever may be the precise significance of these allegories it is clear that the author is mocking human loquacity, credulity and addiction to nine-day wonders. The theme of love, sacred and carnal, also comes into the third dialogue (and perhaps into the fourth), and Des Periers seems to be condemning all forms of constraint, whether by vows (nuns) or intellect (prudes) in favour of spontaneous obedience to the innocent promptings of nature.

By mocking Catholics and Reformers alike, by preaching the value of reticence in an age of compulsive eloquence, Des Periers pleased no party. In so far as his little book can be satisfactorily explained it offers largely negative advice, rejecting all dogmas and apparently settling for discreet agnosticism, though probably not atheism. Behind the brilliant style and deftness of touch a note of disillusioned pessimism can hardly be missed, and one can see how, in the climate of the age, this was regarded with deep suspicion by zealots.

Satire of a very different kind is provided in HENRI ESTIENNE's *Apologie pour Herodote* (1566). A member of the great printing family, ardently Calvinist and brilliant Classical scholar, Estienne (1531–98) had just published a Latin edition of Herodotus, with a preface rebutting the usual charges of mendacity and exaggeration. In the foreword to this French work he explains that he had originally intended to translate his own Latin, but had then decided instead to compose a new preparatory treatise, or first book, in defence of Herodotus. The book is divided into two parts (and was to have had a third) and is of some six to seven hundred pages in forty chapters. The twenty-six chapters of the first part meet the objection that people cannot have been as wicked as Herodotus said by making a detailed comparison between ancient and modern depravity, cumulatively demonstrating the superior wickedness of later ages. Most of the chapters are devoted to a particular vice, for example, lechery, sodomy, blasphemy and larceny, and the last six are given up to a study of these (and other) vices practised by the clergy, especially the friars. The fourteen chapters of the second part are entirely concerned with the falsehood and stupidity of modern times, again worse than in Herodotus' day, and all the examples are drawn from Catholic preaching and malpractice. The result is, to say the least, colourful, so much so that Estienne got into trouble with the puritanical authorities of Geneva for excessive zeal in his self-appointed task of moral sewage-inspector.

There is nothing subtle or Lucianic about the *Apologie*, indeed the chapter on blasphemy condemns Rabelais and Des Periers specifically as worthy heirs to Lucian, but the sheer volume of Estienne's invective, tirelessly sustained over such a range of topics, is imposing and very characteristic of Renaissance polemic. In the course of his indictment of modern vice (in practice going back sixty to eighty years) he draws on a variety of sources, Classical and recent, but shows a predilection on the one hand for historians (relevant to his defence of Herodotus) and on the other for preachers whom his Catholic opponents could not disown. His favourite sources are the French Franciscans Olivier Maillard (died 1502) and Michel Menot (died 1518) and the Italian Dominican Gabriel de Bareleta, whom he constantly quotes as unimpeachable witnesses to the depravity in clergy and people that they denounce. Whether he himself believed them is beside the point. The usual procedure is simply to catalogue examples of vice by stringing together stories and *exempla* of all kinds and in numerous languages and dialects. Estienne explains in his preface that he had been criticized for some of the more unseemly stories, but claims that he only brought them in to illustrate his thesis, never just as entertainment. However that may be, a number of them were incorporated into later editions of Des Periers's *Joyeux Devis* and many more would earn a place in anthologies with publishers willing to risk prosecution.

Given that his declared aim was to out-Herodotus Herodotus, Estienne undeniably succeeds. His repertory of sins and wickedness is as varied as it is bizarre, nor does it lack exuberant humour, but repetition eventually palls, the stories are just too bad to be true and in the end propaganda succumbs beneath its own weight. The *Apologie* is written in a virile and truculent style, and the main satirical device is a sometimes ponderous irony, but Estienne's acute sense of the outrageous continually produces fresh surprises for the reader. The book is an excellent example of the kind of encyclopaedic charge sheet so popular with sixteenth-century polemists, and its parade of vice and folly belongs to the same satirical tradition as that of Luther and even his medieval predecessors.

A third example of satire announces in its title the class to which it belongs: the SATIRE MENIPPÉE (1594) recalls Varro's work of the same name (taken from the Cynic Menippus and also used by Lucian) and conforms to the original definition of satire as a mixture, a work in free form, prose or verse, criticizing some aspect of society. The work was jointly composed by six friends belonging to the party of moderate Catholics known as *politiques*, Pierre le Roy, Pierre Pithou, Nicolas Rapin, Florent Chrestien, Jean Passerat and Jacques Gillot, two of them minor poets, but otherwise clerical and legal men of scholarly bent, not writers at all. Its occasion and subject was the meeting of the States General in 1593, and its object was to ridicule the Holy League, backed by Spain, and advocate the cause of Henri de Navarre, who though a heretic had legitimately succeeded to the throne as Henri IV on the assassination of his cousin Henri III in 1589. More directly topical than the other works discussed, the *Satire* was also far more successful with the public, both as propaganda and as literature, for it continued to be re-edited long after the cause was won. Despite the amateur status of most of its authors, the fervour of their patriotism inspired a work which has not unfairly been described as the transition between *Gargantua* and Pascal's *Provincial Letters* (1657).

The ideological conflict, whose early stages are satirized in the *Cymbalum Mundi*, and to which Estienne contributed just after it had flared up into civil war, had by 1593 inflicted appalling wounds on France and sickened all men of feeling. The brutal and cynical exploitation of French domestic weakness by Spain, acting through the alien Guises, recently naturalized Lorrainers, now threatened national survival. The choice was quite simply between a puppet or viceroy imposed by Spain or, regardless of his religion, a King who was legitimate, French and – welcome change – a man. Henri IV represented the only hope for national unity, dignity and order against the mercenaries and time-servers of the League.

This is the theme of the *Satire*, and it is presented in a variety of ways. The first section introduces two charlatans, one Spanish and the other from Lorraine, extolling the virtues of Catholicon, a wonder drug common in contemporary pharmacopoeias but also obviously standing for Catholic extremism. The claims made by the Spaniard are more extravagant, for the Lorrainer lacks the magic ingredient, gold. There follow four brief sections setting the scene for the assembly, and full of allusions to persons and events. The greater part of the book, and the best, is the series of seven speeches supposedly delivered at the meeting. First comes Mayenne, leader of the Guises and Lieutenant General, then the Cardinal Legate, speaking in a weird mixture of Latin and Italian, followed by Cardinal Pellevé, claimant to the see of Reims, also partly in Latin, the Archbishop of Lyon, the Rector of the Sorbonne, and, for the Second Estate, a soldier of fortune, de Rieux by name. These speeches are at once parody and inadvertent confession, for each in his way declares what he would normally be at pains to conceal: Mayenne only wants the crown for himself, regardless of the people's suffering, the prelates promote their own interests with equal blatancy, and even de Rieux puts himself forward as a candidate for the throne.

After so much brilliant, but wholly destructive, satire, the seventh speech by d'Aubray, deputy for the Third Estate, comes as a shock and a revelation. As long as all the other speeches put together (some 100 pages) it is apparently modelled on the actual speech for which d'Aubray was briefly exiled by the League. In its gravity and sincerity it rises above all partisan considerations, and is still today deeply moving. The greater part of the speech consists of a factual, and remarkably fair, account of events since family rivalry between Guises and Bourbons plunged France into a nominally religious war. It is noteworthy that d'Aubray's royalism shows itself as much in his condemnation of Henri III's assassination (instigated by the League) as in his support for Henri IV, and it is almost as an afterthought that he professes his own Catholic faith. In his moral revulsion for the methods of the Guises and their Spanish paymasters and, for instance, in his comparison between Paris under siege by Henri IV and Jerusalem by Titus, he recalls d'Aubigné's tones in the *Tragiques*, but it was of course only when a sufficient number of Frenchmen of all parties rallied round their rightful King that a return to decency and sanity could be expected, and his sentiments were by then general.

The dozen or so pages of epilogue, and a few poems, which conclude the book come as an anti-climax after this splendid performance, so profoundly and eternally French that the very turn of phrase can be applied with equal aptness to national catastrophes throughout the centuries down to the present day. The *Satire Ménippée* is a historical document, but like the *Provincial Letters* it has transcended its immediate moment to become literature.

The religious and national struggles in the Low Countries threw up one author of international stature who may fittingly close this account of satire which began with Erasmus. PHILIPPE MARNIX DE SAINTE-ALDEGONDE (1540–98) was born in Brussels of a Franc-Comtois father and a mother from Hainault. After studying at Louvain and in Italy, he was converted to Protestantism and spent two years studying theology in Geneva, whence he returned in 1562 to join William of Orange in Holland and become his close friend. War and diplomacy, interspersed with periods of enforced retirement, filled his eventful life, of which the saddest act was handing over Antwerp to the besieging Spaniards (1585). His literary output includes Latin works on husbandry and education, a Dutch translation of the Psalms, numerous polemical pamphlets and two major satires, one in Dutch, the other in French.

The genesis of these two works is complicated, and has only recently been fully cleared up. In 1561 and 1562 one Gentian Hervet, canon of Reims, published two undistinguished pamphlets in letter form against the Huguenots. These were translated into Dutch, and answered in 1569 by a book of some 500 pages by the pseudonymous Isaac Rabbotenu, *De Biencorf der Heiligen Roomsche Kercke* (*The Beehive of the Holy Roman Church*). The book was an enormous success; it had numerous editions, was translated into English (1579) and German (1576 and again, by Fischart, in 1579), and set off a whole series of pamphlets, in both Dutch and French, from Catholics and Protestants.

It is now known (from Hervet's own answer of 1581) that this Dutch book had been preceded by a French version, a *Commentaire* (1567) under the name Jomlaiela, and that this too was by Marnix. Hervet had divided his work into six sections, attacking the Protestants on charges of incredulity, sexual licence and excessive reliance on Scripture, and defending Catholic teaching on the sacraments, invocation of saints and, above all, papal authority, and Marnix follows the same plan. His book, addressed to the Bishop of 'sHertogenbosch, takes its title from an epilogue of some twenty-five pages, allegorically comparing the Roman Church to a beehive, but the rest of it purports to be the work of a Catholic priest reinforcing the arguments of Hervet who, he feels, has not gone far enough. Anticipating Pascal's technique, Marnix makes his Catholic so overstate his case as to ruin it, and with devastating irony adduces evidence from Scripture, the Fathers and Councils supposedly in support of Hervet but actually reducing his argument to absurdity. The satire is often savage, especially when moral questions are involved, and Marnix is not tender in his burlesque account of Catholic ceremonies and beliefs, but now and then he drops the mask and represents the Protestant case directly. In these ecumenical days the bitterness of Marnix's attack and the violence of his language may shock some readers, but the lucidity of the argument and pungency and vigour of the style have long been recognized as making *De Biencorf* one of the literary masterpieces of Dutch.

Meanwhile Marnix went on working at the original (now lost) French version, and by the time he died had completed the first part of the work now retitled *Tableau de différends de la religion*, published 1599. A friend saw to the publication of the second part (1605) but this contains a lot of much earlier material that Marnix had not had time to rework. Thirty years on more serious adversaries than Hervet had arisen, and Marnix is one of the first writers in French to attack the Jesuits, and especially their great theologian, Robert Bellarmine. He aimed, he says, at a comprehensive presentation of the arguments for each side, in the spirit of debate rather than passion, but the irony and parody of the earlier work are no less conspicuous in this, though accompanied by even more erudition and detailed arguments. The Protestant case is closely argued, with attacks on papal claims and insistence on Scriptural authority and liberty of conscience, but the most readable parts of this huge work (nearly 1,300 pages in a modern edition) are the comic stories and descriptions. The debt to Rabelais is constantly evident, often through direct quotation, but mainly through a wealth of verbal invention and dexterity in the master's tradition. Proverbs, archaisms, dialect forms, neologisms, and a magnificent rhythm make Marnix's French reminiscent of Elizabethan English at its best. Specialists have described the book as the most important linguistic document in French of its period, and it is certain that despite its great length, the remoteness of the theological issues and the frequent affronts to modern sensibilities, it is the one work of the century to recapture for page after page the joyous exuberance of Rabelais's style. 'La saincte et solemnelle entreboucleure, concatenation, et circonvolubilipatenotrization des beatissimes Papes de Rome, entreavemariés du cordon rouge . . .' is an untranslatable sample of Marnix warming to his theme. As much of a Netherlander as the Breughels, Marnix had the same love of colour, movement and detail, and if he is not more widely known and appreciated it is largely because he was bilingual and, for nationalistic critics, born on the wrong side of the frontier.

NINE

Vives (1493–1540)

PROBABLY the two Spanish writers of greatest intellectual stature in the first half of the sixteenth century were Juan de Valdés and Juan Luis Vives. Juan de Valdés wrote mainly at Naples. Vives was the most outstanding of those Spaniards who spent some time in the Spanish Netherlands and produced there, mainly in the years before 1566, so much interesting writing on the intellectual and spiritual issues of the age.

Vives was born at Valencia in 1493, the year after the expulsion of professing Jews from Spain, into a prominent *converso* family which had suffered severely, and would continue to do so, from the attentions of the Inquisition. Several of its members were burnt alive, among them Vives's father in 1523/4. When he was sixteen he went off to the University of Paris and three years later made his first visit to the Low Countries. From 1514 onwards Bruges and Louvain were his home. At Louvain he taught Classical literature. He now met Erasmus and became his devoted admirer, just as, later, he became one of Guillaume Budé. By 1519 he was bringing out one work after another, several times attacking what he regarded as the intellectually corrupt and barren university teaching of his day. His *Attack on the Pseudo-Dialecticians*, written that year, was soon read and highly praised by Sir Thomas More. Erasmus, engaged on an edition of St Augustine, persuaded Vives to edit and write a commentary on the *City of God*. The task seriously injured his health. In the month in which Vives dedicated his edition of this work to Henry VIII (July 1522), Antonio de Nebrija, the great Spanish humanist and grammarian, died at Alcalá, where the Complutensian Bible had at last gone on sale. Vives was offered Nebrija's chair of Latin but declined it and in fact never returned to Spain after first leaving it, though his memories of Valencia always remained affectionate. Instead, he came to England. Here, until 1528, he spent most of each year in London, returning each summer to Bruges, where he married in 1524. He also, for two or three years, travelled to Oxford, where, at Corpus Christi College, he held one of the six new lectureships founded by Wolsey and taught Classical literature and law. In London Vives became a close friend of More and often visited him in his new home at Chelsea. He was also the devoted friend of Catherine of Aragon and wrote two books of instruction for the young Princess Mary. His support for the Queen in the question of the divorce eventually cost him the favour of Henry and Wolsey, and in 1528 he finally left England for Bruges, where he lived and wrote until his death in 1540.

The sheer bulk of Vives's writings remains daunting even when, as now, they can all be read in Spanish translation. (Vives always wrote in Latin.) These writings include translations and imitations of works of Classical antiquity as well as commentaries on them, major treatises of moral instruction and educational reform, long exhortations to peace among the princes and peoples of Europe, a project for dealing with the problem of the poor, an extensive and systematic study of the human mind and soul, and a reasoned defence of the Christian faith. The range of subjects is matched by the author's vigour of mind. Vives approached issues with a critical alertness and a readiness to discard old ideas and put forward new and better ones. He wrote enthusiastically in various works of the powers of the human mind. It is an idea which finds extreme statement in his *Fable concerning Man* (1518). Here he shows man taking on the form of each of the orders of creation, thus signifying his mastery of the world. He assumes the aspect even of his Creator himself, and man is admitted to the company of the gods. However, this work, although perhaps the most often reprinted of Vives's works, can mislead in the same way that a work to which he was indebted here, Pico della Mirandola's *Oration on the Dignity of Man*, can mislead when, as so often happens, only its first part is printed. A balanced view of Vives's attitude to human nature will take into account, for example, what he wrote a decade later in his treatise *On Concord and Discord among Mankind* (Book IV, chapters 3, 4 and 5). Here, in terms that call to mind Sánchez de Arévalo's very popular *Mirror of Human Life*, of the mid fifteenth century, Vives speaks of the human body as a foul mess veiled by skin and stresses the transitoriness and hollowness of all earthly concerns. The human mind, as he often says, has become sick. It is this conviction which, together with his sense of what the mind at its best can be, makes him so uneasy about imaginative literature. This, he fears, can all too easily have the effect of a 'sweet poison'. The mind needs to be guided and strengthened; right reason must be established in it; and this is the task of religion, virtue and sound learning. For Vives, learning and the exercise of the powers of the mind are not ends in themselves: they are to serve and promote religion and virtue. Perhaps his most abiding concern is to hold these things together. His conviction that this is critically important derives from his reading of the moralists of Classical antiquity as well as from his Christian beliefs, from both Italian humanists and Erasmus.

Three works that illustrate different aspects of his thought are: *The Instruction of a Christian Woman* (1523); *On the Care of the Poor* (1526); and *On Studies* (1531).

In the first of these he sets himself the practical aim of not only exhorting to feminine virtue but showing both how it may be acquired and what it means in daily living. In its practicability and its concern with the married woman, the work has been described as being of revolutionary novelty. The modern reader may not immediately appreciate the fact. Quite apart from Vives's occasional suggestions that he still accepts the celibate life as intrinsically more excellent than the married, he still draws a great part of his material from the early Fathers of the Church, preoccupied with questions of principle though he says they are. The letters of St Jerome are ever before us, as are Chrysostom, Hilary, Ambrose and Augustine, in addition to the New Testament and especially St Paul. So too are the pagan moral philosophers of Greece and Rome, and the exemplary tales of the historians. The views Vives puts forward are likely to strike the modern reader as narrow and rigid. There is a constant stress on chastity, modesty, plain living and obedience to the husband. Romances of chivalry must not be read. Indeed, all books dealing with erotic love and, in effect, all imaginative literature are proscribed: the good wife will read only the works Vives himself draws on here. He even sees dolls as images of idolatry and believes they stimulate a love of vain adornment. This work reminds one that moral Puritanism was by no means an exclusively Protestant phenomenon. Vives is severe not only on Ovid's *Art of Love* but on the whole courtly-love idea too.

He repeatedly warns against devotion to things which appear attractive but which poison the soul or are dissolved away by time.

On the other hand, this book contains many amusing observations on the behaviour of husbands and wives, and its tone can be deeply human, especially when Vives sets down his idea of what a wife's love should be for her husband. He speaks with affection of his own parents and writes movingly of the devotion his mother-in-law showed to her husband throughout the latter's ten years of illness. The loving care a wife should give to her husband Vives sees as a major part of her Christian living, and holds that it should come even before attendance at Mass and certainly before other religious practices and ceremonies. Here one comes upon a way of thinking strongly reminiscent of Erasmus.

The first part of the next work, the *De subventione pauperum*, sets out the individual Christian's duty to take compassion on those who are stricken with poverty. Vives says that, for him, the chief dogma of all is contained in the words: 'This is my command, that ye love one another.' A man who does not help his brother in need is no Christian. Vives's ideal of Christian society is that state of affairs described in the Acts of the Apostles, when all things were shared together in common concern. In his words on this there are echoes of the Pauline preoccupation with the idea of the Church as the Body of Christ, about which Erasmus wrote with so much feeling. One thinks of Erasmus, too, when Vives stresses that Christians are themselves the Temple of God and rebukes those who spend large sums building churches and endowing Masses while they leave their fellow men hungry. Vives's compassion comes out notably when he parts company with the majority of his age in urging that insanity should not be thought comic and made a matter for entertainment. He condemns precisely the treatment that Don Quixote receives from the Duke and Duchess in Part II of the *Quixote*. However, he is not content simply to exhort. The second part of his work is mainly taken up with an account of the steps city authorities must take to relieve the needy. It is not enough that Church and clergy should give their own money to the poor. Beggars represent a threat to public health and public order, and so on these grounds, apart from others, are the concern of secular authorities. The latter should seek out those who cannot support themselves and help those who have a claim on their care. These, in return, will be obliged to work. Vives dreads the dangers of idleness and holds strongly with St Paul that if a man will not work, neither shall he eat. Those who have brought their troubles on themselves will be given harder work and plainer food than the rest. Those who have suffered sudden misfortune will also be helped. Poor children will be educated at the public expense in schools run by the public authority. The schoolmasters will be chosen with the greatest care and will teach their pupils not only to read and write but, more important still, 'Christian piety and a true judgement of things'. The boys will either be helped on to more advanced education or placed in trades 'according to the inclination of each'. Girls will be trained to be good housewives.

The way in which Vives sketches out social arrangements for the solution of a social problem to some extent recalls More's *Utopia*, a work to which Vives refers with approval in more than one of his writings. One might add that it is difficult to establish how far the *Utopia* was known in Spain, especially since no edition of the Latin, and no translation, was published there during the century. The Spaniards who do refer to it tend to be those who went to the New World in a lay or clerical capacity (pre-eminently Vasco de Quiroga, high court judge and later bishop) and decided that the Utopian arrangements were highly applicable to the organization of peoples who, if they lacked Christianity and divine grace, nevertheless enjoyed the moral advantage of living still in the age of gold.

In his treatise *On Studies* (*De disciplinis*), Vives undertakes a survey of the university teaching of his day, giving a long account of what he sees as its faults and making suggestions for its improvement. Thus he embarks on the discussion of an enormous sweep of subjects: grammar, dialectics, rhetoric, metaphysics, mathematics, medicine, moral philosophy, history and civil law. Above all, he attacks the practitioners of dialectic, those who devoted themselves to studying and propounding logic, inquiring into the possibilities of knowledge and of metaphysical and theological statement. These concerns had become predominant in the university Schools of the fourteenth and fifteenth centuries. The great intellectual energy they stimulated was analytical rather than creative, and on these grounds those who involved themselves in these matters, pre-eminently the scholastics, came under heavy criticism from those who wanted university studies to have a more practical moral or Christian relevance. Renaissance and Reformation, over this point at least, are at one, and both impulses make themselves strongly felt in this work of Vives. He attacks the scholastic philosophers for setting up subjects as ends in themselves, for seeking not only subtlety and complication but also disputation and disagreement for their own sakes. All this makes for the trivialization of knowledge. It is the work of intellectual pride, arrogance and material greed. It goes with an over-assertiveness that is ready to pronounce on everything in heaven and earth and makes for aggressiveness and factiousness. (Vives, especially at the end of the work, gives a vivid account of the diseases that threaten the academic mind.) He attacks the scholastics for ignorance, unscholarly inaccuracy, excessive categorization of knowledge, a reliance on second-hand material, a passive acceptance of doctrines derived from 'authorities', and a refusal to interpret statements in relation to their context and with regard to the intention and situation of the writer.

By contrast, Vives wants simplicity and straightforwardness. Subjects should be introduced to the young attractively and in such a way that they can easily be grasped. Believing this, Vives sets out courses of reading for nearly all the subjects of which he speaks. Above all he wants 'usefulness' – that concept so much urged in the sixteenth century. This, for him, means the fostering of virtue and Christian piety. He stresses that learning is not its own end, that it flourishes best when it is directed towards, and sustained by, what he calls moral and Christian 'wisdom', just as the achievements of the intellect are best commended by humble and courteous scholars whose learning is seen to make them better men. He does not intend, in saying this, to diminish the freedom or dignity of the operation of the mind. Repeatedly and enthusiastically he praises the powers of the intellect that has separated man from the beasts. His wish here is to help stimulate the minds of men to further achievements. He repudiates the view that modern men, in relation to those of Classical antiquity, are as dwarfs on the shoulders of giants. They are all, he says, of the same stature; many things can be understood better now than in the past, and many discoveries still remain to be made.

To a very large extent this treatise embodies the principles and practice that Vives urged upon others. It shows an extraordinary range of first-hand knowledge. It also displays a remarkable combination of independence of outlook and fairness of judgement. At a time when Aristotle generally divided men into antagonistic camps, Vives is happy to praise him as one of the finest intellects in the history of mankind but still determined to point out particular shortcomings of matter and manner in his writings. Though Vives believes that Europe has recently witnessed the rebirth of letters, he takes a detached view of the achievement of this or that Italian humanist while showing a real measure of respect for St Thomas Aquinas. He has some blind spots. He finds it impossible to accept the philosophical neologisms of the Schoolmen, even when they are such words as *realitas, identificatio* or *relationes*. He shows little willingness to consider that these men may, in however unsatisfactory a manner, have been concerned with philosophically respectable questions. His impatience with them can produce entertaining passages of satirical description and amusing moments, as when he turns the tables on his arch-enemies by attributing Luther's errors to the fact that he was a scholastic theologian. This treatise is not only one of the major intellectual works of the sixteenth century but one of the most readable. Its discussions of such issues as imitation in poetry, or the relation of poetry to truth, or the vexed question of the attitude the Christian is to take towards the teachings of the pagan moral philosophers of antiquity are probably as interesting as one will find in any Spanish writer of the century. The work as a whole illustrates the complexity and many-sidedness of north European Christian humanism and warns of the dangers of trying to fit such men as Vives into simple categories. In this respect it seems appropriate that the collection of prayers published in 1535 by Vives, that devoted admirer of More and Catherine of Aragon, and a man who never left the Roman communion, should, later in the century, have been one of the chief sources of a *Book of Christian Prayers* published for use by members of the Church of England.

TEN

Spanish Satire

Alfonso de Valdés (c. 1490–1532)

THE earliest known translation into Spanish of a work by Erasmus dates from 1516; but the years in which he made such an extraordinary impact on Spanish spirituality are the later 1520s and early 1530s. In 1526 the Archdeacon of Alcor's translation of Erasmus' *Enchiridion* had been published, and in 1527 the translator was justly telling the author that no other book of the time had enjoyed such instant success and wide circulation. It was, he said, to be found everywhere, from emperor's court to country inn.

By 1527 the leader among Erasmus' Spanish disciples was Alfonso de Valdés. He was then Latin Secretary to Charles V and remained so until his death from the plague at Vienna in 1532, when he was probably a little past forty. It is the letters he wrote in his official capacity that have survived most securely among his writings – letters such as his vigorous retort to Clement VII when the latter had sent the Emperor an impolite brief, or his exhortation to the cardinals to call a General Council even against the Pope's wishes, or his communication to the princes of Europe claiming that the Emperor was not responsible for the Sack of Rome in May 1527. His own personal Erasmian compositions are themselves *pièces de circonstance*. The *Diálogo de las cosas ocurridas en Roma*, dealing with this same Sack of Rome and written within two or three months of the event, argues that the blame for it rested with the Pope and curia themselves, who had ignored the warnings of Erasmus and Luther. It was God's judgement. The *Diálogo de Mercurio y Carón*, written quite soon afterwards, seeks to show up the perfidy of the King of France, supported later by the scheming Wolsey, during the years 1521–8. These were works written for the interested minority and were probably not printed until about 1545, after which they went on the Index and stayed there. They were rediscovered only in the mid nineteenth century. But in the late 1520s copy after copy was made of them and circulated all over Spain. This was the time when the enthusiasts for Erasmus in Spain included the Emperor himself, the Primate of Spain and the Inquisitor General. Against them the papal nuncio, Baldassare Castiglione, had difficulty in giving his protests against Valdés any effect.

His displeasure with the *Diálogo de las cosas ocurridas en Roma* is not surprising. It is a most powerful attack on Pope and curia. Clement VII, it alleges, is not only not a peace-maker but by his involvement in power politics actually brings about more wars and more spilling of Christian blood. The curia cares only about money and running the Church as a legalistic bureaucracy. By contrast, Valdés portrays the Emperor as one devoted to the cause of Christian peace and the concord and well-being of the peoples of Europe. To achieve this he will go to any trouble and suffer any vexation. Valdés's second dialogue insistently presents the same idea. It was not an idea peculiar to Valdés, though he adopts it with exceptional fervour. Negatively, his hostility to Clement VII owes not a little to Erasmus's detestation of war and his disgust with Julius II leading his own armies into battle. Positively, it was from Erasmus that Valdés had learnt devotion to the idea of men living together in peace, concord and Christian love.

But his debt to Erasmus goes beyond this. Most powerfully in the *Diálogo de Mercurio y Carón*, he attacks religion that has become a matter of empty outward forms, devotion to inanimate objects, and good works undertaken on a *quid pro quo* basis. Against this he sets the ideal of Christianity being a devotion to the things of the spirit, a living out of what he calls 'the Christian doctrine' in the whole of one's daily life, which thus becomes in its entirety an activity of loving God and one's fellow men. He comes, in this way, to write an expressive apologia for an ideal of lay Christianity which went on finding eloquent defenders in Spain well past the time of Trent and at least to the end of the sixteenth century.

Like Erasmus, Alfonso de Valdés does not go into the deep places of the soul, and he does not discuss technical questions of theology or ecclesiology. Rather does he express a mood. And although, like Erasmus, he can sometimes sound glib, that mood is basically one of deep emotion and sincerity. Moreover, his art as a writer gives it a force and attractiveness that have compelled the admiration even of those who do not share his point of view. He is a master of the setpiece, the sustained speech of denunciation, but also of a prose that is less declamatory and more intimate; a prose that is balanced, harmonious, smooth-flowing, and yet close to the structures and tones of private conversation and capable of communicating a sense of deep but quiet emotion. It has much in common with the prose of the Archdeacon of Alcor's translation of the *Enchiridion* and comes well in works cast in the form of dialogues. Moreover, from the *Dialogues* of Lucian and the *Colloquies* of Erasmus, Valdés has learnt how to handle colloquial and comic exchanges between characters which have an appeal that often goes beyond their satirical function. The sometimes outrageous prosecuting-counsel technique of Valdés's spokesman in the *Diálogo de las cosas ocurridas en Roma* is indeed part of the general *brío* of the work but also leaves one with the hope that the author was capable, on occasion, even of laughing at himself.

'El Crotalón'

The dialogue form attracted many writers in Spain after Alfonso de Valdés, especially from the middle of the century onwards. Some took Plato and Castiglione as their chief models, and among them Luis de León's *Nombres de Cristo* gives him a pre-eminent place. Other writers followed Erasmus and Lucian, and, among these, two others besides Valdés are particularly important: the authors of the *Crotalón* and the *Viaje de Turquía*.

Professor Bataillon has shown that the attribution of these works to a sixteenth-century Spanish humanist called Cristóbal de Villalón cannot be sustained. Who wrote the *Crotalón* remains a mystery. What can be established is that it was written about 1552, probably at Valladolid.

The book consists of a series of conversations between Micilo, a shoemaker, and a cock which has lived a thousand lives and now tells Micilo about some of his roles and adventures, and what he has seen of human life. Although Erasmianism as a movement had largely faded out in Spain in the previous years, the stories the cock tells serve to express a strongly Erasmian way of thinking about true and false Christianity. This, however, tends to come through in single remarks or quite brief passages. The author's debt to Lucian is more immediately striking, since from him he took not only the framework of his book but also a good deal of material. In this respect this work is probably the most obviously Lucianic work of sixteenth-century Spanish literature. Its author, for example, uses Lucian's *Alexander* as a basis for a vivid chapter about a priest who travels from place to place making money out of popular credulity and superstition. He follows the *Icaromenippus* quite closely in taking his readers up to the moon so that they can look down and see the truth about the way in which people on earth live. Here, as elsewhere, he changes Lucian's contemporary allusions, making the stories apply to the Spain and Europe of his own day. This chapter illustrates how its author took over, and perhaps even reinforced, Lucian's insistence on the comic absurdity of the aims and ambitions to which men devote their lives, the absurdity of their self-importance, their rivalries and discord, when these are set against the inevitability of the death that will soon come to them all. Sometimes the passages of the *Crotalón* on this subject, like certain passages in Vives, bring to mind those works warning against the unreal, superficial attractions of this world that become so prominent in Spanish literature of the later sixteenth century and the seventeenth.

Nevertheless, the author of this work, in his Prologue, stresses that he wishes not only to teach but to entertain, adding that the word he takes as his title is the Greek for clapper, rattle or castanet. His aim is to give pleasure by means of diversity of matter, and this he takes generously from a variety of authors. His third chapter contains a whole page copied from the *Diálogo de las cosas ocurridas en Roma*. He also borrows from such sources as Boccaccio, Aretino's *Raggiomenti* and the *Orlando furioso*. On the basis of such borrowings he sometimes constructs the extensive descriptions of scenes, historical or imagined, which are so prominent in this work. These descriptions are often overloaded and slow, but most clearly come alive when they deal with episodes and scenes of a sensual kind. This sensual responsiveness sometimes relates to situations of an overtly sexual kind, as in chapters 5–7, taken largely from the *Orlando*, but it is seen very clearly too in the descriptions of the tortures and torments of hell (chapter 15). Here one comes upon a moral ambiguity that lies deep in this work. It is not simply that the author's advocacy of the views of Erasmus and Lucian was insincere. It seems rather that there was a conflict between his moral and religious sense and his imaginative life. For the modern reader this is not among the least interesting facets of the work.

Andrés de Laguna (c. 1511–59)

The *Viaje de Turquía* (*Journey to Turkey*) stands as one of the most fascinating and delightful discoveries of this century. Although it was written in the mid-1550s, it had to wait until 1905 to be published, and then, as has already been said, it was wrongly ascribed to Cristóbal de Villalón. In fact, as Bataillon has shown, it was written by Andrés de Laguna, whose life reflects the interest of the man himself.

His career was that of an exceptionally successful doctor, frequently attending the great and in 1550 appointed physician to the new Pope, Julius III. His career was also international. Having studied at Salamanca and Paris, he left Spain in 1539, at the age of twenty-eight or so, and returned there only when he was about forty-six, not more than about two years before his death. In the meantime he had been five years at Metz, nearly a decade in Italy, mainly at Rome, and also in Cologne and the Low Countries. His interests were wide-ranging. At Salamanca he studied arts, and, at Paris, philosophy and Greek in addition to medicine. He brought out many Latin translations of works of medical interest by Aristotle and Galen, and a Spanish translation of the renowned *De materia medica* of Dioscorides. Amidst this activity he also made Latin versions of some Lucian and Theophrastus, and a Spanish version of Cicero's *Catiline Orations*. A lecture he gave at Cologne in 1543 on the troubles of war-ravaged Europe shows his familiarity with Erasmus' *Adages* and *Complaint of Peace*. He was also fascinated by the Eastern Mediterranean and so well read in books on the subject that scholars were for some time misled into accepting as true Laguna's assertions that his *Viaje de Turquía* was a genuine autobiographical narrative and an eyewitness account not only of the cities and life of Italy but also of Turkey and the Aegean Islands.

In this book one Pedro de Urdemalas tells two friends how he was captured at sea by the Turks in 1542 and taken to Constantinople. There he made his life more tolerable by passing himself off as a doctor, and with considerable success. But life could still be harsh and eventually he escaped. After a journey full of dangers and difficulties

which took him to Greece and various of the islands, he succeeded in returning to Italy and finally to Valladolid (or possibly Burgos),
where, on arrival, he met his two friends.

The narrative of these events is itself full of interest and often makes
a lively adventure story. More striking still, however, is the descriptive
aspect of the account. This is as vivid when Pedro de Urdemalas is
talking about Turkey as when he is commenting on various cities of
Italy, and shows the intensity of the author's interest not only in the
places he himself had visited but also in those which he knew only at
second hand, through books and, probably, from accounts he obtained
at Venice from diplomats and traders.

The book as a whole gives an impression of immense curiosity
regarding what there is in the world and how people live. Pedro
takes equal interest in telling his friends of the religion or dress of the
Turks, what ships call at Chios, or how the foundations of Venetian
buildings are laid. With this curiosity goes a notable lack of prejudice,
an unwillingness to fall in uncritically with accepted attitudes of
praise and blame. He is, for example, determined to challenge current
misrepresentations of the Turkish character. If Turks are cruel, so,
he says, can Spaniards be; on the other hand, the Turks have virtues
which are perhaps more evident than those of Spaniards. He looks at
his fellow-countrymen with a dispassionate gaze. He remarks more
than once that Spaniards are much disliked in Italy, a land where,
moreover, they will find a number of things managed more effi-
ciently than at home. He refuses to regard Nebrija's *Introduction to
Latin* as the best of its kind just because its author was a Spaniard,
and in fact thinks more highly of the works of Erasmus, Melanchthon
and Donatus on the subject. He takes a detailed and sympathetic
interest in the Eastern Orthodox Church, and it is when he writes
on such a subject that one finds him suggesting more than he actually
says, remarking, for example, on the scrupulousness of Eastern monks
in keeping their Rule, and on the fact that the Eastern Church allows
a married clergy. He speaks, without comment, of Spanish Moors
who have left Spain and gone to Constantinople for fear of the
Inquisition.

At one point Pedro angrily protests against the fact that he is
living in an age when a man has only to speak out a particular truth
and he will be declared a satirical fellow, a slanderer and a bad

Christian. If you say you want to hear Mass prayed rather than sung, everyone with a single voice will call you a heretic. In part this is a protest against narrowness and rigidity of outlook in general, for Pedro is not only vastly curious about facts but also interested in discussing questions of an intellectual kind, whether it be the development of the romance languages or the forms of liturgical practice. But still more is it the protest of a man in the 1550s who is still deeply indebted for his religious values and outlook to Erasmus and, probably, some of the works of Vives. Pedro, when he makes this protest, has just been speaking of the gardens which Julius II laid out at Rome. He observes how much better the money would have been spent freeing Christian prisoners of the Turks. His Erasmian outlook comes out in a number of ways: perhaps not so much in what he says about curial simony and ease of living as in his observations on pilgrimages and the efficacy of relics, his mockery of preachers who get lost chasing figurative meanings in the Old Testament, his criticism of the irrelevant subtleties of the scholastic theologians, his preference for what he calls the 'theology of Christ', which is also that of the New Testament and the Fathers, his compassionate concern for the poor and sick, his sense of the destructiveness of war, his insistence that the Commandments are more important than ceremonies and that a single brief prayer from the heart is better than a series of Paternosters told off on a rosary.

In addition to this element of deep religious sincerity one finds moments of grim seriousness, as when Pedro tells of his physical sufferings and despair when undergoing forced labour as a Turkish prisoner. The concreteness yet lack of heroics with which he speaks of this give his account great force. At such a moment one sees with what vividness and wealth of circumstantial detail Laguna can present a situation which he has either imagined in its entirety or drawn from his reading. This concreteness and vividness which he so regularly achieves carry one through the book despite the sheer bulk of description and certain serious defects of form. More important still, however, in this respect, is Laguna's skill at comic writing. To his three interlocutors – Pedro de Urdemalas, Juan de Votadiós and Mátalascallando – he gives names which are all drawn from Spanish folklore and suggest amusing rogues. Pedro, at Constantinople, displays a cunning, a resourcefulness and energy in obtaining money and dealing with awkward situations that is quite picaresque. He is an appropriate creation for an author whose very assertion in his Epistle Dedicatory that he was himself an eye-witness of all that follows is an almost literal translation of a passage from another writer. Pedro and his colleagues together make many satirical comments on society and religious practice. These give the book a further element of comedy which can sometimes be very forthright and boisterous. However, perhaps most entertaining of all is the conversation of the three speakers. Laguna possessed an exceptional ability to capture the tones of colloquial speech. Repeatedly he gives one the impression of looking in on a real situation, of overhearing three likeable and convincing individuals talking together, teasing each other and exchanging banter. The effect is reminiscent of Erasmus' *Colloquies* at their best, and also of Rabelais. Certain passages and details seem almost certainly to be derived from *Pantagruel*, and it is an interesting possibility that Laguna may have met Rabelais at Rome in 1548. The *Viaje de Turquía* is not another *Pantagruel*, but, in the whole of sixteenth-century Spanish prose, is probably the work closest to it. It is also, perhaps, the best single memorial to those lively, intelligent, questioning, open-minded Spaniards of the sixteenth century whose lives were sometimes hardly less interesting than Laguna's and whose existence is still too little remembered today.

ELEVEN

Juan de Valdés (c. 1490–1541)

UNLIKE the dialogues so recently composed by his twin brother Alfonso, Juan de Valdés's *Diálogo de doctrina cristiana*, printed in January 1529, arose not out of external events of political and religious significance but directly out of the religious situation of the time. It stands as the fullest theological and spiritual statement produced in Spain by the Erasmian movement at its height. It sets out, in order, Juan de Valdés's views on the Creed, the Ten Commandments, the Seven Deadly Sins, Four Cardinal Virtues and Three Theological Virtues, the Five Precepts of the Church, the Lord's Prayer and the chief events in man's salvation recounted in the Old and New Testaments. It thus has much of the character of a catechism but is cast in the form of a dialogue, in which the Archbishop of Granada, Fray Pedro de Alba, explains to a priest what instruction he should give to the children of his parish. The priest has been taken to see the Archbishop by one Eusebio, who represents Valdés himself. Pedro de Alba was chosen for the role he plays because, as the *Diálogo* explains, he had learnt much of his Christianity from his predecessor in the see, Hernando de Talavera, and the latter was regarded by various Spanish Erasmians as the model of a Christian bishop in both doctrine and pastoral care. This is nowhere more apparent than in the biography of him composed in 1530 or soon afterwards by his old pupil, the Archdeacon of Alcor, translator of the *Enchiridion*.

There is a strong Erasmian element in the *Diálogo de doctrina cristiana*: a concern with a Christianity that is in spirit and in truth, and for the layman rather than the monk; a conviction that, in comparison with this, outward forms, observances and devotions are 'accessory'; an insistence on the duty and joy of Christian brotherly love. Juan de Valdés sees Christianity as summed up in the Sermon on the Mount, and of this he gives us a translation, based on Erasmus' Greek text and Latin version of 1516; he also follows Erasmus' exposition of the Creed. He praises Erasmus himself, his *Colloquies* and his *Enchiridion*. The Erasmianism of the *Diálogo* is that of this latter work rather than of the *Praise of Folly* – which Juan de Valdés kept chiefly for his letters and, it seems, his conversation.

The work is dedicated to Diego López Pacheco, Marqués de Villena. He, too, was an admirer of Erasmus and, despite his years, had wanted to help defend him against the friars at their conference at Valladolid in 1527. Earlier in the 1520s, however, his palace at Escalona, in New Castile, had been one of the centres of the illuminist movement. Juan de Valdés had been attached to his household, and it may be that one catches echoes of what he had heard taught there in his insistence that Christian perfection must be achieved, or at the least earnestly sought, by every Christian; that through grace it is possible never to fall into mortal sin; and that the centre of the Christian life is the prayer that seeks perfection and the keeping of the Commandments. But the *Diálogo* contains another element still: a preoccupation with man's relation to God and the centrality in this of Christ's saving death; a sense of God's power and greatness, and of man's weakness through the ravages of sin; a sense, too, that man is dependent on divine grace and will surely obtain it if he approaches God in hope and the trustful faith that 'makes him just' before God. All this has a distinctly Lutheran sound and gives the *Diálogo* a tone that sometimes departs from the characteristically Erasmian one. Like the illuminist element, it was significant for the future.

The anonymity of this work, when published, did not deceive. Both it and its author survived the first inquiry into its orthodoxy. However, hearing that the Inquisition was planning proceedings against the *Diálogo*, Juan de Valdés left Alcalá university, where he had been studying, for Rome, probably in 1531. Condemnation in Spain did not necessarily mean condemnation at Rome. Juan de Valdés seems to have acted as an Imperial agent at the papal court and became a chamberlain to the pro-Imperial Pope Clement VII. After the latter's death in September 1534, Juan de Valdés moved to Naples and remained there until his death in 1541, the centre of one of the many groups of people then seriously devoting themselves to living a truly Christian life outside the cloister. Early in 1536 he underwent some profound religious experience – just at the time when Garcilaso, in the same city, was very probably working on his *Third Eclogue*.

Now Juan de Valdés became one of the many who, up to the time of the Colloquy of Ratisbon (1541), were able to give a major role to Luther's teaching on Justification by Faith in their own religious thinking while remaining within the Roman communion. This teaching, together with a preoccupation with interior Christianity that seems to go back to the Spanish illuminist tradition, became the basis for the works that Juan de Valdés now wrote: at least four commentaries on books of the Bible; the *Alfabeto cristiano* (1536), which, again, aims at setting out the rudiments of Christianity and not infrequently takes over almost literally passages from the *Diálogo*; and, finally, the *CX Divine Considerationi* (c. 1540), the original Spanish of which, as of the *Alfabeto cristiano*, is lost. The influence he exercised across Europe, especially through this last work, reached as far as the Quakers. It seems to have been important, too, for the tone and balance of one of the most read and attacked religious treatises of the sixteenth century: the *Trattato utilissimo del beneficio di Giesù Christo crocifisso, verso i Christiani*.

Among Juan de Valdés's disciples at Naples were Abbot Peter Martyr Vermigli, later canon of Christ Church, Oxford, and Bernardino Ochino, subsequently Vicar General of the Capuchins and prebendary of Canterbury. The lasting attachment of Cardinal Pole and the future Primate of Spain, Bartolomé de Carranza, the restorers of Roman Catholicism in England under Mary, to some at least of Valdés's ideas seems to have contributed to their notorious troubles with the Roman and Spanish Inquisitions. In the seventeenth century, Nicholas Ferrar, the Anglican founder of the community at Little Gidding, translated the *Considerationi* into English, and George Herbert, with reservations, praised them.

In the last years of his life Juan de Valdés prepared a Spanish version of the Psalter, partly because it was, he said, the worst translated book in the Vulgate, and principally because he wished to assist his distinguished disciple at Naples, Julia Gonzaga, in cultivating further the reverence she owed to God. He had probably not achieved a very deep knowledge of Hebrew at Alcalá, but the boldness with which he treats Spanish in his determination to keep as close and as faithfully as possible to the original, and his sense of rhythm, above all, result in versions which, in their range of tone and expressiveness (see, for example, Psalms lxviii, xc and cxliii) sometimes invite comparison with Coverdale's. This first Castilian translation of the Psalter by a known hand, and the best, was never published.

Juan de Valdés had a philologist's interest in language. When first in Italy, he discussed literary questions with humanists there. In 1535, probably, he wrote his *Diálogo de la lengua*. His motive in writing, as he sometimes playfully admits, was partly patriotic: he was proud of Castilian as a medium of expression, and speaks of himself as having been brought up 'in the kingdom of Toledo and at the Court of Spain'. His pride in Castilian lies behind his scorn for the Andalusian Antonio de Nebrija, whose *Spanish Grammar* he says he has not read and whose *Latin–Spanish Dictionary* he mocks. He has read Bembo's *Prose della volgar lingua*, printed in 1525, but shows little enthusiasm for it. Bembo's exhortations to use Tuscan as a literary language are not easily transferred to the situation of Castilian, which lacks accepted stylistic models such as Tuscan has in Petrarch and Boccaccio. Juan de Valdés is very aware of the problem he faces in trying to outline a linguistic and stylistic norm. He expounds his ideas in the form of a modest explanation and defence of his own practice in letters written from Rome to friends at Naples. Several times he makes clear his desire not to be pedantic. His repeated assertion is that, in spelling as in style, his wish is to write as he speaks. This is an over-simplification. As regards spelling, he aims at a balance between a respect for the original forms of words in, above all, Latin, and current pronunciation. But the latter must be that of the linguistically conscious and discriminating. As for style, the qualities he desires are clarity, simplicity, directness, euphony of an unpretentious kind, and the avoidance of all 'affectation'. His ideal could scarcely be more remote from that of his contemporary Antonio de Guevara, whom sixteenth-century Europe so much admired. Juan de Valdés's *Diálogo* should be seen in relation to the contemporary debate concerning Ciceronianism and, particularly, Erasmus' satirical attack on the latter in his *Ciceronianus* (1528). The *Diálogo de la lengua* was not published until the eighteenth century; but its stylistic ideal was one which many sixteenth-century Spaniards learnt, directly or indirectly, from Spanish disciples of Erasmus, forming a tradition which finds its finest exemplification in the *Quixote*.

Juan de Valdés's discussion offers many points of literary interest: his love of Spanish proverbs (because, in their compact simplicity, they show Castilian at its purest); his admiration for punning and *ingenio* in verse; his comments on courtly-love *coplas*; his general lack of enthusiasm for fictional writing; his observations on the *Celestina* and *Amadís de Gaula*; and his desire that historians should treat their sources more critically than they often do. Taken together with his other works, the *Diálogo de la lengua* does much to bring out the extraordinary many-sidedness of Juan de Valdés, his strength of interest, his determination to think things out, and his desire to lay hold of what was true and excellent, whether in letters or religion.

TWELVE

Spanish Religious Writers

Luis de Granada (1504-88)

IT is part of the interest of Luis de Granada that he shows clearly how the legacy of Erasmus in Spain continued even when the official religious mood had turned against him. As a Dominican, Luis de Granada was a member of the Order specially responsible for the operation of the Inquisition. Later in his life he counted the Duke of Alba among his penitents and received extravagant praise from both St Charles Borromeo, that 'new model of a catholic bishop', and Pope Gregory XIII. He died in the year of the Spanish Armada. It was at the time he became Provincial of the Dominicans in Portugal, that is, 1556, that he published his *Guía de pecadores* (*Guide for Sinners*), explaining why one should live virtuously, what virtuous living means in practical terms, and how grace for it is to be obtained. At one point he makes a detailed distinction between spiritual, interior virtues and those which consist in particular, outwardly visible, activities. The former include – most important of all – charity, humility, chastity, compassion, long-suffering and the like; the latter, fasting, discipline, silence, enclosure, reading, praying, going on pilgrimages, hearing Mass, attending sermons and divine office, 'together with all the other corporal observances and ceremonies of the Christian or religious life'. Without the former, he says, all the latter are vain. Here we find ourselves back at the famous Rule V of the *Enchiridion*, where Erasmus sets out some of his most central and deeply held convictions. Even the second version of the *Guía de pecadores* reveals one clear borrowing after another from the same work; not that Erasmus' name is ever mentioned: he remains 'a certain doctor'. The first version ran into trouble with the Inquisition and was put on the Index of 1559. Luis de Granada had in any case intended to write a fuller version, and soon did so. It was first printed in 1567 and was omitted from the next Index, that of 1583. The chapter where he borrows so extensively from the *Enchiridion* passed from the first version to the second almost without change (Book II, chapter xix). This fact becomes all the more important in view of the extraordinary success of this work. In the little more than thirty years that remained of the century, it was printed about forty times in Spanish and upwards of twenty-six in Italian. In the seventeenth century there were twenty-five editions in Spain and no less than fifty-six in France. Judged by such a criterion, this was one of the most significant religious works ever to be written by a Spaniard.

Its appeal cannot be attributed in any simple or exclusive way to its Erasmian character, which is only partial, even though it seems to have contributed in a diffused manner to the general mood of the work. This owes much to Luis de Granada's avowed intention, in his revised and much expanded version, of giving more emphasis than, he claimed, was usual to 'the peace, light, true liberty and joy of a good conscience, together with the consolations of the Holy Spirit (enjoyed by the just) which virtue commonly brings with it'. To the Christian leading the life of virtue he promises (and nowhere more persuasively than in Book I, chapter xiv) a sense of confidence, Christian wisdom, liberation from sin, illumination and transformation by the Holy Spirit. It is, very largely, an optimistic, encouraging work and plainly addresses itself, beyond the monk or friar, to the layman. A Jesuit in the 1580s made it a special point of praise that the works of Luis de Granada, 'who is the light and mirror of our days', 'are not only of benefit to spiritual persons dedicated to the service of God but are also marvellously helpful to those submerged in the ocean of the world.' The number of editions that the *Guía de pecadores* went through suggests that very many others thought the same.

Nevertheless, it remains the case that if – as he does – Luis de Granada holds that 'outward' virtues and practices are vain unless they become the expression of 'inward' virtues, of worship in spirit, he also strongly holds that the former are valuable when this condition is fulfilled. In this emphasis he departs rather noticeably from Erasmus. Luis de Granada was, in any case, a writer who drew on many sources. Thus his *Libro de la oración* (*Book on Prayer*, 1554), which has been described as the most important Spanish treatise on prayer to be written in the sixteenth century, is much indebted to the works of

Savonarola on the same subject. In the *Guía de pecadores* the more modern of his sources include St Vincent Ferrer, St Catherine of Siena, Serafín de Fermo, Harph, Tauler and Thomas à Kempis, a translation of whose *Imitation of Christ* was Luis de Granada's first publication. Kempis no doubt was one of those who encouraged Luis de Granada in his marked preference for moral and spiritual wisdom over speculative knowledge; but others could have been the Classical Stoic philosophers, to whose ideas he responds enthusiastically, relating them often to the Christian attitude of *contemptus mundi*. Luis de Granada is not reluctant to urge upon his readers the transitoriness of human life and its pleasures, the foulness of the flesh and the horrors of the grave (see Book II, chapter iv). He writes readily of divine justice and eternal punishment. The doctrines of predestination (albeit to life rather than damnation) and of justification have a marked attraction for him. Passages of his chapters on death and the pains of hell (Book I, chapters vii, viii) may well be found peculiarly capable of inducing a sense of *timor mortis* even while they recall some of the more horrific writing of the fifteenth century. Very noticeably, though, such concerns as these do not lead him to approach the pagan writers of antiquity with that unease and agitation which similar concerns often produced in Spaniards, perhaps especially towards the end of the century. In any case, the predominant tone of the work, as has been suggested, is very different. Few, if any, sixteenth-century Spanish writers have written with greater beauty or more feeling of the loveliness of creation in its ordered variety (Book I, chapter i), or the glory of paradise (I, ix), or more convincingly of the joy of being brought along the road of Christian perfection in this life (I, ii), or more movingly of Christ's atonement (I, iv).

Luis de Granada was one of the finest writers of Spanish prose of the century. For the most part he gives his writing the character of flowingly simple speech, conveying a sense of sympathetic but intent explanation and persuasion. It is well suited to his intention of providing, as he said, a kind of domestic preacher to whom one could listen any time one wished. His absorption in what he is saying does quite often lead him to give his writing greater dramatic force and a more obviously calculated literary aspect, but without losing entirely or for very long the conversational, spoken tone of the rest. Perhaps his literary art is nowhere seen to better effect than in his many biblical quotations. Luis de Granada was a man in love with the Scriptures, particularly the New Testament epistles, the Old Testament prophets, and the Psalms. These are introduced with a keen sense of relevance and emotional effectiveness. They are commonly rendered in a beautifully cadenced prose. His versions of the psalms, in their rhythmical sensitivity, recall the Spanish version of them made by Juan de Valdés. Alike in the character of his style and in his delight in bringing biblical passages into his writing, he carries one's mind back to Erasmus' Spanish disciples and forward to Luis de León.

Luis de León (1527/8–91)

Luis de Granada's *Libro de la oración* was one of the books that Luis de León was allowed to have with him in prison. Thus he drew strength from one of the most outstanding works to be written by a member of the Order which was so largely responsible for his loss of liberty. Luis de León had professed as an Augustinian friar in 1544, when about seventeen, and had been appointed to his first chair in theology in his earlier thirties. This was in 1561, two years after Valdés's Index had banned many Latin and all vernacular versions of the Bible, and three years before the Tridentine decree declaring the Vulgate Latin version alone to be authoritative in the Church. In this situation, enthusiasm such as Luis de León had for studying the Scriptures in the original Greek and Hebrew and for translating them into Spanish could be dangerous. In 1572 he was accused of questioning the accuracy of the Vulgate, translating the Song of Songs, setting up scriptural study against scholastic theology, and having erroneous views on predestination and grace. Behind this lay academic and personal rivalries and antagonisms, as well as hostility between Orders, and not surprisingly a connection was suggested between these allegedly heretical tendencies and the Jewish element in his blood. Arrested in March 1572, he was at length almost totally exonerated and emerged from the Inquisition's cells in December 1576, after intervention by Gaspar de Quiroga, Inquisitor General since 1573. Luis de León returned to his chair at Salamanca, soon changed it for another, and in the year of his death, 1591, was elected Provincial of the Castilian Augustinians. Apart from his poetry, he wrote much prose, in Latin as well as in Spanish. One of his best known works is on the then favourite subject of *The Perfect Wife* – a commentary on the final chapter of Proverbs. He also edited the works of St Teresa, whose reform he favoured. In prison he began on the most famous of his works: *De los nombres de Cristo* (*On the Names of Christ*).

A work on *Nine Names of Christ* had recently been composed by a fellow Augustinian, Alonso de Orozco, and Luis de León may well have been indebted to it. However, the tradition went back to the *Divine Names* of Dionysius the pseudo-Areopagite, written in the sixth century and so influential in the thought of Aquinas. Luis de León takes in turn fourteen biblical names applied to Christ, such as 'The Way', 'Shepherd', 'Prince of Peace', 'Husband', 'Son of God', and 'Jesus', and reflects upon their meanings.

One finds him repeatedly returning to certain favourite themes. The most prominent is that of transformation through Christ. By the grace that Christ bestows the ravages of sin are repaired and human nature is restored to the image of God: grace brings healing, glory, immortality, rest, peace, spiritual riches and abiding joy. Scarcely less emphasized is the idea of the Body of Christ: that of Christ uniting his followers to himself by grace in so deep and inward a manner that they with him and with each other become 'one body'. The appeal of this idea for Luis de León relates in part to his enthusiasm for the notion of cosmic harmony. In him, as in Luis de Granada, one finds the most intense delight taken in the thought of the all-embracing ordered variety of this world and the whole universe. It is seen in the harmony of the countryside as well as in the movements of the heavens. It finds its flowering and recapitulation in the cosmic Christ, by whose grace, moreover, this same order is re-established in the inner being of man. The opening pages of the 'Prince of Peace' chapter set out a number of ideas on this theme which not only provided the matter for some of his greatest poetry but afford us as vivid a statement as one is likely to find of what the notion of cosmic harmony meant to Ficino, Leone Ebreo, Castiglione and so many sixteenth-century Spaniards. How far Luis de León, in writing of this, gives us the neo-Platonism of the Italian Renaissance and how far that of Dionysius is, perhaps, an open question.

Luis de León stresses that outward order, as it bears on the individual and society, is not enough. An admirer of the Stoic philosopher Epictetus, he gives priority of importance to 'interior' rather than 'exterior' realities, to those that really concern a man and lie within the realm of the inner self, which Luis de León sees as being also the realm of grace. Thus, in contrast to the ordinances of the Old Testament, of pagan philosophers and secular law-givers, he sets Christ's law of love and grace and individual care, by which he enables men to desire and perform and become what he requires them to do and be for their own good. He recalls St Paul on this, and St Augustine on *The Letter and the Spirit*. The reader will also recall Erasmus. This contrast, and the distinction he draws between religious practices and true religion in the 'Jesus' chapter, are strongly reminiscent of the major earlier sections of the *Enchiridion*, just as Luis de León's very unhierarchical notion of Christ's kingdom as it exists among his followers in this world recalls Erasmus' treatise *On the Education of a Prince*. The connection, whatever its precise character, reaches to Luis de León's whole enthusiasm for the Gospel and the joyous experience of the loving, illuminating and transforming grace of Christ, and places the *Nombres de Cristo* in that tradition which, coming down largely, though not exclusively, from the writings of Erasmus, played so important a part, as Marcel Bataillon has shown, in Spanish Counter-Reformation religion.

Another way in which the *Nombres de Cristo* joins this tradition is in the love it shows for the early Fathers and, even more, the Scriptures – above all, St Paul and the Old Testament prophets where they speak of the loving care of God. Nothing gives Luis de León more joy than to reproduce at length the great passages of Paul and Isaiah and Ezekiel on this. The *Nombres de Cristo* is a biblical, and, to a lesser extent, a patristic, anthology, as the *Enchiridion* had been. In the important Epistle Dedicatory to Part I, Luis de León acquiesces with a sorrowful and angry reluctance in the decision of Trent to ban vernacular versions of the Scriptures, and looks back with envy to the early days of the Church, when they could be safely read in every tongue. It is his aim, in writing the *Nombres de Cristo*, to put something, in Spanish, in their place. (With regard to secular imaginative literature his attitude is severely disapproving.) His own love of the Scriptures comes out in the beautifully rhythmic translations that he makes of them.

This is also one aspect of his concern with style. In the Epistle Dedicatory to Part III of the *Nombres*, he makes an important defence of the potential stylistic resources of Spanish as against Latin. To write of weighty matters in Spanish requires, he says, the most careful attention to the sound, rhythm and ordering of words. His own practice has given us some of the most lovely prose in Spanish. Its beauty is not monotonous. The meaning of the names of Christ is set out by a monk speaking to two others as they spend some hours together in an agreeably pastoral setting. There are interruptions, questions, and some donnish humour. It is an exposition rather than a meditation: one senses, in the general progress as in the details, an unflagging intellectual control. This is not unfailingly fascinating. The rather legalistic treatment of the Atonement has its longueurs, and the allegorical exegesis can be unsettling. There is a scholarly interest in establishing the meaning of terms in the original tongues. But much more striking is the combination of intellectual and emotional response within a mood of serene joyfulness. Luis de León's artistry as a writer communicates a sense of the sheer beauty of the truth he describes. It can lead to passages of extraordinary intensity and loveliness, as in the opening pages of the 'Prince of Peace', or in the description of the soul being overwhelmed by the sweetness of possession by God in the chapter on the name 'Husband'. If there is one chapter that brings all these things together, it is perhaps the one entitled 'Pastor'.

St Ignatius Loyola (c. 1491–1556)

No Spanish work has exerted so great an influence on the lives of men as the *Spiritual Exercises* of St Ignatius Loyola. They were set down in their main lines at Manresa in 1523, two years after Loyola, now about thirty, had been seriously wounded defending Pamplona against the French and, in the course of recovering, had resolved to give himself to the service of God, performing deeds worthy of St Francis of Assisi, St Dominic and Amadis of Gaul. These *Exercises* show what sustained the spirit of their author in all the tribulations and exertions of the years ahead. Slightly antedating the main vogue of Erasmus in Spain, they come a good decade before Loyola, with nine companions, formed the first nucleus of what was to be the Society of Jesus, and seventeen years before the formal recognition of the new Order by Paul III. They were first published in 1548.

Their aim is to bring a man to choose to give his life to the glory of God and service of Christ, and particularly to resolve whether this shall be in religion or as a layman. Beyond this, their purpose is to give a man strength of will to continue in the life of self-dedication and obedience issuing from that choice. As the Preface says, these are 'Spiritual Exercises for overcoming oneself and for regulating one's life without being swayed by any inordinate attachment'. To this end they encourage a powerfully emotional attachment to Christ in his humiliation, suffering and glory while, on the other hand, vigorously discouraging 'inordinate attachments' to the attractions of this world. The history of the Order, which was one of astonishing growth and achievement even by the time Loyola died in 1556, shows what power lay in this combination of attitudes; and in that history, especially after the first years, the influence of the *Exercises* was very great.

Practical and systematic in their conception and elaboration, the *Exercises* lack literary appeal. Nevertheless, directly and indirectly, they made a deep impact on the sensibility, imagination and writing of Spain, especially as the sixteenth century gave way to the seventeenth. This impact was all the greater since the Society not only played an outstanding role in preaching and spiritual direction but was also uniquely active in education at all its levels. It derived, moreover, from certain recurring elements in the *Exercises*. In these one regularly prays to respond appropriately and adequately to the scene or event on which one is to meditate. Thus one may ask for 'great and intense sorrow and tears for my sins'. This comes after the *compositio loci*, the visualizing of a particular scene in the life of Christ, recreated in all its details with the mind's eye. This is a regular part of the *Exercises*. Prominent too is an exercise which goes further: the applying of each of one's five senses (or rather, their analogues in the imagination) to the scene in question. In the case of Christ's Nativity one not only 'sees' the place and people and 'hears' what is said but one also smells and tastes 'with the sense of smell and that of taste the infinite fragrance and sweetness of the Godhead, of the soul and its virtues', finally applying the sense of touch, 'embracing and kissing the place where such persons tread and sit, always contriving to gather profit thence'. The application of the senses to the apprehension of hell (Week I, Exercise 5) is one of the most famous passages of the work.

One cannot say that the *Exercises*, or the Jesuits, were alone responsible for the emotionalism of Counter-Reformation religion. However, they did much to encourage it, in a systematic and conscious way, not for its own sake but to inculcate certain attitudes and to direct and control the will. On the other hand, their concern with 'indifference', with liberating men from any attachment not duly related to man's final end – the praise and service of God – strengthened and drew strength from the appeal of neo-Stoicism and Seneca. In general terms their influence seems to have made an important contribution to the concern shown by Spanish writers in the later sixteenth century and the seventeenth with the idea of detachment from the false allurements of this world, with the importance of rightly ordering one's life and affections by acts of understanding and the will, clearly and resolutely distinguishing between appearance and reality. But their influence is also seen in, for example, the emotional excitability of their pupil Quevedo (1580–1640), his readiness to turn moral reflection into visual terms and even to develop allegorical techniques on the basis of them. (Gracián (1601–58), himself a Jesuit, was later to take this much further.) In Quevedo particularly one sees a further sign of the influence of the *Exercises* and Jesuit spirituality: the combination of two very different emotional attitudes, or rather the cultivation of emotion and the pursuit of 'indifference' almost at the same time, and the emotional tension and even moral unease that resulted from this.

St Teresa of Jesus (1515–82)

It was only by bringing marble to express an intensity of emotion never before achieved in that medium that Bernini was able, in his renowned *Ecstasy of St Teresa*, to capture what in any age will probably be the most immediately impressive aspect of this saint's religious experience. Most vividly in her *Life* (chapter 29), she speaks of her love and apprehension of God, and her yearning for him, as causing her a pain like that of arrows and fiery golden darts plunged into her heart, a pain with which no pleasure can compare and which she wishes would never cease. She writes also of her torturing sense of not possessing God, which she says is like the agony of death, like being 'crucified between heaven and earth' (chapter 20). Linking such passages with her preoccupation with the suffering humanity of Christ, her grave illnesses, her enthusiastic account of the inhuman mortifications that St Peter of Alcántara, once her confessor, inflicted on himself, the impact on her of St Augustine's *Confessions*, and her debt, both direct and indirect, to fifteenth-century pietism, the modern reader may well find himself reflecting on the psychology of sanctity. Her writings provide an exceptionally rich store of material for such a study. And yet their characteristic tone is very distinctly one that is not self-indulgent and not self-regarding. They were mostly written not by choice but under obedience. Her *Life*, or *Libro de la vida*, which dates from 1562, was composed to assist her confessor in his task of giving her spiritual direction. She wrote her *Camino de perfección* (*Way of Perfection*) shortly afterwards to give guidance in the life of prayer to the nuns of her new reformed Order of Discalced Carmelites. Instructed by another confessor to compose an account of her founding of her religious houses, the *Libro de las fundaciones*, she protested that she was both unwell and desperately busy, only to be told, as she says, by God: 'Daughter, obedience gives strength.' It was likewise with her *Moradas del castillo interior* (*Mansions* (or *Dwelling-Places*) *of the Interior Castle*), which she wrote, in effect, in two months of 1577. Nevertheless, this work above all is responsible for her being, in 1970, declared a Doctor of the Church. It sets out the stages of the life of prayer, the progress of the soul as it moves towards God and achieves union with Him in the mystical marriage, with a fullness and exactness probably never equalled save by St John of the Cross, twenty-seven years younger than she, a recruit to her Order, and her confessor for rather over a year, in 1572–3. What spiritual influence the one had on the other is one of the most fascinating and tantalizing of questions. She described him as the father of her soul. But he was learned, instructed in theology; she, as she often reminds us, was unlearned. In 1576, when she was sixty-one, she was insisting that she had written about prayer what the Lord had given her to understand – 'I understand it because I cannot do otherwise' – but declared that she had never *sought* to understand any matter and feared that, if she did, the devil would deceive her. Repeatedly she says she is writing about facts of her own experience; how or why they come about, she does not know.

Her lack of formal learning and of pretensions to it is seen in her style of writing, which is, to an extraordinary and even puzzling degree, a 'spoken' one, where syntax not infrequently gives way before a breathless rush of words. And yet it very often achieves a powerful effect through simple directness and its rendering of spiritual experiences in the concrete terms of everyday life. It leaves a vivid impression of honesty, humility and matter-of-factness. These qualities are seen in her whole approach to mystical experience. Thus she insists that, while the pain of knowing God is sweet, it is so because God is God and she loves him: it is this, not the experience in itself, that is important. Nowhere does she state this more vigorously than in the remarkable fifth chapter of her *Libro de la fundaciones*. Here she stresses that perfection lies not in spiritual pleasures or mystical experiences but in obedience: 'true union . . . is the making of my will one with God's'. This life of obedience will probably be one of activity, with few opportunities to be alone with God. This was certainly her life from 1567 onwards, when, through her fifties and sixties, up to the time of her death, she was travelling endlessly, founding and directing the religious houses of her Reform.

Her achievement both in the mystical and the practical sphere is one of the triumphs of Counter-Reformation religion. One thinks of her belief in the value of religious Orders, her dependence on confessors, the centrality of the veneration of the Host in her religious life. Her confessors included three Jesuits, and her stress on the importance of self-sacrificial obedience of the will to Christ in his service often brings to mind the *Exercises* of Loyola. However, she embodies the Counter-Reformation less in its opposition to the Protestant Reformers than in its deeper reality as an expression of the passionate desire for radical religious renewal that in different ways animated Protestants and Roman Catholics alike. In her own day she encountered not only strong ecclesiastical opposition to her reforming zeal but also the difficulties that in sixteenth-century Spain awaited anyone who laid emphasis on interior religion. The Inquisition retained her *Life* for twelve years. Luis de León, who at the request of the reformed Carmelites was responsible for the publishing of the first collected works of Santa Teresa, in 1588, subsequently wrote a spirited defence of her orthodoxy in the matter of visions and the prayer of union. He remarks that it would be better if her critics turned their attention to the romances of chivalry and the *Celestina*. Santa Teresa was canonized in 1622.

THIRTEEN

Spanish Essayists

Antonio de Guevara (c. 1481–1545)

ANTONIO DE GUEVARA was, in the sixteenth century, perhaps the best known of all Spanish writers in Europe at large; he remains, when one returns to his works, a highly intriguing one. The work with which he achieved literary fame was his *Marco Aurelio con el Reloj de príncipes*, published in 1529. The *Marco Aurelio* part of this work claims to be a translation of a manuscript found in the library of Cosimo de' Medici preserving a biography of that Emperor by a contemporary. It summarizes his life, reproduces letters he wrote, and recounts improving stories about him. The *Dial of Princes* part of the work (to use the sixteenth-century English title) belongs to the 'Mirrors of Princes' tradition of writing, and sets out Guevara's counsel to princes seen as individuals, heads of families, and as rulers. Amidst a mass of exemplary tales it exhorts the prince, in very largely traditional terms, to care for his people, above all by maintaining justice among them. Its combination of conventional moral instruction and curious information gave it extraordinary success in sixteenth-century Europe, carrying it through more than forty editions in France before 1600. Montaigne recalls his father's particular devotion to it. Its literary style was also much admired. Far from the ideal of simplicity implicit in Boscán's translation of Castiglione's *Courtier*, and the norms recommended by Juan de Valdés, it reveals a love of literary elaboration on Guevara's part which he probably owed to a medieval stylistic ideal. The syntax remains clear, but great play is made with carefully contrived effects of verbal repetition, parallelism, accumulation and contrast, interior rhyme and assonance, rhythmic balance and variation. The effectiveness of this technique can well be seen in perhaps the most famous part of the work, the protest by 'a Peasant from the Danube' against the Romans who have conquered his people. He condemns the cruelty, greed and injustice of their rule as administered by corrupt and stupid officials. It was appreciated at the time that the reference was really to Spanish conquests in the New World. Vasco de Quiroga, in 1535, wrote back from Mexico reminding the Emperor that the latter had read this section of the work, and much praised it, before it was printed, on his way from Burgos to Madrid (1528). It shows Guevara expressing the frequently voiced sixteenth-century moral opposition (fortified by Ovid and Horace) to colonization and the pursuit of trade in new lands when the Spanish expansion across the Atlantic was still in its early days.

Guevara had begun writing this work in 1518, when still Father Guardian of the Franciscan House at Soria. By the time his next most famous works appeared (the *Epístolas familiares* and the *Menosprecio de corte y alabanza de aldea* (*Court Condemned and Village Praised*), in 1539), Guevara had returned to the Court he had left when about twenty-five to become a friar and had been appointed royal preacher, historiographer to Charles V, and Bishop of Guadix, near Granada. He had gone with the Emperor's expedition to Tunis, in 1535, as Garcilaso had done, and was in Provence when Garcilaso was fatally injured. In 1538 he had been appointed to the remote Galician bishopric of Mondoñedo, where, as at Guadix, he showed himself pastorally active, puritan, and energetic in litigation.

The *Epístolas familiares* are, very largely, essays on a variety of moral topics: for example, the mercy the victor must show to the vanquished, the right attitude towards illness and old age, and the character of life at Court. Some of the *Letters* are, in effect, sermons in which one finds the pietistic concentration on the sufferings of Christ prominent in his later *Monte Calvario*. The *Letters* are dated and addressed to particular individuals; nevertheless, for the most part they were never sent but were in fact conceived as literary exercises. Their epistolary form is not their only misleading aspect. What Guevara tells us about himself – for example, the part he played in the revolt of the *comuneros* – often lacks a foundation in fact. Thus he speaks of his crushing scholarly labours in composing his works; and yet, as was notorious at the time, his learning, particularly as regards the Classics, is often simply bogus. He did not hesitate to invent books for authors and authors for books, or to base statements on the evidence of inscriptions and coins which, for all his detailed references to them, did not exist. The *Marco Aurelio* was of his own devising and not taken from a manuscript: the *Meditations* of Marcus Aurelius were not discovered until thirty years after the *Marco Aurelio* was printed. On the other hand, in the *Epístolas*, and still more in the *Menosprecio de corte*, there are passages which possess an arresting degree of truthfulness – as when Guevara writes with satirical vividness of the realities of day-to-day existence at Court. When he praises life in a village in the country, the picture he paints of it is strikingly remote from the world of pastoral literature and gives one an impression of being close to life as it really was in a Spanish village of his time. The *Menosprecio de corte y alabanza de aldea* ends with three chapters in which Guevara looks back on his life at court, passes judgement on it and on himself as he has emerged from it, and bids farewell to the world. It is a passage which presents itself as the expression of a man in a moment of moral crisis in which he at last sees the truth about himself and recognizes that moral wisdom has come too late in life. How far all this answered to Guevara's real state of mind is hard to say. Nowhere are his literary art and literary consciousness more vividly apparent. The note of self-dramatization he achieves sometimes makes one think of Quevedo. At this point in his book, however, the question of factual accuracy ceases to matter: these chapters stand as a general poetic statement of a truth of human experience. They represent one of the most remarkable virtuoso passages in sixteenth-century Spanish literature.

Pedro Mexía (1497–1551)

Pedro Mexía, like Antonio de Guevara, is now among the least read of sixteenth-century Spanish writers, and yet in his own age was one of the most famous. His *Silva de varia lección* (1540), put into English as *The Forest or Collection of Historyes*, went through more than thirty editions during the sixteenth century in Spain and enjoyed exceptional success in France, where it possibly encouraged Boaistuau to compose his *Histoires prodigieuses*. It was also translated into Italian as well as English. It stands as one of the most important of Spanish witnesses to the taste of the time for compilations and miscellanies of random information – the taste that prompted Erasmus to put together his *Apophthegms* and *Adages*, carried the *Nine Books of Memorable Deeds and Sayings* of Valerius Maximus through over a hundred editions, and lay behind Montaigne's *Essais*. Mexía explains his title by saying that he has brought together his material 'without arrangement or order' so that it is like many different kinds of trees in a wood. It is, indeed, there to be wandered through this way and that. He may tell us how the empire of the Turk arose, or about Diogenes the Cynic, or of strange things found in mountains and rocks, or about Tamberlain the Great, the wisdom of animals or the ages of the world – and all in a straight-forward prose which, though lacking outstanding excellence, invites one to read on. Mexía shares the sixteenth-century love of extraordinary and amazing events and its delight in curious information, drawn often from ancient writers, the 'authorities', and pointing to a practical moral lesson.

If this is usually traditional, his enthusiasms sometimes have the distinctive ring of the Italian Renaissance, as when one finds him writing, in one of his longest chapters (Book I, chapter xxxii), a defence of the life of activity in society, an ideal which owed so much to the commendation of the Florentines. He himself drew a pension from Charles V as a 'cosmographer' (as he later did as chronicler of the Emperor's reign), and is said to have been consulted by pilots of ships setting out across the Atlantic from his native Seville, where he spent almost the whole of his life. He writes in praise of printing, admires the great library built up at Seville by his friend Hernando de Colón, son of Christopher Columbus, and joins the number of those who, since the fifteenth century in Spain, had been championing the cause of 'letters and the liberal arts' against those who thought only skill in arms important. If this tempts one to regard Mexía as modern in his outlook, one should remember his frequently expressed interest in the influence of the planets, which (as he explains, conventionally enough), even if they do not destroy the freedom of the will, profoundly affect the characters and behaviour of men. This interest, in itself, would not make him any the less representative of the Renaissance outlook; but it remains the case that, despite his enthusiasms, and even though he had been an eager correspondent of Erasmus in the early 1530s, he does not put across a clearly defined or distinctly weighted point of view. Nevertheless, he does give expression to a number of the chief intellectual concerns of the sixteenth century, and in this respect, perhaps most vividly strikes one as a man of his age in the way he writes on the issues of fortune and divine providence.

These are topics to which he frequently returns, declaring, with some agitation, that the very notion of the former is absurd foolishness, and asserting the reality of the latter with a good deal of emphasis. And yet he complicates matters by writing of how very important it is to recognize and seize the right occasion or opportunity if one is to bring one's plans to a successful fulfilment. This was to become a matter of great interest and discussion among Spanish moralists as the century went on.

FOURTEEN

Michel de Montaigne (1533–92)

MONTAIGNE is as much the product of his age as Rabelais, but his influence coloured seventeenth-century thought to a degree which inevitably affects modern judgement of the *Essays*. He sums up as no other Renaissance writer does the attitudes of an epoch in the reactions of an individual. Even by sixteenth-century standards he is a confusing, and confused, writer, and the appeal of his work derives at least as much from its anti-systematic form as from its basic content.

Like Erasmus and many others Montaigne took immense pleasure in collecting anecdotes, proverbs and *sententiae*, principally from ancient authors, but considerably reinforced by modern historians and personal testimony. Thus, in their original form the *Essays* were something like Erasmus' *Adages*, and a number of those in Book I retain this character (for example, xxii: 'One man's profit is another man's loss', which is less than a page long). Cicero, Seneca, and Plutarch (translated into French by Amyot in 1559) were his favourite sources, and such philosophy as there is has a distinct Stoic ring. Had he continued along such lines we should have little more than a Classical commonplace book. However a series of events shaped his view of life and thus of his work. In 1563 he lost his friend Etienne de la Boétie, never again enjoying with anyone, man or woman, so profoundly satisfying a relationship (movingly described in I, xxviii, 'On Friendship'); in 1568 he lost his father, and in 1571 he retired from public life 'into the bosom of the learned virgins (Muses)', as he put it, at his country house near Bordeaux.

If seclusion thus gave him the opportunity for composition, the loss of his friend provided a major incentive. A. Thibaudet aptly describes the *Essays* as the continuation of a conversation which would not have had to be written down if La Boétie had lived, and while it is obvious that what began as a specific need to conclude unfinished business may ultimately have become a habit, Thibaudet's interpretation is a healthy corrective to the view that Montaigne was just an egocentric exhibitionist. At all events, by the time he began seriously to write his book he had moved on considerably from the original concept of a collection of moral reflections towards a more personal view and, from the first, his comments on a wide variety of topics were accompanied by revelations of often startling candour about himself. Though some of these early essays relate to particular situations (v, 'Whether the commander of a place under siege should come out to parley'; xlv, 'On the battle of Dreux') the great majority treat general moral problems (ii, 'On sadness'; viii, 'On idleness'; xx, 'To philosophize is to learn how to die'). The heroes and captains of antiquity, like Alexander or Epaminondas, are held up as examples, the Stoic virtues of fortitude and self-discipline are extolled, and the appeal to reason, common sense and moderation runs like a watermark through the jumble of themes.

It used to be fashionable to divide Montaigne's life and work into three neat packages succinctly labelled Stoic, Sceptic and Epicurean, but even in the Renaissance, when definitions tend to fit only where they touch, such a classification raises more problems than it solves. As far as Stoicism is concerned, there is no doubt that Montaigne was deeply interested in Stoic writers, and under the influence of La Boétie adopted a broadly Stoic attitude to moral questions such as pain and death. The idea that 'there's nothing either good nor bad but thinking makes it so' appealed to him, and he had personal reasons for needing a set of ethical guidelines such as Stoicism provided. The horrors of civil war, his often painful duties as a magistrate, the example of men like La Boétie and, perhaps most of all, his conviction (confirmed by events) that he would eventually be stricken by the same dreaded affliction of the gall-stone as his father before him, all these considerations attracted him to a way of life which had enabled so many men throughout the ages successfully to assert the mastery of mind over matter. So long as this philosophy met his needs he was content to try it out, but it would be incorrect to describe him even at this stage as a committed Stoic; the empirical vein in him was always too strong.

Whatever one may think of the old tripartite division of Montaigne's thought, the one point on which evidence permits of no disagreement is that in 1575–6 he underwent a genuine crisis, commonly called Sceptical or Pyrrhonist. A good deal of the first book of *Essays* had already been composed in the year or two following his retreat, but political affairs made pressing demands on Montaigne's time and he was very active in both Bordeaux and Paris. In a mood no doubt already favourable to change he then came across the work of Sextus Empiricus, a third-century (A.D.) Greek in whose writings the teaching of Pyrrho is preserved. The main tenet of that brand of philosophical scepticism to which Pyrrho gave his name was that, in the absence of any infallible criteria, the only sensible thing to do is to suspend judgement on all issues, moral or epistemological. This simple rule made a tremendous impression on Montaigne. He took the revelation so seriously that in 1576 he struck a personal medal with the device in Greek ἐπέχω, 'I abstain', and about the same time began writing his longest and most influential essay, the *Apology for Raymond Sebond*.

For no apparent reason, Montaigne's father had conceived so high a regard for the *Theologia Naturalis* of the fifteenth-century Catalan Sebond, that his son translated it to give him pleasure and published his version in 1569. Essentially what Sebond attempts is a theology based not on books or dogma, but on the rational interpretation of the works of nature, 'the book of creatures' as he calls it. The book, and Montaigne's not entirely faithful translation, incurred a good deal of criticism, which the so-called *Apology* was ostensibly designed to refute. In fact this book (it is just one sixth of *all* the *Essays* in their final form) mentions Sebond very little, and far from defending his views is hardly compatible with them.

The essay begins with a somewhat perfunctory defence of Sebond against the charge that reason should not be enlisted in support of faith, but soon passes to the second charge, that Sebond's arguments are not in any case effective, and do not resist rational objections. This is Montaigne's excuse for mounting a massive assault on human reason, the faculty above all others on which men base their arrogant pretensions. The rambling argument pursues a course so serpentine that it is hardly useful to speak of stages, but rather of recurrent themes. First of these is the comparison of man with the animals, to his detriment. A picturesque selection of anecdotes and alleged facts from Plutarch and other Classical writers is adduced as proof that animals are superior to men not only physically, but intellectually and morally as well. A second main theme is that of the great diversity of opinions among philosophers, who for all their proud claim to rational certainty cannot even agree on the nature of the sovereign good. At this point Pyrrho comes in, and the injunction to suspend judgement is accompanied by the standard story of the pig whom Pyrrho observed during a storm at sea completely unconcerned in the midst of so much human panic. This appeal to suspend judgement is accompanied by the fideist argument for which Montaigne was condemned a century or so later; given the inadequacy of reason, Montaigne says that faith should be taken literally on trust from God, through the teaching of the Church, and neither examined nor buttressed by reason.

This leads him on to the argument from relativism that so impressed Pascal. In default of any reliable criterion Montaigne claims that customs and institutions, ranging from formal justice to primitive taboos, are merely self-affirmative: they exist and are respected simply because they are customs, while across a frontier a totally different set of rules may obtain and be enforced with equal rigour. Here Montaigne's innate conservatism finds its strongest plea, for the only argument in favour of change is the appeal to reason. Once this is rejected one course of action is as good as another, so that there can never be any practical justification for altering the *status quo*.

Having thus attacked human claims to pre-eminence Montaigne launches his final blow, to win a Pyrrhic rather than a Pyrrhonist victory. Lest his opponents should take refuge in some sort of pragmatism, he points out that not only are all customs and laws relative and variable according to time and place, but that the very basis of human knowledge is unreliable. Turning a stock Aristotelian argument against its exponents, he says that the only contact we have with the outside world is through our senses, and these, as a series of familiar illustrations about illusions (jaundice, etc.) shows, are notoriously fallible, and may therefore at any given moment be transmitting false data to our fondly trusting minds. In an orgy of self-destructive paradox, Montaigne introduces the then fashionable problem of life as a dream, the impossibility of establishing any independent criterion of truth, and, in short, asserts: 'Finally there is no such thing as constant existence, whether of our being or of that of objects', for everything is in a state of perpetual flux.

Though there is nothing particularly original about these ideas thus baldly presented, the highly personal style and amateur status of Montaigne gave the *Apology* an influence far exceeding that of formal treatises on the same subject. To some extent this attack on reason, by deliberately adopting kill-or-cure tactics, distorts the later essays, but equally this was something he had to get out of his system and it enabled, indeed obliged, him to undertake the self-study, which, together with his scepticism, is his most characteristic feature. Philosophers, lawgivers, even historians being all equally unsure guides, the foundations of knowledge and the constancy of existence being destroyed, all that was left to salvage was that fragment of uncertainty where the risk of error could at least be reduced to a minimum: knowledge of ourselves. Each man's problem is to live his life according to the best lights available; henceforth Montaigne seeks them solely in himself.

The rejection of Stoicism brought about by this sceptical crisis was soon reinforced by actual experience of the gall-stone, by which, after years of apprehension, he was first attacked in about 1577. Thereafter, with the wisdom born of experience, he could write of pain as it related to himself, not just as an abstract concept. At about the same time he was writing the greater part of Book II of the *Essays*, and those which sound the most personal note in the first two books probably belong to as late a period as 1579–80: 'On friendship' (I, xxviii), 'On cannibals' (I, xxxi), 'On books' (II, x), 'On presumption' (II, xvii) and 'On the resemblance of children to their fathers' (II, xxxvii). By 1580 the second book was completed and the *Essays* were published at Bordeaux. It is a measure of his changed conception of the form that the fifty-seven essays of Book I occupy little more space than the thirty-six of Book II (excluding the *Apology*).

The five essays just mentioned as being the most personal are far more typical of the Montaigne who has come down through the centuries than the often rather scrappy musings written earlier. Montaigne's titles are, to say the least, misleading as a guide to content, and the last essay of this first edition only deals in passing with parents and children. It is in fact almost wholly concerned with Montaigne's interim report on the long dreaded disease which he had now known for some eighteen months, and apart from a page or two on the hereditary nature of this and other conditions, the essay discusses at length medical science (which he despised) and the problem of pain. Realizing how much pleasure is enhanced by contrast with pain, Montaigne is led to quote Epicurus, where a few years earlier it would probably have been Seneca, but there is no question of substituting one philosophy for another; henceforth experience is to be the guide. The essay on friendship is self-explanatory, so too is that on books, where he professes particular enthusiasm for Cicero, Seneca and, above all, Plutarch among moralists, but prefers history to anything else. The essay on presumption turns out to be a detailed self-portrait, revealing Montaigne's weaknesses (indecision, poor memory, incorrect speech) and qualities (modesty, endurance, adaptability), and is the first fruit of the decision to put self-study before abstract or dogmatic theorizing. The essay on cannibals refers immediately to the natives of Brazil, some of whom Montaigne had met at Rouen in 1562, and of whom he had learned a lot from one of his servants who had been with Villegagnon in the New World. This essay is a perfect example of Montaigne's relativism, for, seizing on the unfamiliar and even shocking ways of these natives (their heedless nudity seemed to contradict both Genesis and instinct), he extols the harmony and virtue of their society. They are, he says, wild in the sense that fruit or flowers are wild ('sauvage' in French means both savage and wild). This leads him on to a somewhat Utopian account of their customs, from which he concludes that, barbaric as they are, Europeans are worse, for they have corrupted the rough innocence of nature with the polished vice of civilization.

Thus in these five essays all the main themes of the book combine: nature is the surest guide, whether in morals, medicine or education (better to form judgement than instil learning); self-knowledge shows us our own nature; history and travel put ourselves and our society in a wider perspective; friendship, freely chosen, is the most satisfying of human relationships, and is a positive step towards a human solidarity threatened by bigotry, selfishness and misunderstanding.

Shortly after his book appeared, Montaigne went on an extended tour through Germany and Switzerland to Italy, meeting Tasso (unhappily deranged) in Ferrara and spending several months in Rome before returning to Bordeaux, of which town he had been elected mayor in absence in 1581. A new edition of the *Essays* in 1582 incorporated a certain number of reminiscences of this journey, for example a passage on some thermal establishments where he had sought relief from the stone, and there is also a *Journal*, composed partly in Italian, which gives valuable biographical material. A very intense period of civic and diplomatic activity followed, and Montaigne had to cope with the increasingly bitter civil war (he was the personal friend of the future Henri IV, and also enjoyed the confidence of Henri III), with serious outbreaks of plague, and with his continuing ill health. After a second term as mayor (1583–85) he had more time for his book again, and immersed himself in history, ancient and modern. By 1588 he had completed a third book (its twelve essays cover much the same space as each of the two earlier books) also adding considerably to those already published (his policy was normally to insert, not erase, and this leads to sometimes bewildering inconsistency in the same sentence) and the new edition of the complete *Essays* was published, this time in Paris. Montaigne was still working on a further expanded version of this edition when he died in 1592, and his admirer, Mlle de Gournay, published the last edition of the *Essays* in 1595, incorporating most of his additions.

The titles of these last essays are as uninformative as ever, but the essays contain more and more autobiographical matter. 'On repentance' (III, ii) considers whether there is any point in having second thoughts, which, as far as Montaigne is concerned, is senseless, for he learns by trial and error and would not wish to change the past. The theme of flux and inconsistency, already found in the *Apology*, is now predominant, and his earlier admiration for men of action or poets (Homer, Alexander and Epaminondas head the list in II, xxxvi) gives way to a new respect for Socrates as the ideal man, frequently cited in this book, from the first essay to the last. What he admires in Socrates is his 'médiocrité', that is, his exemplification of the golden mean, and his flexibility. In 'On repentance' Montaigne makes much of the epitome of humanity contained within each man ('each man bears the entire form of the human condition') and at the same time stresses the unique personality, 'a form of one's own', which makes each one of us, with all our faults and virtues, ourselves and no one else. To regret this defect or that action, he says, is as foolish as to regret not having wings.

In another Book III essay (viii, 'On the art of conversation')

Montaigne wrote 'our condition is physical to a wonderful degree', and this realization more than any other is a key to the last essays. All men, he says, are his brothers, and those of his nation or province no more nor less than the others. Constantly in the last book he recounts his eating habits, his propensity to travel sickness, his sex life, his health, every intimate detail by which he can fix the unique coordinates of his own personality. We read indeed of his preference for particular types of conversation, or of books, or for individual men or women, but what most clearly emerges is a three-dimensional portrait of himself. Even the style contributes to this effect, for, claiming to write as he speaks, Montaigne ignores all accepted rules of composition and indulges in a highly idiosyncratic, disjointed, parenthetical style which constitutes much of the charm of the book. This racy, colloquial approach certainly attracts the reader as much as it reveals the author. Where earlier essays had been concerned with speculation, opinion, moral lessons, in short the works of reason (always liberally reinforced by anecdote), now personal and physical elements outweigh the rest. The feeling for the brotherhood of man, although it had always formed part of Stoic teaching, is the direct consequence of this shift of emphasis. The problems of life have to be solved in the here and now; as Montaigne says, 'my art and my craft is living.' Reason only makes man presumptuous, stiffens opinion, strengthens barriers; only experience, whether of pleasure or pain, identifies the individual to himself and makes him aware of the inalienable human heritage he shares with all mankind.

While the *Apology* is the longest and most influential of the essays, the last one in the book, 'On experience', is as near as Montaigne comes to a definitive statement. He has already shown from numerous examples how the most trivial bodily phenomena (sneezing, headache) distract the gravest philosophers from the exercise of vaunted reason, and this essay repeats once more the familiar details of his own habits which he rates of greater importance than opinions. We read once more the arguments about relativism and inconstancy, but this time in a less negative form. Experience, he begins, is no more a homogeneous series of events than a row of apparently identical eggs. No two men ever feel or think exactly alike, no one man has the same experience more than once, for with the passage of time, however short, he himself has changed significantly, so that no absolute, universal rules can ever be valid for an individual, let alone for the generality of mankind. Instead of merely suspending judgement Montaigne now accepts experience, trial and error, as the only guide, and by no means a bad one. In this sense, of course, experience means the record of nature kept up to date. Now that he is old and sick he no longer fears pain, but enjoys relief from it as a positive good, nor death, which can only rob him of that small portion of his life remaining after the ravages of age and illness. By being ourselves we are fulfilling our humanity and entering into real communion with the rest of mankind. He concludes that there is no greater perfection than that of being true to oneself, that it requires more effort to stay in the middle way than to drift to extremes and, in a typical phrase, 'seated on the loftiest throne on earth we are still sitting on our own backsides.'

The most original feature of the *Essays* was also the most successful, and though Pascal was not alone in condemning Montaigne's enterprise of self portrayal, it is primarily for this that the book is still read. Perhaps St Augustine's *Confessions* (which Montaigne seems not to have known) come closest in conception and execution, but never before had Montaigne had anyone attempted so minute a self-study just for its own sake. His scepticism and relativism would never have influenced later generations if their vehicle had been less personal, as one can see from the fate of Charron's book *De la Sagesse* (1601), which reproduces in tabulated form the ideas, and nothing but the ideas, of the *Essays*.

The very nature of the work, and the man, make any summing up only tentative, and even so vital a question as that of Montaigne's religion remains hotly disputed. He was a practising Catholic by the standards of his time, and such essays as that 'On prayers' (I, lvi: his own favourite was the Lord's Prayer) as well as the *Journal* of his travels show some sympathy for Catholic teaching; but he was not intolerant of reforming ideas in principle (several of his family were Protestants), and his religion was much more concerned with God, good, just and wise, than with any particular dogma, even with a Mediator. His humanism is extracted from, rather than based on, the ancients, and while he accepted no ready-made philosophy, especially after the sceptical crisis, his examples of admirable men were all of pagans, above all of Socrates. In the terms of his and the next century he seems to have made little or no provision for the working of grace, and if he ever worried about salvation this is not evident from his work. When the controversy about grace and pagan virtue reached its height in the seventeenth century these attitudes of his were of considerable importance.

In the last analysis it is not for his learning or his ideas, nor even for his distinguished role in public affairs, that Montaigne survives, but for what he calls 'my universal being, Michel de Montaigne', as portrayed in the *Essays*, which, as he says, formed him as much as he formed them. Neither as magistrate, Frenchman, nor immortal soul, but as himself, warts and all, was how he wanted to come down to posterity, and in this he succeeded to an incomparable degree.

PART VI

Popular Literature

Introduction

PERHAPS nowhere else in this volume has a division been created more arbitrarily. Everyone can recognize learned literature, and unpopular literature defines itself, but what exactly is popular literature in the Renaissance? First and foremost it is to be found in the oral tradition, whether written down or not, and the process of natural selection over very long periods, often several centuries, is a rough-and-ready guarantee of quality. In all countries songs, ballads, stories, proverbs, hedgerow philosophy, some dramatic material, sometimes even more ambitious genres like the epic, belong in this sense to popular literature. It may happen that something that started on a comparatively erudite level, lives of the saints for example, survives most strongly in popular form; it may equally happen that strictly literary, that is written, crystallization of popular material, as in comedy or short story, illustrates the contrary effect. If this is obvious enough, in the Renaissance it is complicated by the extreme self-consciousness of vernacular writers who were often forced into false positions in their attempt to prove that Latin (or Italian in the case of French and Spanish writers) was not necessarily a better medium for poetry or elevated discourse than their own tongue. One definition of popular literature would therefore cover those works despised by cultural élitists, and indeed regarded as non-literature, precisely because their appeal was to the majority, learned or unlearned, if not necessarily to the masses. Such a definition would be most relevant for Italy, then for France, rather less so for Spain and England and almost not at all for Germany, the Netherlands and Scandinavia, because of the very different levels of cultural development obtaining in each country at a given moment. At the same time it must not be supposed that kings, popes and other top people were ignorant or unappreciative of the literature enjoyed by their humbler fellow citizens. The well-publicized cultural snobbery of the Renaissance is no more reliable as an index of actual consumer habits than similar phenomena today. A further complication arises from the fact that intense piety or patriotism may, as in the sixteenth century, inspire propaganda directed at the widest audience but attaining genuinely literary quality, as is notably the case with much Protestant literature. This section, brief as it has to be, attempts to underline what might otherwise be forgotten, namely the constant and fruitful interaction between popular and literary forms, especially in poetry and drama. It should be added that the largely spurious account of popular literature invented by the Romantic movement, not to mention still more modern attempts to canonize popular taste, is only a hindrance to the understanding of Renaissance literature, whatever ideological purpose it may be thought to serve.

ONE

Germany

Sebastian Brant (1457–1521)

WHEN Sebastian Brant, who was for many years a professor of law at Basle and latterly became town clerk at Strasbourg, published his *Narren schyff* (*Ship of Fools*) in 1494, German vernacular literature had for almost a century suffered a period of unparalleled neglect. To modern eyes the text of Brant's pedantic and censorious little book is scarcely such as to establish him as an author of European stature, yet it achieved a success which was unmatched in German literature until the appearance of Goethe's *Werther*: it passed through six editions and six reprints (not to mention the pirated editions) between 1494 and 1521 and was reprinted fourteen times in the course of the sixteenth century. In the Latin translation of Jacob Locher (1497) it enjoyed international status, was re-translated into the principal European vernaculars, inspired the vogue of 'folly literature' and for the next two centuries was to exercise a marked influence on moral satirists.

The success of the work was primarily due to Brant's thematic exploitation of the folly legacy of the later Middle Ages with their societies of fools and Shrovetide processions in which folly figures traditionally played a considerable role. The conceit on which the review of human failings is based is that all the fools in the Empire have been assembled in a ship for transportation to Narragonia ('Foolonia'), each particular 'folly' being reviewed in an individual chapter. Recent research has revealed that the 112 chapters which go to make up the work are not quite so haphazard and formless as has usually been assumed: each chapter can be shown to possess a distinct rhetorical form (for example, *ratiocinatio*, and *expolitio*) and the whole work seems to have been conceived as an *oratio suasoria*. It is unlikely, however, that most contemporaries – any more than modern scholars – realized that the work was constructed according to Classical rhetorical principles and the popularity of the book undoubtedly derived in large measure from the intriguing woodcuts which accompanied the text and in the production of which the young Dürer probably collaborated. Next to this felicitous exploitation of the legacy of the fifteenth-century block-book, one of the chief attractions must have lain in the episodic nature of the text itself. Each chapter could conveniently be read independently of the whole and positively invited the reader to 'skip and dip' as fancy and the illustrations prompted him. The individual chapters, written in rather wooden *Knittelvers* (rhyming couplets of four stresses per line), vary in length, but the standard disposition of the text is three or four lines of preamble above the woodcut on the left page followed by four lines beneath it and the remaining thirty lines of the normal chapter on the right-hand page. There is no attempt to disguise the review technique: with monotonous regularity Brant introduces his fools with the formula 'Der ist ein narr der . . .' ('He is a fool who . . .') or some suitable variant ('Noch findt man narren manigfalt die . . .': 'You can still find a lot of fools who . . .'), but occasionally the fool is allowed to speak for himself: 'Myn narrheyt loßt mich nit syn gryß' ('My folly won't let me be my [old] age').

Rather surprisingly for a man who associated with humanists such as Locher and Wimpheling, Brant is relatively untouched by the spirit of the Renaissance. There is little trace of *joie de vivre* in his work or of that readiness to question authority which is the hallmark of humanism. Quite the contrary. In almost every chapter Brant anxiously quotes examples from sacred and profane history in order to lend his arguments conclusive weight, and on occasion he specifically rejects the pursuit of learning for its own sake and the investigation of the physical universe as examples of frivolous curiosity which distract mankind from the real business of saving their souls. Nor, in spite of the intention to improve his fellow men, does a reading of the work convey the impression that Brant really felt that the fools he describes were actually worth his efforts on their behalf. Equally, Brant clearly has little sense of the sublime nature of folly such as was to characterize Erasmus' subsequent treatment of his theme, nor does he possess any well-developed sense of humour. Folly for him is largely synonymous with sin and any genuinely humorous treatment is precluded – both, one suspects, because of Brant's own temperament and because he rightly senses the dangers inherent in the ascription of the motto 'castigat ridendo mores' to the comic muse. The author's purpose is unashamedly didactic and he does not share the humanists' sneaking belief in the innate goodness of man: the latter will not naturally incline to that which is right and must be chivvied into goodness by the threat of hell-fire. As a spokesman of the conservative South German bourgeoisie he advocates a sound, puritanical, middle-class ethic and indiscriminately condemns as foolish all deviations from his own norm, whether it be taking part in shooting matches, bibliomania, adultery, failing to follow doctor's orders, or imposing on the faithful by selling forged relics; and, in spite of the equation of foolishness and sin, in good middle-class fashion, the common denominator of the follies he attacks is seen as improvidence – either with regard to the world to come or in the light of their economic and social consequences here on earth.

Notwithstanding the rather wooden pedantry and obscurantism which speak from many chapters, Brant could achieve a surprising emotional intensity when the issues involved affected him really profoundly. Chapters such as 'Von abgang des gloubens' ('On the decay of the faith') and 'Vom Endchrist' ('On Antichrist') introduce us to a devoutly pious conservative, who, full of evident grief at the secular and religious decay of his times, passionately clings to the medieval ideal of the twin authority of pope and Emperor and despairingly appeals for a greater measure of unselfishness and sincerity in the ordering of political and religious life – an appeal which in the light of subsequent events gains a heightened pathos.

Thomas Murner (1475–1537)

The chapters of the *Narrenschiff* were to awaken echoes in German moral satire (Sachs, Fischart, Moscherosch, Abraham a S. Clara) for decades to come, but Brant's most important immediate disciple was the witty Franciscan, Thomas Murner. Murner is massively indebted to Brant. Many of his lines are evident reminiscences of his reading of the *Narrenschiff* and in his first work, *Doctor murners narrenbeschwerung* (*Doctor Murner's exorcism of Fools*, 1512) he borrows not only themes from Brant, but the actual woodcuts as well. Even in his other works – *Der schelmen zunfft* (*The guild of rogues*, 1512); *Die Geuchmatt* (*The meadow of the fools of love*, 1515); *Die*

Mühle von Schwindelshaim (The mill of Schwindelsheim, 1515) – his combination of woodcut and text and his castigation of moral failing as 'folly', together with the essentially episodic nature of his work, bear witness to the source of his inspiration. However, unlike other imitators of Brant (for example, Johann von Morsheim, d. 1516) Murner possesses a liveliness and a sense of fun which distinguish him markedly from his model. Whether he appears as the learned conjuror who is going to exorcize the follies of mankind or as the chancellor of the rogues' guild – devices which conveniently enable him to engage in a Brantian review of common human failings – he replaces the rather bloodless and schoolmasterish censoriousness of his model by a sense of personal involvement and waggish humour. The donnish scholar yields to the popular preacher: in a way that is completely alien to Brant, Murner confesses himself a fool with the rest and evidently enjoys the odd scurrility for its own sake. Gone is the rather depressing Micawberish note which informs the *Narrenschiff*: folly still equals sin, but ultimately, in spite of the waggishness, it is sin as an offence against God rather than as a lack of good sense which Murner attacks – so much so that a recent critic has spoken of his diabolization (*Verteufelung*) of folly. The recital of authorities and examples from the Bible and history has equally disappeared: Murner's examples, as befits a popular preacher, are drawn from everyday life and expressed in the vigorous idiom of normal speech with its images and proverbs, and his waggish, Eulenspiegel-like character colours everything he writes.

The occasional scurrilities and the verve with which Murner describes moral failings should not be allowed to obscure the fundamental seriousness with which he approaches his task. However, his tragedy – and that is hardly too strong a word – was that the very effectiveness of his 'laughing satire' prevented contemporaries (and many a nineteenth-century literary historian) from taking him entirely seriously. His attacks on ecclesiastical abuses, for instance, and the manner in which they were made tended to be taken as evidence of a lack of moral earnestness, with the result that the underlying concern to preserve the fabric of the faith was ignored. Consequently, both friend and foe looked askance at the series of anti-Lutheran pamphlets he published in the years 1519–20 and regarded them as evidence of venality or of simple contrariness. Yet to read these pamphlets or the fine lyric poem 'Ain new lied vom dem vndergang des christlichen glaubens' ('A new song on the decay of the Christian faith', 1522) is to meet a man who, in the midst of acrimonious disputes, which so often produced more heat than light, had the rare faculty of distinguishing between the essential faith and the excrescent abuses from which the faith suffered. Murner's past association with fools and folly dogged him to the end, however, and appropriately enough it was in a work entitled *Von dem großen lutherischen narren* (*On the great Lutheran Fool*, 1522) that Murner said his last word on the issues involved in the Reformation controversy.

This rather sprawling mock epic, rich in references to Murner's previous career and to contemporary controversy, falls into three main parts. In the opening chapters Murner appears as the learned exorcist who conjures the follies of the Great Fool, an allegorical figure in whom the errors of Lutheranism are embodied. In the second part, strikingly prophetic in its anticipation of the Peasants' War of 1525 and the political consequences of the Reformation, Murner, in an image dear to his heart, plays the role of the defender of the castle of the Old Faith against the assaults of the Lutheran cohorts; and finally, in the scurrilous closing chapters, he compromises with Lutheranism, going through a form of marriage with Luther's daughter (the Reformed Church?), until, finding in the bridal chamber that she is impetiginous, he rejects her, since marriage is after all not a sacrament in the Lutheran view! Luther is so upset that he dies refusing extreme unction and is buried to the accompaniment of a cats' chorus in the latrine, while the Great Fool, by contrast, recants on his death-bed and is given more suitable interment. Throughout the work, which is richly illustrated with woodcuts, Murner appears as a tom-cat dressed in a cowl (a reference to the ironical pun on his name: Murrnarr = tom-cat + fool) and in quite characteristic fashion finally claims the cap of the Great Fool as his due.

Owing to difficulties with the printer and the Strasbourg censors *Von dem großen lutherischen narren* never achieved any real measure of popularity, but in its biting and accurate satire and its inventive exploitation of the folly theme, in its scurrilous sense of fun and its very real concern with the great religious issues of the day, it is by no means an unsuitable monument both to its author and to the folly theme itself. The latter lived on and until well into the seventeenth century fools continued to be cured of their folly by a variety of literary horse-cures, but increasingly, under the influence of Lutheranism and the heavily theological climate of the age, moral satirists replace the fool by the devil – the *Saufnarr* and the *Buhlnarr* (drink-fool and lechery-fool) yield to the *Saufteufel* and the *Buhlteufel*; the term 'folly literature' changes its meaning and refers more and more to the Eulenspiegel or Claus Narr type of character, highly amusing in their own way , but almost entirely devoid of serious moral content.

Hans Sachs (1494–1576)

Heine's famous dismissal of Hans Sachs as nothing more than a 'Nürnberger Spießbürger' ('a philistine of limited mental horizon') is not without a certain justification. Sachs brings to poetry the same conscientiously practical outlook and the same respect for the rules of the *Meistersinger* as he brought to his calling as a shoe-maker and the rules of his guild. Poetry for him is neither a blessing nor a curse, but a trade to be followed for the amusement and betterment of his fellows, and his fundamental attitude is one of common-sense practicality flavoured by a highly developed sense of humour. In spite of their unpromising nature when viewed from the modern standpoint, it was these qualities which made him perhaps the most characteristic and certainly the most prolific German writer of his age (he published something like 6,000 titles) and which enabled him to survive as a living force in German popular literature for the greater part of a century.

We are not concerned here with Sachs's dramatic works – even though many of the Shrovetide plays (see p. 509) fall into the category of moral satire and often are simply dramatized versions of anecdotes also treated in verse – but with his use of the *Spruch* and the verse *Schwank*. The *Spruch*, a poem of a single – often very long – strophe cast in any one of a number of metrical forms (*Töne*) and intended to be sung, had been widely used in the Middle Ages as a vehicle for religious, moral, political and didactic themes and was admirably suited for Sachs's purposes. The *Schwank*, by contrast, is not so much a genre as a description of the humorous content, but even here Sachs's didacticism manifests itself in the tendency to draw morals from the often very broad anecdotes he relates. Often, it is true, he is content to tell the anecdote simply for the laughs, but like all his generation he is a moralist at heart and in the main the *Schwänke* as well as the *Sprüche* are made to serve as vehicles for a common-sense and perhaps rather shallow but basically sound moral message. Sachs's ideals are those of his class, and everything which militates against domestic harmony and decorum and a life of modest prosperity in the state to which God has called a man is condemned, whether it be sexual immorality, avarice, prodigality or simple shrewishness. There is, however, no bitterness in Sachs, and even his particular *bêtes noires*, the shrewish wife and the incontinent priest, are treated with a human warmth and degree of good-humoured sympathy which is in striking contrast to the vinegary self-righteousness which speaks from the pages of, for instance, the *Narrenschiff*.

Unlike Brant and Murner, Sachs did not subsume all moral failings in one convenient idiom or topos. Everything he writes is conditioned by an anecdotal episodic approach and in quite uninhibited fashion he draws his material from the whole range of older and contemporary literature. Indeed, it is in his function as a purveyor and popularizer of Renaissance and late medieval themes that a great measure of his historical significance lies: Stainhöwel's rendering of Aesop and Petrarch, Schlüsselfelder's translation of the *Decameron*, Pforr's version of Bidpai, the *Gesta Romanorum*, Wickram's adaptation of Ovid's *Metamorphoses*, Schedel's *World Chronicle*, the native *Schwank* and *Volksbuch*, medieval legends of the saints (especially St Peter), Brant and Murner all provided him with the material from which he fashioned the jingling rhymes which delighted and edified his contemporaries. Like the Shrovetide plays, the *Sprüche* and *Schwänke* introduce us to the whole range of contemporary society, parsons and princes, serving-wenches and merchants. In the main, however, he moves in his own middle-class milieu and for preference treats the traditional butts of popular satire, the hen-pecked husband and his shrewish wife, the incontinent priest and the stupid and gullible peasant.

In spite of his introduction of new *Töne*, Sachs is essentially a traditionalist, in formal matters as from the point of view of content, and his work is virtually untouched by the spirit of the Renaissance lyric. The latter began to exert an influence in Germany only at the beginning of the next century and even then long remained the preserve of learned, upper-class poets. Sachs was not in any real sense a lyricist; poetry for him serves to express ideas not emotions, and his innovations were no more than technical modifications of medieval forms. Similarly, traditional allegorical figures – Truth, Carnival, Winter, etc. – abound in his poems, a fact which makes them peculiarly suitable for illustration and many of them did indeed appear first in broadsheet form accompanied by woodcuts designed by such artists as Georg Pencz and Erhard Schoen. For all his prolific output too, Sachs is not an ingenious or inventive writer, and in many of the *Sprüche* falls back on traditional stock devices to introduce his theme: chance meetings in the course of the poet's evening walk, conversations he happens to overhear, the dreams he has or even simple requests for information directed to older acquaintances all serve repeatedly to launch the poet on his topic.

Sachs thus in many ways exemplifies the German literary situation in the sixteenth century: Renaissance themes are being imported *en masse*, but they are being grafted on to the native literary stock rather than giving rise to new forms or even a new concept of literature. Compared with his contemporaries in other European lands Sachs inevitably appears old-fashioned and limited in outlook and literary know-how; he does, however, possess a naïve spontaneity, a genial good humour and a sincere concern for his fellow men, warts and all, without which German literature would be the poorer and for which one looks in vain amongst many of his more distinguished fellow poets.

Folksong and hymn

With the exception of Luther, Germany in the sixteenth century brought forth no vernacular poet of European stature, and the actual texts of such lyrics as were produced were probably less important than is the case in other European lands, since the words were never intended to be read or recited, but to be sung, and thus constituted an indivisible whole with the music. This applies not only to the folksong and the hymn, but also to the more esoteric products of the Mastersingers – later to be immortalized by Richard Wagner – whose 'schools', while seeking to conserve the legacy of the courtly lyric with a frighteningly pedantic apparatus of prosodic rules and guild snobbery, could never deny their derivation from the lay brother-hoods devoted to the cultivation of choral music.

The exact relationship of the folksong to classical Middle High German poetry has long been a subject of academic dispute. There have probably always been folksongs of one kind and another which of necessity have concentrated on a limited range of topics, and it may well be that the folksong exercised a certain influence on the courtly lyric. In the main, however, the influence probably ran the other way and the folksong's use of colours and bird symbols, and above all its concern with the joys, disappointments and partings of lovers (the 'Dawn Song' is still a living genre!) suggest strongly that in their themes, if not always in their diction, many folksongs are in fact debased and popularized descendants of the poetry of courtly love. The folksong is thus not the anonymous product of the 'folk soul', as the Romantics tended to believe, except in the sense that oral tradition inevitably tended to modify the words in which the 'stout *Landsknecht*', the 'wandering journeyman' or the 'poor sinner' (who not infrequently 'sign' their songs in the last stanza) treat their traditional themes. The other common fallacy, that the sixteenth century witnessed a great outburst of folksong production, is a mistaken conclusion drawn from the fact that it was now that collec-tions began to appear in print (the most famous is Georg Forster's *Frische Teutsche Liedlein*, published in five parts between 1539 and 1556). But although the printers no doubt modified the texts in places, many of the songs they published antedate the sixteenth century considerably, even if they were still very much alive at the time of printing.

Love was not the exclusive theme of the sixteenth-century folk-song. Songs welcoming spring or summer, complaints at the ap-proach of winter, songs in praise of wine and the gay life alternate with historical folksongs, which tell of battles and sieges, and ballads in which sad tales of infidelity and vengeance, captivity and home-coming after many years are given easily memorable form.

The keynote of all types of folksong is simplicity. Parataxis is preferred to hypotaxis, clause and line tend to coincide, assonance is freely used and metrical and rhyme schemes are generally un-sophisticated: four- or eight-line stanzas of four stresses in rhyming couplets or rhyming alternately are most common, although rhyme-less l ines (*Waisen*) are not infrequent. A predilection for stock formu-lae and epithets is very evident – virgins are always tender, valleys deep, mountains high, wine cool, eyes brown, etc., while especially in the final stanza a certain note of resignation is quite characteristic: 'iez far ich ins elend' ('and now I am going to distant countries'), 'Ich seh euch nimmermer' ('I will never see you again'), etc.

*

Although there had been German hymns from medieval times, Luther in a very real sense is the creator of the German hymnological tradition which was to culminate in the choral music of Schütz, Bach and Händel. With rather uncharacteristic modesty he decried the idea that he was a 'poet', but almost against his will his unusual feeling for the poetic qualities of the German language and his musical talents combined to produce a series of hymns which were ultimately to become part of the cultural inheritance of every Protestant German and – in translation – of Protestants throughout the world. As with most of Luther's innovations, his hymns were produced in response to an evident need – the need to replace 'love lyrics and carnal songs' with more edifying matter on the one hand, and to substitute sound Evangelical doctrine for the teachings of the Roman Church on the other. Accordingly, many of Luther's hymns repre-sented an extreme popular counterpart, suitably sugared with music, to his weightier theological treatises and, as the learned Jesuit Con-zenius remarked, 'Luther's songs killed more souls than all his books and sermons.' Perhaps even more important than the success of Luther's own hymns, which rapidly achieved the status of religious folksongs, was the fact that his example was followed by others – notably Paul Speratus, Justus Jonas, Albrecht von Preussen and Johannes Mathesius – who vied with each other in providing a host of religious songs which, as the Riga hymnbook puts it, 'the labourer might sing at his work, the serving-girl while washing dishes, the farmer while working in his fields and the mother as she rocks her crying infant'.

Most of Luther's hymns circulated first in broadsheet form before being brought together in the various compilations published by Luther, initially in collaboration with the musician Johann Walther (the *Geystliches gesangk Büchleyn* of 1524 contains thirty-two German hymns, twenty-four of them from the pen of Luther; the *Geistliche Lieder* of 1529 adds another four by Luther, while of the 105 *Geistliche Lieder* of 1545 some thirty-six are by Luther). Very few of the forty-one hymns we can with certainty ascribe to Luther are entirely original productions. For preference, he translated and adapted established Latin and German models, infusing them with his own spirit and fashioning from them vehicles for his own message: thus the medieval antiphon 'Media vita in morte sumus' becomes in Luther's rendering ('Mitten wyr im leben sind mit dem tod umbfangen') a prayer for release from *spiritual* death, etc. Occasionally too, as in the case of the charming and delicate children's carol 'Vom himel hoch da kom ich her', he adapted a folksong for religious purposes; but it was in the Psalms (xii, lxvii, cxxx, etc.) that he found inspiration for his most memorable hymns, including his celebrated 'Marseillaise of the sixteenth century', 'Ein feste burg ist unser Gott' (Psalm xxxxvi), usually known in English as 'A safe stronghold our God is still'.

From the point of view of prosody Luther draws on both the folksong ('Nu frewt euch, lieben Christen, gmein') and the *Meistergesang* ('Ein feste burg') and, while occasionally simply stressing alternate syllables, normally allows the stress to be dictated by the natural rhythm of the sentence. Although rooted in Luther's personal experience, his hymns are essentially expressions of community experience: 'we', 'our' and 'us' are the characteristic pronouns, and in spite of their function as vehicles of Protestant theology it is not this aspect which in the end predominates. The abiding impression is of rugged simple strength and a robust and manly trust in God. The adoption of 'Ein feste burg' as a battle hymn by Catholic as well as Protestant regiments in the First World War is a striking tribute not so much to Luther's powers of subliminal *propaganda fidei* – which he would have scorned – as to this manliness and Christian confidence, which are typical for him both as a man and as a writer.

Fable

It was perhaps inevitable that the combination of ethics and literature which is characteristic not only of Brant, Murner and Sachs, but of the whole sixteenth century in Germany, should lead to a revival of interest in that ancient vehicle of literary didacticism, the fable. The latter had enjoyed considerable popularity in medieval Germany and manuscripts of such fabulists as der Stricker (*c.* 1250), Ulrich Boner (*c.* 1350) and Gerhard von Minden (*c.* 1370) continued to circulate long after the invention of printing. It was not from this native German tradition that the sixteenth century revival derived its main impetus, however, but from the humanist town doctor of Ulm, HEINRICH STAINHÖWEL (1412–83), who amongst his numerous translations of Latin and Italian classics produced a version of Aesop which on its publication in 1476 became a contemporary best-seller and continued to be reprinted frequently until well into the eighteenth century. For all its boldness as a translation – Stainhöwel anticipates Luther as a translator in his intention, as stated in the 'blurb', to translate 'simply and intelligibly, not word for word but sense for sense' – Stainhöwel's version was only the most successful of several contemporary collections: Boner's *Der Edelstein* (*The Jewel*) had been printed in 1461, and an edition of the 'Cyrillic' anthology appeared in 1490 (reprinted 1520 and 1529), a year which also saw the appearance of Ulrich von Pottenstein's *Spiegel der Wahrheit* (*The Mirror of Truth*), whence Sachs was to take much of his material. The fable was thus firmly established as a popular genre, and there is scarcely a satirist of the sixteenth century who did not make occasional use of it as a vehicle for his didactic message.

Perhaps the best tribute to the esteem in which the fable was held lies in the fact that Luther himself, while at Coburg at the time of the Diet of Augsburg (1530) when the momentous discussions on the famous Confession were taking place, saw fit to embark on a new translation of Aesop, whom as an outstanding moral teacher he could mention in the same breath as the Prophets and the Psalter ('faciemus Sion ex iste Sinai aedificabimusque ibi tria tabernacula, Psalterio unum, Prophetis unum et Aesopo unum'*). Compared with Stainhöwel's rather woolly rendering, Luther's forty-nine fables – which were published posthumously in 1557 – are characterized by an extreme simplicity both in language and syntax which brings the German version strikingly close to the spirit of the Greek original. This direct and almost limpid quality is emphasized by the divorce

---

* 'Let us make out of this **Sinai** a Sion and build there three tabernacles: one for the Psalter, one for the **Prophets** and one for Aesop.'

of fable and moral: unlike Stainhöwel and his original, Luther never uses the moral as an opening gambit, but prints it – often expanded quite considerably – beneath the actual narrative under a separate heading.

While Luther thus tends to prune and stream-line his model, the two greatest fabulists of the century, ERASMUS ALBERUS (*c.* 1500–53) and BURKHARD WALDIS (*c.* 1490–1556), achieved fame precisely because, like La Fontaine at a later date, they were able to clothe the traditional narrative framework inherited from Aesop with a wealth of detail and in the process create genuine characters out of the animal abstractions who originally peopled Aesop's narrative. As a Protestant divine and personal friend of Luther, Alberus was not above introducing an occasional polemical note into his fables, but he saw in them above all 'sweet parables' ideally suited for the moral education and edification of the common people. The collected edition of his forty-nine fables, many of which had appeared earlier, bears the characteristic title *Das buch von der Tugent vnd Weißheit* (*The Book of Virtue and Wisdom*, 1550). The 'sweetening' of the parables is achieved partly by casting them into the traditional four-stressed rhyming couplets of popular German poetry and by working with a much larger canvas – the average length of his fables is some two hundred lines. In imitation of the *Meistersinger*, he loves to localize the action in Germany, often appending detailed geographical descriptions; above all, however, he greatly expands the dialogue, enriching the sparse direct speech of the original with a host of contemporary references and turns of phrase. The result is often a certain moralizing garrulity – in the fable of the thief and the dog, for instance, 'panem porrigens' becomes twenty-two lines of speech including eight lines of accumulated proverbial imagery for 'never', while the dog, in reply, harangues the thief in best parsonical style. Occasionally too, a note of involuntary humour creeps in, as when it is the old donkey who is made the defender of the prevailing social order ('The Donkey and the Horse'), but the more successful passages (for example, the delightful account of the attempts of the town mouse to restore the confidence of her country cousin, or the brilliant description of the origins of the quarrel between the birds and the quadrupeds) achieve a charm and a dramatic liveliness which more than compensate for the occasional long-windedness.

Waldis emerged as a fabulist after Alberus, whose earliest fables were published in 1534, and had clearly learnt from his predecessor. In many respects there is little to choose between them. In contrast to Alberus's rural outlook, Waldis is very much a townsman, with a townsman's tendency to social criticism, but in the main his values are the same as Alberus's and from all his works there speaks the same common-sense, practical morality which holds in high esteem the traditional middle-class virtues of modesty, providence, industry and charity. In common with his age he sees the stratification of society as being willed by God, but as a man of generous disposition and considerable political experience (he represented Riga at the Diet of Nürnberg), he is not slow to warn the powerful and comfort the poor by reminding them that reeds withstand storms which uproot oak trees and that small stones can upset big waggons. Like Alberus, Waldis was a Protestant parson and can never entirely deny the parson's love of moralizing: thus he prefaces his version of the 'Cock and the Pearl' with a somewhat unrelated discourse on the goodness of God and the necessity of labour, and the moral normally takes up between twenty and thirty lines of the sixty-odd lines of the average fable. Like Alberus too, Waldis uses *Knittelvers*, often localizes his fables and uses the dialogue effectively to create personalities out of animal ciphers. Where he excels his model is in the economy and pithy directness of his style – characteristically he loves to introduce proverbial and idiomatic expressions and the moral often culminates in a series of rhymed proverbs. We still have not got a German equivalent of the polished conciseness of La Fontaine, but compared to Alberus's rather heavy approach, Waldis exhibits a lightness and sureness of touch which give the narrative a rare buoyancy. Even in the moralizing passages he can usually retain a certain 'throw-away' quality which keeps the reader on his toes and retains his interest. Characteristically too, he occasionally inserts minor narratives into his morals to prevent our attention from wandering, and by using proverbs which the reader knows and subconsciously accepts as vehicles of truth, appeals, as it were, to the converted and so avoids any undue tendency to preach at us.

A genre which is closely related to the fable is the 'animal epic'. The most important German example of the genre, *Reinke de Vos* (*Reinke the Fox*), is a version of the common European theme, dating back to the early Middle Ages and subsequently to be treated by Goethe, of the fortunes of the crafty fox at the court of the lion. This was published in Low German in Lübeck in 1498 (High German, 1544); but amongst some minor examples the sixteenth century proper also saw the production of two notable animal epics, JOHAN FISCHART's *Flöh Haz, Weiber Traz* (1573, 1577) and GEORG ROLLENHAGEN's *Froschmeuseler* (1595). The former, which draws on the venerable tradition of the mutual hostility of women and fleas, is perhaps the most attractive of all Fischart's verse satires in its good humour and uninhibited exuberance: the metre skips along and incident chases incident with a liveliness worthy of the very animals to which the work is dedicated. The first part, which is heavily indebted to the version of Matthias Holtzwart, consists of a dialogue between a flea and a fly, in which the flea explains the terrible fate which has overtaken his whole clan as a result of their attempt to implement his suggestion that they desert their previous sluttish host in favour of a more attractive upper-class young lady. The complete destruction of his kith and kin, already anticipated in the fate of a similar expedition in which his father had participated as a youngster and which the old man vainly recounts in an attempt to warn his son against his daring undertaking, moves the flea to appeal to Jupiter for an injunction against the bloody persecution of his race by the human female. This naturally introduces the somewhat less interesting second part in which Fischart, in a modification of a traditional conceit, appears as the Flea Chancellor and plenipotentiary of Jupiter and announces the latter's verdict: fleas must expect women to act in self-defence and are in future only to bite women when they are gossiping, dancing or sojourning in the bath-house (in the fifteenth and sixteenth centuries bath-houses enjoyed an evil reputation as hotbeds of immorality).

Not uncommonly the element of social satire in *Flöh Haz* has been exaggerated by critics. It has been suggested, for instance, that the fleas represent the Imperial knights or the Roman clergy in the German body politic, or that the fate of the fleas in trying to change their host constitutes an affirmation of Fischart's belief that rigid social stratification is a good thing and is to be seen as a serious warning against inappropriate social ambitions! It is hardly necessary to comment on the inherent absurdity and improbability of such interpretations, and while it is true that Fischart has a sharp eye for detail and with a few strokes can capture and castigate undesirable social phenomena, whether it be inattention in church, gossiping or exaggerated fashions, to concentrate on such details is to miss the essential point. Fischart is here at his most gay and invites us to share freely in the gaiety and good humour which speak not only from the delightful basic conceit, but from a hundred and one tiny inimitable touches – often untranslatable in their dependence on puns and idioms – but which stick in the mind long after. One thinks of the names he gives to his fleas: Senfimhemd ('Mustard-in-the-shirt'), Keckimschlaf ('Bold-in-sleep'), Nachtzwacker ('Night-nipper'), or the way in which the market woman who puts slaughtered fleas on her plate alongside the bread and wine 'which one should honour' is compared to the necrophagous Dracula, or Jupiter's threat to cure the carnal lusts of the fleas by subjecting them to the same treatment which St Francis and St Benedict reputedly used on themselves to such good effect. This is not to suggest that the work lacks any satirical point, of course, but merely to insist that rather than being concerned with any specific historical abuse or social evil, the satirical crux of Fischart's poem lies in the humorous anthropomorphism – in the laughing revelation of the ultimate insignificance of human affairs and human passions by attributing them to such a humble and despised animal as *pulex irritans*.

In keeping with his magisterial position and inclinations (he was for many years headmaster of the Magdeburg grammar school), Rollenhagen strikes a much more heavily didactic note in his adaptation of the pseudo-Homeric *Batrachomyomachia*. It is not easy to summarize the action of this vast sprawling work of some 20,000 lines, in which Rollenhagen set out to paint a picture of his age and provide a 'useful' alternative to *Eulenspiegel* and the other *Schwankbücher* by taking care that there should be 'no laughter without a lesson'. The central theme of the nature and recent history of the two kingdoms of the mice and the frogs and the war between them is embedded in a web of fable, discourses (often admittedly charming) on popular customs and superstitions, and accurately observed details of animal behaviour. For all the evident interest in the animal kingdom, however, Rollenhagen's frogs and mice are a thinly disguised conceit whereby he can represent the men and women of his own age. Like the good Protestant citizens of Magdeburg, they are hard-headed and successful businessmen, albeit with the rather disturbing habit of quoting Latin, Greek and Hebrew and a regrettable tendency to alchemical speculation. Nor are they free from religious strife and discord: the frog priest Beißkopf ('Bite-head'; like Fischart, Rollenhagen loves to invent names) has recently sought with the aid of toads and the liberal use of excommunication to establish his sole authority over the frogs – an attempt which has come to grief on the rock of popular resistance suitably hardened by the teachings of Elbmarx ('Elbe–Warrior': Wittenberg is on the Elbe!) and the political skill of Prince Mortz (Maurice of Saxony). Politically, although the Hanseatic frogs and the Swiss mice give them pause, Rollenhagen's frogs and mice are monarchists rather than republicans, with the proviso that the monarch must rule under the law, and are in favour of a sharp distinction between secular and ecclesiastical authority.

It is this political element which distinguishes Rollenhagen from his middle-class predecessors. With the latter he shares a common belief in the inherent worth of a life of honest industry and modest prosperity in the condition to which God has called a man. However, as Gervinus pointed out, virtue is no longer absolute, but is seen in its relationship to society and social political considerations ultimately predominate over moral and theological ones. This means that the Pope, for instance, is condemned not so much on theological grounds as because the political power of the papacy is an infringement of the rights of the secular state.

Hans Sachs and the 'Fastnachtspiel'

The term *Fastnachtspiel* (Shrovetide play) is a piece of folk etymology – it should be 'Fassnacht' and derives from 'faseln' ('to blather, talk nonsense') rather than 'fasten' ('to fast') and represents an accommodation of the spring and fertility cults of pagan times to the festivals of the Christian year. The pagan festivals from which the *Fastnachtspiel* ultimately derives probably consisted of a procession in which fertility symbols were carried around the fields to the accompaniment of impromptu songs, dances and recitations, and culminated in the beating, burning or drowning of a figure representing winter. In more sophisticated times the procession, such as we find it surviving in the *Schembartlaufen* (a sort of carnival procession) in Nürnberg, included *tableaux vivants* mounted on drays; the first plays probably resulted from an innovation by which the 'actors' supplemented the activities of a commentator by explaining their own significance – a device which lives on in the review technique of many a literary *Fastnachtspiel*. Naturally in the course of time new meanings were supplied for the ritual acts which had with their Christianization lost all real significance. Thus the joy at the rebirth of spring survives in the general atmosphere of tom-foolery and jollification which, as the name *Fastnachtspiel* indicates, is now seen as a last fling before the abstentions of Lent, while the fertility cult persists in the broad humour and obscenity and the preoccupation with the problems of married life. The crux of the original ceremonies, the beating out of Winter, lives on in the frequent horse-play – fights between peasants, punch-ups between husband and wife, etc. The original cult significance is thus translated into slapstick comedy with an admixture of social and domestic satire; by the sixteenth century the *Fastnachtspiel* is simply a brief dramatized anecdote of everyday life.

Undoubtedly the most successful exponent of the *Fastnachtspiel* was Hans Sachs (see p. 498). As in his other writings Sachs often borrows from a host of Renaissance and medieval sources (Boccaccio, Lucian, the *Volksbuch*, etc.); but the same qualities which made his excursions into high drama so unfortunate – his flat-footed unpretentious homeliness, his preoccupation with the story-line, and the unpolished nature of his diction – were, when allied with his abundant sense of fun, admirably suited to the Shrovetide farces of which his native Nürnberg was one of the principal centres. His earliest *Fastnachtspiele*, such as *Das Hoffgesindt Veneris* (*The Courtiers of Venus*, 1517) or the pseudo-Lucianic *Charon mit den abgeschiedenen gesten* (*Charon and the departed guests*, 1518) still retain the review technique of the older tradition; but by the great period of the fifties (sixty-five of his eighty-five *Fastnachtspiele* were written between 1550 and 1560) he had outgrown this static convention and in playlets which rarely exceed 400 lines in length or introduce more than six characters he presents us with a rapidly developing action expressed with an admirable economy of dialogue in which the homespun nature of the four-stressed doggerel is a perfect match for the rough-hewn and often slapstick nature of the plot.

The *Fastnachtspiele* introduce us to almost the whole range of contemporary society from the higher clergy and the robber-knight down to the urban merchant and the artisan – always seen, of course, from the necessarily limited standpoint of the good, respectable, Lutheran citizen of a prosperous Imperial city. In this latter capacity, partly no doubt due to the force of tradition, partly also because like most city-dwellers he was uneasily aware of the agrarian discontent just outside the city walls which periodically had resulted in bloody uprisings, he naturally tends to direct his social satire against the peasant; he never tires of showing the peasant as a brutish, mean and stupid clod-hopper, crafty in his way, yet a ready prey for any smart alec who happens to come along. His other *bête noire* is the shrewish wife who, contrary to the laws of God and man, has set herself up to rule over her husband and must be reduced to obedience, if necessary by physical violence. Yet his characters are never reduced simply to sociological ciphers, and for all his predilection for stock types he almost invariably gives his characters individual traits which make them live as personalities in their own right. In this he not uncommonly excels his models: Heintz Düppel ('Harry Twerp') in *Der pawr in dem Fegfewr* (*The Peasant in Purgatory*, 1552) – loud-mouthed, mean, disingenuous, full of self-pity and petulant recriminations against his wife – lives for us in a way to which his ancestor in Boccaccio (*Decameron*, III, 8), for instance, cannot even aspire.

As a respectable master of his craft and a convinced Lutheran, Sachs is not content simply to amuse his audience, and not infrequently the closing lines of his plays draw a moral from the action; yet there is no trace of acidity in his moralizing and his fundamental seriousness is cloaked in robust good humour. There are few real villains in Sachs: men, he realizes, are foolish and limited in their mental capacities and not infrequently lack moral rectitude; but Sachs is an optimist and insists on man's capacity for improvement. He may deal with vices such as lechery, greed and dishonesty, but he sets them in a minor key in which their tragic potential is overlaid by the absurdity of their practitioners, who seldom suffer anything more serious than the blackening of an eye or the loss of a cow, the pettiness of the punishment usually matching the effective pettiness of the crime.

Like everything about him, Sachs's humour is generally lacking in subtlety. He loves the broad anecdote, has a sharp eye for the ludicrous and the absurd and not infrequently operates with comedy of situation: a peasant who has allowed the calf to drown sits on a cheese, hissing like a goose, in the hope of hatching out a new calf (*Das Kelberbrüten, Calf-hatching*, 1551); a thief due to be hanged is released on parole, because the gallows is in the middle of a field of corn and the spectators would trample the crop down, while it would cost the parish too much to keep the thief in gaol until after the harvest (*Der Rosdieb zu Fünssing, The horse-thief of Fünssing*, 1554); Neidhart, in a treatment of the common European theme, having discovered the first violet of the year, covers it with his hat and brings his lady to see it, only to find that a peasant has plucked it and left a turd in its place (*Neidhart mit dem feyhel, Neidhart and the violet*). Such humour is not for the sophisticated and the over-sensitive; but it is thanks to such humour and the sheer dramatic liveliness of the *Fastnachtspiele* that Sachs continues to be numbered amongst the tiny band of sixteenth-century dramatists who can still hold a modern audience.

TWO

Italy

'COMMEDIA DELL'ARTE'

THE *commedia dell'arte* implies troupes of professional actors who relied on the barest outline of plot, with improvisation, a repertoire of jokes, set speeches, and comic, even obscene, action. In all this, it appears completely opposed to the *commedia erudita*, which sought its pedigree in antiquity and its justification in the supposedly moral effects of ridicule directed at men's foibles, while, like tragedy, it depended on a fixed text performed by amateurs for special occasions. The origins of the *commedia dell'arte* have been much disputed: it seems clear, however, that it was in the main an Italian creation of the sixteenth century which kept certain links with the ancient *fabulae altellanae*, Latin comedy, and medieval farce. As in the work of Ruzante and others, dialect was used – a mixture of dialects, more or less true to life, each associated with a stock character (Venetian for Pantalone, Bolognese for the Doctor, a bastard form of Bergamask for Arlecchino). The character's popularity was helped by immediate recognition of his distinctive costume and mask. For us, the latter would seem to make for artificiality and a lack of individuality. Even modern audiences, however, prefer their heroes to run true to type, and this was assured by the masks of the *commedia dell'arte*, where the mask itself was no hindrance to the expression of emotion, since the actor was trained to exploit every possibility of limb or gesture. The great Scaramouche, so admired by Molière, was able to keep an audience in fits of laughter by his miming of fear, without uttering a word for a full thirty minutes, while David Garrick was struck by the 'expressiveness' of Bertinazzi's back in his portrayal of Arlecchino.

Pantalone, the Venetian merchant, is mentioned by Shakespeare in *As You Like It* (II, vii). His name may be derived from the phrase 'pianta leone' ('plant the lion'), which referred to the city's emblem and Venetian economic imperialism. Pantalone himself is a merchant, sometimes bankrupt, always old and given to the senile passions of avarice and lust. His costume is made up of a red woollen cap, tight jacket and breeches, with a long black cape. His profile is particularly striking, with his brown mask, jutting white beard, bony face, arched eyebrows, the purse at his belt, his prominent sword and phallus. If married, he is invariably a cuckold; as a father, he is both authoritarian and incredibly careless, losing his children at the drop of a hat and having to resort to birthmarks or the promptings of his long-lost paternal instinct in order to identify them. He is hunched with age, yet capable of astounding feats of agility, chases the maid-servants and usually ends up by getting a beating from Arlecchino and being forced to agree to his son's marriage with the beautiful young girl he had set aside for his own lechery or promised to his friend, the Doctor.

The Doctor comes from Bologna, famous for its university and fine cuisine. He is the most loquacious of all the masks, but fat and perhaps the least agile. He is, of course, a pedant after the tradition of the comic stage, a presumptuous busybody and an insufferable bore. His vast-ranging erudition is hardly skin-deep, and his numerous Greek and Latin quotations are mangled with superb aplomb. Like his Venetian crony, the Doctor represents the older generation, usually in conflict with the young, while his black academic dress is in deep contrast with Pantalone's characteristic red. When he first appeared on the stage (*c.* 1560), the Doctor wore a half-mask, black or flesh-coloured, with a bulbous nose, red cheeks, and a short beard. From this self-satisfied mountain of legal or medical science we get magnificent truisms and never-ending tirades on the most incongruous subjects. In the eighteenth century, Prospero Lambertini, a famous interpreter of the mask, had been elected Supreme Pontiff as Benedict XIV, when he had occasion to remind the Venetian ambassador, who had dared to interrupt him, that Pantalone must keep silent while the Doctor speaks.

After the adaptation of the Classical pedant, we find the Captain – Plautus' *miles gloriosus* – reborn as a satire of the rascally mercenaries and Spanish soldiery who swarmed over Italy in the sixteenth century. His name (Spavento, 'Terror'; Sangre y Fuego, Spanish for 'Blood and Fire') is calculated to strike fear into the hearts of his numerous, but often invisible, opponents. His mask is flesh-coloured, with a huge nose and a bristling moustache; his costume follows the whims of military fashion, but with the great ruff and plumed hat favoured by the Spaniards. In a cocktail of Spanish and basic Italian, he boasts of his descent from all the great captains of antiquity and the incredible feats of valour performed with his sword, inherited from Alexander the Great or Roland. First into a fight, he is always the first to leave or lie down, pretending to be dead or imploring the mercy of his terrible opponents – who usually turn out to be Arlecchino with a wooden stick in his hand. His military vainglory is accompanied by superb conceit in his dealings with the fair sex: seeing himself as a reincarnation of Mars, he takes it for granted that all the Venuses of this world will swoon over his good looks and prowess. The creator of Capitano Spavento della Valle Inferna, Francesco Andreini (*c.* 1548–1624) is one of the most famous names in the history of the *commedia dell'arte*. He was himself a soldier, before being captured by the Turks. On his return from a long period of imprisonment, he made his stage début as a Lover with the famous Gelosi troupe and went on to create new roles, including the famous satire on his former profession. Andreini became director of the Gelosi in 1600 when they went to France, where he was applauded by the public and honoured at court.

Much of the action and verve of the *commedia dell'arte* depended on the wit and resourcefulness of Arlecchino and his cousins. Arlecchino came from the lower town of Bergamo, where everyone was supposed to be a dunce, whereas Brighella, the other *zanni* (a nickname for Giovanni, John, which has given us the epithet 'zany'), came from the upper town, where all the inhabitants were endowed with craft and quick wits. Arlecchino has perhaps the most difficult role of all. He takes little direct part in the plot, but must try to add zest and prevent any drop in dramatic temperature or rhythm. For this, he must possess exceptional acrobatic agility and the gift of adapting himself, chameleon-like, to a whole series of different circumstances. He may walk on stilts or on his hands, somersault across the stage, shin up and fall from the highest walls, pretend to chase and eat flies piecemeal, parody his master, Pantalone, in a grotesque love affair with a maidservant – but always he must think of saving his skin and filling his permanently empty stomach. Arlecchino's famous costume was originally a haphazard collection of dark patches, sewn on to his breeches and long jacket, while on his close-cropped head he wore a soft cap, decorated with a fox's brush or some other symbol of ridicule. His half-mask, usually made of leather, had a wrinkled forehead, bushy eyebrows, tiny holes for the eyes, and a snub nose; but its most striking feature was its colour, black, with all the connotations that have lasted down to the nigger minstrel shows of the present century.

Brighella's name, on the other hand, is redolent of the intrigue and deceit (*imbroglio*, *brigare*) that characterize his resourceful nature and are reflected in the crooked nose and cynical olive green of his half-mask. Towards the end of the sixteenth century, his white costume took on green trimmings, with a dagger to add a forceful note to his cunning exterior. His slit eyes typify his manner of acting: he lets the other *zanni* do all the work, as he prowls around, ever-ready to pounce on some profitable victim. The most vigilant innkeeper cannot stop him from speedily satisfying his hunger and thirst, while he never misses an opportunity to revenge himself on those who try to outwit him. As soon as he manages to lay his hands on some food and money, he is ready to dance and sing, for he is a gifted musician, especially with the guitar. He respects two things in life: his own pleasure and the superior strength of others.

The Lovers were the official centre of the play, but hardly ever remained there. Playing without masks, they were young, goodlooking, elegantly dressed, and spoke 'literary' or 'stage' Tuscan. They would deliver long lists of Petrarchan similes and laments, with all the trappings of Renaissance love rhetoric, expressing their misery and happiness, jealousy and mutual fidelity, in complete contrast to the rough and ready speech of the *zanni*, who frequently parodied the complicated love affairs of their betters. The Lovers had style, but little personality, and, unless played by actors of great skill and imagination, they tended to be eclipsed by the other masks.

The Church had always forbidden women to appear on the stage, and in 1558 a new papal edict was issued in an attempt to put a stop to this immoral practice. Some Italian states, however, had begun to lift the ban against actresses, who were thus able to take their place in the *commedia dell'arte*, although their roles never developed to the same extent as those of the leading male masks. There were in fact no true female 'masks', for the women were no doubt unwilling to hide their features, but sought to set off their beauty with the occasional aid of a tiny black velvet mask, similar to the *loup* used at carnival time. Their dress followed the dictates of fashion, while their charm had to be enhanced by an ability to sing and dance with grace. The most famous actress of the century was Isabella Andreini, born in Padua in 1562. Married to Francesco Andreini, she bore him seven children, wrote poetry and plays, was an expert musician and spoke fluent Latin. Her virtue, beauty, and skill were universally admired and praised by such poets as Tasso, Marino and Chiabrera. After her death, when she was honoured by the leading citizens of Lyon, Isabella gave her name to the typical *innamorata* of Italian comedy.

The influence of the *commedia dell'arte* has been so widespread that Shakespeare, Molière, Marivaux, Watteau, Picasso, Stravinsky, are but a few of the names that spring to mind. It gave the nascent theatre of modern Europe professional zest and polish. It combined dramatic skill of a special order with all the resources of improvisation and a feeling for the general rhythm and speed necessary for great comic acting. Now, we must make an effort to recapture its spirit through the empty *canovacci*, which were pinned up backstage and contain only the barest outline of the action, through the testimony of a few spectators down the ages, and the illustrations of the *Recueil Fossard* and Jacques Callot. Nevertheless, its appeal to all classes and its immense popularity throughout Europe for well over two centuries show that the effort is well worth while.

THREE

France

WHATEVER definition of popular one cares to adopt, it is clear that the preceding pages have only rarely involved discussion of a French popular work. In a negative sense the Pléiade and their contemporaries help to put the concept 'popular' in perspective, because for them it was synonymous with 'vulgar' and as such represented one of the things true literature could not be. In those genres which they sought to establish in France refinement, learning and deliberate rejection of mass appeal were essential. Although Malherbe early in the next century protested against the intrusion into the language of so much that was alien and artificial, seventeenth-century insistence on *bienséance* (seemliness) perpetuated the split between the cultural élite and the rest of the community, which was further widened by the domination of Classicism as an aesthetic norm. Consequently it is not so much the positive influence, or survival, of popular forms that proved significant as their systematic rejection and disappearance from literary histories covering the next two centuries.

Yet the cultural pyramid of which we habitually see only the tip had as broad a base in France as, for instance, in Germany, as literature throughout the century constantly illustrates. The advent of printing together with the Renaissance dramatically changed consumer habits, but even so an author like Montaigne can profess to model his style on the spoken word, and in some cases the oral tradition remained supreme. In poetry folksongs (or what are now so called) of very real merit did not reach print for years, even centuries, after their composition, and at all times popular songs must have been known to a far wider audience than ever saw them on the printed page. The great collection published just a century ago by Le Roux de Lincy is the appropriate context for considering the *chansons* of a poet like Marot and hundreds of others are still extant in rare printed copies. In France, as in Germany, when Protestantism began to spread, psalms and hymns had to be composed which everyone, even illiterates, could learn and sing, often to secular tunes. It should be added that this was not a Protestant invention, for early in the century the Franciscan Olivier Maillard is known to have improvised from the pulpit words (still extant) to contemporary popular songs. This popular element in French Protestantism, with its insistence on the vernacular, touched only a minority of the population directly, but its indirect effect on devotional literature of all kinds, including Catholic, must be taken into account.

In a sense the most influential form of popular literature had for centuries been the sermon. Preachers, especially friars, were trained specialists, and for many of the ignorant laity a course of Advent or Lenten sermons by some leading preacher must have represented the most highly organized form of literature with which they came into contact. We still know far too little about preaching in the sixteenth century, but to judge from the substantial body of material available in print by such men as the Franciscans Maillard (d. 1502), Menot (d. 1518) and Messier (d. 1546) the techniques were still medieval, and no less effective for that. Learning, piety, emotion and frequent crudity characterize these very Gothic productions, but they are seldom dull. Erasmus often ridicules these preachers, Rabelais learnt a great deal from them, Estienne draws on them heavily for his denunciation of Catholic vices, mock sermons were regularly composed, and no account of satire in the century can ignore their influence. From a literary point of view their principal importance is in the transmission of countless *exempla*, on which many short stories (for example, by Des Periers) and anecdotes in more serious works are based, and there is evidence that the preachers in their turn borrowed from story-tellers. Their role in forming (or deforming) public taste is analogous to that of the mass media today, especially in the emphasis on the spoken against the written word. Apart from sermon parodies, traditional at carnival time, it is hardly conceivable that the preachers' oratorical and histrionic tricks (one of them took a skull with him into the pulpit to point a moral) failed to influence actors, and not necessarily only comedians.

Serious popular drama, as we have seen, suffered from the prohibition of 1548, but comedy and farce continued to flourish. The coming from Italy of the *commedia dell'arte* at the end of the century constituted no such break in tradition as occurred with the serious genres, and Molière is the direct inheritor of a genuinely popular acting tradition which he transformed into literature. For reasons already discussed, the groundlings in France did not influence the serious genres as early as they did in England, but at the end of the century, and in the first decades of the next, one can speak of a popular theatre in the box-office sense. The perfection of Classical drama in the seventeenth century demanded a major change in audience as much as in playwrights, but such total estrangement from popular tradition may in the long term have been too high a price to pay, even for the glories of a Corneille or a Racine.

The one genre in which the popular element could survive strongly was fiction, since it was not governed by rules laid down in antiquity and could thus be treated as mere entertainment. Crude versions of tales of chivalry retained their popularity for centuries, but in fiction, as in comedy, it was the presence of lower classes, from bourgeois down to peasant, that encouraged a realism in language and description which would not be tolerated in higher genres. Rabelais, Des Periers and du Fail are often only one stage removed from the chapbook or oral tradition that gave them their raw material, and all have a keen eye and ear for setting, dress, speech and so on. For every written tale, or recorded *exemplum*, there must have been many hours of story-telling which only modern devices could preserve. Here one can really talk of popular literature, since it presents the people, just as they are. Nearly all story-tellers in the century adopt an oral technique, and often stage a story-telling session as setting for their fiction. Grandgousier telling his family tales by the fire in *Gargantua* or du Fail eavesdropping on similar sessions on the village green in Brittany, even Marguerite de Navarre, remind us of the universal habit, applicable to every class, of oral entertainment. Much of this (as in du Fail) may have been no more than taproom gossip about people and events, but it is the same du Fail who mentions the books from which the old schoolmaster would read aloud to his appreciative audience: the Shepherd's Calendar, Aesop's *Fables*, the *Roman de la Rose*. The taste for didacticism did not lessen as one descended the social scale, and those for whom Seneca or even Montaigne were too advanced made do with hedgerow philosophy. Proverbs conditioned style and thought as much as Erasmus' *Adages*, in which indeed the comparison is often drawn between Classical sayings and their modern popular analogues. The solid fund of common sense (and occasional lunacy) represented by such proverbs made a lasting impression on language, and thus on literature.

A sub-literary form which enjoyed enormous popularity all through the century was the almanach, in prose or verse, burlesque or otherwise. Rabelais and Des Periers are two of those who were not ashamed to turn a relatively honest penny by composing such almanachs and prognostications (in their case burlesque) and the influence of this pseudo-scientific prediction was immense. Travellers' tales, broadsheets of journalistic appeal, propaganda for political or religious causes, printed versions of favourite tales of long ago were among the tons of paper annually retailed by booksellers or itinerant pedlars, and incomparably more people could be influenced by a fact (or fiction) than had been possible a generation or two before. While the oral tradition long persisted, the new authority of the printed word soon imposed itself. If much ephemeral material, without literary merit, has thus been preserved, it would be wrong to overlook the new opportunities for prestige and profit eagerly seized by authors who would hardly have bothered with the audience or the reward of pre-printing days. But for the economic inducement of exploiting the profitable and popular chapbook market Rabelais would almost certainly have foundered in the obscurity of a learned tongue; without the inspiration of a live popular tradition Des Periers and du Fail would probably never have given literary form to the spoken word.

In poetry, and in drama as a branch of poetry, the Pléiade largely succeeded in shaping and consolidating a literary language, divorced from everyday usage, which served as the basis for the great leap forward into the standard literary French of the next century. In prose Calvin was the first of a long series of writers who rehabilitated the vernacular by expressing in French the most elevated thoughts, and this again helped to create a gap between the technical language, previously Latin, and ordinary speech, though in his shorter polemical works Calvin does not shrink from farmyard talk. The more vigorous earthy, vulgar forms of speech survived in literature wherever comic realism was appropriate, but for the rest, what people below a certain rank or level of education did or said ceased to interest the increasingly refined and aristocratic society of the next century, whose canons of taste have inevitably, and sometimes imperceptibly, affected our own.

The revolution accomplished in language and style in the first fifty years of the seventeenth century is at once apparent if one compares the first French–English dictionary, by Cotgrave (1611), bursting with treasures of popular idiom drawn from sixteenth-century authors, with that of the Academy, begun under Richelieu and belatedly published in 1694. Literature, oral or written, is only words, after all, and when the words and phrases are no longer officially recognized the literature which they compose simply becomes non-literature. The importance of popular literature in the sixteenth century is not so much that the common man read it, let alone wrote it, but that it could still appear, suitably adapted, in respectable company and even inspire masterpieces. The sheer vigour of French language and literature in the sixteenth century is due in large measure to its roots in traditional soil, however cultivated or exotic the blossoms at the top.

FOUR

Spain

THE establishing in Spain of a tradition of verse written in metres derived from Italian and following Italian models did not put an end to the Spanish national tradition of verse. On the contrary, the latter continued to flourish throughout the century. Its two main forms were the octosyllabic *romance*, or ballad, in which even-numbered lines rhyme in assonance while the others remain un-rhymed, and the *villancico*, a lyrical form, usually in lines of eight or six syllables, in which a basic idea, set out at the start of the poem, normally in two to four lines, is glossed, or enlarged and varied, in a series of stanzas, each of which returns to a refrain provided by the opening statement, or *estribillo*. These poems are prominent in anthologies of the time. In their own day they circulated in the form of *pliegos sueltos*, or broadsheets, sold in the street or at markets and fairs. In this way they reached a wider audience than Italianate verse did, for this tended to be read within a poet's range of acquaintance and to remain, for a considerable time at least, in manuscript. The tradition of verse in national forms represents a continuation of fifteenth-century 'literary' or courtly verse and also popular verse. In the sixteenth century these two deeply influenced each other. Moreover, even the major poets writing in the Italianate metres and forms in many cases continued to write in the Spanish national tradition too, and to move from the one to the other, and even combine them, producing the very attractive results that Góngora and Lope de Vega, particularly, can show. San Juan de la Cruz brings snatches of popular song into his *Cántico espiritual*. There were those who, after the innovations of Boscán and Garcilaso, defended the exclusive use of traditional Spanish verse forms. Among these CRISTÓBAL DE CASTILLEJO (*c.* 1492–1550) is particularly re-membered. One finds him making an attractive rendering in lines of eight and four syllables of Poliphemus' Song, taken from Ovid's *Metamorphoses*. However, it is much more common for

Spanish poets to adopt Italian forms without abandoning Spanish ones.

In sixteenth-century Spanish literature one finds many cases of writers of sophisticated literary culture and learning taking an interest in the lower orders of society and showing a liking for their expression in literature. In *Lazarillo de Tormes* one has a work evidently composed by a man of high literary culture who nevertheless derives the episodes of his book largely from folk-lore and collections of comic tales often involving humble characters. As regards the drama, if the popular element is already present in the plays of Torres Naharro and provides the whole matter of Lope de Rueda's *pasos*, or interludes, it comes to play a very important part in the *comedia* as developed by Lope de Vega, who drew extensively on both popular and Italianate forms and literary traditions in plays whose heroes and heroines are not infrequently peasants and which appealed to audiences that themselves represented a broad range of society. Something of the attitude of humanists like Juan de Valdés and JUAN DE MAL LARA (1524–71) towards popular culture can be seen from the way they regarded Spanish proverbs. They both collected them and both praise them in their writings. Mal Lara in his *Philosophía vulgar* (1568), brings his Classical learning to bear on them, revealing the wisdom they contain by writing glosses on them after the manner of Erasmus in his *Adages*. When the Archdeacon of Alcor translated Erasmus' *Enchiridion*, he deliberately sought to give his version a more popular character than the original possessed. One thinks too of the tendency of much of the sermon literature of the age to render spiritual teaching in the concrete terms of common experience of the most down-to-earth level – as Mateo Alemán was to do in *Guzmán de Alfarache*. These are some indications of the considerable measure of social harmony or unity as regards literary attitudes and taste that one often finds in sixteenth-century Spanish writers.

This is perhaps particularly obvious where religious literary expression is concerned. It appears in the enthusiasm shown for the *autos* performed on the Feast of Corpus Christi. But it shows itself too in the fashion that became marked in the second half of the century for turning secular verse, the Italianate and still more the popular, *a lo divino* – adapting it so as to give it a religious character.

San Juan de la Cruz writes *a lo divino coplas* and *romances* on theological subjects. (There is one on the three Persons of the Trinity.) Others, notably Franciscans, had done this before him. Both he and Santa Teresa gloss in a religious sense what was originally a secular love song belonging to the fifteenth-century courtly tradition: 'Que muero porque no muero' – 'I die because I die not'. It was common among the nuns of Teresa's Reform to write short religious poems in the form of popular songs and to send them to other convents of the Order. One reads of occasions when particular monks, including San Juan de la Cruz, were found singing such poems, and even dancing, in their monastic churches, before the Blessed Sacrament. One finds rubrics to the effect that a given *a lo divino* poem is to be sung to the tune of this or that popular, non-religious song. This *a lo divino* technique might be regarded as an inversion of that of parody, where religious statements and sentiments are applied to profane matters or situations in such a way as to produce a comic lowering of effect. Such parody was much enjoyed in the earlier part of the century in Spain, before the moral earnestness of Counter-Reformers, as of Reformers, largely succeeded in putting an end to it.

For the modern reader the most important example of popular verse enjoying enormous success in sixteenth-century Spain and also undergoing a thorough transformation is that of the ballad. Ballads on subjects relating to persons and events of Spanish history and epic were composed in considerable numbers before 1500. They generally came into being through a process of oral and anonymous composition. By the end of the fifteenth century they had obtained a favourable reception at court and from the musicians and poets there. These, both then and later, often refined such ballads, giving them a more effective and concentrated form. The period of their greatest success runs from about 1515 to about 1580, although few ballads of the 'traditional', pre-1500 type were composed after about 1525. The first anthology entirely given to ballads, the *Cancionero de romances*, was published (at Antwerp) in the late 1540s. Well-known musicians wrote settings for them – the ballads were sung to the accompaniment of the *vihuela*, an instrument combining features of the lute and the guitar. It was in the 1580s that the *romance* was most radically transformed, above all by Góngora and Lope de Vega. The ballad now becomes a form of lyrical verse, a means of giving delicate portrayal to refined and elegant amorous feeling. The tone is often serious, sometimes playful. Sometimes this 'new' or 'artistic' ballad presents the themes, situations and sentiments expressed in pastoral literature – the eclogues and the pastoral novel. Sometimes it transforms the fifteenth-century 'frontier ballad', which had recounted frontier incidents between warring Christians and Moors in the last years of the kingdom of Granada, into the *romance morisco*, where, against a background of exotic colour and elegance and in an atmosphere of refined emotion, the Moorish knights and their ladies become analogues of the pastoral shepherds and shepherdesses. Such ballads prolonged the incomparable success that this form of verse enjoyed at all levels of Spanish society.

Chronological Table

	General including British	Italy	France	Spain	Germany and Netherlands
1499	Cabral discovers Brazil	Ficino d.		Rojas, Comedia de Calisto y Melibea (16 acts)	
1500		Venice Academy of Fillelfeni founded			Erasmus, Adagia
1	Anglo-Portuguese expedition to Newfoundland				Erasmus, Enchiridion (pub. 1503)
2					
3	Julius II Pope	Leonardo, Mona Lisa			
4		Sannazaro, Arcadia			
5		Bembo, Asolani	J. Lemaire de Belges, Epîtres de l'Amant Vert		Reuchlin, Hebrew Grammar and Dictionary
6	Columbus d.	Bramante begins St Peter's			
7		Indulgence proclaimed for rebuilding St Peter's		Rojas, Tragicomedia de Calisto y Melibea (21 acts)	
8	Maximilian I Emperor	Michelangelo begins decoration of ceiling in Sistine Chapel		Rodríguez de Montalvo, Amadís de Gaula	Erasmus, Adagiorum Chiliades Bebel, Facetiae
9	Henry VIII King	Ariosto, I Suppositi Raphael begins decorating the Vatican Stanze			Erasmus, Praise of Folly; Fortunatus (Volksbuch)

529

	General including British	Italy	France	Spain	Germany and Netherlands
1510	Colet founds St Paul's School Albuberque at Goa				
11	Albuberque at Malacca				Murner, Narrenbe-schwörung
12		Michelangelo's Sistine ceiling unveiled			
13	Balboa crosses Panama Leo X Pope	Machiavelli, The Prince Bibbiena, La Calandria			
14					Erasmus, Adagia (Froben ed.); Epistolae Obscurorum Virorum; Eulenspiegel (Volksbuch)
15	François I King	Trissino, Sofonisba	Budé, De Asse		
16	More, Utopia	Ariosto, Orlando furioso (first ed.) Raphael, Sistine Madonna (or 1513)			Erasmus, New Testament (Greek)
17		Folengo, Baldus		Ximénez de Cisnerosd	Luther, Ninety-five Theses
18		Machiavelli, Mandragola Titian, Assumption of Virgin		Vives, Fabula de homine	Erasmus, Colloquia
19	Charles V Emperor Magellan begins circumnavigation (-1522)	Leonardo d.			Hutten, Dialogues

1520		Raphael d.	Josquin des Prés d.	Loyola converted	Luther excommunicated: Babylonish Captivity etc. Melanchthon, Loci communes
21	Conquest of Mexico				
22	Adrian VI Pope, last non-Italian			Complutensian Bible pub. Nebrija d.	Luther, New Testament (German) Reuchlin d.; Zwingli begins reform
23	Clement VII Pope			Vives, Institutio feminae christianae Loyola composes Spiritual Exercises	Hutten d.
24	German Peasants' War				Erasmus, De libero arbitrio
25	Tyndale's Bible Battle of Pavia	Bembo, Prose della volgar lingua Aretino, La Cortegiana			Luther, De servo arbitrio
26		Sannazaro, De partu Virginis		Erasmus, Enchiridion in Spanish	
27	Imperial troops sack Rome	Machiavelli d. Vida, Poeticorum libri tres		A. de Valdés, Diálogo de las cosas ocurridas en Roma	
28		Castiglione, Il Cortegiano		A. de Valdés, Diálogo de Mercurio y Carón	Erasmus, Ciceronianus Dürer d.
29			Budé, Commentarii Linguae Graecae	J. de Valdés, Diálogo de doctrina cristiana Guevara, Marco Aurelio con el Reloj de principes	

	General including British	Italy	France	Spain	Germany and Netherlands
1530		Bembo, *Rime* Sannazaro, *Rime*	Lecteurs royaux (Collège de France) founded		Diet and Confession of Augsburg
31	Henry VIII proclaimed head of Church of England		Marguerite de Navarre, *Miroir de l'âme pecheresse*	Vives, *De Disciplinis*	
32		Ariosto, *Orlando furioso* (definitive ed.)	Marot, *Adolescence clementine* Rabelais, *Pantagruel* R. Estienne, *Thesaurus*	A. de Valdés d.	
33	Conquest of Peru	Ariosto d.	Marot edits Villon	Boscán translates Castiglione's *Cortegiano*	Cranach d.
34	Paul III Pope Jesuits founded Cartier in Canada	Correggio d.	Placards Rabelais, *Gargantua*		Anabaptists seize Münster
35	More executed	Aretino d. Leone Ebreo, *Dialoghi d'amore*		Garcilaso, *Egloga I* J. de Valdés, *Diálogo de la lengua*	Anabaptists destroyed
36	Dissolution of English monasteries begins	Michelangelo begins *Last Judgement*, unveiled 1541	Calvin, *Institutio Christiana* Dolet, *Commentarii Linguae Latinae*	Garcilaso d. J. de Valdés, *Alfabeto cristiano*	Erasmus d. John Secundus d.
37			Des Periers, *Cymbalum Mundi*		
38			Calvin forced to leave Geneva for Strasbourg		Naogeorg, *Pammachius*

					J. Secundus, *Basia* pub.
39			Edict of Villiers-Cotterets makes French legal language	J. de Valdés translates Psalter Guevara, *Epistolas familiares* and *Menosprecio de corte y alabanza de aldea* pub.	
1540	Pope approves Jesuits	Guicciardini, *Storia d'Italia* and d.	*Amadis de Gaule* in French	Mexía, *Silva de varia lección* J. de Valdés, *CX Divine Considerationi* Vives d.	Paracelsus d.
41	Knox begins reform in Scotland Colloquy of Ratisbon	Giraldi, *Orbecche* (first regular Italian tragedy performed on stage)	Calvin returns to Geneva Fr. trans. of *Inst. Chrétienne* Marot, Psalms in French	J. de Valdés d.	
42	Francis Xavier begins mission to Japan	Speroni, *Dialogo delle lingue*; *Canace*		Boscán d.	
43		*Tratato utilissimo del beneficio di Giesù Christo crocifisso*		Vesalius, *De corporis humani fabrica* Boscán–Garcilaso, *Obras*	Holbein d. Copernicus, *De revolutionibus* and d.
44			Scève, *Délie* Marot d.		
45	Council opens at Trent (–1563)	*Rime diverse* published at Venice, first anthology of Italian lyrics	Paré, *Manière de traiter les plaies*	Guevara d.	
46	Christ Church, Oxford and Trinity College, Cambridge, founded		Dolet executed in Paris Rabelais, *Third Book*		Luther d.

	General including British	Italy	France	Spain	Germany and Netherlands
47	Edward VI King Henri II King	Bembo d. Trissino, *L'Italia liberate dai Gotti*			Charles defeats Protestants at Mühlberg
48	Interim of Augsburg concedes married clergy and cup to laity	B. Segni, Italian translation of Aristotle's *Poetics*		Loyola, *Spiritual Exercises* pub.	Interim of Augsburg concedes married clergy and cup to laity
49	First Book of Common Prayer Jesuits in South America Julius III Pope		du Bellay, *Défense* and *Olive* Marguerite de Navarre d.		
1550		Straparola, *Piacevoli notti*	Ronsard, *Odes*; Bèze, *Abraham* Calvin, *Scandales*		Sebastian Münster, *Cosmographia*; Univ. of Louvain pub. *Catalogues des livres reprouvés*
51	*Utopia* in English	Vasari, *Lives of Painters*, I		Mexía d.	
52	Second Book of Common Prayer Xavier d.		Ronsard, *Amours*; Jodelle, *Cléopâtre*; Rabelais, *Fourth Book*	*El Crotalón* written (or 1553)	Treaty of Passau gives Lutherans freedom of worship
53	Mary Queen		Rabelais d. Servetus burnt at Geneva		
54		Bandello, *Novelle* Palestrina's first Masses		Luis de Granada, *Libro de la oración* (first version); *Lazarillo de Tormes*	
55	Paul IV Pope Latimer and Ridley burnt at Oxford		Ronsard, *Hymnes*; Louise Labbé, *Sonnets*	? Laguna writes *Viaje de Turquía*	Sleidan, *History of Charles V's reign* (first contemporary history based on documents) Peace of Augsburg

	History	Italian	French	Spanish	German
56	Charles V abdicates Spain to Philip II, Empire to Ferdinand I Cranmer burnt at Oxford			Luis de Granada, *Guía de pecadores* (first version) Loyola d.	Wickram, *Rollwagenbüchlein; Von Guten und bösen Nachbarn*
57	Portugese settle Macão				Wickram, *Goldaden*
58	Elizabeth Queen Charles V d.		du Bellay, *Regrets*; Des Periers, *Nouvelles Récréations*		
59	Pius IV Pope François II King Peace of Cateau-Cambrésis Valladolid *auto de fe*: Primate of Spain imprisoned by Inquisition		Marguerite de Navarre, *Heptaméron*; Amyot, *Plutarch* in French Calvinist Synod in Paris	Montemayor, *Diana* Valdés's Index of Prohibited Books Laguna d.	
1560	Charles IX King	B. Tasso, *Amadigi*	Grévin, *Jules Cesar* du Bellay d.		
61		J. C. Scaliger, *Poetics* Guicciardini, *Storia* pub.	Grévin, *Les Esbahis*		
62	Maximilian II Emperor Hawkins starts slave trade Sackville and Norton, *Gorboduc* (first English blank-verse tragedy)		Wars of Religion begin (-1594)	St Teresa, *Libro de la vida*	
63	Foxe, *Book of Martyrs* Council of Trent closes				

				'El Brocense', Commentary on Garcilaso	Fischart, Geschichtklitterung
74	Henri III King	Tasso, Gerusalemme liberata finished		'El Brocense', Commentary on Garcilaso	Fischart, Geschichtklitterung
75					Spaniards sack Antwerp Hans Sachs d.
76	Rudolf II Emperor Drake circumnavigates world	Titian d.	Bodin, Republique Belleau, Amours		
77			d'Aubigné begins Tragiques	St Teresa, Moradas del castillo interior	
78	Sebastian of Portugal defeated and killed at Alcazar Kebir		Ronsard, Sonnets pour Hélène; du Bartas, Semaine	St John of the Cross, composes most of Cántico espiritual Ercilla, La Araucaria (Pt II) Aldana d.	
79	North, Plutarch in English		Garnier, Troade		
1580		Teatro Olimpico begun, Vicenza	Montaigne, Essais, I and II	Camões d. Herrera, Anotaciones a Garcilaso	
81		Tasso, Gerusalemme liberata pub.			
82	Edinburgh University founded Gregorian Calendar introduced 4–15 October	Bruno, Il Candelaio Accademia della Crusca founded	Garnier, Bradamante	St Teresa d. Herrera, Algunas Obras Luis de León, De los nombres de Cristo and La perfecta casada	

	General including British	Italy	France	Spain	Germany and Netherlands
83			Garnier, Les Juives		
84	Raleigh discovers Virginia	Bruno, La Cena		St John of the Cross, Subida del Monte Carmelo and 'Llama de amor viva' now completed	
85	Sixtus V Pope	Guarini, Pastor Fido Bruno, Eroici Furori	Ronsard d.	Cervantes, Galatea	
86	Mary Queen of Scots executed Marlowe, Tamburlaine			El Greco, Burial of Count Orgaz	Dr Faust (Volksbuch)
87	Defeat of Armada		Barricades in Paris Montaigne, Essais, III	Luis de Granada d. St Teresa, Works pub. Malón de Chaide, Conversión de la Magdalena	
88		Veronese d.			
89	Catherine de' Medici d. Henri IV King Marlowe, Faustus				
1590	Urban VII Pope (15–27 Sept.) Gregory XIV Pope Sidney, Arcadia; Spenser, Faerie Queene			Ercilla, La Araucana (Pt III)	Rollenhagen, Spiel vom reichen Manne

91	Innocent IX Pope Shakespeare *Henry VI*			St John of the Cross d. Luis de León d.	
92	Clement VIII Pope		Montaigne d.		
93	Marlowe d.	Palestrina d.	Henri IV converted		
94			*Satire Ménippée* Henri IV enters Paris, Wars of Religion end	Ercilla d.	Heinrich Julius von Braunschweig, *Vincentius Ladislaus*
95	Shakespeare, *Romeo and Juliet, MND*	Tasso d.			Rollenhagen, *Froschmeuseler*
96				López Pinciano, *Philosophia antigua poética*	Kepler, *De Admirabili Proportione Coelestium Orbium*
97	Shakespeare, *Richard II, Merchant of Venice*	First opera performed: *Dafne* by Peri and Rinuccini		Herrera d.	St Peter Canisius d.
98	Philip III King		Edict of Nantes		
99	Shakespeare, *Julius Caesar*			Alemán, *Guzmán de Alfarache* (Pt I)	Marnix d.
1600	Shakespeare, *Henry V, As You Like It, Much Ado*	Bruno burnt at Rome			Marnix, *Tableau des différends*

Bibliographies

Bibliography 1

Works of reference and standard bibliographies.

General

Cassell's Encyclopaedia of Literature, 2 vols., London, 1953.
New Cambridge Modern History, Cambridge, 1957–8, Vols. I–II.
Oxford Dictionary of the Christian Church, Oxford, 1958.
Penguin Companion to Literature, Vol. 2, *European*, Harmondsworth, 1969.

France

Oxford Companion to French Literature, Oxford, 1959.
A. Cioranesco, *Bibliographie de la littérature française du XVIe siècle*, Paris, 1959.
A Critical Bibliography of French Literature, Vol. 2, *Sixteenth century*, ed. Cabeen, Syracuse, New York, 1956.
L. Febvre, *Le Problème de l'incroyance au XVIe siècle. La Religion de Rabelais*, Paris, 1947 (massive bibliography for history of ideas).
A. Renaudet, *Préréforme et Humanisme à Paris*, 2nd ed., Paris, 1953 (valuable humanist bibliography).

Germany

K. Goedeke, *Grundriss zur Geschichte des deutschen Dichtung*, especially Vol. II, Dresden, 1886.
P. Merker and W. Stammler, *Reallexikon der deutschen Literatur-Geschichte*, new ed., Berlin 1955– .
J. G. Boeckh, *Geschichte der deutschen Literatur von 1480 bis 1600*, Berlin, 1960.
W. A. Coupe, *A Sixteenth-Century German Reader*, Oxford, 1971 (contains selection of representative writers and movements, with glossary, notes and introduction).

Bibliographies

R. Pascal, *German Literature in the Sixteenth and Seventeenth Centuries*, London, 1968.

W. Stammler, *Von der Mystik zum Barock*, 2nd ed., Berlin, 1950.

Italy

Dizionario enciclopedico della letteratura italiana, ed. G. Petronio, 5 vols., Bari–Rome, 1966–8.

Storia della letteratura italiana, ed. E. Cecchi and N. Sapegno, Vol. IV, *Il Cinquecento*, Milan, 1966.

G. Toffanin, *Il Cinquecento*, 5th ed., Milan, 1965.

For individual authors and bibliographies see: *La letteratura italiana. I Maggiori*, Vol. I, Milan, 1956 and *La letteratura italiana. I Minori*, Vols. I–II, Milan, 1961.

Spain

E. Arnaud and V. Tusón, *Guide de bibliographie hispanique*, Toulouse, 1967.

J. Simón Díaz, *Bibliografía de la literatura hispánica*, Madrid, 1950– .

G. Bleiberg and J. Marías, *Diccionario de literatura española*, 3rd ed., Madrid, 1964.

M. Bataillon, *Erasmo y España. Estudios sobre la historia espiritual del siglo XVI*, Mexico, 1966. (Second Spanish edition, corrected and extended, of original French *Erasme et l'Espagne*, Paris, 1937.) Fundamental for an understanding of sixteenth-century Spanish writing. Very extensive bibliography.

G. Díaz Plaja (ed.), *Antología mayor de la literatura española*, 4 vols., Barcelona, 1958–62, Vol. II, *Renacimiento*.

G. Díaz Plaja (ed.), *Historia general de las literaturas hispánicas*, 6 vols., Barcelona, 1949–67, Vols. II–III (extensive bibliographical information).

P. E. Russell (ed.), *Spain. A Companion to Spanish Studies*, London, 1971.

Bibliography 2

These suggestions for further reading refer primarily to the chapters on the cultural and historical background; only books in English, and readily available, if possible in paperback editions, are listed. Many of them have useful bibliographies.

J. W. Allen, *A History of Political Thought in the XVIth Century*, London, 1960.

R. Bainton, *Here I Stand; A Life of Martin Luther*, London, 1952.

R. R. Bolgar, *The Classical Heritage and Its Beneficiaries*, Cambridge, 1954.

C. M. Bowra, *From Virgil to Milton*, London, 1945.

K. Brandi, *The Emperor Charles V*, London, 1939.

J. Burckhardt, *The Civilisation of the Renaissance in Italy*, London, 1965.

P. Burke, *The Renaissance*, London, 1964.

E. Cassirer and others, *The Renaissance Philosophy of Man*, Chicago, 1948.

A. Chastel, *The Age of Humanism, 1480–1530*, London, 1963.

J. Cruickshank (ed.), *French Literature and Its Background*, Vol. I, *The Sixteenth Century*, Oxford, 1968.

A. G. Dickens, *Reformation and Society in Sixteenth-Century Europe*, London, 1966.

A. G. Dickens, *The Counter-Reformation*, London, 1968.

S. Dresden, *Humanism in the Renaissance*, London, 1968.

J. H. Elliott, *Europe Divided: 1559–1598* (Fontana History of Europe), London, 1968.

W. K. Ferguson, *The Renaissance in Historical Thought*, Boston, 1948.

W. K. Ferguson and others, *The Renaissance: Six Essays*, New York, 1962.

M. P. Gilmore, *The World of Humanism*, New York, 1962.

D. Hay, *The Italian Renaissance in Its Historical Background*, Cambridge, 1966.

D. Hay (ed.), *The Age of the Renaissance*, London, 1967.

T. Helton (ed.), *The Renaissance: A Reconsideration of the Theories and Interpretations of the Age*, Madison, Wisconsin, 1964.

Bibliographies

C. H. Herford, *Studies in Literary Relations of England and Germany in the Sixteenth Century*, London, 1966.

J. H. Hexter, *Reappraisals in History*, London, 1961.

G. Highet, *The Classical Tradition*, New York, 1957.

J. Huizinga, *The Waning of the Middle Ages*, London, 1968.

J. Huizinga, *Men and Ideas*, London, 1959.

M. D. Knowles, *The Religious Orders in England*, Vol. III, Cambridge, 1959.

H. G. Koenigsberger and G. L. Mosse, *Europe in the Sixteenth Century*, London, 1968.

P. O. Kristeller, *Renaissance Thought*, New York, 1961.

P. O. Kristeller, *Studies in Renaissance Thought and Letters*, Rome, 1956.

P. Laven, *Renaissance Italy 1464–1534*, London, 1966.

J. Lynch, *Spain under the Habsburgs*, Vol. I, Oxford, 1965.

J. T. McNeill, *The History and Character of Calvinism*, New York, 1954.

G. Mattingly, *Renaissance Diplomacy*, Penguin Books, Harmondsworth, 1965.

G. Mattingly, *The Defeat of the Spanish Armada*, Penguin Books, Harmondsworth, 1959.

J. A. Mazzeo, *Renaissance and Revolution*, London, 1969.

J. E. Neale, *The Age of Catherine de Medici*, London, 1963.

F. C. Nelson, *Renaissance Theory of Love*, New York, 1958.

E. Panofsky, *Renaissance and Renascences in Western Art*, London, 1970.

J. H. Parry, *The Age of Reconnaissance*, London, 1963.

B. Penrose, *Travel and Discovery in the Renaissance*, New York, 1962.

J. H. Plumb, *The Penguin Book of the Renaissance*, Harmondsworth, 1964.

R. H. Popkin, *The History of Scepticism from Erasmus to Descartes*, Assen, 1960.

E. F. Rice, *The Renaissance Idea of Wisdom*, Cambridge, Massachusetts, 1958.

N. A. Robb, *Neoplatonism of the Italian Renaissance*, London, 1969.

J. Sparrow, 'Latin Verse of the High Renaissance', in E. F. Jacob (ed.), *Italian Renaissance Studies*, London, 1960.

L. W. Spitz, *The Religious Renaissance of the German Humanist*, London, 1963.

C. Trinkaus, *In Our Image and Likeness . . . Italian Humanist Thought*, 2 vols., London, 1970.

D. Weinstein, *The Renaissance and the Reformation, 1400–1600*, New York, 1965.

R. Weiss, *The Spread of Italian Humanism*, London, 1964.

J. S. Whale, *The Protestant Tradition*, Cambridge, 1959.

J. H. Whitfield, *A Short History of Italian Literature*, Penguin Books, Harmondsworth, 1969.

W. P. Wightman, *Science and the Renaissance*, Aberdeen, 1962.

E. H. Wilkins, *A History of Italian Literature*, London, 1954.

E. Wind, *Pagan Mysteries in the Renaissance*, Penguin Books, Harmondsworth, 1967.

W. H. Woodward, *Studies in Education during the Age of the Renaissance, 1400–1600*, Aberdeen, 1962.

F. A. Yates, *French Academies of the Sixteenth Century*, London, 1946.

Fine Arts

O. Benesch, *The Art of the Renaissance in Northern Europe*, London, 1966.

B. Berenson, *Italian Painters of the Renaissance*, 2 vols., London, 1968.

A. Blunt, *Art and Architecture in France, 1500–1700*, Penguin Books, Harmondsworth, 1953.

A. Blunt, *Artistic Theory in Italy, 1450–1600*, Oxford, 1962.

A. Chastel, *Italian Art*, London, 1963.

A. Einstein, *A Short History of Music*, New York, 1965.

L. D. Ettlinger, 'The North Transformed: Art and Artists in Northern Europe', in D. Hay (ed.), *The Age of The Renaissance*, London, 1967.

S. J. Freedberg, *Painting of the High Renaissance . . .*, 2 vols., Cambridge, Massachusetts, 1961.

E. H. Gombrich, *The Story of Art*, London, 1967.

C. Gould, *An Introduction to Italian Renaissance Painting*, London, 1957.

D. J. Grout, *A History of Western Music*, London, 1962.

Grove's Dictionary of Music and Musicians, ed. E. Blom, 5th ed., 10 vols., London, 1954–61.

A. Hauser, *The Social History of Art*, Vol. II, New York, 1959.

E. G. Holt, *A Documentary History of Art*, 2 vols., New York, 1957–8.

R. Klein and H. Zerner, *Italian Art, 1500–1600*, New Jersey, 1966.

G. Kubler and M. Soria, *Art and Architecture in Spain and Portugal and their American Dominions: 1500–1800*, Penguin Books, Harmondsworth, 1959.

P. H. Lang, *Music in Western Civilisation*, London, 1963.

E. Lowinsky, 'Music in the Culture of the Renaissance', *Journal of the History of Ideas*, XV, 1954.

G. Masson, *Italian Villas and Palaces*, London, 1959.

L. Murray, *The High Renaissance*, London, 1967.

Bibliographies

L. Murray, *The Late Renaissance and Mannerism*, London, 1967.

P. Murray, *The Architecture of the Italian Renaissance*, London, 1969.

P. Murray and L. Murray, *The Art of the Renaissance*, London, 1963.

New Oxford History of Music, Vols. III–IV, Oxford, 1968–9.

J. Pope-Hennessy, *Italian High Renaissance and Baroque Sculpture*, 3 vols., London, 1963.

G. Reese, *Music in the Renaissance*, London, 1954.

A. Robertson and D. Stevens, *A History of Music*, Vol. II, *Renaissance and Baroque*, London, 1965.

J. Shearman, *Mannerism*, Penguin Books, Harmondsworth, 1967.

W. Stechow, *Northern Renaissance Art, 1400–1600*, New Jersey, 1966.

L. Venturi, *History of Art Criticism*, New York, 1964.

R. Wittkower, *Architectural Principles in the Age of Humanism*, 3rd ed., London, 1962.

H. Wölfflin, *Classic Art. An Introduction to the Italian Renaissance*, 3rd ed., London, 1968.

H. Wölfflin, *Renaissance and Baroque*, London, 1964.

For monographs on individual artists, see: P. and L. Murray, *Dictionary of Art and Artists*, revised ed., Penguin Books, Harmondsworth, 1968; J. Fleming, H. Honour, N. Pevsner, *The Penguin Dictionary of Architecture*, Penguin Books, Harmondsworth, 1966.

Bibliography 3

Texts

The editions given are normally those referred to in the text. In general, recent available editions have been given rather than the bulkier authoritative library editions, and where accessible English translations exist these have been listed. Apart from a number of general works on criticism, monographs and critical studies have been omitted, with a few special exceptions, as the discrepancies between the different literatures discussed is very great and in any case full bibliographies will be found in the books indicated in the first section of this Bibliography.

PART ONE

2.

Italy

C. S. Baldwin, *Renaissance Literary Theory and Practice*, New York, 1939.

R. A. Hall Jr, *The Italian Questione della Lingua*, Chapel Hill, 1942.

V. Hall Jr, *Renaissance Literary Criticism*, New York, 1945.

B. Hathaway, *The Age of Criticism. The late Renaissance in Italy*, Ithaca, New York, 1962.

B. Migliorini, *The Italian Language*, London, 1966.

G. Saintsbury, *A History of Criticism*, 6th ed., Vol. II, London, 1949.

J. E. Spingarn, *Literary Criticism in the Renaissance*, New York, 1963.

B. Weinberg, *A History of Literary Criticism in the Italian Renaissance*, 2 vols., Chicago, 1961.

There is a useful selection of texts in translation in A. Gilbert, *Literary Criticism: Plato to Dryden*, New York, 1940.

Texts:

P. Bembo, *Prose e rime*, 2nd ed., Turin, 1966.

G. Bruno, *De gli eroici furori*, in *Opere di G. B. e di Tommaso Campanella*, Milan-Naples, 1961; tr. P. E. Memmo, Chapel Hill, North Carolina, 1964.

L. Castelvetro, *Poetica*, Vienna, 1570; reprinted Munich 1967.

B. Castiglione, *Il libro del Cortegiano*, Florence, 1947; tr. G. Bull, Penguin Classics, Harmondsworth, 1967.

G. De Nores: see B. Guarini, *Opere*, Verona, 1737.

G. B. Giraldi, *Scritti estetici*, 2 vols., Milan, 1864.

G. Guarini, *Opere*, Verona, 1737.

N. Machiavelli, 'Discorso o dialogo intorno alla nostra lingua', in *Opere*, Vol. VIII, Milan, 1965; tr. J. R. Hale, *Machiavelli's Literary Works*, Oxford, 1961.

Minturno (A. Sebastiani), *De poeta*, Venice, 1559.

Minturno (A. Sebastiani), *Arte poetica thoscana*, Venice, 1563.

F. Robortello, *Poetica*, Florence, 1548.

J. C. Scaliger, *Poetices libri septem*, Lyon, 1561; reprinted Stuttgart, 1964.

A. Segni, *Ragionamento . . .* , Florence, 1581.

Sperone Speroni, *Dialogo delle lingue*, Lanciano, 1912.

Sperone Speroni, *Opere*, Venice, 1740.

T. Tasso, *Discorsi dell'arte poetica e del poema eroico*, Bari, 1964.

T. Tasso, *Apologia*, in *Opere*, ed. B. Maier, Vol. V, Milan, 1965.

G. Trissino, *Il Castellano*, Milan, 1864.

G. Trissino, transl. of Dante's *De Vulgari Eloquentia* is reprinted in D. Alighieri, *Opere*, ed. F. Chiappelli, Milan, 1965.

M. G. Vida, *Poemata omnia*, Padua, 1731.

France

J. du Bellay, *Deffence et Illustration de la langue françoyse*, ed. H. Chamard, Paris, 1948.

H. Estienne, *De la Precellence du langage françoys*, ed. E. Huguet, Paris, 1896.

J. de La Taille, *L'Art de la tragédie*, ed. F. West, Manchester, 1939.

J. Peletier du Mans, *Art poétique*, ed. A. Boulanger, Paris, 1930.

P. de Ronsard, *Abrégé de l'art poétique françoys*, in *Œuvres*, ed. G. Cohen, Pléiade, Paris, 1950.

T. Sébillet, *Art poétique*, ed. F. Gaiffe, Paris, 1932.

See also:

G. Castor, *Pléiade Poetics*, Cambridge, 1964.

Spain

F. de Herrera, *Anotaciones a Garcilaso*, in *Garcilaso de la Vega y sus comentaristas*, ed. A. Gallego Morell, Granada, 1966.

Bibliographies

R. Lapesa, *Historia de la lengua española*, 4th ed., Madrid, 1959.

A. López Pinciano, *Philosophía antigua poética*, ed. A. Carballo Picazo, 3 vols., Madrid, 1953.

J. de Valdés, *Diálogo de la lengua*, ed. J. F. Montesinos, Clásicos Castellanos, Vol. 86, Madrid, 1953; extracts with useful annotation by R. Lapesa, Biblioteca Clásica Ebro, Zaragoza, 1960.

A. Vilanova, *Historia general de las literaturas hispánicas*, Barcelona, 1949–67, Vol. 3 (survey chapter).

PART TWO

1.
Italy

L. Ariosto, *Orlando furioso*, Bologna, 1960; tr. A. Gilbert, 2 vols., New York, 1954.

T. Tasso, *Gerusalemme liberata*, in *Opere*, ed. B. Maier, Vol. I, Milan, 1963; tr. E. Fairfax, London, 1962.

The third volume of Antonelli's *Parnaso italiano*, Venice, 1835, contains: Alamanni, *Girone il cortese*, B. Tasso, *Amadigi*, and Trissino, *L'Italia liberata* . . . . Other works mentioned are only available in sixteenth-century editions.

Spain and Portugal

L. de Camões, *Os Lusíadas*, in *Obra completa*, ed. A. Salgado Júnior, Aguilar, Rio de Janeiro, 1963; *The Lusiads*, tr. Sir Richard Fanshawe (1655), ed. G. Bullough, London, 1963; also *The Lusiads*, tr. W. C. Atkinson, Penguin Classics, Harmondsworth, 1952.

A. de Ercilla, *La Araucana*, ed. C. de Salamanca, Madrid, 1968; tr. G. Carew, *The Historie of Araucana*, transcribed with introduction and notes by F. Pierce, Manchester, 1964.

2.
Italy

A good anthology is L. Baldacci, *Lirici del Cinquecento*, Florence, 1957; see also D. Ponchiroli, *Lirici del Cinquecento*, Turin, 1958, and G. Spagnoletti, *Il petrarchismo*, Milan, 1959.

T. d'Aragòna, *Le rime*, Bologna, 1891.

T. d'Aragona, *Dell'infinità dell'amore*, in *Trattati d'amore del Cinquecento*, ed. G. Zonta, Bari, 1912.

L. Ariosto, *Opere minori*, Milan–Naples, 1954.

P. Bembo, *Prose e rime*, 2nd ed., Turin, 1966.

F. Berni, *Poesie e prose*, Geneva–Florence, 1934.

Michelangelo Buonarroti, *Rime*, Bari, 1961; some translations in *Penguin Book of Italian Verse*, Harmondsworth, 1958.

B. Castiglione and G. Della Casa, *Opere*, Milan, 1937.

V. Colonna, *Rime e lettere*, Florence, 1860.

G. Cotta, *Latina carmina*, Verona, 1798.

G. Della Casa: see B. Castiglione and G. Della Casa, *Opere*, Milan, 1937.

T. Folengo, *Le 'Maccheronee' di Merlin Cocai*, 2nd ed., 2 vols., Bari, 1927–8.

G. Fracastoro, *Opera omnia*, Venice, 1555; *Naugerius*, tr. R. Kilso, Urbana, 1924.

V. Franco and G. Stampa, *Rime*, Bari, 1913.

V. Gambara, *Rime e lettere*, Florence, 1879.

C. Matraini, *Rime e prose*, Lucca, 1555.

I. Morra, *Canzoniere*, Matera, 1961.

A. Navagero, *Opera omnia*, Padua, 1718.

J. Sannazaro, *Opere volgari*, Bari, 1961.

J. Sannazaro, *Arcadia and Piscatorial Eclogues*, Detroit, 1966.

G. Stampa and V. Franco, *Rime*, Bari, 1913.

T. Tasso, *Opere*, ed. B. Maier, Vols. I–II, Milan, 1963–4.

M. Vida, *De arte poetica*, Oxford, 1722; tr. C. Pitt, in A. S. Cook, *The Art of Poetry*, Boston, 1892.

France

A. M. Schmidt (ed.), *Poètes du XVIe siècle*, Pléiade, Paris, 1953 is an excellent anthology of all the main lyric poets, except Ronsard and d'Aubigné, and contains notably a full selection from Belleau, Pernette du Guillet and Louise Labbé.

R. Belleau, *Les Bergeries*, ed. D. Lacourcelle, Geneva, 1954. See *Poètes du XVIe siècle*, above.

P. Desportes, *Amours*, ed. V. Graham, 7 vols., Geneva, 1958–63.

J. du Bellay, *Œuvres*, ed. H. Chamard, 6 vols., Paris, 1907–31.

J. du Bellay, *Les Regrets* and *Les Antiquitez* have been frequently re-edited, most recently by M. A. Screech, Geneva, 1965.

Pernette du Guillet, *Rimes* in *Poètes du XVIe siècle*, above.

Louise Labbé, *Œuvres*, ed. B. Jourdan, Paris, 1953. See *Poètes du XVIe siècle*, above.

C. Marot, *Œuvres*, ed. C. A. Mayer, London, 1958– .

C. Marot, *Les Psaumes*, ed. S. J. Lenselink, Assen, 1968.

P. de Ronsard, *Œuvres*, ed. G. Cohen, 2 vols., Pléiade, Paris, 1950.

M. Scève, *Œuvres*, ed. B. Guégan, Paris, 1927.

M. Scève, *Délie*, ed. I. D. McFarlane, Cambridge, 1966.

John Secundus (Jean Second), *The Love Poems* (Latin text with English version), ed. F. A. Wright, London, 1930.

John Secundus, *Les Baisers* . . . (Latin text with French version), ed. M. Rat, Paris, 1938.

Spain

A. Terry (ed.), *An Anthology of Spanish Poetry, 1500–1700* (Part I: 1500–1580, Part II: 1580–1700), Oxford, 1965, 1968. This provides an excellent survey of sixteenth-century Spanish poetry together with valuable introductory material.

J. Boscán, *Obras poéticas*, ed. M. de Riquer, A. Comas and J. Molas, Barcelona, 1957.

G. de Cetina, *Obras*, ed. J. Hazañas y la Rúa, 2 vols., Sevilla, 1895.

Garcilaso de la Vega, *Obras*, ed. T. Navarro Tomás. Clásicos Castellanos, Vol. 3, 4th ed., Madrid, 1966. A textually superior ed., with sixteenth-century spelling, is that of E. L. Rivers, Madrid, 1964; paperback ed., Madrid, 1969.

L. de Góngora, *Obras completas*, ed. J. and I. Millé y Jiménez, Madrid, 1962 (reprint). (A valuable annotated anthology of Góngora's verse is found in Vol. 1 of D. Alonso, *Góngora y el 'Polifemo'*, 5th ed., 3 vols., Madrid, 1967.

F. de Herrera, *Poesías*, ed. V. García de Diego, Clásicos Castellanos, Vol. 26, Madrid, 1962 (reprint).

F. de la Torre, *Poesías*, ed. A. Zamora Vicente, Clásicos Castellanos, Vol. 124, Madrid, 1956 (reprint).

3.
Italy

G. Bruno, *Dialoghi italiani*, 3 vols., Bari, 1923–7.

G. Bruno, *Opere latine* . . ., ed. naz., 3 vols., 1880–91; also a critical edition in progress, by G. Aquilecchia.

T. Campanella, *Opere di Giordano Bruno e di Tommaso Campanella*, Milan–Naples, 1956.

T. Campanella, *La città del Sole e scelte di poesie filosofiche*, Milan, 1963; also critical edition in progress, by L. Firpo.

Palingenius (P. A. Manzolli), *Zodiacus vitae*, Amsterdam, 1722.

J. Sannazaro, *De partu virginis*, Naples, 1948.

Bibliographies

L. Tansillo, *Le lagrime di San Pietro*, Venice, 1738.

T. Tasso, *Il mondo creato*, in *Opere*, ed. B. Maier, Vol. IV, Milan, 1964.

M. Vida, *Poemata omnia*, Padua, 1731.

France

T. C. Cave, *Devotional Poetry in France*, Cambridge, 1969, is an in-dispensable introduction to a considerable and still imperfectly known body of verse which has been omitted completely from this volume rather than given cursory treatment.

A. d'Aubigné, *Œuvres*, ed. H. Weber, Pléiade, Paris, 1969.

G. du Bartas, *Works*, ed. U. T. Holmes, 3 vols., Chapel Hill, 1935–40.

Marguerite de Navarre, *Les Marguerites de la Marguerite des Princesses*, ed. F. Frank, 4 vols., Paris, 1873.

Marguerite de Navarre, *Dernières Poésies*, ed. A. Lefranc, Paris, 1896.

Marguerite de Navarre, *La Navire*, ed. R. Marichal, Paris, 1956.

M. Scève, *Le Microcosme*, ed. Valéry Larbaud, Paris, 1928.

Spain

A. Terry (ed.), *An Anthology of Spanish Poetry, 1500–1700*, see above, p. 553.

F. de Aldana, *Poesías*, ed. E. L. Rivers, Clásicos Castellanos, Vol. 143, Madrid, 1957.

John of the Cross, St, *Vida y obras completas de San Juan de la Cruz*, ed. Matías del Niño Jesús, O.C.D. and Lucinio del SS. Sacramento, O.C.D., Biblioteca de autores cristianos, Vol. 15, 4th ed., Madrid, 1960.

John of the Cross, St, *Complete Works of St John of the Cross*, tr. E. A. Peers, 3 vols., 2nd ed., reprint London, 1964; further translation by K. Kavanaugh, O.C.D. and O. Rodríguez, O.C.D., London, 1966.

Luis de León, *Poesías*, ed. A. C. Vega, O.S.A., Madrid, 1955; see also the more readily accessible *Fray Luis de León. The Original Poems*, ed. E. Sarmiento, Manchester, 1953 (the text of this edition is inferior to that of Vega's).

PART THREE

1.
Tragedy

M. T. Herrick, *Italian Tragedy in the Renaissance*, Urbana, 1965. (This, like the similar volumes on Comedy and Pastoral, contains synopses of the main plays.)

An anthology of texts in: F. Doglio, *Il teatro tragico italiano*, Parma, 1960; also, *Teatro italiano antico*, Milan, 1808–12.

P. Aretino, *Teatro*, 2 vols., Lanciano, 1914.

G. B. Giraldi, *Tragedie*, Venice, 1583.

S. Speroni, *Opere*, Venice, 1740.

T. Tasso, *Torrismondo*, in *Opere*, ed. B. Maier, Vol. II, Milan, 1964.

G. G. Trissino, *Opere*, Verona, 1729.

Comedy

M. T. Herrick, *Italian Comedy in the Renaissance*, Urbana, 1960.
Anthologies:
   I. Sanesi, *Commedie del Cinquecento*, 2 vols., Bari, 1912.
   A. Borlenghi, *Commedie del Cinquecento*, 2 vols., Milan, 1959.
   N. Borsellino, *Commedie del Cinquecento*, 2 vols., Milan, 1967.

P. Aretino, *Teatro*, 2 vols., Lanciano, 1914.

L. Ariosto, *Opere minori*, Milan–Naples, 1954.

A. Beolco (Ruzante), *Teatro*, Turin, 1967.

G. Bruno, *Il Candelaio*: see Borsellino, above; tr. in E. Bentley, *The Genius of the Italian Theatre*, London, 1965.

B. Dovizi ('Il Bibbiena'): see Sanesi and Borlenghi, anthologies quoted; tr. in E. Bentley, *The Genius of The Italian Theatre*, London, 1965.

A. Grazzini ('Il Lasca'), *Le commedie*, Bari, 1953.

N. Machiavelli, *Opere*, Vol. VIII, *Il teatro . . .*, Milan, 1965; tr. in J. R. Hale, *Machiavelli's Literary Works*, Oxford, 1961.

Pastoral

M. T. Herrick, *Tragicomedy*, Urbana, 1961.

A. De' Beccari, *Sacrificio*, Ferrara, 1555.

B. Guarini, *Il pastor fido e il Compendio della poesia tragicomica*, Bari, 1914.

T. Tasso, *Opere*, ed. B. Maier, Vol. I, Milan, 1963.

T. Tasso, *Amyntas*, tr. in E. Bentley, *The Genius of the Italian Theatre*, London, 1965.

2.

The only convenient anthology is D. Stone (ed.), *Four Renaissance Tragedies*, Harvard, 1966, containing Buchanan, *Jephté*, Bèze, *Abraham*, Jodelle, *Didon*, and la Taille, *Saul*.

B. K. Jeffery, *Renaissance Comedy*, Oxford, 1970, is far the best treatment of the subject in English and contains synopses of ten of the best comedies of the century.

T. de Bèze, *Abraham sacrifiant*, ed. K. Cameron and others, Geneva, 1967; see also above.

G. Buchanan, *Jephté*, see above.

R. Garnier, *Œuvres*, ed. L. Pinvert, Paris, 1923; and ed. R. Lebègue, 3 vols., Paris, 1949–52.

J. Grévin, *Théâtre*, ed. L. Pinvert, Paris, 1922.

E. Jodelle, *Œuvres*, ed. H. Balmas, 2 vols., Paris, 1964.

Marguerite de Navarre, *Théâtre profane*, ed. V. L. Saulnier, Geneva, 1946.

A. Montchrestien, *Tragédies*, ed. Petit de Julleville, Paris, 1891.

3.

H. J. Chaytor, *Dramatic Theory in Spain. Extracts . . .* , Cambridge, 1925.

A. Hermenegildo, *Los trágicos españoles del siglo XVI*, Madrid, 1961.

N. D. Shergold, *History of the Spanish Stage from Medieval Times until the end of the Seventeenth Century*, Oxford, 1967.

J. P. Wickersham Crawford, *Spanish Drama before Lope de Vega*, revised ed. with bibliographical supplement by W. T. McCready, Philadelphia, 1967. The most convenient survey of the subject.

J. de la Cueva, *Comedias y tragedias*, ed. F. A. de Icaza, 2 vols., Madrid, 1917.

J. de la Cueva, *El Infamador, Los Siete Infantes de Lara, y el Ejemplar poético*, ed. F. A. de Icaza, Clásicos Castellanos, Vol. 60, Madrid, 1965 (reprint).

L. de Rueda, *Obras*, ed. E. Cotarelo, 2 vols., Madrid, 1908.

L. de Rueda, *Obras*, ed. J. Moreno Villa, Clásicos Castellanos, Vol. 59, 2nd ed., Madrid, 1958, contains *Comedia Eufemia*, *Comedia Armelina* and *El Deleitoso* (7 pasos).

L. de Rueda, *Pasos completos*, ed. F. García Pavón, Madrid, 1966.

B. de Torres Naharro, *Propalladia and Other Works*, ed. J. E. Gillet, Pennsylvania, 1943–61, 4 vols.

B. de Torres Naharro, *Tres comedias: Soldadesca, Ymenea, Aquilana*, ed. H. López Morales, New York, 1965.

4.

N. Frischlin, *Julius redivivus*, ed. W. Janell, Berlin, 1912.

N. Frischlin, *Frau Wendelgart*, ed. P. Rothweiler, Tübingen, 1912.

N. Frischlin, *Deutsche Dichtungen*, ed. D. F. Strauss, BlV,★ 1857.

P. Gengenbach, *Werke*, ed. K. Goedeke, Hanover, 1856; reprint Amsterdam, 1966.

Heinrich Julius von Braunschweig, *Schauspiele*, ed. W. L. Holland, BlV, 1855.

Heinrich Julius von Braunschweig, *Selection*, ed. W. Flemming, DLER,† 1931.

N. Manuel, *Sämtliche Dichtungen*, ed. J. Bächtold, *Bibliothek älterer Schriftsteller der deutschen Schweiz*, 1878.

N. Manuel, *Vom Papst und seiner Priesterschaft*, ed. A. Berger, DLER, Reformation, 5.

N. Manuel, *Der Ablasskrämer*, ed. P. Zinsli, Zurich, 1960.

T. Naogeorg, *Pammachius*, ed. J. Bolte, Berlin, 1891; German translation, ed. R. Froning, DNL‡ 22, 1894.

G. Rollenhagen, *Froschmeuseler*, ed. K. Goedeke, Hanover, 1872.

G. Rollenhagen, *Spiel vom reichen Mann und vom armen Lazaro*, ed. J. Bolte, NDL 270–73, 1929.

G. Rollenhagen, *Spiel vom Tobias*, ed. J. Bolte, NDL§ 285–7, 1930.

B. Waldis, *De Parabell vam verlorn Szohn*, ed. H. Berger, DLER, Reformation, 5.

PART FOUR

1.

P. Jourda (ed.), *Conteurs du XVIe siècle*, Pléiade, Paris, 1966, contains the complete texts of Marguerite de Navarre, *Heptaméron*, Des Periers, *Nouvelles Récréations et Joyeux Devis* and du Fail, *Propos rustiques* and *Baliverneries*, as well as tales by other authors.

A. J. Krailsheimer (ed.), *Three Sixteenth-Century Conteurs*, Oxford, 1966, contains a good sample of tales from the above works with notes and introductions in English.

Marguerite de Navarre, *L'Heptaméron*, ed. M. François, Paris, 1943.

F. Rabelais, *Œuvres*, ed. J. Boulenger, Pléiade, Paris, revised 1955; ed. P. Jourda, 2 vols., Paris, 1962; *Gargantua and Pantagruel*, tr. J. M. Cohen, Penguin Classics, Harmondsworth, 1955.

2.

A good anthology is G. B. Salinari, *Novelle del Cinquecento*, 2 vols., Turin, 1955.

★BlV: Bibliothek des literarischen Vereins.
†DLER: Deutsche Literatur in Entwicklungsreihen.
‡DNL: Deutsche Nationalliteratur.
§NDL: Neudrucke deutscher Literaturwerke des 16 und 17 Jahrhunderts.

M. Bandello, *Tutte le opere*, 3rd ed., 2 vols., Milan, 1952.

A. Firenzuola, *Opere*, Florence, 1958.

G. C. Giraldi, *Gli Ecatommiti*, Turin, 1879.

A. F. Grazzini ('Il Lasca'), *Le Cene*, Milan, 1945.

G. F. Straparola, *Le piacevoli notti*, 2 vols., Bari, 1927.

Hieronymus Morlini, *Novellae, Fabulae, Comoedia*, 3rd ed., Paris, 1855.

N. Machiavelli, *Belfagor*, in *Opere*, Vol. VIII, Milan, 1965; tr. in J. R. Hale, *Machiavelli's Literary Works*, Oxford, 1961.

3.

M. Alemán, *Guzmán de Alfarache*, ed. S. Gili y Gaya, Clásicos Castellanos, Vols. 73, 83, 90, 93, 114, Madrid, 1926–36, with reprints.

M. Alemán, *The Rogue, or the Life of Guzman de Alfarache . . . done into English by James Mabbe anno 1623*, reprint with introduction by J. Fitzmaurice Kelly, London, 1924.

Amadís de Gaula, ed. E. B. Place, 4 vols., Madrid, 1959–69.

M. de Cervantes, *La Galatea*, ed. J. B. Avalle-Arce, Clásicos Castellanos, Vols. 154–5, Madrid, 1961.

G. Gil Polo, *Diana enamorada*, ed. R. Ferreres, Clásicos Castellanos, Vol. 135, Madrid, 1962.

J. de Montemayor, *Los siete libros de la Diana*, ed. F. López Estrada, Clásicos Castellanos, Vol. 127. 2nd ed., Madrid, 1954.

F. de Rojas, *Tragicomedia de Calixto y Melibea. Libro también llamado La Celestina*, ed. M. Criado de Val and G. D. Trotter, Madrid, 1958.

F. de Rojas, *Celestina, or the tragicke-comedy of Calisto and Melibea englished from the Spanish . . . by James Mabbe anno 1631*, reprint with introduction by J. Fitzmaurice Kelly, London, 1894.

La vida de Lazarillo de Tormes y de sus fortunas y adversidades, ed. R. O. Jones, Manchester, 1963.

4.

H. Bebel, *Facetien*, ed. C. Bebermeyer, BlV 276, 1931.

Eulenspiegel (Ein kurtzweilig lesen von Dyl Vlenspiegel), ed. H. Knust, NDL 55–6, 1885.

Faust (Historia von D. Johann Fausten), ed. R. Petsch, NDL 7–8, 1911.

J. Fischart, *Sämtliche Dichtungen*, ed. H. Kurz, Leipzig, 1866–7.

J. Fischart, *Selection*, ed. K. Goedeke, NDL 18, 1895.

J. Fischart, *Geschichtklitterung*, ed. U. Nyssen, Düsseldorf, 1965.

Fortunatus, ed. H. Günther, NDL 240–41, 1914.

J. Pauli, *Schimpf und Ernst*, ed. H. Osterley, BlV 85, 1866.

J. Wickram, *Sämtliche Werke*, ed. J. Bolte, BIV 222 and ff., 1901–6.

J. Wickram, *Der jungen Knaben Spiegel* and *Von guten und bösen Nachbarn*, ed. F. Podleiszek, DLER, Volks-und Schwankbücher, 7, 1933.

Bibliographies

PART FIVE

1.

G. Bruno, *Dialoghi italiani*, 3 vols., Bari, 1923–7.

G. Bruno, *Expulsion of the Triumphant Beast*, tr. A. Imerti, New Brunswick, N.J., 1964.

G. Bruno, *The Heroic Frenzies*, tr. P. Memmo, Jr., Chapel Hill, N.C., 1965.

G. Bruno, *The Infinite Universe of Worlds*, annotated translation in: D. W. Singer, *Giordano Bruno. His Life and Thought*, New York, 1950.

B. Castiglione, *Il libro del Cortegiano*, 4th ed., Florence, 1947; tr. G. Bull, in Penguin Classics, Harmondsworth, 1967.

B. Cellini, *Vita*, Milan, 1959; tr. G. Bull, in Penguin Classics, Harmondsworth, 1956.

F. Guicciardini, *Dialogo e discorsi del reggimento di Firenze*, Bari, 1932.

F. Guicciardini, *Ricordi*, Florence, 1951.

F. Guicciardini, *Scritti autobiografici e rari*, Bari, 1936.

F. Guicciardini, *Storia d'Italia*, 5 vols., Bari, 1929; tr. S. Alexander, New York, 1969 and C. Grayson, London, 1966.

F. Guicciardini, *Storie fiorentine*, Bari, 1931.

F. Guicciardini, *History of Italy and History of Florence*, selections, tr. C. Grayson, London, 1966.

F. Guicciardini, *Selected Writings*, tr. M. Grayson, Oxford, 1965.

N. Machiavelli, *Opere*, Milan, 8 vols., 1960–65.

N. Machiavelli, *The Prince*, tr. G. Bull, in Penguin Classics, Harmondsworth, 1961.

N. Machiavelli, *The Discourses*, tr. L. J. Walker, 2 vols., London, 1950.

N. Machiavelli, *Art of War* and *Florentine History* in *Tudor Translations*, London, 1905.

G. Vasari, *Le vite*, 10 vols., Florence, 1966; excerpts tr. G. Bull, in Vasari, *Lives of the Artists*, Penguin Classics, Harmondsworth, 1965.

2.

Erasmus, *Opera Omnia*, 10 vols., Leyden, 1703–6. (A new complete edition has just been begun but will be many years in preparation.)

Erasmus, *Adages*, excellent selection tr. Margaret Mann Phillips, Cambridge, 1964.

Erasmus, *Colloquies*, tr. C. R. Thompson, Chicago and London, 1965.

Erasmus, *Enchiridion*, tr. R. Himelick, Bloomington, Indiana, 1963.

Erasmus, *Julius Exclusus*, text with French translation, Paris, 1873.

See also J. Huizinga, *Erasmus of Rotterdam*, London, 1952, for an interesting selection of letters in English translation.

Erasmus, *Praise of Folly*, tr. Betty Radice, Penguin Classics, Harmondsworth, 1971.

3.
Thomas More, *Utopia*, Vol. IV of *Complete Works*, New Haven and
London, 1964; tr. E. Surtz in *Selected Works*, Yale, 1964, Vol. II.

4.
A. Berger (ed.), *Die Sturmtruppen der Reformation*, DLER, Reformation,
2, 1931.
Epistolae Obscurorum Virorum, ed. and tr. F. G. Stokes, reprint London,
1964.
U. von Hutten, *Opera*, ed. E. Böcking, Leipzig 1859–70; reprint
Aachen, 1963.
O. Schade (ed.), *Satiren und Pasquillen aus der Reformationszeit*,
Hanover, 1863.

5.
M. Luther, *Werke, Kritische Gesamtausgabe*, Weimar, 1883– .
M. Luther, *Werke in Auswahl*, ed. O. Clemen, Berlin, 1950–55.
M. Luther, *Selected Works* in translation, ed. B. L. Woolf, London, 1952.
H. Zwingli, *Sämtliche Werke*, ed. G. Finsler, in *Corpus Reformatorum*,
Vol. 88 seq., 1904– .

6.
S. Franck, *Ketzerchronik* (Preface) and selection of other writings in
H. Fast, *Der Linke Flügel der Reformation*, Bremen, 1963.
S. Franck, *Chronicon Germaniae* (Preface), DLER, Reformation, 7.
S. Franck, *Paradoxa*, ed. T. Ziegler, Strasbourg, 1909.
Paracelsus, *Sämtliche Werke*, ed. K. Sudhoff and others, Wiesbaden,
1922– .

7.
J. Calvin, *Opera* in Vols. I–LIX of *Corpus Reformatorum*, ed. G. Baum,
etc., 1863– .
J. Calvin, *Institution chrétienne* (1541 ed.), ed. J. Pannier, 4 vols., Paris,
1961.
J. Calvin, *Institution chrétienne* (1560 ed.), ed. J. D. Benoît, 5 vols.,
Paris, 1957–63.
J. Calvin, *Institutes of the Christian Religion*, ed. J. T. McNeill, in Vols.
XX–XXI of Library of Christian Classics, Philadelphia, 1960.
(Vols. XXII and XXIII contain English translations of some shorter
works.)
J. Calvin, *Avertissement contre l'Astrologie, Traité des Reliques*, Paris,
1962.

8.

B. Des Periers, *Cymbalum Mundi*, ed. P. H. Nurse, Manchester, 1958.

H. Estienne, *Apologie pour Hérodote*, ed. F. Ristelhuber, Paris, 1879.

P. Marnix de Sainte-Aldegonde, *Œuvres*, ed. E. Quinet, 6 vols., Brussels, 1857–60.

Satire Menippée, ed. E. Tricotel, 2 vols., Lyon, 1877.

9.

J. L. Vives, *Opera omnia*, ed. G. Mayans y Siscar, 8 vols., Valencia, 1782–90; reprint by Gregg, 1964.

J. L. Vives, *Obras completas*, Spanish translation and ed. by L. Riber, 2 vols., Aguilar, Madrid, 1947–8.

J. L. Vives, *Vives and the Renascence Education of Women*, a translation of parts of *De institutione feminae christianae* by Richard Hyrde (?1529), ed. Foster Watson, Cambridge, 1912.

J. L. Vives, *Vives on Education*. A translation of the *De tradendis disciplinis* with an introduction by Foster Watson, Cambridge, 1913.

El Crotalón, see 'C. de Villalón'.

10.

A. de Laguna, *Viaje de Turquía*, see 'C. de Villalón'.

A. de Valdés, *Diálogo de las cosas ocurridas en Roma*, ed. J. F. Montesinos, Clásicos Castellanos, Vol. 89, Madrid, 1956 (reprint); tr. and ed. J. E. Longhurst (*Alfonso de Valdés and the Sack of Rome: Dialogue of Lactancio and an Archdeacon*), Albuquerque, 1952.

A. de Valdés, *Diálogo de Mercurio y Carón*, ed. J. F. Montesinos, Clásicos Castellanos, Vol. 96, Madrid, 1954 (reprint).

'C. de Villalón', *El Crotalón*, ed. A. Cortina, 2nd ed., Colección Austral, Buenos Aires, 1945.

'C. de Villalón', *Viaje de Turquía*, ed. A. G. Solalinde, 3rd ed., Colección Austral, Buenos Aires, 1947.

11.

J. de Valdés, *Diálogo de doctrina christiana y el salterio traducido del hebreo en romance castellano*, ed. D. Ricart, Mexico, 1964.

J. de Valdés, *Diálogo de la lengua*, see, above, p. 551.

J. de Valdés, *The Hundred and Ten Considerations* ..., tr. by Nicholas Ferrar, Oxford, 1638; reprint by F. Chapman, *Valdeso's Divine Considerations, The Sacred Treasury*, Vol. 2, London, 1905.

12.

P. Groult (ed.), *Anthologie de la littérature spirituelle du XVIe siècle*, Paris, 1959, is a useful bi-lingual collection of extracts from seventeen Spanish religious writers of the sixteenth century.

L. de Granada, *Guía de pecadores*, ed. L. G. Alonso Getino, Aguilar, Madrid, 1962.

L. de Granada, *Obra selecta. Una suma de la vida cristiana*, ed. A. Trancho, O.P., Biblioteca de autores cristianos, Vol. 20, Madrid, 1947. An arrangement of passages drawn from different works of Granada's.

L. de León, *De los nombres de Cristo*, ed. F. de Onís, Clásicos Castellanos, Vols. 28, 33, 41. 4th ed., Madrid, 1956.

I. Loyola, St, *The Spiritual Exercises, Spanish and English*, tr. with commentary by J. Rickaby, S.J., 2nd ed., London, 1923.

I. Loyola, St, *The Spiritual Exercises . . . and Directorium in Exercitia*, tr. with commentary by W. H. Longridge, S.S.J.E., 2nd ed., London, 1922.

I. Loyola, St, *Obras completas*, ed. C. de Dalmases and I. Iparraguirre, S.J., Biblioteca de autores cristianos, Vol. 86, 2nd ed., Madrid, 1963.

Teresa of Jesus, St, *Obras completas*, ed. Efrén de la Madre de Dios, O.C.D. and O. Steggink, O.carm., Biblioteca de autores cristianos, Vol. 212, Madrid, 1962; English translation by E. A. Peers of the *Works*, 3 vols., London, 1946; and o1 the *Letters*, 2 vols., London, 1951.

13.

A. de Guevara, *Libro aureo de Marco Aurelio con el Relox de principes*, Anvèrs, 1550; English translation by T. North, *The Diall of Princes (with the famous booke of Marcus Aurelius)*, London, 1557; reprint London, 1919 and Amsterdam, 1968.

A. de Guevara, *Libro primero de las Epístolas familiares*, ed. J. M. de Cossío, 2 vols., Madrid, 1950, 1952.

A. de Guevara, *Menosprecio de corte y alabanza de aldea*, ed. M. Martínez de Burgos, Clásicos Castellanos, Vol. 29, Madrid, 1952 (reprint).

P. Mexía, *Silva de varia lección*, 2 vols., Madrid, 1933–4.

14.

M. de Montaigne, *Essais*, ed. A. Thibaudet, Pléiade, Paris, 1950.

PART SIX

I.

E. Alberus, *Fabeln*, ed. W. Braune, NDL 104–7, 1892.

S. Brant, *Das Narrenschiff*, ed. F. Zarncke, reprint Hildesheim, 1961; illustrated ed. by F. Bobertag, DNL* 16, 1889.

G. Forster, *Frische Teutsche Liedlein*, ed. M. E. Marriage, NDL 203–6, 1903.

Bibliographies

T. Murner, *Deutsche Schriften*, ed. F. Schultz, Strasbourg, 1918–31.

H. Sachs, *Sämtliche Werke*, ed. A. V. Keller, BlV 102–127, 1870–1908.

H. Sachs, *Sämtliche Fastnachtspiele*, ed. E. Goetze, NDL, 1893–1913.

B. Waldis, *Esopus*, ed. H. Kurz, Leipzig, 1862.

2.

P. L. Duchartre, *The Italian Comedy*, New York, 1966.

K. M. Lea, *Italian Popular Comedy*, 2 vols., Oxford, 1934.

A. Nicoll, *The World of Harlequin*, Cambridge, 1963.

G. Oreglia, *The Commedia dell'Arte*, London, 1968.

V. Pandolfi, *La commedia dell'arte. Storia e testi*, 5 vols., Florence, 1957–8.

W. A. Smith, *The Commedia dell'Arte*, New York, 1964.

3.

Les Croniques admirables de ... Gargantua, ed. M. Françon, Rochecorbon, 1956.

A. J. V. Leroux de Lincy, *Recueil de chants historiques*, Paris, 1841.

O. Maillard, *Œuvres françaises*, ed. A. de la Borderie, Nantes, 1877.

M. Menot, *Sermons choisis*, ed. J. Nève, Paris, 1924.

Le Recueil Trepperel, les Farces, ed. E. Droz, Geneva, 1961.

4.

See under Part Three, chapter 3, p. 556.

Selections of popular verse will be found in: D. Alonso and J. M. Blecua (eds.), *Antología de la poesía española. Poesía de tipo popular*, Madrid, 1956; C. C. Smith, *Spanish Ballads*, Oxford, 1964; A. Terry (ed.), *An Anthology of Spanish Poetry, 1500–1700*, see above, p. 553.

D. Alonso (ed.), *Góngora y el 'Polifemo'*, 5th ed., Madrid, 1967, Vol. I.

G. Correas, *Vocabulario de refranes*, 2nd ed., Madrid, 1924.

R. O. Jones (ed.), *Poems of Góngora*, Cambridge, 1966. This work, as also the preceding one, gives a selection of poems by Góngora written in popular forms.

Lope de Vega, *Poesías líricas*, ed. J. F. Montesinos, Clásicos Castellanos, Vols. 68, 75, 2 vols., Madrid, 1953 (reprint).

J. de Mal Lara, *Filosofía vulgar*, ed. A. Vilanova, 4 vols., Barcelona, 1958–9.

R. Rodríguez Moñino, *Construcción crítica y realidad histórica en la poesía española de los siglos XVI y XVII*, 2nd ed., Madrid, 1968.

Bibliographies

M. de Santa Cruz de Dueñas, *Floresta española de apothegmas o sentencias, sabiamente y graciosamente dichas, de algunos españoles*, Toledo, 1574; reprint Madrid, 1953.

E. M. Wilson, *Some Aspects of Spanish Literary History* (Taylorian Lecture for 1966), Oxford, 1967.

Index

In the space available it is unfortunately impossible to provide a full analytical index. Modern writers and critics, whether or not mentioned in the Bibliographies, have not been included, nor have individual works, with a few exceptions. All authors, artists and anonymous works dealt with in the text are listed, so are a few important literary characters (e.g. from Ariosto and Ronsard) and most foreign technical terms explained in the text on their first occurrence (e.g. *autos*). Page references in italics indicate extended treatment of the subject.